Big Data Quantification for Complex Decision-Making

Chao Zhang
Shanxi University, China

Wentao Li
Southwest University, China

A volume in the Advances in Systems Analysis, Software Engineering, and High Performance Computing (ASASEHPC) Book Series

IGI Global
PUBLISHER of TIMELY KNOWLEDGE

Published in the United States of America by
IGI Global
Engineering Science Reference (an imprint of IGI Global)
701 E. Chocolate Avenue
Hershey PA, USA 17033
Tel: 717-533-8845
Fax: 717-533-8661
E-mail: cust@igi-global.com
Web site: http://www.igi-global.com

Library of Congress Cataloging-in-Publication Data

CIP PENDING

Big Data Quantification for Complex Decision-Making
Chao Zhang, Wentao Li
2024 Engineering Science Reference

ISBN: 9798369315828
eISBN: 9798369315835

This book is published in the IGI Global book series Advances in Systems Analysis, Software Engineering, and High Performance Computing (ASASEHPC) (ISSN: 2327-3453; eISSN: 2327-3461)

British Cataloguing in Publication Data
A Cataloguing in Publication record for this book is available from the British Library.

For electronic access to this publication, please contact: eresources@igi-global.com.

Advances in Systems Analysis, Software Engineering, and High Performance Computing (ASASEHPC) Book Series

Vijayan Sugumaran
Oakland University, Rochester, USA

ISSN:2327-3453
EISSN:2327-3461

Mission

The theory and practice of computing applications and distributed systems has emerged as one of the key areas of research driving innovations in business, engineering, and science. The fields of software engineering, systems analysis, and high performance computing offer a wide range of applications and solutions in solving computational problems for any modern organization.

The **Advances in Systems Analysis, Software Engineering, and High Performance Computing (ASASEHPC) Book Series** brings together research in the areas of distributed computing, systems and software engineering, high performance computing, and service science. This collection of publications is useful for academics, researchers, and practitioners seeking the latest practices and knowledge in this field.

Coverage

- Enterprise Information Systems
- Software Engineering
- Engineering Environments
- Storage Systems
- Performance Modelling
- Distributed Cloud Computing
- Computer Graphics
- Computer System Analysis
- Human-Computer Interaction
- Metadata and Semantic Web

IGI Global is currently accepting manuscripts for publication within this series. To submit a proposal for a volume in this series, please contact our Acquisition Editors at Acquisitions@igi-global.com or visit: http://www.igi-global.com/publish/.

The Advances in Systems Analysis, Software Engineering, and High Performance Computing (ASASEHPC) Book Series (ISSN 2327-3453) is published by IGI Global, 701 E. Chocolate Avenue, Hershey, PA 17033-1240, USA, www.igi-global.com. This series is composed of titles available for purchase individually; each title is edited to be contextually exclusive from any other title within the series. For pricing and ordering information please visit http://www.igi-global.com/book-series/advances-systems-analysis-software-engineering/73689. Postmaster: Send all address changes to above address.

Titles in this Series

For a list of additional titles in this series, please visit: www.igi-global.com/book-series

Technological Advancements in Data Processing for Next Generation Intelligent Systems
Shanu Sharma (ABES Engineering College, Ghaziabad, India) Ayushi Prakash (Ajay Kumar Garg Engineering College, Ghaziabad, India) and Vijayan Sugumaran (Oakland University, Rochester USA)
Engineering Science Reference • © 2024 • 357pp • H/C (ISBN: 9798369309681) • US $300.00

Advanced Applications in Osmotic Computing
G. Revathy (SASTRA University, ndia)
Engineering Science Reference • © 2024 • 370pp • H/C (ISBN: 9798369316948) • US $300.00

Omnichannel Approach to Co-Creating Customer Experiences Through Metaverse Platforms
Babita Singla (Chitkara Business School, Chitkara University, Punjab, India) Kumar Shalender (Chitkara Business School, Chitkara University, India) and Nripendra Singh (Pennsylvania Western University, USA)
Engineering Science Reference • © 2024 • 223pp • H/C (ISBN: 9798369318669) • US $270.00

Uncertain Spatiotemporal Data Management for the Semantic Web
Luyi Bai (Northeastern University, China) and Lin Zhu (Northeastern University, China)
Engineering Science Reference • © 2024 • 518pp • H/C (ISBN: 9781668491089) • US $325.00

Bio-Inspired Optimization Techniques in Blockchain Systems
U. Vignesh (Vellore Institute of Technology, Chennai, India) Manikandan M. (Manipal Institute of Technology, India) and Ruchi Doshi (Universidad Azteca, Mexico)
Engineering Science Reference • © 2024 • 288pp • H/C (ISBN: 9798369311318) • US $300.00

Enhancing Performance, Efficiency, and Security Through Complex Systems Control
Idriss Chana (ESTM, Moulay Ismail University of Meknès, Morocco) Aziz Bouazi (ESTM, Moulay Ismail University of Meknès, Morocco) and Hussain Ben-azza (ENSAM, Moulay Ismail University of Meknes, Morocco)
Engineering Science Reference • © 2024 • 371pp • H/C (ISBN: 9798369304976) • US $300.00

Frameworks for Blockchain Standards, Tools, Testbeds, and Platforms
Yanamandra Ramakrishna (School of Business, Skyline University College, Sharjah, UAE) and Priyameet Kaur Keer (Department of Management Studies, New Horizon College of Engineering, India)
Engineering Science Reference • © 2024 • 244pp • H/C (ISBN: 9798369304051) • US $285.00

IGI Global
PUBLISHER of TIMELY KNOWLEDGE

701 East Chocolate Avenue, Hershey, PA 17033, USA
Tel: 717-533-8845 x100 • Fax: 717-533-8661
E-Mail: cust@igi-global.com • www.igi-global.com

Table of Contents

Detailed Table of Contents

This chapter proposes group-oriented multi-attribute decision-making based on mixed advantage-disadvantage degree (GOMADMMADD) method to deal with group-oriented decision analysis. Based on the strict attribute relationship between group members, this method proposes the concepts of "local advantage-disadvantage degrees" and "advantage-disadvantage degrees," which solves the challenge of group-oriented multi-attribute decision-making (GOMADM). However, this method still has the problem that the number of groups to be evaluated increases exponentially. Therefore, the authors first improved the GOMADMMADD method and proposed decision-making method based on dominance-based rough sets (GMADMDRS). Then, the "advantage" neighborhood operators and "disadvantage" neighborhood operators of groups are introduced to define the "advantage-disadvantage neighborhood degree" (ADND), and the GMADMDRS method is optimized by using ADND. The experimental results show that both GOMADMMADD method and GMADMDRS method effectively evaluate the population, and the optimized GMADMDRS algorithm is consistent in the experimental results, and the time performance has been greatly improved, and the computational performance has been significantly improved, which has practical significance to solve the problem of exponential growth of the number of groups to be evaluated. These methods provide a novel perspective and effective method for group oriented multi-attribute decision-making.

This chapter focuses on the issue of selecting a blood glucose meter for diabetic patients. To address this problem, the authors have developed a comprehensive evaluation model that combines triangular fuzzy (TF) logic, multi-granularity (MG), three-way decision (TWD), and rough set theory. The evaluation model takes into consideration the performance indicators of the blood glucose meter and user requirements. The authors utilize TF logic to model the indicators and determine their weights, while integrating the TWD method to handle incomplete and uncertain information. Subsequently, they introduce the PROMETHEE method to comprehensively evaluate and rank various alternatives. Finally, within this evaluation model, they select the optimal choice based on its score. Experimental results demonstrate the effectiveness of our proposed method in resolving the blood glucose meter selection problem and providing personalized recommendations for diabetic patients.

Voice disorders are one of the incipient symptoms of Parkinson's disease (PD). Most of the existing PD severity prediction methods are based on baseline features, and generally select features with high relevance for dimensionality reduction. To further improve the prediction performance, the LDFSF and GWT-RF-Att methods are proposed respectively from the perspective of feature selection and feature transformation. The LDFSF method utilizes dynamic feature selection strategy based on SOM clustering to select feature subsets with high correlation, low redundancy, and high complementarity from voice features. The GWT-RF-Att method uses graph wavelet transform to extract the more effective feature set based on the baseline features, and uses random forest improved by attention mechanism to improve the prediction performance of the model. The results on the Parkinson's telemonitoring dataset show that the performance of the two methods is better than that of the existing comparison methods, thus verifying their effectiveness.

The Durban University of Technology is now engaged in a project to create a data lake house system for a Training Authority in the South African Government sector. This system is crucial for improving the monitoring and evaluation capacities of the training authority and ensuring efficient service delivery. Ensuring the high quality of data being fed into the lakehouse is crucial, since low data quality negatively impacts the effectiveness of the lakehouse system. This chapter examines quality control methods for ingestion-layer pipelines in order to present a framework for ensuring data quality. The metrics taken into

in data by means of reasoning, based on the current representation. The existing research in logic and data aspects of decision implication proposes a set of decision implications with information integrity and extreme simplicity (non-redundancy and optimality), i.e., decision implication canonical basis (DICB), which lays a solid foundation for constructing a knowledge representation and reasoning framework in formal contexts. This chapter conducts a systematic and in-depth study on the important issues of knowledge representation capability, and incomplete formal context adaptability of decision implication, and reasoning based on decision implications.

Preface

In an era where data reigns supreme, the imperative for decision-makers to grapple with the vast and intricate landscape of information has become an unparalleled challenge. *Big Data Quantification for Complex Decision-Making* emerges as a beacon in this data-centric age, unraveling the methodologies, techniques, and frameworks essential for distilling profound insights from colossal datasets. As editors, we embark on this intellectual journey with the conviction that understanding and harnessing big data is not just a technological evolution but a fundamental transformation in the way decisions are made.

The core aspiration of this book is to illuminate the dynamic interplay between big data and the nuanced process of decision-making, particularly in uncertain contexts. Our scope encompasses a spectrum of objectives, each contributing synergistically to the advancement of research and knowledge in this field. We delve into the significance of big data in decision-making, unravel methodological intricacies, adeptly handle uncertainty, merge theoretical underpinnings with real-world applications, contribute meaningfully to ongoing research, provide pragmatic guidance for practitioners, and shed light on prospective directions and implications. At its essence, this book seeks to endow readers with a comprehensive toolbox, empowering effective navigation through the data-rich landscape of modern decision-making.

The unique blend of theoretical frameworks, practical applications, and forward-thinking perspectives forms the cornerstone of our approach. By seamlessly integrating these elements, our goal is to deepen comprehension of how big data can be strategically leveraged to address multifaceted challenges and facilitate well-considered decisions in a world characterized by pervasive uncertainty.

Our intended audience is diverse, reflecting the broad impact of big data on decision-making across various domains. Researchers and academics in data science, decision science, machine learning, artificial intelligence, and related fields will find this book to be a valuable reference, offering insights into challenges, techniques, and prospects inherent in harnessing big data. Practitioners and professionals engaged in data analytics, business intelligence, risk management, and strategic decision-making stand to gain pragmatic insights and methodologies for crafting well-informed decisions within volatile contexts. Lastly, graduate students exploring data science, decision analysis, and related realms will discover in this book a foundational resource that equips them with the knowledge and tools to address intricate real-world challenges.

The thematic breadth of this book is vast, covering topics such as big data analytics, uncertainty modeling, decision-making under uncertainty, fuzzy decision-making, formal concept analysis, rough set theory, deep learning models, neural network models, natural language processing, three-way decisions, multi-granularity analysis, and intelligent control systems. Each chapter contributes a unique perspective, enriching the collective understanding of how big data can be quantified for complex decision-making.

As editors, we express our sincere appreciation to the contributors who have brought their expertise to this endeavor. We believe that "Big Data Quantification for Complex Decision-Making" will serve as a catalyst for advancing both scholarly inquiry and practical applications in this dynamic intersection of big data and decision-making.

Chapter 1: Group-oriented Multi-attribute Decision-Making Method based on Dominance Rough Set Theory

Authored by Bin Yu, Zeyu Xiao, and Yinglong Dai from China, this chapter introduces the Group-oriented Multi-attribute Decision-Making based on mixed advantage-disadvantage degree (GOMADMMADD) method. The GOMADMMADD method addresses the challenge of group-oriented decision analysis by proposing concepts such as "local advantage-disadvantage degrees" and "advantage-disadvantage degrees." The authors go on to enhance this method, introducing the decision-making method based on dominance-based rough sets (GMADMDRS), which optimizes the GMADMDRS method using "advantage" and "disadvantage" neighborhood operators. This optimization involves defining the "advantage-disadvantage neighborhood degree" (ADND), providing a solution for group-oriented multi-attribute decision-making with enhanced efficiency.

Chapter 2: A Multi-Granularity Triangular Fuzzy Approach for Diabetes Blood Glucometer Selection using PROMETHEE and Three-Way Decision

This chapter, authored by Liyin Wang, Yuting Cheng, Xueqing Fan, Anna Wang, and Hansen Zhao address the selection of a blood glucose meter for diabetic patients. Combining triangular fuzzy (TF) logic, multi-granularity (MG) three-way decision (TWD), and rough set theory, the authors develop a comprehensive evaluation model. TF logic models indicators and determines weights, while TWD handles incomplete and uncertain information. The PROMETHEE method is then introduced to evaluate and rank alternatives, providing personalized recommendations for diabetic patients based on the model's effectiveness in resolving the blood glucose meter selection problem.

Chapter 3: Prediction of Parkinson's Disease Severity Based on Feature Optimization

Authored by Tao Zhang, Zaifa Xue, and Zesheng Huo from Yanshan University, China, this chapter focuses on predicting the severity of Parkinson's disease (PD) using voice features. The authors propose the LDFSF and GWT-RF-Att methods for feature selection and transformation, respectively. The LDFSF method uses a dynamic feature selection strategy based on SOM clustering, while the GWT-RF-Att method leverages graph wavelet transform and random forest with an attention mechanism. These methods outperform existing comparison methods, demonstrating their effectiveness in improving prediction performance on the Parkinson's telemonitoring dataset.

Chapter 4: Creating a Data Lakehouse for a South African Government-Sector Learning Control Enforcing Quality Control for Incremental Extract-Load-Transform Pipe

In this chapter, authored by Dharmesh Dhabliya, Vivek Veeraiah, Sukhvinder Singh Dari, Jambi Ratna Raja Kumar, Ritika Dhabliya, Sabyasachi Pramanik, and Ankur Gupta from India, the focus is on creating a data lakehouse system for a South African Government sector. The Durban University of Technology is engaged in this project, emphasizing the importance of data quality in the efficiency of the lakehouse system. The chapter explores quality control methods for ingestion-layer pipelines, assessing metrics such as completeness, accuracy, integrity, correctness, and timeliness. The framework's efficiency is demonstrated through implementation on a sample semi-structured dataset, with suggestions for future development and integration of data from diverse sources.

Chapter 5: Decision Making based on Partition Order Product Space

Authored by Yi Xu from Anhui University, China, this chapter introduces the concept of partition order product space, combining multilevel granular structure with multiview granular structure. Two search algorithms, depth-first searching and breadth-first searching, are proposed to find solutions in this space. The chapter also explores three-way decisions based on partition order product space, presenting four multiview sequential three-way decisions. The approach represents an effective and reasonable way to describe and solve problems through granular computing principles.

Chapter 6: Strategy Selection and Outcome Evaluation of Change-Based Three-Way Decisions Based on Reinforcement Learning

Chunmao Jiang from Fujian University of Technology, China, enhances the trisecting-acting-outcome (TAO) model of three-way decision-making (3WD) in this chapter. The novel approach introduces Q-learning in reinforcement learning for strategy selection and outcome prediction. Changes in tripartition and actions are reinterpreted as states and actions, with cumulative prospect theory used to quantify rewards. The Q-learning algorithm iteratively determines action sets to achieve target rewards efficiently, offering a cost-effective and psychologically attuned action set for predicting utility in change-based 3WD.

Chapter 7: The Extension of MAIRCA Based on Fuzzy Number: Smart Supplier Selection

Hatice Özensel and Burak Efe from Necmettin Erbakan University, Turkey, address the supplier selection phase in supply chain management. They propose an interval-valued q-rung orthopair fuzzy (IVqROF) number-based MAIRCA method for ranking alternative suppliers. This extension of the MAIRCA method utilizes fuzzy numbers but introduces IVqROF numbers, enhancing the evaluation of expert opinions. The study examines smart supplier selection under Industry 4.0 criteria, providing insights into the supplier selection problem faced by an automotive sub-industry company.

Chapter 8: Review of Chinese Text Mining in Agriculture

Xinyue Zhao and Yunsheng Song, from China, conduct a comprehensive review of text mining in Chinese agriculture. The chapter analyzes the characteristics of agricultural text, covers preprocessing of Chinese agricultural text, text representation, agricultural text classification, and text matching. Additionally, the authors delve into the application scenarios of agricultural text mining, agricultural intelligent service, and the current research status in this field.

Chapter 9: A Snapshot Survey of Data Acquisition Forms in Multi-Attribute Decision-Making Studies

Authored by Yuge Niu, Kexin Liu, Fanghui Lu, and Jiayi Zhang, this chapter addresses the need for large-scale data collection in Multi-Attribute Decision-Making (MADM) analysis. The authors provide a snapshot survey, summarizing classic papers, open datasets, remote sensing data, sentiment analysis, and questionnaire survey data collection forms in MADM research. By evaluating classic papers, open datasets, and various data collection methods, the chapter aids researchers and professionals in selecting and designing effective data collection approaches, ensuring reliable and impactful decision-making.

Chapter 10: Research on Knowledge Representation and Reasoning Based on Decision Implication

Shaoxia Zhang from Shanxi University of Finance and Economics, China, explores knowledge representation and reasoning based on decision implication. The Decision Implication Canonical Basis (DICB) is introduced, offering a set of decision implications with information integrity and extreme simplicity. The chapter conducts a systematic and in-depth study on the capability of knowledge representation, focusing on the adaptability of decision implication to incomplete formal context. The research extends to reasoning based on decision implications, providing insights into the effectiveness of this approach in formal contexts.

In the closing pages of "Big Data Quantification for Complex Decision-Making," we reflect upon the extensive exploration into the symbiotic relationship between big data and the intricate process of decision-making. As the landscape of information continues to evolve, the imperative for decision-makers to navigate the complexities of data has become paramount. This book, conceived as a guiding light in the era of data dominance, has unfolded an array of methodologies, techniques, and frameworks essential for extracting profound insights from colossal datasets.

The essence of our collective effort lies in recognizing that grappling with big data is not merely a technological evolution but a fundamental shift in the very fabric of decision-making. The core aspiration of this book was to shed light on the dynamic interplay between big data and nuanced decision-making, especially in the face of uncertainty. Each chapter has been meticulously crafted to contribute synergistically, advancing research and knowledge in this transformative field.

From decoding the significance of big data in decision-making to untangling methodological intricacies, handling uncertainty adeptly, and bridging theoretical foundations with real-world applications, this book seeks to empower its readers. The comprehensive toolbox provided within these pages equips individuals across various domains with the skills to navigate the data-rich landscape and make well-informed decisions.

Our unique approach, fusing theoretical frameworks, practical applications, and forward-thinking perspectives, has aimed to deepen the comprehension of strategically leveraging big data to address multifaceted challenges. This book stands as a testament to the belief that understanding the interplay of big data and decision-making is pivotal for ushering in a new era of informed choices amid pervasive uncertainty.

The intended audience, ranging from seasoned researchers to practitioners and aspiring graduate students, reflects the book's broad impact on decision-making across diverse domains. As editors, we express our gratitude to the contributors who have infused their expertise into this collective work. We envision "Big Data Quantification for Complex Decision-Making" as not just a compilation of knowledge but a catalyst for future exploration and innovation in the dynamic realm where big data intersects with decision-making.

In closing, we invite readers to embark on their own intellectual journeys, armed with the insights and tools provided in this book, as they navigate the uncharted waters of big data and continue to shape the future landscape of decision-making.

Chao Zhang
Shanxi University, China

Wentao Li
Southwest University, China

Chapter 1
Group-Oriented Multi-Attribute Decision-Making Method Based on Dominance Rough Set Theory

Yu Bin
College of Information Science and Engineering, Hunan Normal University, China

Xiao Zeyu
College of Information Science and Engineering, Hunan Normal University, China

Dai Yinglong
College of Information Science and Engineering, Hunan Normal University, China

ABSTRACT

This chapter proposes group-oriented multi-attribute decision-making based on mixed advantage-disadvantage degree (GOMADMMADD) method to deal with group-oriented decision analysis. Based on the strict attribute relationship between group members, this method proposes the concepts of "local advantage-disadvantage degrees" and "advantage-disadvantage degrees," which solves the challenge of group-oriented multi-attribute decision-making (GOMADM). However, this method still has the problem that the number of groups to be evaluated increases exponentially. Therefore, the authors first improved the GOMADMMADD method and proposed decision-making method based on dominance-based rough sets (GMADMDRS). Then, the "advantage" neighborhood operators and "disadvantage" neighborhood operators of groups are introduced to define the "advantage-disadvantage neighborhood degree" (ADND), and the GMADMDRS method is optimized by using ADND. The experimental results show that both GOMADMMADD method and GMADMDRS method effectively evaluate the population, and the optimized GMADMDRS algorithm is consistent in the experimental results, and the time performance has been greatly improved, and the computational performance has been significantly improved, which has practical significance to solve the problem of exponential growth of the number of groups to be evaluated. These methods provide a novel perspective and effective method for group oriented multi-attribute decision-making.

DOI: 10.4018/979-8-3693-1582-8.ch001

INTRODUCTION

Problem Background

Group evaluation and ranking have always been required. In the team ranking, it is necessary to evaluate the team as a whole, in financial investment, portfolio investment is a favorable way to avoid risks, portfolio investment needs to evaluate the financial products of the portfolio as a whole, when the feature selection reveals the correlation between the decision variables and the description variables, consider the interaction between the decision variables, and the overall evaluation of the combination decision variables has far-reaching significance. Evaluate and rank groups as a whole, which are widely used in team ranking, portfolio investment, feature selection, group identification, and more.

A Brief Review of DRSA

In real-life scenarios, decision-makers often encounter problems involving imprecise or fuzzy information. To address such Multi-Attribute Decision Making (MADM) problems, Pawlak introduced rough sets (Pawlak, 1982), later extended by various scholars due to its equivalence relationship limitations. In dealing with dual-level hesitant fuzzy language elements (DHHFLTS), Yu et al. proposed a λ-Rough set model, applying it to multi-attribute decision-making (Yu et al., 2019a; Yu et al., 2019b). Gireesha et al. addressed the uncertainty in cloud service provider evaluation by proposing a method based on improved interval-valued intuitionistic fuzzy set weighted aggregation and product evaluation (Gireesha et al., 2020). In the context of bone transplantation selection, Zhang et al. obtained criteria weights using the variable precision intuitionistic fuzzy rough set (CVPIFRS) model and proposed a new MADM method combining CVPIFRS with TOPSIS (Zhang et al., 2020b). Gou et al. introduced an extended probabilistic dual-level language VIKOR method for MCDM in smart healthcare (Gou et al., 2021). Dogan proposed a fuzzy MCDM method based on spherical fuzzy AHP for technology group screening (Dogan, 2021). Zhang et al. addressed the limitations of distance and similarity in DHHFLTS based on algebra and proposed the DHHFL-ELECTRE II method using cosine similarity for financial logistics enterprises' MADM (Zhang et al., 2022). Kang et al. presented a multi-attribute prediction analysis model in fuzzy information systems based on a new fuzzy rough set theory (Kang et al., 2022).

Greco et al. introduced an extension of rough sets called Dominance-based Rough Set Approach (DRSA), where condition attributes are criteria ranked by preference (Greco et al., 1999; Greco et al., 2001). Later, they proposed the dominance rough fuzzy set model by integrating DRSA into the fuzzy neighborhood (Greco et al., 2006). Zhang et al. established a general framework of hesitant fuzzy language rough set, constructing decision rules based on hesitant fuzzy language information (Zhang et al., 2018). In the context of hesitant fuzzy language, they proposed a hybrid model incorporating multi-granularity decision theory rough set into the dual universe framework (Zhang et al., 2020d). Ahmad et al. addressed the key step of calculating upper and lower approximations in DRSA by proposing an effective method that directly computes them without considering irrelevant objects (Ahmad et al., 2020). Huang et al. focused on applying DRSA to process composite ordered decision systems, including categorical, numerical, set-valued, interval-valued, and missing attributes (Huang et al., 2020). Palangetić et al. advanced the theory by considering additional properties and explored the application of Ordered Weighted Average (OWA) operators to fuzzy DRSA (Palangetić et al., 2021). Błaszczyński et al. tested a new dataset for auto loan applications using the Dominance-based Rough Set Balanced Rule Ensemble

(DRSA-BRE) for financial fraud prediction (Błaszczyński et al., 2021). Kusunoki et al. addressed the issue of too strict approximation under classified data by using variable precision DRSA (VP-DRSA) and variable consistency DRSA (VC-DRSA) parameters to enhance lower approximation in empirical risk minimization (Kusunoki et al., 2021).

A Brief Review of GOMADM

In recent decades, the field of Multi-Attribute Decision Making (MADM) has undergone significant developments, finding applications across various domains. Real-world decision-making problems are often intricate and cannot be adequately addressed through a single criterion. To tackle multi-attribute problems, MADM methods have been developed, greatly enhancing the efficacy of decision-making processes. As a cognitive process, MADM involves selecting the optimal solution by evaluating alternatives in the presence of multiple attributes. Broadly, MADM methods can be categorized into two groups (Figueira et al., 2005): (1) Outranking Techniques: Outranking methods rely on pairwise comparisons of alternatives. Examples include TOPSIS (Technique for Order Preference by Similarity to an Ideal Solution) (Behzadian et al., 2012; Opricovic & Tzeng, 2004), VIKOR (Vlsekriterijumska Optimizacija I Kompromisno Resenje) (Opricovic & Tzeng, 2004), ELECTRE (Elimination Et Choix Traduisant la Realit) (Roy, 1991), and PROMETHEE (Preference Ranking Organization Method for Enrichment Evaluations) (Brans & Vincke, 1985; Murat et al., 2015). (2) Multi-Attribute Utility and Value Theories: This category involves assigning utility to each alternative, encompassing methods such as UTA (UTilites Additives) (Jacquetlagreze & Siskos, 1982), AHP (Analytic Hierarchy Process) (Saaty, 1977), ANP (Analytic Network Process) (Saaty, 2004), and MACBETH (Measuring Attractiveness by a Categorical Based Evaluation Technique) (Costa, 2010).

With the increasing level of detail in data analysis, Group-Oriented Multi-Attribute Decision Making (GOMADM) is emerging as a trend compared to traditional multi-attribute decision-making. In team ranking, the evaluation of the entire team is essential. Portfolio investment, as a risk-avoidance method in financial investment, requires evaluating combined financial products as a whole. The significance of evaluating combined decision variables as a whole becomes apparent when feature selection reveals correlations between decision variables and descriptive variables. Cohorts are evaluated and ranked as a whole, leading to extensive research in team ranking (Das et al., 2022), portfolio investing (Zhang et al., 2020c; Vo et al., 2019; Paiva et al., 2019), feature selection (Mnich & Rudnicki, 2020; Pedersen & Vatn, 2022), group identification (Zhang et al., 2018; Leng et al., 2022), among others.

Group evaluation often involves ranking individuals using multi-attribute decision-making methods and then deriving overall performance based on individual performance. Various methods have been proposed to address the limitations of traditional MADM in group evaluation and ranking problems. These include the MADM integration method proposed by Hussain et al. (Hussain et al., 2020), average formula ranking aggregation, and weighted average consensus ranking aggregation methods by Tidke et al. (Tidke et al., 2020), a new MADM method proposed by Yu et al. to mitigate the influence of attribute weight (Yu et al., 2022b), and a group-oriented multi-attribute decision-making method proposed by Yu et al. (Yu et al., 2022a), further optimized in (Yu et al., 2023b).

The Motives and Contribution of This Chapter

In this chapter, a group oriented multi-attribute method is designed to solve the problem by using the dominant rough set theory. Specifically, we list several main research motivations of this chapter below.

1. With the improvement of the level of detail of data analysis, compared with traditional multi-attribute methods, GOMADM methods are becoming a trend.
2. Rough set theory is an effective tool to compare the advantages and disadvantages between groups. Therefore, it is necessary to design a group oriented multi-attribute decision-making method based on rough set theory.
3. After designing the GOMADMMADD method, the method has the problems that the number of groups to be evaluated increases exponentially and it is not easy to optimize, and the GOMADMMADD method is improved.

In light of the above study motives, we further sum up evident contributions of this chapter below.

1. Based on the dominance rough set theory, the GOMADM MADD method is designed to meet the challenge of decision analysis, and expand the application prospect of dominance rough set.
2. In order to solve the problem that GOMADMMADD method cannot optimize the exponential explosion problem, the GOMADMMADD method is improved to GMADMDRS method. The experimental results show that the GMADMDRS method is reasonable and lays a solid foundation for solving the exponential explosion problem.
3. In order to optimize the GMADMDRS method, this paper designs the superior and inferior potential neighborhood degree (ADND) which is suitable for the GMADMDRS method based on the dominance rough set, and fully studies the properties of the measure, which expands the applicability of the dominance rough set model.
4. In order to solve the problem that the number of candidate groups increases exponentially, the GMADMDRS method is optimized by using the characteristics of ADND. While ensuring the consistency of the results before and after the optimization of the GMADMDRS method, the time performance of the optimized GMADMDRS method has been greatly improved compared with the optimized GMADMDRS method.

Based on the above literature analysis, we have arranged the structure of this chapter as follows. In Section 2, we reviewed information systems and proposed Advantage (Disadvantage) Neighborhood and (Local) Advantage Disadvantage Degrees based on the advantage of rough sets. In the next section, in order to further optimize, we proposed the Advantage (Disadvantage) Neighborhood Operators and Advantage Disadvantage Neighborhood Degrees. In Section 4, we designed the GOMADMMADD method based on the Advantage (Disadvantage) Neighborhood and (Local) Advantage Disadvantage Degrees, and further improved the GMADMDRS method, and further optimize this method based on Advantage (Disadvantage) Neighborhood Operators and Advantage Disadvantage Neighborhood Degrees. In Section 5, a real case study was conducted using a UCI dataset extracted from real data. Finally, some conclusions were summarized and future research issues were proposed.

BASIC KNOWLEDGE

Information System

Given the apparent advantages possessed by information system (IS) in describing research objects primarily characterized by symbolic values, the basic description of IS is as follows.

An information system (IS) is described as a 4-tuple $\{U,Q,V,f\}$, where

U, called the universe of discourse, is a non-empty finite object set;
Q is a non-empty finite attribute set;
$V=\bigcup_{a\in Q}V_a$, where V_a is the set of values of the attribute a;
f: $U\times Q\rightarrow V_a$, is a map such that $f(x,a)\in V_a$ for every $x\in U$ and $a\in Q$.

For any $x\in U$, we use the notation $\mathcal{A}_x$ to represent the set $\{a\in Q|f(x,a)=1\}$, that is, $\mathcal{A}_x$ is the set of all attributes possessing the object x. The cardinality of a finite set X in this study is written as $|X|$.

Advantage (Disadvantage) Neighborhood and (Local) Advantage-Disadvantage Degrees

This section constitutes the core theoretical foundation for implementing the GOMADMMADD method, including the advantage (disadvantage) neighborhood, the (local) advantage-disadvantage degrees.

Based on the comparison of advantages (disadvantages) between the objects, the definition of the advantage (disadvantage) neighborhood is as follows.

Definition 2.1: Let $S=\{U,A,f,V\}$ be an IS and $x\in U$. Then,

(1) $\uparrow x:=\{y\in U\#\ \mathcal{A}_x\subseteq\mathcal{A}_y\}$ and $\downarrow x:=\{y\in U\#\ \mathcal{A}_y\subseteq\mathcal{A}_x\}$.

(2) $\uparrow_+ x:=\{y\in U\#\ \mathcal{A}_x\subset\mathcal{A}_y\}$ and $\downarrow_+ x:=\{y\in U\#\ \mathcal{A}_y\subset\mathcal{A}_x\}$.

Remark: In Definition 2.1(1), if $\mathcal{A}_x\subseteq\mathcal{A}_y$, $x,y\in U$, then we call the object y is better than object x (or object x is worse than object y), and we are more satisfied with y. From the perspective of inclusion between attribute subsets, the advantages and disadvantages between objects are strictly described. A subset $\uparrow x$ of U is called an advantage neighborhood of object x, that is, $\uparrow x$ describes all objects that are better than or the same as x. A subset $\downarrow x$ of U is called a disadvantage neighborhood of object x, that is, $\downarrow x$ describes all objects that are worse than or the same as x.

In Definition 2.1(2), A subset $\uparrow_+x$ of U is called an advantage neighborhood of object x, that is, $\uparrow_+x$ describes all objects that are better than x. A subset $\downarrow_+x$ of U is called a disadvantage neighborhood of object x, that is, $\downarrow_+x$ describes all objects that are worse than x.

According to Definition 2.1, We define some special objects.

Definition 2.2: Let $S=\{U,Q,V,f\}$ be an IS, and $x,y\in U$.

(1) If for any $y\in U$, $x\in\uparrow y$ or $y\in\downarrow x$, then x is called *a Maximum object*, also called absolute maximum.

(2) If for any $y \in U$, $x \in \downarrow y$ or $y \in \uparrow x$, then x is called *a Minimum object*, also called absolute minimum.
(3) If $x = \uparrow x$, then x is called *a maximum object*, also called local maximum, Max_U is the set of all maximum objects.
(4) If $x = \downarrow x$, then x is called *a minimum object*, also called local minimum, Min_U is the set of all minimum objects.

Based on the above definition, the following properties can be obtained

Theorem 2.1: Let$S = \{U, Q, V, f\}$ be an IS and $x \in U$. Then the followings are established.
(1) If $y \in \uparrow x$ and $z \in \uparrow y$, then $z \in \uparrow x$.
(2) If $y \in \downarrow x$ and $z \in \downarrow y$, then $z \in \downarrow x$.
(3) $x \in \downarrow y$ implies $\downarrow x \subseteq \downarrow y$; $x \in \uparrow y$ implies $\uparrow x \subseteq \uparrow y$.
Proof. According to Definition 2.1, obviously.

According to Definition 2.1, we define a type (local) advantage neighborhood and (local) disadvantage neighborhood of an object group X ($X \subseteq U$).

Definition 2.3: Let $S = \{U, Q, V, f\}$ be an IS and an object group $X \subseteq U$.
(1) The local advantage and local disadvantage neighborhoods of X are respectively defined as:

$$\underline{\uparrow} X = \bigcap_{x \in X} \{y \in U \# \uparrow y \subseteq \uparrow x\} \text{ and } \underline{\downarrow} X = \bigcap_{x \in X} \{y \in U \# \downarrow y \subseteq \downarrow x\}.$$

(2) The advantage and disadvantage neighborhood of X are respectively defined as:

$$\overline{\uparrow} X = \bigcup_{x \in X} \{y \in U \# \uparrow x \cap \{y\} \neq \varnothing\} \text{ and } \overline{\downarrow} X = \bigcup_{x \in X} \{y \in U \# \downarrow x \cap \{y\} \neq \varnothing\}.$$

Remark:For an IS, the advantages and disadvantages of the object groups are analyzed by combining the local advantage and local disadvantage neighborhoods. They illustrate the advantages and disadvantages of object groups from different perspectives. Definition 2.3 (1) provided a method to judge the advantages and disadvantages of an object group. This point can be thoroughly illustrated by assuming two object groups X_1, X_2, in which X_1 is better than X_2. Then $\underline{\uparrow} X_1 \subseteq \underline{\uparrow} X_2$ and $\underline{\downarrow} X_1 \supseteq \underline{\downarrow} X_2$. By contrast, if $\underline{\uparrow} X_1 \supseteq \underline{\uparrow} X_2$ and $\underline{\downarrow} X_1 \subseteq \underline{\downarrow} X_2$, then X_2 is better than X_1. The semantic expression is as follows: the smaller the local advantage neighborhood of the object group is, the better the object group will be; the bigger the local disadvantage neighborhood of the object group is, the better the object group will be. Definition of $\underline{\uparrow} X$ in Definition 2.3 (1) is easy to make people mistakenly believe that $\uparrow x \subseteq \uparrow y$ in order to make the concept and semantic interpretation of the definition consistent. However, the original definition of $\uparrow y \subseteq \uparrow x$ is correct. If $\uparrow y \subseteq \uparrow x$, it means that y contains not only all the properties of x, but may also contain properties that x does not have. Once y has more attributes than x (generally, it is considered that the number of objects with more attributes is less), the value of $|\uparrow y|$ will become smaller, which is why $\uparrow y \subseteq \uparrow x$ is defined. The concepts and semantics of Definition 2.3 (2) are linked through consistency. On the one hand, if x contains many attributes, then y satisfying condition $\uparrow y \subseteq \uparrow x$ is very few, so $|\underline{\uparrow} X|$ is very small. On the other hand, if X contains x with more attributes, X is better as a whole. The situation of other $\underline{\downarrow} X$, $\overline{\uparrow} X$ and $\overline{\downarrow} X$ is similar to that of $\underline{\uparrow} X$.

Combined with the semantics of Definition 2.3, we define the following degrees to analyze object groups.

Definition 2.4: Let $S=\{U,Q,V,f\}$ be an IS and an object group $X \subseteq U$.

Let $S=\{U,Q,V,f\}$ be an IS and $X \subseteq U$.

(1) The local advantage-disadvantage degree (LADD) of X is defined as:

$$\mathrm{LADD}(X)=\frac{|\underline{\uparrow} X|}{|\underline{\downarrow} X|+1}.$$

(2) The advantage-disadvantage degree (ADD) of $X$is defined as:

$$\mathrm{ADD}(X)=\frac{|\overline{\uparrow} X|}{|\overline{\downarrow} X|+1}.$$

(3) The mixed advantage-disadvantage degree (MADD) of X is defined as:

$$\mathrm{MADD}(X)=\frac{|\underline{\uparrow} X|}{|\underline{\downarrow} X|+1}+\frac{|\overline{\uparrow} X|}{|\overline{\downarrow} X|+1}.$$

Remark: By Definition 2.4 (1), the smaller the local advantage neighborhood of the object group is, the better the object group will be; the bigger the local disadvantage neighborhood of the object group is, the better the object group will be. Hence, the smaller the LADD of the object group is, the better the object group in an IS will be.

By Definition 2.4 (2), the smaller the advantage neighborhood of the object group is, the better the object subset will be; the bigger the disadvantage neighborhood of the object group is, the better the object group will be. Hence, the smaller the ADD of the object group is, the better the object group in an IS will be.

By fusing Definitions 2.4 (1) and (2), the smaller the MADD of the object group is, the better the object group in an IS will be.

Advantage (Disadvantage) Neighborhood Operators and Advantage-Disadvantage Neighborhood Degrees

This section is the core of the theoretical basis of the improved GMADMDRS method, including the advantage (disadvantage) neighborhood operator, the advantage-disadvantage neighborhood degree, which are the major changes compared to the method in GOMADMMADD. Therefore, in addition to analyzing their differences and connections, we also explained the purpose of this design.

Definition 2.5: For an IS $S=\{U,Q,V,f\}$, we have

(1) The $C_1=Max_U$ is called a 1st level object set, also called a optimal object set;

(2) The $C_2=\{x\in U \mid \uparrow_+ x\subseteq Max_U\}$ is called a 2nd level object set, also called a suboptimal object set;

(3) The $C_3=\{x\in U \mid \uparrow_+ x\subseteq Max_U\cup C_2\}$ is called a 3rd level object set;

(4) The $C_4=\{x\in U \mid \uparrow_+ x\subseteq Max_U\cup C_2\cup C_3\}$ is called a 4th level object set;

...

(K) The $C_k=\{x\in U \mid \uparrow_+ x\subseteq Max_U\cup C_2\cup C_3\cup\ldots\cup C_{k-1}\}$ is called a *k*-th level object set;

...

Remark: Definition 2.5 is not mentioned in GOMADMMADD's article. This definition divides the entire information system into a hierarchical structure, which provides a framework for the subsequent optimization of GMADMDRS.

According to Definition 2.1, we define two type neighborhood operators of an object subset $X(X\subseteq U)$.

Definition 2.6: Let $S=\{U,A,f,V\}$ be an IS and an object subset $X\subseteq U$.

(1) The advantage lower neighborhood operator and advantage upper neighborhood operator of X are respectively defined as:

$$\underline{D^{\uparrow}}(X)=\bigcap_{x\in X}\uparrow x \text{ and } \overline{D^{\uparrow}}(X)=\bigcup_{x\in X}\uparrow x.$$

(2) The disadvantage lower neighborhood operator and disadvantage upper neighborhood operator of X are respectively defined as:

$$\underline{D^{\downarrow}}(X)=\bigcap_{x\in X}\downarrow x \text{ and } \overline{D^{\downarrow}}(X)=\bigcup_{x\in X}\downarrow x.$$

Remark: For an IS, the advantage and disadvantage of the object subset are analyzed by combining two type neighborhood operators. They illustrate the advantage and disadvantage of object subsets from different perspectives. Definition 2.6 (1) provided a method to judge the advantage and disadvantage of an object subset. This point can be thoroughly illustrated by assuming two object groups X_1, X_2, in which

X_1 is better than X_2. Then $\underline{D}^{\uparrow}(X_1)\subseteq\underline{D}^{\uparrow}(X_2)$ and $\underline{D}^{\downarrow}(X_1)\supseteq\underline{D}^{\downarrow}(X_2)$. By contrast, if $\underline{D}^{\uparrow}(X_1)\supseteq\underline{D}^{\uparrow}(X_2)$ and $\underline{D}^{\downarrow}(X_1)\subseteq\underline{D}^{\downarrow}(X_2)$, then X_2 is better than X_1. The semantic expression is as follows: the smaller is the advantage lower neighborhood of the object subset, the better the object subset; the bigger is the disadvantage lower neighborhood of the object subset, the better the object subset. For Definition 2.6 (2), $\overline{D^{\uparrow}}(X)$ represents the set of object subset that includes in the advantage upper neighborhood of *X*; $\overline{D^{\downarrow}}(X)$ represents the set of object subset that includes in the disadvantage upper neighborhood of *X*. They explain the neighborhood between the object subset in an IS from different perspectives. The semantic expression is as follows: the smaller is the advantage upper neighborhood of the object subset, the better the object subset; the bigger is the disadvantage upper neighborhood of the object subset, the better the object subset.

Theorem 2.2: Let *S*={*U*,*A*,*f*,*V*} be an IS. For any $X, X_1, X_2 \subseteq U$, we have

(1) $\underline{D}^{\uparrow}(\{x\})=\overline{D^{\uparrow}}(\{x\})=D^{\uparrow}(x),\underline{D}^{\downarrow}(\{x\})=\overline{D^{\downarrow}}(\{x\})=D^{\downarrow}(x).$

(2) $\underline{D}^{\uparrow}(X)\subseteq\overline{D^{\uparrow}}(X),\underline{D}^{\downarrow}(X)\subseteq\overline{D^{\downarrow}}(X),X\subseteq\overline{D^{\uparrow}}(X),X\subseteq\overline{D^{\downarrow}}(X).$

(3) $X_1\subseteq X_2\Rightarrow\underline{D}^{\uparrow}(X_2)\subseteq\underline{D}^{\uparrow}(X_1),\underline{D}^{\downarrow}(X_2)\subseteq\underline{D}^{\downarrow}(X_1),$

$\overline{D^{\uparrow}}(X_1)\subseteq\overline{D^{\uparrow}}(X_2),\overline{D^{\downarrow}}(X_1)\subseteq\overline{D^{\downarrow}}(X_2).$

(4) $\underline{D}^{\uparrow}(X_1\cap X_2)\supseteq\underline{D}^{\uparrow}(X_1)\cup\underline{D}^{\uparrow}(X_2)\supseteq\underline{D}^{\uparrow}(X_1\cup X_2)=\underline{D}^{\uparrow}(X_1)\cap\underline{D}^{\uparrow}(X_2).$

(5) $\underline{D}^{\downarrow}(X_1\cap X_2)\supseteq\underline{D}^{\downarrow}(X_1)\cup\underline{D}^{\downarrow}(X_2)\supseteq\underline{D}^{\downarrow}(X_1\cup X_2)=\underline{D}^{\downarrow}(X_1)\cap\underline{D}^{\downarrow}(X_2)$

(6) $\overline{D^{\uparrow}}(X_1\cap X_2)\supseteq\overline{D^{\uparrow}}(X_1)\cup\overline{D^{\uparrow}}(X_2),\underline{D}^{\uparrow}(X_1\cup X_2)=\underline{D}^{\uparrow}(X_1)\cup\underline{D}^{\uparrow}(X_2).$

(7) $\overline{D^{\downarrow}}(X_1\cap X_2)\supseteq\overline{D^{\downarrow}}(X_1)\cup\overline{D^{\downarrow}}(X_2),\underline{D}^{\downarrow}(X_1\cup X_2)=\underline{D}^{\downarrow}(X_1)\cup\underline{D}^{\downarrow}(X_2).$

Proof. We only show (4). The other properties can be proven similarly.

For any $x\in\underline{D}^{\uparrow}(X_1)\cap\underline{D}^{\uparrow}(X_2)$, we have $D^{\uparrow}(x)\subseteq D^{\uparrow}(a)$ for any $a\in X_1$ and $D^{\uparrow}(x)\subseteq D^{\uparrow}(b)$ for any $b\in X_2$. Hence, $x\in\underline{D}^{\uparrow}(X_1\cup X_2)$. So, $D^{\uparrow}(x)\subseteq D^{\uparrow}(a)$ for any $a\in X_1$ or $D^{\uparrow}(x)\subseteq D^{\uparrow}(b)$ for any $b\in X_2$, that is, $x\in\underline{D}^{\uparrow}(X_1)\cup\underline{D}^{\uparrow}(X_2)$. If $x\in\underline{D}^{\uparrow}(X_1)$, then $D^{\uparrow}(x)\subseteq D^{\uparrow}(a)$ for any $a\in X_1$. So, $D^{\uparrow}(x)\subseteq D^{\uparrow}(a)$ for any $a\in X_1\cap X_2$, that is, $x\in\underline{D}^{\uparrow}(X_1\cap X_2)$. If $x\in\underline{D}^{\uparrow}(X_2)$, then $D^{\uparrow}(x)\subseteq D^{\uparrow}(b)$ for any $b\in X_2$. So, $D^{\uparrow}(x)\subseteq D^{\uparrow}(b)$ for any $b\in X_1\cap X_2$, that is, $x\in\underline{D}^{\uparrow}(X_1\cap X_2)$. Therefore, $x\in\underline{D}^{\uparrow}(X_1\cap X_2)$. Hence,

$$\underline{D}^{\uparrow}(X_1\cap X_2)\supseteq\underline{D}^{\uparrow}(X_1)\cup\underline{D}^{\uparrow}(X_2)\supseteq\underline{D}^{\uparrow}(X_1\cup X_2)\supseteq\underline{D}^{\uparrow}(X_1)\cap\underline{D}^{\uparrow}(X_2).$$

For any $x \in \underline{D^{\uparrow}}(X_1 \cup X_2)$, we have $D^{\uparrow}(x) \subseteq D^{\uparrow}(a)$ for any $a \in X_1 \cup X_2$. So, $D^{\uparrow}(x) \subseteq D^{\uparrow}(a)$ for any $a \in X_1$ and $D^{\uparrow}(x) \subseteq D^{\uparrow}(b)$ for any $b \in X_2$. Hence, $x \in \underline{D^{\uparrow}}(X_1) \cap \underline{D^{\uparrow}}(X_2)$. So, $\underline{D^{\uparrow}}(X_1 \cup X_2) \subseteq \underline{D^{\uparrow}}(X_1) \cap \underline{D^{\uparrow}}(X_2)$.

For any $x \in \underline{D^{\uparrow}}(X_1 \cup X_2)$, we have $D^{\uparrow}(x) \subseteq D^{\uparrow}(a)$ for any $a \in X_1 \cup X_2$. So, $D^{\uparrow}(x) \subseteq D^{\uparrow}(a)$ for any $a \in X_1$ and $D^{\uparrow}(x) \subseteq D^{\uparrow}(b)$ for any $b \in X_2$. Hence, $x \in \underline{D^{\uparrow}}(X_1) \cap \underline{D^{\uparrow}}(X_2)$. So, $\underline{D^{\uparrow}}(X_1 \cup X_2) \subseteq \underline{D^{\uparrow}}(X_1) \cap \underline{D^{\uparrow}}(X_2)$. Therefore,

$$\underline{D^{\uparrow}}(X_1 \cap X_2) \supseteq \underline{D^{\uparrow}}(X_1) \cup \underline{D^{\uparrow}}(X_2) \supseteq \underline{D^{\uparrow}}(X_1 \cup X_2) = \underline{D^{\uparrow}}(X_1) \cap \underline{D^{\uparrow}}(X_2).$$

Combined with the semantics of Definition 2.6, we define the following degree to analyze an object subset.

Definition 2.7: Let $S=\{U,A,f,V\}$ be an IS and $X \subseteq U$. The advantage-disadvantage neighborhood degree (ADND) of X is defined as:

$$\text{ADND}(X) = \frac{\left|\underline{D^{\uparrow}}(X)\right|+1}{\left|\underline{D^{\downarrow}}(X)\right|+1} \cdot \frac{\left|\overline{D^{\uparrow}}(X)\right|}{\left|\overline{D^{\downarrow}}(X)\right|}.$$

Remark: According to the semantics of Definitions 2.7 (1) and (2), the smaller is the $|D|$ of the object subset, the better the object subset in an IS. In particular, $\underline{D^{\uparrow}}(X)$ and $\underline{D^{\downarrow}}(X)$ become empty sets, $\overline{D^{\uparrow}}(X)$ and $\overline{D^{\downarrow}}(X)$ not become empty sets.We add 1 after $\left|\underline{D^{\uparrow}}(X)\right|$ and $\left|\underline{D^{\downarrow}}(X)\right|$ to avoid that the denominator and numerator are 0 and affect the meaning of ADND .

In the GOMADMMADD method, firstly, the group metric is constructed by using the object's advantage set ($\uparrow x$) and disadvantaged neighborhood set ($\downarrow x$) combined with the idea of rough set approximation. These include local advantage neighborhoods ($\underline{\uparrow} X$) and local disadvantage neighborhoods ($\underline{\downarrow} X$), advantage neighborhoods ($\overline{\uparrow} X$) and disadvantage neighborhoods ($\overline{\downarrow} X$). Secondly, the local advantage-disadvantage neighborhood degree (LADD) is constructed with the help of local advantage and disadvantage neighborhood, and the advantage-disadvantage neighborhood degree (ADD) is constructed with the help of advantage and disadvantage neighborhood. Finally, the subject group's mixed advantage-disadvantage degree (MADD) was constructed by linear combination of LADD and ADD. It is not difficult to see that the idea of MADD is to measure groups from a local and global perspective. The advantage of this is that more comprehensive information can be used, but the disadvantage is that the designed MADD lacks some properties that are conducive to optimization. In the GMADMDRS method of this paper, firstly, the advantage set ($D^{\uparrow}(x)$) and disadvantage set ($D^{\downarrow}(x)$) of the object are combined with the approximation idea of rough set to construct a group metrics. Include advantage lower neighborhood operator ($\underline{D^{\uparrow}}(X)$) and advantage upper neighborhood operator ($\overline{D^{\uparrow}}(X)$), disadvantage lower neighborhood operator ($\underline{D^{\downarrow}}(X)$) and disadvantage upper neighborhood operator

$\left(\overline{D^{\downarrow}}(X)\right)$. Secondly, the groups are measured separately from the perspective of advantage and disadvantage, which are important because they have similar properties, and then the advantage and disadvantage measures are combined nonlinearly to obtain the advantage-disadvantages neighborhood degree (ADND). It can be seen that ADND considers the advantages and disadvantages, but also considers the local and global, which is reflected in the lower and upper neighborhoods. To sum up, the essential difference between ADND and MADD lies in the different angles of consideration and the different forms of combination, and the resulting change in properties is the real purpose. This is also the reason to consider improving MADD to ADND. Using the properties of ADND can optimize the method and reduce the problems caused by exponential explosion, which MADD cannot.

In order to better understand the ADND, we study their related properties as follows:

Theorem 2.3: Let $S=\{U,A,f,V\}$ be an IS, $x,y,z\in U$, $X_1, X_2 \subseteq U$. Then

(1) If $x\leq y$, then ADND($\{x\}$)≥ADND($\{y\}$).

(2) If $x\in Max_U$ and $X \subseteq U$, then $\exists y\in U\backslash Max_U$, s.t. $ADND\left(X\cup\{x\}\right)\leq ADND\left(X\cup\{y\}\right)$. In particular, if $x\in U$, $z\in U\backslash Max_U$, then $\exists y\in Max_U$, s.t. ADND($\{x,y\}$)≤ADND($\{x,z\}$); if $z\in U\backslash Max_U$, then $ADND\left(Max_U\right)\leq ADND\left(Max_U\cup\{z\}\right)$.

(3) If $x\in Min_U$ and $X \subseteq U$, then $\exists y\in U\backslash Min_U$, s.t. $ADND\left(\mathrm{X}\cup\{\mathrm{y}\}\right)\leq ADND\left(\mathrm{X}\cup\{\mathrm{x}\}\right)$. In particular, if $x\in U$, $z\in U\backslash Min_U$, then $\exists y\in Min_U$, s.t. ADND($\{x,y\}$)≥ADND($\{x,z\}$);if $z\in U\backslash Min_U$, then $ADND\left(Min_U\right)\geq ADND\left(Min_U\cup\{z\}\right)$.

(4) If $y\in C_k$, then $\exists x\in C_{k-1}$, s.t. $ADND\left(\bigcup_{i=1}^{k-2}C_i\cup\{x\}\right)\leq ADND\left(\bigcup_{i=1}^{k-2}C_i\cup\{y\}\right)$.

(5) If $x,y\in Max_U$ with ADND($\{x\}$)≤ADND($\{y\}$), then ADND($\{x\}$)≤ADND($\{x,y\}$).

(6) If $x,y,z\in Max_U$ with ADND($\{x\}$)≤ADND($\{y\}$)≤ADND($\{z\}$), then ADND($\{x,y\}$)≤ADND($\{x,z\}$).

(7) If $x,y\in Max_U$, then $|D^{\downarrow}(x)|\geq|D^{\downarrow}(y)|$ if and only if ADND($\{x\}$)≤ADND($\{y\}$).

(8) If $x,y\in Min_U$, then $|D^{\uparrow}(x)|\geq|D^{\uparrow}(y)|$ if and only if ADND($\{x\}$)≥ADND($\{y\}$).

(9) If x is a Minimum object, then ADND($\{x\}$)=$|U|$; If x is a Maximum object, then $ADND\left(\{x\}\right)=\frac{2}{|U|+1}$. In particular, $\frac{2}{|U|+1}\leq ADND\left(\{y\}\right)\leq|U|$, $\forall y\in U$.

(10) For any $X\subseteq U\backslash\left(Min_U\cup Max_U\right)$,

$$ADND\left(X\right)\leq ADND\left(Min_U\right)=\frac{2|U|}{|Min_U|+1}, ADND\left(X\right)\geq ADND\left(Max_U\right)=\frac{2|Max_U|}{|U|+1}.$$

In particular, $\frac{2|Max_U|}{|U|+1}\leq ADND\left(X\right)\leq\frac{2|U|}{|Min_U|+1}$.

Proof. (1) Suppose $y\in D^{\uparrow}(x)$. Then $D^{\uparrow}\left(y\right)\subseteq D^{\uparrow}\left(x\right) and D^{\downarrow}\left(y\right)\supseteq D^{\downarrow}\left(x\right)$ by Theorem 2.1 (3) and (4). By Theorem 2.2 (1),

$$\underline{D^{\uparrow}}(\{x\}) = \overline{D^{\uparrow}}(\{x\}) = D^{\uparrow}(x), \underline{D^{\downarrow}}(\{x\}) = \overline{D^{\downarrow}}(\{x\}) = D^{\downarrow}(x).$$

Hence, $\dfrac{|D^{\uparrow}(x)|+1}{|D^{\downarrow}(x)|+1} \cdot \dfrac{|D^{\uparrow}(x)|}{|D^{\downarrow}(x)|} \geq \dfrac{|D^{\uparrow}(y)|+1}{|D^{\downarrow}(y)|+1} \cdot \dfrac{|D^{\uparrow}(y)|}{|D^{\downarrow}(y)|}$.

Therefore, ADND($\{x\}$)≥ADND($\{y\}$).

(2) Since $x \in Max_U$, there exist $y \in U \backslash Max_U$ with $y \leq x$. Then $D^{\downarrow}(y) \subseteq D^{\downarrow}(x)$ and $D^{\uparrow}(x) \subseteq D^{\uparrow}(y)$. By Definition 2.7, $X \subseteq U$, we have

$$ADND(X \cup \{x\}) = \frac{|\underline{D^{\uparrow}}(X \cup \{x\})|+1}{|\underline{D^{\downarrow}}(X \cup \{x\})|+1} \cdot \frac{|\overline{D^{\uparrow}}(X \cup \{x\})|}{|\overline{D^{\downarrow}}(X \cup \{x\})|}$$

$$= \frac{\left|\bigcap_{z \in X} D^{\uparrow}(z) \cap D^{\uparrow}(x)\right|+1}{\left|\bigcap_{z \in X} D^{\downarrow}(z) \cap D^{\downarrow}(x)\right|+1} \cdot \frac{\left|\bigcup_{z \in X} D^{\uparrow}(z) \cup D^{\uparrow}(x)\right|}{\left|\bigcup_{z \in X} D^{\downarrow}(z) \cup D^{\downarrow}(x)\right|}$$

$$\leq \frac{\left|\bigcap_{z \in X} D^{\uparrow}(z) \cap D^{\uparrow}(y)\right|+1}{\left|\bigcap_{z \in X} D^{\downarrow}(z) \cap D^{\downarrow}(y)\right|+1} \cdot \frac{\left|\bigcup_{z \in X} D^{\uparrow}(z) \cup D^{\uparrow}(y)\right|}{\left|\bigcup_{z \in X} D^{\downarrow}(z) \cup D^{\downarrow}(y)\right|}$$

$$= ADND(X \cup \{y\}).$$

Therefore, $ADND(X \cup \{x\}) \leq ADND(X \cup \{y\})$. Other proofs are obviously.

(3) The proof is similar to (2).

(4) Since $y \in C_k$, there exist $\exists x \in C_{k-1}$ with $y \leq x$ by Definition 2.5. Then $D^{\downarrow}(y) \subseteq D^{\downarrow}(x)$ and $D^{\uparrow}(x) \subseteq D^{\uparrow}(y)$. By Definition 2.7, $X \subseteq U$, we have

$$ADND\left(\bigcup_{i=1}^{k-2} \circ C_i \cup \{x\}\right) = \frac{\left|\underline{D^{\uparrow}}\left(\bigcap_{i=1}^{k-2} \circ C_i \cup \{x\}\right)\right| + 1}{\left|\underline{D^{\downarrow}}\left(\bigcap_{i=1}^{k-2} \circ C_i \cup \{x\}\right)\right| + 1} \cdot \frac{\left|\overline{D^{\uparrow}}\left(\bigcup_{i=1}^{k-2} \circ C_i \cup \{x\}\right)\right|}{\left|\overline{D^{\downarrow}}\left(\bigcup_{i=1}^{k-2} \circ C_i \cup \{x\}\right)\right|}$$

$$= \frac{\left|\bigcap_{z \in \bigcap_{i=1}^{k-2} \circ C_i} D^{\uparrow}(z) \cap D^{\uparrow}(x)\right| + 1}{\left|\bigcap_{z \in \bigcap_{i=1}^{k-2} \circ C_i} D^{\downarrow}(z) \cap D^{\downarrow}(x)\right| + 1} \cdot \frac{\left|\bigcup_{z \in \bigcup_{i=1}^{k-2} \circ C_i} D^{\uparrow}(z) \cup D^{\uparrow}(x)\right|}{\left|\bigcup_{z \in \bigcup_{i=1}^{k-2} \circ C_i} D^{\downarrow}(z) \cup D^{\downarrow}(x)\right|}$$

$$\leq \frac{\left|\bigcap_{z \in \bigcap_{i=1}^{k-2} \circ C_i} D^{\uparrow}(z) \cap D^{\uparrow}(y)\right| + 1}{\left|\bigcap_{z \in \bigcap_{i=1}^{k-2} \circ C_i} D^{\downarrow}(z) \cap D^{\downarrow}(y)\right| + 1} \cdot \frac{\left|\bigcup_{z \in \bigcup_{i=1}^{k-2} \circ C_i} D^{\uparrow}(z) \cup D^{\uparrow}(y)\right|}{\left|\bigcup_{z \in \bigcup_{i=1}^{k-2} \circ C_i} D^{\downarrow}(z) \cup D^{\downarrow}(y)\right|}$$

$$= ADND\left(\bigcup_{i=1}^{k-2} \circ C_i \cup \{y\}\right).$$

Therefore, $ADND\left(\bigcup_{i=1}^{k-2} \circ C_i \cup \{x\}\right) \leq ADND\left(\bigcup_{i=1}^{k-2} \circ C_i \cup \{y\}\right)$.

(5) Since $x, y \in Max_U$ with ADND($\{x\}$)≤ADND($\{y\}$), we have $|D^{\downarrow}(x)| \geq |D^{\downarrow}(y)| \geq 1$, and $|D^{\downarrow}(x)|, |D^{\downarrow}(y)| \in Z^+$ (Z^+ is a set of positive integers). By Definition 2.7 and Theorem 2.2, we have

ADND($\{x\}$) – ADND($\{x,y\}$)

$$= \frac{\left|\underline{D^{\uparrow}}(\{x\})\right| + 1}{\left|\underline{D^{\downarrow}}(\{x\})\right| + 1} \cdot \frac{\left|\overline{D^{\uparrow}}(\{x\})\right|}{\left|\overline{D^{\downarrow}}(\{x\})\right|} - \frac{\left|\underline{D^{\uparrow}}(\{x, y\})\right| + 1}{\left|\underline{D^{\downarrow}}(\{x, y\})\right| + 1} \cdot \frac{\left|\overline{D^{\uparrow}}(\{x, y\})\right|}{\left|\overline{D^{\downarrow}}(\{x, y\})\right|}$$

$$= \frac{\left|D^{\uparrow}(x)\right| + 1}{\left|D^{\downarrow}(x)\right| + 1} \cdot \frac{\left|D^{\uparrow}(x)\right|}{\left|D^{\downarrow}(x)\right|} - \frac{\left|D^{\uparrow}(x) \cap D^{\uparrow}(y)\right| + 1}{\left|D^{\downarrow}(x) \cap D^{\downarrow}(y)\right| + 1} \cdot \frac{\left|D^{\uparrow}(x) \cup D^{\uparrow}(y)\right|}{\left|D^{\downarrow}(x) \cup D^{\downarrow}(y)\right|}$$

$$= \frac{2}{\left|D^{\downarrow}(x)\right| + 1} \cdot \frac{1}{\left|D^{\downarrow}(x)\right|} - \frac{1}{\left|D^{\downarrow}(x) \cap D^{\downarrow}(y)\right| + 1} \cdot \frac{2}{\left|D^{\downarrow}(x) \cup D^{\downarrow}(y)\right|}$$

Suppose that $\left|D^{\downarrow}(x) \cap D^{\downarrow}(y)\right| = t\left|D^{\downarrow}(x)\right|$, $t \in (0,1)$. Since

$$\left|D^{\downarrow}(x)\cup D^{\downarrow}(y)\right|=\left|D^{\downarrow}(x)\right|+\left|D^{\downarrow}(y)\right|-\left|D^{\downarrow}(x)\cap D^{\downarrow}(y)\right|,$$

we have

$$\frac{2}{\left|D^{\downarrow}(x)\right|+1}\cdot\frac{1}{\left|D^{\downarrow}(x)\right|}-\frac{1}{\left|D^{\downarrow}(x)\cap D^{\downarrow}(y)\right|+1}\cdot\frac{2}{\left|D^{\downarrow}(x)\cup D^{\downarrow}(y)\right|}$$

$$=\frac{2}{\left|D^{\downarrow}(x)\right|+1}\cdot\frac{1}{\left|D^{\downarrow}(x)\right|}-\frac{1}{t\left|D^{\downarrow}(x)\right|+1}\cdot\frac{2}{\left|D^{\downarrow}(x)\right|+\left|D^{\downarrow}(y)\right|-t\left|D^{\downarrow}(x)\right|}$$

$$=2\cdot\frac{\left|D^{\downarrow}(x)\right|^{2}t^{2}-\left|D^{\downarrow}(x)\right|^{2}t+\left|D^{\downarrow}(x)\right|^{2}-\left|D^{\downarrow}(x)\right|\left|D^{\downarrow}(y)\right|t+\left|D^{\downarrow}(x)\right|t-\left|D^{\downarrow}(y)\right|}{\left|D^{\downarrow}(x)\right|\left(\left|D^{\downarrow}(x)\right|+1\right)\left(\left|D^{\downarrow}(x)\right|t+1\right)\left(\left|D^{\downarrow}(x)\right|t-\left|D^{\downarrow}(x)\right|-\left|D^{\downarrow}(y)\right|\right)}$$

Since

$$\left|D^{\downarrow}(x)\right|\left(\left|D^{\downarrow}(x)\right|+1\right)\left(\left|D^{\downarrow}(x)\right|t+1\right)\left(\left|D^{\downarrow}(x)\right|t-\left|D^{\downarrow}(x)\right|-\left|D^{\downarrow}(y)\right|\right)<0,$$

and

$$\min\left\{\left|D^{\downarrow}(x)\right|^{2}t^{2}-\left|D^{\downarrow}(x)\right|^{2}t+\left|D^{\downarrow}(x)\right|^{2}-\left|D^{\downarrow}(x)\right|\left|D^{\downarrow}(y)\right|t+\left|D^{\downarrow}(x)\right|t-\left|D^{\downarrow}(y)\right|\right\}$$

$$=\begin{cases}0, & \left|D^{\downarrow}(x)\right|=\left|D^{\downarrow}(y)\right|=1,\\ \dfrac{3\left|D^{\downarrow}(x)\right|^{2}}{4}-1, & \left|D^{\downarrow}(y)\right|=1 \text{ and } \left|D^{\downarrow}(x)\right|>\left|D^{\downarrow}(y)\right|,\\ \dfrac{1}{4\left(3\left|D^{\downarrow}(x)\right|^{2}-2\left|D^{\downarrow}(x)\right|\left(\left|D^{\downarrow}(y)\right|-1\right)-\left(\left|D^{\downarrow}(y)\right|+1\right)^{2}\right)}, & \left|D^{\downarrow}(y)\right|>1 \text{ and } \left|D^{\downarrow}(x)\right|\geq\left|D^{\downarrow}(y)\right|,\end{cases}$$

then

$$\min\left\{\left|D^{\downarrow}(x)\right|^{2}t^{2}-\left|D^{\downarrow}(x)\right|^{2}t+\left|D^{\downarrow}(x)\right|^{2}-\left|D^{\downarrow}(x)\right|\left|D^{\downarrow}(y)\right|t+\left|D^{\downarrow}(x)\right|t-\left|D^{\downarrow}(y)\right|\right\}\geq 0.$$

So,

$$\frac{2}{\left|D^{\downarrow}(x)\right|+1}\cdot\frac{1}{\left|D^{\downarrow}(x)\right|}-\frac{1}{\left|D^{\downarrow}(x)\cap D^{\downarrow}(y)\right|+1}\cdot\frac{2}{\left|D^{\downarrow}(x)\cup D^{\downarrow}(y)\right|}\leq 0,$$

that is, ADND($\{x\}$) – ADND($\{x,y\}$)$\leq$0, where $|D^{\downarrow}(x)|\geq|D^{\downarrow}(y)|\geq 1$, and $|D^{\downarrow}(x)|$, $|D^{\downarrow}(y)|\in Z^{+}$, $t\in(0,1)$.

In particular, when t=0, that is,

$$\begin{aligned} D^{\downarrow}(x)\cap D^{\downarrow}(y) &= ADND(\{x\})-ADND(\{x,y\}) \\ &= \frac{2}{\left|D^{\downarrow}(x)\right|+1}\cdot\frac{1}{\left|D^{\downarrow}(x)\right|}-\frac{2}{\left|D^{\downarrow}(x)\right|+\left|D^{\downarrow}(y)\right|} <;, \end{aligned}$$

when t=1, that is, $D^{\downarrow}(x)=D^{\downarrow}(y)$, ADND($\{x\}$) – ADND($\{x,y\}$) = 0.

Therefore, ADND($\{x\}$)$\leq$ADND($\{x,y\}$), $x,y\in Max_U$ with ADND($\{x\}$)$\leq$ADND($\{y\}$).

(6) The proof is similar to (5)

(7) By Definition 2.7 and Theorem 2.2 (1),

$$ADND(\{x\})=\frac{\left|\underline{D}^{\uparrow}(\{x\})\right|+1}{\left|\underline{D}^{\downarrow}(\{x\})\right|+1}\cdot\frac{\left|\overline{D}^{\uparrow}(\{x\})\right|}{\left|\overline{D}^{\downarrow}(\{x\})\right|}, ADND(\{y\})=\frac{\left|\underline{D}^{\uparrow}(\{y\})\right|+1}{\left|\underline{D}^{\downarrow}(\{y\})\right|+1}\cdot\frac{\left|\overline{D}^{\uparrow}(\{y\})\right|}{\left|\overline{D}^{\downarrow}(\{y\})\right|}.$$

Since $|D^{\downarrow}(x)|\geq|D^{\downarrow}(y)|$, $x,y\in Max_U$, we have

$$\text{ADND}(\{x\})=\frac{\left|\underline{D}^{\uparrow}(\{x\})\right|+1}{\left|\underline{D}^{\downarrow}(\{x\})\right|+1}\cdot\frac{\left|\overline{D}^{\uparrow}(\{x\})\right|}{\left|\overline{D}^{\downarrow}(\{x\})\right|}$$

$$=\frac{\left|D^{\uparrow}(x)\right|+1}{\left|D^{\downarrow}(x)\right|+1}\cdot\frac{\left|D^{\uparrow}(x)\right|}{\left|D^{\downarrow}(x)\right|}\leq\frac{\left|D^{\uparrow}(y)\right|+1}{\left|D^{\downarrow}(y)\right|+1}\cdot\frac{\left|D^{\uparrow}(y)\right|}{\left|D^{\downarrow}(y)\right|}$$

$$=\frac{\left|\underline{D}^{\uparrow}(\{y\})\right|+1}{\left|\underline{D}^{\downarrow}(\{y\})\right|+1}\cdot\frac{\left|\overline{D}^{\uparrow}(\{y\})\right|}{\left|\overline{D}^{\downarrow}(\{y\})\right|}=\text{ADND}(\{y\}),$$

so ADND($\{x\}$)$\leq$ADND($\{y\}$).

Since ADND($\{x\}$)$\leq$ADND($\{y\}$), $x,y\in Max_U$ and Definition 2.7, we have

$$\frac{\left|\underline{D^{\uparrow}}(\{x\})\right|+1}{\left|\underline{D^{\downarrow}}(\{x\})\right|+1}\cdot\frac{\left|\overline{D^{\uparrow}}(\{x\})\right|}{\left|\overline{D^{\downarrow}}(\{x\})\right|}\leq\frac{\left|\underline{D^{\uparrow}}(\{y\})\right|+1}{\left|\underline{D^{\downarrow}}(\{y\})\right|+1}\cdot\frac{\left|\overline{D^{\uparrow}}(\{y\})\right|}{\left|\overline{D^{\downarrow}}(\{y\})\right|}.$$

Then,

$$\frac{\left|D^{\uparrow}(x)\right|+1}{\left|D^{\downarrow}(x)\right|+1}\cdot\frac{\left|D^{\uparrow}(x)\right|}{\left|D^{\downarrow}(x)\right|}\leq\frac{\left|D^{\uparrow}(y)\right|+1}{\left|D^{\downarrow}(y)\right|+1}\cdot\frac{\left|D^{\uparrow}(y)\right|}{\left|D^{\downarrow}(y)\right|}$$

by Theorem 2.2 (1). So, $|D^{\downarrow}(x)|\geq|D^{\downarrow}(y)|$.

Therefore, $x,y\in Max_U$, then $\left|D^{\downarrow}(x)\right|\geq\left|D^{\downarrow}(y)\right|\Leftrightarrow ADND(\{x\})\leq ADND(\{y\})$.

(8) The proof is similar to (7)

(9) Suppose that x is a Minimum object. Then, $D^{\uparrow}(x)=U$, $D^{\downarrow}(x)=\{x\}$. Hence,

$$ADND(\{x\})=\frac{|U|+1}{|\{x\}|+1}\cdot\frac{|U|}{|\{x\}|}=\frac{|U|(|U|+1)}{2}.$$

Suppose that x is a Maximum object. Then, $D^{\uparrow}(x)=\{x\}$, $D^{\downarrow}(x)=U$. Hence,

$$\text{ADND}(\{x\})=\frac{|\{x\}|+1}{|U|+1}\cdot\frac{|\{x\}|}{|U|+1}=\frac{2}{|U|(|U|+1)}.$$

Obviously, $\forall y\in U$, $|D^{\uparrow}(y)|\leq|U|$, $|D^{\downarrow}(y)|\geq1$.

So, $\dfrac{2}{|U|(|U|+1)}\leq\text{ADND}(\{y\})\leq\dfrac{|U|(|U|+1)}{2}$.

(10) The proof is similar to (9).

On the whole, ADND is a measure based on dominance relations of object subsets, which is mainly used to measure the advantages and disadvantages of object subsets. In an IS, if an object x is worse than or the same as an object y, then ADND($\{x\}$)≥ADND($\{y\}$). For an object subset X, if an object x is selected from the first layer and added to X, then there must be an object y in other layers, so that $ADND(X\cup\{x\})\leq ADND(X\cup\{y\})$;Similarly, combining (2) and (4), we get the method of selecting objects, that is, we start from the first layer and select layer by layer to meet the number of selected objects. If the number of selected objects is less than the number of the first layer, we only need to select in the first layer. According to (5), (6) and (7), we select objects from small to large according to the ADND value of the first layer objects.

GOMADMMADD

In this section, we compare the advantages and disadvantages between groups, propose "local advantage-disadvantage degrees" and "advantage-disadvantage degrees", and design an algorithm based on them.

Algorithm 1: Group-oriented multi-attribute decision-making based on mixed advantage-disadvantage degree (GOMADMMADD)

Input: k object groups $X_1 = \{x_{11}, x_{12}, \ldots, x_{1m_1}\}, X_2 = \{x_{21}, x_{22}, \ldots, x_{2m_2}\}, \ldots, X_k = \{x_{k1}, x_{k2}, \ldots, x_{km_k}\}$, ($m_1, m_2, \ldots, m_k$ denote the number of group members), and k ISs $S_1=\{X_1,A,V,f\}$, $S_2=\{X_2,A,V,f\}$, ..., $S_k=\{X_k,A,V,f\}$.
Output: An object group X.
Step 1: For each object $x \in X_1 \cup X_2 \cup \ldots \cup X_k$, calculate $\uparrow x$ and $\downarrow x$ by Definition 2.1;
Step 2: For each object group X_t, $t=1,2,\ldots,k$, comp $\underline{\uparrow} X_t, \underline{\downarrow} X_t, \overline{\uparrow} X_t$, and $\overline{\downarrow} X_t$ by Definition 2.3;
Step 3: For each object group X_t, $t=1,2,\ldots,k$, compute the LADD and ADD of X_t by Definition 2.4(1), (2);
Step 4: For each object group X_t, $t=1,2,\ldots,k$, compute the MADD of X_t by Definition 2.4 (3);
Step 5: Rank the object groups according to the MADD of each object group. The smaller the MADD(X_t) is, the better the object group X_t will be $X_i < X_j \Longleftrightarrow$ MADD(X_i)>MADD(X_j), $i,j=1,2,\ldots,k$.

Note: Analysis of Algorithm 1

(1) Principle: According to Definitions 2.1, 2.3, and 2.4, and related Notes, the principle of Algorithm 1 is obvious.

(2) Optimizations: (a) According to Definitions 2.2 (1) and (2), judge whether the object is Maximum or Minimum. If x is a Maximum or Minimum object, then, in Step 1 $\underline{\downarrow}\{x\} = \overline{\downarrow}\{x\} = U$ or $\underline{\uparrow}\{x\} = \overline{\uparrow}\{x\} = U$.

(3) Limitations: The more complex the object group's neighborhood is, the better the decision-making effect will be, that is, the disadvantage and advantage neighborhoods of each object group are different.

(4) Advantages: (a) There is no need to predict the original data, just know the dominance and inferiority between attribute values. (b) Algorithm 1 is easy to understand according to the intuitive thinking mode of human beings, and does not rely on information outside the IS, such as attribute weights.

(5) the time complexity is $O(k^2)$

GMADMDRS

Based on the semantics of ADND, we design a group-oriented multi-attribute decision-making method to select the optimal group with k objects or more in an IS. The specific method is as follows.

Algorithm 2: Group-oriented multi-attribute decision-making method based on dominance-based rough set(GMADMDRS)

```
Input: An IS S={U,A,f,V}, k.
Output: Set AOS consist of optimal group with k objects or more.
  AOS ← ∅, AS ← ∅ // {all subsets of U }
  for j←k; j < |U|;j++ do
    AS^j←Subsets(U,j) // Subsets(U,j) return subset of all j objects in U
    for i←1; i≤|AS^j|; i ++ do
If ADND(AS_i^j) =min(ADND(AS^j)) then
          AOS^j ← {AOS^j, AS_i^j}
    AOS←{AOS,AOS^j}
    return AOS
```

Optimization of GMADMDRS

For Algorithm 2, the time complexity is $O(2^{|U|})$. When the number of objects increases, the time complexity of Algorithm 2 increases exponentially. To simplify the time complexity of Algorithm 2, we propose the following optimized algorithm according to Theorem 2.3.

Algorithm 3: Optimization of GMADMDRS

```
Input: An IS S={U,A,f,V}, k.
Output: Set AOS consist of optimal group with k objects or more.
ADID ← zeros(|U|,|U|); AOS ← ∅; detSet ← ∅
 for i←1; i≤|U|; i++ do
  for j←1; j≤|U|; j++ do
   if x_i≥x_j then
     ADID(i,j)←1
   else
     ADID(i,j)←0
 for i←1; i≤|U|; i++ do
  if sum(ADID(:,i))=1 then
     C_1 ← C_1 ∪ x_i
 allSet←C_1
 D_+^↑(x_i) ←{x_j|ADID(j,i)=1, 1≤j≤|U|, j≠i}
 for l←2; l ≤|U|; l++ do
   for i←1; i≤|U|; i++ do
if D_+^↑(x_i) ≠ ∅ and D_+^↑(x_i) ∈ allSet then
     C_l ← C_l ∪ x_i
   allSet ← allSet ∪ C_l
 if k≤|C_1| then
   [value,index]←sort(ADND(C_1))
   for t←k; t≤|U|-1; t++ do
      AOS^t ← {AS_i^t | i ∈ index(mint(value))}
   AOS←{AOS,AOS^t}
   k←|C_1|+1
 l=1
 for t←k; t≤|U|-1; t++ do
    if size(detSet)<t
       repeat
          detSet ← detSet ∪ C_l
          l++
until size(detSet ∪ C_l) > t
    len←(k – size(detSet))
    AS^len←Subsets(C_l,len)
    for i←1; i≤size(AS^len); i++
       AS_i^t ← detSet ∪ AS_i^len
    [value,index]←sort(ADND(AS^t))
    AOS^{t} ← {AS^{t}_{i} | i ∈ index(min(value))}
    AOS←{AOS,AOS^t}
  return AOS
```

Algorithm 3 continued

Note: Optimization principle of Algorithm 3

(1) According to Definition 2.5, objects are layered. According to Theorem 2.3 (4), the process of selecting objects is from the first layer to the last layer.

(2) According to Definition.2.5 and Theorem 2.3 (4), the number of selected objects is the minimum number of group selection requirements.

(3) According to Theorem 2.3 (2), (5), and (6), if the number of selected objects is less than or equal to the number of objects in the first layer, it only needs to calculate the ADND value of each object in the first layer, sort from large to small according to the ADND value, and then select the first k objects.

(4) According to Theorem 2.3 (7), if only the first level objects need to be sorted, they are sorted according to $|D^1(x)|$.

(5) the time complexity is $O(|U|^2)$

CASE ANALYSIS

In this section, two examples will be used to verify algorithm 1 and optimized algorithm 3 respectively.

Case Descriptions (Assessment of sales team)

Company T is another kind of private fund company, its main business is real estate investment, equity investment, and wealth management. The company T has set up private affairs department (PAD), major customer department (MCD), and business division (BD) 1,2,3,4, and each department has set up a sales group (team) (SG). The detailed structure is shown in Figure 1.

Figure 1. Local organization chart of the company T

Note: PAD: contact high net worth people, to provide asset allocation and asset management services for investors, and build ''private bank'' for investors. MCD: to serve the third party institutional clients, cooperate with institutions, and achieve win-win wealth.BD 1,2,3,4: provide financial consultation, asset management, and asset allocation services for the QFII.

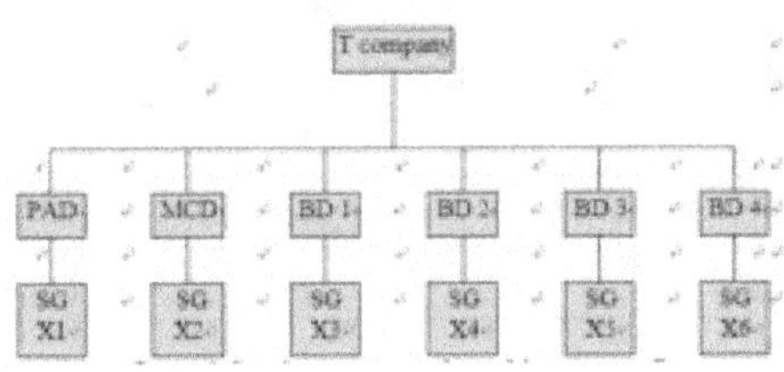

To improve the management level of the company T, it is necessary to strengthen the assessment of the 6 sales groups (teams) (X_1, X_2, X_3, X_4, X_5, X_6) of the company T. The evaluation of sales group (team) is generally based on group (team) members. The indicators of the appraisal members are shown in Table 1. According to the indicators of the appraisal members in Table 1, the 6 information systems of 6 sales groups (teams) are established, as shown in Tables 2-7. In particular, a_0 is not considered in the process of building an information system, because each member must contain a_0.

In the following, we apply the GOMADMMADD to the assessment of the 6 sales groups (teams). According to Tables 2-7, a new IS $S=\{U,A,V,f\}$ with $U = U_1 \cup U_2 \cup U_3 \cup U_4 \cup U_5 \cup U_6$ is established, as shown in Table 8.

Table 1. The indicators of the appraisal members

Attribute	Description of attribute features
Sales task completion rate a_0	Actual sales / planned sales ×100%, the assessment standard is 100%, and the reduction is not less than 2%.
Quarterly sales growth rate a_1	Compared with the sales performance of the previous quarter. If it is increased by 10% or more, recorded as 1, otherwise as 0.
Industry application sales a_2	Develop intentional enterprises. If 2 or more enterprises are successfully developed, recorded as 1, otherwise as 0.
Market analysis a_3	Complete the collection and analysis of market information within the specified time. If the market analysis report is consistent with the actual situation, recorded as 1, otherwise as 0.
Completion rate of training plan a_4	If the test score is higher than or equal to 60 after the completion of the training, recorded as 1, otherwise as 0.
Completion rate of training plan a_5	If the sales situation is reported to the person in charge and statistician in time, the communication with the virtual agent customer service, the timely feedback of customer demand, etc., recorded as 1, otherwise as 0.
Teamwork a_6	If the work of the whole team is affected due to personal reasons, recorded as 0, otherwise as 1.
Professional knowledge a_7	If business knowledge and other related knowledge are mastered, recorded as 1, otherwise as 0.
Analysis and judgment ability a_8	If the objective neighborhood to make a more correct judgment quickly, and flexibly applied to the actual work to achieve better sales performance, recorded as 1, otherwise as 0.
Communication skills a_9	If multiple conversation skills are used flexibly, recorded as 1, otherwise as 0.
Flexibility and adaptability a_{10}	In response to changes in the objective neighborhood, flexibly take appropriate measures, recorded as 1, otherwise 0.
Employee attendance a_{11}	If the attendance rate of employees reaches 100%, recorded as 1, otherwise as 0.
Responsibility a_{12}	If in addition to doing well in one's job, the company also takes the initiative to undertake additional work, recorded as 1, otherwise as 0.
Service consciousness a_{13}	If there is a customer complaint, recorded as 0, otherwise as 1.

Table 2. An IS $S_1=\{U_1,A,V,f\}$ of X_1 of PAD

S_1	a_1	a_2	a_3	a_4	a_5	a_6	a_7	a_8	a_9	a_{10}	a_{11}	a_{12}	a_{13}
x_1	0	1	1	1	0	1	0	1	1	1	1	1	1
x_2	1	0	1	1	0	1	1	1	1	1	1	0	1
x_3	0	1	1	1	1	1	1	1	0	1	1	1	0
x_4	0	1	1	1	1	1	1	1	1	1	1	0	1
x_5	1	0	1	1	1	1	1	1	1	1	0	1	1

Table 3. An IS $S_2=\{U_2,A,V,f\}$ of X_2 of MCD

S_1	a_1	a_2	a_3	a_4	a_5	a_6	a_7	a_8	a_9	a_{10}	a_{11}	a_{12}	a_{13}
x_6	1	1	1	1	1	1	1	1	1	1	1	1	1
x_7	1	1	1	1	1	1	0	1	1	1	1	1	1
x_8	1	1	1	1	1	1	1	1	0	1	1	1	1
x_9	0	1	1	1	0	1	1	1	1	1	1	1	1
x_{10}	1	1	1	1	1	1	1	1	1	1	1	1	1
x_{11}	0	1	1	1	1	1	1	1	0	1	1	1	1

Table 4. An IS $S_3=\{U_3,A,V,f\}$ of X_3 of BD 1

S_1	a_1	a_2	a_3	a_4	a_5	a_6	a_7	a_8	a_9	a_{10}	a_{11}	a_{12}	a_{13}
x_{12}	1	1	1	1	0	1	1	1	0	1	1	0	1
x_{13}	0	1	1	1	1	1	1	1	1	1	1	1	1
x_{14}	1	1	1	1	1	1	1	1	1	1	0	0	1
x_{15}	1	1	1	1	1	1	1	1	1	1	1	1	1

Table 5. An IS $S_4=\{U_4,A,V,f\}$ of X_4 of BD 2

S_1	a_1	a_2	a_3	a_4	a_5	a_6	a_7	a_8	a_9	a_{10}	a_{11}	a_{12}	a_{13}
x_{16}	1	1	1	1	1	1	1	1	1	1	1	1	1
x_{17}	1	1	1	1	1	0	1	1	1	1	1	1	0
x_{18}	0	1	1	0	1	1	1	0	1	1	1	0	1
x_{19}	1	1	1	0	1	1	1	1	1	0	1	1	1
x_{20}	1	1	1	1	1	1	0	1	1	1	1	1	1

Table 6. An IS $S_5=\{U_5,A,V,f\}$ of X_5 of BD 3

S_1	a_1	a_2	a_3	a_4	a_5	a_6	a_7	a_8	a_9	a_{10}	a_{11}	a_{12}	a_{13}
x_{21}	1	1	1	1	1	1	1	1	1	1	1	1	1
x_{22}	1	1	1	1	1	1	1	1	1	1	0	1	1
x_{23}	1	1	1	1	1	1	1	1	1	1	1	1	1
x_{24}	1	1	1	1	1	0	1	1	1	1	1	1	1

Table 7. An IS $S_6=\{U_6,A,V,f\}$ of X_6 of BD 4

S_1	a_1	a_2	a_3	a_4	a_5	a_6	a_7	a_8	a_9	a_{10}	a_{11}	a_{12}	a_{13}
x_{25}	1	1	0	1	1	0	1	1	1	1	0	1	1
x_{26}	1	1	1	1	1	1	0	0	0	0	1	0	1
x_{27}	1	1	1	1	1	1	1	1	1	0	1	1	1
x_{28}	1	1	1	1	1	1	1	1	1	0	1	1	1

Table 8. An IS $S=\{U,A,V,f\}$ of X_1-X_6

S_1	a_1	a_2	a_3	a_4	a_5	a_6	a_7	a_8	a_9	a_{10}	a_{11}	a_{12}	a_{13}
x_1	0	1	1	1	0	1	0	1	1	1	1	1	1
...	...	...	...	...	...	...	...	...	...	...	...	...	...
x_{11}	0	1	0	1	1	1	1	1	0	1	1	1	1
...	...	...	...	...	...	...	...	...	...	...	...	...	...
x_{21}	1	1	1	1	1	1	1	1	1	1	1	1	1
...	...	...	...	...	...	...	...	...	...	...	...	...	...
x_{28}	1	1	1	1	1	1	1	1	1	0	1	1	1

By Step 1 of Algorithm 1, we have

$\uparrow x_1=\{x_1,x_6,x_7,x_9,x_{10},x_{13},x_{15},x_{16},x_{20},x_{21},x_{23}\},\uparrow x_2=\{x_2,x_6,x_{10},x_{15},x_{16},x_{21},x_{23}\}$,

$\uparrow x_3=\{x_3,x_6,x_8,x_{10},x_{13},x_{15},x_{16},x_{21},x_{23}\},\uparrow x_4=\{x_4,x_6,x_{10},x_{13},x_{15},x_{16},x_{21},x_{23}\}$,

$\uparrow x_5=\{x_5,x_6,x_{10},x_{15},x_{16},x_{21},x_{22},x_{23}\},\uparrow x_6=\{x_6,x_{10},x_{15},x_{16},x_{21},x_{23}\}$,

$\uparrow x_7=\{x_6,x_7,x_{10},x_{15},x_{16},x_{20},x_{21},x_{23}\},\uparrow x_8=\{x_6,x_8,x_{10},x_{15},x_{16},x_{21},x_{23}\}$,

$\uparrow x_9=\{x_6,x_9,x_{10},x_{13},x_{15},x_{16},x_{21},x_{23}\},\uparrow x_{10}=\{x_6,x_{10},x_{15},x_{16},x_{21},x_{23}\}$,

$\uparrow x_{11}=\{x_6,x_8,x_{10},x_{11},x_{13},x_{15},x_{16},x_{21},x_{23}\},\uparrow x_{12}=\{x_6,x_8,x_{10},x_{12},x_{15},x_{16},x_{21},x_{23}\}$,

$\uparrow x_{13}=\{x_6,x_{10},x_{13},x_{15},x_{16},x_{21},x_{23}\},\uparrow x_{14}=\{x_6,x_{10},x_{14},x_{15},x_{16},x_{21},x_{22},x_{23}\}$,

$\uparrow x_{15}=\{x_6,x_{10},x_{15},x_{16},x_{21},x_{23}\},\uparrow x_{16}=\{x_6,x_{10},x_{15},x_{16},x_{21},x_{23}\}$,

$\uparrow x_{17}=\{x_6,x_{10},x_{15},x_{16},x_{17},x_{21},x_{23},x_{24}\},\uparrow x_{18}=\{x_4,x_6,x_{10},x_{13},x_{15},x_{16},x_{18},x_{21},x_{23}\}$,

$\uparrow x_{19}=\{x_6,x_{10},x_{15},x_{16},x_{19},x_{21},x_{23},x_{27},x_{28}\},\uparrow x_{20}=\{x_6,x_7,x_{10},x_{15},x_{16},x_{20},x_{21},x_{23}\}$,

$\uparrow x_{21}=\{x_6,x_{10},x_{15},x_{16},x_{21},x_{23}\},\uparrow x_{22}=\{x_6,x_{10},x_{15},x_{16},x_{21},x_{22},x_{23}\}$,

$\uparrow x_{23}=\{x_6,x_{10},x_{15},x_{16},x_{21},x_{23}\},\uparrow x_{24}=\{x_6,x_{10},x_{15},x_{16},x_{21},x_{23},x_{24}\}$,

$\uparrow x_{25}=\{x_6,x_{10},x_{15},x_{16},x_{21},x_{22},x_{23},x_{24},x_{25}\}$,

$\uparrow x_{26}=\{x_6,x_7,x_8,x_{10},x_{15},x_{16},x_{20},x_{21},x_{23},x_{26},x_{27},x_{28}\}$,

$\uparrow x_{27}=\{x_6,x_{10},x_{15},x_{16},x_{21},x_{23},x_{27},x_{28}\},\uparrow x_{28}=\{x_6,x_{10},x_{15},x_{16},x_{21},x_{23},x_{27},x_{28}\}$;

$\downarrow x_1=\{x_1\}$, $\downarrow x_2=\{x_2\}$, $\downarrow x_3=\{x_3\}$,$\downarrow x_4=\{x_4,x_{18}\}$, $\downarrow x_5=\{x_5\}$, $\downarrow x_6=U$, $\downarrow x_7=\{x_1,x_7,x_{20},x_{26}\}$,

$\downarrow x_8 = \{x_3, x_8, x_{11}, x_{12}, x_{26}\}$, $\downarrow x_9=\{x_1, x_9\}$, $\downarrow x_{10}=U$, $\downarrow x_{11}=\{x_{11}\}$, $\downarrow x_{12}=\{x_{12}\}$,

$\downarrow x_{13} = \{x_1, x_3, x_4, x_9, x_{11}, x_{13}, x_{18}\}$, $\downarrow x_{14}=\{x_{14}\}$, $\downarrow x_{15}=U$, $\downarrow x_{16}=U$, $\downarrow x_{17}=\{x_{17}\}$, $\downarrow x_{18}=\{x_{18}\}$,

$\downarrow x_{19}=\{x_{19}\}$, $\downarrow x_{20} = \{x_1, x_7, x_{20}, x_{26}\}$, $\downarrow x_{21}=U$, $\downarrow x_{22} = \{x_5, x_{14}, x_{22}, x_{25}\}$, $\downarrow x_{23}=U$,

$\downarrow x_{24} = \{x_{17}, x_{24}, x_{25}\}$, $\downarrow x_{25}=\{x_{25}\}$, $\downarrow x_{26}=\{x_{26}\}$, $\downarrow x_{27} = \{x_{19}, x_{26}, x_{27}, x_{28}\}$,

$\downarrow x_{28} = \{x_{19}, x_{26}, x_{27}, x_{28}\}$.

By Step 2 of Algorithm 1, we have

$\underline{\downarrow} X_1 = \varnothing, \underline{\uparrow} X_1 = \{x_6, x_{10}, x_{15}, x_{16}, x_{21}, x_{23}\}, \overline{\downarrow} X_1 = \{x_1, x_2, x_3, x_4, x_5, x_{18}\}$,

$\overline{\uparrow} X_1 = \{x_1, x_2, x_3, x_4, x_5, x_6, x_7, x_8, x_9, x_{10}, x_{13}, x_{15}, x_{16}, x_{20}, x_{21}, x_{22}, x_{23}\}, \underline{\downarrow} X_2 = \varnothing$,

$\underline{\uparrow} X_2 = \{x_6, x_{10}, x_{15}, x_{16}, x_{21}, x_{23}\}, \overline{\downarrow} X_2 = U$,

$\overline{\uparrow} X_2 = \{x_6, x_7, x_8, x_9, x_{10}, x_{11}, x_{13}, x_{15}, x_{16}, x_{20}, x_{21}, x_{23}\}, \underline{\downarrow} X_3 = \varnothing$,

$\underline{\uparrow} X_3 = \{x_6, x_{10}, x_{15}, x_{16}, x_{21}, x_{23}\}$, $X_3=U$,

$\overline{\uparrow} X_3 = \{x_6, x_8, x_{10}, x_{12}, x_{13}, x_{14}, x_{15}, x_{16}, x_{21}, x_{22}, x_{23}\}, \underline{\downarrow} X_4 = \varnothing$,

$\underline{\uparrow} X_4 = \{x_6, x_{10}, x_{15}, x_{16}, x_{21}, x_{23}\}, \overline{\downarrow} X_4 = U$,

$\overline{\uparrow} X_4 = \{x_4, x_6, x_7, x_{10}, x_{13}, x_{15}, x_{16}, x_{17}, x_{18}, x_{19}, x_{20}, x_{21}, x_{23}, x_{24}, x_{27}, x_{28}\}, \underline{\downarrow} X_5 = \{x_{25}\}$,

$\underline{\uparrow} X_5 = \{x_6, x_{10}, x_{15}, x_{16}, x_{21}, x_{23}\}, \overline{\downarrow} X_5 = U$,

$\overline{\uparrow} X_5 = \{x_6, x_{10}, x_{15}, x_{16}, x_{21}, x_{22}, x_{23}, x_{24}\}, \underline{\downarrow} X_6 = \varnothing$,

$\underline{\uparrow} X_6 = \{x_6, x_{10}, x_{15}, x_{16}, x_{21}, x_{23}\}, \overline{\downarrow} X_6 = \{x_{19}, x_{25}, x_{26}, x_{27}, x_{28}\}$,

$\bar{\uparrow} X_6 = \{x_6, x_7, x_8, x_{10}, x_{15}, x_{16}, x_{20}, x_{21}, x_{22}, x_{23}, x_{24}, x_{25}, x_{26}, x_{27}, x_{28}\}$.

By Step 3 of Algorithm 1, we have LADD(X_1)=6.00, ADD(X_1)=2.4286, LADD(X_2)=6.00, ADD(X_2)=0.4138, LADD(X_3)=6.00, ADD(X_3)=0.3793, LADD(X_4)=6.00, ADD(X_4)=0.5517, LADD(X_5)=3.00, ADD(X_5)=0.2759, LADD(X_6)=6.00, ADD(X_6)=2.5000.

By Step 4 of Algorithm 1, we have MADD(X_1)=8.4286, MADD(X_2)=6.4138, MADD(X_3)=6.3793, MADD(X_4)=6.5517, MADD(X_5)=MADD(X_6)=8.500.

By Step 5 of Algorithm 1, we have $X_5 > X_3 > X_2 > X_4 > X_1 > X_6$. Thus, the sales group (team) X_5 is the best.

Experimental Analysis (Assessment of Sales Team)

For the 6 sales groups (teams), we make a comparative analysis from the following two perspectives:

(1) The commonly used MADM methods (TOPSIS, VIKOR, TODIM, PROMETHEE, MOORA) are directly used. Before showing the ranking results, we provide Table 9 to illustrate the values of the parameters of some methods. In TOPSIS, we measure the distance from the optimal solution and the worst solution by using Euclidean distance. In VIKOR, v is a threshold parameter that can be set by the decision-maker. We suggest the value of 0.5 for the parameter v. In TODIM, θ is a threshold parameter that can be set by the decision-maker. We suggest the value of 1.0 for the parameter θ.

TOPSIS, VIKOR, TODIM, PROMETHEE, MOORA are used to rank 28 members of all sales groups (teams). The ranking results are shown in Figure 2.

In the results of the above 5 methods, we see that the ranking results of 28 members are the same, but the ranking positions of 6 sales groups (teams) members are relatively scattered, and it is not easy to integrate into the ranking of 6 sales groups (teams). Next, we use a method to integrate, stack the ranking of each sales group (team) member based on Figure 2, and then sort the 6 sales groups (teams). The ranking results are shown in Figure 3.

For Figure 3, we see that the sorting results of the 5 methods are quite similar, but the results of our method are different from those of these 5 methods. This is also consistent with our previous analysis, that is, if the traditional MADM method is directly used, the team ranking is not easy.

Table 9. The parameters of different methods

Methods	Parameters
TOPSIS	Euclidean Distance
VIKOR	$v = 0.5$
TODIM	$\theta = 1.0$

(2) Preprocess the information system of 6 sales groups (teams). For Tables 2-7, we take the attributes owned by the group (team) members directly as the attributes owned by the groups (teams) to get a new IS $S=\{U_7, A, V, f\}$ with $U_7=\{X_1, X_2, X_3, X_4, X_5, X_6\}$, as shown in Table 10.

Figure 2. The parameters of different methods

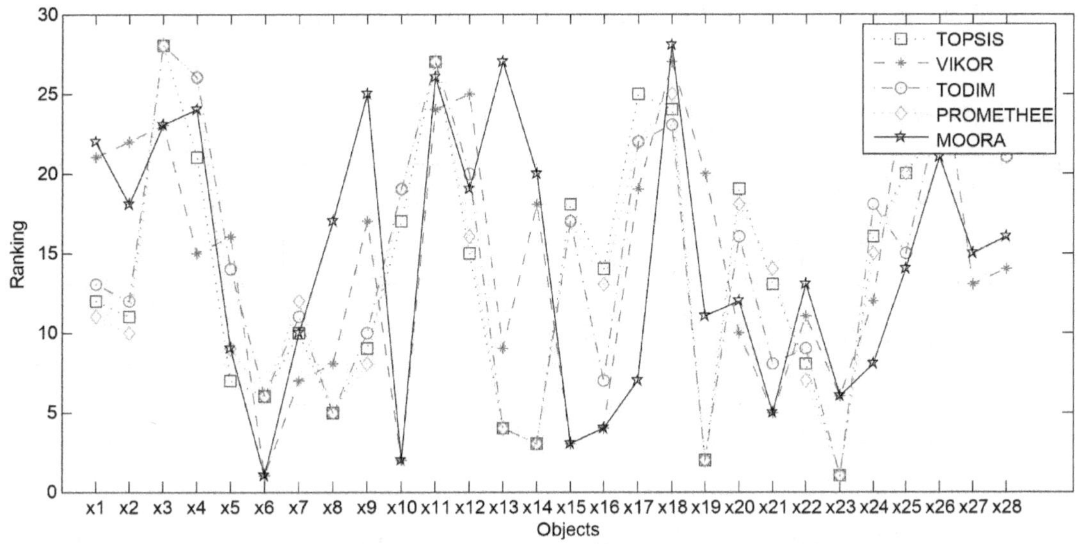

Figure 3. Ranking of the six sales groups based on Figure 2

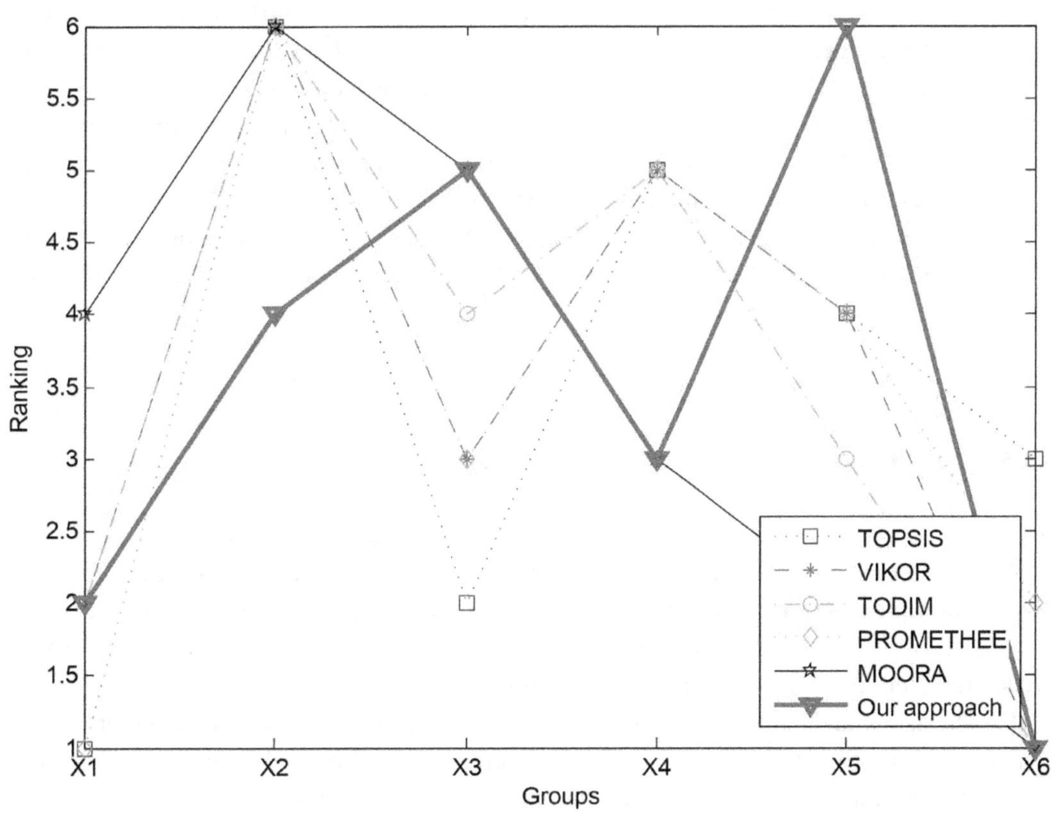

From Table 10, we see that all sales groups (teams) have the same attributes, so it is impossible to sort the sales groups (teams).

From the above two perspectives, the traditional method is ineffective.

Table 10. An IS $S=\{U_7,A,V,f\}$ of X_1-X_6

S	a_1	a_2	a_3	a_4	a_5	a_6	a_7	a_8	a_9	a_{10}	a_{11}	a_{12}	a_{13}
X_1	1	1	1	1	1	1	1	1	1	1	1	1	1
X_2	1	1	1	1	1	1	1	1	1	1	1	1	1
X_3	1	1	1	1	1	1	1	1	1	1	1	1	1
X_4	1	1	1	1	1	1	1	1	1	1	1	1	1
X_5	1	1	1	1	1	1	1	1	1	1	1	1	1
X_6	1	1	1	1	1	1	1	1	1	1	1	1	1

Next, we analyze the effectiveness of our method for the specific situations illustrated in Tables 2-7 as follows:

(a) The number of members in each sales group (team) who have all the attributes. X_1 has no, X_2 has 2, X_3 has 1, X_4 has 1, X_5 has 2, X_6 has no, so X_2 and X_5 are the best groups (teams).

(b) The effectiveness of the number of the sales team. For a group (team), the smaller the number of members is, the higher the effectiveness will be. X_4, X_5, and X_6 have the least number of members, all of them are 4, so the 3 groups (teams) have the highest effectiveness.

(c) The average number of attributes owned by group (team) members. The average number of attributes owned by X_1 members is 11.00, the average number of attributes owned by X_2 members is 11.83, the average number of attributes owned by X_3 members is 11.50, the average number of attributes owned by X_4 members is 11.20, the average number of attributes owned by X_5 members is 12.50, and the average number of attributes owned by X_6 members is 10.50. X_5 has the largest average attribute, so X_5 is the best.

To sum up, X_5 is the best sales group (team), which is consistent with our method.

Case Descriptions (Select of Investment Company)

In the following, we apply the proposed Algorithm3 to a real data set from UCI Machine Learning Repository. The data set is about Qualitative Bankruptcy Data Set (https://archive.ics.uci.edu/ml/datasets/Qualitative_Bankruptcy).The data set description is shown in Table 11 and the attribute set information is described as Table 12. The Qualitative Bankruptcy Data Set is used to predict the Bankruptcy from Qualitative parameters from experts based on attribute characteristics. For this data set, we analyze the attribute characteristics and select companies to invest. Purpose of investment: 1. Guarantee income. Invest in a company that is not bankrupt. If the company goes bankrupt, then it means that the income is zero; 2. Reduce risk and invest in multiple companies, that is, diversify investment and reduce risk. In short, we choose k or more non bankrupt companies to invest.

Table 11(a). Data set description

Data Set Characteristics:	Multivariate	Number of Instances:	250	Area:	Computer
Attribute Characteristics:	Real	Number of Attributes:	7	Date Donated	2014-02-09
Associated Tasks:	Classification	Missing Values?	Yes	Number of Web Hits:	90729

Table 11(b). Data set description

Attribute	Attribute Description	Attribute Grade
Industrial Risk (IR):	Government policies and international agreements, Cyclicality, Degree of competition, The price and stability of market supply, The size and growth of market demand, The sensitivity to changes in macroeconomic factors, Domestic and international competitive power, Product Life Cycle.	P, A, N
Management Risk (MR)	Ability and competence of management, Stability of management, The relationship between management owner, Human resources management, Growth process / business performance, Short and long term business planning, Achievement and feasibility.	P, A, N
Financial Flexibility (FF):	Direct financing, Indirect financing, Other financing.	P, A, N
Credibility (CR):	Credit history Reliability of information The relationship with financial institutes.	P, A, N
Competitiveness (CO):	Market position, The level of core capacities, Differentiated strategy	P, A, N
Operating Risk (OP):	The stability and diversity of procurement, The stability of transaction, The efficiency of production, The prospects for demand for product and service, Effectiveness of sale network.	P, A, N
Class (C):	Bankruptcy, Non-Bankruptcy	B, NB

(Note: P=Positive, A=Average, N=Negative, B=Bankruptcy, NB=Non-Bankruptcy)

Next, we try to use Algorithm 3 for company selection. To apply Algorithm 3 to the Qualitative Bankruptcy Data set, firstly, we delete the instances with duplicated information of the Qualitative Bankruptcy Data set, then we obtain a new data set with 103 instances, where 25 represents bankrupted companies, 78 firms that did not bankrupt in the prediction, as shown in Table 12.

According to the impact of IR, MR, FF, CR, CO, and OP on the company, it is generally believed that: the greater the industry risk, the easier the company is to go bankrupt; The greater the company's management risk, the easier the company is to go bankrupt; The worse the financial flexibility of the company, the easier the company is to go bankrupt; The worse the credibility of the company, the easier it is to go bankrupt; The weaker the competitiveness of the company, the easier it is to go bankrupt; The greater the operating risk of the company, the easier it is to go bankrupt. According to the above cognition, Table 12 is transformed into Table 13.

Table 12. Qualitative bankruptcy data

	IR	MR	FF	CR	CO	OP	C
x_1	P	P	A	A	A	P	NB
x_2	N	N	A	A	A	N	NB
…	…	…	…	…	…	…	…
x_{30}	N	N	A	P	P	P	NB
…	…	…	…	…	…	…	…
x_{50}	N	A	N	N	N	P	B
	…	…	…	…	…	…	…
x_{103}	P	N	N	N	A	A	B

Table 13. An information system S based on qualitative bankruptcy data

	IR	MR	FF	CR	CO	OP	C
x_1	0	0	0.5	0.5	0.5	0	NB
x_2	1	1	0.5	0.5	0.5	1	NB
…	…	…	…	…	…	…	…
x_{30}	1	1	0.5	1	1	0	NB
…	…	…	…	…	…	…	…
x_{50}	1	0.5	0	0	0	0	B
	…	…	…	…	…	…	…
x_{103}	0	0	0	0	0.5	0.5	B

Experimental Analysis (Select of Investment Company)

Combined with the investment purpose, selection requirements: the selected companies will not go bankrupt as much as possible, and the number of selected companies shall be as large as possible. In order to effectively verify the validity of Algorithm 3, according to the prediction of bankruptcy (B) and non bankruptcy (NB) in Table 13, we analyze the effectiveness of the object selected by Algorithm 3. In the selected companies, the higher the proportion of non bankruptcy, the better the effectiveness of Algorithm 3. To analyze the effectiveness of Algorithm 3, we select two groups of data, {1,3,9,22,42,58,72} and {1,11,21,31,41,51,61,71}, respectively. The results are shown in Figures 4 and 5.

In Figures 4 and 5, we take the proportion of non bankrupt companies in the Qualitative Bankruptcy Data set as the benchmark (the benchmark value 0.7573). For Algorithm 3, if the proportion of non bankrupt companies in the selection result is higher than the benchmark, it shows that the selection result of Algorithm 3 is effective. In Figure 4, the k values are chosen according to the object levels. In

Figure 5, the *k* value are taken in equal steps. According to the number of non bankrupt companies in the Qualitative Bankruptcy Data set, the *k* value does not exceed 78. In Figures 4 and 5, Effective value = number of non bankrupt companies in the selected companies / number of selected companies, the effective values are higher than the benchmark, reaching mòre than 0.90. Overall, the effectiveness of Algorithm 3 is excellent.

Remark:(1) In the calculation process, we use Algorithm 3. If Algorithm 2 is used, it needs to calculate 2^{103} times. It is difficult to calculate in the existing calculation force.

(2) When calculating the effective value, because the selected result is not unique, the average of the effective values of all results is used.

Figure 4. The effective rate based on k value of layer by layer

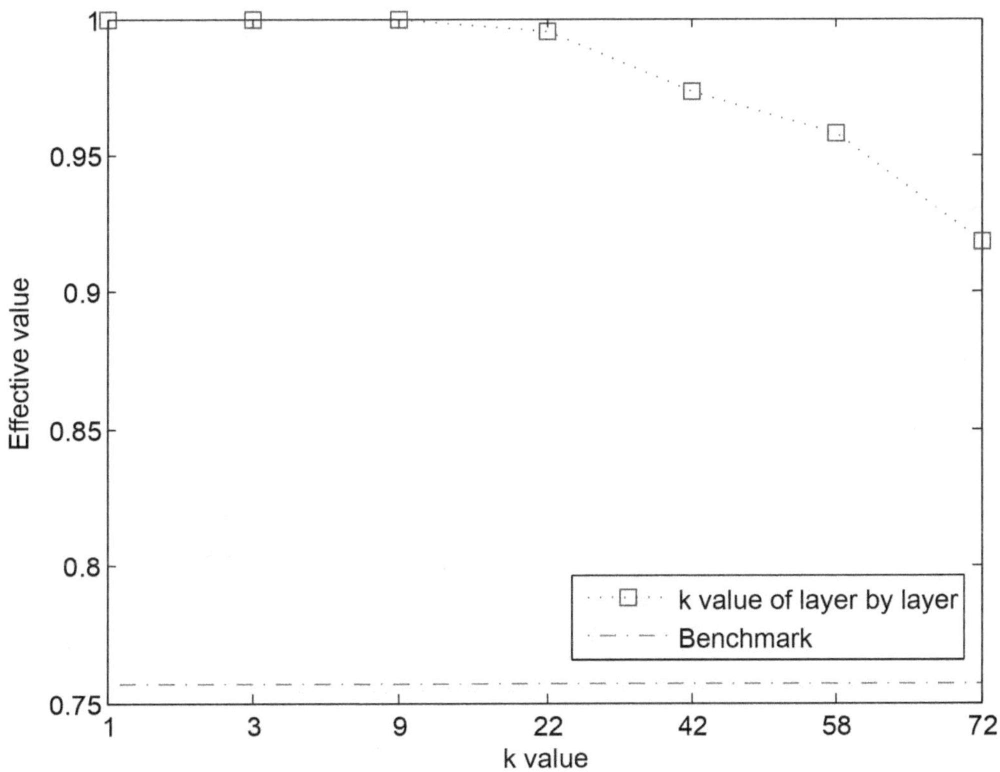

CONCLUSION

This chapter proposes a new GOMADMMADD method based on dominance rough set theory, and proves its effectiveness in evaluating and ranking groups through the evaluation of sales teams. However, it faces two problems: one is the exponential explosion in the number of evaluation and sorting groups, and the other is the lack of optimality in the degree of mixed advantages and disadvantages of this method, which puts it at a bottleneck. To address these issues, the GOMADMMADD method was improved, and the GMADMDRS method was proposed and optimized. In numerical examples, compared with the sorting results of various traditional methods, the sorting results of GMADMDRS are reasonable. Once again, the GMADMDRS method was optimized using the ADND characteristics, and the results before and after optimization remained consistent. The comparison of time performance with numerical examples shows that the optimized GMADMDRS has significantly improved its time performance before optimization. Finally, the optimized GMADMDRS was used to solve the securities investment problem on the bankruptcy company dataset.

Figure 5. The effective rate based on k value of equal step

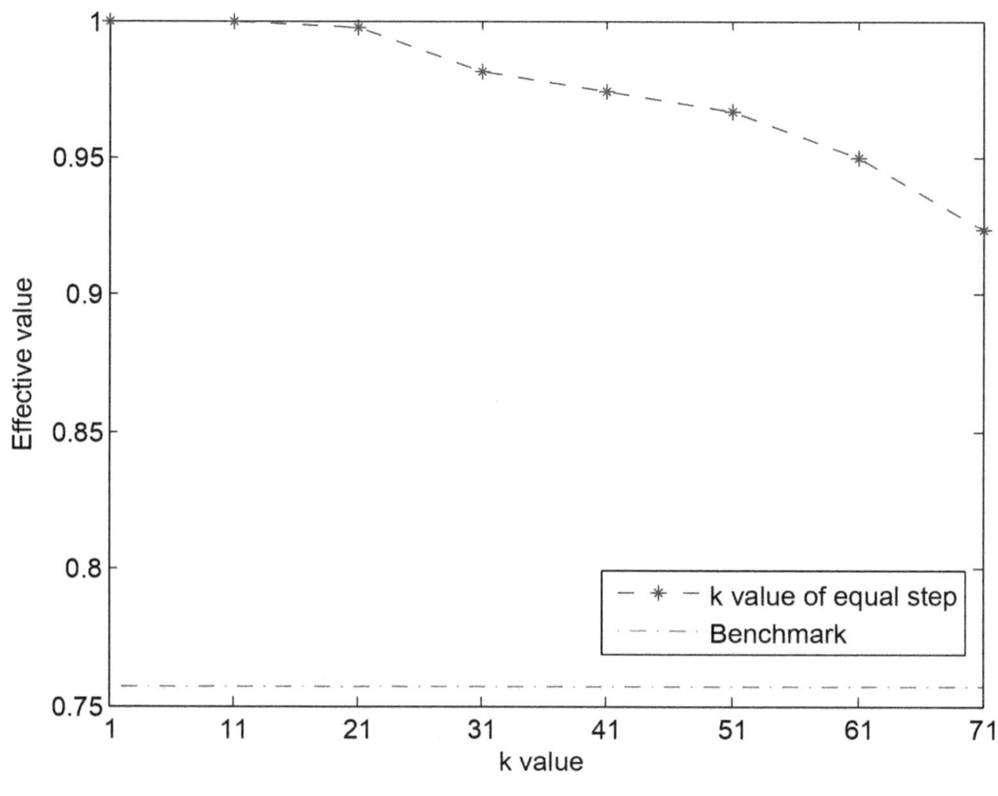

The main contribution of this chapter lies in the dominance based rough set theory, which proposes the GOMADMMADD method, improves it, proposes the GMADMDRS method, and optimizes the GMADMDRS method, significantly improving its performance. The GOMADMMADD method can evaluate each group of groups (such as sales groups), and the optimized GMADMDRS method can effectively select the optimal group, which can be applied to practical problems such as portfolio investment problems, queue checking, and queue segmentation. Analyzing the limitations of our proposed method, the algorithms before and after optimization are only suitable for ordinal information systems, not for categorical data.

As for future research directions, we will investigate the following three aspects. First, we will extend GMADMDRS to the fuzzy environment and design the corresponding method in this environment. Second, we will design a new operator to make GMADMDRS suitable for categorical data, and expand the range of data types that GMADMDRS can handle. Finally, we apply GMADMDRS to group-oriented multi-attribute decision-making problems such as group checking, group partitioning, cohort checks, and cohort segmentation by virtue of the validity and time performance of GMADMDRS.

REFERENCES

Ahmad, A., Qamar, U., & Raza, M. S. (2020). An optimized method to calculate approximations in Dominance based rough set approach. *Applied Soft Computing*, *97*, 106731. doi:10.1016/j.asoc.2020.106731

Behzadian, M., Otaghsara, S. K., Yazdani, M., & Ignatius, J. (2012). A state-of the-art survey of TOPSIS applications. *Expert Systems with Applications*, *39*(17), 13051–13069. doi:10.1016/j.eswa.2012.05.056

Biswas, T. K., Abbasi, A., & Chakrabortty, R. K. (2022). A two-stage VIKOR assisted multi-operator differential evolution approach for Influence Maximization in social networks. *Expert Systems with Applications*, *192*, 116342. doi:10.1016/j.eswa.2021.116342

Błaszczyński, J., de Almeida Filho, A. T., Matuszyk, A., Szeląg, M., & Słowiński, R. (2021). Auto loan fraud detection using dominance-based rough set approach versus machine learning methods. *Expert Systems with Applications*, *163*, 113740. doi:10.1016/j.eswa.2020.113740

Brans, J. P., & Vincke, P. (1985). Note—A Preference Ranking Organisation Method: (The PROMETHEE Method for Multiple Criteria Decision-Making). *Management Science*, *31*(6), 647–656. doi:10.1287/mnsc.31.6.647

Das, N. R., Ghosh, S., Mukherjee, I., & Paul, G. (2023). Adoption of a ranking based indexing method for the cricket teams, *Expert Systems with Applications, 213*, 118796. e Costa, C. A. B., & Vansnick, J. C. (1994), MACBETH—An interactive path towards the construction of cardinal value functions. *International Transactions in Operational Research*, *1*(4), 489–500.

Dogan, O. (2021). Process mining technology selection with spherical fuzzy AHP and sensitivity analysis. *Expert Systems with Applications*, *178*, 114999. doi:10.1016/j.eswa.2021.114999

Fu, Y., Cai, R., & Yu, B. (2022). Group decision-making method with directed graph under linguistic environment. *International Journal of Machine Learning and Cybernetics*, *13*(11), 3329–3340. doi:10.1007/s13042-022-01597-5

Gireesha, O., Somu, N., & Krithivasan, K., & VS, S. S. (. (2020). IIVIFS-WASPAS: An integrated multi-criteria decision-making perspective for cloud service provider selection. *Future Generation Computer Systems*, *103*, 91–110. doi:10.1016/j.future.2019.09.053

Gou, X., Xu, Z., Liao, H., & Herrera, F. (2021). Probabilistic double hierarchy linguistic term set and its use in designing an improved VIKOR method: The application in smart healthcare. *The Journal of the Operational Research Society*, *72*(12), 2611–2630. doi:10.1080/01605682.2020.1806741

Greco, S., Figueira, J., & Ehrgott, M. (2016), *Multiple criteria decision analysis, 37.* New York: Springer.

Greco, S., Inuiguchi, M., & Slowinski, R. (2006). Fuzzy rough sets and multiple-premise gradual decision rules. *International Journal of Approximate Reasoning*, *41*(2), 179–211. doi:10.1016/j.ijar.2005.06.014

Greco, S., Matarazzo, B., & Slowinski, R. (1999). Rough approximation of a preference relation by dominance relations. *European Journal of Operational Research*, *117*(1), 63–83. doi:10.1016/S0377-2217(98)00127-1

Greco, S., Matarazzo, B., & Slowinski, R. (2001). Rough sets theory for multicriteria decision analysis. *European Journal of Operational Research*, *129*(1), 1–47. doi:10.1016/S0377-2217(00)00167-3

Huang, Q., Li, T., Huang, Y., Yang, X., & Fujita, H. (2020). Dynamic dominance rough set approach for processing composite ordered data. *Knowledge-Based Systems*, *187*, 104829. doi:10.1016/j.knosys.2019.06.037

Hussain, A., Chun, J., & Khan, M. (2020). A novel customer-centric Methodology for Optimal Service Selection (MOSS) in a cloud environment. *Future Generation Computer Systems*, *105*, 562–580. doi:10.1016/j.future.2019.12.024

Jacquet-Lagreze, E., & Siskos, J. (1982). Assessing a set of additive utility functions for multicriteria decision-making, the UTA method. *European Journal of Operational Research*, *10*(2), 151–164. doi:10.1016/0377-2217(82)90155-2

Jiang, H., Zhan, J., & Chen, D. (2021). PROMETHEE II method based on variable precision fuzzy rough sets with fuzzy neighborhoods. *Artificial Intelligence Review*, *54*(2), 1281–1319. doi:10.1007/s10462-020-09878-7

Kang, Y., Yu, B., & Cai, M. (2022). Multi-attribute predictive analysis based on attribute-oriented fuzzy rough sets in fuzzy information systems. *Information Sciences*, *608*, 931–949. doi:10.1016/j.ins.2022.07.006

Kusunoki, Y., Błaszczyński, J., Inuiguchi, M., & Słowiński, R. (2021). Empirical risk minimization for dominance-based rough set approaches. *Information Sciences*, *567*, 395–417. doi:10.1016/j.ins.2021.02.043

Leng, Y., Yu, L., & Niu, X. (2022). Dynamically aggregating individuals' social influence and interest evolution for group recommendations. *Information Sciences*, *614*, 223–239. doi:10.1016/j.ins.2022.09.058

Luo, H., Li, L., Zhang, Y., Fang, S., & Chen, X. (2021). Link prediction in multiplex networks using a novel multiple-attribute decision-making approach. *Knowledge-Based Systems*, *219*, 106904. doi:10.1016/j.knosys.2021.106904

Mnich, K., & Rudnicki, W. R. (2020). All-relevant feature selection using multidimensional filters with exhaustive search. *Information Sciences*, *524*, 277–297. doi:10.1016/j.ins.2020.03.024

Murat, S., Kazan, H., & Coskun, S. S. (2015). An application for measuring performance quality of schools by using the PROMETHEE multi-criteria decision making method. *Procedia: Social and Behavioral Sciences*, *195*, 729–738. doi:10.1016/j.sbspro.2015.06.344

Opricovic, S., & Tzeng, G. H. (2004). Compromise solution by MCDM methods: A comparative analysis of VIKOR and TOPSIS. *European Journal of Operational Research*, *156*(2), 445–455. doi:10.1016/S0377-2217(03)00020-1

Paiva, F. D., Cardoso, R. T. N., Hanaoka, G. P., & Duarte, W. M. (2019). Decision-making for financial trading: A fusion approach of machine learning and portfolio selection. *Expert Systems with Applications, 115*, 635–655. doi:10.1016/j.eswa.2018.08.003

Palangetić, M., Cornelis, C., Greco, S., & Słowiński, R. (2021). Fuzzy extensions of the dominance-based rough set approach. *International Journal of Approximate Reasoning*, *129*, 1–19. doi:10.1016/j.ijar.2020.10.004

Pawlak, Z. (1982). Rough sets. *International journal of computer & information sciences, 11*, 341-356.

Pedersen, T. I., & Vatn, J. (2022). Optimizing a condition-based maintenance policy by taking the preferences of a risk-averse decision maker into account. *Reliability Engineering & System Safety*, *228*, 108775. doi:10.1016/j.ress.2022.108775

Purohit, L., & Kumar, S. (2018). A classification based web service selection approach. *IEEE Transactions on Services Computing*, *14*(2), 315–328. doi:10.1109/TSC.2018.2805352

Roy, B. (1991). The outranking approach and the foundations of ELECTRE methods. *Theory and Decision*, *31*(1), 49–73. doi:10.1007/BF00134132

Saaty, T. L. (1977). A scaling method for priorities in hierarchical structures. *Journal of Mathematical Psychology*, *15*(3), 234–281. doi:10.1016/0022-2496(77)90033-5

Saaty, T. L. (2004). Decision making—The analytic hierarchy and network processes (AHP/ANP). *Journal of Systems Science and Systems Engineering*, *13*(1), 1–35. doi:10.1007/s11518-006-0151-5

Sahu, R., Dash, S. R., & Das, S. (2021). Career selection of students using hybridized distance measure based on picture fuzzy set and rough set theory. *Decision Making: Applications in Management and Engineering*, *4*(1), 104–126. doi:10.31181/dmame2104104s

Sharma, H. K., Kumari, K., & Kar, S. (2021). Forecasting Sugarcane Yield of India based on rough set combination approach. *Decision Making: Applications in Management and Engineering*, *4*(2), 163–177. doi:10.31181/dmame210402163s

Tidke, B., Mehta, R., & Dhanani, J. (2020). Consensus-based aggregation for identification and ranking of top-k influential nodes. *Neural Computing & Applications*, *32*(14), 10275–10301. doi:10.1007/s00521-019-04568-0

Vo, N. N., He, X., Liu, S., & Xu, G. (2019). Deep learning for decision making and the optimization of socially responsible investments and portfolio. *Decision Support Systems*, *124*, 113097. doi:10.1016/j.dss.2019.113097

Yu, B., Cai, M., & Li, Q. (2019b). A λ-rough set model and its applications with TOPSIS method to decision making. *Knowledge-Based Systems*, *165*, 420–431. doi:10.1016/j.knosys.2018.12.013

Yu, B., Guo, L., & Li, Q. (2019a). A characterization of novel rough fuzzy sets of information systems and their application in decision making. *Expert Systems with Applications*, *122*, 253–261. doi:10.1016/j.eswa.2019.01.018

Yu, B., Xu, R., Fu, Y., & Xu, Z. (2022a). A Novel Dominance-Based Rough Set Model with Advantage (Disadvantage) Neighborhoods and Its Applications to Assess Sales Group. *International Journal of Fuzzy Systems*, *24*(8), 3501–3512. doi:10.1007/s40815-022-01342-8

Yu, B., Xu, R., Xu, Z., & Dai, J. (2023b). Optimizing group-oriented multiple attribute decision-making method based on dominance-based rough set model with advantaged (disadvantaged) neighborhoods. *Engineering Applications of Artificial Intelligence*, *124*, 106602. doi:10.1016/j.engappai.2023.106602

Yu, B., Xu, Z., Dai, J., & Yang, T. (2022b). A novel multi-attribute decision-making method based on neighborhood approximations and its application. *Expert Systems with Applications*, *199*, 116946. doi:10.1016/j.eswa.2022.116946

Yu, B., Zheng, Z., Xiao, Z., Fu, Y., & Xu, Z. (2023a). A large-scale group decision-making method based on group-oriented rough dominance relation in scenic spot service improvement. *Expert Systems with Applications*, *233*, 120999. doi:10.1016/j.eswa.2023.120999

Zareie, A., Sheikhahmadi, A., & Khamforoosh, K. (2018). Influence maximization in social networks based on TOPSIS. *Expert Systems with Applications*, *108*, 96–107. doi:10.1016/j.eswa.2018.05.001

Zhang, C., Li, D., & Liang, J. (2018). Hesitant fuzzy linguistic rough set over two universes model and its applications. *International Journal of Machine Learning and Cybernetics*, *9*(4), 577–588. doi:10.1007/s13042-016-0541-z

Zhang, C., Li, D., & Liang, J. (2020d). Multi-granularity three-way decisions with adjustable hesitant fuzzy linguistic multigranulation decision-theoretic rough sets over two universes. *Information Sciences*, *507*, 665–683. doi:10.1016/j.ins.2019.01.033

Zhang, C., Zhang, H., & Wang, J. (2018). Personalized restaurant recommendation method combining group correlations and customer preferences. *Information Sciences*, *454*, 128–143. doi:10.1016/j.ins.2018.04.061

Zhang, F., Hao, X., Chao, J., & Yuan, S. (2020a). Label propagation-based approach for detecting review spammer groups on e-commerce websites. *Knowledge-Based Systems*, *193*, 105520. doi:10.1016/j.knosys.2020.105520

Zhang, L., Zhan, J., & Yao, Y. (2020b). Intuitionistic fuzzy TOPSIS method based on CVPIFRS models: An application to biomedical problems. *Information Sciences*, *517*, 315–339. doi:10.1016/j.ins.2020.01.003

Zhang, R., Xu, Z., & Gou, X. (2023). ELECTRE II method based on the cosine similarity to evaluate the performance of financial logistics enterprises under double hierarchy hesitant fuzzy linguistic environment. *Fuzzy Optimization and Decision Making*, *22*(1), 23–49. doi:10.1007/s10700-022-09382-3

Zhang, Y., Jiang, J., Xiang, Y., Zhu, Y., Wan, L., & Xie, X. (2020c). Cloud-assisted privacy-conscious large-scale Markowitz portfolio. *Information Sciences*, *527*, 548–559. doi:10.1016/j.ins.2018.12.055

Chapter 2
A Multi-Granularity Triangular Fuzzy Approach for Diabetes Blood Glucometer Selection Using PROMETHEE and Three-Way Decision

Liyin Wang
Shanxi University, China

Xueqing Fan
Shanxi University, China

Yuting Cheng
Shanxi University, China

Anna Wang
https://orcid.org/0009-0001-5196-9132
Shanxi University, China

Hansen Zhao
Georgia Institute of Technology, USA

ABSTRACT

This chapter focuses on the issue of selecting a blood glucose meter for diabetic patients. To address this problem, the authors have developed a comprehensive evaluation model that combines triangular fuzzy (TF) logic, multi-granularity (MG), three-way decision (TWD), and rough set theory. The evaluation model takes into consideration the performance indicators of the blood glucose meter and user requirements. The authors utilize TF logic to model the indicators and determine their weights, while integrating the TWD method to handle incomplete and uncertain information. Subsequently, they introduce the PROMETHEE method to comprehensively evaluate and rank various alternatives. Finally, within this evaluation model, they select the optimal choice based on its score. Experimental results demonstrate the effectiveness of our proposed method in resolving the blood glucose meter selection problem and providing personalized recommendations for diabetic patients.

DOI: 10.4018/979-8-3693-1582-8.ch002

INTRODUCTION

Problem Background

The advancement of modern medical technology has significantly improved the ability of diabetes patients to manage and monitor their blood glucose levels (Domingo-Lopez, 2022). Glucometers, being convenient medical devices, are extensively utilized in both home and clinical environments. Nonetheless, the market is saturated with a wide array of glucometer models and brands, which presents a challenge for patients in selecting the most suitable one. Factors such as accuracy, quality, after-sales support, and pain sensation must be taken into consideration. Patients must carefully evaluate these factors to choose a glucometer that aligns with their specific needs and preferences. Consequently, in order to aid patients in making well-informed decisions, it is essential to thoroughly comprehend the challenges associated with selecting a glucometer and provide corresponding solutions. Such research endeavors contribute to enhancing the effectiveness of diabetes management, improving patients' quality of life, and guiding medical device manufacturers in meeting the needs and expectations of patients, thus fostering product improvement and innovation.

When selecting a glucometer, patients must take into account various factors, including price, accuracy, and convenience. However, these factors introduce a level of ambiguity and uncertainty that complicates the decision-making process. In order to tackle these challenges, this study presents a comprehensive model that integrates triangular fuzzy sets (TFSs), the TWD, and the PROMETHEE multi-attribute decision-making method to improve the efficiency and accuracy of selecting glucometers.

A Brief Review of TFSs

In 1965, Zadeh (Zadeh, 1965) introduced the concept of fuzzy sets, expanding the representation of uncertain information beyond binary values in real-life scenarios. Fuzzy sets improve the accuracy and reliability of decision-making and have played a vital role in the advancement of fuzzy mathematics. Nevertheless, fuzzy sets also possess certain limitations. For instance, there is often difficulty in setting and selecting appropriate membership functions, and dealing with large datasets and complex problems can result in computational complexity.

To address these limitations, several generalizations of fuzzy sets have been proposed, such as intuitionistic fuzzy sets (Atanassov, 1986), hesitant fuzzy sets (Torra, 2010), and others (Turksen, 1986; Peng & Selvachandran, 2019; Zhang et al., 2019). These generalizations broaden the scope of fuzzy mathematics and offer additional approaches to handle uncertainty. These generalizations have found extensive application across diverse fields and problem domains. Ecer (2022) introduced a novel extension of the MAIRCA framework, namely intuitionistic fuzzy MAIRCA, designed to assess coronavirus vaccines according to specific evaluation criteria. Mishra et al. (2022) proposed a multi-attribute decision making method based on hesitant fuzzy sets and the modified VIKOR method, which effectively addresses the limitations of existing MADM methods. Chai et al. (2023) combined intuitionistic fuzzy sets, interval-valued fuzzy sets, and cumulative prospect theory to propose a novel fuzzy multi-attribute decision making method for selecting the most sustainable supplier. Wang et al. (2022) proposed a novel method for measuring the entropy of Pythagorean fuzzy set, considering both the Pythagorean fuzziness entropy based on membership and non-membership degrees, and the Pythagorean hesitation entropy based on the degree of hesitation. Zhang et al. (2021a, 2022a) introduced q-ROFSs into the framework of MG TWD and explored a novel approach for multi-attribute group decision making (MAGDM) in q-rung orthopair fuzzyinformation systems. Its main focus was on exploring MAGDM with imprecise and incomplete q-rung orthopair fuzzy information.

TFSs (Van Laarhoven & Pedrycz, 1983) are a commonly employed type of fuzzy set that adeptly captures the fuzzy nature of variables. Their extensive utilization in multi-attribute decision-making problems arises from their capacity to precisely portray the fuzzy characteristics of variables. Yue et al. (2023) integrated TFSs and intuitionistic fuzzy sets, redefined and validated the algorithm, expectation function, and distance measure of triangular intuitionistic fuzzy numbers, and introduced a new theory of triangular intuitionistic fuzzy sets (TIFSs). Garg and Rani (2022) presented novel distance measures for intuitionistic fuzzy sets in decision-making, utilizing different triangle centers, and validated their effectiveness through various patterns and challenges, while also providing a clustering algorithm for object matching based on confidence levels. In contrast, this paper utilizes a fusion approach that combined TFSs with MG TWD to assess different indicators of glucometer products. The objective is to identify the most suitable product for patients.

A Brief Review of MG TWD

Granular computing is a computational model that focuses on granularity in understanding and processing data and information. It treats them as complex systems consisting of elements at various levels of granularity. Through operations like grouping, classification, and aggregation, the relationships and mappings between different granularities are established, facilitating efficient information processing and management. Among the techniques used in granular computing, TWD stand out as a prominent tool. Unlike traditional two-way decisions, TWD incorporate the concept of delayed decision-making (Wang et al., 2021). This allows decision-makers (DMs) to gather ample information and grasp the associated risks of different choices, leading to more precise decision-making processes.

TWD was originally proposed by Yao (2010) in 2010 and have since undergone further expansion and development through subsequent research (Yao, 2016, 2018, 2020). Indeed, there has been a significant amount of research conducted on TWD in recent years. Wang et al. (2023) proposed a new decision-making method that combined regret theory with TWDs in fuzzy incomplete information systems. Yi et al. (2022) successfully accomplished the effective integration of Pythagorean fuzzy theory and TWD, thereby enhancing three-way decision-making by incorporating risk preference. Liu et al. (2022) introduced interval-valued intuitionistic fuzzy sets into the loss functions of decision-theoretic rough sets and proposed an optimization-based approach for interval-valued intuitionistic fuzzy TWDs. Furthermore, in the research of some scholars (Zhang et al., 2020b; Lei et al., 2020b; Zhang et al., 2023a; Han et al., 2022), they have combined the TWD approach with linguistic sets to address a wider range of problems and domains. Qian et al. (2010) proposed MG rough sets as an extension to the single-granularity granular computing model, acknowledging that a single-granularity approach can offer only a limited perspective on complex problems. By incorporating multiple equivalence relations from diverse viewpoints, MG rough sets provide advantages in information fusion and analysis. By integrating TWDs with MG computing, some scholars (Zhang et al., 2020a; Pang et al., 2020; Zhang et al., 2021b; Zhang et al., 2022b; Zhang et al., 2022c; Zhang et al., 2023b) offered a multidimensional solution approach for MAGDM. Therefore, this paper adopts the MG TWD method, enabling flexible adjustments and improvements tailored to the specific problem. It offers an effective decision support and guidance mechanism.

A Brief Review of PROMETHEE

MG TWDs have limitations, and certain simplified models of MG TWDs may encounter issues such as a singular threshold or a singular decision matrix. These problems can hinder the effectiveness of the decision-making process.

In response to the above issues, Akram et al. (2023) developed two effective and practical multi-criteria group decision-making approaches by leveraging the groundbreaking theory of the PROMETHEE family of outranking methods. Li et al. (2022) introduced a new DEMATEL method that is based on grey relation analysis using objective data within a decision matrix. Ridha et al. (2023) have introduced a new integration of the best worst method and preference ranking organization for enrichment evaluations method, along with a group decision making mechanism, to sort and rank optimal sets of pareto optimal front solutions based on expert opinions with full consistency ratios and stable ranking configurations. In addition, many scholars have also discussed their applications (Seikh & Mandal, 2023; X. Sang et al., 2022; Moreira et al., 2022; Ahmadi & Peivandizadeh, 2022). Therefore, this paper employs the PROMETHEE method, which enables the evaluation and selection of multiple DMs and multiple decision matrices to achieve optimal decision outcomes.

The Motives and Contribution of This Chapter

Based on the comprehensive literature review, this research aims to integrate TFSs with MG techniques to propose a new MG TWD method within the PROMETHEE framework. The motivation for this study is as follows:

1. Traditional rough set models have limitations when dealing with uncertainty and complexity, necessitating models that are better suited for high-dimensional, complex, and uncertain data. The concepts of TFSs and MG play crucial roles in describing uncertain information. Constructing a MG TFS information system allows for a more accurate completion of the information description process.
2. It is necessary to introduce the concept of adjustable MG TFSs in the information fusion process of glucometers. This is because the MG TWD paradigm provides an effective tool for integrating multi-source information, thereby minimizing the overall decision-making risk.
3. In the application of MG TWD, determining the thresholds is an additional critical task for classifying all objectives. Thus, the integration of effective MAGDM tools is necessary to complete the information analysis process. By utilizing MAGDM, challenges stemming from uncertainty in attribute weights, attribute values, decision preferences, and complex interactions among attributes can be addressed, ultimately improving decision efficiency and accuracy.

Based on the mentioned study motives, we can now summarize the significant contributions of this chapter as follows:

1. In order to enhance the information description capability of TFSs, the concept of the MG TFS information system is introduced.
2. To merge the MG TWD paradigm with TFSs, the concept of adjustable MG triangular fuzzy probabilistic rough set (PRS) is introduced.

3. The MABAC method is employed to determine the most suitable thresholds, forming the foundation for the development of a TF MAGDM method that incorporates MG TWD.

Based on the aforementioned literature analysis, we have organized this chapter as follows. In Section 2, we present several key concepts. Section 3 introduces the concept of an adjustable MG TF PRS model. Section 4 focuses on the development of a novel glucometer selection decision model based on this theoretical framework. In Section 5, we apply the proposed selection decision method to a real-world case study for practical analysis. Finally, we summarize the key findings and conclusions, and provide an outlook on future research directions.

BASIC KNOWLEDGE

TFNs

Triangular fuzzy numbers (TFNs) are valuable in representing uncertain information in diabetes diagnosis, aiding doctors in evaluating the multifactorial aspects of the disease. The following presents the fundamental definition of TFNs.

Definition 2.1: (Gilbey, 2009; Van Laarhoven, & Pedrycz, 1983) Let a real number $x=(x^L,x^M,x^U)$ satisfy $0<x^L\leq x^M\leq x^U$, then x is called a TFN with a membership degree of:

$$f_x(a)=\begin{cases}\dfrac{a-x^L}{x^M-x^L}, a\in\left[x^L,x^M\right]\\ \dfrac{x^U-a}{x^U-x^M}, a\in\left[x^M,x^U\right]\\ 0, other\end{cases} \tag{1}$$

In the above formula, x^L and x^U respectively represent the lower and upper bounds of the TFN x, x^M represents the internal maximum possible value. When $x^L=x^M=x^U$, the TFN x is equivalent to a fixed value of real numbers.

In practical decision-making, uncertain information is frequently encountered. Making judgments solely based on real numbers is challenging. TFN offers a partial solution to this problem by integrating the concept of fuzzy sets.

Definition 2.2: (Mallak et al., 2022) Let U be a non-empty finite domain, and let A be a TFS on U. It can be represented as $A=\{\langle x, A(x)\rangle \mid x\in U\}$, where $A(x)=(x^L,x^M,x^U)$.

To investigate the TF rough set in multiple granularities, the concept of triangular fuzzy relation (TFR) is introduced.

Definition 2.3: Let U and V be two non-empty finite domains. The TFR R is defined as $R=\{\langle (x,y), R(x,y)\rangle \mid (x,y)\in U\times V\}$, where for any $(x,y)\in U\times V$, $R(x,y)$ represents the possible degree of membership of the relationship between x and y.

The concept of a score function for TFNs has been introduced to facilitate the comparison and analysis of distinct TFNs.

Definition 2.4: (Das, 2022; Mao, 2022) Given two TFNs $x=(x^L,x^M,x^U)$ and $y=(y^L,y^M,y^U)$, then the following rules hold:

$$(1)\ x\oplus y=\left[x^L+y^L,x^M+y^M,x^U+y^U\right] \tag{2}$$

$$(2)\ x-y=\left(x^L+\left(-y^L\right),x^M+\left(-y^M\right),x^U+\left(-y^U\right)\right) \tag{3}$$

Among which $-y=(-y^L,-y^M,-y^U)$ defined y as the opposite quantity;

$$(3)\ \frac{1}{x}=\left[\frac{1}{x^U},\frac{1}{x^M},\frac{1}{x^L}\right],x^L,x^M,x^U\neq 0 \tag{4}$$

$$kx=[kx^L,kx^M,kx^U],\ k\geq 0 \tag{5}$$

$$(5)\ x\otimes y=\left[x^Ly^L,x^My^M,x^Uy^U\right] \tag{6}$$

For a TFS A, the complement of set A is denoted as:

$$A^c=\left\{\left\langle x,\left(1-x^U,1-x^M,1-x^L\right)\right\rangle \mid x\in U\right\} \tag{7}$$

Definition 2.5: (F. Feng, 2020) For a specific TFN x, the score function for x is $s(x)=\frac{1}{l_x}\sum_{\gamma\in x}\gamma$, where l_x represents the number of elements contained within x.

Considering that TF distance measures play a crucial role in constructing complex TF information fusion and analysis models, the Euclidean distance is commonly employed when dealing with TFNs.

Definition 2.6: (Coscia, 2022) If we consider two TFNs, x and y, the Euclidean distance from x to y can be calculated as follows:

$$d(x,y)=\left\{\frac{1}{3}\left[\left(x^L-y^L\right)^2+\left(x^M-y^M\right)^2+\left(x^U-y^U\right)^2\right]\right\}^{\frac{1}{2}} \tag{8}$$

The TWD model based on decision-making

In fuzzy information systems, we define $U=\{x_1,\ldots,x_j,\ldots,x_m\}$ as the set of alternative solutions and $V=\{y_1,\ldots,y_k,\ldots,y_n\}$ as the set of attributes. Additionally, we have $u=\{u_1,\ldots,u_k,\ldots,u_n\}^T$ as the set of attribute weights, where $u_k\in[0,1]$ and $\sum_{k=1}^{n}u_k=1$. DM assess each alternative solution based on individual attributes to generate an assessment matrix $p=(q_{jk})_{m\times n}$, where q_{jk} represents the fuzzy evaluation value of x_j relative to y_k. Within the evaluation matrix P, $q_{\min}^k$ and $q_{\max}^k$ respectively indicate the minimum and maximum values relative to $q_{jk} \in \left[q_{\min}^k, q_{\max}^k\right]$.

The TWD model based on decision-making usually consist of two states and three actions. Firstly, let us define the state set $\Omega=\{V,\neg V\}$, which includes two mutually exclusive states representing belonging to the state or not belonging to let the state. The action set is represented as $A=\{a_P,a_B,a_N\}$, which includes three actions for classification: a_P, a_B and a_N. These actions respectively represent x_j belonging to the $POS(V)$, x_j belonging to the $BND(V)$, and x_j belonging to the $NEG(V)$. The parameter $\sigma\in[0,0.5]$ represents the DM's risk preference. When $\sigma=0$, the DM tends to fully embrace risk. When $\sigma=0.5$, the DM tends to completely avoid risk. When $\sigma\in[0,0.5]$, the DM's risk preference gradually transitions from fully embracing risk to completely avoiding risk. According to the decision rules of classical loss functions and the parameter σ, we can calculate the loss functions for the positive region, negative region, and boundary region. Thus, the relative loss function for each alternative solution can be represented as shown in Table 1 below.

Table 1. The relative loss function of x_j

	$V(P)$	$\neg V(N)$
a_P	0	$1 - q_j$
a_B	σq_j	$\sigma(1 - q_j)$
a_N	q_j	0

By utilizing the relative loss functions presented in Table 1 and the established TWD model, the thresholds for x_j are represented as α_j and β_j, respectively:

$$\alpha_j = \frac{(1-\sigma)(1-q_j)}{(1-\sigma)(1-q_j)+\sigma q_j} \tag{9}$$

$$\beta_j = \frac{\sigma(1-q_j)}{\sigma(1-q_j)+(1-\sigma)q_j} \tag{10}$$

PROMETHEE

Given a set of alternative solutions, U, a set of attributes, V, a set of attribute weights, u, and a set of DM's weights, ω, the specific steps of the PROMETHEE evaluation method are as follows:

Step 1: Standardize the decision matrix.

$$h_{ij} = \frac{x_{ij} - \min\left(x_{ij}\right)}{\max\left(x_{ij}\right) - \min\left(x_{ij}\right)} \tag{11}$$

x_{ij} is a positive criterion;

$$h_{ij} = \frac{\max\left(x_{ij}\right) - x_{ij}}{\max\left(x_{ij}\right) - \min\left(x_{ij}\right)} \tag{12}$$

x_{ij} is a negative criterion.

Step 2: Determine the preference function.

After normalizing the matrix, taking into account the bounded rationality of the DMs, establish the suitable preference function.

$P_j(h_{ij},h_{kj})=F_j(d_j(h_{ij},h_{kj}))$, among, $d_j(h_{ij},h_{kj})=h_{ij}-h_{kj}$. $P_j(h_{ij},h_{kj})$ represents a function that measures the evaluation difference of h_{ij} compared to h_{kj} across various attributes within the range of [0,1].

Step 3: Calculate the preference index.

Afterward, aggregate the preference functions of all attributes to obtain the multi-attribute preference index. If weights are assigned, the preference index should be multiplied by their respective weight values.

$$I\left(h_{ij}, h_{kj}\right) = \sum_{j=1}^{n}\left(\omega_j P\left(h_{ij}, h_{kj}\right)\right) \tag{13}$$

Step 4: Calculate the net flow values.

Let $\phi^{+}(A_i)$ and $\phi^{-}(A_i)$ be the positive and negative flows, respectively:

$$\phi^{+}\left(A_i\right) = \frac{1}{m-1}\sum_{k=1}^{m} I\left(A_i, A_k\right) \tag{14}$$

$$\phi^{-}\left(A_i\right) = \frac{1}{m-1}\sum_{k=1}^{m} I\left(A_k, A_i\right) \tag{15}$$

Step 5: Ranking of alternatives.

The alternatives are ranked based on their net flow values, which can be calculated using the following formula:

$$\phi(A_i)=\phi^{+}(A_i)-\phi^{-}(A_i) \tag{16}$$

where, the greater the value of $\phi(A_i)$, the more favorable the alternative.

ADJUSTABLE MG TF PRS

In the TF group decision-making, let us assume there are f DMs. Each DM needs to provide a decision matrix consisting of the set of alternative options, attribute set, attribute weight set, and DM weight set. Assuming U represents the set of alternative options, V represents the set of attributes, U represents the set of attribute weights, $\omega=\{\omega_1,\omega_2,\ldots,\omega_f\}^T$ represents the set of DM weights, where $\omega_i\in[0,1]$ and $\sum_{i=1}^{f}\omega_i=1$. R_i denotes the TFR on $U\times V$, and A represents the set of standard evaluation. In conclusion, a MG triangular fuzzy information system (TFIS) (U,V,R_i,A) can be established.

Definition 3.1: Given a MG TFIS (U,V,R_i,A), for any given $x_j\in U$ $(j=1,2,\ldots,m)$, $y_k\in V$ $(k=1,2,\ldots,n)$, initially determine the attribute weights

$$u_{ij}^{R_i}=\frac{\sum_{j=1}^{m}\sum_{l=1}^{m}\left(d\left(R_i\left(x_j,y_k\right),R_i\left(x_l,y_k\right)\right)\right)}{\sum_{k=1}^{n}\sum_{j=1}^{m}\sum_{l=1}^{m}\left(d\left(R_i\left(x_j,y_k\right),R_i\left(x_l,y_k\right)\right)\right)}$$

for each consumer using the method of maximizing deviations. Subsequently, employ the method of maximizing deviations to ascertain the reviewer weights, defined as follows:

$$\omega_i=\frac{\sum_{j=1}^{n}\sum_{o=1}^{n}\left(d\left(u_{ij}^{R_i},u_{io}^{R_i}\right)\right)}{\sum_{i=1}^{f}\sum_{j=1}^{n}\sum_{o=1}^{n}\left(d\left(u_{ij}^{R_i},u_{io}^{R_i}\right)\right)} \tag{17}$$

To effectively construct MG TF TWD models, the following MG TF membership degree is presented.

Definition 3.2: Given a MG TFIS (U,V,R_i,A), let $\varphi_A^{R_i}\left(x_j\right)$ represent the MG TF membership of x_j with respect to R_i, defined as follows:

$$\varphi_A^{R_i}\left(x_j\right)=\left(\frac{\sum_{y_k\in V}u_kR_i\left(x_j,y_k\right)\left(A\left(y_k\right)\right)^c}{\sum_{y_k\in V}u_kR_i\left(x_j,y_k\right)}\right)^c \tag{18}$$

In what follows, the concept of adjustable TF membership degrees is further developed.

Definition 3.3: Given a MG TFIS (U,V,R_i,A), let $\varphi_A^{R_i}(x_j)$ represent the MG TF membership degrees. Assuming that all values in $\varphi_A^{R_i}(x_j)$ are arranged in ascending order, the value $\varphi_A^{R_{\sigma(i)}}(x_j)$ at the i-th position is referred to as the adjustable TF membership degree of x_j with respect to (U,V,R_i,A).

Based on the adjustable TF membership degree, it is possible to further construct the adjustable MG TF PRS.

Definition 3.4: Given a MG TFIS (U,V,R_i,A), with ξ and ζ as two thresholds where ζ<ξ, the upper and lower approximations of the adjustable MG TF PRS of the TFS A with respect to (U,V,R_i,A) can be expressed as follows:

$$\underline{\sum_{i=1}^{f} R_i}^{\varphi,\xi,\eta}(A)=\left\{\varphi_A^{R_{\sigma(i)}}(x_j)\geq\xi \mid x_j\in U\right\} \tag{19}$$

$$\overline{\sum_{i=1}^{f} R_i}^{\varphi,\zeta,\eta}(A)=\left\{\varphi_A^{R_{\sigma(i)}}(x_j)>\zeta \mid x_j\in U\right\} \tag{20}$$

$\left(\underline{\sum_{i=1}^{f} R_i}^{\varphi,\xi,\eta}(A),\overline{\sum_{i=1}^{f} R_i}^{\varphi,\zeta,\eta}(A)\right)$ is referred to as the adjustable MG TF PRS of the TFS A with respect to (U,V,R_i,A). The parameter $\eta=\frac{i}{f}$ represents the DM's risk coefficient. When η=1, the DM tends to fully pursue risk. When $\eta=\frac{i}{f}$, the DM tends to fully avoid risk. When $\eta=\left[\frac{1}{f},1\right]$, the DM's risk preference gradually adjusts from fully risk-averse to fully risk-seeking. The positive region, negative region, and boundary region of the adjustable MG TF PRS can be expressed as follows:

$$POS_{\xi,\zeta}^{\varphi}(A)=\underline{\sum_{i=1}^{f} R_i}^{\varphi,\xi,\eta}(A) \tag{21}$$

$$NEG_{\xi,\eta}^{\varphi}(A)=U-\overline{\sum_{i=1}^{f} R_i}^{\varphi,\zeta,\eta}(A) \tag{22}$$

$$BND_{\xi,\zeta}^{\varphi}(A)=\overline{\sum_{i=1}^{f} R_i}^{\varphi,\zeta,\eta}(A)-\underline{\sum_{i=1}^{f} R_i}^{\varphi,\xi,\eta}(A) \tag{23}$$

This model mitigates the pitfalls of complete optimism and complete pessimism, enabling the DMs to fine-tune their risk coefficient. This flexibility proves advantageous in addressing issues pertaining to the selection of blood glucose monitors.

Remark: *In the context of glucometer decision-making, given a MG TFIS information system, we can obtain MG TFS PRSs by combining MG PRSs. The model proposed in this section integrates the data from DMs with higher efficiencies and fault tolerances, making it suitable for handling risk-based MAGDM problems.*

THE SELECTION OF GLUCOMETERS BASED ON THE ADJUSTABLE MG TF PRS MODEL

In the context of choosing a glucometer, this section presents a method for MAGDM using TFSs based on (U, V, R_i, A). Firstly, consumers identify the attributes associated with each brand $\varphi_A^{R_{\sigma(i)}}(x_j)$. Subsequently, an objective approach is provided to calculate the relative loss functions. Finally, the classification and ranking results for brand performance are determined.

A TF MAGDM BASED ON MG TWD

To objectively calculate the relative loss function, we need to utilize the TF membership $\varphi_A^{R_i}(x_j)$ of each x_j with respect to (U, V, R_i, A), forming a new evaluation matrix P. In addition, within the evaluation matrix P, for each $\varphi_{ji} \in \left[\varphi_{\min}^i, \varphi_{\max}^i\right]$, $\varphi_{\min}^i$ and $\varphi_{\max}^i$ represent the lower and upper bounds, respectively, relative to R_i.

Moreover, the relative loss function from classical fuzzy information systems has been generalized to the context of TF systems. The TF relative loss function of x_j is illustrated in Table 2. Additionally, by incorporating the parameter $\sigma \in [0,0.5]$ to capture DM's risk preferences, the loss functions for the positive domain, negative domain, and boundary domain can be computed.

Table 2. The aggregated TF relative loss functions

	$R(P)$	$\neg R(P)$
a_P	0	$\neg\varphi_j$
a_B	$\sigma\varphi_j$	$\sigma(\neg\varphi_j)$
a_N	φ_j	0

Based on the relative loss function of x_j in Table 2 and the MG TWD framework, the two thresholds for x_j, denoted as ξ_j and ζ_j, are represented as follows:

$$\xi_j = \frac{(1-\sigma)(\neg\varphi_j)}{(1-\sigma)(\neg\varphi_j)+\sigma\varphi_j} \tag{24}$$

$$\zeta_j = \frac{\sigma(\neg\varphi_j)}{\sigma(\neg\varphi_j)+(1-\sigma)\varphi_j} \tag{25}$$

With the obtained thresholds, we can compute adjustable TF memberships to classify the evaluation results for different brands. Moreover, by applying the ranking structure $POS^{\varphi}_{\xi,\zeta}(A) \succ BND^{\varphi}_{\xi,\zeta}(A) \succ \mathrm{NEG}^{\varphi}_{\xi,\zeta}(A)$, we can rank the performance evaluations of all brands and sort the evaluation results using a scoring function.

TF MAGDM Steps

Based on the above analysis, the specific steps of the TF MAGDM method can be summarized as follows:

Input: A MG TFIS (U,V,R_i,A).
Output: The brand of glucometer chosen.

Step 1: The weights of each consumer attribute are determined using the maximization of deviation method, followed by determining the weights of the experts using the same method, and finally, the parameter σ is determined.
Step 2: Compute the MG TF memberships of each attribute with respect to (U,V,R_i,A).
Step 3: Compute the adjustable MG TF memberships.
Step 4: Calculate the TFR loss function for each x_j.
Step 5: Calculate the three thresholds corresponding to each consumer.
Step 6: Integrate the thresholds using the TF PROMETHEE method.
Step 7: Determine the positive domain, boundary domain, and negative domain based $\underline{\sum_{i=1}^{f} R_i}^{\varphi,\xi,\eta}$ and $\overline{\sum_{i=1}^{f} R_i}^{\varphi,\zeta,\eta}$.

Moreover, the algorithm of the presented method is shown below.

In the aforementioned decision steps of the TFS MAGDM method, assuming the number of all backup options is denoted as m, the number of all attributes as n, and the total number of DMs as f, the complexity of Steps 1 to 8 is presented as follows: $O(mmm)$, $O(mmm)$, $O(nmf)$, $O(mf)$, $O(mf)$, $O(mf)$, $O(mf)$, $O(mf)$. Based on the above analysis, the overall complexity of the proposed TFS MAGDM method is $O(nmm)$.

CASE ANALYSIS

Case Descriptions

This study introduces the adjustable multi-granularity triangular fuzzy PRS model to assist diabetic patients in making informed decisions. The proposed method establishes a three-way decision-making approach based on adjustable multi-granularity TF PRS, aiming to enhance the decision-making process. The model is described as follows:

Algorithm 1: The algorithm of TFS MAGDM

Input: A MG TFIS (U,V,R_i,A)
Output: The brand of glucometer chosen
For i=1 to n, j=1 to m, and k=1 to m do
Obtain the attribute weight
For i=1 to n, j=1 to m, and k=1 to m do
Obtain the expert weight.
For i=1 to f, j=1 to m, and k=1 to n do
Calculate the single TFS membership degree $\varphi_A^{R_i}\left(x_j\right)$, according to Definition 3.2.
For i=1 to f, j=1 to m do
Compute the adjustable TFS membership $\varphi_A^{R_{\sigma(i)}}\left(x_j\right)$.
For i=1 to f, j=1 to m do
Compute aggregated TFS relative loss function based on Table 2.
For i=1 to f, j=1 to m do
Compute aggregated TFS relative loss function based on Table 2.
For i=1 to f, j=1 to m do
Calculate two thresholds ξ_j and ζ_j, according to Section 4.1.
For i=1 to f, j=1 to m do
Positive, boundary and negative regions are determined by adjustable MG TF PRS and thresholds.
For i=1 to f, j=1 to m do
Obtain classification and ranking of all alternatives.

We begin with a TF information system, denoted as (U, V, R_i, A), which represents online reviews. In this system, $U=\{x_1,x_2,x_3,x_4,x_5\}$ represents the brand set, with x_1 representing Fish Jump, x_2 representing Roche, x_3 representing Wenjie, x_4 representing Abbott, and x_5 representing Sanno. The consumer-determined attribute set comprises y_1 (repurchase), y_2 (accuracy), y_3 (low blood collection), y_4 (after-sale degree), and y_5 (low pain perception). Assuming a consumer's choice set

$$A=\{\langle y_1,0.5\rangle,\langle y_2,0.4\rangle,\langle y_3,0.7\rangle,\langle y_4,0.3\rangle,\langle y_5,0.6\rangle\},$$

the adjustable multi-granularity TF PRS model for selecting glucose meter brand performance is established based on U, V, R_i, and A.

In the context of evaluating glucose meter performance, a triangular fuzzy information system is established to determine the objective weights of experts and set the parameter $\sigma=\{0.25,0.25,0.25\}^T$. By computing TF membership and constructing new matrices based on individual membership, we derive adjustable TF membership and build a new matrix.

Next, the expert group, with a value of $\eta=\frac{2}{3}$, obtains the relative loss function of the triangular fuzzy numbers. Subsequently, the final diagnostic threshold is calculated using the relative loss function of the triangular fuzzy numbers and the PROMETHEE method, as depicted in Table 3. Finally, the final ranking results are obtained based on the scoring mechanism of the model.

Overall, the adjustable MG TF PRS model offers a framework for decision-making in glucose meter selection, utilizing a combination of fuzzy mathematics and rough set theory, the ranking results are listed as follows: $x_3 \succ x_1 \succ x_5 \succ x_2 \succ x_4$.

Table 3. Final thresholds

	ξj	ζj
x_1	[0.7494,0.7595,0.773]	[0.2495,0.2597,0.2745]
x_2	[0.75,0.7822,0.7168]	[0.25,0.2852,0.2195]
x_3	[0.7494,0.7802,0.7782]	[0.2495,0.2829,0.2805]
x_4	[0.75,0.7922,0.7721]	[0.25,0.2976,0.2735]
x_5	[0.75,0.7939,0.7409]	[0.25,0.2998,0.2412]

Comparison Analysis

In this section, we demonstrate the effectiveness of the proposed method by comparing it with similar MAGDM methods. Specifically, we compare it with the classical MAGDM method, as well as specific methods such as VIKOR, TOPSIS, TODIM, MABAC, and ensemble operator methods. The results of these comparisons are presented in Figure 1. Additionally, we compare the proposed method with VIKOR, TOPSIS, TODIM, and MABAC under the TWD model, and the results are illustrated in Figure 2.

From Figure 1, it is evident that the results of VIKOR and the ensemble operator methods align with those of the proposed method, all achieving optimal insert values. Although MABAC, TODIM, and TOPSIS show some variation from our results, the optimal values in our method closely resemble those in MABAC, TODIM, and TOPSIS. Overall, the numerical trends of these classical MAGDM methods are similar to our proposed method, thus validating its effectiveness.

Figure 1. Comparative analysis with classic MAGDM methods

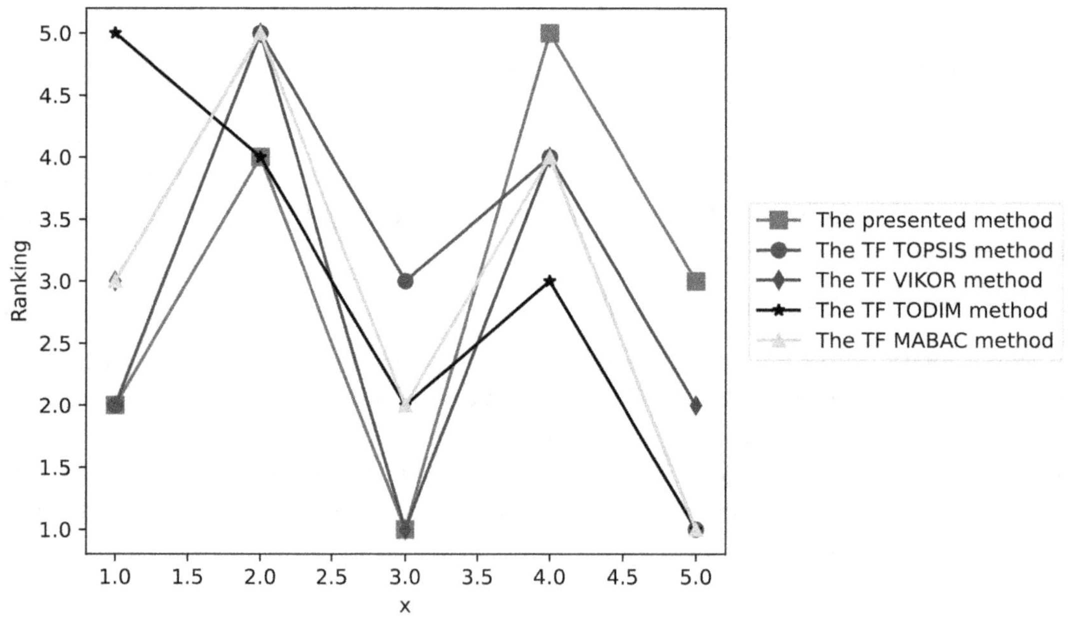

Figure 2 demonstrates that the optimal values obtained by the VIKOR, TOPSIS, and TODIM methods under the TWD model coincide with the results of the proposed method, further substantiating its effectiveness.

Figure 2. Comparison of our method with the classic MAGDM methods under TWD

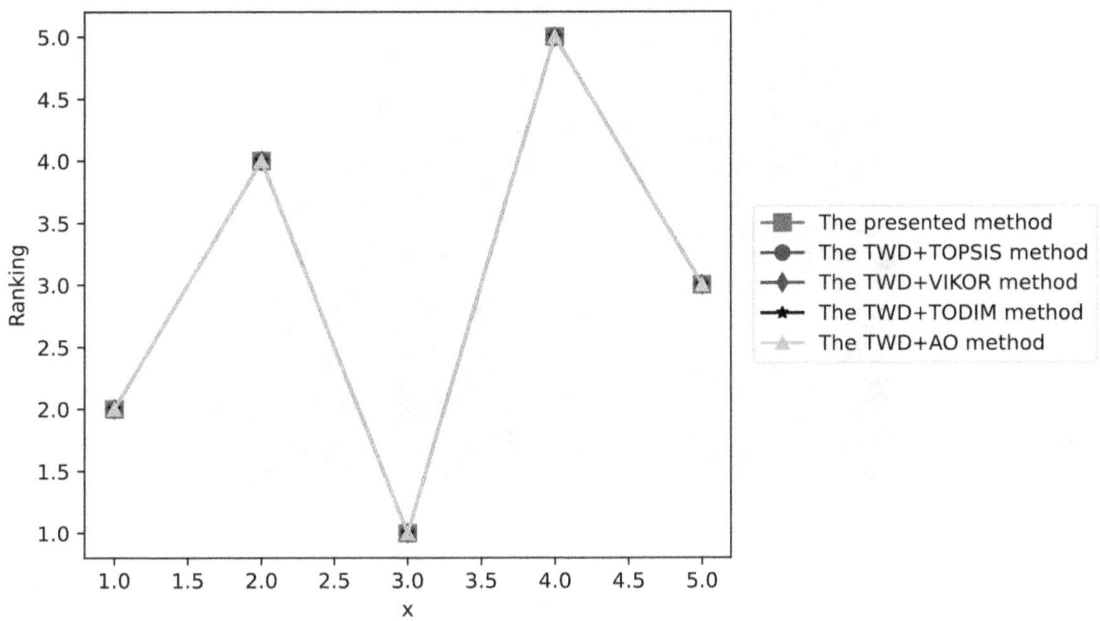

Furthermore, we conducted an analysis of Spearman's correlation coefficient, the results of which are depicted in Figure 3. Spearman correlation coefficients ranging from 0.8 to 1.0 indicate an extremely strong correlation, while coefficients between 0.6 and 0.8 indicate a strong correlation. As shown in Figure 3, the proposed method exhibits a strong correlation with other methods, providing an additional confirmation of its effectiveness.

Sensitivity Analysis

Sensitivity analysis is an analytical method that involves modifying parameters, variables, or assumptions in a study and observing the impact of these variations on model outputs or results. Its core purpose is to assess the sensitivity of a model or system to changes in input parameters or variables, aiming to gain insights into the stability, reliability, and feasibility of the model or system.

In order to gain a deeper understanding of the impact of various parameters, a sensitivity analysis was conducted on the parameters discussed in the preceding sections. Specifically, we examined the influence of two parameters: η, which represents the risk coefficient of the decision maker, and σ, which represents the risk preference of the decision maker.

Figure 3. The Spearman coefficient with different methods

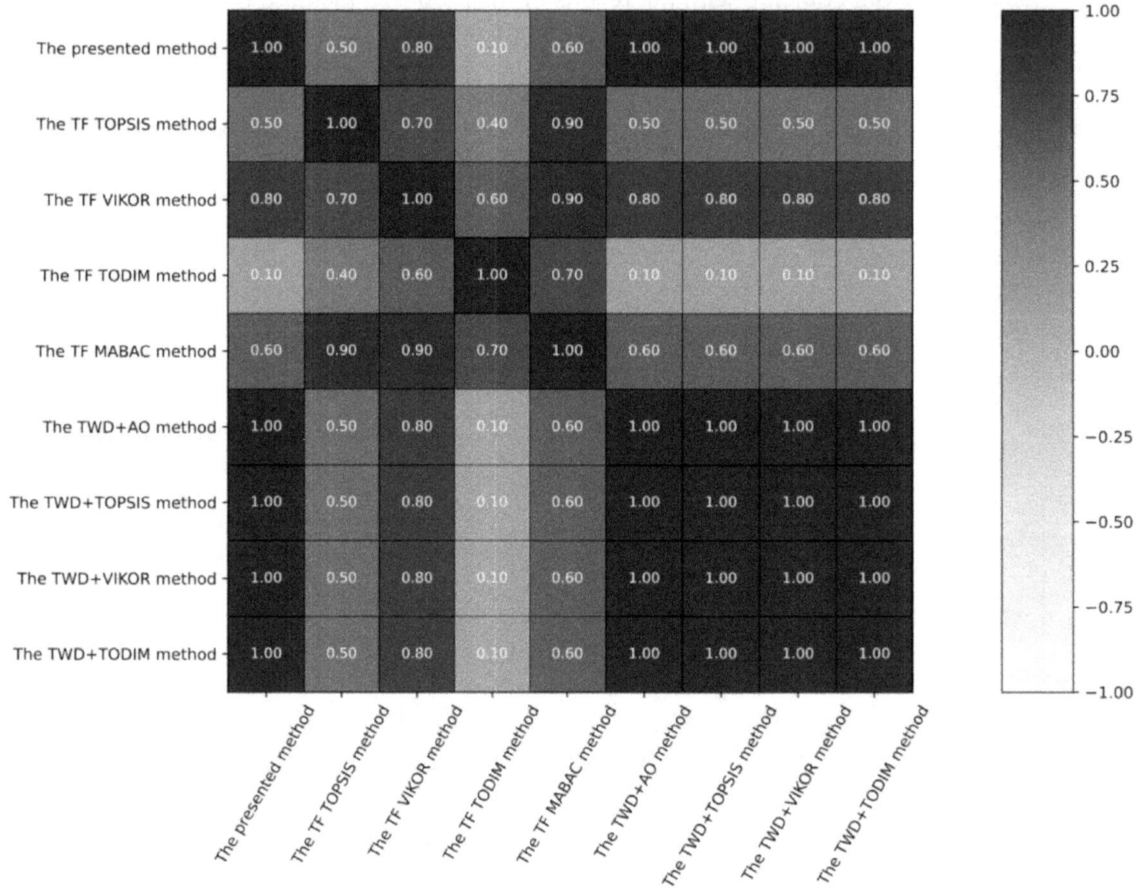

Table 4. Classification results of different η

	$POS^{\psi}_{\xi,\varsigma}(B)$	$BND^{\psi}_{\xi,\varsigma}(B)$	$NEG^{\psi}_{\xi,\varsigma}(B)$
$\eta=\frac{1}{3}$	$\varnothing$	x_1,x_2,x_3,x_4,x_5	$\varnothing$
$\eta=\frac{2}{3}$	$\varnothing$	x_1,x_2,x_3,x_4,x_5	$\varnothing$
η=1	$\varnothing$	x_1,x_2,x_3,x_4,x_5	$\varnothing$

Table 4 presents the results obtained by varying the value of η, while Table 5 displays the results obtained by varying the value of σ. These tables offer valuable insights into how different values of η and σ affect the outcomes of our analysis.

By conducting this sensitivity analysis, we can better comprehend the significance of these parameters and their implications for decision making. This information will contribute to a more comprehensive understanding of the overall decision-making process.

Table 5. Classification results of different σ

	$POS^{\psi}_{\xi,\varsigma}(B)$	$BND^{\psi}_{\xi,\varsigma}(B)$	$NEG^{\psi}_{\xi,\varsigma}(B)$
σ=0	∅	x_1,x_2,x_3,x_4x_5	∅
σ=0.25	∅	x_1,x_2,x_3,x_4x_5	∅
σ=0.5	∅	x_1,x_2,x_3,x_4x_5	∅

CONCLUSION

Glucometers are essential products for diabetic patients as they play a crucial role in managing their condition. Therefore, selecting the right glucose meter is of utmost importance. This study aims to develop a decision-making method to assist diabetic patients in choosing appropriate glucose meter products. To address the challenge of MAGDM, the study introduces the adjustable MG TF PRS model within a TFIS.

The proposed method is built upon the adjustable MG-TF-PRS model and utilizes a three-way decision-making approach. This model has demonstrated effectiveness in addressing the inherent uncertainty and fuzziness encountered during the decision-making process for selecting new glucometer products. Furthermore, its applicability in this specific context has been established. In terms of potential future research applications, the tunable MG-TF-PRS model can be extended to other domains involving decision-making under uncertainty and fuzziness.

Further research can be extended in the following areas:

Consideration of additional decision factors: Apart from the mentioned attributes, other factors such as data management functions and persistence should be taken into account to provide a more comprehensive decision support system.

Exploration of alternative decision models: In addition to the adjustable MG TF PRS model, other decision models, such as trapezoidal fuzzy set theory and fuzzy comprehensive evaluation methods, can be investigated to compare their performance, strengths, and weaknesses.

Incorporation of actual needs and user preferences: By incorporating the actual needs and user preferences of individuals with diabetes, it is possible to develop more specific and personalized metrics that better align with their requirements.

Validation and verification methods: The proposed decision-making method should undergo validation to assess its accuracy and reliability. This can be achieved through field investigations, case studies, or by comparing its performance against existing decision-making methods.

By conducting in-depth research in these areas, the scientific and practical aspects of glucometer selection can be further enhanced. This will enable better decision support for diabetic patients, assisting them in choosing the most suitable product that aligns with their specific needs.

ACKNOWLEDGMENT

The chapter was supported by grants from the National Natural Science Foundation of China (62272284, 61972238, 62072294), the Special Fund for Science and Technology Innovation Teams of Shanxi Province (202204051001015), the Graduate Education Innovation Programs of Shanxi University, Research Project Supported by Shanxi Scholarship Council of China (2022-007), the Training Program for Young Scientific Researchers of Higher Education Institutions in Shanxi, and the Cultivate Scientific Research Excellence Programs of Higher Education Institutions in Shanxi (CSREP) (2019SK036).

REFERENCES

Ahmadi, S. A., & Peivandizadeh, A. (2022). Sustainable portfolio optimization model using promethee ranking: A case study of palm oil buyer companies. *Discrete Dynamics in Nature and Society*, *8935213*, 1–11. doi:10.1155/2022/8935213

Akram, M., Zahid, K., & Kahraman, C. (2023). A PROMETHEE based outranking approach for the construction of Fangcang shelter hospital using spherical fuzzy sets. *Artificial Intelligence in Medicine*, *135*, 102456. doi:10.1016/j.artmed.2022.102456 PMID:36628791

Atanassov, K. T. (1986). Intuitionistic fuzzy sets. *Fuzzy Sets and Systems*, *20*(1), 87–96. doi:10.1016/S0165-0114(86)80034-3

Chai, N., Zhou, W., & Jiang, Z. (2023). Sustainable supplier selection using an intuitionistic and interval-valued fuzzy MCDM approach based on cumulative prospect theory. *Information Sciences*, *626*, 710–737. doi:10.1016/j.ins.2023.01.070

Cheng, Y. T., Zhang, C., Sangaiah, A. K., Fan, X. Q., Wang, A. N., Wang, L. Y., & Liu, Y. X. (2023). Efficient Low-Resource Medical Information Processing Based on Semantic Analysis and Granular Computing. *ACM Transactions on Asian and Low-Resource Language Information Processing*, *3626319*, 3626319. doi:10.1145/3626319

Coscia, M. (2022). Generalized euclidean measure to estimate distances on multilayer networks. *ACM Transactions on Knowledge Discovery from Data*, *16*(6), 1–22. doi:10.1145/3529396

Das, S. K. (2022). An approach to optimize the cost of transportation problem based on triangular fuzzy programming problem. *Complex & Intelligent Systems*, *8*(1), 687–699. doi:10.1007/s40747-021-00535-2

Domingo-Lopez, D. A., Lattanzi, G., Schreiber, L. H. J., Wallace, E. J., Wylie, R., O'Sullivan, J., Dolan, E. B., & Duffy, G. P. (2022). Medical devices, smart drug delivery, wearables and technology for the treatment of diabetes mellitus. *Advanced Drug Delivery Reviews*, *185*, 114280. doi:10.1016/j.addr.2022.114280 PMID:35405298

Ecer, F. (2022). An extended MAIRCA method using intuitionistic fuzzy sets for coronavirus vaccine selection in the age of COVID-19. *Neural Computing & Applications*, *34*(7), 5603–5623. doi:10.1007/s00521-021-06728-7 PMID:35017795

Feng, F., Zheng, Y. J., Alcantud, J. C. R., & Wang, Q. (2020). Minkowski weighted score functions of intuitionistic fuzzy values. *Mathematics*, *8*(7), 1143. doi:10.3390/math8071143

Garg, H., & Rani, D. (2022). Novel distance measures for intuitionistic fuzzy sets based on various triangle centers of isosceles triangular fuzzy numbers and their applications. *Expert Systems with Applications*, *191*, 116228. doi:10.1016/j.eswa.2021.116228

Gilbey, J. (2009). Valuing the digital economy. *Nature*, *462*(7270), 165. doi:10.1038/462165a

Han, X. R., Zhang, C., & Zhan, J. M. (2022). A three-way decision method under probabilistic linguistic term sets and its application to Air Quality Index. *Information Sciences*, *617*, 254–276. doi:10.1016/j.ins.2022.10.108

Lei, W. J., Ma, W. M., & Sun, B. Z. (2020). Multigranulation behavioral three-way group decisions under hesitant fuzzy linguistic environment. *Information Sciences*, *537*, 91–115. doi:10.1016/j.ins.2020.05.025

Li, P., Xu, Z. W., Wei, C. P., Bai, Q. G., & Liu, J. (2022). A novel PROMETHEE method based on GRA-DEMATEL for PLTSs and its application in selecting renewable energies. *Information Sciences*, *589*, 142–161. doi:10.1016/j.ins.2021.12.090

Liu, J. B., Huang, B., Li, H. X., Bu, X. Z., & Zhou, X. Z. (2022). Optimization-based three-way decisions with interval-valued intuitionistic fuzzy information. *IEEE Transactions on Cybernetics*, *53*(6), 3829–3843. doi:10.1109/TCYB.2022.3151899 PMID:35275831

Mallak, S., Attili, B., & Subuh, M. (2022). Numerical Treatment of Hybrid Fuzzy Differential Equations Subject to Trapezoidal and Triangular Fuzzy Initial Conditions Using Picard's and the General Linear Method. *Computation (Basel, Switzerland)*, *10*(10), 168. doi:10.3390/computation10100168

Mao, Z. J., Shi, S. J., Li, H., Zhong, J. X., & Sun, J. W. (2022). Landslide susceptibility assessment using triangular fuzzy number-analytic hierarchy processing (TFN-AHP), contributing weight (CW) and random forest weighted frequency ratio (RF weighted FR) at the Pengyang county, Northwest China. *Environmental Earth Sciences*, *81*(3), 86. doi:10.1007/s12665-022-10193-3

Mishra, A. R., Chen, S. M., & Rani, P. (2022). Multiattribute decision making based on Fermatean hesitant fuzzy sets and modified VIKOR method. *Information Sciences*, *607*, 1532–1549. doi:10.1016/j.ins.2022.06.037

Moreira, M. Â. L., Gomes, C. F. S., Dos Santos, M., da Silva Júnior, A. C., & de Araújo Costa, I. P. (2022). Sensitivity analysis by the PROMETHEE-GAIA method: Algorithms evaluation for COVID-19 prediction. *Procedia Computer Science*, *199*, 431–438. doi:10.1016/j.procs.2022.01.052 PMID:35136460

Pang, J. F., Guan, X. Q., Liang, J. Y., Wang, B. L., & Song, P. (2020). Multi-attribute group decision-making method based on multi-granulation weights and three-way decisions. *International Journal of Approximate Reasoning*, *117*, 122–147. doi:10.1016/j.ijar.2019.11.008

Peng, X., & Selvachandran, G. (2019). Pythagorean fuzzy set: State of the art and future directions. *Artificial Intelligence Review*, *52*(3), 1873–1927. doi:10.1007/s10462-017-9596-9

Qian, Y. H., Liang, J. Y., Yao, Y. Y., & Dang, C. Y. (2010). MGRS: A multi-granulation rough set. *Information Sciences*, *180*(6), 949–970. doi:10.1016/j.ins.2009.11.023

Ridha, H. M., Hizam, H., Mirjalili, S., Othman, M. L., Ya'acob, M. E., & Ahmadipour, M. (2023). Innovative hybridization of the two-archive and PROMETHEE-II triple-objective and multi-criterion decision making for optimum configuration of the hybrid renewable energy system. *Applied Energy*, *341*, 121117. doi:10.1016/j.apenergy.2023.121117

Sang, X. Z., Yu, X. Y., Chang, C. T., & Liu, X. W. (2022). Electric bus charging station site selection based on the combined DEMATEL and PROMETHEE-PT framework. *Computers & Industrial Engineering*, *168*, 108116. doi:10.1016/j.cie.2022.108116

Seikh, M. R., & Mandal, U. (2023). Interval-valued fermatean fuzzy dombi aggregation operators and SWARA based PROMETHEE II method to bio-medical waste management. *Expert Systems with Applications*, *226*, 120082. doi:10.1016/j.eswa.2023.120082

Torra, V. (2010). Hesitant fuzzy sets. *International Journal of Intelligent Systems*, *25*, 529–539. doi:10.1002/int.20418

Turksen, I. B. (1986). Interval valued fuzzy sets based on normal forms. *Fuzzy Sets and Systems*, *20*(2), 191–210. doi:10.1016/0165-0114(86)90077-1

Van Laarhoven, P. J., & Pedrycz, W. (1983). A fuzzy extension of Saaty's priority theory. *Fuzzy Sets and Systems*, *11*(1-3), 229–241. doi:10.1016/S0165-0114(83)80082-7

Wang, W. J., Zhan, J. M., & Zhang, C. (2021). Three-way decisions based multi-attribute decision making with probabilistic dominance relations. *Information Sciences*, *559*, 75–96. doi:10.1016/j.ins.2021.01.028

Wang, W. J., Zhan, J. M., Zhang, C., Herrera-Viedma, E., & Kou, G. (2023). A regret-theory-based three-way decision method with a priori probability tolerance dominance relation in fuzzy incomplete information systems. *Information Fusion*, *89*, 382–396. doi:10.1016/j.inffus.2022.08.027

Wang, Z., Xiao, F. Y., & Cao, Z. H. (2022). Uncertainty measurements for Pythagorean fuzzy set and their applications in multiple-criteria decision making. *Soft Computing*, *26*(19), 9937–9952. doi:10.1007/s00500-022-07361-9 PMID:35966347

Yao, Y. Y. (2010). Three-way decisions with probabilistic rough sets. *Information Sciences*, *180*(3), 341–353. doi:10.1016/j.ins.2009.09.021

Yao, Y. Y. (2016). Three-way decisions and cognitive computing. *Cognitive Computation*, *8*(4), 543–554. doi:10.1007/s12559-016-9397-5

Yao, Y. Y. (2018). Three-way decision and granular computing. *International Journal of Approximate Reasoning*, *103*, 107–123. doi:10.1016/j.ijar.2018.09.005

Yao, Y. Y. (2020). Three-way granular computing, rough sets, and formal concept analysis. *International Journal of Approximate Reasoning*, *116*, 106–125. doi:10.1016/j.ijar.2019.11.002

Yi, J. H., Liu, Y., Forrest, J. Y. L., Guo, X. G., & Xu, X. J. (2022). A three-way decision approach with S-shaped utility function under Pythagorean fuzzy information. *Expert Systems with Applications*, *210*, 118370. doi:10.1016/j.eswa.2022.118370

Yue, Q., Zou, W. C., & Hu, W. (2023). A new theory of triangular intuitionistic fuzzy sets to solve the two-sided matching problem. *Alexandria Engineering Journal*, *63*, 57–73. doi:10.1016/j.aej.2022.07.018

Zadeh, L. A. (1965). Fuzzy sets. *Information and Control*, *8*(3), 338–353. doi:10.1016/S0019-9958(65)90241-X

Zhang, C., Bai, W. H., Li, D. Y., & Zhan, J. M. (2022a). Multiple attribute group decision making based on multigranulation probabilistic models, MULTIMOORA and TPOP in incomplete q-rung orthopair fuzzy information systems. *International Journal of Approximate Reasoning*, *143*, 102–120. doi:10.1016/j.ijar.2022.01.002

Zhang, C., Ding, J. J., Li, D. Y., & Zhan, J. M. (2021a). A novel multi-granularity three-way decision making approach in q-rung orthopair fuzzy information systems. *International Journal of Approximate Reasoning*, *138*, 161–187. doi:10.1016/j.ijar.2021.08.004

Zhang, C., Ding, J. J., Zhan, J. M., & Li, D. Y. (2022b). Incomplete three-way multi-attribute group decision making based on adjustable multigranulation Pythagorean fuzzy probabilistic rough sets. *International Journal of Approximate Reasoning*, *147*, 40–59. doi:10.1016/j.ijar.2022.05.004

Zhang, C., Ding, J. J., Zhan, J. M., Sangaiah, A. K., & Li, D. Y. (2022c). Fuzzy intelligence learning based on bounded rationality in IoMT systems: A case study in Parkinson's disease. *IEEE Transactions on Computational Social Systems*, *10*(4), 1607–1621. doi:10.1109/TCSS.2022.3221933

Zhang, C., Li, D. Y., & Liang, J. Y. (2020a). Interval-valued hesitant fuzzy multi-granularity three-way decisions in consensus processes with applications to multi-attribute group decision making. *Information Sciences*, *511*, 192–211. doi:10.1016/j.ins.2019.09.037

Zhang, C., Li, D. Y., & Liang, J. Y. (2020b). Multi-granularity three-way decisions with adjustable hesitant fuzzy linguistic multigranulation decision-theoretic rough sets over two universes. *Information Sciences*, *507*, 665–683. doi:10.1016/j.ins.2019.01.033

Zhang, C., Li, D. Y., Liang, J. Y., & Wang, B. L. (2021b). MAGDM-oriented dual hesitant fuzzy multigranulation probabilistic models based on MULTIMOORA. *International Journal of Machine Learning and Cybernetics*, *12*(5), 1219–1241. doi:10.1007/s13042-020-01230-3

Zhang, C., Li, D. Y., Zhai, Y. H., & Yang, Y. H. (2019). Multigranulation rough set model in hesitant fuzzy information systems and its application in person-job fit. *International Journal of Machine Learning and Cybernetics*, *10*(4), 717–729. doi:10.1007/s13042-017-0753-x

Zhang, C., Li, X. C., Sangaiah, A. K., Li, W. T., Wang, B. L., Cao, F., & Shangguan, X. K. (2023a). *Collaborative fuzzy linguistic learning to Low-Resource and robust decision system based on bounded rationality*. ACM Transactions on Asian and Low-Resource Language Information Processing. doi:10.1145/3592605

Zhang, C., Zhang, J. J., Li, W. T., Pedrycz, W., & Li, D. Y. (2023b). A regret theory-based MG three-way decision model with incomplete T-spherical fuzzy information and its application in forest fire management. *Applied Soft Computing*, *110539*, 110539. doi:10.1016/j.asoc.2023.110539

Chapter 3
Prediction of Parkinson's Disease Severity Based on Feature Optimization

Tao Zhang
https://orcid.org/0000-0003-0450-724X
Yanshan University, China

Zaifa Xue
Yanshan University, China

Zesheng Huo
Yanshan University, China

ABSTRACT

Voice disorders are one of the incipient symptoms of Parkinson's disease (PD). Most of the existing PD severity prediction methods are based on baseline features, and generally select features with high relevance for dimensionality reduction. To further improve the prediction performance, the LDFSF and GWT-RF-Att methods are proposed respectively from the perspective of feature selection and feature transformation. The LDFSF method utilizes dynamic feature selection strategy based on SOM clustering to select feature subsets with high correlation, low redundancy, and high complementarity from voice features. The GWT-RF-Att method uses graph wavelet transform to extract the more effective feature set based on the baseline features, and uses random forest improved by attention mechanism to improve the prediction performance of the model. The results on the Parkinson's telemonitoring dataset show that the performance of the two methods is better than that of the existing comparison methods, thus verifying their effectiveness.

DOI: 10.4018/979-8-3693-1582-8.ch003

INTRODUCTION

Parkinson's disease (PD) is a common degenerative nervous system disorder characterized by trembling, slow movement, postural balance disorder, and other motor symptoms. And PD patients will also be accompanied by symptoms such as voice disorders (Xue et al., 2022; Zhang et al., 2023a). Fortunately, voice disorders are one of the earliest symptoms of PD, which can generally be observed five years before clinical diagnosis (Zhang et al., 2023b). By analyzing the voice features of subjects, it is possible to use machine learning methods to analyze the severity of the diagnosed patients' conditions, which is of great significance for the early diagnosis and treatment of PD patients.

For the regression tasks for Parkinson's disease, using voice data for severity assessment of PD has shown promising results. The Unified Parkinson's Disease Rating Scale (UPDRS) is an internationally recognized measure for assessing the severity of Parkinson's disease symptoms (Yoon & Gaw, 2021). It consists of two components: motor-UPDRS and total-UPDRS, which assess motor symptoms and overall assessment of PD symptoms. In the past few decades, simple linear regression (LR), nonlinear classification regression tree, k-nearest neighbors (KNN) regression, and support vector regression (SVR) are commonly used traditional prediction methods for Parkinson's disease symptom severity due to their computational efficiency. However, these models may not achieve the desired prediction accuracy (Tsanas et al., 2010). In recent years, machine learning and neural network methods have gained popularity in UPDRS prediction. Mayo & Frank (2017) applied Bayesian regression and its modified version to improve prediction accuracy and generalization ability. Neural networks, such as feed-forward neural networks (Xiang et al., 2016) and adaptive network-based fuzzy inference systems (ANFIS) (Nilashi et al., 2017), have also been employed due to their ability to handle nonlinear relationships. However, neural networks require large datasets and careful parameter tuning, and may be prone to overfitting and lack of generalization ability (Hlavica et al., 2016).

To enhance the generalization ability of the PD severity prediction model, Tunc et al. (2020) proposed a combined approach of feature selection and extreme gradient boosting (XGBoost) based on decision trees (DT) to predict UPDRS scores in PD patients. Despotovic et al. (2020) used the automatic relevance determination (ARD) method to rank PD voice feature weights. In the study by Tsanas et al. (2021), random forest (RF), SVR, and XGBoost were used to evaluate PD severity, and RF exhibits superior prediction performance compared to SVR and XGBoost. RF has been found to possess higher effectiveness, stability, and robustness compared to artificial neural networks (Dong et al., 2021), making it a suitable choice for predicting UPDRS scores in PD patients. Furthermore, the selection of different input features for RF can impact the model's prediction performance (Liu et al., 2018).

However, the above method has the following two problems, which may increase the prediction error of the model. On the one hand, while these methods consider the correlation of the feature to the target value, relying solely on the property may be insufficient. The redundancy and complementarity between features are conducive to the selection of feature subsets that can improve the performance of the model. On the other hand, most of the existing methods for predicting the severity of Parkinson's disease are based on baseline features and the RF regressor, but the information of baseline features is limited, and some decision trees in RF have poor prediction results, which may affect the performance of the model.

To address the above two issues, this chapter proposes two methods to address the aforementioned issues in PD research. Firstly, the local dynamic feature selection fusion (LDFSF) method is introduced for feature selection based on relevance, redundancy, and complementarity in PD symptom severity prediction tasks. This method introduces the maximal information coefficient (MIC) as an effective measure of feature relevance (Reshef et al., 2011). To reduce computational complexity, the proposed method utilizes self-organizing map (SOM) (Nilashi et al., 2019) clustering to select features within each cluster. This method also designs a dynamic feature selection (DFS) strategy based on clustering, which can dynamically update the importance between candidate features and the selected feature subset. The selected features are input into the random forest model to predict the disease severity of the patients. The advantage of the LDFSF method is that the feature subset selected by relevance, redundancy, and complementarity is more universal. The experiment evaluation was conducted on the Parkinson's telemonitoring dataset (PTDS) to compare the proposed LDFSF method with the traditional FS method and the existing literature. The results demonstrate that the LDFSF method effectively selects a small subset of features, leading to superior prediction performance when combined with appropriate regressors. Secondly, this chapter proposes the GWT-RF-Att method that combines the graph wavelet transform (GWT) with attention-weighted RF, which extracts a more effective feature representation and achieve better PD severity prediction results. Based on PD voice features, the GWT-RF-Att method extracts effective frequency features by using GWT, and adaptively selects the decision tree model with better performance in random forest for prediction by using the attention-improved random forest model, thus improving the prediction accuracy. Therefore, the advantage of the GWT-RF-Att method in this paper is that more features related to the target values are obtained and the performance of RF in predicting the severity of PD condition is further improved.

The main contributions of this chapter are as follows:

(1) From the perspective of feature selection and feature transformation, this chapter proposes the LDFSF and GWT-RF-Att methods to optimize voice features of patients to achieve better PD severity prediction performance.
(2) The LDFSF method not only considers the correlation between features and target value, but also designs a dynamic feature selection method based on clustering for analyzing the redundancy between features and the complementarity between features and feature sets.
(3) The GWT-RF-Att method transforms the baseline features by GWT to obtain effective features that are more relevant to the target value, and improves the prediction performance by introducing the attention mechanism into random forest.
(4) Experiment results on the PTDS dataset show that the proposed LDFSF and GWT-RF-Att methods obtain superior performance in PD severity prediction compared to existing methods, thus validating the effectiveness of optimizing patient voice features from the perspective of feature selection and feature transformation.

RELATED WORKS

Feature Selection

Scholars have proposed various feature selection (FS) methods for the tasks of PD severity prediction. Tunc et al. (2020) utilized the Boruta algorithm to establish feature significance by exploring relationships among all relevant features and analyzed the selected features. They concluded that vocal fold vibration patterns were crucial indicators for assessing PD severity. Tsanas et al. (2021) evaluated the features using four FS algorithms to obtain features with high importance and tested three regression models, namely SVR, XGBoost and RF regressors. The results show that the prediction performance of RF consistently outperformed SVR and XGBoost, which verifies its superiority in PD severity prediction. Despotovic et al. (2020) ranked PD voice feature weights using the ARD method and selected eight features with the high relevance with the target value. Gaussian process can extend multivariate Gaussian distribution to infinite many random variables, which has been successfully used in latent variable modeling of high-dimensional data. By combining ARD with Gaussian process, the number of PD voice features was reduced, and prediction accuracy was improved.

The above FS methods based on relevance and redundancy have analyzed the intrinsic relationships between PD voice features and combined with suitable classifiers and regressors to obtain good prediction models. However, the FS analysis using only these two properties is not sufficient. This is because a single feature with low classification ability may have a high dependency on other features, that is, there is complementarity between features, and adding them to the feature subset may help to enhance the recognition ability of the model (Chen et al., 2021). Therefore, in order to select effective features and improve the accuracy of the prediction model, it is necessary to analyze the relevance, redundancy and complementarity of features at the same time.

Graph Wavelet Transform

The graph wavelet transform is a method that utilizes data to construct a weighted path graph, consisting of vertices and edge weights. These edge weights represent the similarity information between connected vertices. By transforming known data into a graph representation, the GWT enhances the input information (Dong et al., 2021). Prior to the application of GWT, the wavelet transform (WT) is a widely used multi-scale analysis method in signal processing. It decomposes the original sequence into sub-series at different frequency scales, extracting important information from the signal. The wavelet coefficients obtained from WT decomposition provide detailed information about the frequency changes in the sequence. In the context of PD pathological signals, WT is commonly employed to extract the time-frequency characteristics. Utilizing these features, predictive models for PD can be developed, improving accuracy (Chakraborty & Nandy, 2020).

Furthermore, WT can also extract sequence information by decomposing the sequence into coefficient vectors of different scales. By analyzing the relationship between these coefficient vectors and the target value, the impact of different sequences on the target value can be determined. Consequently, WT can extract frequency features from the PD feature vector. Lai et al. (2016) proposed a method using graph wavelet transform, which involved sorting the features in the sequence, extracting sequence information, and generating a new feature vector. The effectiveness of the features extracted by the wavelet transform was subsequently verified.

To effectively represent pathological signals in PD patients, the GWT method is employed in this chapter to extract frequency features from PD feature vectors. However, the PD feature vector is high-dimensional data, and different arrangements of features represent different information of frequency. To address this challenge, the chapter considers different feature arrays.

Prediction Methods: Machine and Deep Learning

Machine learning (ML) algorithms have been widely utilized for PD diagnosis, providing reliable and early detection of the disease (Senturk, 2020). Tsanas et al. (2010) compared the performance of the

LR method and classification and regression trees (CART) in mapping PD voice features to UPDRS values. CART outperformed linear predictors, indicating that linear combinations of voice features are not effective for UPDRS prediction. Since then, researchers have proposed more effective prediction models. Ji et al. (2018) and Yoon & Li (2019) combined transfer learning with ML algorithms to account for differences in disease trends among PD patients. Jain & Shetty (2016) found that KNN achieved the lowest error compared to multivariate LR and regression tree methods. Nilashi et al. (2020) utilized SVR with processed PD voice features, both achieving the best performance among the compared methods. XGBoost and RF have also been employed for PD severity estimation. Tunc et al. (2020) utilized the Boruta method to select informative features and fed them into XGBoost, resulting in the lowest mean absolute error. RF, known for its ensemble learning voting mechanism, finds wide application in biomedical informatics (Xu & Pan, 2020). Sharma et al. (2019) and Tsanas et al. (2021) combined RF with their proposed models, all achieving improved prediction results, which highlight the reliability of RF in predicting PD severity and its significant potential.

In addition to ML techniques, deep learning (DL) has gained significant attention due to its powerful automatic feature extraction capabilities (Zhang et al., 2022). In PD classification tasks, Oung et al. (2018) analyzed audio signals using empirical wavelet transform and empirical wavelet packet transform. They employed KNN, probabilistic neural network, and extreme learning machine as classifiers, achieving high classification accuracy. Kadam & Jadhav (2019) proposed a feature ensemble learning method based on sparse autoencoders, verifying its validity and practical value in PD research by comparing it with various classification methods. For predicting symptom severity in PD patients, Xiang et al. (2016) designed a three-layer feedforward neural network structure and utilized a Gaussian mixed regression model for nonlinear prediction, which achieved smoother results compared to KNN and regression tree predictions. Nilashi et al. (2019) developed a method that combined singular value decomposition and adaptive ANFIS to predict disease progression in PD patients. This method improved the time complexity and accuracy of the PD diagnosis system. Nilashi et al. (2020) constructed a prediction model based on a deep belief network and integrated the prediction results using SVR, further enhancing the accuracy of PD severity prediction. However, DL models require careful tuning of hyperparameters to avoid underfitting and overfitting issues (Shahid & Singh, 2020). Moreover, DL models are data-driven and known for their data-consuming nature, requiring larger datasets to demonstrate their excellent performance (Nilashi et al., 2020). In contrast, the Parkinson's telemonitoring dataset is relatively small, which limits the common use of DL methods in PD symptom severity prediction tasks. However, as the PD voice dataset continues to expand, DL methods still hold great potential.

PROPOSED METHOD

Problem Definition

The aim of this chapter is to predict the severity of Parkinson's disease symptoms. Let the PD dataset be $D=\{X,Y\}$, where Y with dimension $M\times1$ represents the PD severity score of motor-UPDRS or total-UPDRS for M samples. $X=\{x_1,x_2,\cdots,x_m\}_{m=1}^{M}$ with dimension $M\times N$ represents the feature of all samples. x_m with dimension $N\times1$ represents the N-dimensional feature vector of the mth sample. One of this chapter of objective is to predict the severity Y of Parkinson's disease patients based on their voice feature vector X. Due to the absence of a straightforward linear relationship between the voice features and the target values (i.e., motor-UPDRS or total-UPDRS), this experiment employs a nonlinear function $f(\bullet)$to capture the complex relationship between them. Denoting the true target value as Y and the corresponding predicted value as Y', then the PD symptom severity estimation problem can be formulated as:

$$Y' = f(X, Y). \tag{1}$$

LDFSF Model

In this chapter, the proposed LDFSF method consists of three main components: MIC relevance analysis, DFS strategy based on SOM clustering, and regression model prediction. The detailed process is depicted in Figure 1.

Relevance-Based Feature Selection

The MIC is not limited to specific function types and can capture linear, nonlinear, functional, and non-functional relationships. Among them, functional relationships include linear functional relationships, nonlinear parabolic, periodic, exponential functional relationships, etc., and the superposition of various functions belongs to non-functional relationships. Thus, MIC is an effective method to evaluate the relevance between variables. Given the nonlinear nature of Parkinson's voice data, MIC can be used to effectively measure the relationship between PD voice features and the target value.

Figure 1. Schematic diagram of local dynamic feature selection fusion method

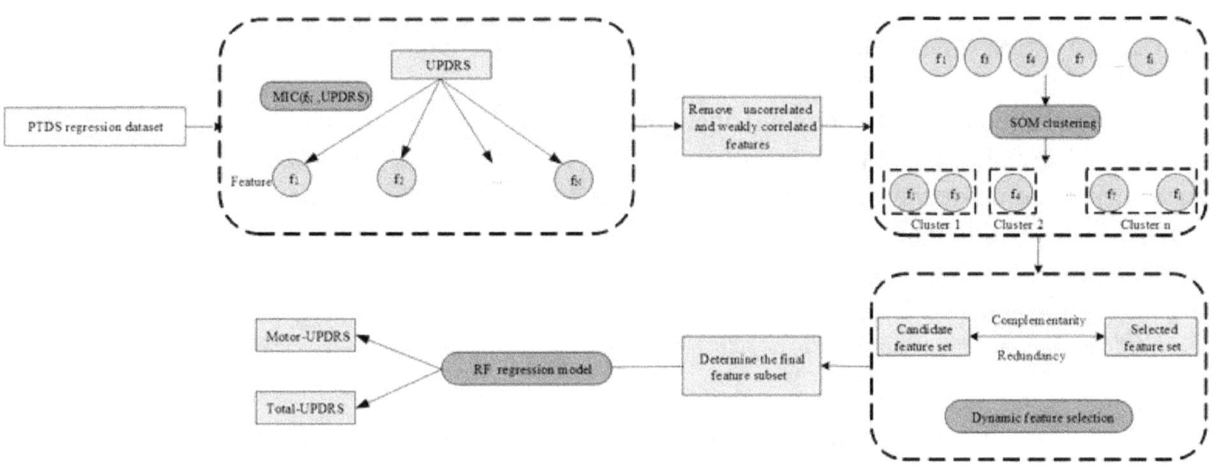

PD dataset can be represented as $D=\{X,Y\}$, where $X = \{f_1, f_2, \cdots, f_i, \cdots, f_N\}_{i=1}^{N}$, $f_i \in \mathbb{R}^{M\times 1}$ represents the feature vector of the sample, N and M represent the feature dimension and the number of samples, respectively. Y = {motor-UPDRS, total-UPDRS} denotes the target value. To begin with, this chapter calculates the MIC score between features and the target value. The main concept of MIC is to divide the scatter diagram grid between the feature variable f_i and the target value Y, and then calculate the relevance between variable f_i and target value Y in each grid using mutual information. The specific steps are as follows:

Step1: Grid division. Suppose that all the data between PD voice features and the target value in the dataset is a finite set of ordered pairs $D' = \{(f_k, y_k), k = 1, 2, \cdots, M\}$. MIC aims to identify all the relationships between variables by dividing the value range of feature f into a segments and the value range of target value y into b segments. The grid of $a\times b$ is defined as G. The division of the variable space has a significant impact on the MIC results and consequently affects the relevance between features and the target value.

Step 2: Mutual information is calculated after the grid is divided. MIC computes the relevance of variables within each grid using mutual information. The mutual information MI(f,y) represents the degree of association between the feature variable f and the target value y within a specific grid. It is defined as:

$$\mathrm{MI}(f, y) = -\sum_{y_k \in y} \sum_{f_k \in f} p(f_k, y_k) \log \frac{p(f_k, y_k)}{p(f_k)p(y_k)}. \tag{2}$$

The joint probability distribution function between variables f and y, denoted as $p(f_k,y_k)$, is approximated by the proportion of samples falling into specific grids. The marginal probability distribution functions of f and y are denoted as $p(f_k)$ and $p(y_k)$, respectively.

Step3: Calculate the maximum MI. The maximum MI is calculated by varying the number of divisions a and b in grid G, changing the location of divisions in the grid and repeating the calculation of mutual information. The MIC value obtained under different division methods is denoted as MI' and represents the mutual information value of the grid G. The maximum mutual information formula of D' under a given grid G is obtained:

$$\mathrm{MI}'(D',a,b) = \max \mathrm{MI}(D'|G). \tag{3}$$

Where $D'|G$ represents different distributions of data D' for a given grid G.

Step 4: Normalize the mutual information value. To compare MI' in different grid divisions, it is necessary to normalize them, so as to obtain the feature matrix $C(D')_{a,b}$ of normalized mutual information values under different grid divisions as follows:

$$C(D')_{a,b} = \frac{\mathrm{MI}'(D', a, b)}{\log \min\{a, b\}}. \tag{4}$$

Step 5: The result of the MIC is defined as the maximum value obtained for the information coefficient between the feature variable f and the target value y It is defined as:

$$\mathrm{MIC}(D') = \max_{a\times b<B(M)} C(D')_{a,b}. \tag{5}$$

Where $B(M)$ refers to the upper limit value of the division within the grid G. The value range of MIC(D') is [0,1]. The larger the MIC value, the stronger the relevance between f and y, that is, f is a strong relevant feature. The smaller the MIC value indicates that the relevance between f and y is weaker, and the f is more likely to be removed. When MIC=0, f is irrelevant and should be removed.

Dynamic Feature Selection Based on Redundancy and Complementarity

The feature selection methods consider both relevance and redundancy to select the optimal subset of features. However, in some cases, the interaction between highly redundant features and other features may have a positive impact on the model. This chapter proposes an approach to select the optimal feature subset. Firstly, PD voice features with high relevance are clustered using SOM to obtain candidate features from different clusters. Then, features are dynamically selected from the candidate features based on their relevance, redundancy, and complementarity to form the final feature subset. Among them, SOM clustering can divide the candidate features into several clusters, and DFS selects the features of each cluster, which can greatly reduce the number of candidate features and decrease the complexity of the model.

Algorithm 1. PD voice feature clustering based on SOM

Input: feature vector $X' = \{f_1, f_2, \cdots, f_i\}_{i=1}^{N'}$, initial weight vector W of neurons in competition layer, output grid size $\dim_x \times \dim_y$, maximum number of iterations T and learning rate ç(t,d).
Output: the weight vector W of neurons in the competition layer.
Process:
Initialize W and ç, and normalize feature vector X'
for time step t=1,…,T **do**
Select an input vector $f_i(t)$ from X'
dis=0
for neuron v=1,…,$\dim_x \times \dim_y$ **do**
if dis=0 **then**
Update the distance between $f_i(t)$ and v:
$d(f_i(t)-W_v(t)) = \|f_i(t)-W_v(t)\|$
$dis = d(f_i(t)-W_v(t))$
BMU: $u=v$
else
if $d(f_i(t)-W_v(t))<dis$ **then**
$dis = d(f_i(t)-W_v(t))$
Update BMU: $u=v$
end for
for neuron v=1,…,$\dim_x \times \dim_y$ **do**
Update the weight vector: $W_v(t+1) = W_v(t) + \eta(t,d)(f_i(t) - W_v(t))$
end for
end for

Self-Organizing Mapping Network Clustering

To better approximate the complex relevance between PD multivariate voice features (Chen et al., 2021), this chapter uses SOM to cluster the voice features with high relevance with the target value. Algorithm 1 outlines the process of clustering PD features using SOM. The SOM network comprises an input layer and a competition layer. The input layer represents the feature vectors, while the competition layer consists of $\dim_x \times \dim_y$ neurons. The relevance between feature vectors and neurons is determined by distance, and neurons are activated through competitive learning. The best matching unit (BMU) is the activated neuron at each moment. The weight vectors of neurons within the BMU's neighborhood are updated based on the learning rate $\eta(t,d)$. The learning rate η decreases as training time t and topological distance d between neurons and the BMU increase. This process updates the weight vectors of the winning neuron and its neighbors to make them closer to the input vectors, effectively mapping high-dimensional PD voice features onto a low-dimensional space.

After obtaining the weight vector W for each neuron in the output layer, the high-dimensional features are mapped to the two-dimensional plane of the output layer. Clustering is performed by determining the shortest distance between the feature vector and each neuron in the output layer. In this method, the similarity of the input PD voice feature data is expressed through the feature mapping of nearest neighbors in the SOM clustering, while preserving the topology of the data.

Dynamic Feature Selection

The dynamic feature selection (DFS) strategy in this section considers both the relevance between features and the target value, as well as the impact of feature redundancy on the importance of candidate features. It can select the those features that are highly relevant, minimally redundant, and exhibit high complementarity. Figure 2 illustrates the process of dynamic feature selection based on SOM clustering.

Figure 2. The dynamic feature selection process based on SOM clustering

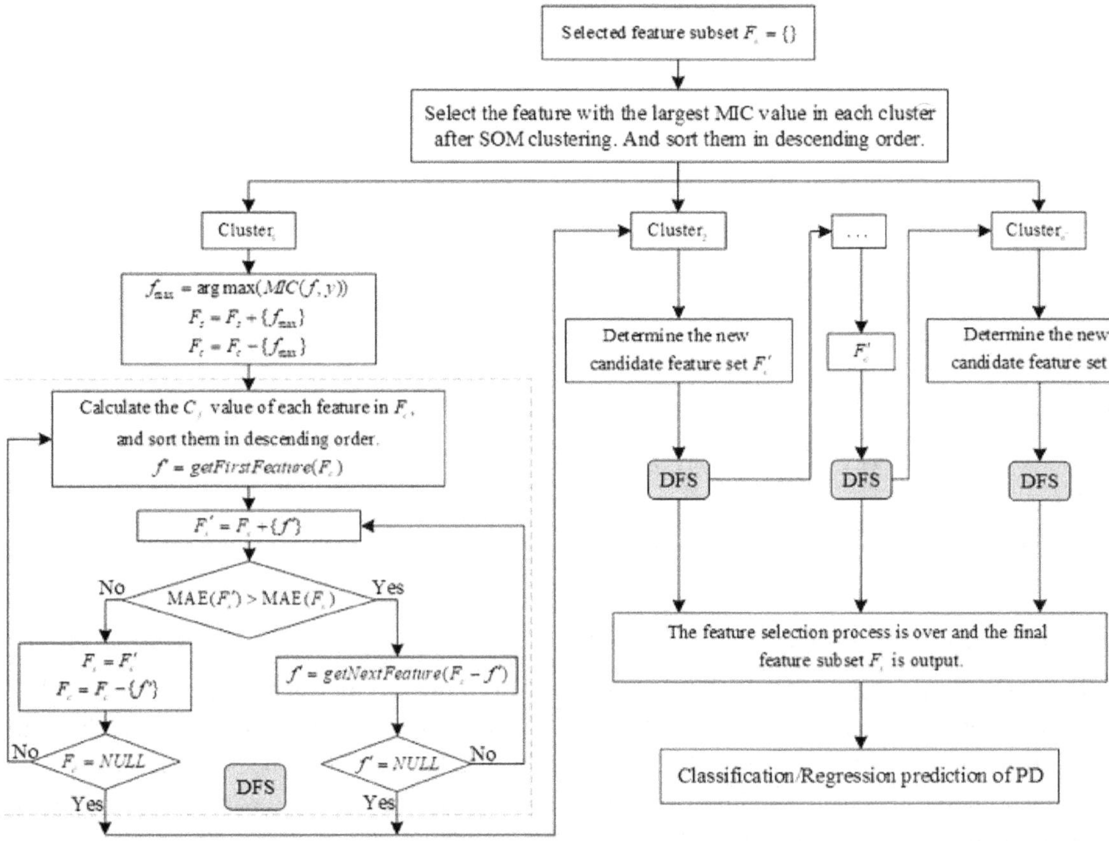

The DFS strategy in Figure 2 starts by selecting features with the highest MIC value from each cluster in SOM clustering. These features are then sorted based on relevance and added to the selected subset. To choose features with low redundancy and high complementarity from the cluster, the proposed DFS strategy considers the MIC(f,y) between candidate features f and the target value y, as well as the average redundancy R_f between candidate features and the selected subset F_s. This approach allows for dynamic updating of the complementarity C_f between candidate features and the selected subset. The redundancy between features f_i and f_j is defined as MIC(f_i,f_j). A higher value indicates a smaller difference in information among features, indicating a stronger level of redundancy. The average redundancy R_f and complementarity C_f are defined as follows:

$$R_f = \frac{\sum_{i=1}^{|F_s|} \mathrm{MIC}(f, f_i)}{|F_s|}, \tag{6}$$

$$C_f = \frac{\mathrm{MIC}(f, y)}{R_f}. \tag{7}$$

Where F_s represents the selected feature subset, and $|F_s|$ represents the number of features in the set F_s. C_f combines relevance and redundancy to assess the significance of candidate features and represents the level of complementarity between candidate features and the selected subset. The larger C_f value indicates a stronger degree of complementarity between candidate features and the selected subset.

In the current clustering method, a dynamic feature selection strategy is employed. This strategy calculates the complementarity C_f between each candidate feature f and the selected feature set F_s using Eqs. (6) and (7). The candidate feature set F_c is then sorted in descending order based on the C_f value. The feature f with the highest C_f value is added to the selected feature subset F_s, creating a new set F_s'. Both F_s and F_s' are input into the RF regressor, and the mean absolute error MAE(F_s) obtained by each is denoted as MAE(F_s) and $\mathrm{MAE}(F_s')$, respectively. If $\mathrm{MAE}(F_s') \leq \mathrm{MAE}(F_s)$, the feature f is added to the selected feature subset F_s, and it is removed from the candidate feature set F_c. However, if $\mathrm{MAE}(F_s') > \mathrm{MAE}(F_s)$, the second feature in F_c is added to F_s to determine the error. This process continues until F_c is empty. At this point, all the features in the next cluster are considered as a new candidate subset F_c', and the features with the highest complementarity with the selected feature subset are selected from F_c' and added to F_s. The above process is repeated until all candidate features have been tested or the number of features in F_s reaches the predetermined upper limit set by the experiment. In such case, F_s becomes the final output feature subset.

GWT-RF-Att Model

This section provides a detailed description of each module in the proposed GWT-RF-Att model. Figure 3 illustrates the workflow of the method. The proposed GWT-RF-Att method calculates the similarity among all PD samples, transforms the features in the similar samples to obtain more efficient information, and finally uses the improved RF model to predict PD severity. To illustrate the flow of the GWT-RF-Att method presented in this chapter more concretely, we expand each module appropriately, as shown in Figure 4.

Figure 3. Workflow of the GWT-RF-Att method for motor- and total-UPDRS prediction

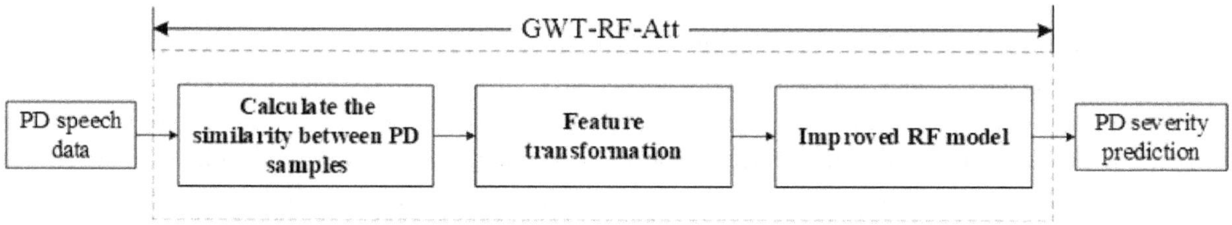

Figure 4 GWT-RF-Att model architecture

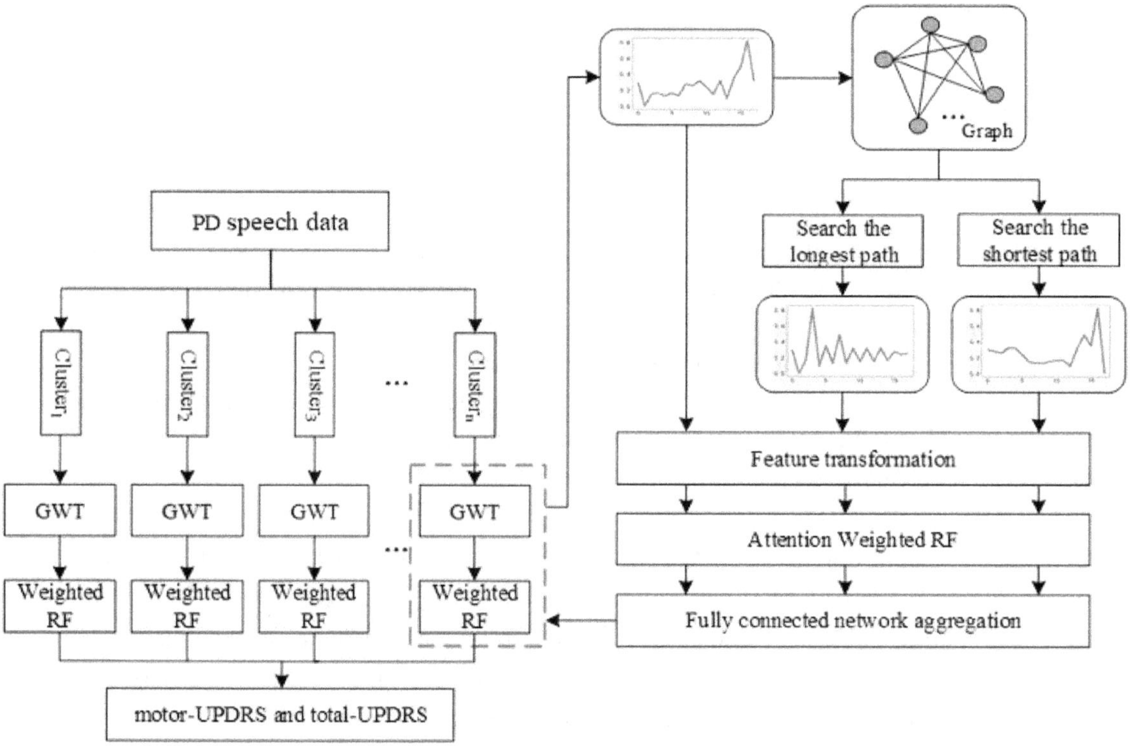

Standardized Clustering

This clustering algorithm can effectively divide the PD samples in the dataset into different clusters, which helps reduce the dimensions of the data and minimize the prediction error of the model (Nilashi et al., 2020). To enhance the efficiency of the clustering process and reduce the number of iterations, this chapter incorporates data standardization on the PD sample data. Prior to clustering, the standardized K-means algorithm performs maximum and minimum standardization on the sample data, thereby simplifying the data processing complexity:

$$x_{:,n} = \frac{x_{:,n} - \min(x_{:,n})}{\max(x_{:,n}) - \min(x_{:,n})}, \tag{8}$$

where $x_{:,n}$ represents the sample feature in the nth column of X. $\min(x_{:,n})$ and $\max(x_{:,n})$ represent the minimum and maximum values in $x_{:,n}$, respectively. In order to cluster M samples into K clusters, an initial mean vector set $C = \{c_1, c_2, \cdots, c_k\}_{k=1}^{K}$ of M samples is randomly selected in initial sample space. The Euclidean distance, represented by D_{mk} in Eq. (9), is then computed between the M samples and the K centroid points. Based on this distance, the samples are automatically assigned to the cluster $clus_m$ that is closest to its respective centroid:

$$clus_m = \arg\min_{1 \le k \le K} D_{mk}(x_m, c_k) = \arg\min_{1 \le k \le K} \left\| x_m - c_k \right\|, \tag{9}$$

where ||•|| represents the 2-norm. After all samples are grouped into their respective clusters, the average vector of each cluster is updated, and clustering is repeated based on Eq. (9). The clustering steps are iterated continuously until the average vector no longer changes, resulting in K clusters of the final PD samples.

Figure 5. Schematic diagram of graph wavelet transform

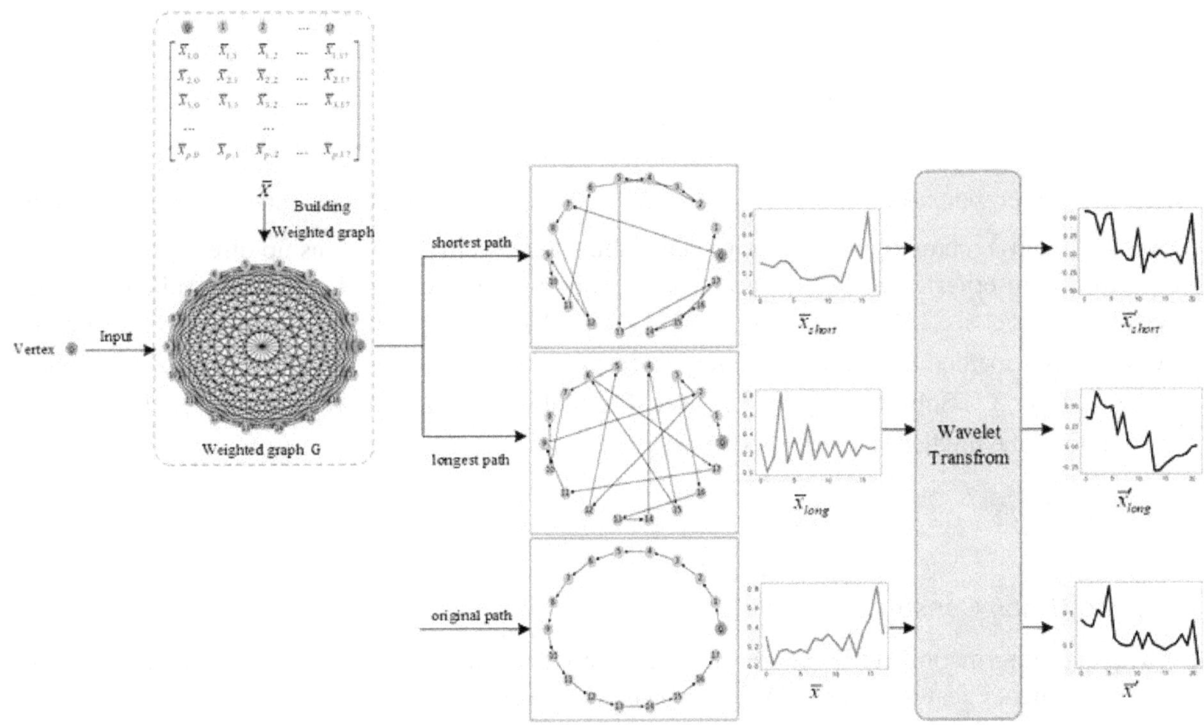

Graph Wavelet Transform

The initial step of the GWT-RF-Att model involves extracting various frequency features from the PD feature vectors using the graph wavelet transform, as illustrated in Figure 5.

The GWT method is used to obtain frequency features from different sequence information of vectors. It starts by constructing a weighted graph G and then applies wavelet transform to extract the frequency features. The construction of G is based on analyzing the correlation between features in the original feature matrix $\overline{X}$ of PD.

Once the initial vertex is determined, the shortest and longest path search method can be used to obtain the smoothest and the most oscillatory vectors $\overline{x}_{short}$ and $\overline{x}_{long}$ from G, which represent different order information of the vectors. To obtain multiple frequency features of the PD vector, wavelet transform is applied to $\overline{x}, \overline{x}_{short}$, and $\overline{x}_{long}$ respectively. Here, $\overline{x}$ represents the original feature vector before sorting.

Assuming the training set of the PD subset is $\overline{D} = (\overline{X}, \overline{Y}) = \{(\overline{x}_i, \overline{y}_i)\}_{i=1}^{\overline{M}}$, where $\overline{M}$ represents the number of PD patients in the training set, and $\overline{Y} = (\overline{y}_1, \overline{y}_2, \cdots, \overline{y}_{\overline{M}})^{\mathrm{T}}$ is the observed value of the sample motor-UPDRS or total-UPDRS. $\overline{X}$ is a matrix of dimensions $\overline{M} \times N$, containing all the features of the training set samples, and $\overline{x}_i$ with dimension $N\times 1$ is a feature vector of the ith sample.

$$\overline{X} = (\overline{x}_1, \overline{x}_2, \cdots, \overline{x}_{\overline{M}})^{\mathrm{T}} = \begin{bmatrix} \overline{x}_{1,1}, \overline{x}_{1,2}, \cdots, \overline{x}_{1,N} \\ \overline{x}_{2,1}, \overline{x}_{2,2}, \cdots, \overline{x}_{2,N} \\ \cdots \\ \overline{x}_{\overline{M},1}, \overline{x}_{\overline{M},2}, \cdots, \overline{x}_{\overline{M},N} \end{bmatrix}, \tag{10}$$

where $\overline{x}_{\overline{M},N}$ represents the Nth feature of the $\overline{M}^{th}$ sample. Due to the intricate nonlinear correlation between $\overline{X}$ and $\overline{Y}$, employing regression algorithms to learn their relationship directly does not meet the performance criteria and the resulting prediction outcomes cannot be readily applied in clinical practice (Tsanas et al., 2010; Tsanas et al., 2021). To enhance the prediction accuracy, this section employs the GWT method to extract frequency features from the baseline feature vectors in $\overline{X}$, yielding the new feature $\overline{X}'$. Subsequently, $\overline{X}'$ is used to establish the mapping relationship between $\overline{X}'$ and $\overline{Y}$. Therefore, the prediction model becomes:

$$\overline{Y}' = f(\overline{X}', \overline{Y}). \tag{11}$$

Weighted Graph Construction

The sequence information of PD features represents the frequency characteristics of the vector. To extract different frequency features from PD feature vectors, a weighted graph G is constructed based on the correlation between features, and the smoothest and most oscillating vectors $\overline{x}_{short}$ and $\overline{x}_{long}$ are obtained by reordering the features.

The weighted graph is denoted as $G=(V,E,Dis)$, where $V=\{v_0,v_1,\ldots,v_{N-1}\}$ is the set of N features of PD voice, $E=\{v_0v_1,v_1v_2,\ldots,v_{N-2}v_{N-1}\}$ is the set of edges between features, and Dis represents the weighted adjacency matrix formed by the weights of all edges. The correlation between features is described by calculating the Euclidean distance $d_{i,j}$ between all features in $\overline{X}$ using Eq. (12). A smaller distance indicates a stronger correlation, while a larger distance indicates a weaker correlation.

$$d_{i,j} = \begin{cases} \left\| \overline{x}_{:,i} - \overline{x}_{:,j} \right\| & \text{if } i \neq j \\ -1 & \text{if } i = j, \text{and the longest path is searched} \\ \infty & \text{if } i = j, \text{and the shortest path is searched} \end{cases}, \tag{12}$$

where $\overline{x}_{:,i}$ and $\overline{x}_{:,j}$ represent the sample features of the ith and j^{th} columns in $\overline{X}$, respectively. $d_{i,j}$ represents the distance between the ith and j^{th} features in $\overline{X}$. When searching for the shortest (longest) path in G, it is necessary to find the closest (farthest) feature from the current feature, excluding itself. Therefore, when $i=j$, $d_{i,j}$ is ∞ (-1). Thus, the distance between N features can be calculated, and the weighted adjacency matrix Dis in G can be obtained:

$$Dis = \begin{bmatrix} d_{1,1}, d_{1,2}, \cdots, d_{1,N} \\ d_{2,1}, d_{2,2}, \cdots, d_{2,N} \\ \cdots \\ d_{N,1}, d_{N,2}, \cdots, d_{N,N} \end{bmatrix}. \tag{13}$$

Feature Sorting and Wavelet Transform

To capture distinct frequency information from the PD feature vector, we obtained vectors $\overline{x}_{short}$ and $\overline{x}_{long}$ by organizing the feature sequence along the shortest and longest paths, respectively. These vectors were then inputted $\overline{x}, \overline{x}_{short}$, and $\overline{x}_{long}$ into the wavelet transform to extract the corresponding frequency features. Algorithm 2 presents the pseudocode for the shortest and longest path search algorithm.

Compared to the original PD feature vector $\overline{x}$, the vector $\overline{x}_{short}$ exhibits smoother characteristics with a decrease in high-frequency components and an increase in low-frequency components. The vector $\overline{x}_{long}$ displays an increase in high-frequency components and a decrease in low-frequency components. By performing wavelet transforms on $\overline{x}, \overline{x}_{short}$, and $\overline{x}_{long}$, we can achieve fine-grained frequency feature extraction of the PD feature vectors. Taking the feature vector $\overline{x}$ as an example, it is decomposed into an approximate component and a detail component after the wavelet transform:

$$\begin{cases} cA_1 = \sum_k \overline{H}_{n-2k}\overline{x}_k \quad ; cD_1 = \sum_k \overline{G}_{n-2k}\overline{x}_k & j=1 \\ cA_j = \sum_k \overline{H}_{n-2k}cA_{j-1} \; ; cD_j = \sum_k \overline{G}_{n-2k}cD_{j-1} & j=2,3,\cdots,J \end{cases}, \tag{14}$$

where J represents the number of decomposition layers, while $\overline{H}$ and $\overline{G}$ denote the low-pass and high-pass wavelet filtering coefficients, respectively. cA_j and cD_j refer to the wavelet coefficients of the jth approximate component and detail component of the signal decomposition, respectively. The wavelet coefficients of vector $\overline{x}$ obtained after performing wavelet decomposition are concatenated to form a new feature vector representation, denoted as $\overline{x}' = [cD_1, cD_2, \cdots, cD_J, cA_J]$. Similarly, the output $\overline{x}'_{short}$ and $\overline{x}'_{long}$ of vectors $\overline{x}_{short}$ and $\overline{x}_{long}$ after wavelet transform can be obtained. Consequently, after feature transformation, the subset $\overline{X}$ yields three transformed results: $\overline{X}', \overline{X}'_{short}$, and $\overline{X}'_{long}$. The expression of $\overline{X}'$ is as follows:

$$\overline{X}' = (\overline{x}'_1, \overline{x}'_2, \cdots, \overline{x}'_{\overline{M}})^{\mathrm{T}} = \begin{bmatrix} cD_{1,1}, cD_{1,2}, \cdots, cD_{1,J}, cA_{1,J} \\ cD_{2,1}, cD_{2,2}, \cdots, cD_{2,J}, cA_{2,J} \\ \cdots \\ cD_{\overline{M},1}, cD_{\overline{M},2}, \cdots, cD_{\overline{M},J}, cA_{\overline{M},J} \end{bmatrix}. \tag{15}$$

Algorithm 2. Shortest and longest path search algorithm

Input: Weighted graph $G=(V,E,Dis)$, where $V=\{v_0,v_1,\ldots,v_{N-1}\}$, $E=\{v_0v_1,v_1v_2,\ldots,v_{N-2}v_{N-1}\}$
Output: U_{short} and U_{long} are the shortest and longest path sorted sets, respectively.
Process:
for $k=0,1,2,\ldots,N-1$ **do**
While the sorting algorithm is the shortest path search **do**
Add vertex v_k to the set U_{short}: $U_{short}=\{v_k\}$
repeat
The neighbor of vertex v_k is $N(k)=\{v_j \in V-U_{short} \mid v_kv_j \in E\}$
Determine v_j: $v_j = \arg\min_{v_j} d_{k,j} = \arg\min \left\| v_j - v_k \right\| \; s.t. \; v_j \in N(k)$
Add the vertex v_j to the end of the ordered set U_{short};
$v_k=v_j$
until $V - U_{short} = \varnothing$
While the sorting algorithm is the longest path search **do**
Add vertex v_k to the set U_{long}: $U_{long}=\{v_k\}$
repeat
The neighbor of vertex v_j is $N(k)=\{v_j \in V-U_{long} \mid v_kv_j \in E\}$
Determine v_j: $v_j = \arg\max_{v_j} d_{k,j} = \arg\max \left\| v_j - v_k \right\| \; s.t. \; v_j \in N(k)$
Add the vertex v_j to the end of the ordered set $U_{long}=\{v_k\}$;
$v_k=v_j$
until $V - U_{long} = \varnothing$

Random Forest Prediction Based on Attention Weighting

After frequency feature extraction of PD feature vectors, the dimensions of the new feature vectors $\overline{x}', \overline{x}'_{short}$, and $\overline{x}'_{long}$ are all $J+1$. RF is a powerful algorithm for handling high-dimensional data and can effectively reduce the risk of overfitting. Therefore, the multi-dimensional feature matrices $\overline{X}', \overline{X}'_{short}$, and $\overline{X}'_{long}$ are input into RF to predict the motor-UPDRS and total-UPDRS of PD patients. RF regression is an ensemble learning algorithm that consists of multiple decision regression trees. Each decision tree in RF is trained on a random subset of samples and features. Suppose the feature vectors $\overline{x}', \overline{x}'_{short}$, and $\overline{x}'_{long}$ are input into RF to generate T decision trees, then the prediction results of $3T$ decision trees is $Tr = \{Tr_1, Tr_2, \cdots, Tr_t\}_{t=1}^{3T}$, where Tr_t represents the prediction results of tth decision tree.

RF obtains the final prediction value by averaging the results of all decision trees under the assumption that each decision tree's results are accurate. However, since the input feature vectors $\overline{x}', \overline{x}'_{short}$, and $\overline{x}'_{long}$ contain different frequency information and the frequency characteristics of the decision trees are different, the output results of the decision trees will also differ. Due to the randomness of RF, not all decision tree predictions are accurate, and the importance of each decision tree's prediction results may vary. Simply averaging the prediction results of all decision trees may increase the prediction error of RF.

To improve the model performance, attention weights are introduced to the decision trees. Figure 6 illustrates the improved random forest prediction model that incorporates attention weighting. It can adaptively focus on decision trees with higher prediction accuracy and suppress decision trees with poor prediction performance, thereby reducing prediction error. The weight of attention is calculated as follows:

$$w = \tanh(W \bullet Tr + b) \tag{16}$$

$$\alpha_i = \frac{\exp(w_i)}{\sum_{t=1}^{3T} \exp(w_t)}, \tag{17}$$

where $w \in \mathbb{R}^{3T}$ represents the weight vector of FC network training. $W \in \mathbb{R}^{3T \times 3T}$ and $b \in \mathbb{R}^{3T}$ denote the parameters of the attention layer to be trained, $\tanh(\bullet)$denotes the activation function. w_i is the unnormalized weight of the ith decision tree, and α_i is the weight of attention of the ith decision tree. The attention mechanism enhances the predictive impact of key decision trees in RF by assigning distinct weights to each decision tree. The prediction result of the weighted decision trees is Tr':

$$Tr' = \{\alpha_1 Tr_1, \alpha_2 Tr_2, \cdots, \alpha_{3T} Tr_{3T}\}. \tag{18}$$

To improve the prediction accuracy, the weighted results are fed into the FC network to obtain the predicted values, denoted as $\overline{y}'$, for the motor-UPDRS or total-UPDRS of PD patients.

$$\overline{y}' = \delta(W_2 \delta(W_1 \cdot Tr' + b_1) + b_2), \tag{19}$$

where δ represents the ReLU activation function, W_1 and W_2 are the weight matrices of the two FC layers respectively. b_1 and b_2 are the bias terms corresponding to the fully connected layer. Once P samples from the test set are fed into the GWT-RF-Att model, the final prediction outcome is denoted as $\overline{Y}' = \{\overline{y}'_1, \overline{y}'_2, \cdots, \overline{y}'_p\}_{p=1}^{P}$. Where $\overline{y}'_p$ represents the predicted UPDRS score for the pth test sample.

Figure 6. Random forest prediction based on attention weighting

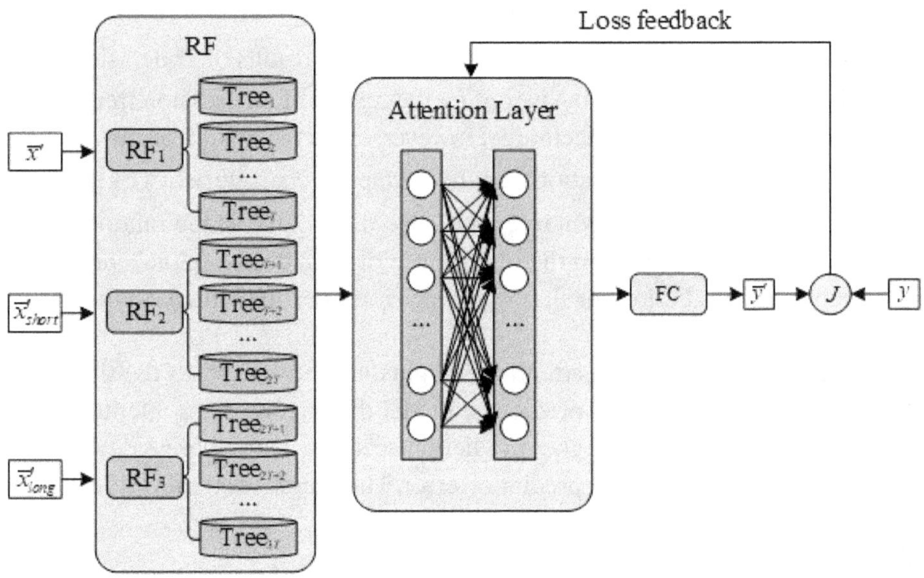

EXPERIMENT

Parkinson's Telemonitoring Dataset

The Parkinson's telemonitoring dataset (PTDS) (Tsanas et al., 2010) originates from the University of Oxford and is widely used for predicting the severity of PD symptoms (Ji et al., 2018; Tsanas et al., 2021; Despotovic et al., 2020; Yoon & Li, 2019). The dataset comprises voice data collected from 42 patients with primary PD, including 28 males and 14 females, each with a 5-year medical history. Patients were required to record 6 sustained vowels /a/ with varying loudness levels on the same day every week, without taking medication during the test. This recording process spanned 6 months, resulting in a total of 5,875 voice samples. Tsanas et al. (2010) applied linear and nonlinear voice signal processing algorithms to extract 16 voice features from the recorded data as shown in Table 1. Additionally, sex and age are considered important factors in predicting PD symptom severity and can be used to track UPDRS values (Xue et al., 2023). Motor-UPDRS and total-UPDRS are commonly used to express different degrees of Parkinson's disease, with a range of 0-108 and 0-176, respectively. The higher their value, the more severe the patient's disease. In this study, the maximum motor-UPDRS and total-UPDRS values observed were 55 and 41, respectively. Thus, all subjects included in the study exhibited moderate Parkinson's symptoms. Previous research has demonstrated a linear increase in UPDRS scores over a 5-year period without drug treatment for early-stage PD patients. Therefore, the UPDRS scores of patients were evaluated at the beginning, after 3 months, and after 6 months during data collection. Using piecewise linear interpolation, the UPDRS values at other time points were estimated based on the actual UPDRS scores at these three stages (Tsanas et al., 2010). In summary, this dataset provides valuable information for studying PD symptom severity prediction and includes voice features, sex, age, and UPDRS scores at different time points for PD patients.

Table 1. Voice features extracted by voice signal processing algorithm

Feature Classification	Feature
Frequency Disturbance	Jitter (%), Jitter (Abs), Jitter:RAP, Jitter:PPQ5, Jitter:DDP
Amplitude perturbation	Shimmer, Shimmer(dB), Shimmer:APQ3, Shimmer:APQ5, Shimmer:APQ11, Shimmer:DDA
Noise-Signal ratio	NHR, HNR
Pitch variation	RPDE, PPE
Noise variation	DFA

Experiment Setup

Experiment Setup of the LDFSF Model

During the experiment, the parameters to be adjusted in the proposed LDFSF method mainly include the determination of grid division mode in MIC and related parameters in SOM. Among them, the number and method of grid division in MIC have a significant impact on the relevance measurement of features. Therefore, this chapter set the upper limit $B(M)$ of grid G division in MIC as $M^{0.6}$, which has been proven to be the most effective in practical applications (Reshef et al., 2011). The parameters of SOM are set as follows: learning rate $\eta=0.9$, output grid size $dim_x=dim_y=4$, and maximum number of iterations $T=1000$. In the process of dynamic feature selection, the training set is used for feature selection, the validation set is used to evaluate the quality of the selected feature subset, and the test set is used to assess the performance of the prediction model that combines the feature selection framework with the regressor.

To assess the model's ability to predict the severity of PD symptoms and validate the accuracy of the prediction results, this chapter employs mean absolute error (MAE) as the evaluation metric for the prediction model. MAE is calculated as follows:

$$\mathrm{MAE} = \frac{1}{M'}\sum_{k=1}^{M'}\left|y_k - y'_k\right|, \tag{20}$$

Where M' represents the number of test samples, y_k and y'_k represent the true value and the predicted value of the model, respectively. The smaller the MAE, the closer the predicted value is to the true value, indicating better prediction performance.

Experiment Setup of the GWT-RF-Att Model

To simplify the modeling process, this chapter utilized the standardized K-means algorithm to cluster similar samples in the Parkinson's telemonitoring dataset. The choice of the number of clusters can impact the performance of the clustering algorithm. A previous study (Nilashi et al., 2019) explored the number of clusters for this dataset and suggested that 4 or 9 clusters would be reasonable. However, considering the relatively small size of the PD dataset, we opted for 4 clusters.

The GWT-RF-Att model employs the GWT method to extract different frequency features from PD feature vectors. The GWT involves two main parameters: the number of wavelet decomposition layers and the selection of wavelet basis. The accuracy of vector decomposition results can be determined by the number of wavelet decomposition layers, which can be chosen by analyzing the length of the PD feature vector. In this case, the length was set to 2 due to its short length. Additionally, a suitable wavelet function needs to be selected for wavelet analysis. The Daubechies (db) wavelet is commonly used due to its orthogonality and satisfaction of Parseval's theorem. Therefore, this chapter selected the popular "db2" wavelet basis.

To improve the performance of the GWT-RF-Att model, the hyperparameters of the attention-weighted RF model were optimized. This includes the number of decision trees in the RF, units in the attention layer, units in the FC layer, and the training batch. The best parameter selection method is adjusting only the relevant parameters while keeping others constant to achieve the best prediction performance (Zhang et al., 2021). The best hyperparameters for predicting motor-UPDRS and total-UPDRS in each cluster are provided in Tables 2 and 3, respectively.

Table 2. Hyperparameter settings in each cluster for motor-UPDRS

Hyperparameter	Cluster1	Cluster2	Cluster3	Cluster4
Num of decision trees	90	75	75	150
Attention layer units	18	18	18	18
FC layer units1	32	32	32	32
FC layer units2	1	1	1	1
Epoch	500	500	500	500
Batch_size	16	16	16	16

Table 3. Hyperparameter settings in each cluster for total-UPDRS

Hyperparameter	Cluster1	Cluster2	Cluster3	Cluster4
Num of decision trees	90	90	150	90
Attention layer units	18	18	18	18
FC layer units1	32	32	32	32
FC layer units2	1	1	1	1
Epoch	500	500	500	1000
Batch_size	16	32	16	32

Experiment Results

Experiment Results of the LDFSF Model

Result of the Selected Feature Set

In this chapter, the proposed LDFSF method is employed to address the regression problems associated with PD diagnosis. By selecting the optimal subset of features and combining them with suitable regressors, the LDFSF framework effectively achieves accurate PD severity prediction. The effectiveness of RF methods on public dataset PTDS has been previously demonstrated. Therefore, this chapter integrates the LDFSF framework with RF to validate the feasibility and reliability of the proposed method.

For PD severity prediction, the LDFSF method initially assesses the relevance between features and the target value using the MIC, as depicted in Figure 7. Features with low relevance to the target value (UPDRS) can degrade the performance of the classification and regression models. To address this, the chapter sorts the MIC(f,y) values of all features in descending order and eliminates the bottom 20% of features with low relevance, retaining the top 80% of features. Subsequently, the SOM method is employed to cluster the selected features. The clustering results of SOM on features are presented in Table 4, revealing high similarity within each cluster and the potential presence of redundant features.

Figure 7. Relevance (MIC) between features and the target value UPDRS

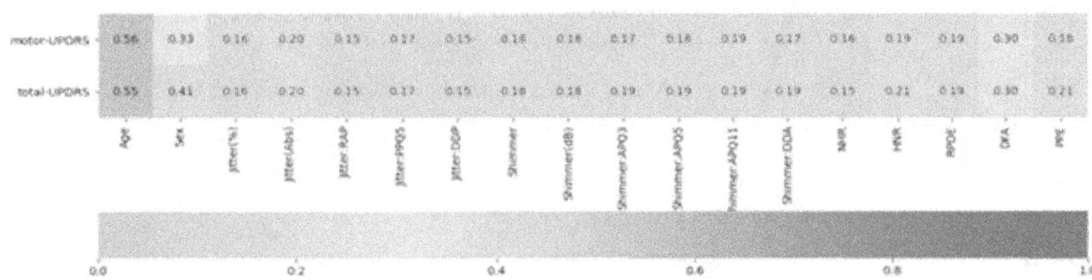

The proposed dynamic feature selection process, combining SOM clustering with RF, derives the optimal feature subset based on redundancy and complementarity. Figure 8 illustrates the accuracy and MAE variation of the validation set during the dynamic feature selection process. Existing FS methods using the same PTDS dataset typically yield the simplest feature sets of 8. To compare with the latest literature, the proposed DFS strategy limits the number of selected features to 8 for PTDS dataset. As shown in Table 4 and Figure 8, the DFS strategy stops running in cluster 3 when the number of selected feature sets reaches 8.

Effect of SOM Clustering

Table 5 presents the performance of the proposed LDFSF model, both before and after incorporating SOM clustering, along with the corresponding time consumption. This analysis aims to highlight the impact of SOM clustering on the prediction model.

Table 4. Clustering results of SOM in PD regression task

Cluster	Feature set
1	{Age, HNR, RPDE, DFA}
2	{Sex}
3	{Jitter (Abs), Jitter: PPQ5, Shimmer, Shimmer (dB), Shimmer: APQ3, Shimmer: APQ5, Shimmer: APQ11, Shimmer: DDA}
4	{PPE}

Figure 8. The dynamic selection process of feature subset
(Each step of the process adds a candidate feature to the feature subset. ◆ indicates that the candidate feature is determined to be added to the subset, and × indicates that the feature added to the subset will be removed. The feature subset (8 features) determined based on RF is {Age, RPDE, DFA, HNR, Sex, Shimmer: APQ3, Jitter (Abs), Shimmer: APQ11})

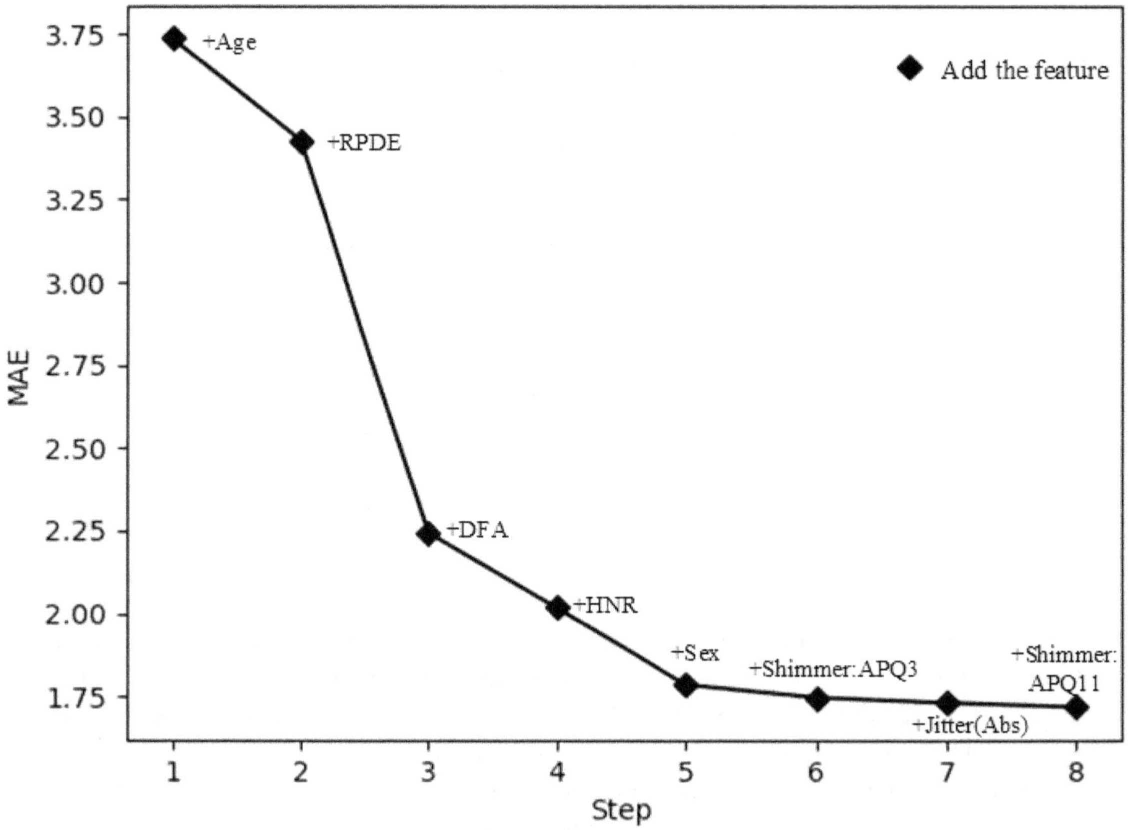

As shown in Table 5, the prediction model's running time is reduced on both datasets after SOM clustering. This can be attributed to the high similarity of features within the same cluster and the low similarity between clusters. The proposed method focuses on the relationship between candidate features within the same cluster and feature subsets during dynamic feature selection, avoiding the consideration of irrelevant features in other clusters, thus reducing the computational cost of the model. For the prediction results, the performance of the model after SOM clustering is improved in both classification and regression prediction, which is consistent with the results of Nilashi et al. (2019) and Nilashi et al. (2020). This outcome may be attributed to SOM clustering's ability to identify feature relevance, and dynamic feature selection methods that incorporate redundancy and complementarity can better analyze the intrinsic connections between features. Specifically, SOM clustering groups features based on similarity, and the high similarity within each cluster suggests potential redundancy. For example, as shown in Table 4, cluster 3 contains features with high inter-feature relevance (Despotovic et al., 2020). Since they measure voice signals similarly, some redundant features may need to be eliminated. However, the dynamic feature selection method based on SOM clustering not only reduces computational costs but also helps remove redundant features, thereby enhancing the prediction performance of PD regression models.

Table 5. Comparison of effects of SOM clustering on prediction model performance and time consumption

Dataset	Evaluation metrics		Not used SOM	Use SOM
PTDS	Motor-UPDRS	MAE	1.64	1.62
		Time (s)	259.15	258.77
	Total-UPDRS	MAE	2.14	1.99
		Time (s)	259.07	258.77

Performance Comparison With Existing Methods

In order to further validate the effectiveness of the proposed LDFSF framework and its combination with RF for prediction, this section compares the LDFSF method with traditional FS methods and recent literature results.

Table 6 presents a comparison of the effects of traditional FS methods and the LDFSF method on model performance. The traditional FS methods, such as ReliefF, mRMR, and Boruta (Tunc et al., 2020), select features based on relevance to the target value and redundancy between features. The LDFSF framework in this chapter adds complementarity to this foundation to explore the intrinsic connections between features. To verify the effectiveness of combining relevance, redundancy, and complementarity for feature selection, Table 6 compares the performance impact of different feature selection algorithms on the prediction model using the same regressor. RF performs well in PD regression prediction (Tsanas et al., 2021). Therefore, in Table 6, each feature selection method is combined with RF to compare the performance of the FS method. Additionally, the same number of features is set in this section to compare the effectiveness of the selected feature subsets. In summary, this section provides a comprehensive comparison of different feature selection methods, highlighting the effectiveness of the proposed LDFSF framework combined with RF for prediction.

Table 6 demonstrates that the proposed LDFSF method outperforms traditional FS algorithms in PD severity progression prediction tasks. ReliefF only considers feature relevance, while mRMR and Boruta focus on selecting features with high relevance and low redundancy. However, these methods do not consider the complementarity between candidate features and feature subsets. In contrast, the LDFSF method combines relevance, redundancy, and complementarity for feature selection, resulting in the proposed prediction model shows superiority with the same regressor RF in Table 6. Specifically, the MAE of motor-UPDRS predicted by the LDFSF method is 10.00%, 8.99% and 10.99% lower than that of ReliefF, mRMR and Boruta respectively, and the MAE of total-UPDRS predicted is 6.13%, 6.13% and 9.13% lower than that of ReliefF, mRMR and Boruta respectively.

Table 6. Comparison of the results between the proposed method and the traditional feature selection methods

FS method	RF regressor	
	Motor-UPDRS	Total-UPDRS
ReliefF	1.80	2.12
mRMR	1.78	2.12
Boruta	1.82	2.19
LDFSF(ours)	**1.62**	**1.99**

Furthermore, Table 7 compares the results of the proposed LDFSF method with those of existing literature. Specifically, this chapter compare the results of Ji et al. (2018), Yoon & Li (2019), Tsanas et al. (2021), and Despotovic et al. (2020) with the results of the proposed LDFSF method on the PTDS dataset.

Table 7 reveals that the LDFSF model achieves better prediction results compared to the literature. For regression, Ji et al. (2018) and Yoon & Li (2019) utilize transfer learning to address the limited data issue in PD patients, but face challenges in measuring similarity across different time dimensions. Tsanas et al. (2021) employ four FS methods combined with RF for PD severity assessment, but potential bandwidth restrictions or transmission errors may affect accuracy. Despotovic et al. (2020) achieve better prediction results with the Gaussian process regression model based on ARD, but ARD does not consider redundancy and complementarity when ARD calculates the weights of individual features and selects the feature with higher weight to form a feature subset. In comparison of Table 7, the LDFSF method surpasses the proposed method by Despotovic et al. (2020) in terms of prediction performance, validating the effectiveness of feature selection based on relevance, redundancy, and complementarity. Overall, the LDFSF method enables the selection of a small yet effective subset of PD voice features, providing certain reference value for accurate PD severity assessment. However, the rough extraction of traditional voice features from the whole voice data makes the model accuracy limited.

Table 7. Performance comparison between the proposed method and the existing methods

Methods	Motor-UPDRS	Total-UPDRS
Ji et al. (2018)	3.00	4.60
Yoon & Li (2019)	2.40	-
Tsanas et al. (2021)	2.65	3.17
Despotovic et al. (2020)	1.65	2.02
LDFSF (ours)	**1.62**	**1.99**

Experiment Results of the Proposed GWT-RF-Att Model

Effectiveness of GWT

To provide further insight into the effectiveness of the GWT proposed features, the Spearman correlation coefficient is calculated to quantify the correlation between the features and UPDRS (Tsanas et al., 2021). Figure 9 displays the Spearman correlation coefficients between PD baseline voice features and UPDRS, as well as between frequency features and UPDRS.

The strength of the correlation between each feature and UPDRS is indicated by the absolute value of Spearman's correlation coefficient. In Figure 9, the deeper the red or blue color, the stronger the correlation between the corresponding feature and UPDRS. It can be observed that compared to the baseline PD features, the frequency features extracted by GWT exhibit a significantly higher number of features with a high Spearman correlation coefficient with UPDRS, confirming the effectiveness of these frequency features.

Figure 9 also reveals that some features extracted by GWT have a weak association with UPDRS. The original RF model averages the results of all decision trees, assuming that each tree is accurate. However, if a decision tree selects a large number of features with little correlation with UPDRS, it may reduce prediction performance. By employing an attention layer to adaptively learn and assign different attention weights to the decision trees generated by RF, the model can focus more on decision trees with better prediction performance. Therefore, the RF model improved by the attention mechanism may build a more accurate prediction model.

Figure 9a. Spearman correlation coefficient between features and UPDRS in cluster1

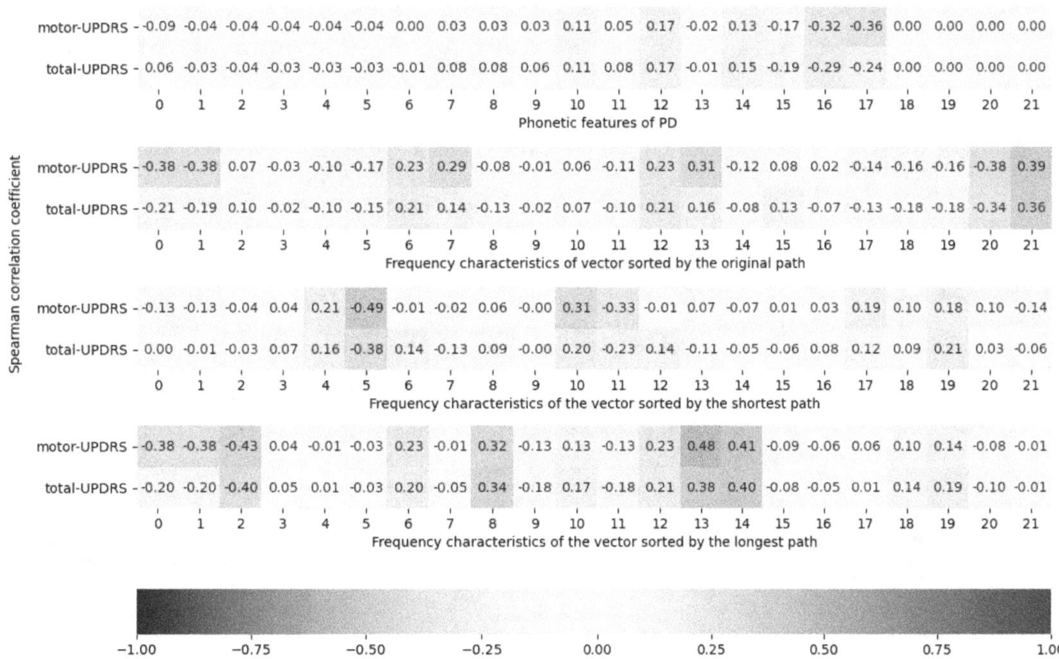

Figure 9b. Spearman correlation coefficient between features and UPDRS in cluster2

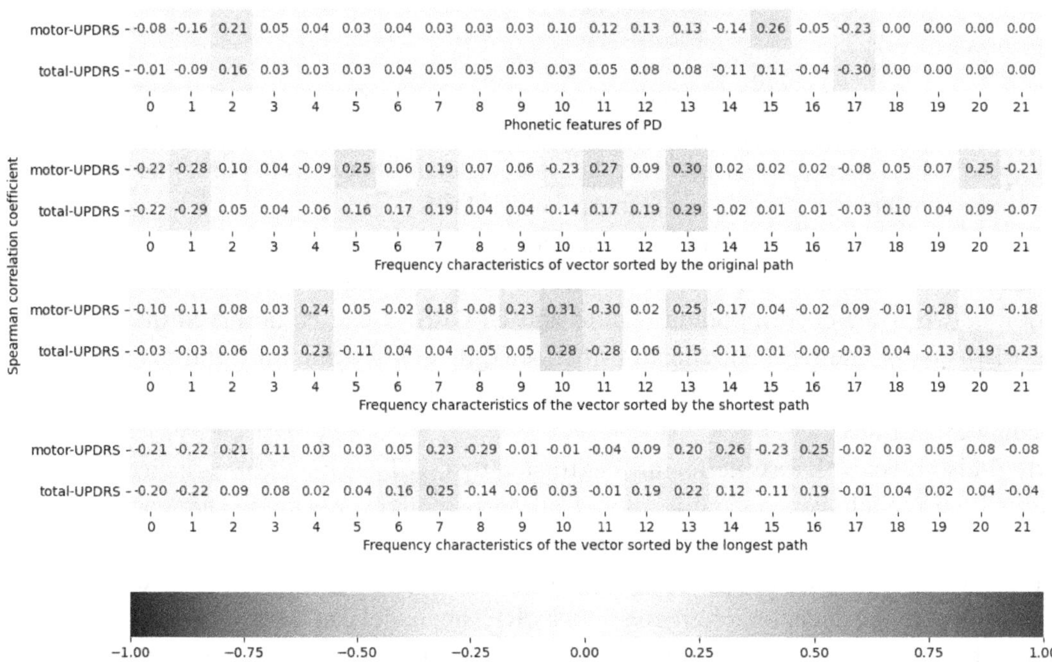

Figure 9c. Spearman correlation coefficient between features and UPDRS in cluster3

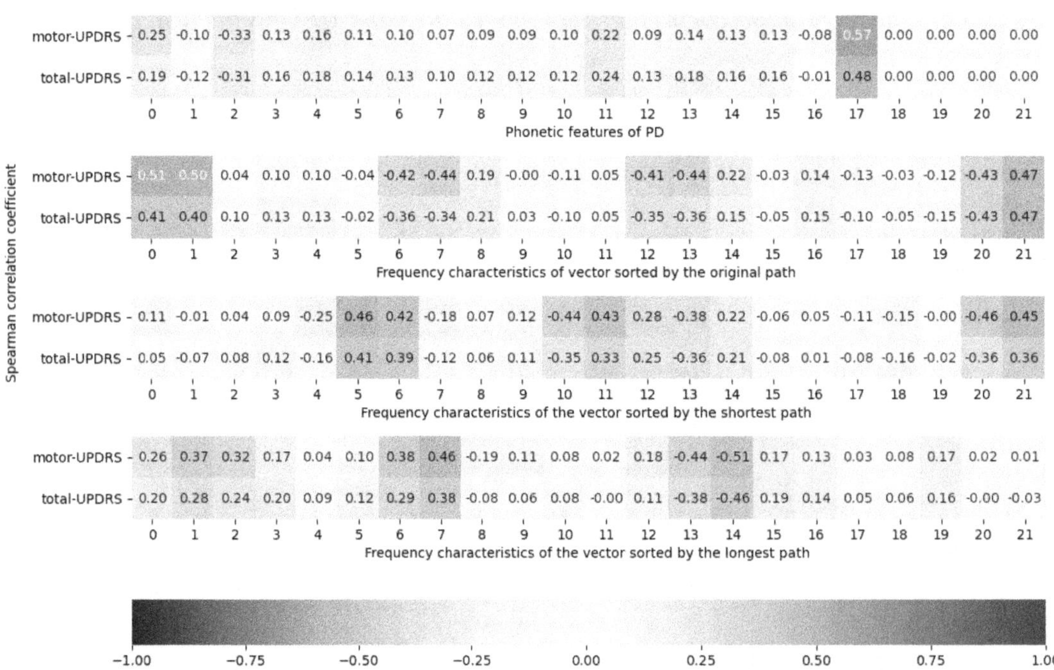

Figure 9d. Spearman correlation coefficient between features and UPDRS in cluster4

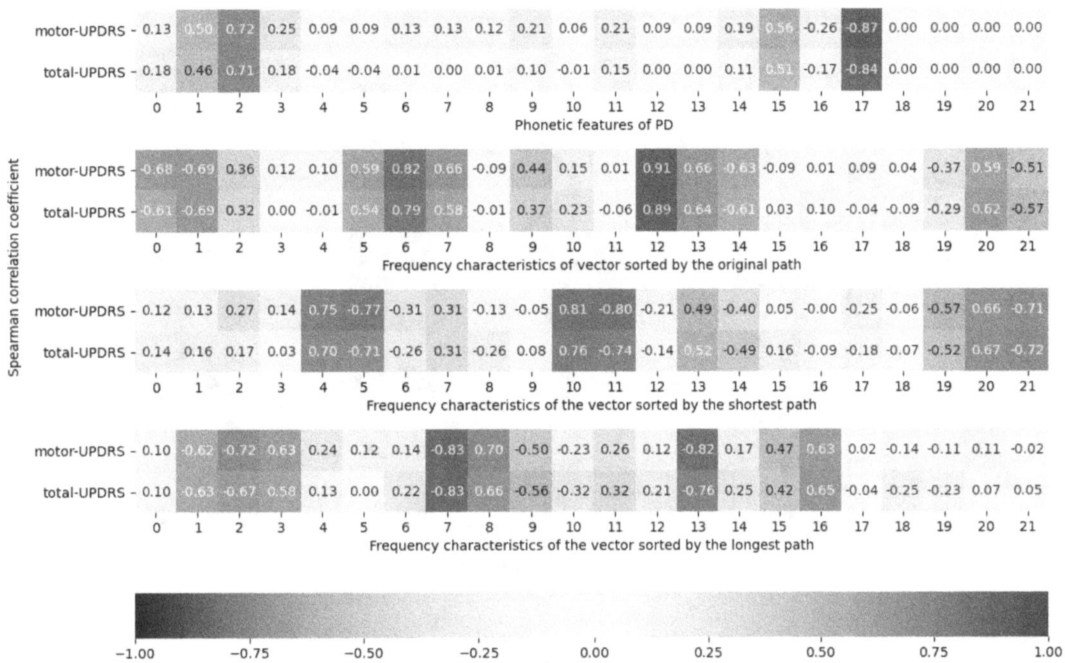

Clustering Results

To validate the clustering results, Figure 10 displays the MAE for each cluster. Tsanas et al. (2021) pointed out that when the MAE of the PD severity prediction model is less than 5 points, this prediction model will be very useful in practice. The bar chart in Figure 10 demonstrates that after dividing the Parkinson's telemonitoring dataset into four clusters, the MAE of the proposed GWT-RF-Att model for the prediction of motor-UPDRS and total-UPDRS are all less than 5, which indicates the practicability of this model.

The UPDRS consists of three main parts: "Mentation, Behavior and Mood," "Activities of Daily Living," and "Motor Examination." The motor-UPDRS is specific to assessing motor signs of Parkinson's disease, including voice features. On the other hand, the total-UPDRS incorporates not only motor-UPDRS but also mental health and daily activities. Therefore, it is assumed that motor-UPDRS is more closely related to voice disorders in sound-generated motor activities compared to total-UPDRS (Despotovic et al., 2020). This explains the lower MAE of predicted motor-UPDRS in each cluster compared to total-UPDRS, as depicted in Figure 10.

The statistical significance of GWT features is assessed using the p-values, as presented in Table 8. The p-value is determined through t-tests to evaluate the significance of the method. It is observed that in all cases, the GWT features exhibit a statistically significant correlation with UPDRS (p-value < 0.05) (Tsanas et al., 2021). Consequently, the GWT features obtained in this chapter are deemed statistically significant.

Figure 10. Performance results for PD progression assessment in each cluster

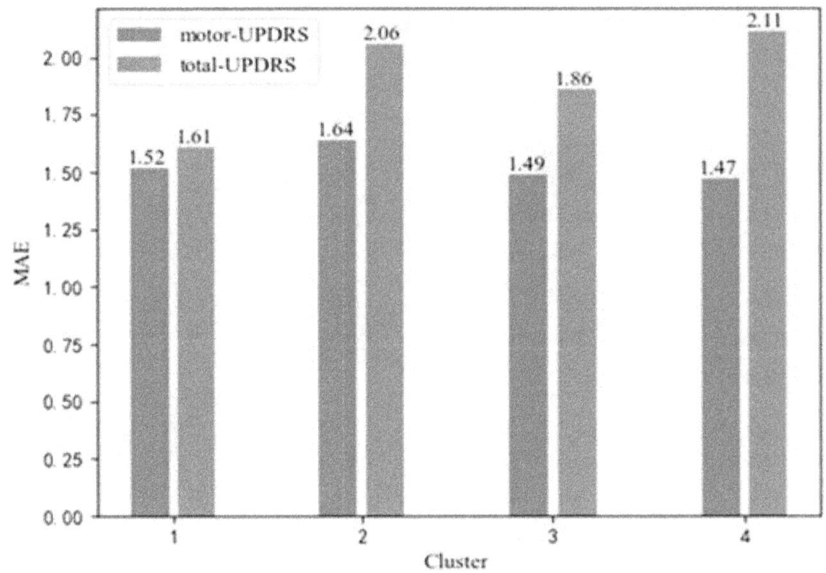

Table 8. The p-value for performing t-test for the GWT features

UPDRS	GWT features			
	Cluster1	**Cluster2**	**Cluster3**	**Cluster4**
Motor-UPDRS	0.0002	0.0058	0.0002	0.0047
Total-UPDRS	0.0197	0.0020	0.0002	0.0107

Comparison of Results

To evaluate the performance of our proposed GWT-RF-Att model, we compared it with traditional machine learning methods and state-of-the-art methods from the literature. Baseline methods including SVR, XGBoost, and RF were used in the experiment. Additionally, we compared our proposed method with GWT combined with SVR, XGBoost, and RF (i.e. GWT-SVR, GWT-XGBoost, GWT-RF) to highlight the influence of GWT-extracted features, and with RF combined with attention mechanism (RF-Att) to assess the impact of attention weights on prediction results. To ensure fairness, all models were trained and tested on the same datasets with optimized parameters.

Table 9 presents the MAE of motor-UPDRS and total-UPDRS predicted by the aforementioned models on the test set. The results indicate that replacing baseline features with GWT-extracted features improves the prediction performance of traditional methods, and the addition of attention weighting reduces the MAE of RF. Furthermore, we compared our proposed model with several advanced methods from the literature, including FDAMF, PTL, FS-RF, and GPR-ARD. The performance of these methods on the same Parkinson's telemonitoring dataset is also reported in Table 9.

Table 9. Comparative results for predicting Parkinson's disease progression assessment

Model		Input feature	Att	Motor-UPDRS	Total-UPDRS
Traditional machine learning methods	SVR	Baseline	No	2.77	3.53
	XGBoost	Baseline	No	1.72	2.44
	RF	Baseline	No	1.69	2.09
	RF-Att	Baseline	Yes	1.66	2.04
	GWT-SVR	GWT	No	2.63	3.33
	GWT-XGBoost	GWT	No	1.71	2.16
	GWT-RF	GWT	No	1.67	2.08
Advanced methods	Ji et al. (2018)	Baseline	No	3.00	4.60
	Yoon & Li (2019)	Baseline	No	2.45	3.02
	Tsanas et al. (2021)	Baseline	No	2.65	3.17
	Despotovic et al. (2020)	Baseline	No	1.65	2.02
Proposed	GWT-RF-Att	GWT	Yes	**1.53**	**1.91**

The specific prediction results of each model in Table 9 can be analyzed as follows. Among traditional machine learning methods, both XGBoost and RF outperform the single prediction model SVR due to their integrated algorithms. Moreover, RF combines bagging and random feature selection, effectively addressing the overfitting issue observed in XGBoost. This not only enhances the robustness of the RF model but also improves its prediction accuracy. Consequently, compared to SVR and XGBoost models, RF demonstrates a reduction in MAE of 40.07% and 40.79% for motor-UPDRS and total-UPDRS, respectively, affirming its effectiveness in predicting PD severity progression. Additionally, compared to SVR, XGBoost, and RF, GWT-SVR, GWT-XGBoost, and GWT-RF models achieve reductions in MAE of 5.05%, 0.58%, 1.18%, and 5.67%, 11.48%, 0.48% for motor-UPDRS and total-UPDRS, respectively. Figure 11 compares the effects of attention mechanisms on the model. It can be seen that the errors are reduced after the addition of attention mechanism. Furthermore, the MAE of motor-UPDRS and total-UPDRS predicted by the GWT-RF and RF-Att models was reduced by 1.18%, 1.78% and 0.48% and 2.39%, respectively, compared to the RF model. Therefore, these results demonstrate that GWT can extract more effective PD features, and the attention-weighting-based RF can focus on the decision trees with better prediction performance. By combining these two methods, the proposed GWT-RF-Att model further reduces the MAE and improves the prediction performance.

Moreover, Table 9 reveals that the proposed model outperforms the existing literature in terms of predicting PD severity, achieving the lowest MAE values. The results show that the MAE of the proposed method for predicting motor-UPDRS and total-UPDRS are 1.53 and 1.91, respectively. The proposed method achieved a significant improvement compared to the best results of the literature in Table 9. The MAE was reduced by 7.27% and 4.05%. In previous studies, methods like FDAMF (Ji et al., 2018) and PTL (Yoon & Li, 2019) attempted to predict the UPDRS score of PD patients by learning from the information of other patients. However, it was challenging to measure the similarity of PD patients in different time dimensions, which limited the reduction of prediction errors. FS-RF (Tsanas et al., 2021) and GPR-ARD (Despotovic et al., 2020) used feature selection algorithms to select important PD features, which improved prediction accuracy. However, this approach may result in the loss of crucial information, affecting the performance of the model. In contrast, the proposed GWT-RF-Att model overcomes these limitations. It utilizes graph wavelet transform to capture more effective PD features and employs an attention weighting mechanism to focus on decision tree models with different prediction performance. As a result, the proposed model effectively enhances the prediction accuracy. Compared with the results of LDFSF method in Table 7, the prediction error of GWT-RF-Att method is lower, which indicates the effectiveness of the features extracted by GWT-RF-Att method. However, since the method requires wavelet transform and attention layer training, the limitation of the proposed model is that the running time of the model may be long.

Figure 11. Attention weighted RF predicts the MAE for motor-UPDRS and total-UPDRS

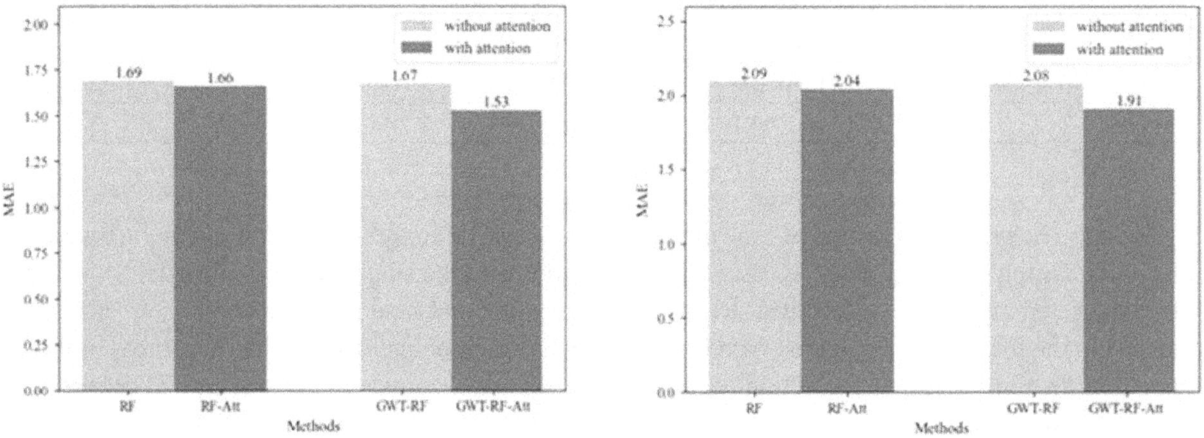

CONCLUSION AND FUTURE WORKS

This chapter proposes LDFSF and GWT-RF-Att methods for PD severity prediction from the perspectives of feature selection and feature transformation, both of which improve prediction performance. The LDFSF method analyzes the relevance, redundancy, and complementarity among PD voice features. It utilizes the maximal information coefficient to determine feature relevance and selects feature subsets with high relevance, low redundancy, and high complementarity using a dynamic feature selection method based on SOM clustering. The GWT-RF-Att method is based on graph wavelet transform and attention weighted random forest. It predicts the severity of current symptoms in PD patients using effective frequency features extracted from PD voice features. This method adaptively focuses on decision tree models with better performance in the random forest for prediction, resulting in improved accuracy. Experimental results on real public PTDS dataset show that both LDFSF and GWT-RF-Att methods have achieved better predictive performance compared to existing methods, thus verifying the effectiveness of these two methods in PD severity prediction.

In future research, combining the two proposed methods to achieve better results is an interesting attempt. Additionally, the causal feature selection method will be introduced to uncover the Markov boundary of the target variable UPDRS. This approach aims to identify voice features that have a causal relationship with UPDRS, thereby enhancing the robustness and practicality of the diagnostic model.

REFERENCES

Chakraborty, J., & Nandy, A. (2020). Discrete wavelet transform based data representation in deep neural network for gait abnormality detection. *Biomedical Signal Processing and Control*, *62*, 102076. doi:10.1016/j.bspc.2020.102076

Chen, Z., Chen, Q., Zhang, Y., Zhou, L., Jiang, J., Wu, C., & Huang, Z. (2021). Clustering-based feature subset selection with analysis on the redundancy–complementarity dimension. *Computer Communications*, *168*, 65–74. doi:10.1016/j.comcom.2021.01.005

Despotovic, V., Skovranek, T., & Schommer, C. (2020). Speech based estimation of Parkinson's disease using Gaussian processes and automatic relevance determination. *Neurocomputing*, *401*, 173–181. doi:10.1016/j.neucom.2020.03.058

Dong, X., Li, G., Jia, Y., & Xu, K. (2021). Multiscale feature extraction from the perspective of graph for hob fault diagnosis using spectral graph wavelet transform combined with improved random forest. *Measurement*, *176*(2), 109178. doi:10.1016/j.measurement.2021.109178

Hlavica, J., Prauzek, M., Peterek, T., & Musilek, P. (2016). Assessment of Parkinson's disease progression using neural network and ANFIS models. *Neural Network World*, *26*(2), 111–128. doi:10.14311/NNW.2016.26.006

Jain, S., & Shetty, S. (2016). Improving accuracy in noninvasive telemonitoring of progression of Parkinson's disease using two-step predictive model. *Third International Conference on Electrical, Electronics, Computer Engineering and their Applications (EECEA)*, (pp. 104-109). IEEE. 10.1109/EECEA.2016.7470774

Ji, W., Lv, Y., Lin, G., & Li, Y. (2018). Filtering-based domain adaptation model fusion method in prediction of Parkinson's disease symptom severity. *Yiqi Yibiao Xuebao*, *39*(06), 104–111.

Kadam, V. J., & Jadhav, S. M. (2019). Feature ensemble learning based on sparse autoencoders for diagnosis of Parkinson's disease. *Proceedings of ICCASP*, *810*, 567–581. doi:10.1007/978-981-13-1513-8_58

Lai, Z., Qu, X., Liu, Y., Guo, D., & Chen, Z. (2016). Image reconstruction of compressed sensing MRI using graph-based redundant wavelet transform. *Medical Image Analysis*, *27*, 93–104. doi:10.1016/j.media.2015.05.012 PMID:26096982

Liu, L., Chen, R., Zhao, Q., & Zhu, S. (2018). Applying a multistage of input feature combination to random forest for improving MRT passenger flow prediction. *Journal of Ambient Intelligence and Humanized Computing*, *10*(11), 4515–4532. doi:10.1007/s12652-018-1135-2

Mayo, M., & Frank, E. (2017). Improving naive bayes for regression with optimised artificial surrogate data. *Applied Artificial Intelligence*, *34*(6), 484–514. doi:10.1080/08839514.2020.1726615

Nilashi, M., Ahmadi, H., Sheikhtaheri, A., Naemi, R., & Zhao, J. (2020). Remote tracking of Parkinson's disease progression using ensembles of deep belief network and self-organizing map. *Expert Systems with Applications*, *159*, 113562. doi:10.1016/j.eswa.2020.113562

Nilashi, M., Ibrahim, O., Samad, S., Ahmadi, H., Shahmoradi, L., & Akbari, E. (2019). An analytical method for measuring the Parkinson's disease progression: A case on a Parkinson's telemonitoring dataset. *Measurement*, *136*, 545–557. doi:10.1016/j.measurement.2019.01.014

Oung, Q. W., Muthusamy, H., Basah, S. N., Lee, H., & Vijean, V. (2018). Empirical wavelet transform based features for classification of Parkinson's disease severity. *Journal of Medical Systems*, *42*(2), 29. doi:10.1007/s10916-017-0877-2 PMID:29288342

Reshef, D. N., Reshef, Y. A., Finucane, H. K., Grossman, S. R., Mcvean, G., Turnbaugh, P. J., Lander, E. S., Mitzenmacher, M., & Sabeti, P. C. (2011). Detecting novel associations in large data sets. *Science*, *334*(6062), 1518–1524. doi:10.1126/science.1205438 PMID:22174245

Senturk, Z. K. (2020). Early diagnosis of Parkinson's disease using machine learning algorithms. *Medical Hypotheses*, *138*, 109603. doi:10.1016/j.mehy.2020.109603 PMID:32028195

Shahid, A. H., & Singh, M. P. (2020). A deep learning approach for prediction of Parkinson's disease progression. *Biomedical Engineering Letters*, *10*(1), 227–239. doi:10.1007/s13534-020-00156-7 PMID:32477610

Sharma, P., Sundaram, S., Sharma, M., Sharma, A., & Gupta, D. (2019). Diagnosis of Parkinson's disease using modified grey wolf optimization. *Cognitive Systems Research*, *54*, 100–115. doi:10.1016/j.cogsys.2018.12.002

Tsanas, A., Little, M. A., Mcsharry, P. E., & Ramig, L. O. (2010). Accurate telemonitoring of Parkinson's disease progression by non-invasive speech tests. *Nature Precedings*, *57*(4), 884–893. PMID:19932995

Tsanas, A., Little, M. A., & Ramig, L. O. (2021). Remote assessment of Parkinson's disease symptom severity using the simulated cellular mobile telephone network. *IEEE Access : Practical Innovations, Open Solutions*, *9*, 11024–11036. doi:10.1109/ACCESS.2021.3050524 PMID:33495722

Tunc, H. C., Sakar, C. O., Apaydin, H., Serbes, G., & Gurgen, F. (2020). Estimation of Parkinson's disease severity using speech features and extreme gradient boosting. *Medical & Biological Engineering*, *58*, 2757–2773. PMID:32910301

Xiang, Z., Xiao, Z., Wang, D., & Li, X. (2016). A Gaussian mixture framework for incremental nonparametric regression with topology learning neural networks. *Neurocomputing*, *194*(19), 34–44. doi:10.1016/j.neucom.2016.02.008

Xu, S., & Pan, Z. (2020). A novel ensemble of random forest for assisting diagnosis of Parkinson's disease on small handwritten dynamics dataset. *International Journal of Medical Informatics*, *144*(2), 104283. doi:10.1016/j.ijmedinf.2020.104283 PMID:33010729

Xue, Z., Lu, H., Zhang, T., Xu, J., & Guo, X. (2023). A local dynamic feature selection fusion method for voice diagnosis of Parkinson's disease. *Computer Speech & Language*, *82*, 101536. doi:10.1016/j.csl.2023.101536

Xue, Z., Zhang, T., & Lin, L. (2022). Progress prediction of Parkinson's disease based on graph wavelet transform and attention weighted random forest. *Expert Systems with Applications*, *203*, 117483. doi:10.1016/j.eswa.2022.117483

Yoon, H., & Gaw, N. (2021). A novel multi-task linear mixed model for smartphone-based telemonitoring. *Expert Systems with Applications*, *164*, 113809. doi:10.1016/j.eswa.2020.113809

Yoon, H., & Li, J. (2019). A novel positive transfer learning approach for telemonitoring of Parkinson's disease. *IEEE Transactions on Automation Science and Engineering*, *16*(1), 180–191. doi:10.1109/TASE.2018.2874233

Zhang, C., Ding, J., Zhan, J., Sangaiah, A. K., & Li, D. (2023a). Fuzzy intelligence learning based on bounded rationality in IoMT systems: A case study in Parkinson's disease. *IEEE Transactions on Computational Social Systems*, *10*(4), 1607–1621. doi:10.1109/TCSS.2022.3221933

Zhang, T., Lin, L., & Xue, Z. (2023b). A voice feature extraction method based on fractional attribute topology for Parkinson's disease detection. *Expert Systems with Applications*, *219*, 119650. doi:10.1016/j.eswa.2023.119650

Zhang, T., Shan, H., & Little, M. A. (2022). Causal GraphSAGE: A robust graph method for classification based on causal sampling. *Pattern Recognition*, *128*, 108696. doi:10.1016/j.patcog.2022.108696

Zhang, T., Zheng, X., & Liu, M. (2021). Multiscale attention-based LSTM for ship motion prediction. *Ocean Engineering*, *230*, 109066. doi:10.1016/j.oceaneng.2021.109066

Chapter 4
Creating a Data Lakehouse for a South African Government-Sector Learning Control Enforcing Quality Control for Incremental Extract-Load-Transform Pipe

Dharmesh Dhabliya
https://orcid.org/0000-0002-6340-2993
Vishwakarma Institute of Information Technology, India

Jambi Ratna Raja Kumar
https://orcid.org/0000-0002-9870-7076
Genba Sopanrao Moze College of Engineering, India

Vivek Veeraiah
Sri Siddharth Institute of Technology, Sri Siddhartha Academy of Higher Education, India

Ritika Dhabliya
ResearcherConnect, India

Sukhvinder Singh Dari
https://orcid.org/0000-0002-6218-6600
Symbiosis Law School, Symbiosis International University, India

Sabyasachi Pramanik
https://orcid.org/0000-0002-9431-8751
Haldia Institute of Technology, India

Ankur Gupta
https://orcid.org/0000-0002-4651-5830
Vaish College of Engineering, India

ABSTRACT

The Durban University of Technology is now engaged in a project to create a data lake house system for a Training Authority in the South African Government sector. This system is crucial for improving the monitoring and evaluation capacities of the training authority and ensuring efficient service delivery. Ensuring the high quality of data being fed into the lakehouse is crucial, since low data quality negatively

DOI: 10.4018/979-8-3693-1582-8.ch004

impacts the effectiveness of the lakehouse system. This chapter examines quality control methods for ingestion-layer pipelines in order to present a framework for ensuring data quality. The metrics taken into account for assessing data quality were completeness, accuracy, integrity, correctness, and timeliness. The efficiency of the framework was assessed by effectively implementing it on a sample semi-structured dataset. Suggestions for future development including enhancing by integrating data from a wider range of sources and providing triggers for incremental data intake.

INTRODUCTION

In South Africa, Sector Education and Training Authorities (SETAs) are government-established entities responsible for managing skills development and training in various sectors of the economy. These entities are referred to as Government-Sector Training Authorities (GTAs), and they play a crucial role in the country's efforts to improve skills and training across many sectors. The Durban University of Technology (DUT) has partnered with a South African Government Technical Agency (GTA) to enhance the data management strategy used by the GTA for an ongoing project. This is achieved by assisting DUT students in developing supplementary talents. In order to enhance the data management capabilities of the GTA, it was recognized that a comprehensive system was required to store data and generate reports automatically. Following the discussion, the DUT team suggested using Microsoft Azure services to establish a data warehousing solution. Additional context for the project is presented by (Mthembu et al. 2024). This chapter focuses on establishing a Data Lakehouse for a Training Authority in the South African Government sector. One crucial aspect is investigating techniques to ensure the integrity of data as it moves through the system, particularly during the Incremental Extract-Load-Transform Pipelines at the Ingestion Layer employing Data Orchestration.

In the age of Big Data, where the vast amount of information poses both advantages and challenges, effectively handling and using data has become essential for organizational success. The wide range of data types, including structured, semi-structured, and unstructured forms, requires a sophisticated approach for data manipulation (Azad et al., 2020). The Extract, Load, Transform (ELT) framework is a versatile tool that is well acknowledged for its efficacy in negotiating the complexities of contemporary data settings (Singhal & Aggarwal, 2022). However, as data pipelines get larger and more complicated, guaranteeing the integrity of data quality (DQ) has become more important.

The emergence of big data has necessitated the use of Distributed Data Warehouses (DLH). Harby and Zulkernine (2022) suggested that the big data age has brought up new issues for traditional Data Warehouses (DWs). The increase in diverse data quantities caused by digital transformation presents a difficulty for traditional data warehouse solutions in businesses (Čuš & Golec, 2022; Giebler et al., 2021). Furthermore, (Barika et al. 2019) highlight the challenges faced by researchers in organizing, controlling, and implementing big data workflows, which differ significantly from typical workflows. After undergoing transformation and being placed into the data warehouse (DW), the original filtered information is no longer retained (Figueira, 2018). According to Conventional, (Nambiar and Mundra 2022), the ETL procedure is deemed inadequate for fulfilling certain data management requirements.

A Data Lake (DL) is a comprehensive storage and exploration system specifically intended to manage large amounts of varied data. It has been widely recognized as the preferred method for processing and storing various data (Begoli et al., 2021).An further research undertaken by the DUT team emphasizes the significance of data governance in establishing authority over data utilization and decision-making via the implementation of processes, rules, organizational structures, and responsibilities (Mthembu et al., 2024).Failure to regularly maintain a data lake might result in expensive and difficult data management. Insufficient execution of data governance in DL systems may result in the creation of a chaotic "Data Swamp," which undermines the worth of information in knowledge management and analytical systems owing to the presence of difficult-to-process and analyze data.

DLH emerged as an innovative concept that integrates the benefits of DL and DW, enabling companies to efficiently handle, analyze, and store vast quantities of data in a versatile and cost-efficient way. According to (Harby and Zulkernine 2022), this is intended to expedite the process of extracting information effectively.

The objective of this chapter is to provide a structured system for managing and incorporating data into a Data Lakehouse (DLH) to guarantee the accuracy and reliability of the data. The research outlines the following goals, which are aligned with the aim:

- Analyze current literature to identify crucial parameters and quality control measures for data orchestration and intake.
- Create and implement a framework that incorporates the essential elements and quality control measures indicated for efficiently managing and integrating data in a distributed ledger healthcare (DLH) system.
- To assess the efficacy of the established framework and provide suggestions for data quality management in the orchestration and ingestion of data for a distributed ledger technology (DLT) healthcare system.

By offering further study data on the use of Azure Data Factory (ADF) for the orchestration and ingestion of data into a data lake it enhances the existing knowledge base to facilitate future study in data orchestration and ingestion using Azure Services. Identify the limitations of establishing a pipeline for data orchestration and ingestion. Furthermore, offering comments for prospective investigations in this domain enhances the importance of our study. The study explores the concept of data orchestration, which is a crucial area that combines data management and quality control. The main objective is to provide quality control procedures in incremental ELT pipelines inside the Ingestion Layer of a Data Warehouse (DW). The research highlights the difficulties associated with using semi-structured data and recognizes the need for specific approaches to guarantee optimal data quality and integrity. The study result describes the creation of a pipeline and framework that allows data from SharePoint to be imported into a specific container inside the data lake architecture. The pipeline includes essential steps for converting semi-structured data into a structured format and utilizes data orchestration methods to ensure the correctness, completeness, and consistency of the data being processed.

Section 1 clearly explains the cause of the gap and offers a strong remedy, which is shown by the objectives and driven by the desire to provide valuable insights to the field of study and achieve specific research outcomes. The explicit references to the study's aims, scope, and delimitations provide a comprehensive understanding of the content and boundaries of this research. The methodology, datasets, matrices, and tools and platforms to be used in the experiment are described in Section 2. This provides sufficient time for thorough preparation for the subsequent Chapter Four. Section 3 demonstrates the results of the experiment and assesses the efficacy of the created artifacts. In addition, Section 3 discusses the constraints and offers an evaluation of the experiment's execution. Section 4 presents the findings of the experiments and evaluates the overall performance of the manufactured artifacts, in line with the experimental aspect of the study.

LITERATURE REVIEW

(Figueira, 2018) posits that the primary objective of the area of big data is to provide a means of managing vast quantities of data in order to generate valuable insights and knowledge. (Gupta, 2023) explains that the concept of big data originated from the three main factors known as the 3V's. These factors include: volume, which refers to the amount of data available (Liu & Zhang, 2020; Pratsri & Nilsook, 2020); variety, which encompasses a wide range of data types and sources, such as structured, semi-structured, and unstructured data (Liu & Zhang, 2020); and velocity, which represents the speed at which new data is generated and transferred (Liu & Zhang, 2020). Subsequently, the 5V's framework emerged, including the original 3V's and incorporating the following additions: The veracity of Big Data is of utmost importance, as ensuring accurate data without duplication is a challenging and time-consuming task. Value refers to data that is valuable and holds significance for business applications, including analysis for summarization and strategic planning, with the aim of enhancing product value and improving competitiveness in the target market. Figure 1, created by Sandhu in 2021, illustrates many instances of the 5V's.

Figure 1. Representation of the 5V's

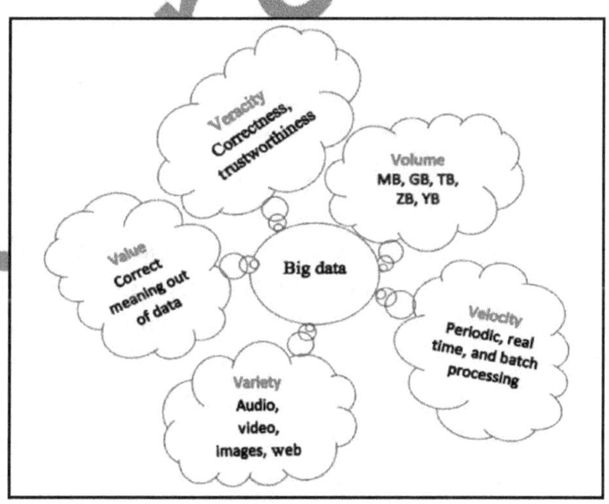

The three categories of content format sources are structured data, semi-structured data, and unstructured data. Structured data pertains to data that is systematically organized in a certain hierarchical pattern. Storing data in this manner facilitates search engines in presenting and comprehending it more effortlessly. Semi-structured data is characterized by an irregular and implicit structure, without a clearly defined data model. In this particular database format, the distinction between data and schema is not readily apparent. In contrast to organized data, unstructured data functions as its complete opposite. The absence of a well-defined framework results in the processing of data being a time-consuming task.

Semi-structured data presents the most difficulty in handling due to its lack of adherence to a pre-established data model and absence of a stable schema. This is a result of its irregular and implicit framework (Dickson & Asagba, 2020). (Nadal et al. 2022) have identified factors that make the ingestion of semi-structured data into a pipeline with schema flexibility challenging presenting difficulties in creating a standardized framework for processing since it may be necessary to accept various data examples.

(Raj, et al. 2020) asserts that ETL and ELT are the primary classifications of data pipelines. Data lakes (DLs) use the Extract, Load, and Transform (ELT) methodology, in which the first step involves loading the "raw data" followed by its subsequent transformation (Cherradi & El Haddadi, 2022).The ELT technique, in contrast to the ETL procedure, follows a similar fundamental idea but differs in terms of sequencing. Instead of doing the transformation before loading, the data is loaded first and then converted afterwards. Data orchestration has a wider range of activities compared to data integration. While data integration mainly concentrates on consolidating data for reporting purposes, data orchestration includes tasks such as resource allocation, monitoring, data discovery, preparation, and integration, processing, and linking enriched data across various landscapes (Dinh & Nguyen, 2022). (Kevin and Ginger 2021) highlight the objective of the system to efficiently handle and combine data, consequently improving or establishing corporate operations.

Data intake is usually the first layer in the design. The primary function of the intake layer is to acquire data from various sources and integrate it into the distributed learning system. (Cherradi & El Haddadi, 2022) have shown that data intake at the ingestion layer may be performed in several ways, depending on the source and destination. These methods include batch processing, real-time processing, or a combination of both. According to (Isah et al. 2019), stream processing involves the handling of continuous or dynamic data, in contrast to batch processing. Stream processing, a technique that allows for real-time data analysis without relying on persistent storage, plays a crucial role in social media platforms such as Twitter and Facebook. The velocity at which data is received greatly impacts this process (Nambiar & Mundra, 2022). Stream processing excels at handling large amounts of data that is constantly flowing at high speeds, and it can be quickly expanded to accommodate increased demands (Hlupić & Puniš, 2021). (Nambiar and Mundra, 2022) provide a hybrid processing strategy that combines batch and stream processing methods. This approach aims to achieve higher accuracy while minimizing processing time.

The chosen DQ qualities are correctness, validity, data integrity, accuracy, completeness, and timeliness. Although the threshold conditions were met, it was considered unnecessary to evaluate consistency for ingestion-layer processes. Consistency guarantees the consistent presentation of data, its alignment with other data, and its freedom from contradiction. This was considered more relevant to source systems and transformation-oriented pipelines. Assessing the comprehensibility of data is primarily important for systems-level governance, rather than being a central concern at the data input layer.

Performing a data integrity check during data import is essential for preserving data dependability and preventing data corruption throughout the transfer process between providers and repositories (Anastasova & Yanev, 2021), assesses whether data values adhere to predetermined criteria, and any variation suggests possible issues in the process of collecting the data. According to (Peng et al. 2015), data validity pertains to the integrity of data, namely its consistency and correctness throughout its existence. Data accuracy refers to the extent to which information precisely and faithfully portrays its intended topic or process (Anastasova & Yanev, 2021). Completeness refers to the state of data including all the anticipated properties and linked instances, which determines the extent of information (Koltay, 2020).

Timeliness refers to the age of the data and is of utmost importance in industrial systems that handle continuous production. Any delays or gaps in the data might lead to inaccurate management choices. (Gabarro and Stewart, 2021) emphasize that the effectiveness of an orchestration's dependability may be assessed using two separate measures. Firstly, by examining its behavioral comprehensiveness measured by the number of its calculated results.

Figure 2. DQ attribute occurrences

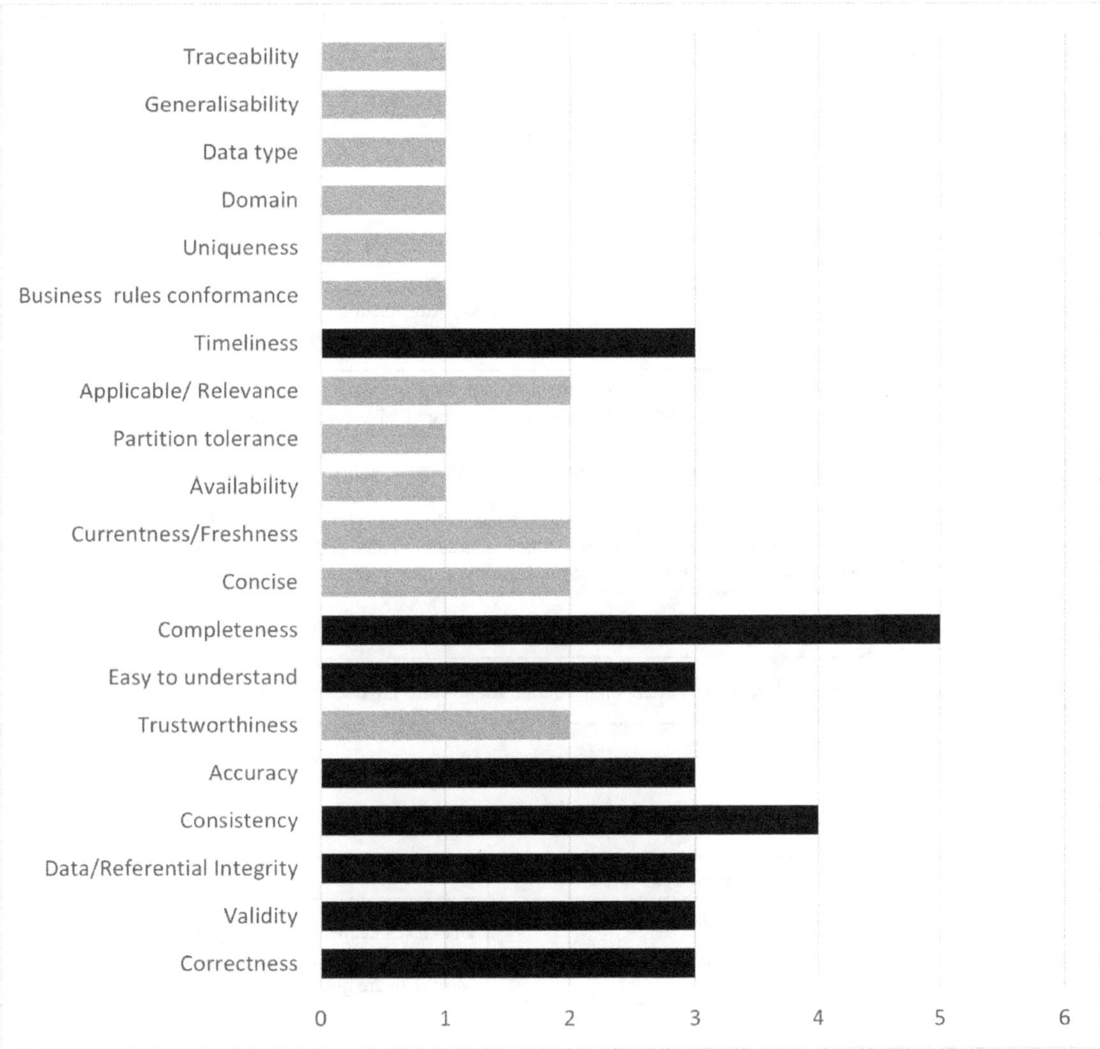

RESEARCH METHODOLOGY

This research used the paradigm of Design Science Research (DSR) as suggested by (Vom Brocke et al. 2020), who argue that DSR is fundamentally a problem-solving paradigm. Figure 3 below depicts the DSR paradigm developed by Ellis and Levy (2010).

Figure 3. DSR paradigm

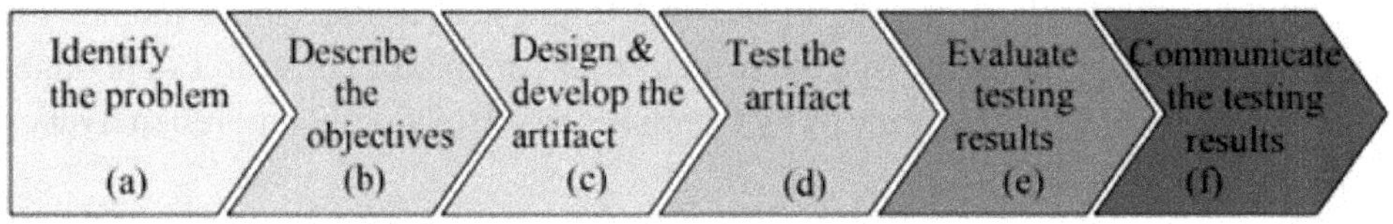

The activities depicted in Figure 3 are adapted to this study as follows in Table 2:

This research use Mixed Method Research (MMR) to enhance the quantitative results by using qualitative methodologies to provide more depth and significance to the findings. The inclusion of this enhanced data will enable this study to provide significant findings that will make a valuable contribution to the existing body of research (Strijker et al., 2020).

Table 1. DSR paradigm research adaptation

Activity	Study Adaptation
Identification of problem	Semi-structured data possess as a challenge for data ingestion
Description of objectives	Due to the flexible nature of semi-structured data, there is a need for a robust pipeline which can ensure that DQ is not compromised, when ingesting semi-structured data from the source to the destination.
Design and development of artifacts	The artefact designed in this study is the DQ frameworks and the data orchestration pipeline.
Testing of artifacts	The artefacts are tested by utilising a mock dataset obtained. The pipeline are developed and tested by transforming the source semi-structured data to structured data and stored in a SQL database table. The DQ framework are utilised to verify the completeness, accuracy, integrity, correctness, and timeliness.
Evaluation of testing results	The evaluation of the effectiveness of the artefacts is evaluated against the DQ framework created.
Communication of testing results	The results of the DQ and data orchestration frameworks are documented and discussed.

Table 2. Differences between data lakes and warehouses

Parameters	*Data warehouse*	*Data lake*
Information	Data warehouses solely pay attention to business procedures.	Data lakes keep all processing information
Processing	Extensively treated data	Most data are not processed
Type of Data	Mostly in tabular and structured forms	they may be classified as semi-structured, structured, or unstructured
Work	optimized to retrieve data	Distribute data stewardship
Agility	Compared to data lakes, this arrangement is fixed and less flexible.	Very flexible and able to adjust and reposition as need
Users	extensively used by business analysts and experts	Data scientists, data developers, and business analysts utilize data lakes.
Repository	Expensive storage with quick reaction times is used	Data lakes are designed for inexpensive storage.
Security	Expensive storage	Low cost storage

Collection of Data

The provided dataset is a CSV file that includes personnel information sourced from datablist.com. The collection includes User ID, First Name, Last Name, Date of Birth, and Job Title for 100 entries. Only the first 80 recordings will be subjected to ingestion for the purpose of this experiment. The following 20 records are allocated for testing data import after the first phase. The data entries are delimited by semi-colons, and these delimiters will be eliminated when converting the CSV file to a SQL database table. It is crucial to recognize that the first row of the CSV denotes the column headings.

Process of Dataflow

Figure 4 depicts the flow of data from the source, which is represented by SharePoint. The dataset being transferred is represented as a CSV file, which contains semi-structured data. Arrows symbolize the conduit that will be used for the transmission of the data. Significantly, Azure Data Factory will be used for this procedure. The data will be transported from the source to the DL and then duplicated in a container known as "Raw". The data contained inside this container will stay in its original, unaltered state, prohibiting any modifications to be made. Data timestamp is used to monitor new instances, indicating the current status of the data. Subsequently, the data residing in the Raw container will be replicated and transformed into a table inside an Azure SQL database, facilitating the implementation of data orchestration. Two more columns will be included, namely hashing and date timestamp. Hashing generates a distinct hash value that serves as a unique identifier for a record, hence preventing record duplication. The date timestamp will record the precise moment that the data was either added or changed. Subsequently, the organized information will be placed in the data lake inside a container referred to as "Curated". However, this study will specifically examine the functionality of data orchestration for curate data. Data orchestration will be used to prevent the duplication of previously added records. This will reduce data duplication caused by hashing. If there are any modifications to the data of an existing record, it will be updated. Furthermore, to enable the gradual intake of data, a trigger mechanism will be deployed to automatically execute the pipeline at certain intervals.

Figure 4. Pipeline Dataflow

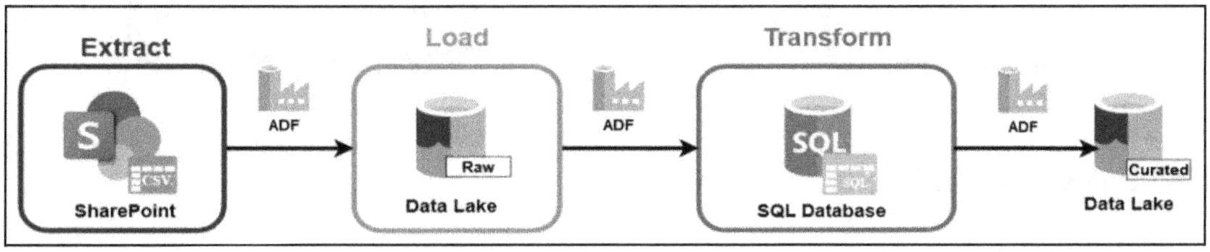

Framework for Ensuring Data Quality

The metrics shown in Figure 5 were derived from the findings presented in Table 1. Considering the analysis of integrity and validity conducted by (Peng et al. 2015), the DQ qualities of integrity and validity are regarded as synonymous.

Figure 5. DQ Framework

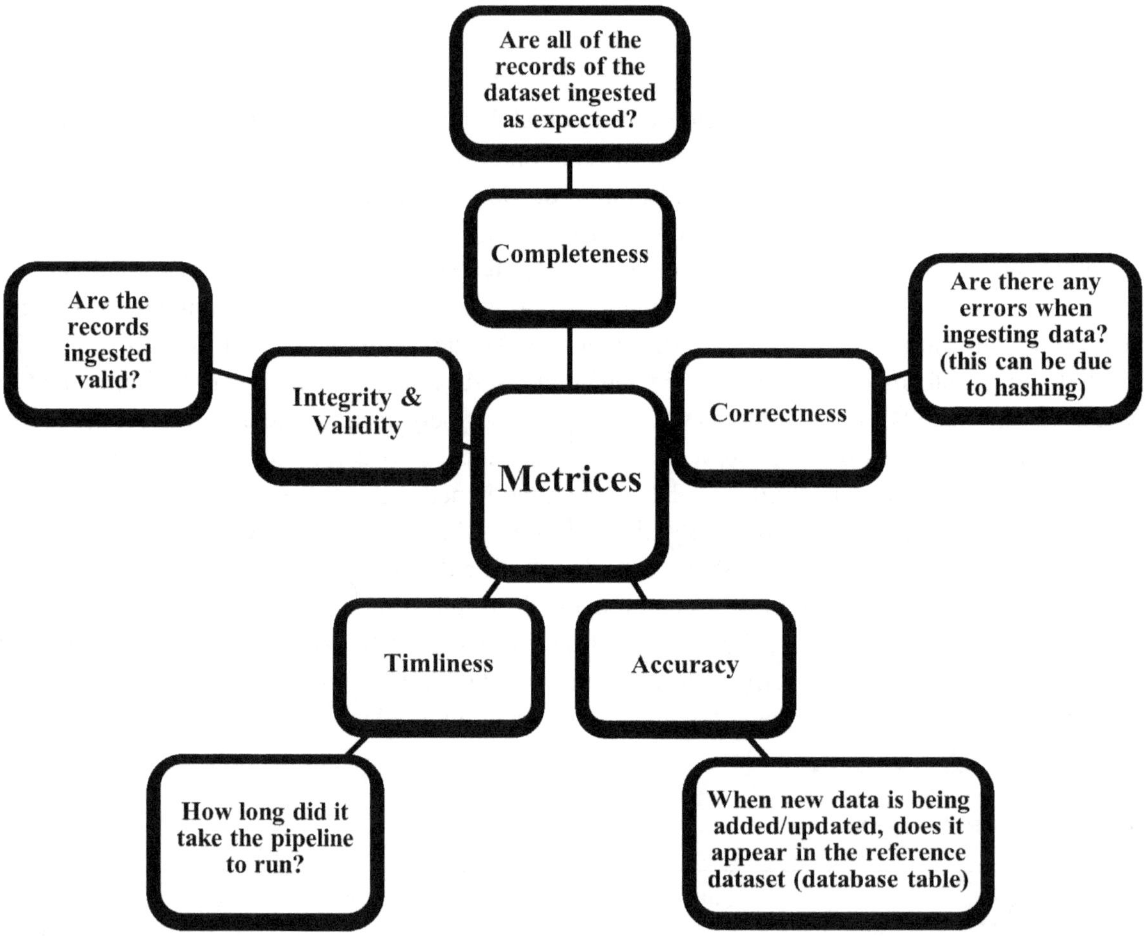

RESULTS AND ANALYSIS

Computation of Metrics

The term "reference dataset" in this study refers to the anticipated quantity of records that should be included in the dataset (Mahanti, 2019). The expected number of records refers to the anticipated number of records, whereas the actual number of records is the outcome obtained after doing the experiment. Frequently, a "benchmark" dataset is used as a reference for comparison. This benchmark is considered to provide a full and accurate depiction of the topic under consideration. The benchmark is a projection of the anticipated quantity of records used to assess the comprehensiveness of the dataset in issue.

Wholeness

Completeness pertains to the degree to which the whole of the anticipated records is acquired. The completeness of the dataset is assessed by calculating the ratio between the actual number of records and the total anticipated number of records. The completeness result might be represented either as a percentage or as N/A. The success criteria for the result are 100%.

The following illustrates the meaning of the symbols in the equation:

- *Comp%*: The rate of completeness of the dataset.
- *Arecords*: The actual number of records presented in the dataset.
- *Erecords*: The expected number of records in dataset.

$$Comp\% = \left(\frac{Arecords}{Erecords}\right) \times 100 \quad (1)$$

If:
Arecords>Erecords; *Comp%= N/A*
No data ingested then; *Acc %* = N/A

Correctness

Data correctness pertains to the absolute lack of mistakes; it adheres to a binary idea where data is classified as either accurate or incorrect, with no middle ground. Accuracy may vary, but for data to be considered accurate, it must mostly be right. Correctness refers to the absolute adherence to truth and accuracy in data, whereas accuracy quantifies the extent to which the data accurately reflects the world it represents. However, in order for any data to be acknowledged as accurate, its fundamental accuracy is indisputable. The measure of accuracy is represented by either a "Yes" or "No" or "Not Applicable". The success criteria for the result are zero.

The following illustrates the meaning of the symbols in the equation: Corr: the degree of data completeness. Arecords: the aggregate count of factual entries included in the dataset. Erecords: the overall anticipated quantity of records inside the collection. The absolute difference between the values of Erecord and Arecords is represented by the variable Corr.

where: Corr > 0; indicates a fault in the accuracy of the dataset.

A correlation coefficient of 0 implies that the ingestion of the dataset is accurate. No data has been processed or included; Correlation is not applicable.

Accuracy

The following depicts what the symbols represent in the equation:

- *Acc%*: The rate of accuracy of the dataset.
- *Trecords*: The total number of records presented in the dataset.
- *Tacc*: The number of accurate records in the dataset.
- *Arecords*: The total number of actual records presented in the dataset.
- *Erecords*: The total number of expected records in the dataset.

$$Acc\% = \left(\frac{Tacc}{Arecords}\right) \times 100 \qquad (3)$$

If:
Arecords≠Erecords then; *Tacc=Erecords*
Arecords=Erecords then; *Tacc=Arecords*
No data ingested then; *Acc%* = N/A

Validity and Integrity

Validity refers to the accuracy and soundness of information, whereas integrity refers to the consistency and reliability of data.

A record would be considered legitimate if the hashing is accurate. Essentially, this is the total number of legitimate records among the total number of records that were consumed. The result of validity and data integrity may be shown either as a percentage or as N/A. The success criteria for the result are a 100% achievement rate.

The follow depicts what the symbols represent in the equation:

- *Vi%*: The rate of the integrity records of the dataset.
- *Tvalid*: The total number of valid records presented in the dataset.
- *Arecords*: The total number of records presented in the dataset.
- *Tinacc*: The total number of inaccurate records presented in the dataset.

$$Tvalid = Arecords - Tinacc \qquad (4)$$

$$Vi\% = \left(\frac{Tvaild}{Arecords}\right) \times 100 \qquad (5)$$

If:
No data ingested then; *Vi%* = N/A

Timeliness

Timeliness, in the context of data management, pertains to the velocity at which data is provided or made available to business users. Essentially, it measures the time difference between the instant data is generated and when it is shown to the user. The "Occurrence Time" is a vital component of timeliness since it precisely identifies the specific instant when a real-world event, represented by the data, occurred. It also represents the moment when a certain characteristic or value associated with an object first became tangible. Essentially, "Occurrence Time" denotes the first time. In order to quantify this, the duration of data transmission is determined by calculating the difference between the end time and the start time, which is expressed in seconds. The success criteria for the result must be achieved within a time frame of 120 seconds. Significantly, several programs provide information on the length of the execution.

The following depicts what the symbols represent in the equation:

- *Time*(*s*): The rate of time it takes to ingest the dataset in seconds.
- *ST*: The Start Time (Occurrence time) of the dataset.
- *ET*: The End Time (Data delivery time) of the dataset.

$$Time(s) = ET - ST \quad (6)$$

If:
$Time(s) < 120s$; then valid
$Time(s) > 120s$; then not valid.

Case Scenarios

Establishing the scenario and its success criteria assists in determining the anticipated outcome and the projected outcomes. In Table 3, the variable "n" denotes the scenario number. The word "aim" refers to the major objective of the scenario. The "description" provides an account of the procedures involved. Lastly, the "success criteria" describes the standards used to decide whether the intended outcomes were accomplished.

Table 3. Scenario Case

Case n	
Aim	**ingesting fresh data**
Explanation	Explain the procedure that will be followed.
	Specify what constitutes a success for the outcomes.

Test Case

Test cases provide a methodical methodology to evaluate data using the previously specified DQ criteria. Users may record the initial data, any changes or additions made throughout the process, and the expected outcomes inside this framework. Additionally, it has a segment for overseeing many test endeavors, assessing their success or failure, and adding supplementary comments. The last part offers a concise overview of the overall effectiveness of the test case. The header provides details on the test case and scenario in the given test case. The test number is denoted by <number>, while the scenario number is indicated by n, and the title is represented by <title>. The dataset contains a count of entries located below the header. The input variable represents the original number of rows in the dataset, while the variable reflects the current number of rows. The process variable indicates the number of new rows that will be added to the dataset. Ultimately, the result accurately portrays the anticipated conclusion of the ingesting process. The next section presents the test results, including the computation of the matrices, which demonstrates the efficiency of the pipeline for that specific situation. Subsequently, the success is judged based on the established criteria for success. This may be indicated by either a positive response (Y) or a negative response (N). Supplementary remarks or observations for each matriculation might be recorded if necessary.

The overall findings represent the last segment of the test case, indicating whether the experiment achieved success or failure. The quantity of favorable results is recorded, and the success rate is computed. Finally, the ultimate determination is made on whether the experiment was ultimately successful or unsuccessful, depending on the specified success criteria.

Success Rate Calculation

The success criterion of the success rate outcome is 100%, thus the verdict will be Success, and otherwise the verdict is Fail.

The follow depicts what the symbols represent in the equation:

- *Srate* represents the Success rate
- *Tsucces* represents the total number of metrices that met the success criteria
- *Tmetrices* represents the total number of metrices

$$Srate = \left(\frac{Tsuccess}{Tmetrices}\right) \times 100 \tag{7}$$

If:
Srate= 100%; success
Srate< 100%; fail

Framework for Managing and Coordinating Data

Figure 6 represents the structure that will facilitate the assessment of data orchestration. Prior to anything else, it is important to finish the scenario instances. In the subsequent stage, it is necessary to document the beginning count of rows, the procedure, and the specific specifics of the conclusion in the test case. After completing the previous procedures, the following step is to execute the pipeline and finally record the outcomes in the test case and assess the overall result of the experiment.

Figure 6. Data Orchestration Framework

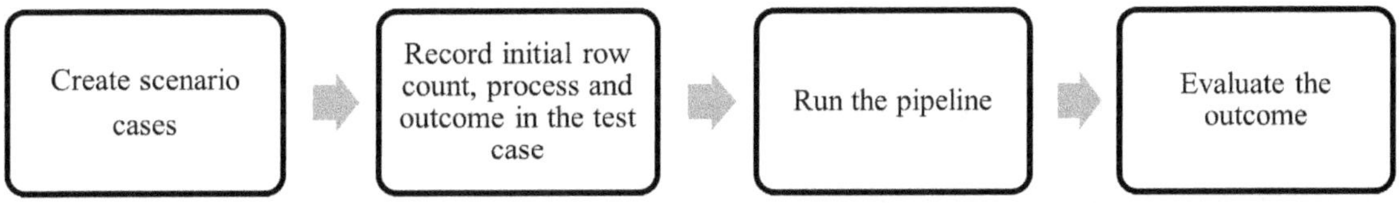

Procedure for establishing the pipeline using Azure services:

Step 1: You need to establish an Azure account.

In order to access the Azure portal and make use of Azure Services, it is necessary to register an Azure account. Moreover, the utilization of certain services necessitates the acquisition of credits, which incur charges commensurate with the nature of the services generated and used.

Step 2: Establishing the environment

Begin by creating a resource group to serve as storage for all the resources that will be used. It is important to pick the resource group that will be used for future purposes, if it is relevant. This resource group should be the one that has been formed. To proceed, the subsequent action involves establishing a storage account to securely retain the source data. After a successful deployment, proceed to establish a container. Then, inside that container, create a folder and upload the necessary files into it. Blob storage was used for testing reasons. Subsequently, establish an Azure SQL Server for the purpose of storing the Azure Database. This study employs SQL authentication as the chosen technique of authentication. Users are required to log in with a password in order to access the contents of the database server. Subsequently, proceed to establish an Azure SQL Database. This location functions as the destination where the semi-structured data, in the form of a CSV file, is converted into structured data and then saved in a table. Building a database incurs costs, but building the database server does not. The configuration of the database is determined by the desired performance and intended use of the database. The cost summary will compute the monthly expenses by considering the chosen database configurations. After creating the database, the Azure Data Factory (ADF) instance is created. Once the deployment is finished, the ADF studio may be launched.

Step 3: Transfer the contents of a CSV file to a database table.

Create connected services for both the source and sink in ADF. Establish a link service for blob storage, where the CSV file is saved as a blob for the purpose of this study. The second service that is connected is an Azure SQL Database, which is linked to the database. Next, build a new pipeline and choose the dataflow activity. A new data flow has to be generated and assigned as the data flow for the data flow activity. Subsequently, generate datasets for each of the associated services. Subsequently, create a new pipeline and opt for the copy action. Assign the source to the dataset containing the CSV file, and assign the sink to the dataset containing the SQL database. Choose the option to automatically build a table if the table does not already exist in the database. Subsequently, verify the pipeline and troubleshoot any issues.

Step 4: Establishing the data orchestration pipeline

Generate a novel data flow, thereafter establish a fresh pipeline, and use the data flow activity. Subsequently, establish the data flow to match the previously generated data flow. Establish two sources: the first source will retrieve data from the blob storage, while the reference source will get data from the database. These sources will be compared. Activating the data flow debug is necessary since it enables the data flow to execute. Generate Link a derived column transformation to the initial source and generate a column for hashing and another for the date timestamp. Given the introduction of two more columns, it is necessary to establish new columns in the database. It is important to note that the data types of the column, the expression returned in the "Dataflow expression builder," and the database must be the same. Subsequently, it is necessary to establish a connection with a Lookup transformation in order to validate if the records already exist or are considered new. To do this, you may configure the lookup stream to match the reference source. The lookup condition is used to provide the criteria for comparing the two sources with each other. In order to ascertain the outcome of the record after comparison, a conditional split transformation was linked to the dataflow. This study encompasses three potential streams: new record, update, and no action. The state of each stream is determined in its respective condition "Dataflow expression builder". The process will follow its respective stream and finally reach the sink, depending on the condition that is satisfied. The fresh record stream is linked to the sink, but the update stream needs an extra transformation in comparison. In order to enable record updates, it is necessary to attach an alter row transformation to the update stream. Finally, the sink determines the target dataset where the records will be stored. The update technique varies between the new record stream and the update stream in terms of the selected choices. In the new record stream, only the insert option is chosen, whereas in the update stream, both the insert and update options are selected. Subsequently, the columns in the data flow must be accurately linked to the corresponding columns in the destination dataset.

Step 5: Implement the pipeline

To start the pipeline, choose the pipeline built thereafter, and verify the pipeline for any potential errors. Assuming there are no issues, execute the pipeline by choosing the debug option. To see the count of rows written, choose the output option and then pick the data flow details.

Assessment of Framework

Before acquiring and using the ADF environment, this research used a theoretical strategy to execute the experiment and evaluate the efficacy of the generated artifacts. This theoretical assessment included both favorable and unfavorable outcomes for each given situation. The same possibilities were assessed both theoretically and practically.

Assessment of Outcomes

Scenario 1 assessed the initial data import process by absorbing a total of 80 records. Significantly, the reference dataset did not include any previous entries. The newly imported records were cross-referenced with the reference dataset to see whether any records already existed (this process was applied to all scenarios). In addition, the records that are ingested would be assigned a date timestamp and undergo hashing to ensure data integrity. Unfortunately, the data timestamp was not visible. Consequently, a total of 80 records were successfully processed, aligning with the anticipated result. The measures of completeness, accuracy, and validity/integrity achieved a perfect score of 100%, while correctness received a score of 0 (Y). Thus, Scenario 1 was deemed successful.

Scenario 2 was used to evaluate the intake of new records. This was achieved by consuming 10 new records. It is worth mentioning that there are a total of 80 entries included in the reference dataset. Consequently, a total of 10 records were successfully swallowed, aligning with the projected outcome of 90 records being eaten. The metrics of completeness, accuracy, and validity/integrity achieved a perfect score of 100%, however correctness received a score of 0 (Y). Thus, Scenario 2 achieved success.

Scenario 3 included the modification of preexisting records.15 new records were tested, with 10 being new and 5 being pre-existing. The success requirements include the absence of any newly ingested data and the updating of five existing records. The completeness and accuracy achieved a score of 100%, while the validity/integrity achieved a score of 95%. However, correctness received a score of 0 (Y).The compromise of validity and integrity implies a problem in the constructed pipeline, since the preservation of data quality is crucial in a real-world context. An error in the data might render a company's system unreliable and could result in financial consequences. Upon examination, the new records were included, but no records were modified. Consequently, a grand total of 100 recordings were swallowed. Consequently, Scenario 3 did not provide the desired outcome.

Scenario 4 included testing the intake of pre-existing records. The initial amount of records ingested was 100, and 10 pre-existing records were used to test this situation. The anticipated outcome did not need the consumption of any documents. The measures of completeness, accuracy, and validity/integrity achieved a perfect score of 100%, while correctness received a score of 0 (Y). Thus, Scenario 4 achieved its objective.

Figure 7 depicts the time it takes for the pipeline to execute and provide outcomes. The pipeline execution did not beyond 120 seconds, indicating that all scenarios resulted in good results. Scenario 3 took the longest time to finish the experiment and provide results. This scenario included the process of entering and modifying data. Significantly, with every iteration of the pipeline, the execution time decreased. However, because the first run of Scenario 3 was successful, this particular duration was recorded.

General Performance

Upon completion of the experiment, the statistical analysis reveals that the total success rate of 84% surpasses the failure rate of 16% by a ratio of 5 to 1 (84:16 = 5.25:1 ⇒ 5:1). Based on the statistics, this resulted in a favorable outcome. Nevertheless, according to the specifications of data quality (DQ), accuracy is a necessary condition. Consequently, this experiment is considered unsuccessful since the pipeline was unable to update records. The pie chart shown in Figure 8 provides a visual representation of the total performance rate.

Figure 7. Timeliness Evaluation

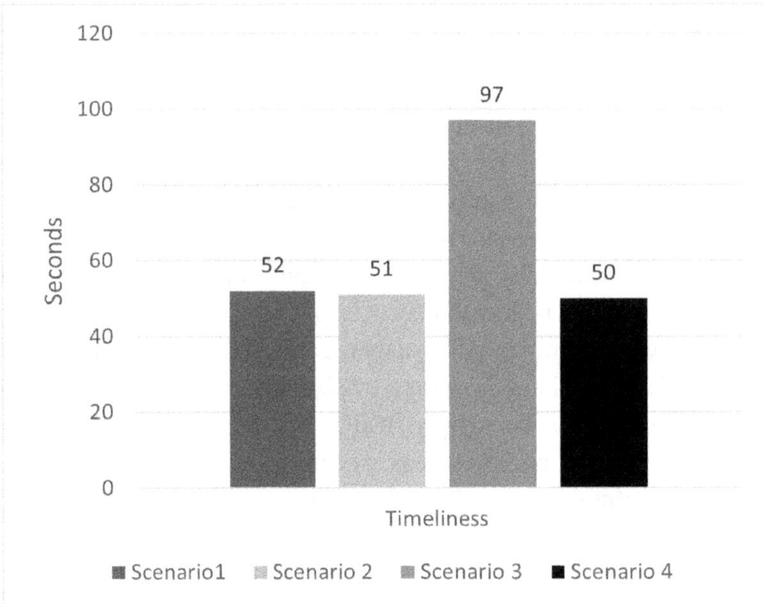

Figure 8. Overall Performance

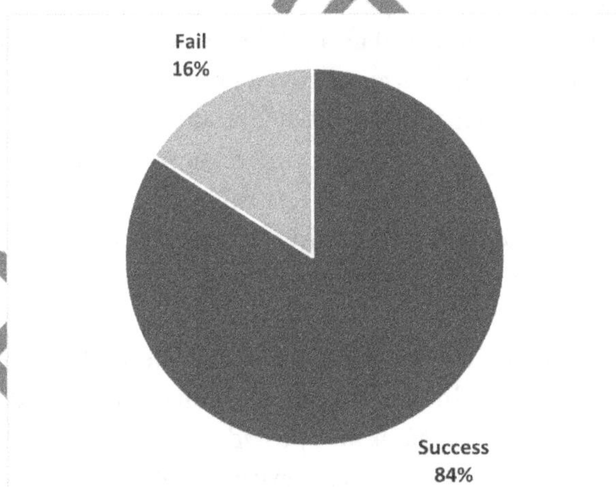

Obstacles

The primary obstacle encountered during the actual execution of the experiment was acquiring the necessary credit to access and exploit resources inside the Azure environment. The credit balance imposed limitations on resource creation, namely on the creation of additional "SQL Databases". In addition, it is necessary to watch the Azure credits while constructing the data flow, since running the debug process incurs costs that depend on the duration of its use. The update stream failed to operate as anticipated, resulting in data that cannot be relied upon. Efforts were undertaken to solve this puzzle; but, the intended result was not achieved. This discrepancy may be attributed to a mismatch in the hashing process. If none of the requirements were satisfied, no records will be impacted. In addition, the date timestamp was successfully implemented in the query editor of the "Azure SQL Database". However, the pipeline failed to incorporate a datetime stamp for the ingested entries.

Application Trends of Data Lakes

Fresh Research Investigation Marketresearch.biz now offers a study of the Data Lake Market 2023 by Market Trends (Drivers, Constraints, Opportunities, Threats, Challenges and Investment Opportunities), Size, Share, and Outlook. The size of the data lake market is predicted to increase from USD 13.9 billion in 2022 to around USD 92.1 billion by 2032, with a compound annual growth rate (CAGR) of 21.4% from 2023 to 2032. Both organized and unstructured data in its original form may be stored centrally in a data lake. Companies may store data in its original form utilizing data lakes, which provide flexibility and simple accessibility for analysis down the road. This is in contrast to conventional data warehousing approaches, which demand that data be processed and arranged before being stored. The market for data lakes includes a variety of goods,

Upon completion of the experiment, it was seen that using the copy activity at the beginning of the procedure was not advisable. This occurs when data is sent from the source to the sink without checking for any duplicate entries. While this study does not specifically focus on data cleansing, it is still an important issue to take into account. It is important to document and acquire the schema for the sink in a more effective manner for future study. The decision to use blob storage as the source, rather than alternative sources like SharePoint, was motivated by the goal of resolving any issues or difficulties. Difficulties arose, making it more convenient to comprehend and retrace the error's origin. This methodology facilitated enhanced comprehension, which has the potential to serve as a roadmap for future implementation using other sources. The sink was not configured for a distributed ledger (DL), since this work would be addressed in future research. The sink was configured to the "Azure SQL Database", facilitating the visualization of the conversion of the data from semi-structured to structured format. Nevertheless, next research will ultimately focus on deep learning (DL). The framework demonstrated efficacy in capturing the outcomes of each scenario event. The design was suitable; nevertheless, it has to be updated due to the identification of defects throughout the trial. Furthermore, it was noted that the remark part was optional, which might be considered a matter of personal taste.

CONCLUSION

The aims of this study were accomplished by identifying crucial criteria and implementing data quality control measures based on available literature. Multiple DQ traits were found, prompting a further in-depth investigation of their occurrence and importance. The DQ features used for this study were specifically intended to guarantee the data's quality throughout the process of intake. After successfully achieving the initial study objective, the discovered data quality criteria were employed as measurements in the design and development of the framework for data orchestration and ingestion. The efficacy of the established framework was assessed by implementing the data orchestration and watching the results of the experiment. Therefore, the final research aim has been accomplished. The efficacy of the created frameworks was first assessed in a theoretical manner and then validated via actual evaluation. Theoretical assessment alone would not have completely corresponded to real-world situations; nonetheless, it did contribute to comprehending the outcomes of using the DQ framework, both in terms of success and failure. To fully understand the efficiency of the study's artifacts, it was necessary to practically apply the pipeline. The experiment's practical execution revealed that the assessment of timeliness should be based on the anticipated quality that would be consumed. The figures given in Section 3 indicate that the experiment was successful, with a success rate of 84% and a failure rate of 16%. Despite the positive outcomes, this experiment is considered a failure based on the criteria of DQ. In order to achieve a Defects Quantification (DQ), it was necessary for the experiment to provide a success rate of 100%. The artifacts produced in this research demonstrated a certain level of efficacy, while the findings indicate that they need more refinement to fully capitalize on their potential and enhance their efficiency. Significantly, another crucial outcome of this investigation included the acquisition curves. It facilitated comprehension and firsthand experience of the intricacies involved in designing and executing pipelines, as well as comprehending the functioning of data orchestration. Utilizing cloud technology incurs significant expenses. The primary constraint of this study is the restricted availability of loans. The economic implications of debugging led to a reduction in the experimentation of data orchestration components. Nevertheless, despite the constraints of this study, it has enhanced the comprehension of DQ maintenance and data orchestration. By presenting a comprehensive set of principles for the design and execution of data orchestration systems, it significantly enhances the current knowledge base. Furthermore, it provides valuable insights for the creation of a data orchestration pipeline. Future research should further investigate the adaptation of data transfer between SharePoint and DL, using the analytical framework and empirical insights offered by this study. Additionally, it would be intriguing to ascertain if the findings of this investigation will yield similar outcomes on other cloud platforms such as Amazon Web Services and Oracle. Future endeavors should prioritize the integration of the study's discoveries with deep learning techniques and improving the process of extracting data from SharePoint. Further study is advised to give priority to the creation of a robust framework for managing metadata activities. Moreover, it is essential to provide a trigger function to enable the gradual intake of data from the source. Conducting thorough testing is crucial to determine the efficiency of the framework in data orchestration. Significantly, future research should specifically target the deficiencies found in this study. This involves efforts to enhance the DQ metrics, test case, and address issues related to data updates. Furthermore, it was determined that there is a need to investigate a more efficient approach for first transferring data from the source to the sink. This technique should only prioritize importing the schema utilized from the source to the sink, since the approach employed just copied the entries without confirming the presence of any duplication. Future work should also include the preservation of updated records in a DLH, without overwriting them, in order to retain a comprehensive historical record. Instead, new entries should be introduced and clearly indicated as a distinct version of the current record. The data timestamp might be used in the future for the development of this solution. According to Table 1, the trait of correctness was recognized as one of the DQ attributes mentioned in the literature. Hence, future study should investigate an additional DQ characteristic. Furthermore, it is crucial to prioritize the analysis of different types of changes in future endeavors, since there is a potential for a multitude of changes to transpire throughout time. It is important to take into account the concept of progressively changing dimensions. Finally, there are still many aspects to be improved and taken into account, since this study just scratches the surface of the potential of data orchestration. Hence, future study should delve into more complex aspects of data manipulation within this domain.

REFERENCES

Anastasova, Y., & Yanev, N. (2021). Models and data quality in information systems applicable in the mining industry. E3S Web of Conferences, Sofia, Bulgaria.

Azad, P., Navimipour, N. J., Rahmani, A. M., & Sharifi, A. (2020). The role of structured and unstructured data managing mechanisms in the Internet of things. *Cluster Computing*, *23*(2), 1185–1198. doi:10.1007/s10586-019-02986-2

Barika, M., Garg, S., Zomaya, A. Y., Wang, L., Moorsel, A. V., & Ranjan, R. (2019). Orchestrating big data analysis workflows in the cloud: Research challenges, survey, and future directions. *ACM Computing Surveys*, *52*(5), 1–41. doi:10.1145/3332301

Begoli, E., Goethert, I., & Knight, K. (2021). A lakehouse architecture for the management and analysis of heterogeneous data for biomedical research and mega-biobanks. 2021 IEEE International Conference on Big Data (Big Data), Orlando, FL, USA

Bjeladinovic, S. (2018). A fresh approach for hybrid SQL/NoSQL database design based on data structuredness. *Enterprise Information Systems*, *12*(8-9), 1202–1220. doi:10.1080/17517575.2018.1446102

Cherradi, M., & El Haddadi, A. (2022). A Scalable framework for data lakes ingestion. *Procedia Computer Science*, *215*, 809–814. doi:10.1016/j.procs.2022.12.083

Čuš, B., & Golec, D. (2022). Data Lakehouse: Benefits in small and medium enterprises. *Mednarodno inovativno poslovanje – Journal of Innovative Business and Management, 14*(2), 1-10.

Datablist. (n.d.). *Download Sample CSV Files for free*. https://www.datablist.com/learn/csv/download-sample-csv-files

Dickson, M. S., & Asagba, P. (2020). The Semi-Structured Data Model and Implementation Issues for Semi-Structured Data. *International Journal of Innovation and Sustainability*, *3*, 47–51.

Dinh, V.-N., & Nguyen, H.-A. (2022). Data Process Approach by Traditional and Cloud Services Methodologies.

Gabarro, J., & Stewart, A. (2021). Modelling web-service uncertainty: The angel/daemon approach. *Computer Science Review*, *39*, 100355. doi:10.1016/j.cosrev.2020.100355

Giebler, C., Gröger, C., Hoos, E., Eichler, R., Schwarz, H., & Mitschang, B. (2021). The data lake architecture framework. *BTW 2021*.

Gupta, P. M. (2023). The Role of Big Data in Smart Healthcare. *International Journal of Internet of Things*, *2023*. Advance online publication. 10.5923

Harby, A. A., & Zulkernine, F. (2022). From Data Warehouse to Lakehouse: A Comparative Review. 2022 IEEE International Conference on Big Data (Big Data), Osaka, Japan

Hlupić, T., & Puniš, J. (2021). An Overview of Current Trends in Data Ingestion and Integration. 2021 44th International Convention on Information, Communication and Electronic Technology (MIPRO).

Isah, H., Abughofa, T., Mahfuz, S., Ajerla, D., Zulkernine, F., & Khan, S. (2019). A survey of distributed data stream processing frameworks. *IEEE Access : Practical Innovations, Open Solutions*, *7*, 154300–154316. doi:10.1109/ACCESS.2019.2946884

Kevin, P., & Ginger, G. (2021). *Managing Data Orchestration and Integration at Scale*. O. R. Media.

Khan, N., Naim, A., Hussain, M. R., Naveed, Q. N., Ahmad, N., & Qamar, S. (2019). The 51 v's of big data: survey, technologies, characteristics, opportunities, issues and challenges. *Proceedings of the international conference on omni-layer intelligent systems*, Crete, Greece. 10.1145/3312614.3312623

Koltay, T. (2020). Quality of open research data: Values, convergences and governance. *Information (Basel)*, *11*(4), 175. doi:10.3390/info11040175

Liu, P., Loudcher, S., Darmont, J., & Noûs, C. (2021). Archaeodal: A data lake for archaeological data management and analytics. *Proceedings of the 25th International Database Engineering & Applications Symposium*, Lyon, France. 10.1145/3472163.3472266

Liu, Z., & Zhang, A. (2020). Sampling for big data profiling: A survey. *IEEE Access : Practical Innovations, Open Solutions*, *8*, 72713–72726. doi:10.1109/ACCESS.2020.2988120

Mahanti, R. (2019). *Data Quality: Dimensions, Measurement, Strategy, Management, and Governance*. ASQ Quality Press.

Mthembu, Z. K., Patel, S. S., Naicker, N., Joseph, S., Madamshetty, L., Moonsamy, D., Akinola, A. T., & Govender, P. (2024 under review). Developing a Data Lakehouse for a South African Government-Sector Training Authority: Governance Framework Design through Systematic Literature Review and Meta-Analysis. In O. S. Ogunleye (Ed.), *Machine Learning and Data Science Techniques for Effective Government Service Delivery*. IGI Global.

Nambiar, A., & Mundra, D. (2022). An Overview of Data Warehouse and Data Lake in Modern Enterprise Data Management. *Big Data and Cognitive Computing*, *6*(4), 132. doi:10.3390/bdcc6040132

Peng, G., Privette, J. L., Kearns, E. J., Ritchey, N. A., & Ansari, S. (2015). A unified framework for measuring stewardship practices applied to digital environmental datasets. *Data Science Journal*, *13*(0), 231–253. doi:10.2481/dsj.14-049

Plano Clark, V. L. (2017). Mixed methods research. *The Journal of Positive Psychology*, *12*(3), 305–306. doi:10.1080/17439760.2016.1262619

Pratsri, S., & Nilsook, P. (2020). Design on Big Data Platform-Based in Higher Education Institute. *Higher Education Studies*, *10*(4), 36–43. doi:10.5539/hes.v10n4p36

Raj, A., Bosch, J., Olsson, H. H., & Wang, T. J. (2020). Modelling data pipelines. 2020 46th Euromicro conference on software engineering and advanced applications (SEAA), Portoroz, Slovenia

Sandhu, A. K. (2021). Big data with cloud computing: Discussions and challenges. *Big Data Mining and Analytics*, *5*(1), 32–40. doi:10.26599/BDMA.2021.9020016

Singhal, B., & Aggarwal, A. (2022). ETL, ELT and Reverse ETL: A business case Study. *2022 Second International Conference on Advanced Technologies in Intelligent Control, Environment, Computing & Communication Engineering (ICATIECE)*, Bangalore, India 10.1109/ICATIECE56365.2022.10046997

Strijker, D., Bosworth, G., & Bouter, G. (2020). Research methods in rural studies: Qualitative, quantitative and mixed methods. *Journal of Rural Studies*, *78*, 262–270. doi:10.1016/j.jrurstud.2020.06.007

Vom Brocke, J., Hevner, A., & Maedche, A. (2020). Introduction to design science research. *Design science research. Cases*, 1-13.

KEY TERMS AND DEFINITIONS

Data Ingestion: The process of collecting and importing information from a variety of sources into an archive, e.g. the Data Lakehouse, so that it can be made available for analysis.

Data Lakehouse: A unified data management architecture that enables organizations to store and analyze structured and unstructured data on a single platform, combining the benefits of Data Lakes and Data Warehouses.

Data Orchestration: This is to ensure efficient data flows and integration into a system, often facilitated through automated working processes, by coordinating and managing different processing tasks.

Data Quality: The degree to which data are accurate, complete, timely, and consistent, providing reliable and meaningful information for decision making.

Semi-Structured Data: Data which has an irregular and implicit structure that lacks a defined data model.

Chapter 5
Decision-Making Based on Partition Order Product Space

Yi Xu
Anhui University, China

ABSTRACT

Granular computing focuses on structured thinking and problem solving, which solves complex problem based on granular structure. Existing studies on granular structures mainly focus on multilevel granular structure and multiview granular structure respectively, without combining multilevel granular structure and multiview granular structure. In order to describe and solve problem in a more effectively and reasonably way, we propose partition order product space by combining multilevel granular structure with multiview granular structure. To obtain a solution for problem solving in partition order product space, we propose two search algorithms: depth-first searching algorithm and breadth-first searching algorithm. From the viewpoint of granular computing, existing three-way decisions cannot effectively combine multiview and multilevel to make decisions. As the partition order product space follows the principles of multiview and multilevel, we discuss three-way decisions based on partition order product space. We propose four multiview sequential three-way decisions.

INTRODUCTION

Zadeh proposed and discussed the concept of fuzzy information granularity, which was the first time the concept of "granularity" was proposed (Zadeh, 1979). Hobbs published a paper directly titled "Granularity" (Hobbs, 1985), discussing the decomposition and merging of granules, and proposing methods and models for generating granules of different granularities. Lin T.Y. proposed "Granular Computing" during a visit in the University of California, Berkeley (Lin, 1998). Granular computing focuses on structured thinking and problem solving, which are viewed as human-inspired paradigms of computing and information processing (Bargiela & Pedrycz, 2008; Pedrycz, Skowron, & Kreinovich, 2008; Yao, 2009; Yao, 2016). It solves complex problem based on granular structure. In granular structure, a set of attributes (features) is often selected as a view to describe objects from a particular angle. In each view, objects can be further described from different levels of granularities (abstraction), and each granularity

DOI: 10.4018/979-8-3693-1582-8.ch005

determines a level. Multiview and multilevel are two basic principles of granular computing (Yao, 2009; Yao, 2016). In real applications, to achieve a more comprehensive and reasonable solution in problem solving, people usually simultaneously solve a problem from both multiple views and multiple levels rather than just solving a problem from either multiple views or multiple levels (Bargiela & Pedrycz, 2008; Yao, 2009; Yao, 2016). We select medical diagnosis as an example to illustrate the importance of combining multiple views and multiple levels. In medical diagnosis, assume that a doctor needs to diagnose whether a patient has influenza or pneumonia. To obtain accurate diagnostic conclusions, patients usually have to undergo several kinds of examinations, such as routine examinations, including assessments of a patient's temperature, cough and sore throat; biochemical examinations, including routine blood tests, C-reactive protein tests and mycoplasma pneumonia tests; and imaging examinations, including X-ray, CT and MRI. Different kinds of examinations provide information about patients from different horizontal perspectives, and each kind of examination can be described as a view. In each view, with an increase in the number of examination items, information about patients becomes increasingly detailed, which constructs multiple levels of information and provides information about patients from different vertical perspectives. First, if a doctor gives the diagnosis conclusion only from a single view, such as routine examinations, there is a great possibility of misdiagnosis. Therefore, to make an accurate diagnosis, the doctor usually makes a decision from multiple views. Second, in a view such as imaging examinations, a patient does not complete all examination items at one time, after which the doctor makes a conclusion. Instead, the patient may first implement an X-ray, and then the doctor tries to make a diagnosis. If a diagnosis cannot be reached, the patient may further implement CT. Namely, in each view, doctors usually make decisions from multiple levels step by step. Last, with multiple views and multiple levels of each view, according to the real needs of the patient, he or she can flexibly implement examinations of different views and different levels. For example, the patient may first undergo examinations to assess temperature, cough and routine blood tests. If the diagnosis conclusion cannot be reached from these examination results, then the patient may undergo an X-ray examination and a C-reactive protein test. The doctor usually simultaneously combines the examination results of multiview and multilevel and flexibly chooses different views and different levels in a view to obtain more reasonable decision results.

The existing studies on granular structures mainly focus on multilevel granular structure and multiview granular structure respectively, without combining multilevel granular structure and multiview granular structure. Granular structure based on multilevel is composed of a linearly ordered family of levels, which only provides one view with multiple levels. Granular structure based on multiview provides multiple views, but each view only consists of one level. In order to understand and describe problem in a more comprehensive way, and then solve the problem more effectively and reasonably, given a universe, we take partition as the granulation method. Combining multilevel granular structure with multiview granular structure, we propose partition order product space. Partition order product space is a new granular computing model that simultaneously follows the principles of multiple views and multiple levels. Based on the partition order product space, we can solve a problem from multiple views and at multiple levels in each view. Linearly ordered multiple levels are utilized to represent a view. A partition order product space is the Cartesian product of many linearly ordered levels, which is a lattice. Each node of the lattice is a solution of problem solving, which is a family of one-level views. To obtain a solution for problem solving in partition order product space, we propose two search algorithms, which are referred to as the depth-first searching algorithm and breadth-first searching algorithm.

The theory of three-way decisions proposed by Yao (Yao, 2011; Yao, 2010) can be motivated, interpreted and implemented from the viewpoint of granular computing (Bargiela & Pedrycz, 2008; Fang,

Gao, & Yao, 2020; Pedrycz, Skowron, & Kreinovich, 2008; Yao, 2013), which is associated with concept learning (Zhi, Qi, Qian, & Wei, 2019), decision making (Li, Zhang, Zhou, & Huang, 2017; Liang & Liu, 2016; Luo, Hu, & Qin, 2020; Yao, 2019; Zhang, Li, & Liang, 2020), classification (Dai, Zhou, Li, & Liu, 2019; Liu, Li, & Liang, 2014; Savchenko, 2016; Yue, Chen, Miao, & Fujita, 2020; Zhang, Xia, & Wang, 2017) and clustering (Wang & Yao, 2018; Xie, Xia, Wang, & Gao, 2023). In real applications, this theory has been successfully applied in many fields, such as image processing (Li, Zhang, Huang, & Zhou, 2016; Savchenko, 2019), text processing (Zhang, 2019; Behzadidoost, Mahan, & Izadkhah, 2024), recommender systems (Zhang & Min, 2016), data mining and knowledge acquisition (Chen, Li, Min, Liu, & Tsang, 2017; Min, Zhang, Zhai, & Shen, 2020; Wang, Shi, Yang, & Mi, 2019; Wei, Liu, Qi, & Qian, 2020; Xu, Miao, Zhang, & Zhang, 2017). Different from the traditional two-way decisions that must culminate in an immediate decision, when the available information is insufficient or the evidence is not strong enough to support an acceptance or a rejection at a particular level of granularity, the third option of non-commitment allows us to defer a decision to the next level of granularity. From the viewpoint of granular computing, there are mainly four kinds of three-way decisions: classical three-way decisions (Yao, 2011; Yao, 2010), sequential three-way decisions (Yao, 2013; Yang, Li, Liu, Chen, & Luo, 2017; Yang, Li, Fujita,Liu, & Yao, 2017), multigranulation three-way decisions (Qian, Zhang, Sang, & Liang, 2014; Qian, Liang, & Lin, 2017; Sang, Liang, & Qian, 2015; Zhou & Yao, 2010) and multigranulation sequential three-way decisions (Qian, Liu, & Yue, 2019; Qian, Liu, & Miao, 2020). Classical three-way decisions and multigranulation three-way decisions are single-step decisions. Sequential three-way decisions and multigranulation sequential three-way decisions are multi-step decisions. Classical three-way decisions are based on a single view with a single level. Sequential three-way decisions are based on a single view with multiple levels (Yao, 2013; Yang, Li, Liu, Chen, & Luo, 2017; Yang, Li, Fujita, Liu, & Yao, 2017). Multigranulation three-way decisions are based on multiple views, and each view has only a single level (Qian, Zhang, Sang, & Liang, 2014; Qian, Liang, & Lin, 2017; Sang, Liang, & Qian, 2015; Zhou & Yao, 2010). Multigranulation sequential three-way decisions are based on multiple views; each view has a single level and the sequential process is formed using a sequence of thresholds (Qian, Liu, & Yue, 2019; Qian, Liu, & Miao, 2020). In summary, sequential three-way decisions only consider multiple levels and do not adequately consider the issue of multiple views. Multigranulation three-way decisions and multigranulation sequential three-way decisions only consider multiple views and do not sufficiently consider the issue of multiple levels. Sequential three-way decisions, multigranulation three-way decisions and multigranulation sequential three-way decisions separately use multiple views or multiple levels. A relative separation of multiple views and multiple levels calls for their integration. Therefore, we discuss three-way decisions based on partition order product space. Combining depth-first and breadth-first searching algorithms with optimistic and pessimistic fusion strategies, we propose four multiview sequential three-way decisions: depth-first optimistic multiview sequential three-way decisions, depth-first pessimistic multiview sequential three-way decisions, breadthfirst optimistic multiview sequential three-way decisions, and breadth-first pessimistic multiview sequential three-way decisions. The proposed four multiview sequential three-way decisions can make decisions not only from multiview but also at multilevel. Existing three-way decisions can be considered special cases of the proposed models.

We introduce partition order product space in Section 2. In Section 3, we propose two types of search algorithms: depth-first searching algorithm and breadth-first searching algorithm, to obtain a solution for problem solving in partition order product space. In Section 4, combining depth-first and breadth-first searching algorithms with optimistic and pessimistic fusion strategies, we propose four multiview sequential three-way decisions. Section 5 is Conclusion.

PARTITION ORDER PRODUCT SPACE

Partition order product space solves a problem from multiple views and at multiple levels in each view (Xu & Yao, 2019), which simultaneously follows the principles of multiple views and multiple levels. Based on the partition order product space, we can more comprehensively understand and describe the problem and then more effectively and reasonably solve the problem. Given a universe, first, partition order product space uses a partition on the universe to define a level. Second, a nested sequence of partitions is employed to define a hierarchy, which represents a view with a linearly ordered relation. Last, given many views that determine many linearly ordered relations, a partition order product space is proposed based on the Cartesian product of multiple linearly ordered relations, which is a lattice. Each node of the lattice is a solution of problem solving, which is a family of one-level views. The descriptions of important notations are presented in Table 1.

Table 1. Notations and descriptions

Notations	Descriptions
U	universe
X	a target concept
x	an object
POS(*X*)	positive region of *X*
NEG(*X*)	negative region of *X*
BND(*X*)	boundary region of *X*
[*x*]	equivalence class of *x*
Pr(*X*|[*x*])	conditional probability of *x* being in *X*
á,â	thresholds
IS= (*U*,*AT*=*C*∪*D*,*V*,*f*)	an information system
ð	a partition on *U*
P= {$ð_1$,$ð_2$,…,$ð_n$}	a partition order
$P_i = \{\pi_i^1, \pi_i^2, \cdots, \pi_i^{n_i}\}$	the *i*-th partition order
v_i= (P_i,≼)	the *i*-th view
π_i^j	the j-th level of the *i*-th view
n_i	number of levels in view v_i
$POPS_m$= (×P_i,$≼_P$)	a partition order product space
m	number of views
$l^k = \left(\pi_1^{k_1}, \pi_2^{k_2}, \cdots, \pi_m^{k_m}\right)$	the k-th problem solving level in $POPS_m$
$[x]_{\pi_i^{k_i}}$	equivalence class of *x* with respect to $\pi_i^{k_i}$
L= {l^1,l^2,…,l^t}	a traversal sequence of problem solving levels
$\alpha_i^{k_i}, \beta_i^{k_i}$	thresholds on the k_i-th level of the *i*-th view

Assume that $\pi = \{A_1, A_2, \ldots, A_k\}$ is a partition on U, satisfying $\bigcup_{i=1}^{k} A_i = U$ and $A_i \cap A_j = \varnothing (i \neq j)$. Given two partitions $\pi_1 = \{A_1, A_2, \ldots, A_k\}$ and $\pi_2 = \{B_1, B_2, \ldots, B_k\}$. If $\forall B_1 \in \pi_2$, $A_i \in \pi_1$, satisfying $B_i \subseteq A_i$, we infer that π_2 is finer than π_1 or π_1 is coarser than π_2, which is denoted as $\pi_2 \preceq \pi_1$.

Definition 1 (Xu & Yao, 2019). A partition order is defined as a family of partitions $P = \{\pi_1, \pi_2, \ldots, \pi_n\}$, satisfying $\pi_n \preceq \pi_{n-1} \preceq \ldots \preceq \pi_1$.

Definition 2 (Xu & Yao, 2019). Given a partition order $P = \{\pi_1, \pi_2, \ldots, \pi_n\}$. A view is defined as the total order set $(P, \preccurlyeq)$, denoted as v. Each π_j is defined as a level.

A partition order can be constructed by a nested sequence of equivalence relations. Assume that $R = \{E_1, E_2, \ldots, E_n\}$ is a nested sequence of equivalence relations on U, satisfying $E_n \subseteq E_{n-1} \subseteq \ldots \subseteq E_1$. Then $U / E_i = \{[x]_{E_i} \mid x \in U\}$ is a partition, where

$$[x]_{E_i} = \{y \in U \mid (x, y) \in E_i\}$$

is the equivalence class of x with respect to E_i, which is referred to as a granule, $1 \leq i \leq n$. If we select U/E_i as π_i, then we can derive the partition order $P = \{\pi_1, \pi_2, \ldots, \pi_n\}$.

A view is defined by a partition order. A partition order can be constructed by a nested sequence of equivalence relations. Thus, how to construct a nested sequence of equivalence relations is a crucial issue for a view. There are many methods (Catanzariti, Chiaselotti, Infusino, & Marino, 2020; Chen, Li, Min, Liu, & Tsang, 2017; Liu, Zhang, Ciucci, Wu, & Min, 2018). Given an information system, based on a nested sequence of attribute sets $C_1 \subset C_2 \subset \ldots \subset C_n \subseteq C$, we can obtain a nested sequence of equivalence relations. Given a multi-scale information system

$$S = (U, A) = (U, \{a_j^k \mid k = 1, 2, \ldots, I, j = 1, 2, \ldots, m\})$$

(Chen, Li, Min, Liu, & Tsang, 2017), based on a multi-scale sequence of attribute value sets $V^I \prec V^{I-1} \prec \ldots \prec V^1$, we can also achieve this aim.

Theorem 1 (Yang, Li, Liu, Chen, & Luo, 2017). Given an $IS = (U, AT = C \cup D, V, f)$ and $C_1 \subset C_2 \subset \ldots \subset C_n \subseteq C$ Suppose

$$E_{C_i} = \{(x, y) \in U \times U \# \ \forall a \in C_i, f(x, a) = f(y, a)\}$$

is the equivalence relation determined by C_i; $1 \leq i \leq n$. Then $E_{C_n} \subset E_{C_{n-1}} \subset \ldots \subset E_{C_1}$ is a nested sequence of equivalence relations.

$$\forall x \in U, [x]_{C_n} \subset [x]_{C_{n-1}} \subset \ldots \subset [x]_{C_1}, \text{ where } [x]_{C_i} = \{y \in U \mid (x, y) \in E_{C_i}\}$$

is the equivalence class of x with respect to C_i.

Theorem 1 indicates that a nested sequence of attribute sets determines a nested sequence of equivalence relations, based on which we can construct a view. In this view, the number of attributes increases with the levels. From the high level to the low level, the quality of granules ranges from coarse to fine, and the size of granules ranges from large to small. Consequently, at a higher level of granularity, one may have a more abstract and compact representation of a decision problem by omitting details, leading to a faster decision process but a less accurate result. On the other hand, at a lower level of granularity, one may have a more concrete and elaborate representation, leading to a slower decision process but a more accurate result.

Theorem 2 (Yang, Li, Liu, Chen, & Luo, 2017). Given a

$$S = (U, A) = (U, \{a_j^k \# \ k = 1, 2, ..., I, j = 1, 2, ..., m\}$$

and $V^I \prec V^{I-1} \prec ... \prec V^1$. Suppose

$$E_{V^k} = \{(x, y) \in U \times U \# \ \forall a_j \in A, f(x, a_j^k) = f(y, a_j^k)\}$$

is the equivalence relation determined by V^k scale of A,$1 \leq k \leq I$. Then $E_{V^I} \subset E_{V^{I-1}} \subset ... \subset E_{V^1}$ is a nested sequence of equivalence relations.

$$\forall x \in U, [x]_{V^I} \subset [x]_{V^{I-1}} \subset ... \subset [x]_{V^1}, \text{ where } [x]_{V^k} = \{y \in U \mid (x, y) \in E_{V^k}\}$$

is the equivalence class of x with respect to V^k scale of A.

Theorem 2 indicates that a multi-scale sequence of attribute value sets determines a nested sequence of equivalence relations, based on which we can construct a view. In this view, the scale of attribute value sets increases with the levels. From the high level to the low level, the quality of granules ranges from coarse to fine, and the size of granules ranges from large to small.

A single view provides multilevel understanding and representation of the reality or a problem from a particular angle, and many views produce multiview with multilevel understanding and representation of the reality or a problem. The partition order product space is defined as follows:

Definition 3 (Xu & Yao, 2019). Given m views $v_i = (P_i, \preceq), P_i = \{\pi_i^1, \pi_i^2, \cdots, \pi_i^{n_i}\}, \pi_i^j$ is the j-th level of the i-th view, n_i is the number of levels in $v_i, 1 \leqslant i \leqslant m, 1 \leqslant j \leqslant n_i$. The partition order product space $POPS_m$ is defined as the Cartesian product of $(P_i, \preccurlyeq)$:

$$POPS_m = \left(\mathop{\times}_{i=1}^{m} P_i, \preceq_P \right) \tag{1}$$

where $\mathop{\times}_{i=1}^{m} P_i = \{(\pi_1^{j_1}, \pi_2^{j_2}, \cdots, \pi_m^{j_m}) \mid \pi_i^{j_i} \in P_i, 1 \leqslant i \leqslant m, 1 \leqslant j_i \leqslant n_i\}, \preceq_P$ is partial order relationship defined as

$$\forall (\pi_1^{j_{11}}, \pi_2^{j_{21}}, \cdots, \pi_m^{j_{m1}}), (\pi_1^{j_{12}}, \pi_2^{j_{22}}, \cdots, \pi_m^{j_{m2}}) \in \mathop{\times}_{i=1}^{m} P_i, (\pi_1^{j_{11}}, \pi_2^{j_{21}}, \cdots, \pi_m^{j_{m1}}) \preceq_P (\pi_1^{j_{12}}, \pi_2^{j_{22}}, \cdots, \pi_m^{j_{m2}}),$$

if and only if $\forall 1 \leqslant i \leqslant m, \pi_i^{j_{i1}} \leq \pi_i^{j_{i2}}$.

A partition order product space $POPS_m = \left(\overset{m}{\underset{i=1}{\times}} P_i, \preceq_P \right)$ can be simply written as $POPS_m=(\times P_i,\preccurlyeq_P)$.

Theorem 3 (Xu & Yao, 2019). The partition order product space $POPS_m=(\times P_i,\preccurlyeq_P)$ is a lattice structure.

The detailed proof is presented in (Xu & Yao, 2019). From Definition 3 and Theorem 3, we discover that $POPS_m$ is based on the Cartesian product of m views and that different views provide an understanding and description of a problem from different perspectives. Each view understands and describes a problem from multiple levels of granularity. Therefore, partition order product space provides a multiview and multilevel understanding and description of a problem.

In partition order product space, each node is defined as a problem solving level, which is a family of one-level views.

Definition 4 (Xu & Yao, 2019). Given

$$POPS_m = \left(\times P_i, \preceq_P\right), \forall \left(\pi_1^{j_1}, \pi_2^{j_2}, \cdots, \pi_m^{j_m}\right) \in \overset{m}{\underset{i=1}{\times}} P_i, \left(\pi_1^{j_1}, \pi_2^{j_2}, \cdots, \pi_m^{j_m}\right)$$

is a problem solving level, denoted as l^j.

In the following part, we give an example to illustrate the partition order product space.

Example 1. Table 2 illustrates a multi-scale information system $S=(U,A)$, which describes 12 patients from 3 views: Blood Pressure, Age and Blood Glucose are expressed as v_1, v_2 and v_3, respectively. $U=\{x_1,x_2,x_3,x_4,x_5,x_6,x_7,x_8,x_9,x_{10},x_{11},x_{12}\}$ is the object set of 12 patients. To simplify the discussion, we assume that each view has one attribute with multi-scale attribute value sets. In v_1, a^1 and a^2 correspond to a two-scale sequence of attribute value sets with respect to blood pressure. a^1 is the first-scale of blood pressure with two attribute values $\{Normal, Abnormal\}$. a^2 is the second-scale of blood pressure with three attribute values {<90, 90-120, >120}. a^1 and a^2 determine a nested sequence of equivalence relations according to Theorem 2, so we can derive the partition order $P_1 = \left\{\pi_1^1, \pi_1^2\right\}$. Next, v_1 can be denoted as $(P_1,\preccurlyeq)$ Similarly, in v_2, b^1, b^2 and b^3 correspond to a three-scale sequence of attribute value sets with respect to age. b^1 is the first-scale of age with two attribute values {≤50, >50}. b^2 is the second-scale of age with three attribute values {18-30, 31-50, 51-100}. b^3 is the third-scale of age with five attribute values {18-30, 31-40, 41-50, 51-65, 66-100}. b^1, b^2 and b^3 determine the partition order $P_2 = \left\{\pi_2^1, \pi_2^2, \pi_2^3\right\}$. Next, v_2 can be denoted as $(P_2,\preccurlyeq)$. In v_3, c^1 and c^2 correspond to a two-scale sequence of attribute value sets with respect to blood glucose. c^1 is the first-scale of blood glucose with two attribute values $\{Normal, Abnormal\}$. c^2 is the second-scale of blood glucose with three attribute values {<6, 6-7.5, >7.5}. c^1 and c^2 determine the partition order $P_3 = \left\{\pi_3^1, \pi_3^2\right\}$. Next, v_3 can be denoted as $(P_3,\preccurlyeq)$. Consequently, the partition order product space $POPS_3= (\times P_i,\preccurlyeq_P)$ can be constructed based on these three views, $1 \leqslant i \leqslant 3$.

For view v_1, the two levels are described as:

$$\pi_1^1 = \left\{\left\{x_1, x_3, x_4, x_5, x_6, x_8, x_{10}, x_{12}\right\}, \left\{x_2, x_7, x_9, x_{11}\right\}\right\},$$

$$\pi_1^2 = \{\{x_1, x_3, x_4, x_5, x_8, x_{12}\}, \{x_2, x_9\}, \{x_4, x_6, x_{10}\}, \{x_7, x_{11}\}\}.$$

For view v_2, the three levels are described as:

$$\pi_2^1 = \{\{x_1, x_3, x_4, x_7, x_8, x_{10}, x_{12}\}, \{x_2, x_5, x_6, x_9, x_{11}\}\},$$

$$\pi_2^2 = \{\{x_1, x_3, x_7, x_{10}\}, \{x_2, x_5, x_6, x_9\}, \{x_4, x_8, x_{12}\}, \{x_{11}\}\},$$

$$\pi_2^3 = \{\{x_1, x_7, x_{10}\}, \{x_2, x_5\}, \{x_3\}, \{x_4\}, \{x_6, x_9\}, \{x_8, x_{12}\}, \{x_{11}\}\}.$$

For view v_3, the two levels are described as:

$$\pi_3^1 = \{\{x_1, x_2, x_6, x_9, x_{10}, x_{11}\}, \{x_3, x_4, x_5, x_7, x_8, x_{12}\}\},$$

$$\pi_3^2 = \{\{x_1\}, \{x_2, x_6, x_9, x_{10}, x_{11}\}, \{x_3, x_4, x_8, x_{12}\}, \{x_5, x_7\}\}.$$

We can see that the levels in v_1 satisfy $\pi_1^2 \preceq \pi_1^1$, and the corresponding equivalence classes satisfy $[x]_{\pi_1^2} \subseteq [x]_{\pi_1^1}$. The levels in v_2 satisfy $\pi_2^3 \preceq \pi_2^2 \preceq \pi_2^1$, and the corresponding equivalence classes satisfy $[x]_{\pi_2^3} \subseteq [x]_{\pi_2^2} \subseteq [x]_{\pi_2^1}$. The levels in v_3 satisfy $\pi_3^2 \preceq \pi_3^1$, and the corresponding equivalence classes satisfy $[x]_{\pi_3^2} \subseteq [x]_{\pi_3^1}$. For each view, from the top level to the bottom level, the granule decreases, and the granularity gradually becomes finer.

The lattice structure of the partition order product space is shown in Fig. 1.

As shown in Fig. 1, there are 12 problem solving levels in the partition order product space, which can solve a problem not only from multiple views but also at multiple levels. According to the actual diagnosis needs, the doctor can flexibly choose different views and different levels in a view, which makes the diagnosis reasonable.

SEARCH APPROACH

Given a partition order product space $POPS_m = (\times P_i, \leqslant_P)$ determined by m views v_i, where each view has n_i levels. Based on Definition 3, $POPS_m$ has $\prod_{i=1}^{i=m} n_i$ problem solving levels. When we solve a problem, how to search in the partition order product space to find suitable problem solving levels is a crucial problem.

Table 2. Multi-scale information system

U	*BloodPressure*(v_1)		*Age*(v_2)			*BloodGlucose*(v_3)		**Heart Disease**
	a^1	a^2	b^1	b^2	b^3	c^1	c^2	
x_1	Normal	90-120	≤50	18-30	18-30	Normal	<6	No
x_2	Abnormal	90-120	>50	51-100	41-50	Normal	>7.5	Yes
x_3	Normal	90-120	≤50	18-30	31-40	Abnormal	6-7.5	No
x_4	Normal	>120	≤50	31-50	18-30	Abnormal	6-7.5	No
x_5	Normal	90-120	>50	51-100	41-50	Abnormal	<6	No
x_6	Normal	>120	>50	51-100	51-65	Normal	>7.5	Yes
x_7	Abnormal	<90	≤50	18-30	18-30	Abnormal	<6	No
x_8	Normal	90-120	≤50	31-50	66-100	Abnormal	6-7.5	Yes
x_9	Abnormal	90-120	>50	51-100	51-65	Normal	>7.5	Yes
x_{10}	Normal	>120	≤50	18-30	18-30	Normal	>7.5	No
x_{11}	Abnormal	<90	>50	18-30	31-40	Normal	>7.5	No
x_{12}	Normal	90-120	≤50	31-50	66-100	Abnormal	6-7.5	Yes

Figure 1. Lattice structure of the partition order product space.

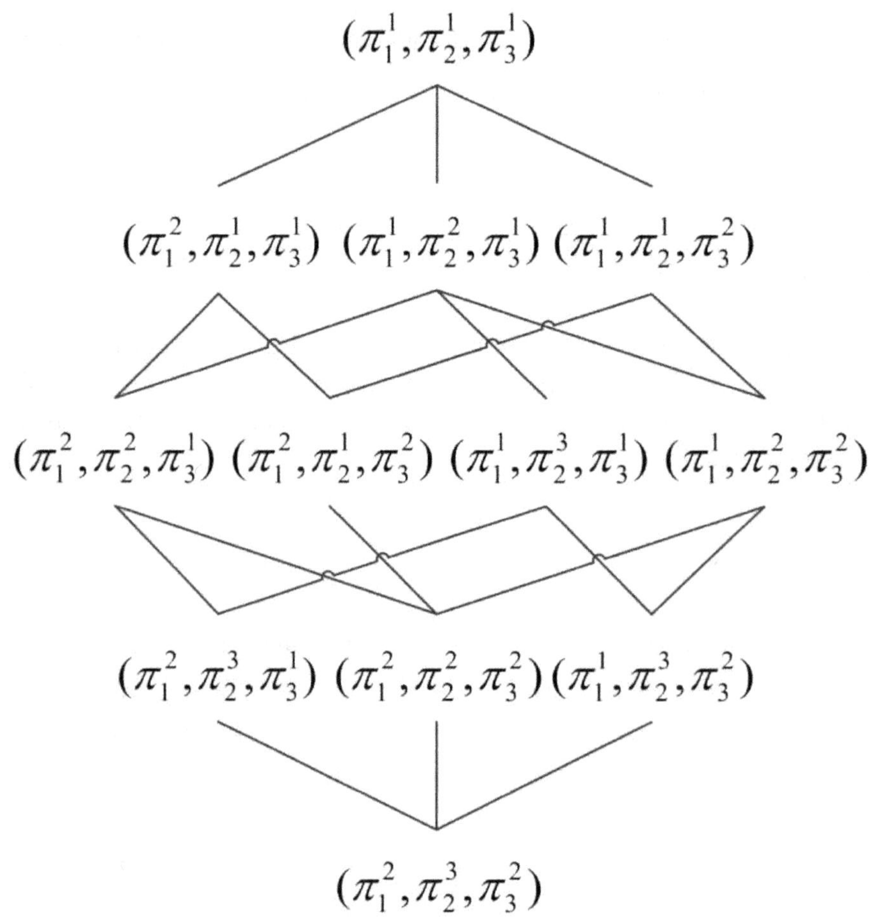

As the topology structure of the partition order product space is a lattice, usually, there are two search strategies. The first search strategy is the depth-first searching strategy, and the second search strategy is the breadth-first searching strategy. In the following part, we give two search algorithms in partition order product space, which are referred to as the depth-first searching algorithm and breadth-first searching algorithm, as shown in Algorithm 1 and Algorithm 2.

Algorithm 1: *Depth-first searching algorithm*

Input: Partition order product space $POPS_m = (\times P_i, \preccurlyeq_P)$ with k problem solving levels. **Output:** A traversal sequence L of problem solving levels.
$L = \varnothing$
Suppose *visited* k is the visited matrix of k problem solving levels, $adj[k][k]$ is the adjacency matrix of k problem solving levels.
//Initialize visited matrix
for $1 \leqslant i \leqslant k$ **do**
$visited[i]=False$
end for
//Initialize adjacency matrix
for $1 \leqslant i \leqslant k$ **do**
for $1 \leqslant j \leqslant k$ **do**
if there is an edge between problem solving level i and problem solving level j **then**
$adj[i][j]=True$
else
$adj[i][j]=False$
end if
end for
end for
//Depth-first traversal in partition order product space
for $1 \leqslant l \leqslant k$ **do**
if $visited[l]=False$ **then**
$DFS(POPS_m, l)$
end if
end for
return L
//Depth-first traversal function using recursive method
function $DFS(POPS_m, l)$:
$visited[l]=Trued$
$L=L\cup$problem solving level l
if $l=k$ **then**

Algorithm 1 continued

break // If l is the finest problem solving level then the algorithm ends
end if
for $1 \leqslant i \leqslant k$ **do**
if $adj[l][i]$=*True* and $visited[i]$=*False* **then**
$DFS(POPS_m, i)$ //Recursive traversal unvisited adjacent vertices of l
end if
end for
end function

Algorithm 2: *Breadth-first searching algorithm*

Input: Partition order product space $POPS_m = (\times P_i, \leqslant_p)$ with k problem solving levels.
Output: A traversal sequence L of problem solving levels.

$L = \varnothing$
Suppose $visited[k]$ is the visited matrix of k problem solving levels, $adj[k][k]$ is the adjacency matrix of k problem solving levels, q is a queue of all problem solving levels, *push*() is the function of putting a problem solving level into the queue, *pop*() is the function of taking a problem solving level out of the queue.
//Initialize visited matrix
for $1 \leqslant i \leqslant k$ **do**
$visited[i]$=*False*
end for
//Initialize adjacency matrix
for $1 \leqslant i \leqslant k$ **do**
for $1 \leqslant j \leqslant k$ **do**
if there is an edge between problem solving level i and problem solving level j **then**
$adj[i][j]$=*True*
else
$adj[i][j]$=*False*
end if
end for
end for
//Initialize queue q
$q = \varnothing$
//Breadth-first traversal in partition order product space
for $1 \leqslant l \leqslant k$ **do**
if $visited[l]$=*False* **then**

Algorithm 2 continued

18:	*visited*[*l*]=*True*
19:	*L*=*L*∪problem solving level *l*
20:	*q.push*(*l*)
21:	**while** $q \neq \varnothing$ **do**
22:	*l*=*q.pop*()//Get the head vertex of the queue
23:	**for** $1 \leqslant i \leqslant k$ **do**
24:	**if** *adj*[*l*][*i*]=*True* and *visited*[*i*]=*False* **then**
25:	*L*=*L*∪problem solving level *i*
26:	*visited*[*i*]=*True* //Traversal unvisited adjacent vertices of *l*
27:	*q.push*(*i*)
28:	end if
29:	end for
30:	end while
31:	end if
32:	end for
33:	**return** *L*

In Algorithm 1 and Algorithm 2, according to the depth-first searching strategy and breadth-first searching strategy, we can obtain a sequence of problem solving levels. Based on the sequence of problem solving levels, we can solve a problem from coarse granularity to fine granularity.

In Algorithm 1, steps 3-5 initialize the visited matrix of k problem solving levels as False. Steps 6-14 initialize the adjacency matrix of k problem solving levels. If problem solving level i and problem solving level j are adjacent, $adj[k][k]$ is True; otherwise, it is False. Steps 15-19 traverse problem solving levels in the partition order product space from the current problem solving level l using the depth-first searching strategy. Steps 21-32 is the depth-first traversal function using the recursive method. In this function, first, the unvisited problem solving level l is visited and added to the traversal sequence L and then recursively visits the unvisited adjacent vertices of l. Note that steps 24-26 indicate that if l is the finest problem solving level then the algorithm ends. Usually, the depth-first traversal method traverses all problem solving levels in partition order product space. However, in Algorithm 1, when the finest problem solving level is visited, there is no need to traverse other coarser problem solving levels.

The time complexity of steps 3-5 is $O(k)$. The time complexity of steps 6-14 is $O(k^2)$. For function DFS with steps 21-32, which traverses problem solving levels in partition order product space from problem solving levels l and where the time complexity is $O(k^2)$, so the time complexity of steps 15-19 is $O(k^2)$. In summary, the time complexity of Algorithm 1 is $O(k^2)$.

In Algorithm 2, steps 3-5 initialize the visited matrix of k problem solving levels as False. Steps 6-14 initialize the adjacency matrix of k problem solving levels. If problem solving level i and problem solving level j are adjacent, $adj[i][j]$ is True; otherwise, it is False. Steps 16-32 traverse problem solving levels in the partition order product space from the current problem solving level l using the breadth-first searching strategy, which is based on a queue. First, the unvisited problem solving level l is visited and added to the traversal sequence L; it is put into the queue. When the queue is not empty, the head of queue l is dequeued and visits the unvisited adjacent vertices of l; the visited adjacent vertex is put in the queue.

The time complexity of steps 3-5 is $O(k)$. The time complexity of steps 6-14 is $O(k^2)$. The time complexity of steps 16-32 is $O(k^2)$. In summary, the time complexity of Algorithm 2 is $O(k^2)$.

Note that the traversal sequence L of problem solving levels based on the depth-first searching algorithm is different from that based on the breadth-first searching algorithm. We illustrate their difference by an example.

Figure 2. A sequence of problem solving levels in the partition order product space based on the depth-first searching algorithm

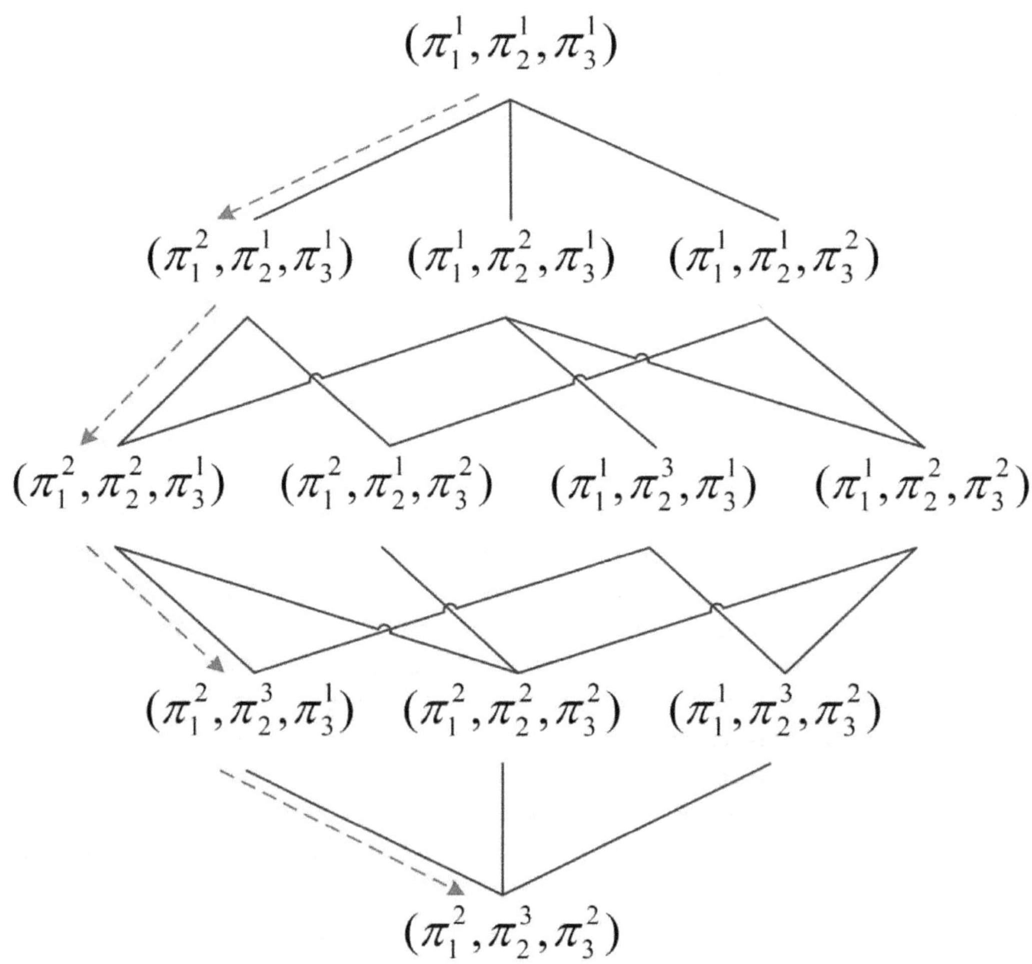

Example 2 (Continuation of Example 1) For the partition order product space in Example 1, based on depth-first searching algorithm, suppose the searching path is expressed as dotted lines with arrows. Then the traversal sequence of problem solving levels $L=\{l^1,l^2,l^3,l^4,l^5\}$, where

$$l^1=\left(\pi_1^1,\pi_2^1,\pi_3^1\right),l^2=\left(\pi_1^2,\pi_2^1,\pi_3^1\right),l^3=\left(\pi_1^2,\pi_2^2,\pi_3^1\right),l^4=\left(\pi_1^2,\pi_2^3,\pi_3^1\right),l^5=\left(\pi_1^2,\pi_2^3,\pi_3^2\right),$$

which is shown in Fig.2. $l^5 \preceq_P l^4 \preceq_P \cdots \preceq_P l^1$ holds.

Figure 3. A sequence of problem solving levels in the partition order product space based on the breadth-first searching algorithm

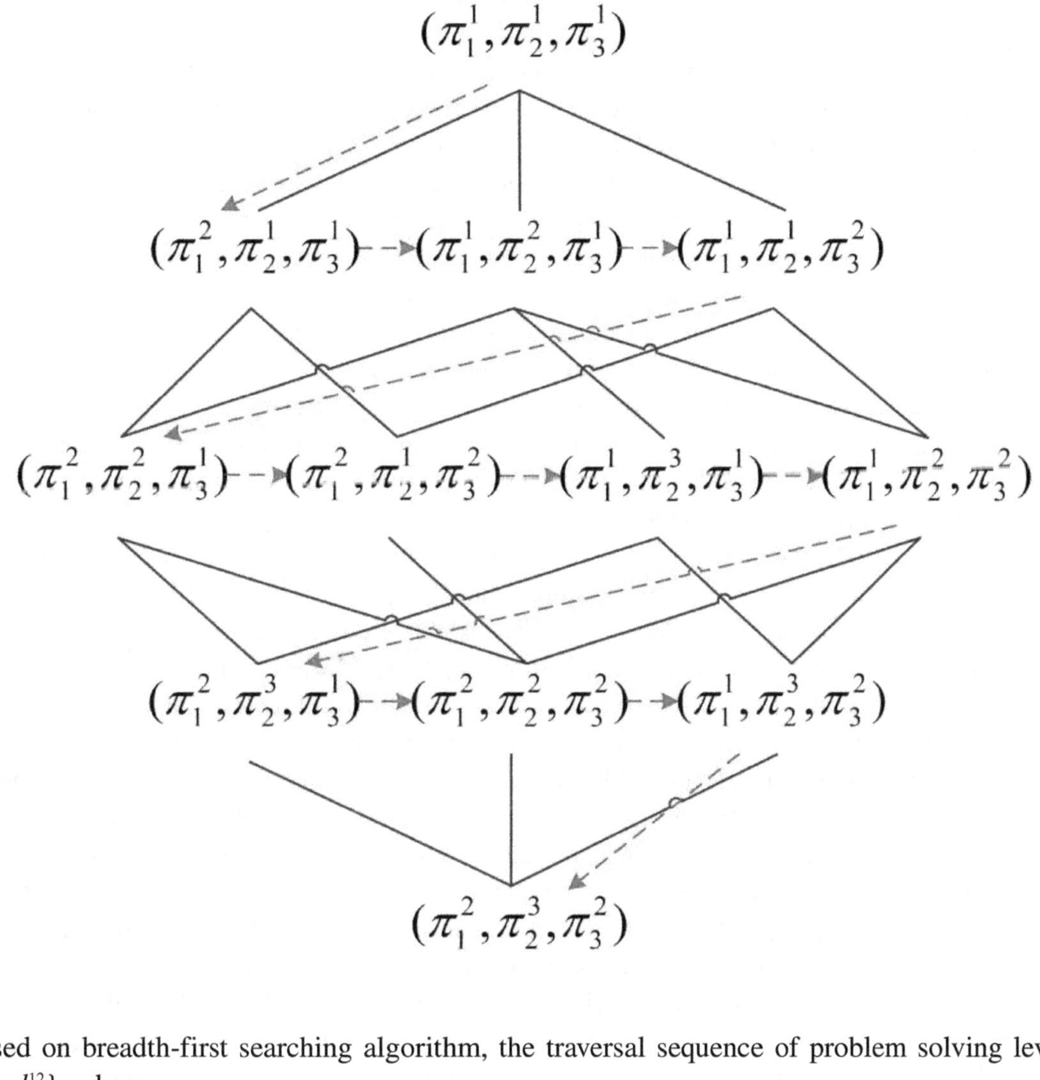

Based on breadth-first searching algorithm, the traversal sequence of problem solving levels $L=\{l^1,l^2,\ldots,l^{12}\}$, where

$$l^1=\left(\pi_1^1,\pi_2^1,\pi_3^1\right),l^2=\left(\pi_1^2,\pi_2^1,\pi_3^1\right),l^3=\left(\pi_1^2,\pi_2^2,\pi_3^1\right),\ldots,l^{12}=\left(\pi_1^2,\pi_2^3,\pi_3^2\right),$$

which is shown in Fig.3. However, as there is no partical order relation between problem solving levels with the same depth, such as

$$l^2=\left(\pi_1^2,\pi_2^1,\pi_3^1\right),\ l^3=\left(\pi_1^1,\pi_2^2,\pi_3^1\right),\ l^4=\left(\pi_1^1,\pi_2^1,\pi_3^2\right),\ l^4\preceq_P l^3\preceq_P l^2,$$

does not hold.

THREE-WAY DECISION BASED ON PARTITION ORDER PRODUCTION SPACE

Three-way decisions are generated from decision-theoretic rough sets (DTRS), which divide the universe into three pair-wise disjoint regions with two thresholds based on the minimum expected overall decision risk (Yao, 2010). From the viewpoint of granular computing, there are mainly four kinds of three-way decisions: classical three-way decisions, sequential three-way decisions, multigranulation three-way decisions and multigranulation sequential three-way decisions.

To clearly illustrate the relationships and differences among these four models, we analyze them from two aspects: the first aspect is their problem description space, and the second aspect is their problem solving space. As classical three-way decisions use one set of attributes to describe objects and there are no multiple levels, the problem description space of classical three-way decisions has only one view, which has only one level. Accordingly, based on the single view and single level problem description space, the problem solving space of classical three-way decisions has only one solution (Yao, 2011; Yao, 2010). The problem description space and problem solving space of classical three-way decisions are shown in Fig.4 (a). As sequential three-way decisions use one set of attributes to describe objects and based on the attribute set to construct multiple levels, its problem description space has one view with multiple levels. Accordingly, based on the single view and multiple levels problem description space, the problem solving space of sequential three-way decisions has multiple solutions and makes decisions from coarse-granularity to fine-granularity constituting a sequential process (Yao, 2013; Yang, Li, Liu, Chen, & Luo, 2017; Yang, Li, Fujita, Liu, & Yao, 2017). The problem description space and problem solving space of sequential three-way decisions are shown in Fig.4 (b). Multigranulation three-way decisions use multiple sets of attributes to describe objects, and there are no multiple levels in each attribute set, so its problem description space has multiple views, but each view only consists of one level. Accordingly, based on multiple views and single level problem description space, multigranulation three-way decisions make decisions by fusing the decision results of multiple views, so its problem solving space has one solution (Qian, Zhang, Sang, & Liang, 2014; Qian, Liang, & Lin, 2017; Sang, Liang, & Qian, 2015; Zhou & Yao, 2010). The problem description space and problem solving space of multigranulation three-way decisions are shown in Fig.4 (c). Multigranulation sequential three-way decisions use multiple sets of attributes to describe objects, and there are also no multiple levels in each attribute set, so its problem description space has multiple views, and each view has only one level. The problem description space of multigranulation sequential three-way decisions is the same as that of multigranulation three-way decisions. However, their problem solving spaces are different. Note that multigranulation sequential three-way decisions use a sequence of thresholds to realize the sequential process instead of constructing multiple levels based on the attribute set. Therefore, the problem solving space of multigranulation sequential three-way decisions has multiple solutions and makes decisions from coarse-granularity to fine-granularity by a sequence of thresholds; each solution is a fusion of the decision results of multiple views (Qian, Liu, & Yue, 2019; Qian, Liu, & Miao, 2020). The problem description space and problem solving space of multigranulation sequential three-way decisions are shown in Fig.4 (d).

Figure 4. Problem description space and problem solving space of different three-way decisions

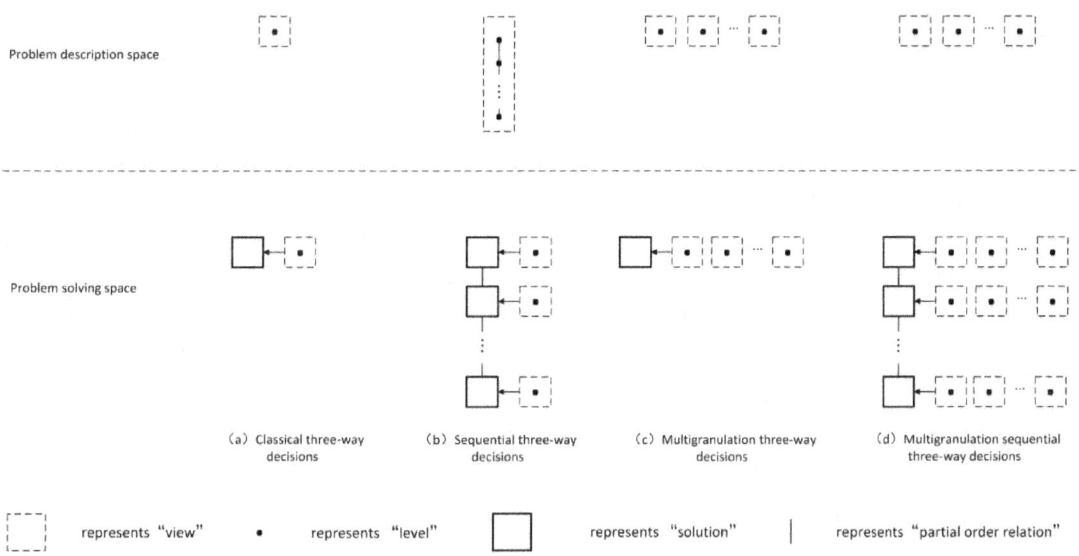

From the above analysis, classical three-way decisions, sequential three-way decisions, and multigranulation three-way decisions do not combine multiple views and multiple levels. Although multigranulation sequential three-way decisions consider multiple views and multiple levels, they only use multiple views to describe objects, but each view still has only one level, that is, the granularity in each view is fixed and unchanged from coarse-granularity to fine-granularity with the sequential process of decision making. Therefore, we discuss three-way decisions based on partition order product space.

Through depth-first or breadth-first searching algorithms, we can obtain a sequence of problem solving levels in partition order product space. Based on a sequence of problem solving levels, we can make sequential decisions. However, as each problem solving level is a family of one-level views, we need to fuse multiple views at the problem solving level. There are many fusion strategies (Wei & Liang, 2018). In the following part, we choose optimistic and pessimistic fusion strategies (Qian, Liang, Yao, & Dang, 2010; Qian, Zhang, Sang, & Liang, 2014; Qian, Liang, & Lin, 2017; Qian, Liu, & Yue, 2019) to fuse multiple views. Optimistic and pessimistic fusion strategies are proposed in multigranulation rough sets (MGRS) (Qian, Liang, Yao, & Dang, 2010), where the target concept is approximated through a family of indiscernibility relations. In the lower approximation (positive region), the word "optimistic" is used to express the idea that in multiple independent indiscernibility relations, we need only at least one of the indiscernibility relations to satisfy the inclusion condition between the equivalence class and the target concept, while the word "pessimistic" is used to express the idea that in multiple independent indiscernibility relations, we need all of the indiscernibility relations to satisfy the inclusion condition between the equivalence class and the target concept (Qian, Liang, Yao, & Dang, 2010; Qian, Zhang, Sang, & Liang, 2014; Qian, Liang, & Lin, 2017). Combining depth-first and breadth-first searching algorithms with optimistic and pessimistic fusion strategies, we propose four multiview sequential three-way decisions: depth-first optimistic multiview sequential three-way decisions, depth-first pessimistic multiview sequential three-way decisions, breadth-first optimistic multiview sequential three-way decisions, and breadth-first pessimistic multiview sequential three-way decisions.

The problem description space and problem solving space of multiview sequential three-way decisions based on partition order product space are shown in Fig.5. In Fig.5, according to Definition 3, the partition order product space consists of multiple views, and each view has multiple levels organized by linearly ordered relations. Therefore, in the problem description space of multiview sequential three-way decisions based on partition order product space, there are multiple rectangles formed by dotted lines, and each one denotes a view. In each view, there are multiple dots, and each dot denotes a level, where multiple levels are organized by linearly ordered relation. Through the Cartesian product of multiple linearly ordered relations, multiple views with multiple levels can be integrated into a lattice, which is the problem solving space of multiview sequential three-way decisions. Each element in the lattice is a problem solving level denoted as a rectangle. Each problem solving level is a family of one-level views, as shown in the circle formed by dotted lines.

Assume that $L=\{l^1,l^2,\ldots,l^t\}$ is a traversal sequence of problem solving levels based on depth-first or breadth-first searching algorithms, $l^k=\left(\pi_1^{k_1},\pi_2^{k_2},\cdots,\pi_m^{k_m}\right)$ is the k-th problem solving level, $1\leqslant k\leqslant t$, and $[x]_{\pi_i^{k_i}}$ is the equivalence class of $x\in U$ with respect to $\pi_i^{k_i}, 1\leqslant k_i\leqslant n_i$. In the following section, we introduce four multiview sequential three-way decisions.

Figure 5. Problem description space and problem solving space of multiview sequential three-way decisions based on partition order product space

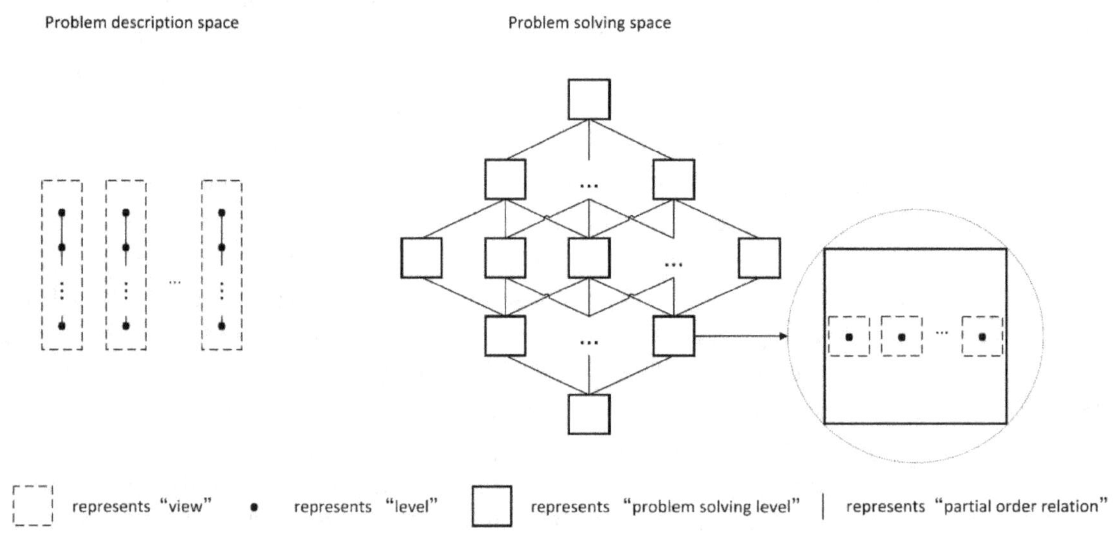

Depth-First Optimistic Multiview Sequential Three-Way Decisions

Based on the depth-first searching algorithm and optimistic fusion strategy, depth-first optimistic multiview sequential three-way decisions are defined as follows:

Definition 5. Let $L = \{l^1, l^2, \ldots, l^t\}$ be a traversal sequence of problem solving levels based on depth-first searching algorithm, $X \subseteq U$ be a target concept. Given m pairs of thresholds $\left(\alpha_i^{k_i}, \beta_i^{k_i}\right)$, the positive region, negative region and boundary region of the k-th problem solving level of depth-first optimistic multiview sequential three-way decisions are defined as:

$$POPSPOS^{D\text{-}O}\left(X^k\right) = \left\{x \in U \mid Pr\left(X \mid [x]_{\pi_1^{k_1}}\right) \geq \alpha_1^{k_1} \vee Pr\left(X \mid [x]_{\pi_2^{k_2}}\right) \geq \alpha_2^{k_2} \vee \cdots \vee Pr\left(X \mid [x]_{\pi_m^{k_m}}\right) \geq \alpha_m^{k_m}\right\} \tag{2}$$

$$POPSPOS^{D\text{-}O}\left(X^k\right) = \left\{x \in U \mid Pr\left(X \mid [x]_{\pi_1^{k_1}}\right) \leq \beta_1^{k_1} \wedge Pr\left(X \mid [x]_{\pi_2^{k_2}}\right) \leq \beta_2^{k_2} \wedge \cdots \wedge Pr\left(X \mid [x]_{\pi_m^{k_m}}\right) \leq \beta_m^{k_m}\right\} \tag{3}$$

$$POPSBND^{D\text{-}O}(X^k) = X^k - POPSPOS^{D\text{-}O}(X^k) - POPSNEG^{D\text{-}O}(X^k) \tag{4}$$

where $X^1 = X$, $X^k = POPSBND^{D\text{-}O}(X^{k-1})$.

From the first problem solving level to the t-th problem solving level of L, the positive region, negative region and boundary region of depth-first optimistic multiview sequential three way decisions are defined as:

$$POPSPOS^{D\text{-}O}\left(X\right) = \bigcup_{1 \leqslant k \leqslant t} POPSPOS^{D\text{-}O}\left(X^k\right) \tag{5}$$

$$POPSNEG^{D\text{-}O}\left(X\right) = \bigcup_{1 \leqslant k \leqslant t} POPSNEG^{D\text{-}O}\left(X^k\right) \tag{6}$$

$$POPSBND^{D\text{-}O}(X) = X - POPSPOS^{D\text{-}O}(X) - POPSNEG^{D\text{-}O}(X) \tag{7}$$

Depth-first optimistic multiview sequential three-way decisions are the combination of the depth-first searching algorithm and optimistic fusion strategy. The depth-first searching algorithm obtains a sequence of problem solving levels to construct a sequential decision process. The optimistic fusion strategy fuses multiple one-level views at the problem solving level to make three-way decisions. At the problem solving level, according to the optimistic fusion strategy, in the positive region, we use the operation "disjunction" to fuse multiple views, which makes three-way decisions from multiview. Based on a sequence of problem solving levels, from the high problem solving level to the low problem solving level, we make three-way decisions from multilevel. Consequently, depth-first optimistic multiview sequential three-way decisions can make decisions not only from multiple different views but also at multiple abstract levels. We can flexibly change views and levels to make decisions more reasonable. The detailed process is described in Algorithm 3.

Algorithm 3: *The algorithm of depth-first optimistic multiview sequential three-way decisions*

Input: (1) A partition order product space $POPS_m=(\times P_i,\preccurlyeq_p)$ defined by an information system $SI=(U,AT=C\cup D,V,f)$ with m views v_i and each v_i has n_i levels, $1\leqslant i\leqslant m$. (2) A traversal sequence of problem solving levels based on depth-first searching algorithm $L=\{l^1,l^2,\ldots,l^t\}$. (3) $n_1\times n_2\times\ldots\times n_m$ pairs of thresholds $\left(\alpha_i^{k_i},\beta_i^{k_i}\right),1\leqslant i\leqslant m,1\leqslant k_i\leqslant n_i$. (4) A target concept $X\subseteq U$. **Output:** Positive region $POPSPOS^{D\_O}(X)$, negative region $POPSNEG^{D\_O}(X)$, boundary region $POPSBND^{D\_O}(X)$.
Initialize $X^1=X$, $POPSPOS^{D\_O}(X)=\varnothing, POPSNEG^{D\_O}(X)=\varnothing, POPSBND^{D\_O}(X)=\varnothing$.
for k=1 to t **do**
if $X^k=\varnothing$ **then**
break;
else
Calculate positive region $POPSPOS^{D\_O}(X^k)$, negative region $POPSNEG^{D\_O}(X^k)$ and boundary region $POPSBND^{D\_O}(X^k)$ of the k-th problem solving level l^k;
//Calculate three regions of sequential process
$POPSPOS^{D\_O}(X)=POPSPOS^{D\_O}(X)\cup POPSPOS^{D\_O}(X^k)$;
$POPSNEG^{D\_O}(X)=POPSNEG^{D\_O}(X)\cup POPSNEG^{D\_O}(X^k)$;
$POPSBND^{D\_O}(X)=X-POPSPOS^{D\_O}(X)-POPSNEG^{D\_O}(X)$;
$X^{k+1}=POPSBND^{D\_O}(X)$;
end if
end for
return $POPSPOS^{D\_O}(X)$, $POPSNEG^{D\_O}(X)$, $POPSBND^{D\_O}(X)$

In the following part, we use an example to illustrate the calculation process of depth-first optimistic multiview sequential three-way decisions.

Example 3 (Continuation of Example 2) Given a traversal sequence of problem solving levels $L=\{l^1,l^2,l^5,l^9,l^{12}\}$ based on depth-first searching algorithm, where

$$l^1=\left(\pi_1^1,\pi_2^1,\pi_3^1\right),l^2=\left(\pi_1^2,\pi_2^1,\pi_3^1\right),l^5=\left(\pi_1^2,\pi_2^2,\pi_3^1\right),l^9=\left(\pi_1^2,\pi_2^3,\pi_3^1\right),l^{12}=\left(\pi_1^2,\pi_2^3,\pi_3^2\right).$$

Let $X=\{x_1,x_2,x_3,x_6,x_7,x_9,x_{11},x_{12}\}$ be a target concept. Suppose the thresholds of π_i^j are α_i^j and β_i^j.

Let $X^1=X$, we calculate its positive region, negative region and boundary region based on problem solving level $l^1=\left(\pi_1^1,\pi_2^1,\pi_3^1\right)$. Suppose three thresholds of problem solving level l^1 are

$$\alpha_1^1=0.7\ and\ \beta_1^1=0.3,\ \ \alpha_2^1=0.7\ and\ \beta_2^1=0.3,\ \ \alpha_3^1=0.7\ and\ \beta_3^1=0.3.$$

From Example 1, we have:

$$\text{À}_1^1 = \{\{x_1, x_3, x_4, x_5, x_6, x_8, x_{10}, x_{12}\}, \{x_2, x_7, x_9, x_{11}\}\},$$

$$\pi_2^1 = \{\{x_1, x_3, x_4, x_7, x_8, x_{10}, x_{12}\}, \{x_2, x_5, x_6, x_9, x_{11}\}\},$$

$$\pi_3^1 = \{\{x_1, x_2, x_6, x_9, x_{10}, x_{11}\}, \{x_3, x_4, x_5, x_7, x_8, x_{12}\}\}.$$

$\forall x \in U$, the conditional probability $\Pr\left(X^1 \mid [x]_{\pi_1^1}\right), \Pr\left(X^1 \mid [x]_{\pi_2^1}\right)$, *and* $\Pr\left(X^1 \mid [x]_{\pi_3^1}\right)$ can be calculated. Taking x_1 as an example.

$$\Pr\left(X^1 \mid [x_1]_{\pi_1^1}\right) = \frac{\left|\{x_1, x_2, x_3, x_6, x_7, x_9, x_{11}, x_{12}\} \cap \{x_1, x_3, x_4, x_5, x_6, x_8, x_{10}, x_{12}\}\right|}{\left|\{x_1, x_3, x_4, x_5, x_6, x_8, x_{10}, x_{12}\}\right|} = 0.5.$$

$$\Pr\left(X^1 \mid [x_1]_{\pi_2^1}\right) = \frac{\left|\{x_1, x_2, x_3, x_6, x_7, x_9, x_{11}, x_{12}\} \cap \{x_1, x_3, x_4, x_7, x_8, x_{10}, x_{12}\}\right|}{\left|\{x_1, x_3, x_4, x_7, x_8, x_{10}, x_{12}\}\right|} = 0.57.$$

$$\Pr\left(X^1 \mid [x_1]_{\pi_3^1}\right) = \frac{\left|\{x_1, x_2, x_3, x_6, x_7, x_9, x_{11}, x_{12}\} \cap \{x_1, x_2, x_6, x_9, x_{10}, x_{11}\}\right|}{\left|\{x_1, x_2, x_6, x_9, x_{10}, x_{11}\}\right|} = 0.83.$$

So

$$\beta_1^1 = 0.3 \le \Pr\left(X^1 \mid [x_1]_{\pi_1^1}\right) = 0.5 \le \alpha_1^1 = 0.7,$$

$$\beta_2^1 = 0.3 \le \Pr\left(X^1 \mid [x_1]_{\pi_2^1}\right) = 0.57 \le \alpha_2^1 = 0.7,$$

$$\Pr\left(X^1 \mid [x_1]_{\pi_3^1}\right) = 0.83 \ge \pm_3^1 = 0.7,$$

that is, there is at least one level À_3^1 of view v_3 satisfying $\Pr\left(X^1 \mid [x_1]_{\pi_3^1}\right) \ge \alpha_3^1$.Then based on formula (2) of Definition 5, x_1 is assigned to positive region $POPSPOS^{D\text{-}O}(X^1)$. For the other objects, we can conduct the similar calculation. Then based on Definition 5, we have:

$POPSPOS^{D\text{-}O}(X^1) = \{x_1, x_2, x_5, x_6, x_7, x_9, x_{10}, x_{11}\}$,

$POPSNEG^{D\text{-}O}\left(X^1\right) = \varnothing$,

$POPSBND^{D\text{-}O}(X^1) = \{x_3, x_4, x_8, x_{12}\}$.

Let $X^2 = POPSBND^{D\text{-}O}(X^1) = \{x_3, x_4, x_8, x_{12}\}$, three thresholds of problem solving level l^2 be

$$\alpha_1^2 = 0.6 \text{ and } \beta_1^2 = 0.4,\ \ \alpha_2^1 = 0.7 \text{ and } \beta_2^1 = 0.3,\ \ \alpha_3^1 = 0.7 \text{ and } \beta_3^1 = 0.3.$$

Then based on Definition 5, we have:

$POPSPOS^{D\text{-}O}(X^2) = \{x_3, x_8, x_{12}\}$,

$POPSNEG^{D\text{-}O}\left(X^2\right) = \varnothing$,

$POPSBND^{D\text{-}O}(X^2) = \{x_4\}$.

Let $X^3 = POPSBND^{D\text{-}O}(X^3) = \{x_4\}$, three thresholds of problem solving level l^5 be

$$\alpha_1^2 = 0.6 \text{ and } \beta_1^2 = 0.4,\ \ \alpha_2^2 = 0.6 \text{ and } \beta_2^2 = 0.4,\ \ \alpha_3^1 = 0.7 \text{ and } \beta_3^1 = 0.3.$$

Then based on Definition 5, we have:

$POPSPOS^{D\text{-}O}\left(X^3\right) = \varnothing$,

$POPSNEG^{D\text{-}O}(X^3) = \{x_4\}$,

$POPSBND^{D\text{-}O}\left(X^3\right) = \varnothing$.

As $POPSBND^{D\text{-}O}\left(X^3\right) = \varnothing$, from the first problem solving level to the third problem solving level of L, the positive region, negative region and boundary region of depth-first optimistic multiview sequential three-way decisions are calculated as:

$$\begin{aligned} POPSPOS^{D\text{-}O}(X) &= \bigcup_{1 \leqslant k \leqslant 3} POPSPOS^{D\text{-}O}\left(X^k\right) \\ &= \{x_1, x_2, x_3, x_5, x_6, x_7, x_8, x_9, x_{10}, x_{11}, x_{12}\}, \end{aligned}$$

$$POPSNEG^{D\text{-}O}(X) = \bigcup_{1 \leqslant k \leqslant 3} POPSNEG^{D\text{-}O}\left(X^k\right) = \{x_4\},$$

$$POPSBND^{D\text{-}O}(X) = U - POPSPOS^{D\text{-}O}(X) - POPSNEG^{D\text{-}O}(X) = \varnothing.$$

Depth-First Pessimistic Multiview Sequential Three-Way Decisions

Based on the depth-first searching algorithm and pessimistic fusion strategy, depth-first pessimistic multiview sequential three-way decisions are defined as follows:

Definition 6. Let $L=\{l^1,l^2,\ldots,l^t\}$ be a traversal sequence of problem solving levels based on depth-first searching algorithm, $X\subseteq U$ be a target concept. Given m pairs of thresholds $\left(\alpha_i^{k_i},\beta_i^{k_i}\right)$, the positive region, negative region and boundary region of the k-th problem solving level of depth-first pessimistic multiview sequential three-way decisions are defined as:

$$POPSPOS^{D\_P}\left(X^k\right) = \left\{x\in U \mid Pr\left(X\mid[x]_{\pi_1^{k_1}}\right)\geq\alpha_1^{k_1}\wedge Pr\left(X\mid[x]_{\pi_2^{k_2}}\right)\geq\alpha_2^{k_2}\wedge\cdots\wedge Pr\left(X\mid[x]_{\pi_m^{k_m}}\right)\geq\alpha_m^{k_m}\right\} \tag{8}$$

$$POPSNEG^{D\_P}\left(X^k\right) = \left\{x\in U \mid Pr\left(X\mid[x]_{\pi_1^{k_1}}\right)\leq\beta_1^{k_1}\vee Pr\left(X\mid[x]_{\pi_2^{k_2}}\right)\leq\beta_2^{k_2}\vee\cdots\vee Pr\left(X\mid[x]_{\pi_m^{k_m}}\right)\leq\beta_m^{k_m}\right\} \tag{9}$$

$$POPSBND^{D\_P}(X^k) = X^k - POPSPOS^{D\_P}(X^k) - POPSNEG^{D\_P}(X^k). \tag{10}$$

where $X^1=X$, $X_k=POPSBND^{D\_P}(X^{k-1})$.

From the first problem solving level to the t-th problem solving level of L, the positive region, negative region and boundary region of depth-first pessimistic multiview sequential three-way decisions are defined as:

$$POPSPOS^{D\_P}\left(X\right)=\bigcup_{1\leqslant k\leqslant t} POPSPOS^{D\_P}\left(X^k\right) \tag{11}$$

$$POPSNEG^{D\_P}\left(X\right)=\bigcup_{1\leqslant k\leqslant t} POPSNEG^{D\_P}\left(X^k\right) \tag{12}$$

$$POPSBND^{D\_P}(X) = X - POPSPOS^{D\_P}(X) - POPSNEG^{D\_P}(X). \tag{13}$$

Depth-first pessimistic multiview sequential three-way decisions are the combination of the depth-first searching algorithm and pessimistic fusion strategy. The depth-first searching algorithm obtains a sequence of problem solving levels to construct a sequential decision process. The pessimistic fusion strategy fuses multiple one-level views at the problem solving level to make three-way decisions. At a problem solving level, according to the pessimistic fusion strategy, in the positive region, we use the operation "conjunction" to fuse multiple views, which makes three-way decisions from multiview. Based on a sequence of problem solving levels, from the high problem solving level to the low problem solving level, we make three-way decisions from multilevel. Consequently, depth-first pessimistic multiview sequential three-way decisions can make decisions not only from multiple different views but also at multiple abstract levels. Compared with depth-first optimistic multiview sequential three-way decisions, the main difference is the fusion strategy for fusing multiple views. The detailed process is described in Algorithm 4.

Algorithm 4*: The algorithm of depth-first pessimistic multiview sequential three-way decisions*

Input:
(1) A partition order product space $POPS_m=(\times P_i,\preccurlyeq_P)$ defined by an information system $IS=(U, AT=C\cup D, V, f)$ with m views v_i and each v_i has n_i levels, $1\leqslant i\leqslant m$.
(2) A traversal sequence of problem solving levels based on depth-first searching algorithm $L=\{l^1,l^2,\ldots,l^t\}$.
(3) $n_1\times n_2\times\ldots\times n_m$ pairs of thresholds $\left(\alpha_i^{k_i},\beta_i^{k_i}\right), 1\leqslant i\leqslant m, 1\leqslant k_i\leqslant n_i$.
(4) A target concept $X\subseteq U$.
Output: Positive region $POPSPOS^{D\_P}(X)$, negative region $POPSNEG^{D\_P}(X)$, boundary region $POPSBND^{D\_P}(X)$.

Initialize $X^1=X$, $POPSPOS^{D\_P}(X)=\varnothing, POPSNEG^{D\_P}(X)=\varnothing, POPSBND^{D\_P}(X)=\varnothing$.
for $k=1$ to t **do**
  if $X^k=\varnothing$ **then**
  break;
  else
Calculate positive region $POPSPOS^{D\_P}(X^k)$, negative region $POPSNEG^{D\_P}(X^k)$ and boundary region $POPSBND^{D\_P}(X^k)$ of the k-th problem solving level l^k;
//Calculate three regions of sequential process
  $POPSPOS^{D\_P}(X) = POPSPOS^{D\_P}(X) \cup POPSPOS^{D\_P}(X^k)$;
  $= POPSNEG^{D\_P}(X) \cup POPSNEG^{D\_P}(X^k)$;
  $POPSBND^{D\_P}(X) = X - POPSPOS^{D\_P}(X) - POPSNEG^{D\_P}(X)$;
  $X^{k+1} = POPSBND^{D\_P}(X)$;
  end if
end for
return $POPSPOS^{D\_P}(X)$, $POPSNEG^{D\_P}(X)$, $POPSBND^{D\_P}(X)$

In the following part, we use an example to illustrate the calculation process of depth-first optimistic multiview sequential three-way decisions.

Example 4 (Continuation of Example 2) Given a traversal sequence of problem solving levels $L=\{l^1,l^2,l^5,l^9,l^{12}\}$ based on depth-first searching algorithm, where

$$l^1=\left(\pi_1^1,\pi_2^1,\pi_3^1\right), l^2=\left(\pi_1^2,\pi_2^1,\pi_3^1\right), l^5=\left(\pi_1^2,\pi_2^2,\pi_3^1\right), l^9=\left(\pi_1^2,\pi_2^3,\pi_3^1\right), l^{12}=\left(\pi_1^2,\pi_2^3,\pi_3^2\right).$$

Let $X=\{x_1,x_2,x_3,x_6,x_7,x_9,x_{11},x_{12}\}$ be a target concept. Suppose the thresholds of π_i^j are α_i^j *and* β_i^j.

Let $X^1=X$, we calculate its positive region, negative region and boundary region based on problem solving level $l^1=\left(\pi_1^1,\pi_2^1,\pi_3^1\right)$. Suppose three thresholds of problem solving level l^1 are

$\alpha_1^1 = 0.7 \text{ and } \beta_1^1 = 0.3,\ \ \alpha_2^1 = 0.7 \text{ and } \beta_2^1 = 0.3,\ \ \alpha_3^1 = 0.7 \text{ and } \beta_3^1 = 0.3.$

From Example 1, we have:

$$\pi_1^1 = \{\{x_1, x_3, x_4, x_5, x_6, x_8, x_{10}, x_{12}\}, \{x_2, x_7, x_9, x_{11}\}\},$$

$$\pi_2^1 = \{\{x_1, x_3, x_4, x_7, x_8, x_{10}, x_{12}\}, \{x_2, x_5, x_6, x_9, x_{11}\}\},$$

$$\pi_3^1 = \{\{x_1, x_2, x_6, x_9, x_{10}, x_{11}\}, \{x_3, x_4, x_5, x_7, x_8, x_{12}\}\}.$$

$\forall x \in U$, the conditional probability $Pr\left(X^1 \mid [x]_{\pi_1^1}\right), Pr\left(X^1 \mid [x]_{\pi_2^1}\right), \text{ and } Pr\left(X^1 \mid [x]_{\pi_3^1}\right)$ can be calculated. Taking x_2 as an example.

$$Pr\left(X^1 \mid [x_2]_{\pi_1^1}\right) = \frac{\left|\{x_1, x_2, x_3, x_6, x_7, x_9, x_{11}, x_{12}\} \cap \{x_2, x_7, x_9, x_{11}\}\right|}{\left|\{x_2, x_7, x_9, x_{11}\}\right|} = 1.0.$$

$$Pr\left(X^1 \mid [x_2]_{\pi_2^1}\right) = \frac{\left|\{x_1, x_2, x_3, x_6, x_7, x_9, x_{11}, x_{12}\} \cap \{x_2, x_5, x_6, x_9, x_{11}\}\right|}{\left|\{x_2, x_5, x_6, x_9, x_{11}\}\right|} = 0.8.$$

$$Pr\left(X^1 \mid [x_2]_{\pi_3^1}\right) = \frac{\left|\{x_1, x_2, x_3, x_6, x_7, x_9, x_{11}, x_{12}\} \cap \{x_1, x_2, x_6, x_9, x_{10}, x_{11}\}\right|}{\left|\{x_1, x_2, x_6, x_9, x_{10}, x_{11}\}\right|} = 0.83.$$

So

$$Pr\left(X^1 \mid [x_2]_{\pi_1^1}\right) = 1.0 \geq \alpha_1^1 = 0.7,$$

$$Pr\left(X^1 \mid [x_2]_{\pi_2^1}\right) = 0.8 \geq \alpha_2^1 = 0.7,$$

$$Pr\left(X^1 \mid [x_2]_{\pi_3^1}\right) = 0.83 \geq \alpha_3^1 = 0.7,$$

that is, all levels: π_1^1 of view v_1, π_2^1 of view v_2 and π_3^1 of view v_3 satisfy

$$Pr\left(X^1 \mid [x_2]_{\pi_1^1}\right) \geq \alpha_1^1, Pr\left(X^1 \mid [x_2]_{\pi_2^1}\right) \geq \alpha_2^1, \text{ and } Pr\left(X^1 \mid [x_2]_{\pi_3^1}\right) \geq \alpha_3^1.$$

Then based on formula (8) of Definition 6, x_2 is assigned to positive region $POPSPOS^{D\_P}(X^1)$. For the other objects, we can conduct the similar calculation. Then based on Definition 6, we have:

$POPSPOS^{D\_P}(X^1) = \{x_2, x_9, x_{11}\}$,

$POPSNEG^{D\_P}\left(X^1\right) = \varnothing$,

$POPSBND^{D\_P}(X^1) = \{x_1, x_3, x_4, x_5, x_6, x_7, x_8, x_{10}, x_{12}\}$.

Let $X^2 = POPSBND^{D\_P}(X^1) = \{x_1, x_3, x_4, x_5, x_6, x_7, x_8, x_{10}, x_{12}\}$, three thresholds of problem solving level l^2 be

$\alpha_1^2 = 0.6$ *and* $\beta_1^2 = 0.4$, $\alpha_2^1 = 0.7$ *and* $\beta_2^1 = 0.3$, $\alpha_3^1 = 0.7$ *and* $\beta_3^1 = 0.3$.

Then based on Definition 6, we have:

$POPSPOS^{D\_P}\left(X^2\right) = \varnothing$,

$POPSNEG^{D\_P}(X^2) = \{x_4, x_6, x_{10}\}$,

$POPSBND^{D\_P}(X^2) = \{x_1, x_3, x_5, x_7, x_8, x_{12}\}$.

Let $X^3 = POPSBND^{D\_P}(X^2) = \{x_1, x_3, x_5, x_7, x_8, x_{12}\}$, three thresholds of problem solving level l^5 be

$\alpha_1^2 = 0.6$ *and* $\beta_1^2 = 0.4$, $\alpha_2^2 = 0.6$ *and* $\beta_2^2 = 0.4$, $\alpha_3^1 = 0.7$ *and* $\beta_3^1 = 0.3$.

Then based on Definition 6, we have:

$POPSPOS^{D\_P}(X^3) = \{x_1\}$,

$POPSNEG^{D\_P}(X^3) = \{x_5\}$,

$POPSBND^{D\_P}(X^3) = \{x_3, x_7, x_8, x_{12}\}$.

Let $X^4 = POPSBND^{D\_P}(X^3) = \{x_3, x_7, x_8, x_{12}\}$, three thresholds of problem solving level l^9 be

$\alpha_1^2 = 0.6$ *and* $\beta_1^2 = 0.4$, $\alpha_2^3 = 0.5$ *and* $\beta_2^3 = 0.45$, $\alpha_3^1 = 0.7$ *and* $\beta_3^1 = 0.3$.

Then based on Definition 6, we have:

$POPSPOS^{D\_P}(X^4) = \{x_3, x_7, x_8, x_{12}\}$,

$$POPSNEG^{D\_P}\left(X^{4}\right)=\varnothing,$$

$$POPSBND^{D\_P}\left(X^{4}\right)=\varnothing.$$

As $POPSBND^{D\_P}\left(X^{4}\right)=\varnothing$, from the first problem solving level to the 4-th problem solving level of *L*, the positive region, negative region and boundary region of depth-first pessimistic multiview sequential three-way decisions are calculated as:

$$POPSPOS^{D\_P}\left(X\right)=\bigcup_{1\leqslant k\leqslant 4} POPSPOS^{D\_P}\left(X^{k}\right)=\left\{x_1,x_2,x_3,x_7,x_8,x_9,x_{11},x_{12}\right\},$$

$$POPSNEG^{D\_P}\left(X\right)=\bigcup_{1\leqslant k\leqslant 4} POPSNEG^{D\_P}\left(X^{k}\right)=\left\{x_4,x_5,x_6,x_{10}\right\},$$

$$POPSBND^{D\_P}\left(X\right)=U-POPSPOS^{D\_P}\left(X\right)-POPSNEG^{D\_P}\left(X\right)=\varnothing.$$

For depth-first optimistic multiview sequential three-way decisions, the positive region is defined by "disjunction" (Equation 2 of Definition 5), and the negative region is defined by "conjunction" (Equation 3 of Definition 5). For depth-first pessimistic multiview sequential three-way decisions, the positive region is defined by "conjunction" (Equation 8 of Definition 6), and the negative region is defined by "disjunction" (Equation 9 of Definition 6). From Example 3 and Example 4, it is evident that compared with depth-first optimistic multiview sequential three-way decisions, depth-first pessimistic multiview sequential three-way decisions have fewer objects in the positive region and a larger number of objects in the negative region.

Breadth-First Optimistic Multiview Sequential Three-Way Decisions

Based on the breadth-first searching algorithm and optimistic fusion strategy, breadth-first optimistic multiview sequential three-way decisions are defined as follows:

Definition 7. Let $L=\{l^1,l^2,\ldots,l^t\}$ be a traversal sequence of problem solving levels based on breadth-first searching algorithm, $X\subseteq U$ be a target concept. Given m pairs of thresholds $\left(\alpha_i^{k_i},\beta_i^{k_i}\right)$, the positive region, negative region and boundary region of the k-th problem solving level of breadth-first optimistic multiview sequential three-way decisions are defined as:

$$\begin{aligned}&POPSPOS^{B\_O}\left(X^{k}\right)\\&=\left\{x\in U \mid Pr\left(X\mid[x]_{\pi_1^{k_1}}\right)\geq\alpha_1^{k_1}\vee Pr\left(X\mid[x]_{\pi_2^{k_2}}\right)\geq\alpha_2^{k_2}\vee\cdots\vee Pr\left(X\mid[x]_{\pi_m^{k_m}}\right)\geq\alpha_m^{k_m}\right\},\end{aligned}\qquad(14)$$

$$POPSNEG^{B\_O}\left(X^k\right)$$
$$=\left\{x\in U\mid Pr\left(X\mid[x]_{\pi_1^{k_1}}\right)\le\beta_1^{k_1}\wedge Pr\left(X\mid[x]_{\pi_2^{k_2}}\right)\le\beta_2^{k_2}\wedge\cdots\wedge Pr\left(X\mid[x]_{\pi_m^{k_m}}\right)\le\beta_m^{k_m}\right\}, \quad (15)$$

$$POPSBND^{B\_O}(X^k)=X^k-POPSPOS^{B\_O}(X^k)-POPSNEG^{B\_O}(X^k). \quad (16)$$

where $X^1=X$, $X^k= POPSBND^{B\_O}(X^{k-1})$.

From the first problem solving level to the t-th problem solving level of L, the positive region, negative region and boundary region of breadth-first optimistic multiview sequential three-way decisions are defined as:

$$POPSPOS^{B\_O}\left(X\right)=\bigcup_{1\leqslant k\leqslant t}POPSPOS^{B\_O}\left(X^k\right) \quad (17)$$

$$POPSNEG^{B\_O}\left(X\right)=\bigcup_{1\leqslant k\leqslant t}POPSNEG^{B\_O}\left(X^k\right) \quad (18)$$

$$POPSBND^{B\_O}(X)=X-POPSPOS^{B\_O}(X)-POPSNEG^{B\_O}(X) \quad (19)$$

Breadth-first optimistic multiview sequential three-way decisions are the combination of the breadth-first searching algorithm and optimistic fusion strategy. The breadth-first searching algorithm obtains a sequence of problem solving levels to construct a sequential decision process. The optimistic fusion strategy fuses multiple one-level views at the problem solving level to make three-way decisions. At the problem solving level, according to the optimistic fusion strategy, in the positive region, we use the operation "disjunction" to fuse multiple views, which makes three-way decisions from multiview. Based on a sequence of problem solving levels, from the high problem solving level to the low problem solving level, we make three-way decisions from multilevel. Consequently, breadth-first optimistic multiview sequential three-way decisions can make decisions not only from multiple different views but also at multiple abstract levels. The detailed process is described in Algorithm 5.

In the following part, we use an example to illustrate the calculation process of depth-first optimistic multiview sequential three-way decisions.

Example 5 (Continuation of Example 2) Given a traversal sequence of problem solving levels $L=\{l^1,l^2,l^3,\ldots,l^{12}\}$ based on depth-first searching algorithm, where

$$l^1=\left(\pi_1^1,\pi_2^1,\pi_3^1\right),l^2=\left(\pi_1^2,\pi_2^1,\pi_3^1\right),l^3=\left(\pi_1^1,\pi_2^2,\pi_3^1\right),\ldots,l^{12}=\left(\pi_1^2,\pi_2^3,\pi_3^2\right).$$

Let $X=\{x_1,x_2,x_3,x_6,x_7,x_9,x_{11},x_{12}\}$ be a target concept. Suppose the thresholds of π_i^j are α_i^j and β_i^j. Let $X^1=X$, three thresholds of problem solving level l^1 be

$$\alpha_1^1=0.7\ and\ \beta_1^1=0.3,\ \ \alpha_2^1=0.7\ and\ \beta_2^1=0.3,\ \ \alpha_3^1=0.7\ and\ \beta_3^1=0.3.$$

Algorithm 5: *The algorithm of depth-first optimistic multiview sequential three-way decisions*

Input:
(1) A partition order product space $POPS_m = (\times P_i, \preccurlyeq_p)$ defined by an information system $IS = (U, AT = C \cup D, V, f)$ with m views v_i and each v_i has n_i levels, $1 \leqslant i \leqslant m$.
(2) A traversal sequence of problem solving levels based on depth-first searching algorithm $L = \{l^1, l^2, \ldots, l^t\}$.
(3) $n_1 \times n_2 \times \ldots \times n_m$ pairs of thresholds $(\alpha_i^{k_i}, \beta_i^{k_i}), 1 \leqslant i \leqslant m, 1 \leqslant k_i \leqslant n_i$.
(4) A target concept $X \subseteq U$.
Output: Positive region $POPSPOS^{B\_O}(X)$, negative region $POPSNEG^{B\_O}(X)$, boundary region $POPSBND^{B\_O}(X)$.

Initialize $X^1 = X$, $POPSPOS^{B\_O}(X) = \varnothing, POPSNEG^{B\_O}(X) = \varnothing, POPSBND^{B\_O}(X) = \varnothing$.
for $k=1$ to t **do**
  if $X^k = \varnothing$ **then**
  break;
  else
Calculate positive region $POPSPOS^{B\_O}(X^k)$, negative region $POPSNEG^{B\_O}(X^k)$ and boundary region $POPSBND^{B\_O}(X^k)$ of the k-th problem solving level l^k;
//Calculate three regions of sequential process
  $POPSPOS^{B\_O}(X) = POPSPOS^{B\_O}(X) \cup POPSPOS^{B\_O}(X^k)$;
  $POPSNEG^{B\_O}(X) = POPSNEG^{B\_O}(X) \cup POPSNEG^{B\_O}(X^k)$;
  $POPSBND^{B\_O}(X) = X - POPSPOS^{B\_O}(X) - POPSNEG^{B\_O}(X)$;
  $X^{k+1} = POPSBND^{B\_O}(X)$;
  end if
end for
return $POPSPOS^{B\_O}(X)$, $POPSNEG^{B\_O}(X)$, $POPSBND^{B\_O}(X)$

Then based on Definition 7, we have:

$POPSPOS^{B\_O}(X^1) = \{x_1, x_2, x_5, x_6, x_7, x_9, x_{10}, x_{11}\}$,

$POPSNEG^{B\_O}(X^1) = \varnothing$,

$POPSBND^{B\_O}(X^1) = \{x_3, x_4, x_8, x_{12}\}$.

Let $X^2 = \{x_3, x_4, x_8, x_{12}\}$, three thresholds of problem solving level l^2 be

$$\alpha_1^2 = 0.6 \text{ and } \beta_1^2 = 0.4, \quad \alpha_2^1 = 0.7 \text{ and } \beta_2^1 = 0.3, \quad \alpha_3^1 = 0.7 \text{ and } \beta_3^1 = 0.3.$$

Then based on Definition 7, we have:

$POPSPOS^{B\_O}(X^2) = \{x_3, x_8, x_{12}\}$.

$POPSNEG^{B\_O}(X^2)=\varnothing$,

$POPSBND^{B\_O}(X^2) = \{x_4\}$.

Let $X^3=\{x_4\}$, three thresholds of problem solving level l^3 be

$\alpha_1^1=0.7$ *and* $\beta_1^1=0.3$, $\alpha_2^2=0.6$ *and* $\beta_2^2=0.4$, $\alpha_3^1=0.7$ *and* $\beta_3^1=0.3$.

Then based on Definition 7, we have:

$POPSPOS^{B\_O}(X^3)=\varnothing$,

$POPSNEG^{B\_O}(X^3) = \{x_4\}$,

$POPSBND^{B\_O}(X^3)=\varnothing$.

As $POPSBND^{B\_O}(X^3)=\varnothing$, from the first problem solving level to the third problem solving level of L, the positive region, negative region and boundary region of breadth-first optimistic multiview sequential three-way decisions are calculated as:

$$POPSPOS^{B\_O}(X)=\bigcup_{1\leqslant k\leqslant 3} POPSPOS^{B\_O}(X^k)=\{x_1,x_2,x_3,x_5,x_6,x_7,x_8,x_9,x_{10},x_{11},x_{12}\},$$

$$POPSNEG^{B\_O}(X)=\bigcup_{1\leqslant k\leqslant 3} POPSNEG^{B\_O}(X^k)=\{x_4\},$$

$$POPSBND^{B\_O}(X)=U-POPSPOS^{B\_O}(X)-POPSNEG^{B\_O}(X)=\varnothing.$$

Breadth-First Pessimistic Multiview Sequential Three-Way Decisions

Based on the breadth-first searching algorithm and pessimistic fusion strategy, breadth-first pessimistic multiview sequential three-way decisions are defined as follows:

Definition 8. Let $L=\{l^1,l^2,\ldots,l^t\}$ be a traversal sequence of problem solving levels based on breadth-first searching algorithm, $X\subseteq U$ be a target concept. Given m pairs of thresholds $(\alpha_i^{k_i},\beta_i^{k_i})$, the positive region, negative region and boundary region of the k-th problem solving level of breadth-first optimistic multiview sequential three-way decisions are defined as:

$$POPSPOS^{B\_P}\left(X^k\right) = \left\{x \in U \mid Pr\left(X \mid [x]_{\pi_1^{k_1}}\right) \geq \alpha_1^{k_1} \wedge Pr\left(X \mid [x]_{\pi_2^{k_2}}\right) \geq \alpha_2^{k_2} \wedge \cdots \wedge Pr\left(X \mid [x]_{\pi_m^{k_m}}\right) \geq \alpha_m^{k_m}\right\}, \quad (20)$$

$$POPSNEG^{B\_P}\left(X^k\right) = \left\{x \in U \mid Pr\left(X \mid [x]_{\pi_1^{k_1}}\right) \leq \beta_1^{k_1} \vee Pr\left(X \mid [x]_{\pi_2^{k_2}}\right) \leq \beta_2^{k_2} \vee \cdots \vee Pr\left(X \mid [x]_{\pi_m^{k_m}}\right) \leq \beta_m^{k_m}\right\}, \quad (21)$$

$$POPSBND^{B\_P}(X^k) = X^k - POPSPOS^{B\_P}(X^k) - POPSNEG^{B\_P}(X^k). \quad (22)$$

where $X^1=X$, $X^k=POPSBND^{B\_P}(X^{k-1})$.

From the first problem solving level to the t-th problem solving level of L, the positive region, negative region and boundary region of breadth-first pessimistic multiview sequential three-way decisions are defined as:

$$POPSPOS^{B\_P}\left(X\right) = \bigcup_{1 \leqslant k \leqslant t} POPSPOS^{B\_P}\left(X^k\right) \quad (23)$$

$$POPSNEG^{B\_P}\left(X\right) = \bigcup_{1 \leqslant k \leqslant t} POPSNEG^{B\_P}\left(X^k\right) \quad (24)$$

$$POPSBND^{B\_P}(X) = X - POPSPOS^{B\_P}(X) - POPSNEG^{B\_P}(X) \quad (25)$$

Breadth-first pessimistic multiview sequential three-way decisions are the combination of the breadth-first searching algorithm and pessimistic fusion strategy. The breadth-first searching algorithm obtains a sequence of problem solving levels to construct a sequential decision process. The pessimistic fusion strategy fuses multiple one-level views at the problem solving level to make three-way decisions. At the problem solving level, according to the pessimistic fusion strategy, in the positive region, we use the operation "conjunction" to fuse multiple views, which makes three-way decisions from multiview. Based on a sequence of problem solving levels, from the high problem solving level to the low problem solving level, we make three-way decisions from multilevel. Consequently, breadth-first pessimistic multiview sequential three-way decisions can make decisions not only from multiple different views but also at multiple abstract levels. The detailed process is described in Algorithm 6.

In the following part, we use an example to illustrate the calculation process of depth-first optimistic multiview sequential three-way decisions.

Example 6 (Continuation of Example 2) Given a traversal sequence of problem solving levels $L=\{l^1,l^2,l^3,\ldots,l^{12}\}$ based on depth-first searching algorithm, where

$$l^1 = \left(\pi_1^1, \pi_2^1, \pi_3^1\right), l^2 = \left(\pi_1^2, \pi_2^1, \pi_3^1\right), l^3 = \left(\pi_1^1, \pi_2^2, \pi_3^1\right), \ldots, l^{12} = \left(\pi_1^2, \pi_2^3, \pi_3^2\right).$$

Let $X=\{x_1,x_2,x_3,x_6,x_7,x_9,x_{11},x_{12}\}$ be a target concept. Suppose the thresholds of π_i^j are α_i^j and β_i^j.

Algorithm 6*: The algorithm of depth-first optimistic multiview sequential three-way decisions*

Input:
(1) A partition order product space $POPS_m = (\times P_i, \preccurlyeq_p)$ defined by an information system $IS = (U, AT = C \cup D, V, f)$ with m views v_i and each v_i has n_i levels, $1 \leqslant i \leqslant m$.
(2) A traversal sequence of problem solving levels based on depth-first searching algorithm $L = \{l^1, l^2, \ldots, l^t\}$.
(3) $n_1 \times n_2 \times \ldots \times n_m$ pairs of thresholds $\left(\alpha_i^{k_i}, \beta_i^{k_i}\right), 1 \leqslant i \leqslant m, 1 \leqslant k_i \leqslant n_i$.
(4) A target concept $X \subseteq U$.
Output: Positive region $POPSPOS^{B\_P}(X)$, negative region $POPSNEG^{B\_P}(X)$, boundary region $POPSBND^{B\_P}(X)$.

Initialize $X^1 = X$, $POPSPOS^{B\_P}(X) = \varnothing, POPSNEG^{B\_P}(X) = \varnothing, POPSBND^{B\_P}(X) = \varnothing$.
for k=1 to t **do**
  if $X^k = \varnothing$ **then**
  break;
  else
Calculate positive region $POPSPOS^{B\_P}(X^k)$, negative region $POPSNEG^{B\_P}(X^k)$ and boundary region $POPSBND^{B\_P}(X^k)$ of the k-th problem solving level l^k;
//Calculate three regions of sequential process
  $POPSPOS^{B\_P}(X) = POPSPOS^{B\_P}(X) \cup POPSPOS^{B\_P}(X^k)$;
  $POPSNEG^{B\_P}(X) = POPSNEG^{B\_P}(X) \cup POPSNEG^{B\_P}(X^k)$;
  $POPSBND^{B\_P}(X) = X - POPSPOS^{B\_P}(X) - POPSNEG^{B\_P}(X)$;
  $X^{k+1} = POPSBND^{B\_P}(X)$;
  end if
end for
return $POPSPOS^{B\_P}(X)$, $POPSNEG^{B\_P}(X)$, $POPSBND^{B\_P}(X)$

Let $X^1 = X$, three thresholds of problem solving level l^1 be

$$\alpha_1^1 = 0.7 \text{ and } \beta_1^1 = 0.3,\ \ \alpha_2^1 = 0.7 \text{ and } \beta_2^1 = 0.3,\ \ \alpha_3^1 = 0.7 \text{ and } \beta_3^1 = 0.3.$$

Then based on Definition 8, we have:

$$POPSPOS^{B\_P}(X^1) = \{x_2, x_9, x_{11}\},$$

$$POPSNEG^{B\_P}(X^1) = \varnothing,$$

$$POPSBND^{B\_P}(X^1) = \{x_1, x_3, x_4, x_5, x_6, x_7, x_8, x_{10}, x_{12}\}.$$

Let $X^2 = \{x_1, x_3, x_4, x_5, x_6, x_7, x_8, x_{10}, x_{12}\}$, three thresholds of problem solving level l^2 be

$$\alpha_1^2 = 0.6 \text{ and } \beta_1^2 = 0.4,\ \ \alpha_2^1 = 0.7 \text{ and } \beta_2^1 = 0.3,\ \ \alpha_3^1 = 0.7 \text{ and } \beta_3^1 = 0.3.$$

Then based on Definition 8, we have:

$$POPSPOS^{B\_P}\left(X^2\right)=\varnothing,$$

$POPSNEG^{B\_P}(X^2) = \{x_4,x_6,x_{10}\}$,

$POPSBND^{B\_P}(X^2) = \{x_1,x_3,x_5,x_7,x_8,x_{12}\}$.

Let $X^3 = \{x_1,x_3,x_5,x_7,x_8,x_{12}\}$, three thresholds of problem solving level l^3 be

$$\alpha_1^1 = 0.7 \text{ and } \beta_1^1 = 0.3,\quad \alpha_2^2 = 0.6 \text{ and } \beta_2^2 = 0.4,\quad \alpha_3^1 = 0.7 \text{ and } \beta_3^1 = 0.3.$$

Then based on Definition 8, we have:

$$POPSPOS^{B\_P}\left(X^3\right)=\varnothing,$$

$POPSNEG^{B\_P}(X^3) = \{x_5\}$,

$POPSBND^{B\_P}(X^3) = \{x_1,x_3,x_7,x_8,x_{12}\}$.

Let $X^4 = \{x_1,x_3,x_7,x_8,x_{12}\}$, three thresholds of problem solving level l^4 be

$$\alpha_1^1 = 0.7 \text{ and } \beta_1^1 = 0.3,\quad \alpha_2^1 = 0.7 \text{ and } \beta_2^1 = 0.3,\quad \alpha_3^2 = 0.6 \text{ and } \beta_3^2 = 0.4.$$

Then based on Definition 8, we have:

$POPSPOS^{B\_P}(X^4) = \{x_1,x_3,x_7,x_8,x_{12}\}$,

$$POPSNEG^{B\_P}\left(X^4\right)=\varnothing,$$

$$POPSBND^{B\_P}\left(X^4\right)=\varnothing.$$

As $POPSBND^{B\_P}\left(X^4\right)=\varnothing$, from the first problem solving level to the 4-th problem solving level of L, the positive region, negative region and boundary region of breadth-first pessimistic multiview sequential three-way decisions are calculated as:

$$POPSPOS^{B\_P}\left(X\right)=\bigcup_{1\leqslant k\leqslant 4} POPSPOS^{B\_P}\left(X^k\right)=\left\{x_1,x_2,x_3,x_7,x_8,x_9,x_{11},x_{12}\right\},$$

$$POPSNEG^{B\_P}(X) = \bigcup_{1 \leqslant k \leqslant 4} POPSNEG^{B\_P}(X^k) = \{x_4, x_5, x_6, x_{10}\},$$

$$POPSBND^{B\_P}(X) = U - POPSPOS^{B\_P}(X) - POPSNEG^{B\_P}(X) = \varnothing.$$

For breadth-first optimistic multiview sequential three-way decisions, the positive region is defined by "disjunction" (Equation 14 of Definition 7), and the negative region is defined by "conjunction" (Equation 15 of Definition 7). For breadth-first pessimistic multiview sequential three-way decisions, the positive region is defined by "conjunction" (Equation 20 of Definition 8), and the negative region is defined by "disjunction" (Equation 21 of Definition 8). As shown in Example 5 and Example 6, compared with breadth-first optimistic multiview sequential three-way decisions, breadth-first pessimistic multiview sequential three-way decisions have fewer objects in the positive region and a larger number of objects in the negative region.

We summarize the advantages and limitations of the proposed multiview sequential three-way decisions. First, as partition order product space simultaneously provides the understanding and description of a problem from multiple views and multiple levels, the proposed four multiview sequential three-way decisions based on partition order product space can solve a problem not only from multiview but also from multilevel. The integration of multiview and multilevel renders the understanding and description of the problem more comprehensive and then solves the problem more effectively and reasonably. Second, note that for the proposed multiview sequential three-way decisions based on partition order product space, when the number of views is one and the number of levels in a view is one, the proposed models degenerate to classical three-way decisions. When the number of views is one, the proposed models degenerate to sequential three-way decisions. When the number of levels in each view is one, the proposed models degenerate to multigranulation three-way decisions. When the number of levels in each view is one and we use different thresholds on different granularity levels of the sequential process, the proposed models degenerate to multigranulation sequential three-way decisions. Therefore, existing three-way decisions can be considered special cases of the proposed multiview sequential three-way decisions. Last, the proposed multiview sequential three-way decisions also have limitations. With an increasing number of views and levels in each view, the complexity of the problem solving space of multiview sequential three-way decisions, which are based on partition order product space, will increase dramatically, resulting in a combinatorial explosion. Therefore, in future work, we will investigate the reduction method of the problem solving space to reduce the complexity of problem solving.

CONCLUSION

Granular computing exploits problem solving and information processing governed by a multiview principle and a multilevel principle. In order to understand and describe problem in a more comprehensive way, and then solve the problem more effectively and reasonably, we propose partition order product space. Partition order product space is a new granular computing model that follows the principles of multiview and multilevel. To obtain a solution for problem solving in partition order product space, we propose two search algorithms, which are referred to as the depth-first searching algorithm and breadth-first searching algorithm. We discuss three-way decisions based on the partition order product space.

By combining depth-first and breadth-first searching algorithms with optimistic and pessimistic fusion strategies, we propose four multiview sequential three-way decisions, which can make decisions not only from multiple different views but also at multiple abstract levels. Existing three-way decisions may be considered special cases of the proposed models. Multiview sequential three-way decisions can make decision from multiview and multilevel to obtain more reasonable decision results, which can be used in intelligent medical, recommender system, management decision. In the future, we can investigate more effective methods to determine the evaluation functions and thresholds under multiview sequential three-way decisions based on partition order product space.

ACKNOWLEDGMENT

This work was supported by the National Natural Science Foundation of China (No.62076002, 61402005, 61972001), the Natural Science Foundation of Anhui Province, China (No.2008085MF194, 1308085QF114, 1908085MF188), the Higher Education Natural Science Foundation of Anhui Province, China (No. KJ2013A015).

REFERENCES

Bargiela, A., & Pedrycz, W. (2008). Toward a theory of granular computing for human-centered information processing, *IEEE.T.Fuzzy. Syst.*, *16*, 320–330.

Behzadidoost, R., Mahan, F., & Izadkhah, H. (2024). Granular computing-based deep learning for text classification. *Information Sciences*, *652*, 119746. doi:10.1016/j.ins.2023.119746

Catanzariti, F., Chiaselotti, G., Infusino, F., & Marino, G. (2020). Object similarity measures and Pawlak's indiscernibility on decision tables. *Information Sciences*, *539*, 104–135. doi:10.1016/j.ins.2020.05.030

Chen, H., Li, J. H., Min, F., Liu, W. Q., & Tsang, E. C. C. (2017). Optimal scale selection in dynamic multi-scale decision tables based on sequential three-way decisions. *Inf. Sci*, *415–416*, 213–232.

Dai, D., Zhou, X. Z., Li, H. X., & Liu, L. F. (2019), Co-training based sequential three-way decisions for cost-sensitive classification, *Proceedings of the 16th International Conference on Networking, Sensing and Control*, 157–162. 10.1109/ICNSC.2019.8743205

Fang, Y., Gao, C., & Yao, Y. Y. (2020). Granularity-driven sequential three-way decisions: A cost-sensitive approach to classification. *Information Sciences*, *507*, 644–664. doi:10.1016/j.ins.2019.06.003

Hobbs, J. (1985), Granularity, *In Proceedings of the Ninth International Joint Conference on Artificial Intelligence (IJCAI)*, 432-435.

Li, H. X., Zhang, L. B., Huang, B., & Zhou, X. Z. (2016). Sequential three-way decision and granulation for cost-sensitive face recognition. *Knowledge-Based Systems*, *91*, 241–251. doi:10.1016/j.knosys.2015.07.040

Li, H. X., Zhang, L. B., Zhou, X. Z., & Huang, B. (2017). Cost-sensitive sequential three-way decision modeling using a deep neural network. *International Journal of Approximate Reasoning*, *85*, 68–78. doi:10.1016/j.ijar.2017.03.008

Liang, D. C., Liu, D., & Kobina, A. (2016). Three-way group decisions with decision-theoretic rough sets. *Information Sciences*, *345*, 46–64. doi:10.1016/j.ins.2016.01.065

Lin, T. Y., Polkowski, L., & Skowron, A. (1998). Granular computing on binary relations II: Rough set representations and belief functions, *Rough Sets in Knowledge Discovery. Berlin. PhysicaVerlag*, *1*, 121–140.

Liu, D., Li, T. R., & Liang, D. C. (2014). Incorporating logistic regression to decision-theoretic rough sets for classifications. *International Journal of Approximate Reasoning*, *55*(1), 197–210. doi:10.1016/j.ijar.2013.02.013

Liu, F., Zhang, B., Ciucci, D., Wu, W., & Min, F. (2018). A comparison study of similarity measures for covering-based neighborhood classifiers. *Information Sciences*, *448–449*, 1–17. doi:10.1016/j.ins.2018.03.030

Luo, J. F., Hu, M. J., & Qin, K. Y. (2020). Three-way decision with incomplete information based on similarity and satisfiability. *International Journal of Approximate Reasoning*, *120*, 151–183. doi:10.1016/j.ijar.2020.02.005

Min, F., Zhang, Z. H., Zhai, W. J., & Shen, R. P. (2020). Frequent pattern discovery with tri-partition alphabets. *Information Sciences*, *507*, 715–732. doi:10.1016/j.ins.2018.04.013

Pedrycz, W., Skowron, A., & Kreinovich, V. (2008). *Handbook of granular computing*. John Wiley & Sons. doi:10.1002/9780470724163

Qian, J., Liu, C., Miao, D., & Yue, X. (2020). Sequential three-way decisions via multi-granularity. *Information Sciences*, *507*, 606–629. doi:10.1016/j.ins.2019.03.052

Qian, J., Liu, C., & Yue, X. (2019). Multigranulation sequential three-way decisions based on multiple thresholds. *International Journal of Approximate Reasoning*, *105*, 396–416. doi:10.1016/j.ijar.2018.12.007

Qian, Y. H., Liang, J. Y., Lin, G. P., Guo, Q., & Liang, J. (2017). Local multigranulation decision-theoretic rough sets. *International Journal of Approximate Reasoning*, *82*(C), 119–137. doi:10.1016/j.ijar.2016.12.008

Qian, Y. H., Liang, J. Y., Yao, Y. Y., & Dang, C. Y. (2010). MGRS: A multi-granulation rough set. *Information Sciences*, *180*(6), 949–970. doi:10.1016/j.ins.2009.11.023

Qian, Y. H., Zhang, H., Sang, Y. L., & Liang, J. Y. (2014). Multigranulation decision-theoretic rough sets. *International Journal of Approximate Reasoning*, *55*(1, 1pt.2), 225–237. doi:10.1016/j.ijar.2013.03.004

Sang, Y.L., Liang, J.Y., & Qian, Y.H. (2015), Decision-theoretic rough sets under dynamic granulation, *Knowl. Based Syst.* 84–92.

Savchenko, A. V. (2016). Fast multi-class recognition of piecewise regular objects based on sequential three-way decisions and granular computing. *Knowledge-Based Systems*, *91*, 252–262. doi:10.1016/j.knosys.2015.09.021

Savchenko, A. V. (2019). Sequential three-way decisions in multi-category image recognition with deep features based on distance factor. *Information Sciences*, *489*, 18–36. doi:10.1016/j.ins.2019.03.030

Wang, P. X., Shi, H., Yang, X. B., & Mi, J. S. (2019). Three-way k-means: Integrating k-means and three-way decision. *International Journal of Machine Learning and Cybernetics*, *10*(10), 2767–2777. doi:10.1007/s13042-018-0901-y

Wang, P. X., & Yao, Y. Y. (2018). CE3: A three-way clustering method based on mathematical morphology. *Knowledge-Based Systems*, *155*, 54–65. doi:10.1016/j.knosys.2018.04.029

Wei, L., Liu, L., Qi, J. J., & Qian, T. (2020). Rules acquisition of formal decision contexts based on three-way concept lattices. *Information Sciences*, *516*, 529–544. doi:10.1016/j.ins.2019.12.024

Wei, W., & Liang, J. Y. (2018). Information Fusion in Rough Set Theory: An Overview. *Information Fusion*, *48*, 107–118. doi:10.1016/j.inffus.2018.08.007

Xie, J., Xia, S. Y., Wang, G. Y., & Gao, X. B. (2023). GBMST: An Efficient Minimum Spanning Tree Clustering Based on Granular-Ball Computing. *Clinical Orthopaedics and Related Research*, *2303*, 01082.

Xu, J. F., Miao, D. Q., Zhang, Y. J., & Zhang, Z. F. (2017). A three-way decisions model with probabilistic rough sets for stream computing. *International Journal of Approximate Reasoning*, *88*, 1–22. doi:10.1016/j.ijar.2017.05.001

Xu, Y., & Yao, Y. Y. (2019). Partition order product space: Partition based granular computing model. *J. Computer Res. Dev.*, *56*(4), 836–843.

Yang, X., Li, T. R., Liu, D., Chen, H. M., & Luo, C. (2017). A unified framework of dynamic three-way probabilistic rough sets. *Information Sciences*, *420*, 126–147. doi:10.1016/j.ins.2017.08.053

Yang, X., Li, T. R., Fujita, H., Liu, D., & Yao, Y. Y. (2017). A unified model of sequential three-way decisions and multilevel incremental processing. *Knowledge-Based Systems*, *134*, 172–188. doi:10.1016/j.knosys.2017.07.031

Yao, Y. Y. (2009), Integrative levels of granularity, A. Bargiela, W. Pedrycz (Eds.), Human-centric information processing through granular modelling, 182, 31–47.

Yao, Y. Y. (2010). Three-way decisions with probabilistic rough sets. *Information Sciences*, *180*(3), 341–353. doi:10.1016/j.ins.2009.09.021

Yao, Y. Y. (2011). The superiority of three-way decisions in probabilistic rough set models. *Information Sciences*, *181*(6), 1080–1096. doi:10.1016/j.ins.2010.11.019

Yao, Y. Y. (2013), Granular computing and sequential three-way decisions, Proceedings of International Conference on Rough Sets and Knowledge Technology (RSKT 2013), LNCS, 8171, 16–27. 10.1007/978-3-642-41299-8_3

Yao, Y. Y. (2016). A triarchic theory of granular computing. *Granul. Comput.*, *1*(2), 145–157. doi:10.1007/s41066-015-0011-0

Yao, Y. Y. (2019). Three-way conflict analysis: Reformulations and extensions of the Pawlak model. *Knowledge-Based Systems*, *180*, 26–37. doi:10.1016/j.knosys.2019.05.016

Yue, X. D., Chen, Y. F., Miao, D. Q., & Fujita, H. (2020). Fuzzy neighborhood covering for three-way classification. *Information Sciences*, *507*, 795–808. doi:10.1016/j.ins.2018.07.065

Zadeh, L. A., Gupta, M. M., Ragade, R. K., & Yager, R. R. (1979). *Fuzzy sets and information granularity*. Advance in Fuzzy Sst Theory and Applications NorthHolland.

Zhang, C., Li, D. Y., & Liang, J. Y. (2020). Interval-valued hesitant fuzzy multi-granularity three-way decisions in consensus processes with applications to multi- attribute group decision making. *Information Sciences*, *511*, 192–211. doi:10.1016/j.ins.2019.09.037

Zhang, H. R., & Min, F. (2016). Three-way recommender systems based on random forests. *Knowledge-Based Systems*, *91*, 275–286. doi:10.1016/j.knosys.2015.06.019

Zhang, Q. H., Pang, G. H., & Wang, G. Y. (2019). A novel sequential three-way decisions model based on penalty function. *Knowledge-Based Systems*, *192*, 105350. doi:10.1016/j.knosys.2019.105350

Zhang, Q. H., Xia, D. Y., & Wang, G. Y. (2017). Three-way decision model with two types of classification errors. *Information Sciences*, *420*, 431–453. doi:10.1016/j.ins.2017.08.066

Zhang, Y. B., Zhang, Z. F., Miao, D. Q., & Wang, J. Q. (2019). Three-way enhanced convolutional neural networks for sentence-level sentiment classification. *Information Sciences*, *477*, 55–64. doi:10.1016/j.ins.2018.10.030

Zhi, H. L., Qi, J. J., Qian, T., & Wei, L. (2019). Three-way dual concept analysis. *International Journal of Approximate Reasoning*, *114*, 151–165. doi:10.1016/j.ijar.2019.08.010

Chapter 6
Strategy Selection and Outcome Evaluation of Change-Based Three-Way Decisions Based on Reinforcement Learning

Chunmao Jiang
Fujian University of Technology, China

ABSTRACT

In this chapter, we enhance the trisecting-acting-outcome (TAO) model of three-way decision-making (3WD) with a novel approach for strategy selection and outcome prediction using Q-learning in reinforcement learning. We reinterpret the changes in tripartition and actions in the TAO model as states and actions in reinforcement learning, respectively. The reward is quantified using cumulative prospect theory, and the Q-learning algorithm iteratively determines action sets that achieve target rewards efficiently. This method offers a cost-effective and psychologically attuned action set for predicting the utility in change-based 3WD, demonstrated through a practical example.

INTRODUCTION

The three-way decision (3WD) model is consistent with human cognition and offers a nuanced semantic framework for understanding decision-making processes. This approach categorizes decisions into three distinct categories: acceptance, non-commitment, and rejection, each derived from the positive, boundary, and negative regions of rough set approximations, respectively (Yao, 2009). In 2012, Yao refined this concept, proposing a model that divides a universal set into three segments to facilitate more precise classifications (Yao, 2012).

Over time, the scope of 3WD has expanded beyond its original probabilistic rough set basis, evolving into a broader conceptual framework, to form a complex research network (Yang & Li, 2019). This more expansive interpretation of 3WD emphasizes a triadic approach to thought and problem solving, a method prevalent across various disciplines and supported by cognitive theory. This approach simplifies complex

DOI: 10.4018/979-8-3693-1582-8.ch006

problems by dividing them into three interconnected but distinct components, reducing cognitive and information overload (Yao, 2019). In its evolution and development, a large number of research results were produced (Fang & Min, 2019; Liu & Liang, 2016; Li & Huang, 2017; Min & Zhu, 2012; Qian & Liu, 2020; Wang & Yao, 2018; Zhang & Li, 2020, Zhang & Pang, 2020; Yu & Wang, 2020; Yang & Li, 2019; Li & Huang, 2017; Zhan & Wang, 2023; Wang & Li, 2022; Wang & Ma, 2022).

A notable example of this expansive interpretation is the trisecting-acting-outcome (TAO) model, where 'trisecting' refers to dividing the universal set into three parts, and 'acting' is the process of selecting and providing the optimal action that fulfills the result and maintains them at a moderate level. On the one hand, based on the required outcome, the decision maker designed appropriate strategies for the tripartition to achieve the expected results. On the other hand, strategies are selected to maintain the outcome at a moderate level. The outcome refers to the effectiveness of the results of trisecting and acting.

Jiang and Yao (2018) introduced a quantitative evaluation method based on a general 3WD model, movement-based 3WD, and Jiang and Guo (2020) developed a probabilistic model for strategy selection based on information entropy. They also introduced the proportional utility function (PUF) for assessing outcomes from dual perspectives in movement-based 3WD (Jiang & Guo, 2021; Jiang & Guo, 2022). In addition, the change-based TAO model (Jiang & Duan, 2022) was proposed to measure effectiveness by integrating interval sets and distinctive utility functions. This framework uses interval sets to represent the impact of strategies or actions, using a utility measurement method to assess changes in three intervals and amalgamating these utilities for a comprehensive effectiveness evaluation.

However, some key issues still need to be adequately addressed when dealing with change-based three-way decisions. The goal of a change-based three-way decision is to change the object from the original tripartition to a more effective one. The three-way decision based on changes explains and answers one type of question: Why do we need to 'Trisecting and Acting'? That is, the three-way decision is intended to produce more satisfactory changes. In this chapter, we develop a method for selecting optimal strategies and calculating future utility based on change-based three-way decisions.

This chapter applies reinforcement learning to predict future utilities and generate a set of strategies to reach the target reward in the shortest cycle during future utility computation using the Q-learning algorithm. During the prediction process, altered tripartition can be treated as states in reinforcement learning. Multiple strategies for applying to the altered tripartition are available and these strategies are referred to as actions in reinforcement learning. Each time the strategy has changed the tripartition, it has produced a utility referred to as a reward for reinforcement learning.

The Motives and Contribution of This Chapter

The primary motivation behind this research is to address critical issues in change-based three-way decisions (C-3WD) and to improve the understanding of the Trisecting-Acting-Outcome (TAO) model in decision-making. While previous studies have mainly focused on the 'trisecting' and 'Acting' phases, little attention has been given to the 'outcome.' Additionally, there is a need to find strategies that can achieve desired utility efficiently in a finite cycle, reducing trial-and-error costs.

To address these challenges, this research proposes a method that leverages reinforcement learning to predict future utilities and generate optimal strategies for change-based three-way decisions. Key contributions of this work include the following:

1. **Focus on change-based three-way decisions:** The research shifts its focus to change-based three-way decisions (C-3WD), which aim to transform the original tripartition into a more effective one. This addresses why 'Trisecting and Acting' must produce more satisfactory changes.
2. **Reinforcement Learning Approach**: The proposed method, specifically the Q-learning algorithm, utilizes reinforcement learning to predict future utilities and select strategies. Changed tripartitions are treated as states and strategies for tripartition changes are regarded as actions. The aim is to achieve the target reward efficiently in the shortest cycle.
3. **Outcome Prediction-Based Strategy Selection**: This research contributes to the field of three-way decision-making by addressing issues in change-based three-way decisions and providing a novel approach to strategy selection and outcome evaluation using reinforcement learning. The goal is to find the best match between trading and acting in terms of effectiveness, efficiency, and interpretability.

According to the above analysis, we arranged the structure of this chapter below. Section 2 reviews the fundamental concepts of change-based three-way decisions and reinforcement learning. Section 3 describes specifically the method of strategy selection and outcome evaluation for change-based three-way decisions using reinforcement learning. Section 4 provides an illustrative example to demonstrate the effectiveness of our method, and Section 5 concludes the chapter with suggestions for future research directions.

BASIC KNOWLEDGE

TAO Model

Figure 1 illustrates the comprehensive processes of the Trisecting-Acting-Outcome (TAO) model in three-way decision making (Yao, 2020). This model comprises three interconnected components: trisecting, acting, and outcome, each with distinct but related functions. The TAO model not only delineates the individual roles of these components but also elucidates their interdependencies. While each part operates independently, they collectively form a cohesive whole and are either distinctly separate or weakly joined.

Trisecting is a crucial step in the three-way decision process, significantly influencing the overall outcome. Its effectiveness lies in its ability to produce varied results based on the method of trisection used, underscoring its role as a fundamental mechanism in achieving a successful trisection, a core concept in three-way decision making.

Acting is another vital aspect of the TAO framework. It involves applying specific strategies to the three-segmented parts to meet predefined objectives. The effectiveness of the three-way decision is highly dependent on the acting step, as different strategies yield different outcomes, affecting the decision-making process's overall efficacy.

Both trisecting and acting are instrumental in determining the success of three-way decisions: the application of the TAO model, whether trisection-driven or action-driven, varies depending on the context. The trisection-driven approach emphasizes optimizing trisecting methods, with subsequent actions and strategies developed based on the trisection results. Conversely, the action-driven approach prioritizes strategy selection from a given set to influence the three-way decision's effectiveness, determining how to divide a whole into three regions best. Often, these two approaches are integrated to enhance the applicability and effectiveness of the three-way decision in various scenarios.

The outcome evaluation component is distinct from trisecting and acting, focusing primarily on assessing the effectiveness of these two processes. Considers the results of both the trisection and the strategies employed, providing valuable feedback that informs future decisions and strategy adjustments. This evaluative step is essential to measure the overall impact and success of the three-way decision-making process.

Figure 1. The TAO of the three-way decision
Source: Yao (2021)

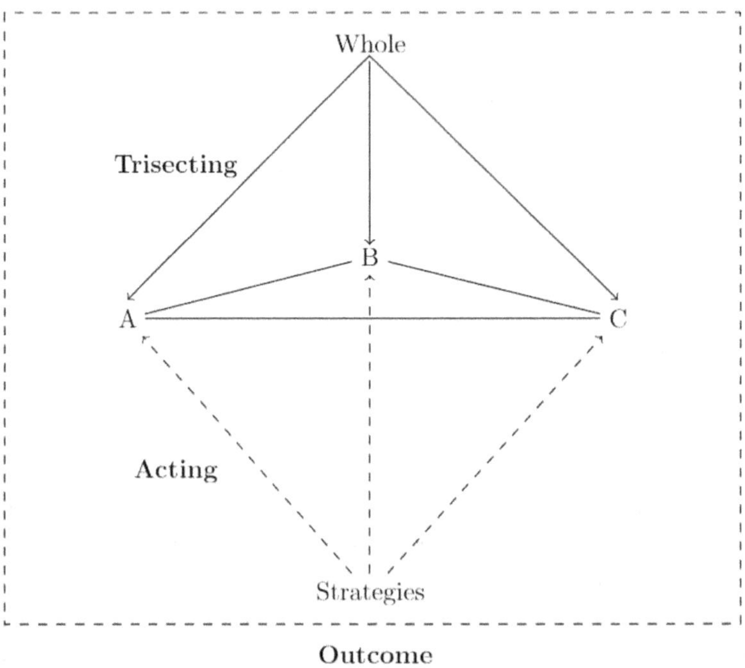

Evaluation of Outcome

The primary function of the outcome in three-way decision making is to assess the process's effectiveness. This assessment focuses on identifying and analyzing the differences that emerge before and after implementing the trisecting and acting steps. To quantify this change, we use the following general formula (Gao & Yao, 2017):

$$Q(\pi'|\pi) = Q(\pi') - Q(\pi).$$

In this equation, $Q(\pi)$ and $Q(\pi')$ denote the initial and subsequent quantified outcomes, respectively. This measurement can evaluate aspects such as benefit, cost, or utility. While a direct calculation of

$Q(\pi)$ and $Q(\pi')$ might not always be feasible, this formula still offers a means to gauge the difference. Occasionally, the measure $Q(\pi'|\pi)$ can be assessed from alternative perspectives.

In existing research, much emphasis is placed on the aspects of tripartition and action, with limited focus on outcome evaluation. Yao and Jiang, in their pioneering work, proposed a comprehensive metric framework for measuring outcomes based on Trisecting and Acting, as indicated in the following equation:

$$Q(\pi) = w_1 Q(P_1) + w_2 Q(P_2) + w_3 Q(P_3).$$

Here, $Q(\pi)$ signifies the overall results, which may encompass cost, benefit, or risk. $Q(P_i)$, $i=1,2,3$ represents the outcome of a specific region P_i, and w_i is the weight assigned to $Q(P_i)$, $i=1,2,3$. This framework facilitates a more nuanced and comprehensive evaluation of the outcomes, contributing significantly to the field of three-way decision-making.

Change-Based Three-Way Decisions

Definition 8.1: (Jiang et al., 2022). An evaluation space is defined by a triplet $E=(U,S,e)$, where U is a finite non-empty set of objects, S is a set of states, and e is an evaluation from $U \times S$ to the set of real number $\mathfrak{R}$, namely, $e: U \times S \cdot \mathfrak{R}$. For a pair of an object $x \in U$ and a state $s \in S$, $e(xs)$ denotes the evaluation value of x in state s.

As a special case of $\mathfrak{R}$, we may use a three-valued set {-1,0,+1} to qualitatively indicate some properties of objects. We may also use the unit interval [0,1]. The evaluation value $e(xs)$ represents the object in states. By looking at the two states, we can observe changes.

Definition 8.2: (Jiang et al., 2022). In an evaluation space $E(U,S,e)$, given a pair of states $(s,s') \in S \times S$, the change of evaluation values of an object $x \in U$ is defined by:

$$c(x \mid (s,s')) = e(x \mid s') - e(xs).$$

In the definition above, we produce a new evaluation method. It does not merely evaluate an object in one state, and it uses the object's values in two different states by calculating their difference. The new evaluation extends the traditional evaluation methods. More specifically, we employ the difference between two values as changes. It does not relate this difference to the initial value $e(xs)$. Sometimes it needs to consider changes relative to the value $e(xs)$.

Definition 8.3: (Jiang et al., 2022). In an evaluation space $E=(U,S,e)$, suppose $e(xs) \neq 0$ for all $x \in U$ and $s \in S$. Given a pair of states $(s,s') \in S \times S$, the relative change of values of an object $s \in U$ is defined by:

$$rc(x \mid (s,s')) = \frac{e(x \mid s') - e(xs)}{abs(e(xs))},$$

where abs (.) denotes the absolute value of a real number.

In some situations, we may want to evaluate the overall changes of a set of objects. The simplest way is to summarize the changes of the objects in the set.

Definition 8.4: (Jiang et al., 2022). Suppose $X \subseteq U$ is a subset of objects. The overall change of objects in X is defined by:

$$\sum_{x \in X} c\left(X \mid (s,s')\right) = c\left(x_1 \mid (s,s')\right) + c\left(x_2 \mid (s,s')\right. + \ldots + c\left(x_n \mid (s,s')\right),$$

$$\sum_{x \in X} rc\left(X \mid (s,s')\right) = rc\left(x_1 \mid (s,s')\right) + rc\left(x_2 \mid (s,s')\right. + \ldots + rc\left(x_n \mid (s,s')\right),$$

where $X = \{x_1, x_2, x_3, \ldots, x_n\}$.

The summation collects the differences of all objects in the set X in two states. If the summation result is over zero, the strategy achieves a positive effect; if the result is zero, there is no change; otherwise, the approach will offer a negative effect, so the summation can provide a qualitative characterization for a strategy.

Reinforcement Learning

Reinforcement Learning (RL) (Kaelbling, 1996), denoted as a method in machine learning, emphasizes how agents learn the optimal strategy in an environment through their actions and the feedback from rewards received. Assuming that the environment possesses Markovian characteristics, sequential reinforcement learning problems can be aptly modeled through Markov Decision Processes (MDPs).

The change of trisecting states by strategy acting adheres to Markovian properties, meaning that the subsequent trisecting state solely depends on the current state and policy, irrespective of history. A Markov Decision Process is represented by the tuple π_c, A,P,R>. Here, π_c is a finite set encompassing all possible trisecting states, while A is a finite set of all applicable strategies. P represents the probability of transition to the next state transition probability $P\left(\pi_c' \mid \pi_c, A\right)$, indicating the likelihood of transitioning to the next state π_c' under the current state π_c and strategy A. The reward function $R\left(\pi_c, A, \pi_c'\right)$ quantifies the reward obtained for transitioning to state π_c' under the conditions of state π_c and strategy A. Owing to its capacity to effectively encapsulate the dynamic interaction between an agent and its environment, MDPs are commonly used to describe reinforcement learning tasks.

The Q-learning algorithm in reinforcement learning seeks the optimal strategy in a Markov Decision Process (MDP) context by continuously updating a Q-table through exploration and learning. This table records the value function for each pair of state-actions, representing the expected return from executing a specific action. The algorithm updates the Q-function $Q(\pi_c,A)$ using the formula:

$$Q\left(\pi_c, A\right) \leftarrow Q\left(\pi_c, A\right) + \alpha\left[R\left(\pi_c, A, \pi_c'\right) + \gamma \max_{A'} Q\left(\pi_c', A'\right) - Q\left(\pi_c, A\right)\right].$$

The balance between exploration and exploitation is managed by strategies like ε-greedy. This Q-learning approach, applied to 3WD, models the evolution of trisecting states under different strategies, optimizing strategy selection based on state dynamics. The algorithm aims to converge the Q-table towards the optimal value function, enabling the best action selection in any given state.

In this chapter, we define utility generated from changes in trisecting states as rewards, denoted as $R(\pi_c, A, \pi_c')$, where π_c and π_c' are the current and subsequent trisecting states, and A is the applied strategy. The Q-function, $Q(\pi_c, A)$, updated with these rewards, guides strategy selection to maximize cumulative rewards. We introduce a target reward value, R_{target}, and consider exploration complete when the sum of rewards $\sum R(\pi_c, A, \pi_c')$ from sequential strategies reaches R_{target}. The process iterates until a stable and efficient strategy path emerges, as indicated by consistent attainment of R_{target} in the fewest cycles.

Integrating reinforcement learning with the study of changes in 3WD, the utility generated by the fluctuation in trisecting states can be utilized as rewards. These rewards serve to calculate and update the Q-function. Decisions are then made based on the Q-function to select strategies that maximize cumulative rewards. Given the ongoing changes in trisecting states under various strategies, this chapter proposes setting a target reward value. The exploration is deemed complete when the cumulative rewards generated by the changes in trisecting states under consecutive strategies reach this target value. Following this methodology, multiple explorations are conducted until a stable and shortest strategy path is consistently identified.

STRATEGY SELECTION AND UTILITY MEASUREMENT BASED ON REINFORCEMENT LEARNING

This section employs the Markov Decision Process to model maximizing utility through continuous optimization of strategy selection in changing trisecting states. Initially, quadratic programming is used to solve for state transition probabilities. Subsequently, the rewards generated by state changes are calculated using the cumulative prospect theory. Finally, the Q-learning algorithm is employed to identify the strategy that maximizes rewards in each cycle.

Figure 2. Three-way decision based on reinforcement learning (RL-3WD)

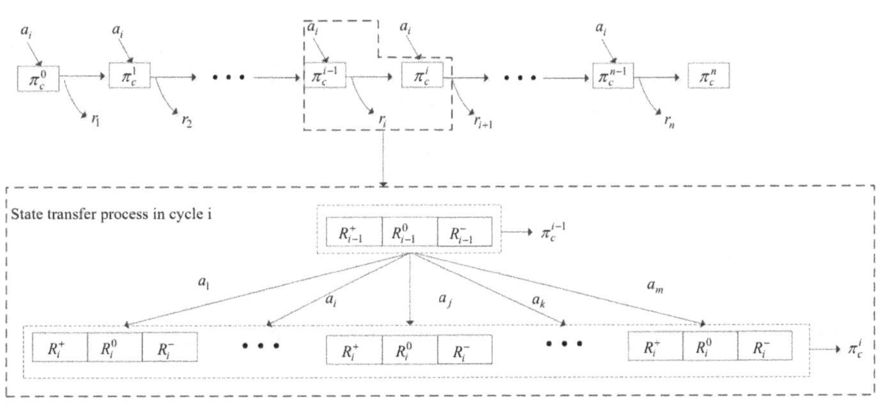

Figure 2 illustrates the process of updating the Q table using the Q-learning algorithm. For a trisecting state π_c^t in cycle *t*, a strategy *A* is chosen using the ε-greedy approach, which, when applied, yields a more effective trisecting state π_c^{t+1} in cycle *t+1*, thus generating a reward r_t. This reward is then used to update the Q-table. This process is repeated through multiple training iterations until the Q-values in the Q-table stabilize. The following outlines the specific approach for a series of strategy trainings on the trisecting states $\{R^+,R^0,R^-\}$:

State Transition Probability Matrix: Calculate the transition probability matrix resulting from the application of each strategy. Based on this matrix, determine the trisecting states for the next cycle.

Use cumulative prospect theory to calculate the utility value of the new trisecting state generated by each strategy application and consider this as a reward in reinforcement learning.

Strategy Selection: Choose the strategy for each trisecting state in each cycle from the Q table using the ε-greedy approach.

Set Training Termination Criteria: Establish a target reward value during strategy training. Training stops when the cumulative reward of the training reaches this target value.

Conduct multiple trainings until the Q values in the Q-table stabilize, then select the strategy with the highest Q value for each cycle.

States and Transition Probability Matrix

In the Markov Decision Process related to three-way changes, the sequence of trisecting states that vary with cycles is considered as the state set. The application of different strategies yields various state-transition probability matrices. These matrices determine the distribution of trisecting states in the next cycle. This section employs quadratic programming to solve for the state transition probability matrix between different cycles.

Suppose there are *n* cycles in a simulation round, each cycle generating a trisecting state after the application of the strategy. The vector representing the distribution of trisecting states in the initial cycle is:

$$\pi_c(0)=\left[\left|R_0^+\right|,\left|R_0^0\right|,\left|R_0^-\right|\right].$$

Where $\left|R_0^\chi\right|$, $\chi=\{+,0,-\}$ indicates the distribution of trisecting regions in the initial cycle.

After k cycles, the estimated probability that an object is in the trisecting region R_k^χ is $\left|R_k^\chi\right|$, hence the state distribution vector after the k step transition is:

$$\pi_c(k)=\left[\left|R_k^+\right|,\left|R_k^0\right|,\left|R_k^-\right|\right].$$

Let $\tilde{P}$ be the estimated value of the state transition probability matrix in the Markov predictive model,

$$\tilde{P} = \begin{bmatrix} \tilde{p}_{++} & \tilde{p}_{+0} & \tilde{p}_{\pm} \\ \tilde{p}_{0+} & \tilde{p}_{00} & \tilde{p}_{0-} \\ \tilde{p}_{\mp} & \tilde{p}_{-0} & \tilde{p}_{--} \end{bmatrix}.$$

Therefore, the estimate $\tilde{\pi}_c(k)$ of $\pi_c(k)$ is:

$$\tilde{\pi}_c(k) = \pi_c(k-1)\tilde{P} = \left[\left|R_{k-1}^{+}\right|, \left|R_{k-1}^{0}\right|, \left|R_{k-1}^{-}\right|\right] \cdot \tilde{P} = \pi_c(0) \cdot \tilde{P}^k$$

$$= \left[\left|R_0^{+}\right|, \left|R_0^{0}\right|, \left|R_0^{-}\right|\right] \cdot \begin{bmatrix} \tilde{p}_{++} & \tilde{p}_{+0} & \tilde{p}_{\pm} \\ \tilde{p}_{0+} & \tilde{p}_{00} & \tilde{p}_{0-} \\ \tilde{p}_{\mp} & \tilde{p}_{-0} & \tilde{p}_{--} \end{bmatrix}^k,$$

$k=1,2,\ldots,n$.

Let $C_\chi(k)$ denote the error between the estimated probability $\left|\tilde{R}_k^\chi\right|$ and the actual value $\left|R_k^\chi\right|$ of the changed tripartition R^χ after the k-step transfer:

$$C_\chi(k) = \left|R_k^\chi\right| - \left|\tilde{R}_k^\chi\right| = \left|R_k^\chi\right| - \sum_{j=\{-,0,+\}}^{|j|} \left|R_{k-1}^j\right| \tilde{P}_{\chi j}.$$

Where $j=\{+,0,-\}$, $\chi=\{+,0,-\}$, and $+ \succ 0 \succ -$.

Then n cycles, the sum of squares of the errors E_χ in region R^χ is given by:

$$E_\chi = \sum_{k=1}^{n} \left(C_\chi(k)\right)^2.$$

In each cycle, the sum of squared errors D in the transition process of objects within the changing trisecting regions is as follows:

$$D = \sum_{\chi=\{-,0,+\}}^{|\chi|} E_\chi = \sum_{\chi=\{-,0,+\}}^{|\chi|} \sum_{k=1}^{n} \left(C_\chi(k)\right)^2 = \sum_{\chi=\{-,0,+\}}^{|\chi|} \sum_{k=1}^{n} \left(\left| R_k^\chi \right| - \sum_{j=\{-,0,+\}}^{|j|} \left| R_{k-1}^j \right| \tilde{P}_{\chi j}\right)^2.$$

We introduce constraints into the model to establish an optimization model to solve the Markov state transition probability matrix by utilizing the concept of the least-squares method. The objective function of this model is to minimize the sum of squared errors D in the transition process at each stage in each state. The constraints of the model are the row-sum conditions and non-negativity conditions. The specific formulation is as follows.

$$\begin{cases} \min D = \sum_{\chi=\{-,0,+\}}^{|\chi|} \sum_{k=1}^{n} \left(\left| R_k^{\chi} \right| - \sum_{j=\{-,0,+\}}^{|j|} \left| R_{k-1}^{j} \right| \tilde{P}_{\chi j} \right)^2 \\ s.t \sum_{j=\{-,0,+\}}^{|j|} P_{\chi j} = 1 \\ P_{\chi j} \geq 0 \end{cases}.$$

There are various methods for solving quadratic programming, such as Lemke, active set, and linear transformation methods. Here, the model is transformed into a linear programming model for the solution, simplifying the complexity of solving the model.

Strategy Selection

For each change-based tripartition state in every cycle, there exist multiple strategies that can be applied, which are considered as the action set in the Markov Decision Process. The objective is to select a strategy that maximizes the cumulative reward from the initial to the terminal state of the change-based tripartition state. To achieve this, we employ the Q-learning algorithm, which continuously explores and learns to update a Q-table. This table records the value function of each pair of state-actions.

In the process of strategy selection, a Q-table is initially constructed with column labels as change-based tripartition states π_c^i and row labels as applicable strategies A_i. At the beginning of the cycle, all values in the Q-table are initialized to zero. For the change-based tripartition state corresponding to the cycle in the Q-table, a -greedy strategy is used to choose the strategy to apply. Specifically, when the action value function $Q(\pi_c,A)$ is greater than ε or all $Q(\pi_c,A)$ values are zero, a strategy is randomly selected for implementation. Otherwise, the strategy corresponding to the maximum value $Q(\pi_c,A)$ in that cycle is chosen.

The values of $Q(\pi_c,A)$ in the Q-table are continuously updated. The specific formula for updating $Q(\pi_c,A)$ is as follows. Suppose strategy A_m is applied to the change based tripartition state π_c^i of cycle i, then the real calculation formula for $Q\left(\pi_c^i, A_m\right)_{Re}$ is

$$Q\left(\pi_c^i, A_m\right)_{\text{Re}} = r_i + \gamma \max_{A'} Q\left(\pi_c^{(i+1)}, A'\right).$$

Here, r_i represents the reward value for the change-based tripartition state π_c^i generated by applying strategy A_m in the i-th cycle, γ is the discount factor, and $\max_{A'} Q\left(\pi_c^{(i+1)}, A'\right)$ denotes the maximum Q value for the change-based tripartition state $\pi_c^{(i+1)}$ in cycle i+1 in the Q-table.

In the Q-table, the value of $Q\left(\pi_c^i, A_m\right)$ at the position corresponding to the application of strategy A_m on the change-based tripartition state π_c^i is the value function updated after previous training, considered as the estimated value $Q\left(\pi_c^i, A_m\right)_{Es}$. $CQ\left(\pi_c^i, A_m\right)$ represents the difference between the estimated and real values:

$$CQ\left(\pi_c^i, A_m\right) = Q\left(\pi_c^i, A_m\right)_{\text{Re}} - Q\left(\pi_c^i, A_m\right)_{\text{Es}}.$$

Based on the above formula, the Q value at the position corresponding to the change based tripartition state π_c^i and strategy A_m in the Q-table is updated by

$$Q\left(\pi_c^i, A_m\right) \leftarrow Q\left(\pi_c^i, A_m\right)_{\text{Es}} + \sigma CQ\left(\pi_c^i, A_m\right),$$

where σ is the learning rate.

For updating the Q-table, manual calculations are impractical; hence the Q-learning algorithm is developed for computation as follows.

Algorithm 1: *Q-Learning for Change-Based Trisecting State Optimization*

Input: Initial change-based tripartition state π_c^0 Number of training episodes E Target reward R Cumulative reward CR Learning rate σ Discount factor γ Output: Optimized Q-table	
1.	Initialize the Q-table with zeros.
2.	Define the dynamics of the tripartition with transfer probabilities and reward functions.
3.	Create a dynamic change environment with transfer probability and reward functions.
4.	For each episode in range(E):
5.	Initialize π_c.
6.	While CR≤R:
7.	Choose A from Q-table using ε -greedy.
8.	Apply action A gets π_c' and r from the environment.
9.	$Q(\pi_c, a) \leftarrow Q(\pi_c, a)_{Es} + \sigma CQ(\pi_c, a)$.
10.	$CR \leftarrow CR + r$.
11.	$\pi_c \leftarrow \pi_c'$.
12.	End while
13.	End for
14.	Return optimized Q-table.

According to Algorithm 1, an updated Q-table can be obtained. The strategy with the highest Q value for each change-based tripartition state in the updated Q-table can be selected to form an optimal strategy sequence to achieve the target reward in the shortest time. This sequence of strategies, learned from experience, represents the strategies that can achieve maximum utility, thus guiding future strategy selection.

Reward and Future Utility

In the Markov Decision Process of three-way decision making, each change in the change-based tripartition state generates a reward to update the Q-table. We employ the cumulative prospect theory to calculate the rewards generated in each cycle.

Cumulative prospect theory describes decision-makers' behavior and attitudes toward risk under conditions of uncertainty and risk. Its principal ideas can be summarized in three aspects: Outcomes are viewed as gains or losses relative to a reference point, rather than as final states of wealth. Second, decision-makers exhibit risk aversion for gains, and risk-seeking for losses, and are more sensitive to losses than gains. Lastly, in the face of low-probability events, decision-makers tend to magnify their impact, while for high-probability events, they tend to downplay it. The Cumulative Prospect Theory suggests that decision-makers prefer decisions with the highest cumulative prospect value. Using the value function $v(x_h)$ and the decision weight function ψ_h, the cumulative prospect value function v is given by:

$$v = \sum_{h=-m}^{n} \psi_h v(x_h).$$

For the change-based tripartition state $\{R_k^+, R_k^0, R_k^-\}$ in the kth cycle, applying strategy A results in a regional change of objects in the universal set U, leading to the change-based tripartition state $\{R_{k+1}^+, R_{k+1}^0, R_{k+1}^-\}$ in the $k+1^{\text{th}}$ cycle. The application of strategy A could lead to ideal, uncertain, or nonideal changes in objects in the R_k^+ region, with similar potential changes in the R_k^0 and R_k^- regions. Let x_k denote the utility generated by objects in the R_k^χ region changing to R_{k+1}^χ.

Decision-makers need to set a reference value $\bar{x}$; if objects in the R_k^χ region under the influence of strategy A undergo ideal or uncertain changes, then $x_k \geq \bar{x}$, indicating a gain. Otherwise, a loss is incurred. As empirically validated, Tversky and Kahneman provided a detailed formula for the value function $v(x_h)$:

$$\begin{cases} (x_h - \bar{x})^{\mu}, & \text{if } x_h \geq \bar{x} \\ -\theta(\bar{x} - x_h)^{\nu}, & \text{if } x_h < \bar{x} \end{cases}$$

Here, let $\mu=\nu=0.88$ and $\theta=2.25$. As shown by the formula above, the value function is a monotonically increasing function.

By substituting the change utility value x_k into the value function formula $v(x_h)$, the value function for each region in the most effective change-based tripartition state of cycle $k+1$, resulting from the change-based tripartition state of cycle k under the influence of strategy A, can be obtained as detailed in Table 1:

Table 1 The value functions for changes in the area of the object

π_c^k \ π_c^{k+1}	R_{k+1}^{+}	R_{k+1}^{0}	R_{k+1}^{-}
R_k^{+}	v_{++}^k	v_{+0}^k	v_{+-}^k
R_k^{0}	v_{0+}^k	v_{00}^k	v_{0-}^k
R_k^{-}	v_{-+}^k	v_{-0}^k	v_{--}^k

In the cumulative prospect theory, the decision-maker's weight functions for gains and losses are computed differently. Therefore, two non-linear transformations of probability are considered, providing the weight function formulas for gains and losses respectively as follows:

$$w^{+}(p_h)=\frac{p_h^{\sigma}}{\left(p_h^{\sigma}+(1-p_h)^{\sigma}\right)^{\frac{1}{\sigma}}},$$

$$w^{-}(p_h)=\frac{p_h^{\delta}}{\left(p_h^{\delta}+(1-p_h)^{\delta}\right)^{\frac{1}{\delta}}}.$$

Where p_h is the probability corresponding to x_{ij}^k. Let σ=0.61, δ=0.69.

In continuous probability transformations, weighting the cumulative probabilities and sorting the change utilities of objects in each change region in ascending order are necessary. The decision weight function ψ_h for each utility, whether gain or loss, can be represented as:

$$\psi_h=\begin{cases} w^{+}(p_h+\cdots+p_n)-w^{+}(p_{h+1}+\cdots+p_n), \\ \qquad h\geq 0; \\ w^{-}(p_{-m}+\cdots+p_h)-w^{-}(p_{-m}+\cdots+p_{h-1}), \\ \qquad h<0. \end{cases}$$

From the above calculations of the value function, it is known that the value function is a monotonically increasing function. Therefore, the value functions generated by the changes can be sorted to obtain the weight functions related to each change. By comparing the magnitudes of the various value functions, the decision weight functions in all scenarios can be represented as follows:

$$\psi_i\left(\Pr\left(R_{k+1}^{\chi} \mid [x]\right)\right)=\begin{cases} w^{+}\left(\Pr\left(R_{k+1}^{+} \mid [x]\right)\right), \chi=+, \\ w^{+}\left(\Pr\left(R_{k+1}^{+} \mid [x]\right)+\Pr\left(R_{k+1}^{0} \mid [x]\right)\right) \\ \quad -w^{+}\left(\Pr\left(R_{k+1}^{+} \mid [x]\right)\right), \chi=0, \\ w^{-}\left(\Pr\left(R_{k+1}^{-} \mid [x]\right)\right), \chi=-. \end{cases}$$

Where $i=\{+,0,-\}$, $\chi=\{+,0,-\}$, $\Pr\left(R_{k+1}^{\chi} \mid [x]\right)$ represents the probability that the equivalence class $[x]$ belongs to the region R_{k+1}^{χ}.

Therefore, according to the cumulative prospect theory, the cumulative prospect value v for each region in the change-based tripartition state of the kth cycle can be calculated as follows.

$$\upsilon\left(R_k^{+} \mid [x]\right)=\psi_{+}\left(\Pr\left(R_{k+1}^{+} \mid [x]\right)\right)v_{++}^{k}+\psi_{+}\left(\Pr\left(R_{k+1}^{0} \mid [x]\right)\right)v_{+0}^{k}+\psi_{+}\left(\Pr\left(R_{k+1}^{-} \mid [x]\right)\right)v_{\pm}^{k}.$$

$$\upsilon\left(R_k^{0} \mid [x]\right)=\psi_{0}\left(\Pr\left(R_{k+1}^{+} \mid [x]\right)\right)v_{0+}^{k}+\psi_{0}\left(\Pr\left(R_{k+1}^{0} \mid [x]\right)\right)v_{00}^{k}+\psi_{0}\left(\Pr\left(R_{k+1}^{-} \mid [x]\right)\right)v_{0-}^{k}.$$

$$\upsilon\left(R_k^{-} \mid [x]\right)=\psi_{-}\left(\Pr\left(R_{k+1}^{+} \mid [x]\right)\right)v_{\mp}^{k}+\psi_{-}\left(\Pr\left(R_{k+1}^{0} \mid [x]\right)\right)v_{-0}^{k}+\psi_{-}\left(\Pr\left(R_{k+1}^{-} \mid [x]\right)\right)v_{--}^{k}.$$

Therefore, the reward generated by the change-based tripartition state π_c^{k+1} obtained from applying strategy A in the kth cycle is:

$$r_k=\upsilon\left(R_k^{+} \mid [x]\right)+\upsilon\left(R_k^{0} \mid [x]\right)+\upsilon\left(R_k^{-} \mid [x]\right).$$

The rewards generated in each cycle during every training process can be determined based on calculated rewards, thereby estimating the future utility of three-way decision changes. The Q-learning algorithm is used to update the Q-table and to identify the shortest path to the target reward through a sequence of strategies based on the Q-table. Combined with the state transition probability matrix, a future sequence of change-based tripartition states can be predicted, and the reward for each cycle is calculated using cumulative prospect theory. In this process, the future utility of three-way changes is given by:

$$G\left(\pi_c\right)=r_1+\gamma r_2+\ldots+\gamma^{n-1}r_n.$$

Where r_i represents the reward obtained in the ith cycle of the shortest simulated cycle.

Since this method employs cumulative prospect theory to calculate rewards generated in each cycle for predicting future utility, it more accurately reflects the decision-maker's behavioral preferences. Future utility calculated using this method can estimate outcomes before a series of strategies are executed and provide relatively accurate predictions.

As delineated in this paper, the three-way decision framework employing reinforcement learning offers an innovative approach to optimizing strategy selection and enhancing utility measurement. The application of reinforcement learning to the three-way decision method enables the maximization of cumulative rewards, demonstrating a significant stride in decision-making methodologies. Nevertheless, this approach presents opportunities for further refinement. Presently, the state transition matrix relies on quadratic programming for its resolution. This aspect could be more efficiently addressed by employing advanced algorithms, such as policy gradient methods inherent in deep reinforcement learning. Moreover, incorporating affective computing into the reward calculation could align the reward function more closely with the decision-maker's preferences, thereby enhancing the model's applicability and accuracy.

While integrating reinforcement learning into the three-way decision framework marks a theoretical advancement, its practical application is still nascent and warrants extensive exploration. Future research should pivot towards applying this model in concrete scenarios, such as medical decision-making or financial investment decisions. This application-oriented approach would involve collecting real-world data and establishing Markov process models specific to the problem at hand. Utilizing the proposed method in these real-life scenarios would validate its effectiveness in practical settings and develop it into a reliable tool for supporting three-way decisions. Empirical analyses stemming from these applications could provide critical insights, thereby enabling further refinement of the method. This evolution would substantially augment its ability to address complex decision problems effectively.

Illustrative Example

This section illustrates the concept of this study using an example of a store operation. The objective here is to select a strategy that enables the store to reach the target reward in the shortest possible time within a limited number of cycles and to predict the store's future revenue under the current state.

The operators regularly conduct various promotions on the platform to increase sales. Depending on the nature of the promotions, the sales volume of the products in the store can change to varying degrees. Based on the change in product sales volume, if the sales increase of a product exceeds 10, it is classified as a hot selling item; if the sales decrease by 10, it is classified as a potential item; otherwise, it is considered a promotional item, represented by R^+, R^-, and R^0, respectively. The process of changing product sales in the store with each planned promotion is considered a cycle, typically lasting 3-5 days.

Currently, there are three traffic-driving activities a_1, a_2, a_3 on the platform. For products in the store, appropriate traffic-driving activities are applied to the three different areas R^+, R^0, R^-. The combination of activities applied to the three areas in each cycle is considered a strategy, and the product sales in the store change differently depending on the strategy implemented. Based on experience, three sets of strategies are now set: $A_1=\{a_1,a_3,a_2\}$, $A_2=\{a_3,a_1,a_2\}$, $A_3=\{a_2,a_2,a_1\}$.

A Single State Transition Process

Now, 76 promotions-sensitive products are selected from the store as sample data. In the store's past data, 20 cycles of data for each strategy A_1, A_2, A_3 are extracted. Based on these data, the initial distribution of hot sales, potential and promotional products for strategies A_1, A_2, A_3 is determined to be [21,30,25], [15,36,25], [28,21,27] respectively. After the 20th cycle, the distribution of these three categories of products changes to [46,14,16], [36,25,15], [42,17,17], respectively. Using the aforementioned method, the state transition probabilities for the store's products under the influence of strategies A_1, A_2, A_3 can be approximately calculated as follows:

$$\tilde{P}_{A_1} = \begin{bmatrix} 0.6037 & 0.1452 & 0.2511 \\ 0.5655 & 0.2231 & 0.2114 \\ 0.6576 & 0.2310 & 0.1114 \end{bmatrix},$$

$$\tilde{P}_{A_2} = \begin{bmatrix} 0.3662 & 0.5242 & 0.1096 \\ 0.5145 & 0.1213 & 0.3642 \\ 0.6576 & 0.2310 & 0.1114 \end{bmatrix},$$

$$\tilde{P}_{A_3} = \begin{bmatrix} 0.5768 & 0.2142 & 0.2090 \\ 0.5484 & 0.2203 & 0.2313 \\ 0.5146 & 0.2141 & 0.2713 \end{bmatrix}.$$

Assuming that in the kth cycle, applying strategy A_1 to the sales volume tripartition region with a product distribution of [17,28,31] will result in a new product tripartition region of [46,16,14] and generate a reward. First, based on the changes in product distribution, the following parameters are listed in Table 2 for each region:

Table 2 Regional parameters

πc	χ=+	χ=0	χ=-
R_k^χ	17	28	31
R_{k+1}^χ	46	16	14
x_k	$1000*\lvert R_k^i \cap R_{k+1}^\chi \rvert$	$500*\lvert R_k^i \cap R_{k+1}^\chi \rvert$	$-200*\lvert R_k^i \cap R_{k+1}^\chi \rvert$

Where $i = \{+, 0, -\}$. Let $\overline{x} = 0.1$. The value function generated by the state change can be obtained, as shown in Table 3.

Then, using Equation above, the weights of changes in each region are calculated, with the results shown in Table 4.

Table 3 Value function generated by change

π_c^k \ π_c^{k+1}	R_{k+1}^+	R_{k+1}^0	R_{k+1}^-
R_k^+	3323.81	441.97	-1045.62
R_k^0	4901.08	1115.21	-1323.80
R_k^-	6138.44	1268.34	-904.53

Table 4 Weight values generated by change in the region

π_c^k \ π_c^{k+1}	R_{k+1}^+	R_{k+1}^0	R_{k+1}^-
R_k^+	0.476	0.0915	0.2943
R_k^0	0.4550	0.1430	0.2656
R_k^-	0.5072	0.2211	0.1815

Based on the value functions and weights, the profit value for the k cycle can be calculated as follows:

$$r^k = \upsilon\left(R_k^+ \mid [x]\right) + \upsilon\left(R_k^0 \mid [x]\right) + \upsilon\left(R_k^- \mid [x]\right)$$

$\approx$1314.85+2037.87+3229.67=6582.39.

Multiple Simulation Results Analysis

Now, we conduct a future utility prediction for the current sales volume change-based tripartition state [12,26,38], assuming the store's target profit is 50,000. Set the ε in the ε-greedy strategy to 0.8, the learning rate σ to 0.1, and the discount factor γ to 0.8. Using the Q-learning algorithm, the Q-table is updated.

Around 300 training iterations, the number of cycles needed to reach the target profit stabilized at nine cycles. Figure 3 shows the trend in the number of cycles required to achieve the target profit over multiple training sessions. It is observed that as the number of training sessions increases, the number of cycles needed to reach the target profit shows a downward trend. After training, the Q-table is exported as shown in Table 5:

Figure 3. Average cycle variation of multiple simulations

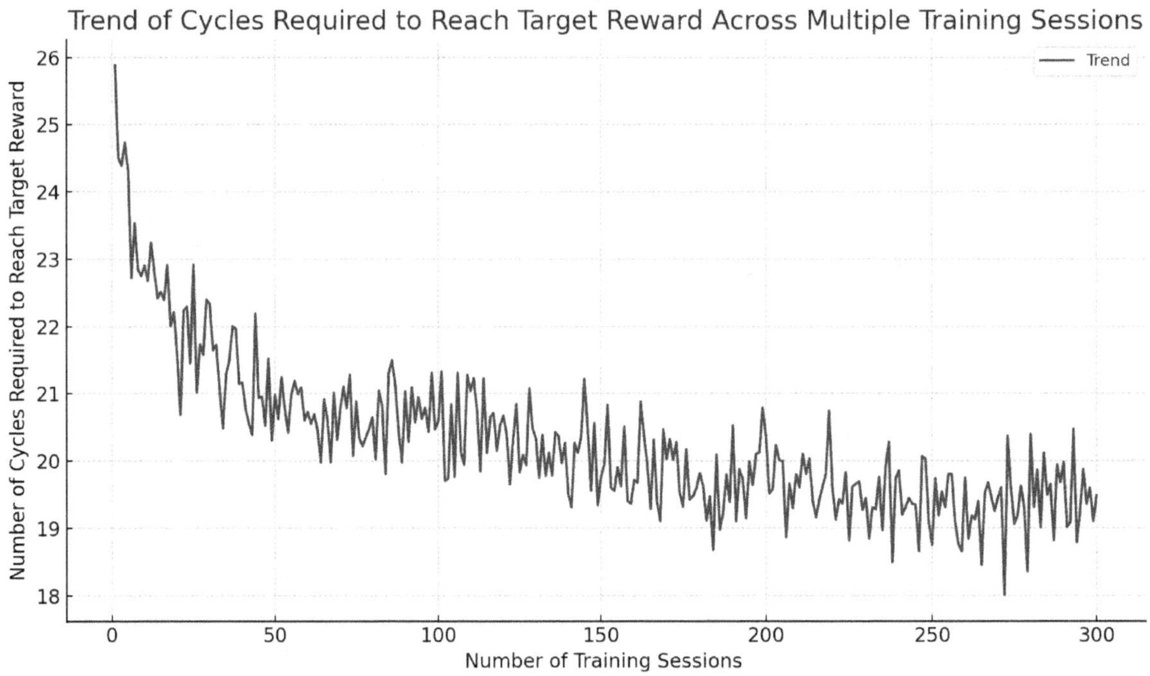

Table 5 Updated Q-table

π_c^k	Strategy		
	A_1	A_2	A_3
π_c^0	25126.68	26025.18	22150.23
π_c^1	24679.51	22530.43	23636.89
π_c^2	20943.68	21041.82	22999.41
π_c^3	21205.15	22118.56	20760.78
π_c^4	19472.07	19443.12	20958.95
π_c^5	19299.01	17351.48	15284.67
π_c^6	16219.77	14032.83	14973.53
π_c^7	12378.92	11154.01	12427.71
π_c^8	8682.98	6834.03	7683.58

As can be seen from Table 5, applying the strategies $\{A_2, A_1, A_3, A_2, A_3, A_1, A_1, A_3, A_1\}$ sequentially over nine cycles can achieve the target profit most quickly, providing guidance for the store's subsequent strategy selection. Following this strategic plan can improve the efficiency and profitability of store operations.

In the last simulation, the rewards generated in cycles 0-8 were approximately 6988.68, 6279.39, 5442.3, 5733.48, 5464.21, 6451.19, 6386.86, 6394.74, and 6393.75, respectively. Therefore, the future utility of the current change-based tripartition state π_c can be calculated as follows:

$$G(\pi) = 6988.68 + 0.8 \times 6279.39 + 0.82 \times 5442.3 + 0.83 \times 5733.48 + 0.84 \times 5464.21 + 0.85 \times 6451.19 + 0.96 \times 6386.86 + 0.87 \times 6394.74 + 0.88 \times 6393.75 \approx 26870.91$$

The above future utility of the change-based tripartition state is based on the maximum profit predicted using the optimal strategy. It holds a significant reference value for assessing the current operational status of the store. The method proposed in this chapter can better assist stores in strategy selection and utility assessment, guiding operators to better manage and run their stores, achieve profit maximization, and enhance market share and competitiveness, thus holding substantial practical significance.

CONCLUSION

This chapter discusses the 'Acting' and 'efficiency' within the TAO model of change-based three-way decision making, introducing reinforcement learning into strategy selection and utility measurement of change-based three-way decisions. Utilizing Cumulative Prospect Theory, it calculates the rewards generated by state transitions in each cycle and uses these as feedback signals. The Q-learning algorithm is then used to update the Q-table, from which the shortest sequence of strategies to reach the target reward is selected and future utility is predicted.

The introduction of reinforcement learning into the three-way the model enhances decision efficiency and quality of the decision, offering novel and effective solutions for other types of decision models. However, this chapter also has some limitations, such as not considering the issue of changing thresholds for trisecting regions with environmental changes and not describing methods to adjust the parameters of the Q-learning algorithm according to specific problems and environments. Future research will further explore these areas.

Data Availability Statement: The data sets generated and analyzed during the current study are available in the database, the UCI repository, http://archive.ics.uci.edu/ml/index.php.

Declaration of Competing Interest: Authors have no financial or non-financial interests that are directly or indirectly related to the chapter submitted for publication.

ACKNOWLEDGMENT

The chapter was supported by grants from the National Natural Science Foundation of China (62272284, 61972238, 62072294), the Special Fund for Science and Technology Innovation Teams of Shanxi Province (202204051001015), the Graduate Education Innovation Programs of Shanxi University, Research Project Supported by Shanxi Scholarship Council of China (2022-007), the Training Program for Young

Scientific Researchers of Higher Education Institutions in Shanxi, and the Cultivate Scientific Research Excellence Programs of Higher Education Institutions in Shanxi (CSREP) (2019SK036).

REFERENCES

Fang, Y., & Min, F. (2019). Cost-sensitive approximate attribute reduction with three-way decisions. *International Journal of Approximate Reasoning*, *104*, 148–165. doi:10.1016/j.ijar.2018.11.003

Gao, C., & Yao, Y. (2017). Actionable strategies in three-way decisions. *Knowledge-Based Systems*, *133*, 141–155. doi:10.1016/j.knosys.2017.07.001

Guo, D., Jiang, C., Sheng, R., & Liu, S. (2022). A novel outcome evaluation model of three-way decision: A change viewpoint. *Information Sciences*, *607*, 1089–1110. doi:10.1016/j.ins.2022.06.022

Jiang, C., Guo, D., & Duan, Y. (2022). Measure effectiveness of change-based three-way decision using utility theory. *Cognitive Computation*, *14*(3), 1009–1018. doi:10.1007/s12559-022-09999-x

Jiang, C., Guo, D., Duan, Y., & Liu, Y. (2020). Strategy selection under entropy measures in movement-based three-way decision. *International Journal of Approximate Reasoning*, *119*, 280–291. doi:10.1016/j.ijar.2020.01.013

Jiang, C., Guo, D., & Sun, L. (2021). Effectiveness measure for TAO model of three-way decisions with interval set. *Journal of Intelligent & Fuzzy Systems*, *40*(6), 11071–11084. doi:10.3233/JIFS-202207

Jiang, C., Guo, D., & Xu, R. (2021). Measuring the outcome of movement-based three-way decision using proportional utility functions. *Applied Intelligence*, *51*(12), 8598–8612. doi:10.1007/s10489-021-02325-2

Jiang, C., & Yao, Y. (2018). Effectiveness measures in movement-based three-way decisions. *Knowledge-Based Systems*, *160*, 136–143. doi:10.1016/j.knosys.2018.07.008

Kaelbling, L. P., Littman, M. L., & Moore, A. W. (1996). Reinforcement learning: A survey. *Journal of Artificial Intelligence Research*, *4*, 237–285. doi:10.1613/jair.301

Li, J., Huang, C., Qi, J., Qian, Y., & Liu, W. (2017). Three-way cognitive concept learning via multi-granularity. *Information Sciences*, *378*, 244–263. doi:10.1016/j.ins.2016.04.051

Liu, D., Liang, D., & Wang, C. (2016). A novel three-way decision model based on incomplete information system. *Knowledge-Based Systems*, *91*, 32–45. doi:10.1016/j.knosys.2015.07.036

Min, F., & Zhu, W. (2012). Attribute reduction of data with error ranges and test costs. *Information Sciences*, *211*, 48–67. doi:10.1016/j.ins.2012.04.031

Qian, J., Liu, C., Miao, D., & Yue, X. (2020). Sequential three-way decisions via multi-granularity. *Information Sciences*, *507*, 606–629. doi:10.1016/j.ins.2019.03.052

Wang, J., Ma, X., Xu, Z., & Zhan, J. (2022). Regret Theory-Based Three-Way Decision Model in Hesitant Fuzzy Environments and Its Application to Medical Decision. *IEEE Transactions on Fuzzy Systems*, *30*(12), 5361–5375. doi:10.1109/TFUZZ.2022.3176686

Wang, P., & Yao, Y. (2018). CE3: A three-way clustering method based on mathematical morphology. *Knowledge-Based Systems*, *155*, 54–65. doi:10.1016/j.knosys.2018.04.029

Wang, T., Li, H., Qian, Y., Huang, B., & Zhou, X. (2022). A Regret-Based Three-Way Decision Model Under Interval Type-2 Fuzzy Environment. *IEEE Transactions on Fuzzy Systems*, *30*(1), 175–189. doi:10.1109/TFUZZ.2020.3033448

Watkins, C. J. C. H., & Dayan, P. (1992). Q-learning. *Machine Learning*, *8*(3), 279–292. doi:10.1007/BF00992698

Yang, B., & Li, J. (2020). Complex network analysis of three-way decision researches. *International Journal of Machine Learning and Cybernetics*, *11*(5), 973–987. doi:10.1007/s13042-020-01082-x

Yang, X., Li, T., Fujita, H., & Liu, D. (2019). A sequential three-way approach to multi-class decision. *International Journal of Approximate Reasoning*, *104*, 108–125. doi:10.1016/j.ijar.2018.11.001

Yao, Y. (2009). Three-way decision: An interpretation of rules in rough set theory. *In LNCS 5589: Proceedings of the 4th International Conference on Rough Sets and Knowledge Technology*, Gold Coast, July 14-16, 2009 (pp. 642-649). Berlin, Heidelberg: Springer. 10.1007/978-3-642-02962-2_81

Yao, Y. (2010). Three-way decisions with probabilistic rough sets. *Information Sciences*, *180*(3), 341–353. doi:10.1016/j.ins.2009.09.021

Yao, Y. (2011). The superiority of three-way decisions in probabilistic rough set models. *Information Sciences*, *181*(6), 1080–1096. doi:10.1016/j.ins.2010.11.019

Yao, Y. (2012). An outline of a theory of three-way decisions. *Lecture Notes in Computer Science*, *7413*, 1–17. doi:10.1007/978-3-642-32115-3_1

Yao, Y. (2016). Three-way decisions and cognitive computing. *Cognitive Computation*, *8*(4), 543–554. doi:10.1007/s12559-016-9397-5

Yao, Y. (2018). Three-way decision and granular computing. *International Journal of Approximate Reasoning*, *103*, 107–123. doi:10.1016/j.ijar.2018.09.005

Yao, Y. (2020). Three-way granular computing, rough sets, and formal concept analysis. *International Journal of Approximate Reasoning*, *116*, 106–125. doi:10.1016/j.ijar.2019.11.002

Yao, Y. (2021). The geometry of three-way decision. *Applied Intelligence*, *51*(9), 6298–6325. doi:10.1007/s10489-020-02142-z

Yu, H., Wang, X., Wang, G., & Zeng, X. (2020). An active three-way clustering method via low-rank matrices for multi-view data. *Information Sciences*, *507*, 823–839. doi:10.1016/j.ins.2018.03.009

Zhan, J., Wang, J., Ding, W., & Yao, Y. (2023). Three-Way Behavioral Decision Making With Hesitant Fuzzy Information Systems: Survey and Challenges. *IEEE/CAA Journal of Automatica Sinica, 10*, 330-350.

Zhang, C., Li, D., & Liang, J. (2020). Multi-granularity three-way decisions with adjustable hesitant fuzzy linguistic multigranulation decision-theoretic rough sets over two universes. *Information Sciences*, *507*, 665–683. doi:10.1016/j.ins.2019.01.033

Zhang, Q., Pang, G., & Wang, G. (2020). A novel sequential three-way decisions model based on penalty function. *Knowledge-Based Systems*, *192*, 105350. doi:10.1016/j.knosys.2019.105350

Chapter 7
The Extension of MAIRCA Based on Fuzzy Number:
Smart Supplier Selection

Hatice Kübra Özensel
Necmettin Erbakan University, Turkey

Burak Efe
Necmettin Erbakan University, Turkey

ABSTRACT

Supplier selection, which is one of the phases of supply chain management, was examined in this chapter. In the line of four expert opinions and literature review, four main criteria, including environmental, economic, social, and smart criteria, and 18 sub-criteria were evaluated in this study. An interval-valued q-rung orthopair fuzzy (IVqROF) number based MAIRCA (multi attributive ideal-real comparative analysis) method is proposed for the ranking of 5 alternative suppliers. In this chapter, fuzzy number was proposed for the MAIRCA method, but unlike the literature, IVqROF number was applied to the MAIRCA method. It has been seen that the IVqROF number, which is the extension of the q-rung orthopair fuzzy number obtained by developing the intuitionistic fuzzy number and the Pythagorean fuzzy number, provides an advantage in evaluating expert opinions. In addition, Industry 4.0 criteria were examined under the smart criterion and contributed to the supplier selection problem. The study examined the smart supplier selection problem of an automotive sub-industry company.

INTRODUCTION

The retail market is growing day by day by becoming global, and the product produced in one continent can be used as raw material in another continent and sold to other continents. In addition to the advantages that this globalization brings, it also makes supply chain management more complex and difficult for companies. It pushes businesses to seek more systematic, technological and faster ways for sustainable supply chain management. Businesses that can build these systematic, sustainable supply

DOI: 10.4018/979-8-3693-1582-8.ch007

chains and realize their competitiveness with error-free supply processes as well as the right product, provide a competitive advantage over other businesses in the same sector. Despite the importance of the supply chain, it is also seen that until a certain time, not many empirical studies have been carried out by experts on the definition and integration of supply chain management within all other business policies. Supplier selection is the first and one of the most significant links in the supply chain to reduce costs. Many businesses aim to establish strong ties and cooperate with their suppliers in order to rise their competitiveness, to comply with the planned delivery dates given to their customers with the least deviation, and to increase the effectiveness of management (Shin et al., 2000).

Supplier selection has become one of the most important management issues. Supplier selection aims to identify the supplier with the highest performance to consistently meet the needs of the business. Choosing the best supplier among many possible suppliers with various qualifications is a complex task (Guarnieri and Trojan, 2019).

Since customer and supplier relationships are very important in businesses, choosing the right suppliers requires much more than cost comparison and the choices are predicted by various quantitative and qualitative factors. Once a supplier is fully integrated into an adequately run and organized supply chain, that relationship has a long-term impact on the competitiveness. Therefore, the supplier selection problem has a very important role in organizing an effective system for the supply chain. The supplier selection problem aims to decrease purchasing risk, maximize value for the customer, and establish short and long term connections between the consumer and suppliers. Developments in smart technologies over the years inevitably affect supply chains. Advanced smart technologies positioned as components of Industry 4.0, such as the internet of things, cyber systems, big data and artificial intelligence, ensure that all links forming the supply chain are more perceptible, interpretable, predictable, controllable and optimized. Supply chains where these smart technologies are integrated are defined as smart supply chains.

Supply chains are subject to increasingly faced with natural, human-induced or technological risks such as natural disasters, transportation accidents, worker strikes, terrorist attacks due to globalization. The consequences of these factors cause supply chain disruptions due to losses in productivity, profit, competition and revenue. Therefore, making supply chains smart and sustainable has become a necessity to protect the customer from shortages and interruptions. A business with a sustainable supply chain perspective needs to both communicate with the supplier and satisfy the customer, government and shareholders. In addition, in order to produce sustainable products in a sustainable supply chain, sustainability criteria must be taken into consideration when selecting suitable suppliers (Hosseini and Khaled, 2019).

In smart supply chain management, smart technologies are used at every stage, from transportation to the analysis of operators' working processes, to provide higher sustainability in social, environmental and economic terms. Sustainable supplier selection is one of the most significant components for the continuity of this sustainability. Because the actions of suppliers have great importance for sub-companies to achieve sustainable competitive advantage. It is very important to use smart technologies in evaluation process to achieve this sustainability in selection of suppliers (Chen et al., 2020; Ghadimi et al., 2019).

Traditional supplier selection is largely based on criteria such as affordable price and close distance. With the use of smart information technologies in supply chains, that smart supplier selection criteria such as supplier information management, warehouse automation, digitalization in the logistics system and data security, have emerged (Hasan et al., 2020; Torğul and Paksoy, 2023).

In general, decision makers face many uncertain factors when providing decision preferences for on-demand suppliers. Supplier selection depends on cost, quality, performance, technology, etc. It is a complex problem involving many criteria. Therefore, in order to obtain a systematic supplier selection process in line with existing criteria, a method is needed in which the criteria can be evaluated and prioritized (Tam and Tummala, 2001).

RELATED WORKS

This chapter uses many abbreviations and it can be seen in Appendix 1. In the dealer selection study for a telecommunication company conducted by Tam et al., a review of the decision-making methods in the literature is presented in order to support the dealer selection process. Based on extensive research in the literature, the study proposes a model based on AHP (Analytic Hierarchy Process) to include decision makers with conflicting goals. The result of the case study shows that AHP ensures decreasing the time for supplier selection (Tam and Tummala, 2001). An approach for supplier classification is proposed by integrating ELECTRE (Elemination and Choice Translating Reality English) TRI, which is used in classification problems, and hesitant fuzzy set. The proposed method is examined in the automotive industry (Galo et al., 2018). Kaya and Yet proposed DEMATEL (Decision Making Trial and Evaluation Laboratory) method to form a knowledge-based Bayesian network in line with the information obtained from multiple experts. The proposed method is applied in a case study of supplier selection at an automobile manufacturer (Kaya and Yet, 2019). Liu et al. examined a hybrid multi criteria decision making (MCDM) model combining fuzzy-based BWM (Best Worst Method), VIKOR (Multi-Criteria Optimization and Compromise Solution), PT (Prospect Theory) methods to make innovative supplier selection in the electric vehicle industry (Liu et al. 2021). Bai et al. examined socially sustainable supplier selection using the fuzzy grey number, BWM (Best Worst Method) and TODIM integration (Bai et al., 2019). Liang et al. proposed the prospect theory-based distributed linguistic ORESTE (Organization Rangement et Syntese de Donnees Relationnelles) method to describe the three superiority relationships (preference, indifference, and incomparability) in terms of the limited rationality of the decision maker in line with flexible and intelligent criteria. It is applied in the selection of battery suppliers in new energy vehicles enterprises (Liang et al., 2022). Ghadimi et al. added Industry 4.0 criteria to the sustainable supplier selection problem (Ghadimi et al., 2019). Chen et al. propose the interval valued type-2 fuzzy set based TOPSIS (Technique for Order of Preference by Similarity to Ideal Solution) and DEMATEL methods for smart supplier selection (Chen et al., 2020). Hasan et al. proposed fuzzy set based TOPSIS method to rank the alternative suppliers under logistics 4.0 (Hasan et al., 2020). Pınar and Boran proposed q rung orthopair fuzzy (q-ROF) number based TOPSIS and ELECTRE methods for supplier selection (Pınar and Boran, 2020). Alavi et al. determined the weights of economic, social and cyclical criteria for sustainable supplier selection by using fuzzy best-worst method (BWM). The supplier with the highest performance is defined by using fuzzy inference system (Alavi et al., 2021). Abdollahzadeh et al. (2023) handled fuzzy best- worst method and fuzzy gray relational analysis methods to select the food suppliers in hospitals. Bisht and Pal (2024) handle social network analysis considering the trust relationships among experts and suggest q rung orthopair fuzzy decision making framework for green supplier selection. Singh et al. (2024) used TODIM (TOmada de Decisao Interativa Multicriterio) method based fuzzy prospect theory for optimal hydrogen fuel cell component supplier selection. Meng et al. (2024) presented TOPSIS approach based on graph neural networks in Pythagorean fuzzy environment.

Although fuzzy sets are very successful in evaluating uncertainties, they are insufficient in explaining the degree of non-membership/hesitancy of decision makers. In order to fill this deficiency of fuzzy sets,

Atanassov presented an intuitionistic fuzzy set model in which both membership and non-membership degrees can be evaluated (Atanassov, 1986; Ali et al., 2022).

Pythagorean fuzzy sets, which are considered an extension of intuitionistic fuzzy set models, were introduced as a result of the need for a wider definition range. In an intuitionistic fuzzy set, the sum of the membership and non-membership degrees is allowed to be at most 1, and if it is less than 1, the difference is defined as hesitancy. In Pythagorean fuzzy sets, the sum of the squares of the membership and non-membership degrees is allowed to be at most 1 for a wider definition range. However, Pythagorean fuzzy sets are also lacking in some real applications. In order to achieve more accurate results in these real practices, a generalized q-ROF sets model can adjust the restriction on membership and non-membership degrees from a parameter type as an extension of Pythagorean fuzzy sets (Ali et al., 2022).

Some studies used q rung orthopair fuzzy number for different areas such as natural gas pipeline project risk assessment (Efe and Efe, 2023b) and glove design (Efe and Efe, 2022). MAIRCA based on q rung orthopair fuzzy number was presented for selecting emergency service of patients. (Efe and Efe, 2023a). It seems that the q-ROF sets model and its hybrid structures, which are a powerful idea, attracted the attention of researchers and caused them to deepen their studies on it. One of these studies presented a hybrid structure integrating interval-valued fuzzy set and q-ROF set (Joshi et al., 2018).

This chapter contributes to the literature as follows:

- MAIRCA is extended by using interval valued q-ROF number unlike existing studies in the literature. This study simultaneously ensures the advantages of MAIRCA and interval valued q-ROF number. It ensures to prevent information loss of the experts for the weights of criteria and criteria based alternative evaluation.
- Smart supplier selection is a new trend. This chapter also handled Industry 4.0 criteria except traditional supplier selection criteria. It used a novel method, which is interval valued q-ROF number based MAIRCA, for smart supplier selection problem.

MAIN FOCUS OF THE CHAPTER

This section presents the steps of MAIRCA method and definitions of interval valued q-ROF number.

The steps of the MAIRCA method are summarized below (Pamucar et al., 2018).

Step 1: Establishing the decision matrix. The criterion (C_j) values for each alternative (A_i) are included in Equation (1).

C1 C2 … Cn

$$x = \begin{bmatrix} x_{11} & x_{12} & \cdots & x_{1n} \\ \vdots & \vdots & \ddots & \vdots \\ x_{m1} & x_{m1} & \cdots & x_{mn} \end{bmatrix} \tag{1}$$

Step 2: It is essential for the decision maker to be impartial. While m is the total number of alternatives, the priority of ith alternative (PAi) is calculated with the help of Equation (2). Since the decision maker is equidistant from each of the alternatives, all priorities are equal as in Equation 3.

$$PA_i = \frac{1}{m};\ £_{i=1}^{m} PA_i = 1;\ i=1, 2, 3,\ldots..m \tag{2}$$

$$PA_1 = PA_2 = \cdots = PA_m \tag{3}$$

Step 3: Establishing of the matrix of theoretical ponder. tp_{ij} matrix is found by multiplying the priorities of the alternatives (PA_i) with weights the criteria (w_j).

$$\text{TP}=\begin{bmatrix} P_{A1}*W_1 & P_{A1}*W_2 & \cdots & P_{A1}*W_m \\ P_{A2}*W_1 & P_{A2}*W_2 & \cdots & P_{A2}*W_n \\ \vdots & \vdots & \ddots & \vdots \\ P_{Am}*W_1 & P_{Am}*W_2 & \cdots & P_{Am}*n \end{bmatrix} \tag{4}$$

Step 4: The matrix of real ponder (Tr) matrix is obtained by making use of the Tp matrix and X matrix. Matrix elements are calculated with the help of equation (5) for maximization type criteria and equation (6) for minimization type criteria.

$$t_{rij} = t_{pij} \times \left(\frac{x_{ij} - x_{ij}^{-}}{x_{ij}^{+} - x_{ij}^{-}} \right) \tag{5}$$

$$t_{rij} = t_{pij} \times \left(\frac{x_{ij} - x_{ij}^{+}}{x_{ij}^{-} - x_{ij}^{+}} \right) \tag{6}$$

x_{ij}^{+} shows the maximum value getting from alternative (x_{ij}^{+} = max $(x_1, x_2, \ldots, x_m)$, x_{ij}^{-} shows the minimum value getting from alternative (x_{ij}^{-} = min $(x_1, x_2, \ldots, x_m)$.

Step 5: The total gap matrix (TG) is obtained by subtracting the matrix of real ponder (Tr) from the matrix of theoretical ponder (Tp) with the help of Equations (7)-(8).

$$G_{ij} = tp_{ij} - tr_{ij} \tag{7}$$

$$TG = T_P - T_R \begin{bmatrix} g_{11} & g & \cdots & g_{1n} \\ \vdots & \vdots & \ddots & \vdots \\ g_{m1} & g_{m2} & \cdots & g_{mn} \end{bmatrix} \tag{8}$$

Step 6: In the last step of the method, the sum of the criterion values in TG matrix is found separately for each alternative with the help of equation (9). The alternative with the smallest value among the values obtained from this equation is considered the best alternative.

$$Q_i = £_{J-1}^{n} g_{ij},\ i=1,2,\ldots,m \tag{9}$$

Yager (2016) proposed the q-ROF number to overcome the shortcomings of the intuitionistic fuzzy number and the Pythagorean fuzzy number. IVqROF number whose definition is given below, has been proposed by expanding q-ROF numbers. Ju et al. (2019) defined IVq-ROF number operators below.

Definition 1: Let X be a non-empty fixed set, an IVq-ROF number on X can be defined as follows:

$$A=\left\{\left\langle x,\left(\left[\mu_A^L(x),\mu_A^U(x)\right],\left[\vartheta_A^L(x),\vartheta_A^U x\right]\right)\right\rangle \middle| x\in X\right\} \tag{10}$$

$\left[\mu_A^L(x),\mu_A^U(x)\right]$ and $\left[\vartheta_A^L(x),\vartheta_A^U x\right]$ show the membership and non-membership degrees for x∈X in set A, respectively. It must be ensured $x\in X:\left[\mu_A^L(x),\mu_A^U(x)\right]\subseteq[0,1]$, $\left[\vartheta_A^L(x),\vartheta_A^U(x)\right]\subseteq[0,1]$, $(\mu_A^U(x))^q+\left(\vartheta_A^U(x)\right)^q\leq 1$ conditions.

$$\left[\pi_A^L(x),\pi_A^U(x)\right]=\left[(1-(\mu_A^U(x))^q-\left(\vartheta_A^L(x)\right)^q)^{\frac{1}{q}},(\mu_A^L(x))^q-\left(\vartheta_A^L(x)\right)^q)^{\frac{1}{q}}\right]$$

shows the hesitancy of x∈X.

$$\left[\mu_A^L(x),\mu_A^U(x)\right],\left[\vartheta_A^L(x),\vartheta_A^U(x)\right]$$

is shown as $a=\left[\mu_a^L,\mu_a^U\right],\left[\vartheta_a^L,\vartheta_a^U\right]$ to ensure the convenience.

Definition 2: Let be $a_1=\left[\mu_1^L,\mu_1^U\right],\left[\vartheta_1^L,\vartheta_1^U\right]$ and $a_2=\left[\mu_2^L,\mu_2^U\right],\left[\vartheta_2^L,\vartheta_2^U\right]$ two IVq-ROF numbers.

$$a_1\oplus a_2=\left[((\mu_1^L)^q+(\mu_2^L)^q-(\mu_1^L)^q\times(\mu_2^L)^q))^{1/q},((\mu_1^U)^q+(\mu_2^U)^q-(\mu_1^U)^q\times(\mu_2^U)^q))^{1/q}\right], \left[(\vartheta_1^L)\times(\vartheta_2^L),(\vartheta_1^U)\times(\vartheta_2^U)\right] \tag{11}$$

$$a_1\otimes a_2=\left[(\mu_1^L)\times(\mu_2^L),(\mu_1^L)\times(\mu_2^L)\right], \left[((\vartheta_1^L)^q+(\vartheta_2^L)^q-(\vartheta_1^L)^q\times(\vartheta_2^L)^q)^{1/q},((\vartheta_1^U)^q+(\vartheta_2^U)^q-(\vartheta_1^U)^q\times(\vartheta_2^U)^q)^{1/q}\right] \tag{12}$$

$$\lambda a_1 = \left[(1-(1-\left(\mu_1^L)^q\right)^\lambda)^{\frac{1}{q}}, (1-(1-\left(\mu_1^U)^q\right)^\lambda)^{\frac{1}{q}}, \left[(\vartheta_1^L)^\lambda, (\vartheta_1^U)^\lambda\right] \right], \lambda>0 \tag{13}$$

$$a_1^\lambda = \left[(\mu_1^L)^\lambda, (\mu_1^U)^\lambda\right], \left[(1-(1-\left(\vartheta_1^L)^q\right)^\lambda)^{\frac{1}{q}}, (1-(1-\left(\vartheta_1^U)^q\right)^\lambda)^{\frac{1}{q}} \right], \lambda>0 \tag{14}$$

Definition 3: If $a = \left[\mu_a^L, \mu_a^U\right], \left[\vartheta_a^L, \vartheta_a^U\right]$ is an IVq-ROF number, score function $S(a)$ and accuracy function $P(a)$ are defined below.

$$S(a) = \frac{1+(\mu_a^U)^q - (\vartheta_a^U)^q + 1 + (\mu_a^L)^q - (\vartheta_a^U)^q}{4} \tag{15}$$

$$P(a) = \frac{(\mu_a^U)^q - (\mu_a^L)^q + (\vartheta_a^U)^q - (\vartheta_a^U)^q}{4} \tag{16}$$

For 0≤ S(a)≤1, the higher the S(a) score point, the higher the IVq-ROF number will be. If S(a)=1 then a=[1,1],[0,0]; if S(a)=0 then a=[0,0],[1,1]. Likewise, for 0≤ P(a)≤1, the higher the P(a) score, the higher the IVq-ROF number will be. The score function is used to rank fuzzy numbers.

Definition 4: IVq-ROF numbers $(a_1, a_2, \ldots, a_n)$ can be combined by using geometric mean aggregation operator below. This operator is used to aggregate the opinions of the experts.

$$= \left[\prod_{j=1}^{n} (\mu_j^L)^{w_j}, \prod_{j=1}^{n} (\mu_j^U)^{w_j} \right], \left[\left(1 - \prod_{j=1}^{n} \left(1-(\vartheta_j^L)^q\right)^{W_j}\right)^{1/q}, \left(1 - \prod_{j=1}^{n} \left(1-(\vartheta_j^U)^q\right)^{W_j}\right)^{1/q} \right] \tag{17}$$

Definition 5: If a_1= $([a_1,b_1],[c_1,d_1])$ and a_2= $([a_2,b_2],[c_2,d_2])$ are two IVq-ROF numbers, the distance among them is calculated as follows:

$$d(a_1, a_2) = \frac{1}{4}\left(\left|a_1^2 - a_2^2\right| + \left|b_1^2 - b_2^b\right| + \left|c_1^2 - c_2^2\right| + \left|d_1^2 - d_2^2\right|\right) \tag{18}$$

SOLUTIONS AND RECOMMENDATIONS

In this part of the study, the application of this new proposed model in a company in the automotive sub-industry sector is shown. The specified business was established in 1988 and is one of the pioneers in its sector. In addition to Automotive, it also has over 1000 types of products in the Marine-Locomotive and Stationary Engine groups. Table 1 shows the pseudo code of the proposed method.

Table 1. The pseudo code

Inputs: The expert group, criteria, alternatives, the judgments of expert group, the value of q
-begin
-Start algorithm and data entries
for each expert, collect the criteria weights judgments
for E1 to E4
- Collect the judgment of each criteria weight by using linguistic terms - Transform to q-ROF numbers from linguistic terms End
Aggregate the judgments of experts
for each expert, collect the criteria based alternative judgments
for E1 to E4
- Collect the judgment of each criteria based alternative by using linguistic terms - Transform to q-ROF numbers from linguistic terms End
Aggregate the judgments of experts
Calculate the criteria based alternative Apply the steps of MAIRCA based on IVqROF number
Rank the alternative suppliers and find the best supplier
End

In the first stage of the application, 18 sub-criteria under 4 main criteria and 5 different alternatives (A1, A2…A5) were determined using the experience of 4 experts (E1, E2, E3, E4). The obtained data through a comprehensive literature research and the opinions of the experts are presented in Table 2. Expert 1 is the general coordinator who has over 20 years of experience in the business and has visited the suppliers determined as alternatives. Expert 2 is the purchasing manager who has been working in the business for 8 years. Expert 3 is the purchasing engineer who currently carries out purchasing activities in the business, Expert 4 is the stock manager who has been working in the industry for 15 years and extensive experience and deep technical knowledge about the product supplied.

The price criterion located under the economical criterion is the minimization type and is used to evaluate the high cost of the product to be supplied. The quality criterion is the maximization type and was utilized to handle the quality standards of supplier. Delivery time is the minimization type and was used to evaluate the length of delivery time offered by the supplier in line with its location and logistics management. The technology capacity is the maximization type and was employed to handle the pace of development and future production capabilities of supplier. The flexibility criterion is the maximization type and was utilized to handle the shortness of lead time, speed of resolving disputes, and adaptability of supplier.

Environment pollution control and environment management systems, which fall under the main environmental criterion, are maximization type criteria and were used to evaluate the abundance of the supplier's documentation on environmental management and the degree of procedures they have implemented to protect the environment from manufacturing waste. Eco-design recycling criterion is the maximization type and are used to evaluate the extent to which production waste is recycled. The green point is the maximization type and was used to evaluate how packaging waste is utilized by suppliers.

Table 2. Smart supplier selection criteria

Main criteria	Subcriteria
Economical (C1)	Price (C11)
	Quality (C12)
	Delivery time (C13)
	Technology capacity (C14)
	Flexibility (C15)
Environmental (C2)	Environment pollution control (C21)
	Environment management system (C22)
	Eco-design recycling (C23)
	Green point (C24)
Social (C3)	Occupational health and safety (C31)
	Staff development (C32)
	Local community effect (C33)
	Information disclosure (C34)
Smart (C4)	Industry 4.0 staff (C41)
	Digital customer relations (C42)
	Smart maintenance (C43)
	Industry 4.0 utilization (C44)
	Prediction ability (C45)

The occupational health and safety criterion, which is under the social main criterion, is the maximization type and is used to evaluate the occupational health and safety documents and procedures of the suppliers. The staff development criterion is the maximization type and was used to evaluate the supplier's personnel training. The local community effect is the maximization type and has been used to assess the supplier's returns to the community in which it resides. Information disclosure is the minimization type and is used to assess the supplier's rate of sharing and dissemination of existing data.

The criteria under the smart criterion are determined for smart supplier selection. Industry 4.0 staff and industry 4.0 utilization criteria are maximization type criteria and were used to evaluate the integration rate of the units and personnel within the supplier into smart technologies. The digital customer relations criterion is the maximization type and was used to evaluate the supplier's current infrastructure and speed that will enable the customer to quickly communicate their demands through the digital environment. The smart maintenance criterion is the maximization type and is used to evaluate the rate at which the supplier maintains the product it provides by using smart technologies such as artificial intelligence and the internet of things, detects its malfunction, repairs it or prevents it. The prediction ability criterion is the maximization type and was employed to handle the ability of supplier to forecast customer demand by analyzing historical customer data through smart technologies.

The weights of criteria were calculated using the interval-valued q-ROF number in line with the linguistic data collected from 4 experts. In the study, q = 3 was accepted. In the first stage, the opinions of experts were received from experts for 4 main criteria and 18 sub-criteria in line with linguistic data.

Table 3 shows the linguistic terms and their IVq-ROF number scales. These scales are used to determine the importance degrees of criteria.

Table 4 and Table 5 show the experts' opinions for the main criteria in linguistic terms and IVq-ROF numbers. Table 6 and Table 7 show the opinions of experts for the sub-criteria in linguistic terms and IVq-ROF numbers.

Table 3. Linguistic terms and fuzzy numbers

Linguistic terms	IVqROF numbers
Very high (VH)	[(0.95, 0.99), (0.20, 0.30)]
High (H)	[(0.80, 0.90), (0.30, 0.40)]
Few high (FH)	[(0.60, 0.70), (0.40, 0.50)]
Medium (M)	[(0.50, 0.60), (0.50, 0.60)]
Few low (FL)	[(0.30, 0.40), (0.70, 0.80)]
Low (L)	[(0.20, 0.30), (0.90, 0.95)]
Very low (VL)	[(0.10, 0.20), (0.96, 0.99)]

Table 4. Linguistic terms for the weights of main criteria according to each expert

	E1	E2	E3	E4
C1	VH	H	VH	FH
C2	FH	M	M	H
C3	VH	H	H	FH
C4	FH	VH	H	H

Table 5. The weights of main criteria according to each expert

	E1	E2	E3	E4
C1	[(0.95, 0.99), (0.2, 0.3)]	[(0.8, 0.9), (0.3, 0.4)]	[(0.95, 0.99), (0.2,0.3)]	[(0.6, 0.7), (0.4, 0.5)]
C2	[(0.6, 0.7), (0.4, 0.5)]	[(0.5, 0.6), (0.5, 0.6)]	[(0.5, 0.6), (0.5, 0.6)]	[(0.8, 0.9), (0.3, 0.4)]
C3	[(0.95, 0.99), (0.2, 0.3)]	[(0.8, 0.9), (0.3, 0.4)]	[(0.8, 0.9), (0.3, 0.4)]	[(0.6, 0.7), (0.4, 0.5)]
C4	[(0.6, 0.7), (0.4, 0.5)]	[(0.95, 0.99), (0.2,0.3)]	[(0.8, 0.9), (0.3, 0.4)]	[(0.8, 0.9), (0.3, 0.4)]

After determining the importance degrees of the criteria, group expert opinions were obtained by using the geometric mean aggregation operator in Eq. (17) for the main and sub-criteria. Table 8 and Table 9 show group expert opinions for the main criteria and sub-criteria.

After obtaining group opinions, the weights of criteria were calculated by multiplying the group expert opinion of the main criterion to which the group expert opinion of each sub-criterion depends, as in Equation 12. Table 10 shows the weights of criteria.

Table 6. Linguistic terms for the weights of subcriteria according to each expert

	E1	E2	E3	E4
C11	M	FH	VH	M
C12	VH	H	H	H
C13	M	H	VH	H
C14	H	VH	VH	M
C15	H	M	H	FH
C21	FH	H	M	FL
C22	M	M	FH	L
C23	H	FH	M	L
C24	FH	M	M	L
C31	H	VH	H	H
C32	H	VH	VH	H
C33	M	M	FH	FL
C34	VH	VH	VH	H
C41	FH	FH	M	FL
C42	H	VH	VH	VH
C43	FL	M	M	FH
C44	M	H	FH	L
C45	H	H	VH	FH

Table 7. The weights of subcriteria according to each expert

	E1	E2	E3	E4
C11	[(0.5, 0.6), (0.5, 0.6)]	[(0.6, 0.7), (0.4, 0.5)]	[(0.95, 0.99), (0.2, 0.3)]	[(0.5, 0.6), (0.5, 0.6)]
C12	[(0.95, 0.99), (0.2, 0.3)]	[(0.8, 0.9), (0.3, 0.4)]	[(0.8, 0.9), (0.3, 0.4)]	[(0.8, 0.9), (0.3, 0.4)]
C13	[(0.5, 0.6), (0.5, 0.6)]	[(0.8, 0.9), (0.3, 0.4)]	[(0.95, 0.99), (0.2, 0.3)]	[(0.8, 0.9), (0.3, 0.4)]
C14	[(0.8, 0.9), (0.3, 0.4)]	[(0.95,0.99), (0.2, 0.3)]	[(0.95, 0.99), (0.2, 0.3)]	[(0.5, 0.6), (0.5, 0.6)]
C15	[(0.8, 0.9), (0.3, 0.4)]	[(0.5, 0.6), (0.5, 0.6)]	[(0.8, 0.9), (0.3, 0.4)]	[(0.6, 0.7), (0.4, 0.5)]
C21	[(0.6, 0.7), (0.4, 0.5)]	[(0.8, 0.9), (0.3, 0.4)]	[(0.5, 0.6), (0.5, 0.6)]	[(0.3, 0.4), (0.7, 0.8)]
C22	[(0.5, 0.6), (0.5, 0.6)]	[(0.5, 0.6), (0.5, 0.6)]	[(0.6, 0.7), (0.4, 0.5)]	[(0.2, 0.3), (0.9, 0.95)]
C23	[(0.8, 0.9), (0.3, 0.4)]	[(0.6, 0.7), (0.4, 0.5)]	[(0.5, 0.6), (0.5, 0.6)]	[(0.2, 0.3), (0.9, 0.95)]
C24	[(0.6, 0.7), (0.4, 0.5)]	[(0.5, 0.6), (0.5, 0.6)]	[(0.5, 0.6), (0.5, 0.6)]	[(0.2, 0.3), (0.9, 0.95)]
C31	[(0.8, 0.9), (0.3, 0.4)]	[(0.95,0.99), (0.2, 0.3)]	[(0.8, 0.9), (0.3, 0.4)]	[(0.8, 0.9), (0.3, 0.4)]
C32	[(0.8, 0.9), (0.3, 0.4)]	[(0.95,0.99), (0.2, 0.3)]	[(0.95, 0.99), (0.2, 0.3)]	[(0.8, 0.9), (0.3, 0.4)]
C33	[(0.5, 0.6), (0.5, 0.6)]	[(0.5, 0.6), (0.5, 0.6)]	[(0.6, 0.7), (0.4, 0.5)]	[(0.3, 0.4), (0.7, 0.8)]
C34	[(0.95, 0.99), (0.2, 0.3)]	[(0.95,0.99), (0.2, 0.3)]	[(0.95, 0.99), (0.2, 0.3)]	[(0.8, 0.9), (0.3, 0.4)]
C41	[(0.6, 0.7), (0.4, 0.5)]	[(0.6, 0.7), (0.4, 0.5)]	[(0.5, 0.6), (0.5, 0.6)]	[(0.3, 0.4), (0.7, 0.8)]
C42	[(0.8, 0.9), (0.3, 0.4)]	[(0.95,0.99), (0.2, 0.3)]	[(0.95, 0.99), (0.2, 0.3)]	[(0.95,0.99), (0.2, 0.3)]
C43	[(0.3, 0.4), (0.7, 0.8)]	[(0.5, 0.6), (0.5, 0.6)]	[(0.5, 0.6), (0.5, 0.6)]	[(0.6, 0.7), (0.4, 0.5)]
C44	[(0.5, 0.6), (0.5, 0.6)]	[(0.8, 0.9), (0.3, 0.4)]	[(0.6, 0.7), (0.4, 0.5)]	[(0.2, 0.3), (0.9, 0.95)]
C45	[(0.8, 0.9), (0.3, 0.4)]	[(0.8, 0.9), (0.3, 0.4)]	[(0.95, 0.99), (0.2, 0.3)]	[(0.6, 0.7), (0.4, 0.5)]

Table 8. Group expert opinions for main criteria

C1	C2	C3	C4
[(0.8113, 0.8864), (0.3001,0.3950)]	[(0.5886, 0.6901), (0.4417, 0.5402)]	[(0.7772, 0.8656), (0.3165, 0.4134)]	[(0.7772, 0.8656), (0.3165, 0.4134)]

Table 9. Group expert opinions for subcriteria

	Group opinion
C11	[(0.6144, 0.7067), (0.4340, 0.5307)]
C12	[(0.8351, 0.9217), (0.2814, 0.3800)]
C13	[(0.7425, 0.8329), (0.3632,0.4576)]
C14	[(0.7751, 0.8529), (0.3511, 0.4432)]
C15	[(0.6620, 0.7637), (0.3950, 0.4926)]
C21	[(0.5180, 0.6236), (0.5306, 0.6315)]
C22	[(0.4162, 0.5244), (0.6953, 0.7795)]
C23	[(0.4681, 0.5803), (0.6828, 0.7662)]
C24	[(0.4162, 0.5244), (0.6953, 0.7795)]
C31	[(0.8351, 0.9217), (0.2814, 0.3800)]
C32	[(0.8718, 0.9439), (0.2599, 0.3575)]
C33	[(0.4606, 0.5635), (0.5558, 0.6575)]
C34	[(0.9100, 0.9667), (0.2338, 0.3314)]
C41	[(0.4821, 0.5856), (0.5401, 0.6418)]
C42	[(0.9100, 0.9667), (0.2338, 0.3314)]
C43	[(0.4606, 0.5635), (0.5558, 0.6575)]
C44	[(0.4681, 0.5803), (0.6828, 0.7662)]
C45	[(0.7772, 0.8656), (0.3165, 0.4134)]

Table 10. The weights of criteria

C11	[(0.4985, 0.6265), (0.4741, 0.5866)]
C12	[(0.6775, 0.8170), (0.3652, 0.4836)]
C13	[(0.6024, 0.7383), (0.4191, 0.5332)]
C14	[(0.6289, 0.7561), (0.4104, 0.5233)]
C15	[(0.5370, 0.6770), (0.4431, 0.5580)]
C21	[(0.3049, 0.4303), (0.6061, 0.7178)]
C22	[(0.2449, 0.3619), (0.7327, 0.8226)]
C23	[(0.2755, 0.4005), (0.7224, 0.8126)]
C24	[(0.2449, 0.3619), (0.7327, 0.8226)]
C31	[(0.6490, 0.7978), (0.3763, 0.4955)]
C32	[(0.6775, 0.8170), (0.3652, 0.4836)]
C33	[(0.3579, 0.4877), (0.5828, 0.6944)]
C34	[(0.7073, 0.8367), (0.3533, 0.4710)]
C41	[(0.3746, 0.5069), (0.5691, 0.6814)]
C42	[(0.7073, 0.8367), (0.3533, 0.4710)]
C43	[(0.3579, 0.4877), (0.5828, 0.6944)]
C44	[(0.3638, 0.5023), (0.6979, 0.7877)]
C45	[(0.6040, 0.7492), (0.3967, 0.5147)]

In the last part of the application, 5 alternatives were ranked with the IVq-ROF number based MAIRCA method. First, 4 experts were asked to evaluate the performance of the alternatives according to the criteria in line with the linguistic term scales in Table 3. Table 11 shows the importance ratings of the alternatives determined by experts in linguistic terms according to the criteria. Group opinions were obtained by using the IVq-ROF number aggregation operator in Eq. 17. Table 12 shows the group opinions of experts for criteria based alternatives.

After obtaining group opinions, the steps of the IVq-ROF numbers based MAIRCA method were applied. The group opinions in Table 12 were multiplied as in Equation 12 to obtain the weighted normalized decision matrix, which is the first stage of IVq-ROF number based MAIRCA. Table 13 shows the weighted normalized decision matrix for the IVq-ROF numbers based MAIRCA method.

Table 11. Criteria based alternatives according to experts

		C11	C12	C13	C14	C15	C21	C22	C23	C24	C31	C32	C33	C34	C41	C42	C43	C44	C45
E1	A1	FL	VH	FL	H	L	H	H	H	FH	VH	FH	FH	VH	H	M	H	H	H
	A2	FL	VH	H	H	M	H	H	H	FH	VH	H	FH	VH	H	FH	H	H	H
	A3	L	FH	VH	M	FH	M	M	FH	M	FH	FH	M	FH	M	H	L	M	H
	A4	FH	H	FL	H	M	M	M	M	M	H	H	M	H	FH	FH	FH	M	L
	A5	H	FH	L	FH	FH	FL	FL	M	L	M	M	M	H	M	FH	L	FL	L
E2	A1	VL	FH	L	VH	FL	VH	H	VH	H	VH	FH	H	VH	H	FL	H	VH	FH
	A2	M	H	VH	VH	L	VH	H	VH	H	VH	VH	H	VH	VH	FH	H	VH	VH
	A3	L	M	H	M	H	M	FH	FH	M	FH	FH	H	M	FH	H	M	M	VH
	A4	H	H	M	H	M	M	L	M	M	M	FH	FH	H	FH	VH	M	FH	L
	A5	VH	H	M	FH	M	FL	FL	L	FL	M	M	FH	H	FH	H	L	M	L
E3	A1	FL	FH	M	H	L	VH	H	VH	H	VH	FH	FH	VH	VH	L	H	H	FH
	A2	M	VH	H	H	FL	VH	H	VH	H	VH	VH	FH	H	H	FH	H	H	H
	A3	L	M	FH	FL	H	FH	M	FH	FH	H	M	FL	FH	FH	H	M	L	H
	A4	H	FH	M	H	M	M	FL	FL	M	H	H	M	FH	FH	H	M	FH	L
	A5	VH	FH	FL	FH	FH	L	L	FL	M	M	M	M	FH	M	FH	FL	L	VL
E4	A1	L	FH	L	FH	L	H	H	H	H	VH	M	FH	VH	H	FL	FH	H	L
	A2	FL	H	FH	H	L	VH	H	H	H	VH	H	FH	VH	H	M	FH	H	FH
	A3	L	FL	FH	FL	FL	M	M	M	FH	FH	FL	FH	M	M	FH	L	M	FH
	A4	FH	FH	M	H	M	L	L	M	L	FH	M	FH	FH	FH	H	FH	M	VL
	A5	VH	M	VL	FL	M	FL	L	FL	L	FH	M	M	FH	FH	FH	VL	M	VL

Since the decision maker is equidistant from each of the alternatives, the priorities of the alternatives are all equal.

$$PA_i = \frac{1}{m}, m = 5; \; P_{Ai} = \frac{1}{5}, P_{Ai} = 0,2$$

The matrix of theoretical ponder is formed by multiplying the priorities of the alternatives (PA_i) and the weights of criteria (w_j) as in Equation 13. Table 14 shows the matrix of theoretical ponder.

The matrix of real ponder was formed by making use of the matrix of theoretical ponder and the decision matrix. Table 15 shows the matrix of real ponder obtained using Eq. (12) and Eq. (18). While forming the matrix of real ponder, Eq. (5) and Eq. (6) were used for maximization and minimization type criteria, respectively.

The total gap matrix was obtained by subtracting the elements of the matrix of real ponder from the elements of the matrix of theoretical ponder as in Eq. (7). Additionally, Eq. (18) was used for distance calculation. Table 16 shows the total gap matrix.

Table 12. Group opinion for criteria based alternatives

	A1	A2	A3	A4	A5
C11	[(0.2060,0.3130), (0.8703, 0.9367)]	[(0.3873, 0.4899), (0.6230, 0.7252)]	[(0.2000, 0.3000), (0.9000, 0.9500)]	[(0.6928, 0.7937), (0.3575,0.4563)]	[(0.9100, 0.9667), (0.2338, 0.3314)]
C12	[(0.6730, 0.7634), (0.3691, 0.4664)]	[(0.8718, 0.9439), (0.2599, 0.3575)]	[(0.4606, 0.5635), (0.5558,0.6575)]	[(0.6928, 0.7937), (0.3575, 0.4563)]	[(0.6160, 0.7172), (0.4134, 0.5120)]
C13	[(0.2783, 0.3834), (0.8177, 0.8892)]	[(0.7772, 0.8656), (0.3165, 0.4134)]	[(0.7232, 0.8129), (0.3450, 0.4417)]	[(0.4401, 0.5422), (0.5703, 0.6721)]	[(0.2340, 0.3464), (0.8590, 0.9281)]
C14	[(0.7772, 0.8656), (0.3165, 0.4134)]	[(0.8351, 0.9217), (0.2814, 0.3800)]	[(0.3873, 0.4899), (0.6230, 0.7252)]	[(0.8000, 0.9000), (0.3000, 0.4000)]	[(0.5045, 0.6086), (0.5233, 0.6247)]
C15	[(0.2213, 0.3224), (0.8715, 0.9306)]	[(0.2783, 0.3834), (0.8177, 0.8892)]	[(0.5826, 0.6901), (0.5020, 0.6018)]	[(0.5000, 0.6000), (0.5000, 0.6000)]	[(0.5477, 0.6481), (0.4563, 0.5559)]
C21	[(0.8718, 0.9439), (0.2599, 0.3575)]	[(0.9100, 0.9667), (0.2338, 0.3314)]	[(0.5233, 0.6236), (0.4793, 0.5791)]	[(0.3976, 0.5045), (0.7029, 0.7873)]	[(0.2711, 0.3722), (0.7794, 0.8623)]
C22	[(0.8000, 0.9000), (0.3000, 0.4000)]	[(0.8000, 0.9000), (0.3000, 0.4000)]	[(0.5233, 0.6236), (0.4793, 0.5791)]	[(0.2783, 0.3834), (0.8177, 0.8892)]	[(0.2449, 0.3464), (0.8330, 0.9029)]
C23	[(0.8718, 0.9439), (0.2599, 0.3575)]	[(0.8718, 0.9439), (0.2599, 0.3575)]	[(0.5733, 0.6735), (0.4302, 0.5298)]	[(0.4401, 0.5422), (0.5703, 0.6721)]	[(0.3080, 0.4120), (0.7573, 0.8416)]
C24	[(0.7445, 0.8452), (0.3314, 0.4302)]	[(0.7445, 0.8452), (0.3314, 0.4302)]	[(0.5477, 0.6481), (0.4563, 0.5559)]	[(0.3976, 0.5045), (0.7029, 0.7873)]	[(0.2783, 0.3834), (0.8177, 0.8892)]
C31	[(0.9500, 0.9900), (0.2000, 0.3000)]	[(0.9500, 0.9900), (0.2000, 0.3000)]	[(0.6447, 0.7454), (0.3800, 0.4793)]	[(0.6620, 0.7637), (0.3950, 0.4926)]	[(0.5233, 0.6236), (0.4793, 0.5791)]
C32	[(0.5733, 0.6735), (0.4302, 0.5298)]	[(0.8718, 0.9439), (0.2599, 0.3575)]	[(0.4821, 0.5856), (0.5401, 0.6418)]	[(0.6620, 0.7637), (0.3950, 0.4926)]	[(0.5000, 0.6000), (0.5000, 0.6000)]
C33	[(0.6447, 0.7454), (0.3800, 0.4793)]	[(0.6447, 0.7454), (0.3800, 0.4793)]	[(0.5180, 0.6236), (0.5306, 0.6315)]	[(0.5477, 0.6481), (0.4563, 0.5559)]	[(0.5233, 0.6236), (0.4793, 0.5791)]
C34	[(0.9500, 0.9900), (0.2000, 0.3000)]	[(0.9100, 0.9667), (0.2338, 0.3314)]	[(0.5477, 0.6481), (0.4563, 0.5559)]	[(0.6928, 0.7937), (0.3575, 0.4563)]	[(0.6928, 0.7937), (0.3575, 0.4563)]
C41	[(0.8351, 0.9217), (0.2814, 0.3800)]	[(0.8351, 0.9217), (0.2814, 0.3800)]	[(0.5477, 0.6481), (0.4563, 0.5559)]	[(0.6000, 0.7000), (0.4000, 0.5000)]	[(0.5477, 0.6481), (0.4563, 0.5559)]
C42	[(0.3080, 0.4120), (0.7573, 0.8416)]	[(0.5733, 0.6735), (0.4302, 0.5298)]	[(0.7445, 0.8452), (0.3314, 0.4302)]	[(0.7772, 0.8656), (0.3165, 0.4134)]	[(0.6447, 0.7454), (0.3800, 0.4793)]
C43	[(0.7445, 0.8452), (0.3314, 0.4302)]	[(0.7445, 0.8452), (0.3314, 0.4302)]	[(0.3162, 0.4243), (0.8005, 0.8731)]	[(0.5477, 0.6481), (0.4563, 0.5559)]	[(0.1861, 0.2913), (0.8991, 0.9543]
C44	[(0.8351, 0.9217), (0.2814, 0.3800)]	[(0.8351, 0.9217), (0.2814, 0.3800)]	[(0.3976, 0.5045), (0.7029, 0.7873)]	[(0.5477, 0.6481), (0.4563, 0.5559)]	[(0.3500, 0.4559), (0.7321, 0.8169)]
C45	[(0.4899, 0.6031), (0.6744, 0.7575)]	[(0.7772, 0.8656), (0.3165, 0.4134)]	[(0.7772, 0.8656), (0.3165, 0.4134)]	[(0.1682, 0.2711), (0.9210, 0.9668)]	[(0.1414, 0.2449), (0.9372, 0.9778)]

Table 13. The weighted normalized decision matrix

	A1	A2	A3	A4	A5
C11	[(0.1027,0.1961), (0.8860, 0.9501)]	[(0.1931, 0.3069), (0.6858 0.7970)]	[(0.0997, 0.1879), (0.9117, 0.9605)]	[(0.3453, 0.4973), (0.5282, 0.6524)]	[(0.4536, 0.6056), (0.4905, 0.6135)]
C12	[(0.4560, 0.6237), (0.4588, 0.5878)]	[(0.5906, 0.7712), (0.4029, 0.5356]	[(0.3120, 0.4604), (0.5963 0.7148)]	[(0.4694, 0.6485), (0.4517, 0.5822)]	[(0.4174, 0.5860), (0.4876,0.6146)]
C13	[(0.1677, 0.2830), (0.8340, 0.9078)]	[(0.4682, 0.6390), (0.4688, 0.5958)]	[(0.4357, 0.6001), (0.4815, 0.6079)]	[(0.2651, 0.4003), (0.6261, 0.7424)]	[(0.1410, 0.2557), (0.8710, 0.9397)]
C14	[(0.4887, 0.6544), (0.4621, 0.5885)]	[(0.5252, 0.6969), (0.4479, 0.5752)]	[(0.2436, 0.3704), (0.5651, 0.7775)]	[(0.5031, 0.6805), (0.4551, 0.5830)]	[(0.3173, 0.4602), (0.5872, 0.7062)]
C15	[(0.1189, 0.2182), (0.8842, 0.9434)]	[(0.1495, 0.2595), (0.8369, 0.9104)]	[(0.3129, 0.4672), (0.5872, 0.7073)]	[(0.2685, 0.4062), (0.5859, 0.7062)]	[(0.2941, 0.4387), (0.5580, 0.6809)]
C21	[(0.2658, 0.4062), (0.6183, 0.7359)]	[(0.2775, 0.4160), (0.6150, 0.7323)]	[(0.1595, 0.2683), (0.5756, 0.7895)]	[(0.1212, 0.2171), (0.7898, 0.8782)]	[(0.0826, 0.1602), (0.8391, 0.9181)]
C22	[(0.1960, 0.3257), (0.7428, 0.8364)]	[(0.1960, 0.3257), (0.7428, 0.8364)]	[(0.1282, 0.2256), (0.7721, 0.8630)]	[(0.0682, 0.1387), (0.8984, 0.9540)]	[(0.0600, 0.1254), (0.9061, 0.9594)]
C23	[(0.2402,0.3780), (0.7294, 0.8232)]	[(0.2402, 0.3780), (0.7294,0.8232)]	[(0.1579, 0.2697), (0.7528, 0.8460)]	[(0.1212, 0.2171), (0.7898, 0.8782)]	[(0.0849, 0.1650), (0.8652, 0.9332)]
C24	[(0.1824, 0.3058), (0.7462, 0.8397)]	[(0.1824, 0.3058), (0.7462, 0.8397)]	[(0.1342, 0.2345), (0.7669, 0.8586)]	[(0.0974, 0.1826), (0.8453, 0.9178)]	[(0.0682, 0.1387), (0.8984, 0.9540)]
C31	[(0.6166, 0.7898), (0.3934, 0.5258)]	[(0.6166, 0.7898), (0.3934, 0.5258)]	[(0.4185, 0.5947), (0.4721, 0.6022)]	[(0.4296, 0.6093), (0.4815, 0.6097)]	[(0.3396, 0.4975), (0.5401, 0.6636)]
C32	[(0.3884, 0.5503), (0.4993, 0.6257)]	[(0.5906, 0.7712), (0.4029, 0.5356)]	[(0.3266, 0.4785), (0.5834, 0.7031)]	[(0.4485, 0.6240), (0.4752, 0.6029)]	[(0.3388,0.4902), (0.5514, 0.6729)]
C33	[(0.2308,0.3635), (0.6231, 0.7417)]	[(0.2308, 0.3635), (0.6231, 0.7417)]	[(0.1854, 0.3041), (0.6824, 0.7949)]	[(0.1961, 0.3161), (0.6496, 0.7658)]	[(0.1873, 0.3041), (0.6590, 0.7742)]
C34	[(0.6719, 0.8284), (0.3726, 0.5048)]	[(0.6436, 0.8089), (0.3833, 0.5156)]	[(0.3874, 0.5423), (0.5129, 0.6368)]	[(0.4900, 0.6641), (0.4444, 0.5745)]	[(0.4900, 0.6641), (0.4444, 0.5745)]
C41	[(0.3129, 0.4672), (0.5872, 0.7073)]	[(0.3129, 0.4672), (0.5872, 0.7073)]	[(0.2052, 0.3285), (0.6397, 0.7570)]	[(0.2248, 0.3548), (0.6184, 0.7379)]	[(0.2052, 0.3285), (0.6397, 0.7570)]
C42	[(0.2178, 0.3447), (0.7716, 0.8610)]	[(0.4054, 0.5636), (0.4935, 0.6194)]	[(0.5265, 0.7072), (0.4289, 0.5602)]	[(0.5497, 0.7243), (0.4206, 0.5515)]	[(0.4560 0.6237), (0.4588, 0.5878)]
C43	[(0.2665, 0.4122), (0.6101, 0.7292)]	[(0.2665, 0.4122), (0.6101, 0.7292)]	[(0.1132, 0.2069), (0.8478, 0.9196)]	[(0.1961, 0.3161), (0.6496, 0.7658)]	[(0.0666, 0.1421), (0.9209, 0.9701)]
C44	[(0.3038, 0.4630), (0.7078, 0.8025)]	[(0.3038, 0.4630), (0.7078, 0.8025)]	[(0.1446, 0.2534), (0.8287, 0.9038)]	[(0.1992, 0.3255), (0.7384, 0.8323)]	[(0.1273, 0.2290), (0.8429, 0.9156)]
C45	[(0.2959, 0.4519), (0.7047, 0.7998)]	[(0.4694, 0.6485), (0.4517, 0.5822)]	[(0.4694, 0.6485), (0.4517, 0.5822)]	[(0.1016, 0.2031), (0.9263, 0.9715)]	[(0.0854, 0.1835), (0.9414, 0.9809)]

Table 14. The matrix of theoretical ponder

	A1	A2	A3	A4	A5
C11	[(0.2966, 0.3800), (0.8613, 0,8988)]	[(0.2966, 0.3800), (0.8613, 0,8988)]	[(0.2966, 0.3800), (0.8613, 0,8988)]	[(0.2966, 0.3800), (0.8613, 0,8988)]	[(0.2966, 0.3800), (0.8613, 0,8988)]
C12	[(0.4156, 0.5264), (0.8175, 0.8648)]	[(0.4156, 0.5264), (0.8175, 0.8648)]	[(0.4156, 0.5264), (0.8175, 0.8648)]	[(0.4156, 0.5264), (0.8175, 0.8648)]	[(0.4156, 0.5264), (0.8175, 0.8648)]
C13	[(0.3638, 0.4608), (0.8404, 0.8818)]	[(0.3638, 0.4608), (0.8404, 0.8818)]	[(0.3638, 0.4608), (0.8404, 0.8818)]	[(0.3638, 0.4608), (0.8404, 0.8818)]	[(0.3638, 0.4608), (0.8404, 0.8818)]
C14	[(0.3816, 0.4748), (0.8368, 0.8785)]	[(0.3816, 0.4748), (0.8368, 0.8785)]	[(0.3816, 0.4748), (0.8368, 0.8785)]	[(0.3816, 0.4748), (0.8368, 0.8785)]	[(0.3816, 0.4748), (0.8368, 0.8785)]
C15	[(0.3211, 0.4152), (0.8498, 0.8899)]	[(0.3211, 0.4152), (0.8498, 0.8899)]	[(0.3211, 0.4152), (0.8498, 0.8899)]	[(0.3211, 0.4152), (0.8498, 0.8899)]	[(0.3211, 0.4152), (0.8498, 0.8899)]
C21	[(0.1790, 0.2544), (0.9047, 0.9358)]	[(0.1790, 0.2544), (0.9047, 0.9358)]	[(0.1790, 0.2544), (0.9047, 0.9358)]	[(0.1790, 0.2544), (0.9047, 0.9358)]	[(0.1790, 0.2544), (0.9047, 0.9358)]
C22	[(0.1435, 0.2130), (0.9397, 0.9617)]	[(0.1435, 0.2130), (0.9397, 0.9617)]	[(0.1435, 0.2130), (0.9397, 0.9617)]	[(0.1435, 0.2130), (0.9397, 0.9617)]	[(0.1435, 0.2130), (0.9397, 0.9617)]
C23	[(0.1616, 0.2363), (0.9370, 0.9594)]	[(0.1616, 0.2363), (0.9370, 0.9594)]	[(0.1616, 0.2363), (0.9370, 0.9594)]	[(0.1616, 0.2363), (0.9370, 0.9594)]	[(0.1616, 0.2363), (0.9370, 0.9594)]
C24	[(0.1435, 0.2130), (0.9397, 0.9617)]	[(0.1435, 0.2130), (0.9397, 0.9617)]	[(0.1435, 0.2130), (0.9397, 0.9617)]	[(0.1435, 0.2130), (0.9397, 0.9617)]	[(0.1435, 0.2130), (0.9397, 0.9617)]
C31	[(0.3955, 0.5094), (0.8225, 0.8690)]	[(0.3955, 0.5094), (0.8225, 0.8690)]	[(0.3955, 0.5094), (0.8225, 0.8690)]	[(0.3955, 0.5094), (0.8225, 0.8690)]	[(0.3955, 0.5094), (0.8225, 0.8690)]
C32	[(0.4156, 0.5264), (0.8175, 0.8648)]	[(0.4156, 0.5264), (0.8175, 0.8648)]	[(0.4156, 0.5264), (0.8175, 0.8648)]	[(0.4156, 0.5264), (0.8175, 0.8648)]	[(0.4156, 0.5264), (0.8175, 0.8648)]
C33	[(0.2106, 0.2899), (0.8976, 0.9297)]	[(0.2106, 0.2899), (0.8976, 0.9297)]	[(0.2106, 0.2899), (0.8976, 0.9297)]	[(0.2106, 0.2899), (0.8976, 0.9297)]	[(0.2106, 0.2899), (0.8976, 0.9297)]
C34	[(0.4373, 0.5447), (0.8121, 0.8602)]	[(0.4373, 0.5447), (0.8121, 0.8602)]	[(0.4373, 0.5447), (0.8121, 0.8602)]	[(0.4373, 0.5447), (0.8121, 0.8602)]	[(0.4373, 0.5447), (0.8121, 0.8602)]
C41	[(0.2207, 0.3019), (0.8934, 0.9261)]	[(0.2207, 0.3019), (0.8934, 0.9261)]	[(0.2207, 0.3019), (0.8934, 0.9261)]	[(0.2207, 0.3019), (0.8934, 0.9261)]	[(0.2207, 0.3019), (0.8934, 0.9261)]
C42	[(0.4373, 0.5447), (0.8121, 0.8602)]	[(0.4373, 0.5447), (0.8121, 0.8602)]	[(0.4373, 0.5447), (0.8121, 0.8602)]	[(0.4373, 0.5447), (0.8121, 0.8602)]	[(0.4373, 0.5447), (0.8121, 0.8602)]
C43	[(0.2106, 0.2899), (0.8976, 0.9297)]	[(0.2106, 0.2899), (0.8976, 0.9297)]	[(0.2106, 0.2899), (0.8976, 0.9297)]	[(0.2106, 0.2899), (0.8976, 0.9297)]	[(0.2106, 0.2899), (0.8976, 0.9297)]
C44	[(0.2141, 0.2990), (0.9306, 0.9534)]	[(0.2141, 0.2990), (0.9306, 0.9534)]	[(0.2141, 0.2990), (0.9306, 0.9534)]	[(0.2141, 0.2990), (0.9306, 0.9534)]	[(0.2141, 0.2990), (0.9306, 0.9534)]
C45	[(0.3648, 0.4694), (0.8312, 0.8756)]	[(0.3648, 0.4694), (0.8312, 0.8756)]	[(0.3648, 0.4694), (0.8312, 0.8756)]	[(0.3648, 0.4694), (0.8312, 0.8756)]	[(0.3648, 0.4694), (0.8312, 0.8756)]

Table 15. The matrix of real ponder

	A1	A2	A3	A4	A5
C11	[(0.2925, 0,3748), (0,8668, 0,9029)]	[(0.2448, 0.3143), (0.9200, 0.9421)]	[(0.2966, 0.3800), (0.8613, 0.8988)]	[(0.1670, 0.2148), (0.9740, 0.9813)]	[(0, 0), (1, 1)]
C12	[(0.3462, 0.4410), (0.8917, 0.9207)]	[(0.4156, 0.5264), (0.8175, 0.8648)]	[(0, 0), (1, 1)]	[(0.3566, 0.4539), (0.8821, 0.9135)]	[(0.3175, 0.4052), (0.9158, 0.9385)
C13	[(0.3528, 0.4472), (0.8536, 0.8919)]	[(0, 0), (1, 1)]	[(0.1473, 0.1881), (0.9888, 0.9919)]	[(0.2852, 0.3629), (0.9206, 0.9419)]	[(0.3638, 0.4608), (0.8404, 0.8818)]
C14	[(0.3670, 0.4571), (0.8539, 0.8915)]	[(0.3816, 0.4748), (0.8368, 0.8785)]	[(0, 0), (1, 1)]	[(0.3745, 0.4662), (0.8453, 0.8849)]	[(0.2559, 0.3204), (0.9487, 0.9624)]
C15	[(0, 0), (1, 1)]	[(0.1726, 0.2245), (0.9754, 0.9823)]	[(0.3179, 0.4113), (0.8539, 0.8930)]	[(0.3104, 0.4017), (0.8634, 0.9001)]	[(0.3211, 0.4152), (0.8498, 0.8899)]
C21	[(0.1773, 0.2521), (0.9073, 0.9376)]	[(0.1790, 0.2544), (0.9047, 0.9358)]	[(0.1532, 0.2179), (0.9392, 0.9593)]	[(0.1070, 0.1524), (0.9789, 0.9860)]	[(0, 0), (1, 1)]
C22	[(0.1435, 0.2130), (0.9397, 0.9617)]	[(0.1435, 0.2130), (0.9397, 0.9617)]	[(0.1292, 0.1918), (0.9557, 0.9719)]	[(0.0518, 0.0769), (0.9971, 0.9982)]	[(0, 0), (1, 1)]
C23	[(0.1616, 0.2363), (0.9370, 0.9594)]	[(0.1616, 0.2363), (0.9370, 0.9594)]	[(0.1431, 0.2094), (0.9558, 0.9716)]	[(0.1227, 0.1796), (0.9720, 0.9820)]	[(0, 0), (1, 1)]
C24	[(0.1435, 0.2130), (0.9397, 0.9617)]	[(0.1435, 0.2130), (0.9397, 0.9617)]	[(0.1327, 0.1970), (0.9520, 0.9696)]	[(0.0983, 0.1460), (0.9802, 0.9875)]	[(0, 0), (1, 1)]
C31	[(0.3955, 0.5094), (0.8225, 0.8690)]	[(0.3955, 0.5094), (0.8225, 0.8690)]	[(0.2757, 0.3581), (0.9372, 0.9545)]	[(0.2783, 0.3615), (0.9355, 0.9532)]	[(0, 0), (1, 1)]
C32	[(0.2849, 0.3642), (0.9387, 0.9554)]	[(0.4156, 0.5264), (0.8175, 0.8648)]	[(0, 0), (1, 1)]	[(0.3327, 0.4242), (0.9035, 0.9295)]	[(0.1938, 0.2485), (0.9804, 0.9859)
C33	[(0.2106, 0.2899), (0.8976, 0.9297)]	[(0.2106, 0.2899), (0.8976, 0.9297)]	[(0, 0), (1, 1)]	[(0.1630, 0.2246), (0.9513, 0.9668)]	[(0.1406, 0.1939), (0.9685, 0.9786)]
C34	[(0, 0), (1, 1)]	[(0.1993, 0.2516), (0.9812, 0.9864)]	[(0.4373, 0.5447), (0.8121, 0.8602)]	[(0.3728, 0.4670), (0.8809, 0.9123)]	[(0.3728, 0.4670), (0.8809, 0.9123)]
C41	[(0.2207, 0.3019), (0.8934, 0.9261)]	[(0.2207, 0.3019), (0.8934, 0.9261)]	[(0, 0), (1, 1)]	[(0.1427, 0.1957), (0.9701, 0.9795)]	[(0, 0), (1, 1)]
C42	[(0, 0), (1, 1)]	[(0.3856, 0.4826), (0.8687, 0.9032)]	[(0.4311, 0.5374), (0.8195, 0.8659)]	[(0.4373, 0.5447), (0.8121, 0.8602)]	[(0.4070, 0.5084), (0.8468, 0.8866)]
C43	[(0.2106, 0.2899), (0.8976, 0.9297)]	[(0.2106, 0.2899), (0.8976, 0.9297)]	[(0.1296, 0.1787), (0.9752, 0.9832)]	[(0.1966, 0.2707), (0.9160, 0.9425)]	[(0, 0), (1, 1)]
C44	[(0.2141, 0.2990), (0.9306, 0.9534)]	[(0.2141, 0.2990), (0.9306, 0.9534)]	[(0.0982, 0.1375), (0.9931, 0.9954)]	[(0.1812, 0.2533), (0.9575, 0.9716)]	[(0, 0), (1, 1)]
C45	[(0.2918, 0.3772), (0.9108, 0.9351)]	[(0.3648, 0.4694), (0.8312, 0.8756)]	[(0.3648, 0.4694), (0.8312, 0.8756)]	[(0.1143, 0.1485), (0.9945, 0.9960)]	[(0, 0), (1, 1)]

Table 16. The total gap matrix

	C11	C12	C13	C14	C15	C21	C22	C23	C24
A1	0,0058	0,0906	0,0151	0,0199	0,1904	0,0024	0	0	0
A2	0,0645	0	0,2152	0	0,1494	0	0	0	0
A3	0	0,2584	0,1913	0,2247	0,0044	0,0335	0,0156	0,0192	0,0121
A4	0,1301	0,0782	0,0956	0,0097	0,0149	0,0745	0,06	0,0363	0,0408
A5	0,1706	0,122	0	0,1393	0	0,1006	0,0645	0,0709	0,0645
	C31	**C32**	**C33**	**C34**	**C41**	**C42**	**C43**	**C44**	**C45**
A1	0	0,1535	0	0,2721	0	0,0535	0	0	0,0352
A2	0	0	0	0,2303	0	0,041	0	0	0
A3	0,1424	0,2584	0,1146	0	0,121	0,0067	0,0214	0,031	0
A4	0,14	0,1058	0,0553	0,0849	0,0815	0	0,013	0,0213	0,0141
A5	0,2461	0,2169	0,0742	0,0849	0,121	0,028	0,0132	0,0311	0,0114

In the total gap matrix, the criterion ratings of each alternative were added as in Eq. (9), the weight degrees of the alternatives were calculated. The alternative with the smallest value among the obtained values was accepted as the best alternative. Table 17 shows the ranking of alternatives. In the ranking obtained by IVqROF numbers based MAIRCA, the most suitable smart supplier alternative for the business was found to be A2. A2 alternative is followed by A1-A4-A3 and A5 alternatives, respectively. A sensitivity analysis is performed on the impact of varying q values and the result is shown in Figure 1. Different q values present the same ranking for suppliers. Figure 2 presents a comparison analysis. The proposed method is compared with classic MAIRCA, VIKOR and TOPSIS methods. The results of the proposed method and classic MAIRCA are the same. The results of the proposed method, classic VIKOR and TOPSIS are the same except A3 and A5. This shows that the proposed method is useful for supplier selection problem.

Figure 1. Sensitivity analysis

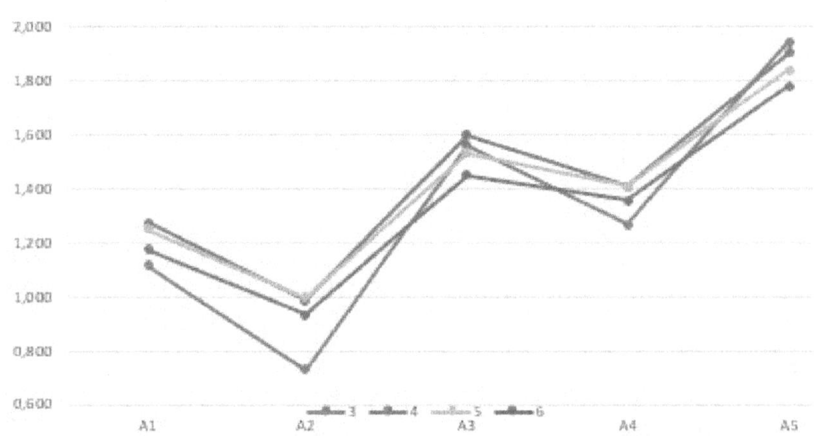

Figure 2. Comparison analysis

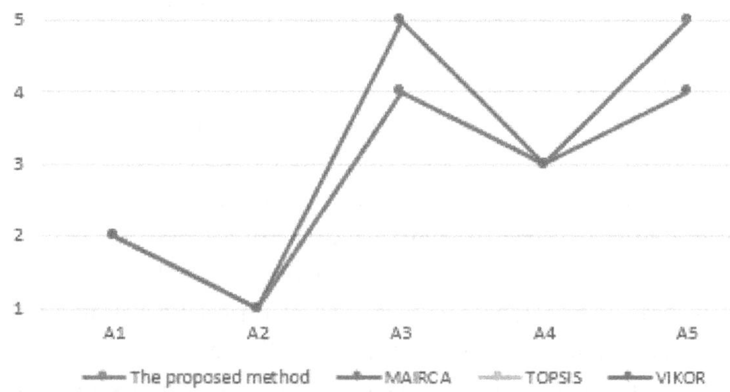

Table 17. The rankings of alternatives

	Total	Ranking
A1	1,1149	2
A2	0,7287	1
A3	1,5636	4
A4	1,2675	3
A5	1,9461	5

FUTURE RESEARCH DIRECTIONS

The limitation of this chapter is to define the weights of the criteria by using an aggregation operator. It aims to use a pairwise comparison matrix among criteria in future studies. This proposed new MCDM (IVqROF numbers based MAIRCA) method can be used in all complex decision making problems involving conflicting and uncertain criteria, except for supplier selection or smart supplier selection problems. There are many MCDM methods in the literature and new methods continue to be added. In future studies, research can be conducted using interval-valued q-ROF number integration of different decision-making methods. Interval valued q-ROF numbers can be developed with new extensions and used as a basis for both MAIRCA method and other MCDM methods in the literature.

CONCLUSION

The concept of supply chain is an indication that no business has complete control over the production and delivery of the products it provides to the customer. The participation of other businesses involved throughout all processes and the interactions between different parties are also important. In this period where increasingly strong competition prevails under the influence of changing environmental and social factors in recent years and businesses strive to provide competitive advantage, a strong supply chain is considered the key to companies' continued success. For this reason, in order to build strong supply chains, businesses examine the links that make up the supply chain and make efforts to improve, strengthen and make each of them sustainable. In this improvement process, they include their suppliers in the process with performance scoring reports and development programs.

Supply chain management has become very important in real life businesses and literature due to increasing globalization. Businesses aim to establish strategic collaborations with the most ideal suppliers in order to increase their competitiveness by building efficient supply chains. Choosing the right supplier will significantly reduce the total cost, as the supplier selection decisions are very effective in the profitability of the business and directly affect the delivery times of the enterprises. However, this process is complex and difficult because supplier selection may involve multiple conflicting and unclear criteria.

In its simplest form, a decision problem can be thought of as making a choice among options according to a goal or criterion. Decision makers need accurate and reliable predictions for the decisions they will make. Taking scientific criteria into consideration while doing this enables them to make better decisions. Classical MCDM techniques are often not sufficient to evaluate these unclear and contradictory criteria.

In this study, MAIRCA method based on interval valued q-ROF numbers, which is not included in the literature, is proposed to evaluate conflicting and uncertain criteria. This new proposal was applied on the smart supplier selection problem in an automotive supplier industry company. In addition to the traditional criteria, smart criteria have been added with the detailed literature study while determining the criteria for smart supplier selection. In the study, interval valued q-ROF numbers were used to reflect the uncertainties in the statements of the experts to the problem. In order to investigate the weights of the criteria constituting the concept of smart supplier selection for alternatives, the linguistic expression definitions of the experts were transformed into fuzzy numerical expressions by using IVqROF numbers based MAIRCA.

REFERENCES

Abdollahzadeh, S., Teymourlu, M., & Amini, A. (2023). Selection of suppliers using FBWM-FGRA hybrid approach in hospital food supply chain. *Journal of Intelligent & Fuzzy Systems*, *45*(6), 9655–9668. doi:10.3233/JIFS-231845

Alavi, B., Tavana, M., & Mina, H. (2021). A dynamic decision support system for sustainable supplier selection in circular economy. *Sustainable Production and Consumption*, *27*, 905–920. doi:10.1016/j.spc.2021.02.015

Ali, G., Afzal, M., Asif, M., & Shazad, A. (2022). Attribute reduction approaches under interval-valued q-rung orthopair fuzzy sof framework. *Applied Intelligence*, *52*(8), 8975–9000. doi:10.1007/s10489-021-02853-x

Atanassov, K. T. (1986). Intuitionistic fuzzy sets. *Fuzzy Sets and Systems*, *20*(1), 87–96. doi:10.1016/S0165-0114(86)80034-3

Bai, C., Kusi-Sarpong, S., Ahmadi, H. B., & Sarkis, J. (2019). Social sustainable supplier evaluation and selection: A group decision-support approach. *International Journal of Production Research*, *57*(22), 7046–7067. doi:10.1080/00207543.2019.1574042

Bisht, G., & Pal, A. (2024). A q-rung orthopair fuzzy decision-making framework considering experts trust relationships and psychological behavior: An application to green supplier selection. *Decision Science Letters*, *13*(1), 67–82. doi:10.5267/j.dsl.2023.12.002

Chen, Z., Ming, X., Zhou, T., & Chang, Y. (2020). Sustainable supplier selection for smart supply chain considering internal and external uncertainty: An integrated rough-fuzzy approach. *Applied Soft Computing*, *87*, 106004. doi:10.1016/j.asoc.2019.106004

Efe, B., & Efe, L. (2023a). Hastaların Acil Servis Seçimi İçin Q Seviyeli Bulanık MAIRCA Yöntemi Önerisi. *Necmettin Erbakan Üniversitesi Fen ve Mühendislik Bilimleri Dergisi*, *5*(2), 288–298.

Efe, B., & Efe, Ö. F. (2023b). Fine-Kinney method based on fuzzy logic for natural gas pipeline project risk assessment. *Soft Computing*, *27*(22), 16465–16482. doi:10.1007/s00500-023-09108-6

Efe, Ö. F., & Efe, B. (2022). A decision support model based on q-rung orthopair fuzzy number for glove design application. *Neural Computing & Applications*, *34*(15), 12695–12708. doi:10.1007/s00521-022-07118-3

Galo, N. R., Calache, L. D. D. R., & Carpinetti, L. C. R. (2018). A group decision approach for supplier categorization based on hesitant fuzzy and ELECTRE TRI. *International Journal of Production Economics*, *202*, 182–196. doi:10.1016/j.ijpe.2018.05.023

Ghadimi, P., Wang, C., Lim, M. K., & Heavey, C. (2019). Intelligent sustainable supplier selection using multiagent technology: Theory and application for Industry 4.0 supply chains. *Computers & Industrial Engineering*, *127*, 588–600. doi:10.1016/j.cie.2018.10.050

Guarnieri, P., & Trojan, F. (2019). Decision making on supplier selection based on social, ethical, andenvironmental criteria: A study in the textile industry. *Resources, Conservation and Recycling*, *141*, 347–361. doi:10.1016/j.resconrec.2018.10.023

Hasan, M. M., Jiang, D., Ullah, A. M. M. S., & Noor-E-Alam, M. (2020). Resilient supplier selection in logistics 4.0 with heterogeneous information. *Expert Systems with Applications*, *139*, 139. doi:10.1016/j.eswa.2019.07.016

Hosseini, S., & Khaled, A. (2019). A hybrid ensemble and AHP approach for resilient supplier selection. *Journal of Intelligent Manufacturing*, *30*(4), 207–228. doi:10.1007/s10845-016-1241-y

Joshi, B. P., Singh, A., Bhatt, P. K., & Vaisla, K. S. (2018). Interval valued q-rung orthopair fuzzy sets and their properties. *Journal of Intelligent & Fuzzy Systems*, *35*(5), 5225–5230. doi:10.3233/JIFS-169806

Ju, Y. B., Luo, C., Ma, J., Gao, H. X., Gonzalez, E., & Wang, A. H. (2019). Some interval-valued q-rung orthopair weighted averaging operators and their applications to multipleattribute decision making. *International Journal of Intelligent Systems*, *34*(10), 2584–2606. doi:10.1002/int.22163

Kaya, R., & Yet, B. (2019). Building Bayesian networks based on DEMATEL for multiple criteria decision problems: A supplier selection case study. *Expert Systems with Applications*, *134*, 234–248. doi:10.1016/j.eswa.2019.05.053

Liang, Y., Ju, Y., Martinez, L., & Tu, Y. (2022). Sustainable battery supplier evaluation of new energy vehicles using a distributed linguistic outranking method considering bounded rational behavior. *Journal of Energy Storage*, *48*(5), 103901. doi:10.1016/j.est.2021.103901

Liu, G., Fan, S., Tu, Y., & Wang, G. (2021). Innovative supplier selection from collaboration perspective with a hybrid MCDM model: A case study based on NEVs manufacturer. *Symmetry*, *13*(1), 143–191. doi:10.3390/sym13010143

Meng, Z., Lin, R., & Wu, B. (2024). Multi-criteria group decision making based on graph neural networks in Pythagorean fuzzy environment. *Expert Systems with Applications*, *242*, 122803. doi:10.1016/j.eswa.2023.122803

Pamucar, D. S., Tarle, S. P., & Parezanovic, T. (2018). New hybrid multicriteria new decision-making dematel-maırca model: Sustainable selection of a location for the development of multimodal logistics centre. *Ekonomska Istrazivanja*, *31*(1), 1641–1665. doi:10.1080/1331677X.2018.1506706

Pınar, A., & Boran, F. E. (2020). A q-rung orthopair fuzzy multi-criteria group decision making method for supplier selection based on a novel distance measure. *International Journal of Machine Learning and Cybernetics*, *11*(8), 1749–1780. doi:10.1007/s13042-020-01070-1

Shin, H., Collier, D. A., & Wilson, D. D. (2000). Supply management orientation and supplier/buyer performance. *Journal of Operations Management*, *18*(3), 317–333. doi:10.1016/S0272-6963(99)00031-5

Singh, R. R., Zindani, D., & Maity, S. R. (2024). A Novel Fuzzy-Prospect Theory Approach for Hydrogen Fuel Cell Component Supplier Selection for Automotive Industry. *Expert Systems with Applications*, *246*, 123142. doi:10.1016/j.eswa.2024.123142

Tam, M. C., & Tummala, V. R. (2001). An application of the AHP in vendor selection of a telecommunications system. *Omega*, *29*(2), 171–182. doi:10.1016/S0305-0483(00)00039-6

Torğul B., Paksoy T., (2023). Smart and sustainable supplier selection using interval type-2 Fuzzy AHP. Politeknik Dergisi, Erken Görünüm Makale.

Yager, R. R. (2016). Generalized orthopair fuzzy sets. *IEEE Transactions on Fuzzy Systems*, *25*(5), 1222–1230. doi:10.1109/TFUZZ.2016.2604005

APPENDIX

Abbreviations

Abbreviation	Definition
MAIRCA	Multi Attributive Ideal-Real Comparative Analysis
IVqROF	Interval-valued q-rung orthopair fuzzy
q-ROF	q rung orthopair fuzzy
AHP	Analytic Hierarchy Process
ELECTRE	Elemination and Choice Translating Reality English
DEMATEL	Decision Making Trial and Evaluation Laboratory
MCDM	Multi criteria decision making
BWM	Best Worst Method
VIKOR	Multi-Criteria Optimization and Compromise Solution
PT	Prospect Theory
ORESTE	Organization Rangement et Syntese de Donnees Relationnelles
TODIM	TOmada de Decisao Interativa Multicriterio
TOPSIS	Technique for Order of Preference by Similarity to Ideal Solution
TG	Total gap
Tr	The matrix of real ponder
Tp	The matrix of theoretical ponder
S(a)	Score function
P(a)	Accuracy function

Chapter 8
Review of Chinese Text Mining in Agriculture

Xinyue Zhao
https://orcid.org/0009-0000-1528-7137
Shandong Agricultural University, Taian, China

Yunsheng Song
Shandong Agricultural University, Taian, China

ABSTRACT

Agricultural text mining refers to the utilization of natural language processing and deep learning techniques to extract and analyse useful information from a vast amount of existing agricultural texts. Nowadays, there is a tremendous quantity of text information related to Chinese agriculture; however, there is a scarcity of summarization and generalization in the field of agricultural text mining. This leads to duplicated and redundant agricultural textual information, making it difficult to obtain a holistic perspective on agricultural texts. Therefore, this chapter aims to categorize and summarize the latest developments in text mining in Chinese agricultural domain. Firstly, following the order of Chinese agricultural text mining, various methods for agricultural text preprocessing and representation are introduced. Then, research work related to Chinese agricultural text classification and matching is discussed in detail. Finally, the chapter concludes with a summary of the current state of research in agricultural intelligent services. This chapter contributes to a better understanding of the research trends in this field and provides suggestions and inspiration for future studies.

INTRODUCTION

With the rapid development of the Internet, the volume of textual information in the agricultural domain continues to increase. The substantial amount of agricultural text data faces challenges such as data dispersion, insufficient text mining, and complex content. Consequently, the efficient extraction and analysis of valuable information from large-scale agricultural datasets have become crucial issues in the agricultural domain.

DOI: 10.4018/979-8-3693-1582-8.ch008

As the world's population continues to grow, how to increase agricultural production on limited land area is crucial. In the current era of globalization and digitization, agricultural text mining is not only a means to enhance agricultural production efficiency but also a key tool providing profound insights for agricultural decision-makers, researchers, and practitioners. By mining textual data in the agricultural domain, we can gain a comprehensive understanding of various aspects such as crop growth, meteorological conditions, market trends, and more. This enables the optimization of agricultural production processes, improvement of crop quality, and even effective responses to global challenges like climate change and food safety.

Text mining can be understood as the process of utilizing computer technology and natural language processing (NLP) methods to discover, extract, analyse, and infer useful information from a large amount of textual data (Guo 2023). The development of text mining can be divided into three stages. The first stage is the rule-based stage, where early text mining primarily relied on manually designed rules used to extract specific information from the text. Rule-based methods include keyword-based searches, information extraction based on vocabulary and grammar rules, among others. Text mining in this stage was mainly applied to information retrieval, keyword search, and simple text classification tasks. The second stage is the statistical-based stage, where text mining gradually shifted towards statistical techniques with the rise of statistical methods, relying more on the statistical distribution of the data itself. This period emphasized the application of probability models and vector space models. Statistical-based text mining is primarily applied to tasks such as text classification, clustering, information retrieval, and various NLP problems. The third stage is the deep learning stage, where deep learning models, through the learning of multiple layers of neural networks, can automatically learn more complex and abstract features and representations from large-scale text data, achieving breakthroughs in the field of text mining. Deep learning-based text mining is mainly applied to complex NLP tasks such as sentiment analysis, machine translation, named entity recognition, and others. Currently, due to the unique characteristics of the agricultural domain, the performance of existing text mining techniques transferred to the agricultural domain is not satisfactory. This paper summarizes relevant research on Chinese agricultural text (CAT) mining up to now, to provide readers with more valuable and targeted information.

Text mining is the key technical support for agricultural intelligent services, and research on CAT mining directly affects the process of digital-driven agricultural development. Although there have been comprehensive literature reviews on CAT mining, the existing English review papers do not cover the mainstream deep learning methods and technologies (Drury, 2019). While the existing Chinese papers provide a summary of various aspects of agricultural text mining, they lack specific elaboration on these topics (Zhao, 2023). This paper will start from the characteristics of CATs to clarify the status of research on CAT mining technology and the development status of agricultural intelligent services. Based on NLP, agricultural intelligent services can be classified into two types: classification and prediction. The former is mainly used for the classification and information extraction of CATs, such as agricultural news classification, agricultural intelligent Question Answering System (Q&A), and agricultural public opinion monitoring. The latter is mainly used for agricultural product price prediction.

CORE TECHNOLOGUES FOR CHINESE CAT MINING

To extract potential information effectively and efficiently from CATs, it is necessary to have a deep understanding of the characteristics of agricultural domain texts. CAT mining should start from the specific features of agricultural datasets. Based on a thorough review of relevant literature, the following four characteristics of CAT can be summarized:

- Agricultural datasets are characterized by their vast scale, wide-ranging scope, and diverse structures. Data encompasses various fields such as crop growth monitoring, soil data, market reports, agricultural research data, and more. Different domains exhibit variation in data formats.
- CATs exhibit periodicity and seasonality. Agricultural data is usually organized around the biological lifecycle of crops, which can be further divided into different growth stages, each with its unique characteristics. For example, in spring, CATs mostly focus on seeding and seedling cultivation, while in the summer, crop pest and disease prevention may be a primary concern. Analyzing the periodicity of CATs can assist agricultural practitioners in making better decisions and planning.
- CATs have strong regional characteristics. From a macro perspective, there are differences in soil types, climate, and crop types across different regions. From a micro perspective, there are also significant differences in crop yields between different plots in the same region. Therefore, any CAT data analysis must be combined with local natural environment and social conditions.
- Agricultural data contains many specialized vocabulary and English abbreviations specific to the agricultural field. CATs typically contain many domain-specific terms, agricultural processes, and technical descriptions. At the same time, some CATs may also involve some abbreviation forms, such as N, P, K, etc.

Constrained by the characteristics of CAT, existing text mining research predominantly targets general domain texts, and the applicability to agricultural domain texts still requires further validation. Therefore, to leverage CAT data comprehensively and profoundly, and to promote the high-quality development of information technology in agriculture, there is an urgent need to explore effective text mining techniques for intelligently extracting agricultural knowledge. This aims to enable users to acquire the desired agricultural knowledge more rapidly, conveniently, efficiently, and accurately. It is precisely because of the characteristics of Chinese CAT mentioned above that text preprocessing is necessary when conducting CAT mining.

Text Preprocessing

Currently, agricultural text data includes, but is not limited to, various structures such as news articles, community Q&A, and scientific research papers. Therefore, preprocessing CAT data is crucial for text mining. Before entering the model, the text corpus needs to undergo a series of preprocessing steps to convert it into a format that meets the requirements of the model's input. CAT data preprocessing has its unique characteristics.

- Chinese text does not have physical spacing between words like English words. Therefore, segmentation cannot be completed solely using the simplest spaces and punctuation marks as in English. Chinese words are considered the smallest semantic units.
- Secondly, there are many homonyms in Chinese, meaning that the same word has different meanings. For example, "笔记本" may refer to paper notebooks in the understanding of elementary school students, but it could mean laptops to computing professionals.

- Chinese CAT has specialized vocabulary specific to the agricultural field. For instance, "济麦22" must be viewed to understand its meaning; otherwise, the agricultural term will lose its original meaning.

Based on the characteristics of Chinese agricultural text data preprocessing, Figure 1 illustrates the basic steps of preprocessing for Chinese agricultural texts.

Figure 1. Fundamental steps of agricultural text preprocessing

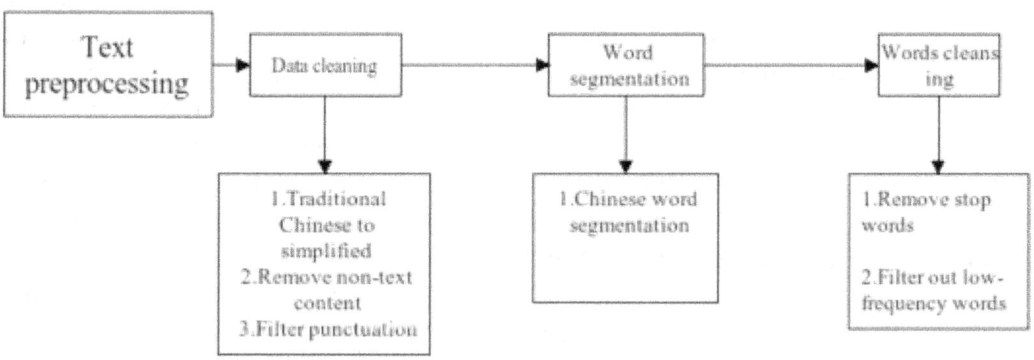

Text preprocessing is the first step in Chinese text mining and it has a crucial impact on the effectiveness of text mining. The results of text preprocessing directly or indirectly affect subsequent research tasks. Most of the work in the data mining process is performed during the data preprocessing stage. Xue stated in "Text Mining Techniques" that the text preprocessing process may account for 80% of the entire system workload (Xue, 2005). The main steps of text preprocessing include data cleaning, word segmentation, and word cleaning.

(1) Data cleaning: Data cleaning is a crucial preprocessing step in addressing problematic data and plays an important role in ensuring data quality (Wu, 2015). Since the corpora we collect are created by Chinese users from around the world on the internet, it is inevitable that the collected text information contains some traditional Chinese characters. This leads to different word embedding vectors for the same word in the subsequent text representation process. Therefore, the first task of data cleaning is to convert the traditional Chinese characters in the dataset into simplified Chinese characters, ensuring that subsequent data mining is performed on unified Chinese texts. Gao (Gao, 2011) has previously implemented traditional to simplified Chinese conversion using the Java language. The idea is to generate 13,053 traditional Chinese character codes based on BIG5 encoding standard, and then use Word software to complete the conversion from these 13,053 traditional Chinese characters to simplified Chinese characters. If there is a change in the encoding before and

after the conversion, a mapping relationship is established between the traditional and simplified character codes and stored in a hash table. Otherwise, it means that the traditional and simplified characters have the same form and no operation is needed. The second step of data cleaning is to remove non-textual content. Since most CAT data comes from web pages, these web documents often contain various HTML tags, scripts, and other unnecessary non-textual content. The presence of such content not only occupies storage space but also leads to inaccurate results in subsequent text mining. Therefore, removing non-textual content is crucial for the subsequent mining process. The final step of data cleaning is to remove punctuation marks. Not only do punctuation marks in the text have no practical meaning for understanding the text, but their presence also increases the complexity of mining algorithms and affects subsequent performance (Shi, 2020).

(2) Word segmentation: For Chinese text mining tasks, word segmentation is usually a crucial step, as the quality of word segmentation directly affects the performance of text mining. Word segmentation involves dividing a sentence, which is composed of a sequence of characters, into a collection of words according to certain rules. Given the unique characteristics of CAT preprocessing as analyzed above, selecting a suitable word segmentation algorithm for the agricultural domain is essential for subsequent mining work. Research on agricultural word segmentation can be divided into four stages: rule-based methods, dictionary-based methods, statistical methods, and deep learning-based methods. Traditional rule-based segmentation relies on a series of rules defined by researchers, but its efficiency and accuracy are limited. With the development of the Internet, researchers have constructed agricultural dictionaries, leading to the emergence of dictionary-based word segmentation methods. With the advancement of machine learning techniques, researchers have started utilizing statistical models for word segmentation, which can alleviate the impact of unknown words on segmentation performance. In recent years, deep learning techniques have gained significant breakthroughs in the field of agricultural word segmentation. This method utilizes neural network models to learn contextual information of words, thereby improving the accuracy and generalization ability of word segmentation. It can automatically learn features and adapt well to different agricultural domains. Yu (Yu, 2022) proposed a BERT-BiLSTM-CRF model for word segmentation in the field of animal husbandry, addressing issues such as many specialized vocabulary and unknown words. The paper utilizes BERT pre-trained models for word embedding and bi-directional Long Short-Term Memory (BiLSTM) to capture contextual features, fully considering the global features of input sequences. Based on the initial word segmentation results, the paper introduces a constructed dictionary for the field of animal husbandry and utilizes the reverse maximum matching algorithm for matching and word segmentation correction. This reduces errors in segmenting disease names and phrases in disease text, thus improving word segmentation performance with an F1 score of 96.38%. Di (Liu, 2021) proposed a keyword extraction method that combines new word discovery and an improved TextRank algorithm. Since word segmentation is the first step in keyword extraction, the paper utilizes mutual information between words and left-right entropy to discover new words, supplementing the agricultural domain word segmentation dictionary. Additionally, by incorporating word features and considering word position and part-of-speech information, the paper improves the calculation method for word importance in TextRank algorithm for keyword extraction. Experimental results show that the proposed algorithm achieves an average F1 score increase of 7.5% compared to traditional Term Frequency-Inverse Document Frequency (TF-IDF) algorithms and 9.8% compared to TextRank algorithm, demonstrating its practicality.

(3) Word cleaning: After tokenizing the text data, there may be many words that have no actual meaning in Chinese text, such as "我", "这儿", "是", etc. These words not only waste storage space but also affect algorithm performance (Shi, 2020). Therefore, to reduce the noise caused by stopwords in text mining, the last step of text preprocessing is to remove low-frequency words that appear infrequently or below a certain frequency in the text dataset. The main idea of using a stopwords list to remove stopwords is to scan the word segmentation list against the stopwords list and filter out the vocabulary that is present in the stopwords list. Currently, the most used Chinese stopwords lists are: Chinese stopwords list (https://gitcode.com/goto456/stopwords/blob/master/cn_stopwords.txt), Baidu stopwords list (https://gitcode.com/goto456/stopwords/blob/master/baidu_stopwords.txt), HIT stopwords list (https://gitcode.com/goto456/stopwords/blob/master/hit_stopwords.txt), and SCU stopwords list from the Machine Intelligence Laboratory (https://gitcode.com/goto456/stopwords/blob/master/scu_stopwords.txt).

Generally, there are three levels of granularity for CAT mining: character-based, word-based, and sentence-based. Text preprocessing work needs to format the original text according to the data requirements on a case-by-case basis, such as using character-based algorithms instead of word segmentation for character-based granularity, while sentence-based granularity does not require word segmentation. Therefore, the actual content of text preprocessing needs to be adjusted according to the specific data requirements. After this process, the text has a unified format, avoiding errors in subsequent text representation steps. However, there is currently no research on the impact of word segmentation and character segmentation on text mining performance, and the performance of both methods still needs further study.

Text Representation

Text representation is a crucial step in NLP. The performance of text representation directly impacts the effectiveness of the entire text mining process. Text representation refers to the process of converting textual information in natural language into numerical forms that can be understood and processed by computers. Looking at the development history of text representation, it has evolved from static word vectors to dynamic word vectors. Currently, widely used methods in research include One-Hot, TF-IDF, Word2Vec, ELMo, BERT, among others.

One-Hot

One-Hot encoding can be traced back to its origin in mathematics and statistics for handling categorical variables. With the rise of data mining, One-Hot encoding has evolved into a commonly used data representation method. In the case of CAT with N vocabulary words, One-Hot encoding utilizes binary vectors of length N to represent each word, with only one digit being 1 at any position, and the rest are 0. Hence, One-Hot encoding is also referred to as One-Hot binary encoding (Liu, 2021). Taking the words {"小麦", "如何", "防止", "病虫草害"} as an example, their One-Hot encoding is shown in Table 1, where One-Hot encodings for these five words are [1,0,0,0], [0,1,0,0], [0,0,1,0], and [0,0,0,1], respectively. By observing One-Hot encoding, it can be noted that the distance between any two words is always $\sqrt{2}$. Therefore, when it comes to studying distance calculations between category values, using One-Hot encoding is more reasonable. However, for datasets with many categories, One-Hot encoding can significantly increase the dimensionality of the data. Additionally, when performing One-Hot encoding, if a discrete variable has missing values, it cannot be encoded. Thus, One-Hot encoding is unable to handle missing value problems.

Table 1. Example of one-hot text representation

	小麦	如何	防止	病虫草害
小麦	1	0	0	0
如何	0	1	0	0
防止	0	0	1	0
病虫草害	0	0	0	1

TF-IDF

The vector space model (VSM) based on bag-of-words model was initially proposed by Salton and his colleagues in the 1970s. VSM simplifies the processing of textual content into vector operations in the vector space, representing semantic similarity through spatial similarity. This method is simple and efficient, relying on pure mathematical calculations without involving complex linguistic knowledge. The classical computational formula is TF-IDF formula:

$$w_{(t,\bar{d})} = \frac{tf(t,d) \times \log(N/n_t + 0.01)}{\sum_{t \in d} tf(t,\bar{d}) \times \log(N/n_t + 0.01)^2}$$

Wei et al. (Wei, 2015) addressed challenges in agricultural data, such as the difficulty of acquiring massive information and the uneven quality of information. They proposed a CAT classification model based on support vector machines (SVM). The model performs feature selection by adjusting document frequency (DF) values according to rules and calculates weights through TF-IDF. The classifier is constructed to achieve automatic classification of agricultural information. The final model achieves an accuracy rate as high as 95.60%, surpassing models such as KNN, neural networks, Bayesian, and SMO. Xiang et al. (Xiang, 2022) tackled the issue of TF-IDF algorithm being affected by imbalanced corpora. They proposed a multi-feature fusion algorithm for Term Frequency-Inverse Word Frequency (TF-IWF) CAT auto-indexing. This algorithm integrates TF-IDF and TF-IWF algorithms, considering both the distribution of text keywords and the impact of imbalanced datasets. The model shows an improvement of 0.80% in F1 value on imbalanced datasets and 0.12% on balanced datasets. Jin et al. (Jin, 2020) focused on challenges in CAT Q&A, such as short sentences, limited vocabulary, and strong feature sparsity. They suggested using TF-IDF algorithm to expand text features. Words with similarity higher than 80.00% and within the top 5 rankings are selected for feature expansion, alleviating the issues of limited vocabulary and feature sparsity.

TF-IDF is a simple and effective text representation method that is easy to understand and implement. However, it neglects the semantic connections between words in natural language, which is the fundamental reason why the model cannot address the problems of synonymous and polysemous word. Additionally, TF-IDF overlooks the sequential information of words in the text. For tasks relying on word order relationships, such as language models or sequence labeling, TF-IDF may not be suitable.

Word2Vec

Mikolov and others proposed Word2Vec in 2013 (Mikolov, 2013), which is a text representation method based on distributed representation. Specifically, it maps each word to a specific location in a high-dimensional vector space, such that semantically similar words are closer in this vector space. The idea behind distributed representation is that each word in the vocabulary can be defined by other words in its context, and similar contexts will result in similar distributed representations. Word2Vec has two main models: Continuous Bag of Words (CBOW) and Skip-Gram. CBOW model attempts to predict the target word from the context words, while Skip-Gram model tries to predict the context words from the target word. Figure 2 (Wang, 2023) depicts the architecture of CBOW and Skip-Gram models proposed by Mikolov.

Figure 2. Diagram of COBW and Skip-Gram model architecture

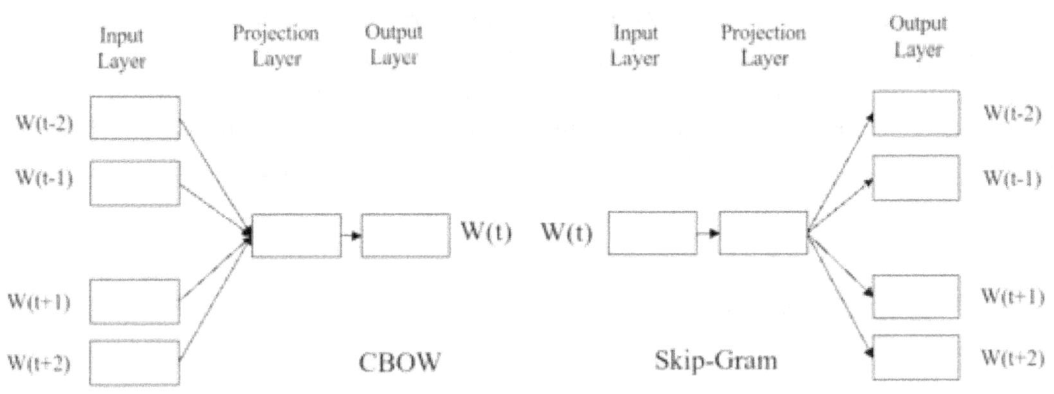

Chen et al. (Chen, 2020) combined Word2Vec with BiLSTM model to learn semantic information from text and employed attention mechanisms to enhance focus on key classification keywords in the text. This approach to some extent addressed the issue of short CATs with insufficient features. Experimental results show that the proposed model outperforms existing machine learning classification models across multiple metrics. Feng et al. (Feng, 2021), focusing on the characteristics of rice knowledge text, employed Word2Vec method for text vectorization and compared it with OneHot, TF-IDF, and Hashing methods. The results indicated that Word2Vec method exhibits higher classification accuracy, with a correctness rate of 86.44%, effectively addressing issues such as sparse text vector representation and incomplete information.

Despite being a powerful text representation method, Word2Vec is a static approach, meaning that once Word2Vec model is trained, the generated word vectors remain fixed for the same word and context. This static nature may limit Word2Vec's ability to capture dynamic changes in word meanings, especially in cases where word semantics vary with context. For instance, a single word may have different meanings in various contexts, and a static Word2Vec model cannot dynamically adjust the corresponding word vector representations in different contexts.

ELMo

The training methods for word embeddings such as Word2Vec and GloVe are generally context-independent, meaning that the vector representation of a word remains the same regardless of its context. This limitation fails to address the problem of ambiguity. In 2018, Matthew Peters et al. proposed Embeddings from Language Model (ELMo) as a solution. ELMo is a feature-based pre-training model that utilizes a BiLSTM. The basic idea behind ELMo is as follows: Firstly, a large-scale corpus is used to pre-train a bi-directional language model (BiLM), with the word embeddings serving as inputs to this model. Then, the weights of BiLM are fixed, and BiLM is run on dataset, recording the representations of each word across all layers. ELMo representation is obtained by concatenating the corresponding word vector with its contextualized representations in all layers (Kong, 2023). The word vectors obtained through ELMo can effectively capture the specific meanings within their corresponding contexts, thus addressing the issue of word sense disambiguation. ELMo model architecture is shown in Figure 3.

Ye (Ye, 2023) proposed an ELMo-TextCNN detection model for addressing the challenges of small cyberbullying datasets and handling polysemous words. The model leverages ELMo encoding to obtain word vectors that incorporate richer contextual information, thereby resolving the issue of word ambiguity. Furthermore, the superior generalization ability of TextCNN model enhances the overall performance of the model in experiments.

Figure 3. ELMo model architecture

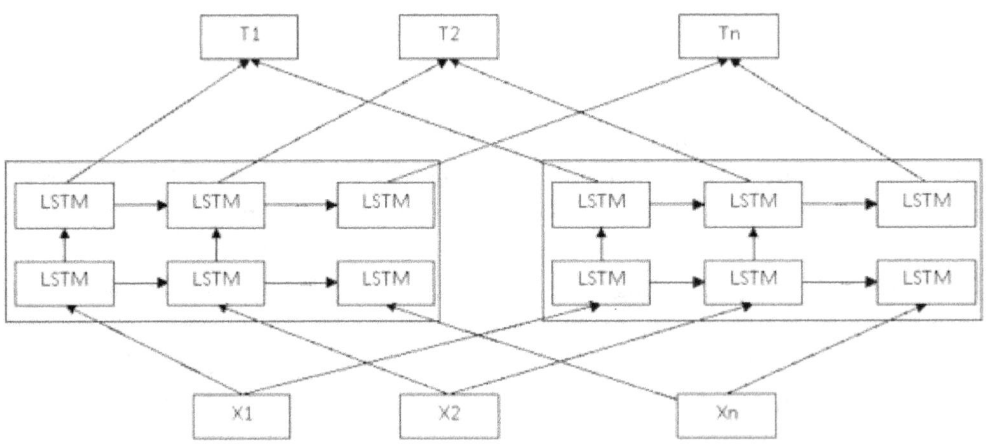

ELMo utilizes a deep learning-based text representation method that considers the semantic variations of words in different contexts. As a result, ELMo can better capture the polysemy of words and contextual information, providing more rich and accurate word vector representations. However, it requires training multiple layers of bidirectional language models simultaneously, resulting in higher computational complexity.

BERT

In 2018, Devlin et al. (Kasneci, 2023) introduced BERT (Bidirectional Encoder Representations from Transformers). BERT is a pre-trained language representation model that differs from previous approaches by using bidirectional Transformer encoders instead of traditional unidirectional language models or shallow concatenation of two unidirectional language models for pre-training. BERT achieves a deep understanding of language context, enabling it to generate context-aware word vectors. Unlike the static word vectors of Word2Vec, BERT represents a dynamic word embedding method that can dynamically adjust word vectors based on context. Therefore, BERT is more suitable for various NLP tasks, such as Q&A, text classification, named entity recognition, and can be fine-tuned for significant performance improvements across different tasks.

BERT text representation is composed of three types of embeddings, as shown in Figure 4. First, token embeddings undergo tokenization processing, inserting two special tokens at the beginning "[CLS]" and end "[SEP]" of the text. "[CLS]" represents a feature used for classification models, and for non-classification models, this symbol can be omitted. "[SEP]" indicates the sentence separation symbol, used to separate two sentences in the input corpus. Then, the token embedding layer maps each word in the input text to a high-dimensional embedding vector, like the word embeddings in Word2Vec. Segment embeddings handle the relationships between different sentences or segments in the input text. In BERT, each input sequence is divided into segments, and each segment is assigned a different embedding vector. Since Transformer model lacks fixed order information, position embeddings are added to capture the sequence information of the input sequence. Finally, Position Embeddings assign a specific embedding vector to each input position, enabling the model to perceive the order of words in the input.

Figure 4. BERT text represents the encoding layer

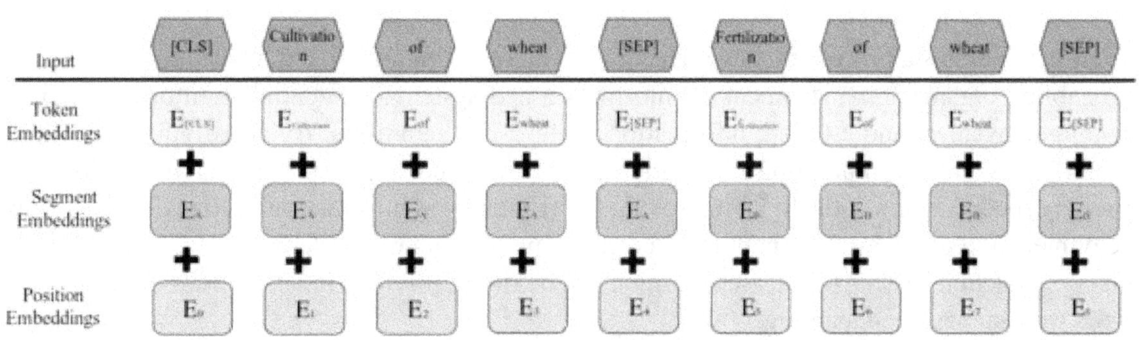

Wang (Wang, 2022) proposed a rice question similarity matching model based on BERT called Coattention-DenseBiGRU. Addressing the characteristics of rice text, the model utilizes a 12-layer Transformer-based Chinese BERT pre-training model to vectorize the text data. Comparative analysis with Word2Vec, Glove, and TF-IDF methods was conducted, revealing that BERT method effectively addresses the issue of polysemy, where a word may have different meanings in different contexts. In another work by Shi (Shi, 2022), aiming to overcome the high cost of manual annotation for agricultural news text, a text classification algorithm combining deep active learning with BERT was proposed. The paper also validated the effectiveness of BERT in combination with three sampling functions—DAL, DBAL, and the lowest confidence degree—and demonstrated that the optimal performance was achieved when BERT was combined with DAL. This provides practical experience and insights for deep active learning in the classification of news text.

BERT is based on Transformer, which enables it to learn rich context-related word vector representations. BERT is a model based on large-scale unsupervised training, and it has strong transferability. However, the large number of model parameters results in high computational complexity and training time.

Based on extensive literature review, paper summaries the advantages and disadvantages of various text representation methods in the following Table 2:

Table 2. Advantages and disadvantages of various text representations

Method	Advantages	Disadvantages
One-Hot	Simple and intuitive, easy to implement	The feature space will increase with the increase of the number of categories, Unable to handle missing values
TF-IDF	Simple and effective, easy to understand and implement	Does not consider the order between words, Unable to solve the problems of synonyms and polysemous words
Word2Vec	Consider contextual information, smaller dimensionality, and faster speed	Unable to solve the problem of polysemous words
ELMo	Solve the problem of polysemous words	High level of complexity, cannot handle out-of-vocabulary words
BERT	Capture contextual information and have contextual understanding ability	High level of complexity, requires truncation for long texts, unable to handle out-of-vocabulary words.

CAT Classification

Text classification is a process of categorizing and summarizing massive CAT data in an orderly manner, enabling organized management of information and systematic accumulation of knowledge, and providing convenient and efficient information retrieval for data users. By classifying CATs, automation and intelligent distribution of information can be achieved, supporting research decision-making, promoting specialization in the field, improving the efficiency of information utilization, and driving the development and progress of agriculture. Currently, mainstream research on CAT classification mainly focuses on machine learning. Machine learning can be further divided into "shallow" machine learning and the well-known deep learning.

CAT Classification Based on "Shallow" Machine Learning

Based on classical machine learning, CAT classification involves using traditional machine learning algorithms to categorize texts in the agricultural domain. This method is simple and effective for CAT classification, especially suitable for relatively standardized classification tasks. However, for semantically complex and highly specialized text data in the agricultural domain, the feature representation capability of this method is limited and may not be as strong as the feature representation capability of methods based on deep learning. "Shallow" machine learning relies on manually extracting text features and is often independent of subsequent modeling. Widely used in the field of text classification are support vector machines, naive Bayes, and FastText.

CAT Classification Based on Support Vector Machine

Support Vector Machine (SVM) is a supervised learning model used for classification and regression analysis. Vatnik et al. (Cortes, 1995) first proposed SVM, systematically introducing the concepts of SVM, including the basic principles of linear SVM and support vector networks. This work laid the foundation for the subsequent development of SVM. Nonlinear SVM was introduced by Vatnik and others, which, using Kernel Trick, mapped data to a high-dimensional space, making linearly inseparable problems in high-dimensional space linearly separable. Cortes et al. (Gunn, 1998) introduced the soft margin version of SVM, known as C-SVM. The C parameter allows for a certain tolerance of classification errors while maximizing the margin, improving the model's robustness. The development of SVM has evolved from linear to nonlinear, from hard margin to soft margin, and introduced the kernel trick. Its successful application in machine learning and continuous improvement of theoretical foundations have made SVM a widely influential learning algorithm.

Wei et al. (Wei, 2015) proposed a Chinese CAT classification model based on Support Vector Machine. The model's purpose is to build a keyword library for the agricultural industry classification. Through rule adjustments of DF values for feature selection and TF-IDF weight calculation, a classifier is built to achieve automatic classification of agricultural information. Lu et al. (Lu, 2021) addressed the issue of SVM being significantly affected by noise or outliers. They proposed an agricultural Chinese text classification model based on center-kernel-aligned fuzzy SVM. This model weakens the impact of the imbalance in classification distribution and the problem of the feature space origin being far from the mapped samples through center-kernel alignment. Additionally, the model uses fuzzy membership degrees, assigns weights to samples, and increases the impact of SVM on the optimal hyperplane. Experimental results show that CKA-FSVM algorithm performs well in CAT classification. Li et al. (Li, 2018) addressed the challenges of large-scale labeled text information in supervised learning-based text classification algorithms. They proposed a semi-supervised CAT classification method based on feature family semantic diffusion kernel and Support Vector Machine. The algorithm addresses the difficulty of labeling a large dataset by introducing semi-supervised learning. Overall, the algorithm thoroughly considers the semantic relationships between words, ensuring that even in cases of sparse samples, the context of words with semantic equivalence or closeness is mapped to similar feature vectors.

CAT Classification Based on Naive Bayes

Bayes classifier is a statistical method based on Bayes theorem for classification. Naive Bayes is the most common and simplest type of Bayes classifier which is mainly used in the field of supervised learning. Naive Bayes classifier adopts the "attribute conditional independent assumption", which means that the features are independent of each other. The CAT classification method based on Naive Bayes assigns the text x to a category that maximizes its probability.

Zhao (Zhao, 2020) and others proposed a naive Bayes-based CAT classification algorithm to address the scarcity of CAT corpora. The algorithm was validated using a news dataset from Ministry of Water Resources of the People's Republic of China, which was divided into four categories: agricultural news, agricultural technology, agricultural market, and agricultural product prices. Naive Bayes classifier was used for classification. The experimental results showed that the performance of naive Bayes CAT classifier was high. However, as the demand continues to increase, there are still many research and exploration questions worth studying. Chen (Chen, 2020) and others addressed the issue of naive Bayes classifier excessively relying on the quality of the classification data and the significant decrease in classification effectiveness when dealing with complex and multi-attribute data. They proposed a combination of multiple naive Bayes classifiers using Adaboost algorithm to design an A_B model. To solve the three-classification problem, A_B model was trained as an A_B classifier, and two A_B classifiers were combined to solve the three-classification problem. The experimental accuracy reached 94.33%. Furthermore, when adding 30% of interfering data to the standard test data, it was found that compared to naive Bayes classifier, A_B classifier exhibited higher tolerance for data quality and still demonstrated good classification performance for complex and multi-attribute data.

Agriculture Text Classification Based on FastText.

FastText is a word vector and text classification tool introduced by Facebook researcher Mikolov in 2016, as outlined in the paper "Enriching Word Vectors with Subworld Information." The paper proposes a method of enhancing word vectors using subworld embeddings, enabling FastText to effectively handle polysemous words, complex morphologies, and out-of-vocabulary terms. As a result, it has proven to be an excellent tool for word vectors and text classification in large-scale text data (Wankhade, 2022).

Wang et al. (Wang, 2022) addressed CAT classification using FastText model, conducting experiments on a dataset of 65,000 records. Comparative experiments led to the conclusion that FastText model outperforms TextRNN, TextCNN, TextDPCNN, and Transformer models, demonstrating higher practical value. Shi [22] combined deep active learning with FastText text classification algorithm. Its advantage lies in the fact that active learning technology requires manual annotation of only a portion of the data to train the model, while the remaining data is annotated by the model, significantly reducing annotation costs. Huo (Huo, 2019), focusing on the issue that FastText, after n-gram feature enhancement, may generate some meaningless low-frequency words that disrupt the effectiveness of text classification, proposed two improvements: "weighted selection of important words" and "integration of news headlines," resulting in algorithms CF-FastText and Title-FastText, respectively. Experimental results indicate that CF-FastText algorithm achieves better classification performance compared to a single improvement.

Chinese Text Classification in Agricultural Based on Deep Learning

Compared to traditional machine learning models, deep learning models attempt to emulate human learning processes by automatically extracting features from vast amounts of data. Introduced in 2006, deep learning involves the integration of multi-layer neural networks, enabling computers to autonomously undergo the learning process, learning higher-level and more abstract language features without relying on manually designed features (Hinton, 2019). Deep learning adopts an end-to-end approach that does not require manual feature extraction. Instead, it uses neural networks to automatically extract features and is closely related to subsequent modeling. In the field of CAT classification, classic algorithms such as CNN, RNN, and their combination algorithm RCNN are widely applied.

CAT Classification Based on CNN

Convolutional Neural Networks (CNNs) originated in the 1980s when Yann et al. [33] proposed LeNet-5 for handwritten digit recognition. This network included convolutional layers, pooling layers, and fully connected layers, laying the foundation for the subsequent development of CNNs. With the advancement of graphic processing units and increased computational capabilities, Krizhevsky et al. (Krizhevsky, 2012) introduced AlexNet in 2012, achieving significant success in image recognition and sparking a renewed interest in CNNs. In 2014, Simonyan proposed VGGNet, enhancing network performance by using small-sized convolutional kernels and a deeper network structure, becoming one of the classics in CNN design (Liao, 2023). In 2018, He et al. (He, 2016) introduced Residual Block to address the vanishing gradient and exploding gradient issues during the training of deep neural networks. ResNet introduced residual connections across layers, allowing information to flow directly through shortcut paths across hierarchical levels, facilitating the learning of identity mappings and supporting deeper network architectures. This work provided an effective method for constructing extremely deep neural networks, profoundly influencing the development of CNNs. Due to the outstanding performance of CNNs, they have been increasingly applied in various fields, such as object detection, semantic segmentation, and facial recognition. In recent years, the combination of self-supervised learning methods with CNNs has automated network design.

In agricultural research, Convolutional Neural Networks have primarily been applied to CAT classification. Bao (Bao, 2022) employed BERT for character encoding of agricultural queries and utilized TextCNN to extract high-dimensional features for query classification. In the subdivision experiments of agricultural queries, BERT-TextCNN achieved F1 values of 86.06%, 90.56%, 95.04%, and 85.55% for the categories of cultivation techniques, field management, soil and water management, and others, outperforming other deep learning models. Wang (Wang, 2022) addressed the limitations of fixed-width convolutional kernels and the lack of consideration for the impact of keywords on classification in current CAT classification methods. Considering the sparse characteristics and noise in rice queries, this study proposed a rice text classification method based on Attention-DenseCNN. Improvements over previous research include using dense-connected CNN to address the sparse feature issue in rice queries and employing attention mechanisms to effectively utilize features obtained through dense-connected convolutional neural networks for classification.

CNNs achieve local perception through convolutional and pooling layers, demonstrating remarkable feature extraction capabilities and adaptability. However, the presence of pooling layers can lead to the loss of valuable information and overlook the correlation between the overall and partial information.

CAT Classification Based on RNN

Recurrent Neural Networks (RNNs) constitute a class of neural networks designed for processing sequential data. In contrast to traditional feedforward neural networks, RNNs incorporate recurrent connections, enabling them to model sequential information with memory and contextual understanding capabilities. Hochreiter et al. (Memory, 2010) introduced Long Short-Term Memory (LSTM), which, through the incorporation of gate mechanisms, addressed the limitations of traditional RNNs, such as the vanishing or exploding gradient problem, when dealing with long sequences. LSTM enhanced RNNs' ability for long-term memory and sequence modeling. Cho et al. proposed Gated Recurrent Units (GRUs) (Zhang, 2023), which simplified the structure of LSTM to some extent by reducing the number of parameters while still effectively modeling sequential information through gate mechanisms. With the continuous advancement of deep learning, research on RNNs has delved deeper. Researchers have enhanced RNNs' performance in NLP, speech recognition, and other domains by stacking multiple layers of RNNs, introducing attention mechanisms, and employing various other methods. Sutskever (Sutskever, 2014) introduced Sequence-to-Sequence (Seq2Seq) model, which utilizes an encoder-decoder structure with RNNs for sequence data processing. Seq2Seq model excelled in tasks like machine translation, providing crucial insights for subsequent NLP research. Vaswani (Vaswani, 2017) and others proposed Transformers model in 2017, introducing self-attention mechanisms to replace traditional RNN and LSTM. Transformers parallelized the processing of sequential data, improving training efficiency and achieving notable success in NLP.

In the field of agriculture, researchers have focused on the application of Recurrent Neural Networks in CAT classification. Chen et al. (Chen, 2020) addressed the issue of insufficient semantic extraction in short CATs by proposing an CAT classification model based on BiLSTM-Attention. This model, built upon LSTM, incorporated bidirectional LSTM to alleviate the limitation of insufficient contextual information for capturing sentence context, to some extent resolving the challenges posed by short CATs with limited features. Additionally, the introduction of attention mechanisms endowed the classifier with a degree of inclusiveness, mitigating sensitivity issues in the classifier to data.

RNN throughs recurrent connections, capture temporal dependencies in sequences, offering memory and contextual understanding capabilities. However, RNNs face challenges such as the vanishing or exploding gradient problem, making it difficult for them to effectively learn long-term dependencies in training long sequences. Furthermore, RNNs incur relatively high computational and memory costs, particularly when dealing with lengthy sequences during training, potentially leading to resource constraints.

CAT Classification Based on the Blend of CNN and RNN

In neural networks, CNN and RNN serve as primary model architectures for classification problems, each having its own advantages and limitations. RNN excels in handling sequential structures, considering the context information of sentences. However, in RNN, the importance of words in a sentence increases as you move further back, which may impact the final classification results. This is because the most influential words for sentence classification could be located at any position in the sentence. CNN, being an unbiased model, can capture crucial features through max-pooling. However, determining the size of the sliding window in CNN is not straightforward. Choosing a window size that is too small may result in the loss of important information, while selecting one that is too large can lead to a massive parameter space. To address these limitations, Lai (Lai, 2015) and others proposed RCNN architecture in

2015. This architecture utilizes a bidirectional recurrent structure to obtain context information, enabling the retention of word order over a broader range during text representation learning compared to CNN. Additionally, it employs a max-pooling layer to capture the essential parts of the text, automatically determining which features play a more crucial role in text classification.

Jin et al. (Jin, 2020) addresses the challenges of short CAT question-answer sentences, limited vocabulary, strong sparsity in features, large data volume, high noise, and poor standardization. They proposed an agricultural question-answer sentence classification model based on BiGRU-MulCNN. The model uses TF-IDF algorithm to expand feature words in the text, and MulCNN algorithm is employed to further extract high-dimensional, multiscale local features from the text. Yang et al. (Yang, 2023) tackled issues in agricultural news text, such as poor specificity and unclear classification. They proposed an agricultural news text classification model based on ERNIE+DPCNN+BiGRU. In comparison to other domains with shorter headlines, this model reduces 2 convolutional layers in DPCNN layer to retain more text features. Experimental results show a 1.29% increase in accuracy compared to the baseline ERNIE model.

Figure 5. Text matching model

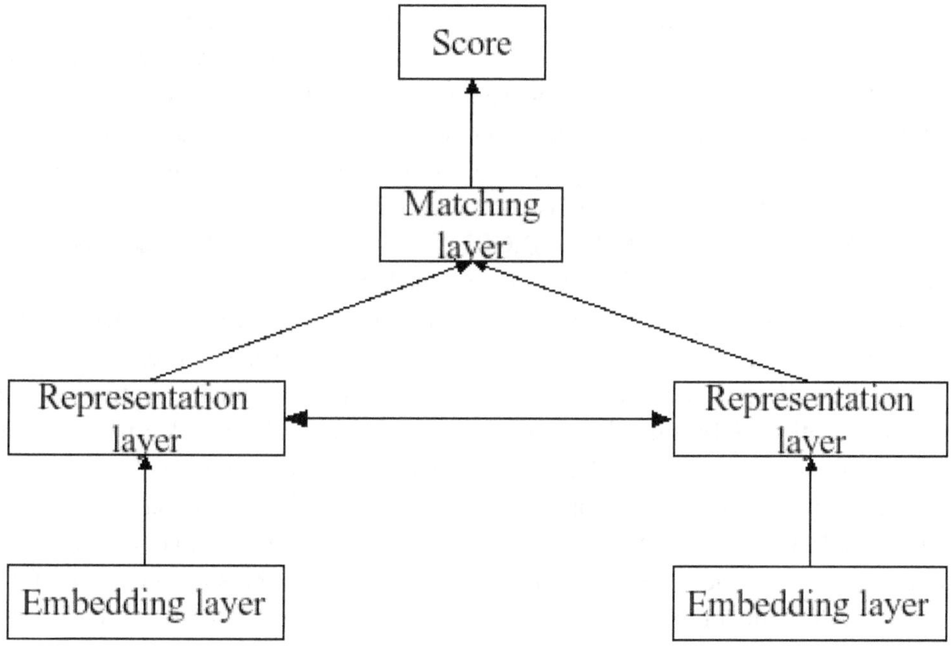

Chinese Text Matching in Agricultural

Text matching is a fundamental problem in NLP that plays a crucial role in various NLP tasks such as information retrieval, Q&A, paraphrase identification, dialogue systems, and machine translation. These NLP tasks can be largely abstracted as text matching problems. Traditional text matching techniques include Bag of Words (BOW), Vector Space Model (VSM), TF-IDF, BM25, Jaccard similarity, SimHash, among others. For instance, BM25 algorithm calculates the matching score between query and document fields based on the coverage of the query field by the document field, where higher scores indicate better matching between web pages and queries. With the continuous development of deep learning, Word Embeddings trained on neural networks have been employed for text matching computations. This training approach is concise, and the semantic interpretability of the obtained word vectors is further enhanced. The text matching process is illustrated in Figure 5.

Chinese Text Matching in Agricultural Based on RNN

Based on RNN, CAT matching is an approach that utilizes Recurrent Neural Networks (RNN) for matching CATs. The basic idea involves transforming CAT into a sequential representation and processing the sequential data using an RNN model. RNN model can capture temporal and semantic information in the text, providing a better representation of the text's intrinsic features. By comparing the representation vectors of two texts, their similarity can be computed, thus achieving text matching

Jin et al. (Jin, 2020) proposed an Attention-DenseBiGRU agricultural question similarity matching model based on BERT. To enhance feature transmission and extraction while reducing feature loss, this study employs a densely connected BiGRU. The Attention DenseBiGRU introduced in this study enhances interaction between two networks through attention mechanisms at the encoding layer, extracting feature correlations between sentence pairs to improve the accuracy of text matching. In the experimental section, BERT-Attention-DenseBiGRU model is compared with six other deep learning models: BiLSTM, Self-attention BiLSTM, TextCNN, ABCNN, BiGRU, and Attention BiGRU. The experiments show that the proposed BERT-Attention-DenseBiGRU achieves the highest precision and F1 score, with precision, recall, and F1 values significantly superior to the other six deep learning models. Liu (Liu, 2022) proposed an approach using character-level Word2Vec representation to initialize query representations. It employs a Siamese neural network as the basic model framework to learn the semantic features of sentences, capturing context information. Subsequently, a BiLSTM recurrent neural network is used to extract semantic temporal features. Finally, sentence similarity is calculated at the semantic level using a cosine function containing semantic information. This approach is compared with other semantic matching models in experimental trials. In the context of agricultural question answering, Zhao et al. constructed a corpus called CCDIP, which is a collection of agricultural similarity paraphrases consisting of 13 categories. They proposed AgrCQS model for studying the similarity matching of Chinese agricultural disease and pest problems. To address the issues of identifying boundaries and insufficient lexical information, the model employed hybrid embedding to generate word vectors. The feature extraction layer utilized MM-CNN to extract local contextual information of different sizes. BiLSTM layer employed a sub-attention mechanism to enhance the ability of BiLSTM in extracting core semantics. Experimental results showed that the model achieved a question classification accuracy of 93.92%.

Chinese Text Matching in Agricultural Based on CNN

The CAT matching method based on Convolutional Neural Networks (CNN) utilizes the convolutional operation of CNN to capture local features in the text, thereby achieving text matching between different instances. Jing et al (Jin, 2022), addressing challenges such as a limited vocabulary, numerous domain-specific terms, poor sentence regularity, and strong feature sparsity in question texts generated in agricultural Q&A communities, proposed a text matching model that integrates multiple semantic features. In the text preprocessing layer, the model constructs a co-occurrence relationship network for words, enabling the calculation of weights for each word co-occurrence pair and enriching the features of short texts. Additionally, the model employs Bidirectional Long Short-Term Memory (BiLSTM), Convolutional Neural Networks (CNN), and densely connected networks to build a text matching model, facilitating the extraction of text features from multiple perspectives. In the experimental section, Co_BiLSTM_CNN model is compared with MaLSTM, ESIM, ABCNN, and CDNN networks based on Siamese networks. Experimental results demonstrate that the proposed Co_BiLSTM_CNN model outperforms the comparative models with significantly improved accuracy, precision, recall, and F1 values, all exceeding 94.00%.

CAT matching finds primary applications in agricultural informatization, agricultural technology dissemination, and agricultural product quality testing. Therefore, researching CAT matching plays a crucial role in advancing intelligent services in agriculture.

CAT MINING APPLICATIONS

The goal of CAT mining is to provide scientific decision-making support to farmers, agricultural enterprises, and government decision-makers by analyzing and mining agricultural-related data. This aims to promote efficiency, quality, and sustainable development in agricultural production. At the beginning of the 21st century, with the rise of information technologies such as internet of things, cloud computing, and big data, agricultural intelligent services have been widely promoted. Currently, agricultural intelligent services have been implemented throughout the entire process of agricultural production, from pre-production to production and post-production stages (Wu, 2022). Agricultural intelligent services are technological systems built by researchers based on the information needs and experiences of agricultural operators. These systems make full use of key technologies such as data science, visual analysis, and artificial intelligence to integrate, correlate, and analyze all data related to agricultural planting and production processes. They provide personalized, accurate, and intelligent service models. Furthermore, with the continuous growth of the population, the role of agricultural intelligent services is becoming increasingly prominent, agricultural intelligent service application and related technologies are shown in Figure 6. Agricultural intelligent services not only meet the growing demand for food due to population growth and provide scientific decision support to agricultural producers but also promote sustainable development in the agricultural sector. Additionally, they bring about more employment opportunities and improve rural economic development through technological advancements, thereby enhancing people's living conditions.

Figure 6. Applications of CAT mining

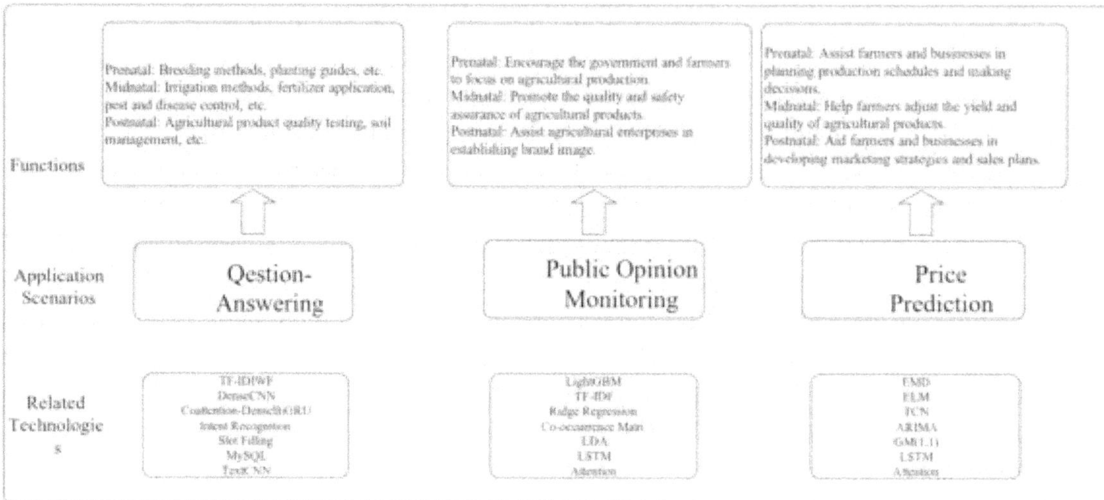

Intelligent Q&A for Agriculture

Intelligent Q&A is an application based on artificial intelligence technology, which aims to extract accurate and meaningful answers from a large amount of information by understanding natural language questions posed by users. Agricultural intelligent service based on knowledge base is an important research task to solve problems by making full use of the data in the knowledge base. In fact, the implementation process is divided into three modules: problem analysis, text retrieval and answer generation, and its basic architecture is shown in Figure 7 (Zhou, 2022). At present, China has established many large-scale knowledge services network platforms for collecting, transmitting, and preserving agricultural digital research results. For example, "Agricultural search", a professional search engine, has 6 million agricultural cooperation websites and realizes an intelligent search engine for full-text and semantic retrieval. Wanfang Data Knowledge Service Platform has constructed an agricultural knowledge service platform based on Chinese literature data. Zhou et al. (Guo, 2023), aiming at the problems of agricultural question classification, such as the lack of corpus, the narrow content range of the corpus or the need for manual labeling, this paper uses crawler technology to obtain 28608 data, and cleans and segments the data, etc., to construct an CAT corpus that can be used for the research of Q&A. Xiang (Xiang,2022) et al., aiming at TF-IDF algorithm is easily affected by unbalanced corpus, this paper proposes an automatic indexing algorithm of CAT based on word frequency-inverse document and inverse word frequency with multi-feature fusion. The algorithm first statistics the features of word frequency, part of speech, word position and word span of the corpus, and then merges the candidate words into synonyms. Finally, the information of part of speech, word position and word span of the candidate words are quantified, the weight of each candidate word is calculated by TF-IDIWF algorithm, and the top N words are selected as keywords. Through the improvement of automatic indexing technology, it is of great significance to realize the effective organization and efficient use of Internet agricultural information resources. Wang (Wang, 2022) used deep learning and NLP technology to construct a rice Q&A, which mainly solved four technical problems: automatic classification of agricultural questions, automatic detection of similar questions, automatic selection of correct answers, and construction of generative question answering models. Guo (Guo, 2023) et al. proposed a joint model, AgIG-IDSF, for intent recognition and slot filling tasks in the field of agricultural pest and disease control. Currently, the predominant approach in this field is the pipeline method, which can lead to error propagation issues. To address this, the authors introduced a model that is based on intent embedding information and gate mechanism. AgIG-IDSF model utilizes attention mechanism to enrich the semantic context and incorporates intent embedding information. It also employs a gate mechanism to fuse the vectors. Experimental results demonstrate that the proposed AgIG-IDSF model outperforms other models in terms of intent recognition and slot filling performance in agricultural pest and disease control. Furthermore, it exhibits certain generalization capabilities.

Figure 7. Intelligent question answering basic framework diagram

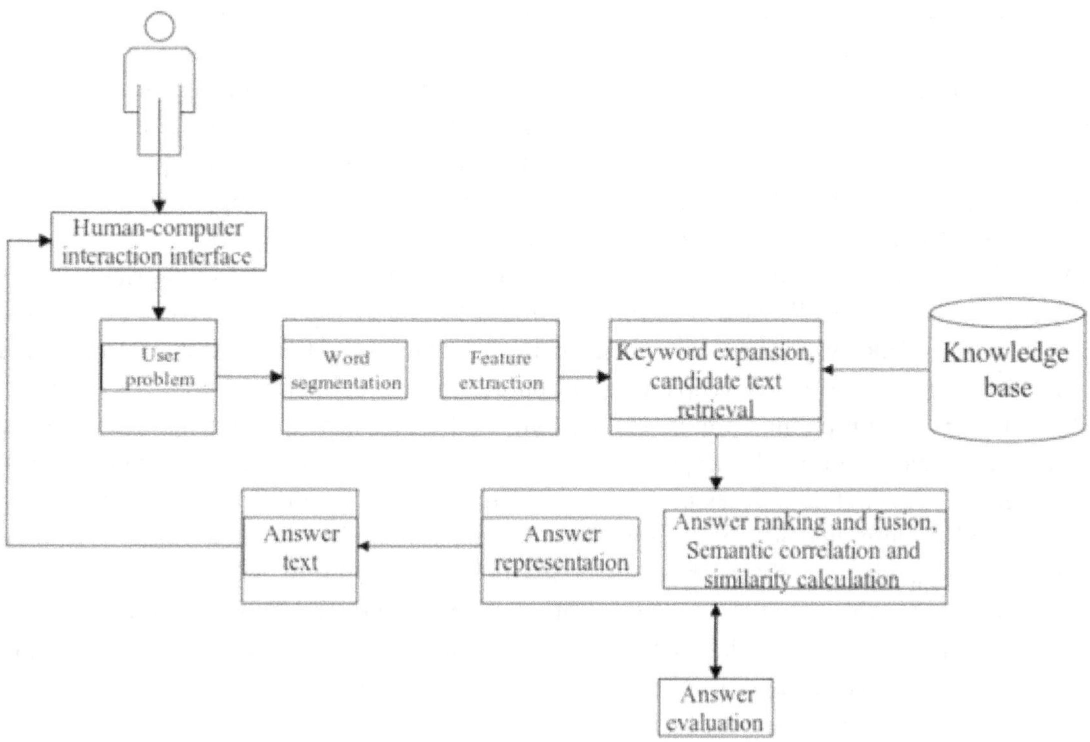

Agricultural Public Opinion Monitoring

With the popularity of the Internet, the number of Internet users in China has reached 5.4 billion people as of 2023, emphasizing the need for enhanced global cooperation (Shang, 2023). Along with the Internet comes online public opinion, which plays an undeniable role in the agricultural sector. Different people have different voices on the same matter, but when agricultural production safety crises occur, netizens spread information through online platforms, often exaggerating negative impacts and causing social panic. Therefore, it is crucial to monitor online public opinion in real-time and control the direction of negative sentiment, utilizing the Internet. After years of development, China's public opinion system has gradually formed a relatively mature monitoring system, including but not limited to the People's Network Public Opinion Monitoring Office, Fudan University's Public Opinion Research Laboratory, and Baidu's public opinion system. However, directly applying existing systems to the agricultural field still poses challenges, prompting many researchers to focus on studying methods for monitoring public opinion in the agricultural domain.

Ren's research (Ren, 2019) focused on studying the hot topics in social media public opinion in the agricultural field. The research designed and implemented an agricultural public opinion detection and analysis system. Firstly, the system classified collected agricultural texts using Naive Bayes algorithm, and experimental results showed an accuracy rate as high as 96%. Additionally, K-means was used to construct agricultural public opinion topic indexing to identify agricultural hotspots in social media texts. Secondly, the research utilized Boson sentiment lexicon to construct sentiment dictionaries for agriculture, including sentiment words, degree adverbs, and negation words. The sentiment dictionary method was employed for sentiment calculation. Finally, the system was designed and implemented with modules for data collection, processing, and analysis. The system processed and analyzed public opinions by collecting information from social media platforms, and provided feedback on public opinion results. Chen (Chen, 2015) and others proposed a public opinion monitoring model. This model includes three main components: public opinion information collection, public opinion analysis, and public opinion service. The information collection component utilizes multiple parallel web crawlers to collect public opinion information and filters out duplicate links. The public opinion segmentation module analyzes agricultural public opinion by constructing the ontology of the agricultural domain, thereby enhancing the model's early warning capability. The public opinion service platform serves as the user interface of the system and presents analysis results to users through visualization techniques. This model strengthens the analysis capabilities of public opinion information, provides comprehensive and accurate agricultural public opinion analysis, allows for real-time monitoring of developments in the agricultural field, and provides important support for agricultural authorities and decision-makers. Chen's research (Chen, 2020) addresses the negative impacts of uncontrolled negative public opinion, proposing a public opinion detection system. The system uses word vectors and LightGBM to identify agricultural-related news and establishes a text classification model for CATs using TF-IDF and ridge regression, thus extracting negative news. In addition, to understand the themes of news articles, a keyword detection method is proposed, which utilizes co-occurrence matrices and co-occurrence graphs to extract keyword phrases from news articles. Experimental results demonstrate that the system achieves an accuracy rate of 93.82% in identifying agricultural news. Finally, to further improve system performance, the paper proposes a TF-IDF-based automatic text summarization method, which combines TF-IDF and sliding window calculations while considering the position features of sentences, achieving better results. Fu's research (Fu, 2021) addresses the problem of the large number of contents and diverse information related to agricultural public opinion on various online platforms, making it difficult to accurately grasp the hotspots and development patterns of public opinion. This paper proposes an LSTM-based agricultural public opinion prediction and analysis model with attention mechanism. The topic mining component adopts LDA topic model to classify keywords and topics in a large amount of text information, facilitating discussions on the probability distribution and heat changes of various subjects. The number of topics is determined through experimentation, with the lowest perplexity achieved at seven topics. The prediction of topic heat is based on LSTM method, with an attention layer added after LSTM layer to focus the model's final decision on historical data that is truly helpful for the ultimate prediction. This model enables a faster grasp of public opinion patterns, facilitating timely adjustments to public opinion trends by external forces.

Agriculture is a matter of national importance and people's livelihoods. Properly guiding online public opinion can prevent individuals from deliberately exaggerating and propagating negative news, which may cause social panic and affect social stability. It also helps government departments to accurately understand the needs and current situation of the people.

Agricultural Product Price Prediction

Price forecasting can assist farmers, agricultural enterprises, and governments in developing better planting and sales strategies to cope with market fluctuations and changes. The fluctuation of agricultural product prices is often influenced by multiple factors, including market supply and demand, climate factors, policy factors, and international markets. As a result, agricultural product prices exhibit seasonality, trends, and random fluctuations, displaying non-linear characteristics. Predicting agricultural product prices falls within the realm of time series forecasting, while agricultural products also have perishability, which adds to the difficulty of price forecasting.

Lv (Lv, 2023) constructed a sentiment analysis model for the network public opinion of small-scale agricultural products using garlic as an example. The model utilizes an optimized BERT model to generate sentiment word vectors. It then employs BiLSTM to extract contextual information and introduces local attention mechanism and global attention mechanism to determine the importance of words and sentences. Finally, the Softmax function is used to score the sentiment polarity of the network public opinion: the closer the score is to 0, the more inclined it is towards negative sentiment, and vice versa. In addition, the article combines network public opinion to predict the prices of small-scale agricultural products and considers the network sentiment index as a factor influencing the decision-making of intermediaries and consumers. It proposes a garlic price prediction analysis framework based on the perspective of stakeholders in the garlic industry chain. The dynamic model averaging theory is introduced to achieve accurate garlic price prediction. Zhang (Zhang, 2023) proposes a combined forecasting model for corn futures prices by integrating sentiment analysis and market indicators derived from multiple dimensions. Firstly, the PDDM model is used for sentiment analysis, where the embedding layer adopts RoBERTa-wwm-ext to generate word vectors. The information extraction layer employs TextCNN and BiGRU parallel dual-channel models to capture different local information and introduces attention mechanisms to assign different weights to different words in the text. Furthermore, based on the model, the PDDM-CFSD model is constructed by incorporating the Chinese Financial Sentiment Dictionary (CFSD), and experimental results show that the introduction of CFSD improves various indicators of the PDDM sentiment classification algorithm to a certain extent. Finally, 33 indicators such as domestic corn import volume and sentiment variables are selected as input features for the LSTM model to predict corn futures prices. Wang (Wang, 2023) uses soybean prices as an example to predict soybean prices based on news headlines. Firstly, BERTopic is applied for topic modeling to analyze the themes and sentiments of soybean news headlines. Then, BERT+BiLSTM is used for sentiment analysis of news headlines. Finally, Bayesian algorithm SVR is employed for hyperparameter optimization and comparative experiments. The experimental results demonstrate that the proposed BO_SVR model based on text topic modeling has higher accuracy in predicting soybean prices compared to traditional RF and XGBoost prediction models.

CONCLUSION AND FUTURE WORK

This paper summarizes the research status, key technologies, and main application scenarios of CAT mining, and introduces the research status of agricultural intelligent service in detail. This paper firstly introduces the uniqueness of CATs, including the large scale of agricultural data sets, the wide range of agricultural data sets, the different structure of CATs, the poor standardization of CAT expression, the uneven quality of text, the existence of many professional words in agricultural data and strong regionality. These characteristics make it challenging to mine and analyze CATs. Then the related technology of CAT mining is introduced in detail, such as text preprocessing, text representation, CAT classification, CAT matching. Finally, it summarized the research status of CAT mining application scenario-agricultural intelligent service.

This article provides a comprehensive review of the current research status of CAT mining, aiming to help researchers understand the status, hot issues, and trend developments in this field. Through the analysis and integration of various text data, the review can provide a systematic knowledge framework to assist researchers in better grasping and understanding relevant issues in the agricultural domain. In addition, CAT mining research can also be used to discover hidden knowledge, rules, and patterns in CATs, which can help researchers identify existing problems and challenges in the field.

CAT mining has a broad development prospect in the future. Its evolution direction and key prospects can be considered from the following aspects:

- CAT mining will pay more attention to the fusion and processing of multi-modal data. With the wide application of agricultural sensors, satellite remote sensing and other technologies, agricultural data have emerged more abundant and diverse forms. Integrating multi-modal information, such as text, image, and time series, will make text mining more comprehensive understanding of agricultural production environment and provide more diversified information for decision-making.
- CAT mining will pay more attention to the construction of domain knowledge graph. Constructing a knowledge graph in the agricultural field will help to better organize and express agricultural information and promote the integration of knowledge across fields.
- International cooperation and data sharing will be the trend of CAT mining in the future. Establishing an international cooperation framework and sharing agricultural data and text mining methods will help to better meet global agricultural challenges and promote global cooperation and innovation in the field of agriculture.

REFERENCES

Bao, T., Luo, R., & Guo, T. (2022). Analysis of agricultural question classification model based on BERT character vector and TextCNN. *Journal of Southern Agricultural Sciences*, *7*, 2068–2076.

Chen, C. (2020). *Application research of NLP technology in Agricultural public opinion analysis system*. Beijing University of Technology.

Chen, P., & Guo, X. Y. (2020). Agricultural short text information classification based on Adaboost and Naive Bayes. *Journal of Software*, *41*(9), 13–18.

Chen, P., & Guo, X. Y. (2020). Agricultural short text information classification based on Adaboost and Naive Bayes. *Journal of Software*, *41*(9), 13–18.

Chen, T., & Liu, S. H. (2015). Research on agricultural network public opinion monitoring system under cloud environment. *Journal of Agricultural Network Information*, *1*, 41–44.

Cortes, C., & Vapnik, V. (1995). Support-vector networks. *Machine Learning*, *20*(3), 273–297. doi:10.1007/BF00994018

Di, X. K., Zhang, H., & Qin, X. T. (2023). Keywords extraction algorithm in agricultural field based on new word discovery and improved TextRank algorithm. *Journal of Agricultural Engineering*, *13*(06), 21–25.

Drury, B., & Roche, M. (2019). A survey of the applications of text mining for agriculture. *Computers and Electronics in Agriculture*, *163*, 104864. doi:10.1016/j.compag.2019.104864

Feng, S., Xu, T. Y., & Zhou, Y. C. (2021). Rice knowledge text classification method based on deep convolutional neural network. *Nongye Jixie Xuebao*, *3*, 257–264.

Fu, L. F., & Zhao, F. F. (2021). Prediction and analysis of agricultural public opinion based on Attention mechanism LSTM model. *Journal of Mathematics in Practice and Understanding*, *51*(17), 64–76.

Gao Q. S., & Zhang X. W. (2011), Implement the traditional/simplified conversion in Java programs. *International Journal of Computer Programming Skills and Maintenance, 13*, 21-24+52.

Gunn S. R. (1998). Support vector machines for classification and regression. *ISIS technical report, 14*(1), 5-16.

Guo S.L., Su X. N., & Fang X. H. (2023), Research on Travel text association knowledge Mining and recommendation service based on NER and Apriori algorithm. *Modern information, 43*(11):123-134.

Guo, X. C., Hao, X., & Yao, X. C. (2023). Research on joint model of intention recognition and slot filling for agricultural pest knowledge answer. *Nongye Jixie Xuebao*, *54*(01), 205–215.

He, K., Zhang, X., & Ren, S. (2016), Deep residual learning for image recognition, In *Proceedings of the IEEE conference on computer vision and pattern recognition,* (pp. 770-778). IEEE.

Hinton, G. E., Osindero, S., & Teh, Y. W. (2006). A fast learning algorithm for deep belief nets. *Neural Computation*, *18*(7), 1527–1554. doi:10.1162/neco.2006.18.7.1527 PMID:16764513

Huo, T. T. (2019). *Research on news Text classification based on FastText and its application in agricultural news*. Jilin University.

Jin, N., Zhao, C. J., & Wu, H. R. (2020). Research on classification Technology of agricultural question Answering based on bigru_mulcnn. *Nongye Jixie Xuebao*, *51*(5), 8.

Jin, N., Zhao, C. J., & Wu, H. R. (2020). Research on classification technology of agricultural question Answering based on BiGRU_MulCNN. *Nongye Jixie Xuebao*, *51*(5), 199–206.

Jin, N., Zhao, C. J., & Wu, H. R. (2022). Agricultural short text matching Technology based on multi-semantic features. *Chinese Journal of Agricultural Machinery*, *5*, 325–331.

Kasneci, E., Seßler, K., Küchemann, S., Bannert, M., Dementieva, D., Fischer, F., Gasser, U., Groh, G., Günnemann, S., Hüllermeier, E., Krusche, S., Kutyniok, G., Michaeli, T., Nerdel, C., Pfeffer, J., Poquet, O., Sailer, M., Schmidt, A., Seidel, T., & Kasneci, G. (2023). ChatGPT for good? On opportunities and challenges of large language models for educatio. *Learning and Individual Differences*, *103*, 102274. doi:10.1016/j.lindif.2023.102274

Kong, L. Y., & Zhou, Z. P. (2023). Aspect level Sentiment analysis of mixed attention networks based on ELMo. *Journal of Chinese Information Processing*, *37*(06), 147–156.

Krizhevsky, A., Sutskever, I., & Hinton, G. E. (2012). Imagenet classification with deep convolutional neural networks. *Advances in Neural Information Processing Systems*, 25.

LeCun, Y., Bottou, L., Bengio, Y., & Haffner, P. (1998). Gradient-based learning applied to document recognition. *Proceedings of the IEEE*, *86*(11), 2278–2324. doi:10.1109/5.726791

Li, W. (2018). *Semi-supervised agricultural text classification Based on semantic diffusion kernel and support vector Machine*. Gannan Normal University.

Liao, Q. J., Liu, T., & Zhang, X. Y. (2023). Research on facial expression recognition based on VGGNet. *Software Engineering*, *26*(11), 59–62.

Liu, H. B., Han, J. J., & Ma, M. X. (2020). Research on agricultural product price prediction based on EMD-ELM model. *Journal of Agricultural Big Data*, *2*(03), 68–74.

Liu, H. L., Tao, J., & Qin, L. (2021). Implementation of One-hot coding based on Python. *Journal of Wuhan Shipbuilding Technical College*, *20*(03), 136–139.

Liu, Z. C., Zhao, C. J., & Wu, H. R. (2022). Research on similarity matching method of rice questions based on BiLSTM-CNN. *Chinese Journal of Agricultural Mechanization*, *43*(12), 125–132.

Lu, H., Qiu, Y., & Dai, X. (2021). Chinese Agricultural text classification based on central kernel alignment fuzzy svm. *Journal of Gannan Normal University*, *042*(006), 57–61.

Lv, X. C. (2023). *Small-scale Agricultural Product Price Forecast based on the Influence of Network Public Opinions*. Northeast Forestry University.

Memory, L. S. T. (2010). Long short-term memory. *Neural Computation*, *9*(8), 1735–1780. PMID:9377276

Mikolov, T., Sutskever, I., & Chen, K. (2013). Distributed representations of words and phrases and their compositionality. *Advances in Neural Information Processing Systems*, 26.

Ren, X. Y. (2019). *Research on Agricultural public Opinion Monitoring and analysis system*. Henan Agricultural University.

Shang, K. Y. (2023). European Union accelerates the development of green industry. *Journal of Theoretical Review*, *6*, 62–63.

Shi G. F. (2020), Implementation of Chinese text corpus preprocessing module based on jieba Chinese word segmentation, *International Journal of Computer Knowledge and Technology, 16*(14), 248-251+257.

Shi Y. L., Cui Y. P., & Du Z. G. (2022). Agricultural News Text Classification Method Based on BERT and Deep active learning, *Journal of agricultural books intelligence 8*, 19-29.

Sutskever, I., Vinyals, O., & Le, Q. V. (2014). Sequence to sequence learning with neural networks. *Advances in Neural Information Processing Systems*, 27.

Vaswani, A., Shazeer, N., & Parmar, N. (2017), Attention is all you need, Advances in neural information processing systems, 30.

Wang, F. J., Wei, L. J., & Zhao, X. (2022). Research on agricultural short text classification based on FastText model. *Software*, *10*, 27–29.

Wang, H. R. Q., Wang, X. M., & Miao, Y. S. (2022). Similarity Matching of agricultural question Answering Community Based on BERT-Attention-DenseBiGRU. *Nongye Jixie Xuebao*, *1*, 244–252.

Wang, K. Y. (2023). *A BO_SVR Method Based on News Headlines on Soybean Price Forecasting Study*. Jilin Agricultural University.

Wang, R. Q., Wan, X. M., & Miao, Y. S. (2022). Similarity Matching of agricultural question Answering Community Based on BERT-Attention-DenseBiGRU. *Nongye Jixie Xuebao*, *1*, 244–252.

Wang, Z. Q., Zhang, Z., & Xia, Y. F. (2023). Fault Alarm Prediction of CNC Machine Tools Based on Word2vec and LSTM-SV. *Combined Machine Tools and Automatic Processing Technology*, *4*, 71–75.

Wankhade, M., Rao, A. C. S., & Kulkarni, C. (2022). A survey on sentiment analysis methods, applications, and challenges. *Journal of Artificial Intelligence Research*, *55*(7), 5731–5780.

Wei, F. F., Duan, Q. L., & Xiao, X. C. (2015). Classification Technique of Chinese Agricultural Text Information Based on SVM. *Journal of Transactions of the Chinese Society for Agricultural Machinery*, *46*(S1), 174–179.

Wu, H. R., Guo, W., & Deng, Y. (2022). A Survey of Semantic Understanding Techniques for Agricultural texts. *Chinese Journal of Agricultural Machinery*, *5*, 1–16.

Wu, L., & Li, S. (2015). The attempt of text mining data preprocessing in TCM prescription database. *International Journal of Chinese Medicine Library and Information*, *39*(03), 8–11.

Xiang, H. M., Bai, T., & Li, Y. D. (2022). Automatic indexing of agricultural text based on word embedding and multi-feature fusion. *Xinjiang Nongye Daxue Xuebao*, *6*, 486–492.

Xue, W. M., & Lu, Y. C. (2005). Dual hesitant fuzzy graphs with applications to multi-attribute decision making. *International Journal of Cognitive Computing in Engineering*, *1*, 18–26.

Yang, S. Q., Duan, X. L., & Xiao, Z. (2023). Agricultural news text classification based on ERNIE+DPCNN+BiGRU. *Computer Applications (Nottingham)*, (05), 1461–1466.

Ye, S. H., Ge, Y. H., & Chen, B. (2023). Cyberbullying detection model based on ELMo-TextCNN. *Journal of Information Security Research*, *9*(09), 868–876.

Yu, L. G., Liu, J. T., & Zhu, J. (2022). Effects of the electrical stimulation on the behavioral and physiological performances of the beef cattle [Transactions of the CSAE]. *International Journal of Chinese Society of Agricultural Engineering*, *38*(13), 221–227.

Zhang, H. (2023). *Research on the forecasting method of China's corn futures market by combining sentiment analysis*. Anhui Agricultural University.

Zhang, K. R., Yang, W. S., & Yan, B. (2023). A multi-step forecasting model for airport terminal cooling load based on VMD-IPSO-GRU. *Heating Ventilating & Air Conditioning*, *53*(S2), 84–88.

Zhao, C. J. (2023). Review on intelligent service technology of agricultural knowledge [Chinese and English]. *Journal of Intelligent Agriculture*, *5*(02), 126–148.

Zhao, Y., & Guo, X. Y. (2020). Research on agricultural text classification method based on Naive Bayes. *Journal of Water Saving Irrigation*, *2*, 98–102.

Zhou, J. M., Li, Y. C., & Lai, C. X. (2022). Research on question classification in question answering system for agricultural field [Natural Science Edition]. *Journal of Henan University of Science and Technology*, *3*, 63–70.

Chapter 9
A Snapshot Survey of Data Acquisition Forms in Multi-Attribute Decision-Making Studies

Yuge Niu
https://orcid.org/0009-0000-5242-8090
Shanxi University, China

Kexin Liu
https://orcid.org/0009-0005-4336-6170
Shanxi University, China

Fanghui Lu
Shanxi University, China

Jiayi Zhang
Trinity College Dublin, Ireland

ABSTRACT

Multi-attribute decision-making (MADM) analysis is an important field widely used in the decision-making process. As the volume of data increases, it becomes critical to have a comprehensive understanding of large-scale data collection. However, current research lacks a holistic approach to obtaining large-scale data. This chapter aims to address this research gap by summarizing classic papers, open datasets, remote sensing data, sentiment analysis, and questionnaire survey data collection forms in MADM research. Classic papers provide a wealth of foundational knowledge, while open datasets provide diverse and large-scale data. Additionally, remote sensing data provides real-time information for urban planning and environmental management decisions. Finally, sentiment analysis leverages social media to gain unique insights, and questionnaire surveys are valid. Overall, this chapter helps researchers and professionals improve their selection and design of data collection methods to ensure reliable and impactful data collection, thereby improving the ability to make informed decisions.

DOI: 10.4018/979-8-3693-1582-8.ch009

INTRODUCTION

With the rapid development of emerging technologies such as Internet technology, cloud computing, and the Internet of Things, the scale of data has grown explosively. The accumulation and storage of massive amounts of data provide huge opportunities and challenges for national decision-making and enterprise operations. This data contains a wealth of information in various fields that can help people better understand how the real world works and evolves. Big data dynamically reflect the development trend of various economic and social indicators, and reflects the effect of policy implementation in multiple dimensions and levels, making social management more refined and intelligent, and providing people with a more scientific and data-based decision-making thinking (Yaqoob et al., 2016; Zhang et al., 2024). MADM is an important part of decision science, which refers to the decision-making process that requires comprehensive consideration of multiple attribute factors in the decision-making process to achieve the optimal decision-making goal (Zanakis et al., 1998). Decision-making problems in real life are often affected by multiple attribute factors, and the influence of multiple attributes needs to be considered comprehensively (Zhang, 2008a; Wang et al., 2021). By comprehensively considering multiple attribute factors, we can evaluate the decision-making object more comprehensively, grasp the decision-making environment more accurately, and make more scientific and reasonable decisions, which is helpful to improve the accuracy and effectiveness of decision-making (Zhang & Yager, 2008b; Zhang et al., 2023).

Data collection is a crucial part of MADM research, as its quality and comprehensiveness directly affect the final decision outcome (Platts et al., 2002). At present, there are five main data collection methods commonly used in academia:

(1) Obtaining Data from Classic Papers: Classic papers refer to research results that have important influence and representation in a certain field. Classic papers contain a wealth of data that can be used for the analysis and decision-making of MADM. Through in-depth analysis and evaluation of this data, decision-makers (DMs) can better understand the nature and context of the problem, so that they can make more accurate decisions (Van Oudenhoven et al., 2018). These data can be used to establish a variety of different types of decision-making models, such as analytic hierarchy process (AHP), fuzzy comprehensive evaluation method, entropy weight method, etc., and can also be used to optimize decision-making schemes, so as to help DMs evaluate and compare different decision-making schemes, so as to choose the optimal scheme and improve the scientificity and efficiency of decision-making (Zhang et al., 2019). However, the data in classic papers may have problems such as update lag, difficulty in obtaining, and lack of multi-dimensional information.

(2) Sentiment Analysis: Sentiment analysis, also known as opinion mining or sentiment analysis, refers to the use of natural language processing and machine learning (ML) techniques to identify and understand the emotions and sentiments expressed in text. There is a close relationship between sentiment analysis and multi-attribute decision making (Ji et al., 2018). Sentiment analysis can help DMs gain a more comprehensive understanding of the emotional tendencies and attitudes of decision objects, thereby better considering the emotional factors of decision objects in MADM (Tan et al., 2022; Awajan et al., 2021). By taking into account the results of sentiment analysis, emotional factors can be incorporated into the consideration scope of MADM, thus enabling a more comprehensive evaluation of the impact of different choices on emotional factors (Wu & Zhang, 2019). This can help in formulating decisions and strategies that better align with market

demands and consumer emotional preferences. Therefore, sentiment analysis provides a more detailed and comprehensive decision basis for MADM, contributing to improved decision accuracy and specificity. However, sentiment analysis can also lead to biased results due to problems such as imperfection of emotional vocabulary, language and cultural biases.

(3) Remote Sensing Data: Remote sensing data are the information of the earth's surface obtained through long-distance means such as satellites and aircraft, including various attributes such as land cover type, temperature, humidity and so on (Zhang et al., 2016). These multi-attribute remote sensing data can be widely used in environmental monitoring, urban planning, agricultural production and other fields. In MADM, you need to consider the correlation and impact between different attributes. Remote sensing data provide information on a variety of attributes, which can provide comprehensive geographic information, real-time information, high accuracy, and cross-regionality, and provide a scientific basis for decision-making. Data support for MADM, e.g., in urban planning, environmental protection, and agricultural resource management. Through the analysis of multi-attribute information of remote sensing data, it can provide DMs with a more comprehensive understanding and more accurate decision-making basis.

(4) Open Datasets: Open datasets refer to publicly available and accessible datasets provided by governments, organizations, or communities. These datasets cover a wide range of topics, such as population statistics, environmental data, economic data, and more. They can contain various attributes relevant to decision-making, providing more comprehensive and accurate information and avoiding subjectivity and bias in the decision-making process. By analyzing these datasets, correlations, trends, and other information can be extracted to help DMs better understand the context of their decisions (Barlas et al., 2015). Open datasets can provide historical and trend data for analysis, foster community engagement, and save time and costs associated with data collection (Zhang et al., 2020a). However, they may have data incompleteness, privacy and security issues, as well as data quality and consistency concerns, which can affect the reliability and accuracy of MADM (Immonen et al., 2018).

(5) Questionnaire Survey: The questionnaire survey method is a scientific approach to accurately grasp the phenomena or problems in the complex macro world through effective use of numbers. It is a research method that provides a realistic basis for solving problems, improving the current situation, and planning for the future. It is a method of studying the objective facts produced by various social forces behind social phenomena. The emergence and widespread use of the survey method provide a feasible way for DMs to obtain objective and effective data. If researchers can effectively use this method, they undoubtedly have a powerful tool to access unknown areas of knowledge. The questionnaire is the most frequently used data collection tool or instrument for quantitative studies especially surveys (Taherdoost, 2016).

The contributions to this chapter are as follows:

(1) This chapter will comprehensively discuss various data collection methods, including open datasets, remote sensing data, sentiment analysis, questionnaire survey, etc. Through a comprehensive comparison of these methods, researchers and practitioners can better choose the appropriate data collection method.

(2) This chapter will focus on the practical application of different data collection methods. By discussing how to access and leverage this data, it is possible to provide practical recommendations for DMs to better use the data to support decision-making analysis.
(3) This chapter will focus on newer data collection methods, such as remote sensing data and sentiment analysis. The application of these methods in MADM research has been relatively seldom explored. Through the discussion of these emerging methods, researchers and practitioners can be provided with new ideas and methods to enrich the data sources of MADM research.

The remainder of the chapter is organized as follows: Section 2 delves into the evolution of the five data collection methodologies within the realm of MADM. Section 3 elaborates on the application of these five data collection techniques to MADM, accompanied by illustrative examples. Section 4 addresses the obstacles associated with these methodologies and suggests potential trends for future research. Lastly, Section 5 provides a summary of the entire text.

LITERATURE REVIEW

Literature Review on Obtaining Data From Classic Papers

Obtaining data from classic papers, which refers to extracting data from published research papers for subsequent analysis and application, is a common research method in which researchers can collect, organize, and analyze data from the existing literature to support their own research (Zahedi-Seresht et al., 2016). This approach is commonly used in study design, such as literature reviews, meta-analyses, and secondary data analysis. In the field of MADM, there are also many researchers who obtain data from classic papers. Operators, fuzzy sets, and granular computation are important mathematical tools in the MADM. In terms of operators, Zhang et al. (2018) used Wei (2017) numerical examples to verify the effectiveness of the proposed method in the study of fuzzy Dombi Heronian mean operators and its application in MADM. In terms of fuzzy sets, Li et al. (2019) used the example of Ju and Wang (2013) as a numerical example in the study of multi-attribute group decision-making. In terms of granular computing, Zhang et al. (2020b) used the data of Zhang et al. (2017) in order to effectively compare and analyze with the existing multi-attribute group decision-making methods in the study of multi-granularity probabilistic models to deal with multi-attribute group decision-making problems and interval neutrosophic information. Obtaining data from classic papers helps policymakers understand historical decision-making processes and outcomes, leading to a better understanding of the current decision-making environment and challenges (Brehmer, 1992; Cobo et al., 2014). This historical data can also be used to predict future trends and directions (Sanchez-Nunez et al., 2021), thereby helping DMs make more accurate and reliable decisions.

Literature Review of Sentiment Analysis

The term "sentiment analysis" was coined by Nasukawa and Yi (2003). Sentiment analysis can be conducted at three levels: sentence level (Tang et al., 2015), document level (Pu et al., 2019), and aspect level (Ma et al., 2019; Nandhini & Pradeep, 2020; Nandwani & Verma, 2021). Sentiment analysis techniques are typically categorized into dictionary-based methods (Bernabe-Moreno et al., 2020), machine learning-based methods (Tiwari et al., 2020; Maslej-Kresnakova et al., 2020), deep learning-based methods (Dashtipour et al., 2020), and hybrid methods (Ersahin et al., 2019). The application of sentiment analysis in MADM can be divided into two categories. One is text-based sentiment analysis, used to extract sentiment information from user feedback, comments, and other text to provide references for decision-making. The other category is emotion recognition-based MADM, which considers emotional factors as one of the decision attributes. Regarding text-based sentiment analysis, previous studies have proposed sentiment analysis methods based on sentiment lexicons. For instance, Cheng et al. (2023) constructed a sentiment lexicon for blood glucose meters and combined text analysis techniques such as text cleaning to extract and analyze user evaluations of different blood glucose meters, using the results as an important indicator for blood glucose meter selection. Additionally, researchers have utilized ML algorithms to conduct sentiment mining on large-scale text data, providing support for product marketing, public opinion monitoring, and other MADM. Rahman and Hossen (2019) used five ML classifiers, including Bernoulli Naive Bayes, decision trees, support vector machines, and maximum entropy, to perform sentiment analysis on collected movie data reviews, thereby supporting the corresponding MADM. Wu et al. (2023) conducted sentiment analysis on medical service reviews using the deep neural network BERT (Bidirectional Encoder Representations from Transformers) to support patient selection of online doctors. As for emotion recognition-based MADM, some studies have combined psychological theories and decision models to explore the influence of emotions on decision outcomes, providing theoretical foundations for decision-making behaviors under different emotional states. Sudhakaran et al. (2022) developed an emotion recognition-based music model by integrating psychological theories, facial expressions, and deep learning technology. In summary, applying sentiment analysis to MADM can help DMs better understand public opinion, improve the objectivity and democracy of decision-making, and thus better meet public needs and optimize decision outcomes.

Literature Review of Remote Sensing Data

The application of remote sensing data in MADM can be classified into qualitative and quantitative categories. Qualitative applications mainly involve using remote sensing data for land cover classification and identification, providing spatial information support for decision-making. Quantitative applications, on the other hand, involve extracting land cover features from remote sensing data and combining them with other attribute data for multi-attribute decision analysis.

In the literature review, researchers have focused on the qualitative application of remote sensing data in MADM, particularly on the classification methods and techniques of remote sensing imagery, as well as the application of different remote sensing data in land cover identification and classification. For instance, studies have been conducted on land use type classification using high-resolution remote sensing imagery (Shao et al., 2020; Cao et al., 2023), as well as on estimating vegetation cover using multi-source remote sensing data (Hu et al., 2017). In terms of quantitative applications, researchers have concentrated on the fusion methods of remote sensing data with other attribute data and the construction of multi-attribute decision analysis models. For instance, research has been conducted on using remote sensing data to extract urban land use information and combining it with economic, social, and other multi-attribute data for urban planning decisions (Liu et al., 2017), as well as on environmental monitoring using remote sensing data and combining it with pollution sources, meteorological, and other multi-attribute data for environmental management decisions (Ehlers et al., 2006).

In conclusion, the application of remote sensing data in MADM covers qualitative and quantitative categories. The relevant literature review demonstrates the wide-ranging application prospects of remote sensing data in land cover identification and classification, multi-attribute decision analysis, and other areas. However, further research and exploration are still needed to enhance the effectiveness and level of application of remote sensing data in MADM.

Literature Review of Open Datasets

The development of open datasets can be traced back to the 1980s. At that time, governments and academic institutions gradually realized the importance of data and began to open up large amounts of data so that more people could access and utilize this information. In this phase, open datasets mainly consisted of government data and academic research data, and were limited by the technology and network conditions of the time, making it relatively difficult to access and utilize the data (Uhlir & Schroder, 2007). With the widespread popularity of the internet and technological advancements, open datasets began to be more widely promoted and applied. In 2007, the US government launched the data.gov website, which made a large number of government datasets available to the public, marking the beginning of open government data. Subsequently, more and more countries and organizations have also launched similar open data platforms. Open datasets in this phase also covered a wider range of fields, including economics, society, environment, and various other aspects of data.

The development of open datasets has also benefited from the open-source community and the rapid development of data science (Janssen, et al., 2012). Open datasets provide rich resources for data scientists, engineers, and researchers, which has promoted the development of data analysis and data mining. At the same time, the application of open data has gradually expanded into commercial and social fields, providing new possibilities for innovation and problem-solving.

With the development of artificial intelligence and big data technology, open datasets have played an important role in intelligent applications and data-driven decision-making. In the early 21st century, an increasing number of governments and non-governmental organizations began promoting the release and utilization of open datasets. Some countries and regions established specialized open data platforms to encourage public and private sectors to share data and promote data reuse and secondary development (Harper & Konstan, 2015).

Entering the mid-21st century, open datasets became a global trend, expanding into various industries and fields. In addition to government-released open datasets, more and more enterprises and research institutions began opening up their own data to promote innovation and collaboration (Molloy, 2011).

In the digital and intelligent age, open datasets have become an important support for promoting economic development, scientific research, and social governance. An increasing number of countries and regions have begun to attach importance to open data policies, intensifying the construction of open datasets, and further expanding the application scope of open datasets in various fields.

Literature Review of Questionnaire Survey

The survey method first appeared in 1882 when British anthropologist Galton established an anthropological testing laboratory in London, printing the questions to be investigated on questionnaires, distributing and collecting these questionnaires to collect relevant data. Since then, survey methods have played a significant role in exploring and understanding the mysteries and regularities of social phenomena.

Researchers analyze and make decisions based on the collected data (Cobanoglu et al., 2003). With the development of new technologies and improvements in various statistical analysis methods, survey methods have become faster and more scientific in collecting and organizing data, which is an important reason for their widespread use. Some scholars refer to the survey method as a "written survey method" and a "fill-in-the-blank method," with the key point being that researchers provide designed questionnaires to relevant individuals in any feasible way according to standardized procedures, and then analyze the results to obtain information, thus making decisions and predictions (Wettergren, et al., 2016).

The mid to late 20th century saw a significant shift towards computer-assisted survey methods, which revolutionized data collection and analysis. The advent of online surveys and data collection platforms in the 21st century further transformed the landscape of survey research, making it more accessible and cost-effective (Wright, 2005).

Today, survey methods continue to be a fundamental tool for collecting and analyzing data in various fields, including social sciences, marketing, public opinion research, and healthcare. The ongoing development of survey techniques, including adaptive survey designs, mobile data collection, and advanced statistical methods, ensures that survey research remains a versatile and powerful approach for understanding human behavior and attitudes.

The survey technique is an efficient way to collect large sample data, making it easy to analyze and present data in a structured way. There are various classification methods in survey research, each with its own advantages and limitations; however, they complement each other. Through survey collection and investigation, researchers can obtain effective and rigorous results, helping them make the most accurate decisions.

SPECIFIC METHODS

Specific Methods of Obtaining Data from Classic Papers for MADM

A specific step to obtain data from a classic paper and apply it to MADM is as follows:

(1) Determine data needs: Determine what data to take from a classic paper, which may involve experimental data, survey results, statistics, etc.
(2) Literature research: Search academic databases, journals or related professional websites (such as Google Scholar, IEEE Xplore, Elsevier, Springer, etc.) to find relevant classic papers to ensure the credibility and academic value of the papers. Obtain experimental data, case data, survey data, etc. from papers to support data analysis and decision-making for MADM.
(3) Organize the data: Organize the data obtained from the paper into a structured form, including attributes, attribute values, weights, and other information. This may require converting the descriptive data in the text into a data format that can be calculated and analyzed, such as converting the description into digital data.
(4) Determine attribute weights: Determine the weight of each attribute according to the method or experimental results proposed in the paper. Common methods include AHP, principal component analysis, etc. According to the specific method in the paper, the data need to be processed and calculated to obtain the weight value of each attribute.

(5) Analyze the data: Use the data and methods in the paper to analyze the data of MADM objects. This may include calculating the score or ranking of individual attributes, calculating the overall score, etc. These analyses can be carried out based on the models or methods proposed in the paper, ensuring the accuracy and reliability of the data analysis.
(6) Make decisions: According to the results of data analysis, combined with the weight of multiple attributes, formulate decision-making strategies or make decision-making recommendations. This may include the evaluation, ranking, or scoring of different decision-making options, as well as the final decision recommendation or decision-making basis.

It is important to note that when obtaining data, it is important to comply with the relevant laws and regulations and data use agreements. Some data may be subject to copyright protection or require special permissions for access and use. Therefore, it is important to be mindful of the relevant legal requirements when obtaining data.

Next, let us take the example of a research in the field of environmental management, with the purpose of evaluating the environmental quality of different cities in order to formulate environmental protection policies, to better explain this form of data collection. Here is an example of a concrete step (The full framework is presented in Figure 1.):

Figure 1. The framework of environmental quality protection MADM.

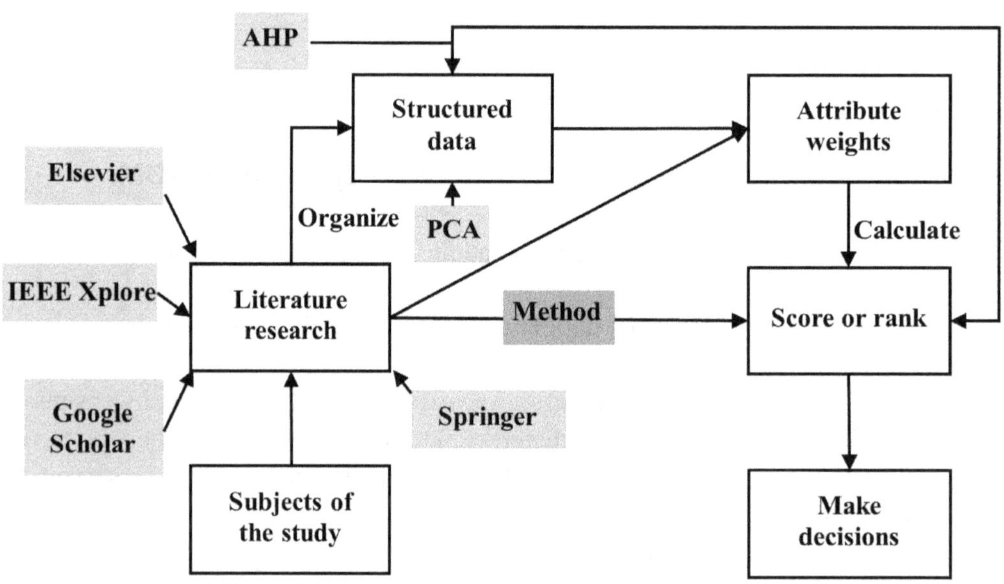

(1) Gather data on the environmental quality of each city, including air quality index, water quality index, garbage disposal, green space coverage, etc.
(2) Conduct a thorough search of academic databases to identify a seminal paper that offers a comprehensive investigation and evaluation of the environmental quality of different cities. The chosen

paper should provide detailed data and analysis results. In order to facilitate a better understanding, we have vividly demonstrated how to search for relevant papers on the IEEE Xplore official website, as shown in Figure 2.

(3) Extract relevant data such as air quality index, water quality index, garbage disposal, and green space coverage of each city from the selected paper. Organize this information into a structured format for further analysis and decision-making.

(4) Determine the weight of each environmental quality attribute based on the methodology or experimental results outlined in the selected paper. This may involve establishing the importance and weight value of each indicator according to survey results and expert opinions presented in the paper.

(5) Utilize the data and methodologies outlined in the selected paper to analyze the environmental quality of each city. Calculate scores or rankings for each index to obtain a comprehensive environmental quality evaluation.

(6) Based on the results of the data analysis and the assigned weight of each index, develop environmental protection policies or decision-making recommendations. This may involve proposing tailored environmental protection measures and policy recommendations for different cities.

Figure 2. Papers on IEEE Xplore.ieee.org.

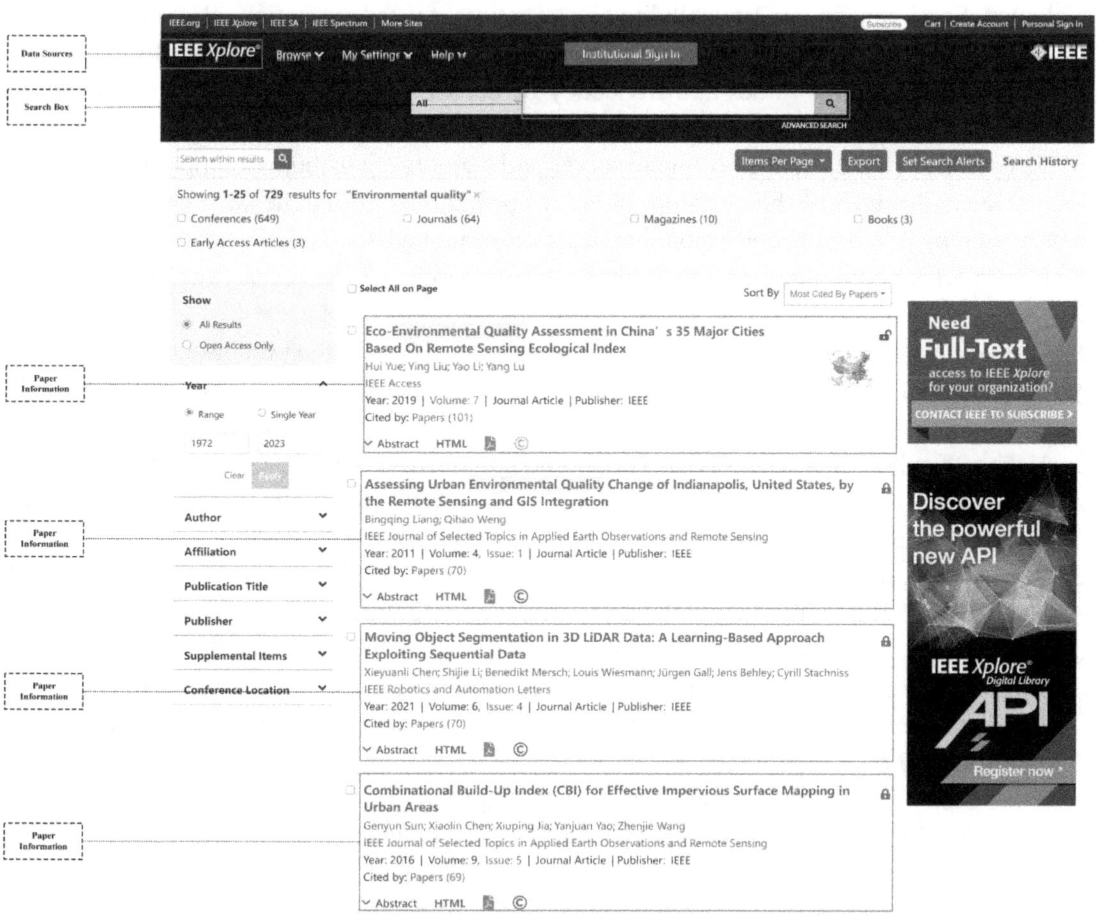

Specific Methods of Sentiment Analysis for MADM

A specific step-by-step application of sentiment analysis to MADM is as follows:

(1) Determine the decision object: Clearly identify the object for MADM, such as a product, service, or brand.
(2) Collect data: Collect relevant text data for MADM, such as user reviews, surveys, social media comments, etc. These data should cover multiple attributes, such as product performance, price, appearance, etc. Researchers also use datasets from the field of emotion and sentiment analysis, such as SemEval, Stanford Sentiment Treebank, International Survey on Affective Reasoning and Emotion, to evaluate the effectiveness of their models. Additionally, using web scraping tools to collect online reviews is also a good form of data collection.
(3) Data preprocessing: Clean and preprocess the collected data, including removing noise, text standardization, and sentiment word extraction, to prepare for sentiment analysis.
(4) Sentiment analysis: Use sentiment analysis techniques to identify and analyze the emotional tendencies in the text data. Sentiment analysis can be based on ML models or deep learning models to recognize the emotional polarity (positive, negative, neutral) and emotional intensity in the text.
(5) Determine attribute weights: Based on the multiple attributes of the decision object, determine the weight of each attribute using methods such as expert evaluation, AHP, data mining, etc.
(6) Calculate Sentiment score: Typically involves sentiment word extraction, classification, and emotional intensity calculation. Then, calculate the sentiment score and polarity of the text based on the emotional intensity values and frequency of occurrence of sentiment words to evaluate the emotional impact of users on each attribute.
(7) Make decisions: Based on the sentiment scores and weights of attributes, comprehensively evaluate the various attributes of the decision object to formulate a comprehensive emotional evaluation result, thereby developing corresponding decision strategies, such as product improvement, adjustment of market positioning, etc., to better meet the emotional needs and expectations of users.

Here, we will use the research conducted by Yang et al. (2023) on the purchase of personalized new energy vehicles as an example to explain how sentiment analysis can be better applied to MADM. The full framework is presented in Figure 3.

Step 1: The "Koubei" interface on the "Autohome" platform provides rich evaluations of purchased new energy vehicles by users. Therefore, Yang et al. chose to use the platform's review information to help "Autohome" improve its personalized product recommendation service.

Step 2: Yang et al. used web scraping tools to select 6 electric vehicles (Lingbao T03, Wuling Hongguang MINIEV, BYD Han, BYD Tang, NIO ES6, and XPeng P7) from the "Autohome" platform (https://www.autohome.com.cn) and categorized the evaluations of these electric vehicles into eight attributes: space, power, handling, energy consumption, comfort, appearance, decoration, and value for money. In order to facilitate understanding, we have displayed the owner reviews of these vehicles on the "Autohome" platform, as shown in Figure 4.

Step 3 and Step 4: Yang et al. utilized Gooseeker (http://www.gooseeker.com/) on the Product Recommendation Platform for each new energy vehicle. They conducted sentiment analysis by cleaning data, establishing sentiment dictionaries, obtaining data trends, and transforming the evaluations of each attribute of the new energy vehicles to obtain the quantity of positive, negative, and neutral comments.

Figure 3. The framework of personalized new energy vehicle purchase MADM

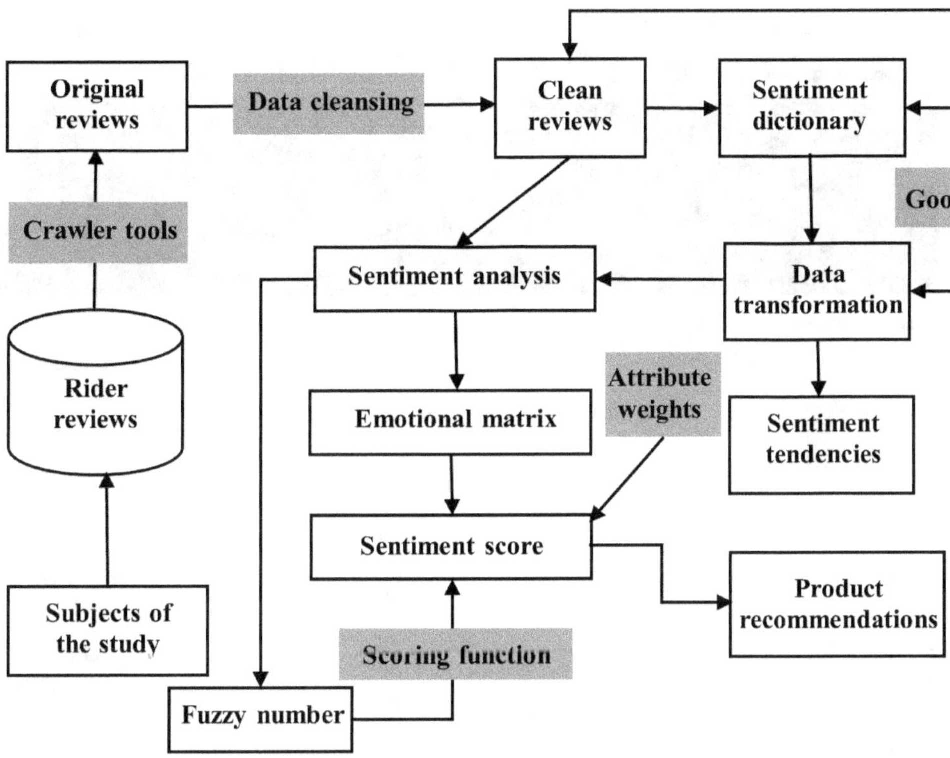

Step 5: Based on a formula, they calculated the proportion of the three different sentiment polarities for each product attribute and converted them into corresponding values. Subsequently, they constructed a multi-attribute integrated sentiment matrix.

Step 6: Using the q-rung orthogonal fuzzy weighted partition Mourehd mean operator, they obtained the q-rung orthogonal fuzzy numbers for each situation by aggregating the information matrix. After that, the attribute is divided into three parts according to its actual meaning, and the weight of each attribute is set by the user. They then calculated the product score according to the equation of the score function.

Step 7: They recommended the new energy vehicle that aligns with the personalized preferences of users based on the comparison rules of the score function.

Specific Methods of MADM With Remote Sensing Data

The application of remote sensing data to MADM typically involves the following specific steps:

(1) Data acquisition: The first step is to obtain relevant remote sensing data, which may include satellite imagery, aerial photography images, lidar data, etc. This data can be used to obtain information on the topography, vegetation cover, land use, etc. of the surface.

Figure 4. Vehicle types and reviews on Autohome.com

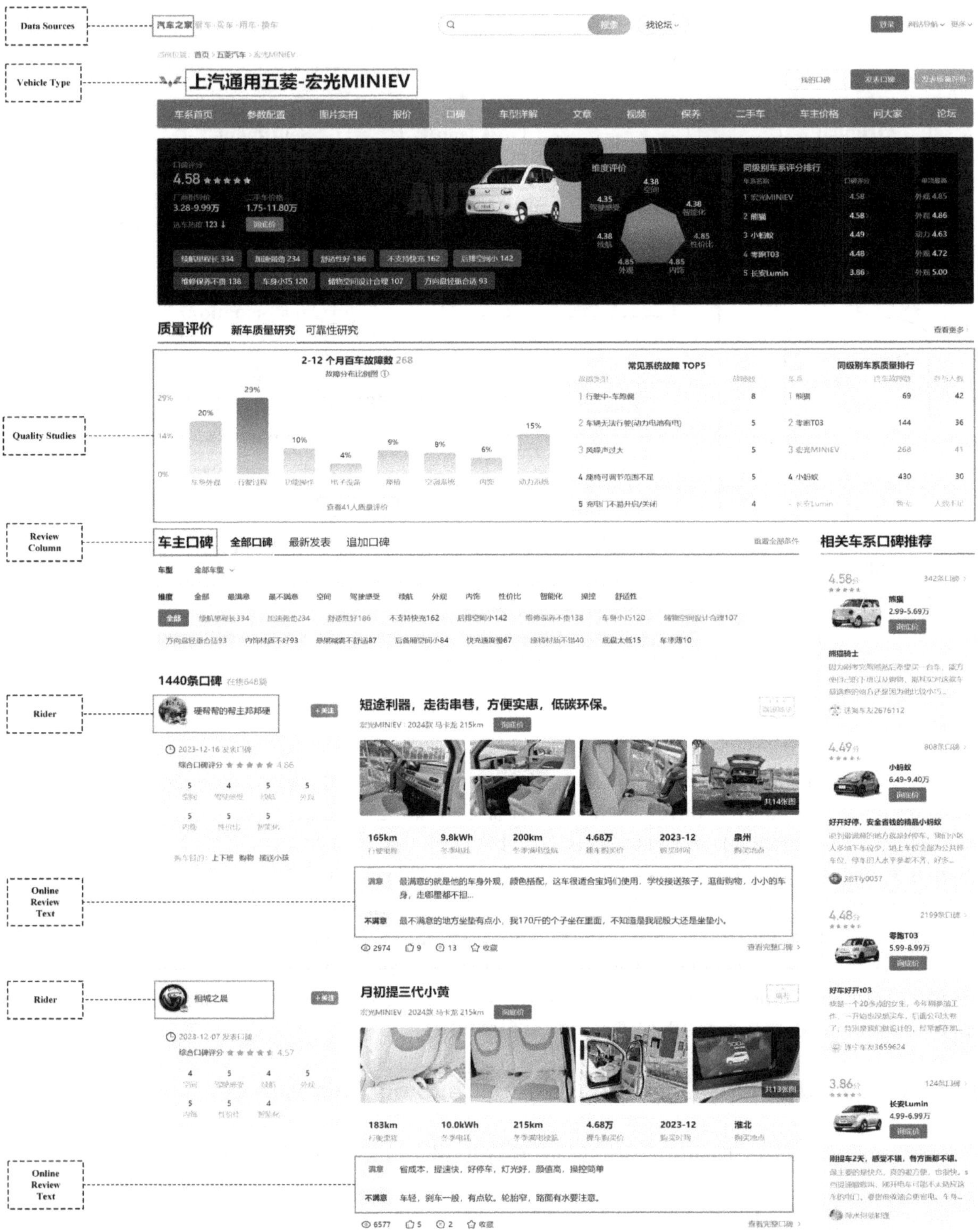

(2) Data preprocessing: The obtained raw remote sensing data may need to be preprocessed, including atmospheric correction, geometric correction, image registration, etc., to ensure the accuracy and availability of the data.
(3) Feature extraction: Use remote sensing data to extract relevant geographic information features, such as vegetation coverage, land type, water distribution, etc. These features are usually achieved through image processing and remote sensing techniques.
(4) Data integration: Different features extracted from remote sensing data are integrated to form a multi-attribute dataset, which may include vegetation cover, land type, terrain undulation, etc.
(5) Attribute weighting determination: For different attributes, you need to determine their importance and weight in the decision. This can be determined by expert evaluation, AHP, fuzzy synthesis evaluation, etc.
(6) Establishment of decision-making model: According to the multi-attribute data and its weight, the MADM model is established, and the common models include weighted linear combination model, fuzzy comprehensive evaluation model, TOPSIS model, etc.
(7) Decision analysis: The established decision model is used to evaluate and analyze different solutions or options to determine the optimal decision-making plan.
(8) Result display: Visualize the results of decision analysis for DMs and stakeholders to understand and reference.

The above steps are the general process of applying remote sensing data to MADM, and may be appropriately adjusted and expanded according to specific problems and data conditions in practical applications.

The specific steps involved in MADM typically include the following (The full framework is presented via Figure 5.):

(1) Data acquisition: Relevant remote sensing data needs to be obtained, which may include satellite images, aerial photographs, LiDAR data, etc. These data can be used to obtain information about the terrain, vegetation cover, land use, etc. Data can be obtained from platforms such as USGS Earth Explore, LAADS, Copernicus Open Access Hub, Geospatial Data Cloud, and more.
(2) Data preprocessing: The acquired raw remote sensing data may need to undergo preprocessing, including atmospheric correction, geometric correction, image registration, etc., to ensure data accuracy and usability.
(3) Feature extraction: Utilize remote sensing data to extract relevant geographic information features, such as vegetation cover, land types, water distribution, etc. These features are typically obtained through image processing and remote sensing techniques.
(4) Data integration: Integrate the different features extracted from remote sensing data to form a multi-attribute dataset, which may include attributes such as vegetation cover, land types, terrain variability, etc.
(5) Attribute weight determination: For different attributes, it is necessary to determine their importance and weight in the decision-making process. This can be achieved through methods such as expert assessment, AHP, fuzzy comprehensive evaluation, etc.
(6) Decision model establishment: Based on the multi-attribute data and their weights, establish a multi-attribute decision model. Common models include weighted linear combination model, fuzzy comprehensive evaluation model, TOPSIS model, etc.

(7) Decision analysis: Use the established decision model to evaluate and analyze different alternatives or options, and determine the optimal decision.
(8) Results presentation: Visualize the results of the decision analysis for the understanding and reference of DMs and stakeholders. This may include maps or other visual representations of the optimal decision outcome.

Figure 5. The framework of MADM with remote sensing data

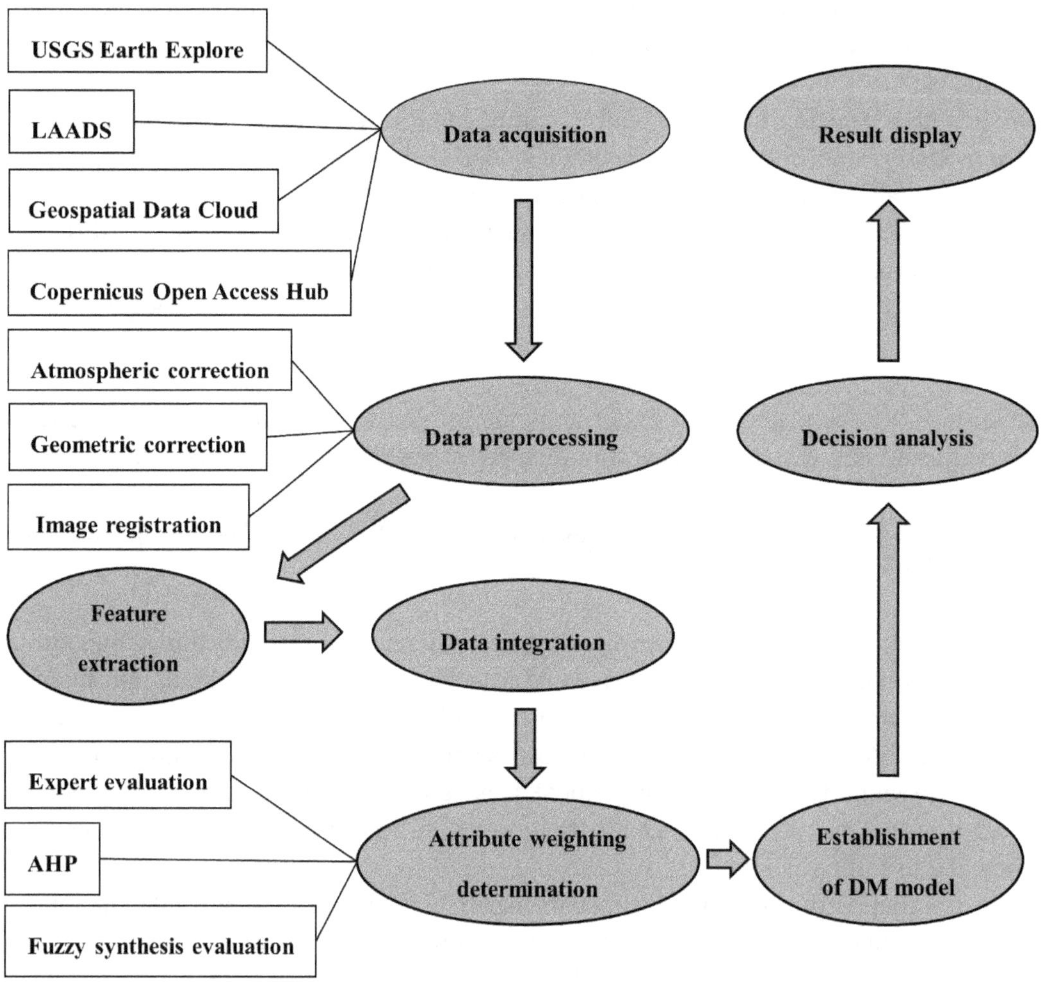

Specific Methods of Open Datasets for MADM

Open datasets can support various types of MADM, whether it is government decision-making, business management, or community development. It is a major method for providing data support for decision-making (Kirchner et al., 2015). There are thousands of data repositories on the Web, providing access to millions of datasets (Zhang et al., 2022). National and regional governments, scientific publishers and consortia, commercial data providers, and others publish data for fields ranging from social science to life science to high-energy physics to climate science and more. Access to this data is critical to facilitating reproducibility of research results, enabling scientists to build on others' work, and providing data journalists easier access to information and its provenance (Uhlir & Schroder, 2007).

The process of obtaining data from open datasets can involve the following steps (The full framework is presented in Figure 6.):

Figure 6. Framework of obtain data from open datasets

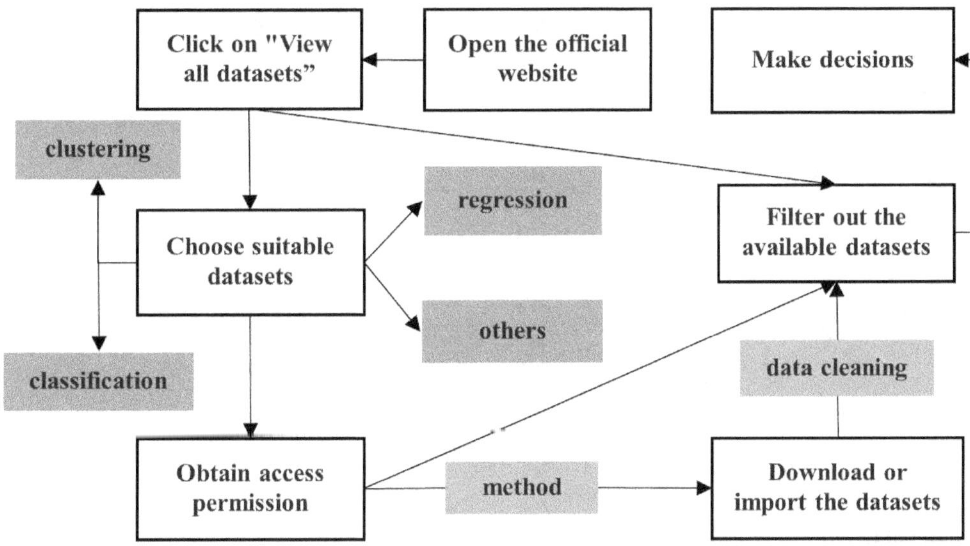

(1) Find relevant open datasets: Search for suitable open datasets using internet search engines, data portals (such as data.gov, Kaggle, etc.), or dedicated data resource platforms.
(2) Understand the content and format of the dataset: Before choosing a dataset, it is important to understand the types of data, the volume, the data structure, and other relevant information (Janssen, et al., 2012). This helps in determining if the data fit the requirements and deciding how to extract and process the data.
(3) Obtain access permission: Some open datasets may require users to register or obtain access authorization in order to download and use the data. In this step, it is important to comply with the rules set by the data provider and adhere to legal and compliance principles.
(4) Download or import the dataset: Depending on the data set's availability, you can choose to directly download the data files or import the data through APIs, database connections, etc.
(5) Data cleaning and processing: After obtaining the data, it may require data cleaning and processing operations. This includes handling missing values, outliers, and standardizing data formats to ensure data quality and consistency. Zhang et al. (2023) used data from open datasets, and after data cleaning and analysis, they used the obtained dataset to support forest fire related decision-making, providing a good example.

Figure 7. Data on healthcare datasets on Kaggle datasets

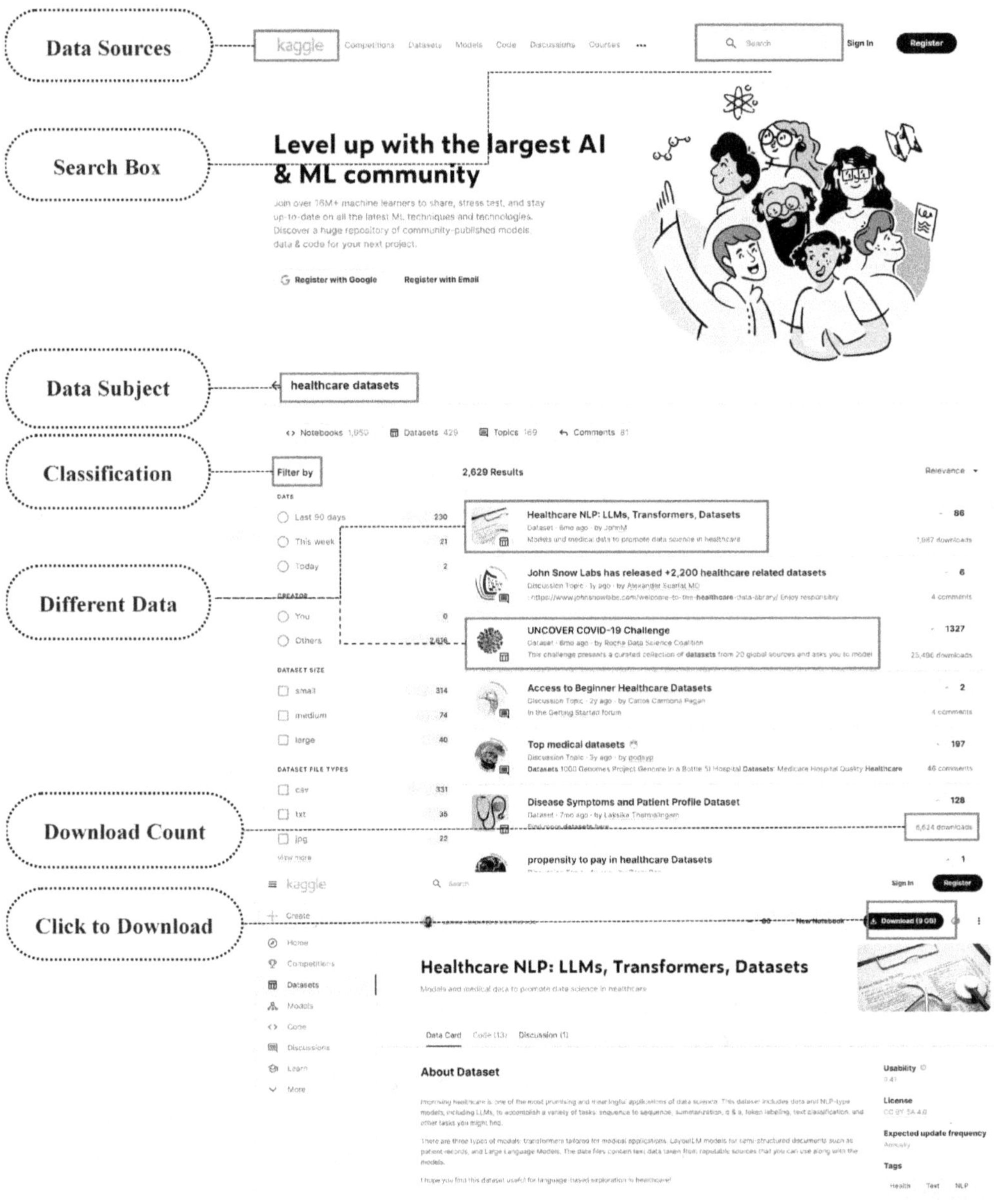

For instance, Kaggle datasets is an open data science competition platform that provides various datasets for data scientists and ML experts. As shown in Figure 7, the open datasets on Kaggle encompass different domains such as finance, healthcare, transportation, etc. Data scientists can utilize these datasets to solve real-world problems, such as predicting stock market trends, diagnosing diseases, optimizing traffic flow, and more. For instance, researchers can use healthcare datasets available on Kaggle to analyze patients' electronic medical records using ML algorithms, identify risk factors for diseases, and provide better decision support in healthcare. Thus, to get started, one can log in to the official Kaggle website, search for relevant keywords to find datasets, and choose the dataset that fits their research methodology and algorithms. As Kaggle datasets are derived from real-world scenarios and have undergone accuracy and reliability verification, researchers can utilize them relatively reliably for analysis and modeling purposes. Nevertheless, Kaggle datasets may have limitations such as incompleteness or biases, thus it is crucial to perform data cleaning and preprocessing after accessing or downloading the dataset. Moreover, the openness of datasets may raise privacy and security concerns, especially when personal data is involved. Therefore, researchers need to comply with relevant regulations and ethical guidelines while using Kaggle datasets and ensure data security and privacy protection.

Specific Methods of Questionnaire Survey for MADM

Questionnaire survey is a popular data collection method for academic or marketing research in a variety of fields. Face-to-face, telephone interviews and postal surveys are traditional approaches of completing questionnaire surveys. However, with the growing access to the internet facility globally (Evans & Mathur, 2005), for instance, internet penetration in Nepal, a low-income country, increased exponentially in the past two decades, from less than 50 users in 1995 to 11.9 million users (about 45% of total population) in 2015 (Wright, 2005) and the price of technology devices (e.g. tablet computers, hardware) and software continuing to reduce (Van Selm & Jankowski, 2006), a novel internet-based data collection technique such as online questionnaire survey has become popular in recent years (Wettergren, et al., 2016). Recently, qualitative data collection through online focus groups is also emerging (Stewart et al., 2016), suggesting, research participants in the digital age can now interact with each other and the interviewer or facilitator in an online- multimedia setting.

Therefore, in order to obtain effective questionnaire data, there are six methodological components that are crucial for successful online surveys when developing and operating online surveys (Lietz, 2010). These are: user-friendly design and layout; selecting survey participants; avoiding multiple responses; data management; ethical issues. Once a survey questionnaire is designed and completed, it is necessary to extract data from it. It is important to understand the nature, structure, and characteristics of the data obtained from a survey questionnaire before analyzing it using available software modules. For example, the proportion of waste in the proportion is usually the most commonly included content in survey reports. In addition to proportions, contingency tables are also one of the main presentation forms and analysis bases for survey data. Therefore, to obtain data from a survey questionnaire (Lietz, 2010), you can follow the steps below (The full framework is presented in Figure 8.):

(1) It is necessary to design a targeted and operational questionnaire, including open-ended and closed-ended questions to obtain comprehensive and specific information, it must be User-friendly design and layout.
(2) Appropriate survey participants need to be selected to ensure that they can genuinely reflect the required data.
(3) Surveys can be conducted through face-to-face, telephone, online, or other methods to ensure the comprehensiveness and accuracy of the data.
(4) The collected data needs to be organized and analyzed to draw conclusions and make recommendations, which includes analyze proportion, set contingency tables and examine ethical issues.

Figure 8. The framework of using data on questionnaire for MADM

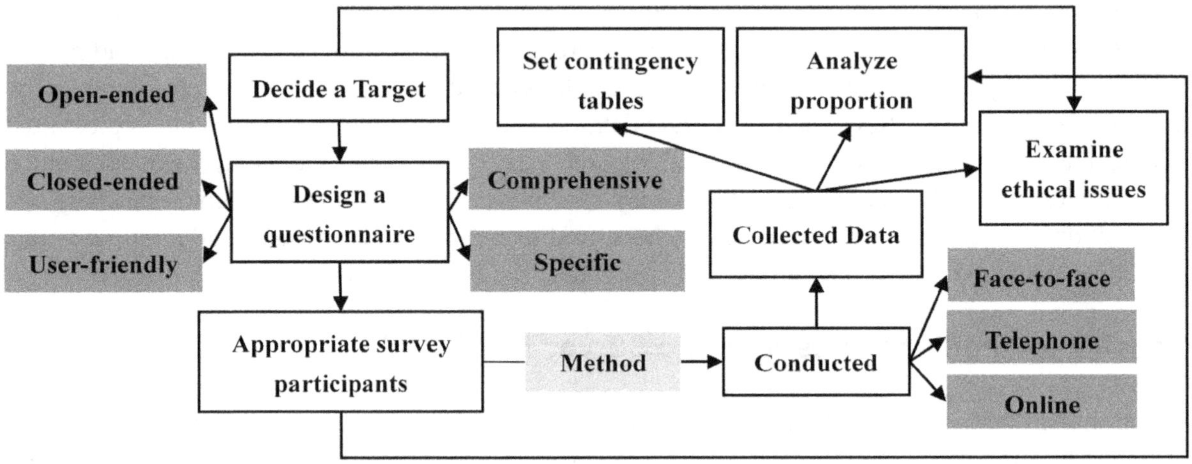

Through these methods, data can be effectively obtained from survey questionnaires, providing strong support for subsequent decision-making, as shown in Figure 9.

QUESTIONS AND EXPECTATIONS

Questions and Expectations of Obtaining Data From Classic Papers

Obtaining data from classic papers is a traditional method of data acquisition. However, with the development of artificial intelligence, metaverse, and ML, this method also faces several challenges. Firstly, the demand for large-scale and diverse data is increasing with the advancement of AI and ML technologies. Traditional classic papers may not provide sufficiently diverse and large-scale data, necessitating the exploration of alternative data sources to meet the needs of algorithms and models. Secondly, data from classic papers may have issues related to quality and accuracy, particularly when it comes to data from virtual worlds such as the metaverse. Future efforts need to address how to ensure the quality and accuracy of data to enhance the precision and robustness of AI and ML models. Additionally, as the demand for large-scale data increases, issues related to data privacy and security become more prominent. Safeguarding user privacy and data security during the data acquisition process presents a significant challenge. Lastly, as AI technology advances, there may be a need for more automated and intelligent data acquisition methods to meet the demand for large-scale data. This will require the integration of AI technology to achieve automated data retrieval, cleaning, and integration.

In summary, the method of obtaining data from classic papers faces numerous challenges when applied in the fields of artificial intelligence, metaverse, and ML. Therefore, there is a need to continuously improve data acquisition methods and technologies to meet the demand for large-scale, diverse, and high-quality data. This will contribute to the advancement of the field of MADM and propel the development of artificial intelligence and ML.

Figure 9. Obtain data from a questionnaire.

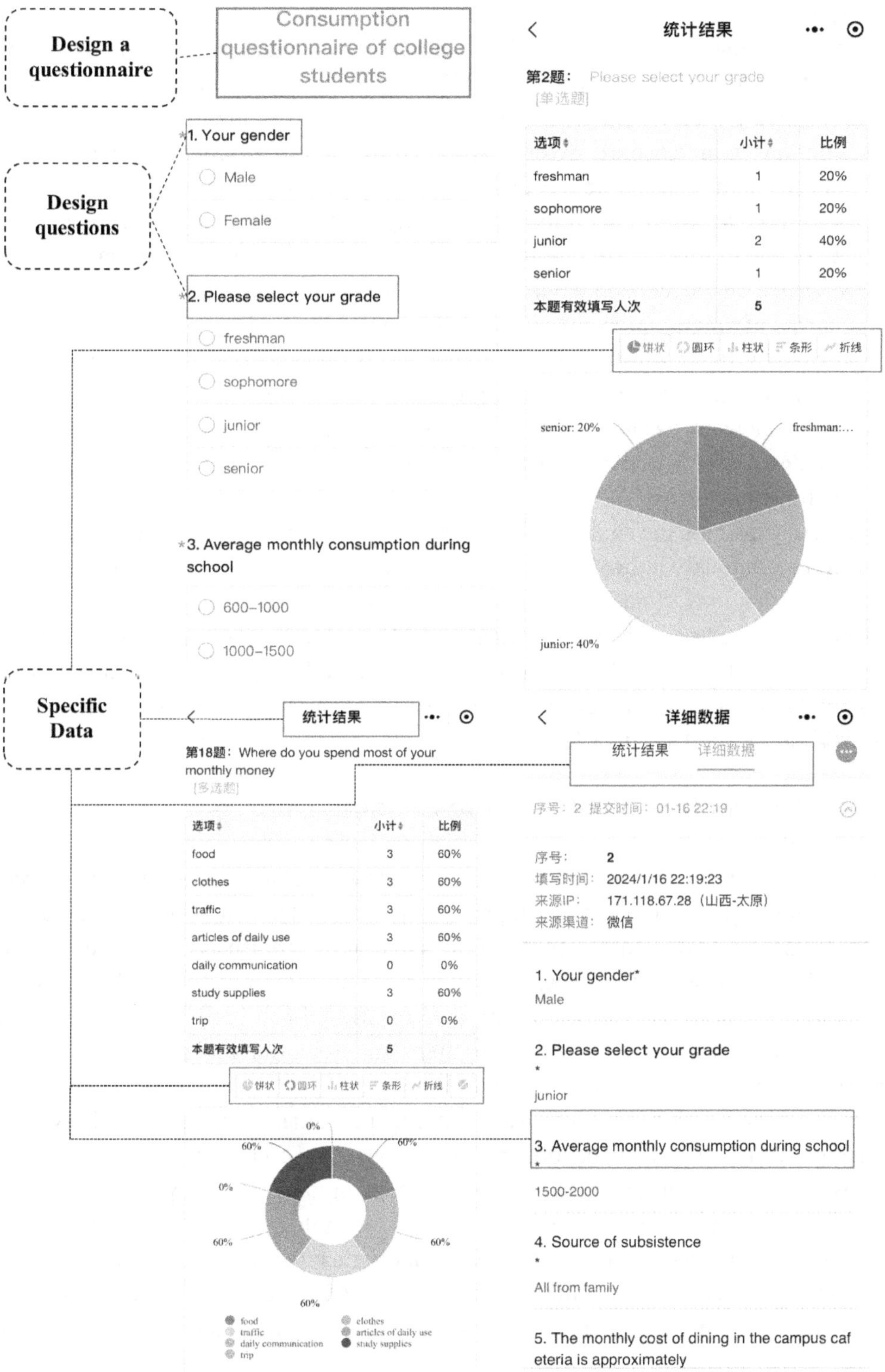

Questions and Expectations of Sentiment Analysis

In the future, sentiment analysis will face a series of challenges, particularly with the continuous development of artificial intelligence, the metaverse, and ML. Initially, sentiment analysis needs to continuously enhance its understanding of diverse contexts and user evaluations. With the advancement of AI technology, users express emotions in increasingly diverse ways in different environments, placing higher demands on sentiment analysis to more accurately capture user emotional needs and evaluations. Secondly, with the rise of the metaverse, sentiment analysis needs to adapt to the emotional experiences and expressions of people in virtual environments. In the metaverse, people may express emotions in different ways, such as through virtual characters and environments. Sentiment analysis needs to understand and interpret these new forms of emotional expression to better support user interaction and experiences in the metaverse. Additionally, the development of ML technology presents both challenges and opportunities for sentiment analysis. With the continuous progress of deep learning and natural language processing technologies, sentiment analysis can better learn and understand emotions from massive data. However, it also needs to address issues such as data bias and model generalization to improve the accuracy and robustness of sentiment analysis.

In conclusion, when facing the challenges of artificial intelligence, the metaverse, and ML, sentiment analysis needs to continuously improve algorithms and models to enhance its understanding of diverse contexts and user evaluations. It needs to adapt to the emotional experiences and expressions of people in the metaverse, while leveraging the advantages of ML technology to more accurately capture user emotional needs and evaluations. This will provide more reliable support for MADM, thereby driving the development of artificial intelligence and metaverse technologies to create more intelligent and personalized experiences and services for people.

Questions and Expectations of Remote Sensing Data

Remote sensing data exhibit certain limitations in MADM, including complex data processing and analysis, which requires professional technology and equipment; Data quality and accuracy are affected by a variety of factors, and errors may occur; At the same time, the use of remote sensing data may involve personal privacy and security issues, and relevant information needs to be handled and protected carefully. Therefore, when using remote sensing data for MADM, it is necessary to carefully evaluate the reliability and accuracy of the data, and strengthen data protection and privacy protection measures to ensure the scientificity and security of decision-making.

In the future, with the development of artificial intelligence and metaverse technology, the application of remote sensing data in MADM will become more intelligent and comprehensive. Artificial intelligence can help process and analyze large amounts of remote sensing data, providing more accurate and rapid information extraction and decision support. Metaverse technology can integrate remote sensing data with virtual reality, augmented reality, and other technologies to achieve a comprehensive simulation and visualization of various Earth attributes, providing DMs with more intuitive and immersive decision support. This will propel human society towards a more intelligent and sustainable direction.

Questions and Expectations of Open Datasets

Obtaining data through open datasets can support MADM, helping DMs gain a more comprehensive and accurate understanding of the decision context, providing scientific evidence, enabling prediction and planning, promoting information sharing, and innovation. This brings more transparency, accuracy, and credibility to the decision-making process.

However, obtaining data from open datasets faces numerous challenges. Attention needs to be given to data quality, privacy and security issues, as well as the adaptability and specificity of the data. Researchers should conduct a comprehensive evaluation when selecting and using datasets and combine other methods and data sources to validate and support research findings. In the field of artificial intelligence, training algorithms and models require a large amount of high-quality data, and the uncertainty and inconsistency of data quality may lead to model instability and inaccurate predictions (Antony & Salian, 2021). In the metaverse field, the construction of virtual environments similarly requires real and accurate data to ensure the realism and authenticity of the virtual world.

Secondly, privacy and security issues related to data cannot be overlooked. With the continuous collection and sharing of data, the protection of personal privacy data becomes particularly important. In the field of artificial intelligence, it is necessary to ensure the reasonable use and protection of sensitive data to prevent data leaks and misuse. In the metaverse field, users' personal information and virtual identities need to be fully protected to prevent privacy infringements and security vulnerabilities in virtual environments.

Additionally, data diversity and interoperability are also challenges. The effective integration and utilization of data from different sources and formats pose a complex problem. In the field of artificial intelligence, interoperability and consistency between different data sources need to be addressed to ensure the effective use and analysis of data. In the metaverse field, the establishment of unified standards and protocols is needed for data exchange and interconnection between different virtual environments to achieve interconnectivity in the virtual world.

Therefore, to overcome these challenges, it is necessary to strengthen data governance and management, while promoting data standardization and sharing. Furthermore, there is a need to enhance technological research and innovation to address the constantly emerging data challenges and promote the development of artificial intelligence and metaverse technologies.

In the future, we can expect open datasets to become more comprehensive, covering a wider range of topics, and being continuously updated. This will enable DMs to access real-time and up-to-date information to make informed decisions (Kirchner et al., 2015). Additionally, advancements in technology, such as artificial intelligence and ML, will further enhance the analysis and utilization of open datasets by automating data processing, extracting valuable insights, and generating predictive models. Furthermore, with increased collaboration and partnerships between different stakeholders, the quality control processes for open datasets will become more robust. This will ensure the reliability and accuracy of the data, building further trust among users. Data standards and interoperability will also be improved, allowing for easier integration and comparison of data from different sources.

Overall, the future of obtaining data from open datasets holds great potential for empowering DMs with valuable information, driving innovation, and improving transparency. With advancements in technology and increased collaboration, open datasets will continue to evolve and play a vital role in shaping-making landscape.

Questions and Expectations of Questionnaire Survey

Obtaining data from surveys faces challenges in the fields of artificial intelligence and metaverse. Firstly, survey data are often static and fragmented, and cannot fully reflect users' real behaviors and emotions in virtual environments. This requires comprehensive analysis by combining other data sources, such as behavioral data in virtual reality environments and social media data, to better understand user behaviors and needs. Secondly, due to the rapid development of AI and metaverse technologies, the topics and areas involved in surveys are also constantly expanding and deepening. This requires survey designers and data analysts to have broader professional knowledge and skills to better respond to complex and changing survey needs (Fenton, et al., 2001). Finally, with the increasing awareness of personal data privacy protection, survey data also need stricter protection and compliance management to ensure the safety and privacy of user data. Therefore, surveying in data acquisition for AI and metaverse fields needs continuous innovation and improvement to meet increasingly complex challenges.

To address these issues, several measures can be taken. Firstly, more advanced statistical methods (such as factor analysis or regression analysis) can be used to analyze the data, in order to identify patterns and relationships in the responses. Secondly, improving questionnaire design to ensure clear and unambiguous questions can enhance respondent understanding and accuracy of responses (Ikart, 2019). Additionally, the adoption of new technologies such as online surveys can facilitate more efficient data collection and easier implementation of randomized experiments and other advanced survey designs. Furthermore, with the increasing awareness of data privacy and security, strengthening measures to protect data privacy and security, including the application of encryption technology and other security measures to prevent the disclosure of sensitive information, is a future development trend.

In conclusion, although there may be some challenges in obtaining data from questionnaires, continuous improvement of methods and technologies can ensure that questionnaire surveys remain an important tool for researchers and practitioners to obtain valuable information.

CONCLUSION

Data collection methods in MADM are one of the important research directions in this field. This chapter systematically discusses the development process of the five data collection methods, and introduces their application in MADM in detail, including example description, data processing, and model building. We put forward the challenges of these methods, such as how to ensure data quality and how to improve data processing efficiency, and discussed the development trend of future research. The research results of this chapter provide a basic framework and reference for future research, and also provide valuable guidance for DMs and practitioners. In future research, we need to further explore how to ensure the accuracy and reliability of data in the data collection process, and how to combine different data collection methods to achieve more comprehensive and accurate MADM.

REFERENCES

Awajan, I., Mohamad, M., & Al-Quran, A. (2021). Sentiment analysis technique and neutrosophic set theory for mining and ranking big data from online reviews. *IEEE Access : Practical Innovations, Open Solutions*, *9*, 47338–47353. doi:10.1109/ACCESS.2021.3067844

Barlas, P., Lanning, I., & Heavey, C. (2015). A survey of open source data science tools. *International Journal of Intelligent Computing and Cybernetics*, *8*(3), 232–261. doi:10.1108/IJICC-07-2014-0031

Bernabe-Moreno, J., Tejeda-Lorente, A., Herce-Zelaya, J., Porcel, C., & Herrera-Viedma, E. (2020). A context-aware embeddings supported method to extract a fuzzy sentiment polarity dictionary. *Knowledge-Based Systems*, *190*, 105236. doi:10.1016/j.knosys.2019.105236

Brehmer, B. (1992). Dynamic decision making: Human control of complex systems. *Acta Psychologica*, *81*(3), 211–241. doi:10.1016/0001-6918(92)90019-A PMID:1462786

Cao, F., Xing, B., Luo, J., Li, D., Qian, Y., Zhang, C., Bai, H., & Zhang, H. (2023). An efficient object detection algorithm based on improved YOLOV5 for High-Spatial-Resolution Remote sensing images. *Remote Sensing (Basel)*, *15*(15), 3755. doi:10.3390/rs15153755

Cheng, Y., Zhang, C., Sangaiah, A. K., Fan, X., Wang, A., Wang, L., & Liu, Y. (2023). *Efficient Low-Resource Medical Information Processing Based on Semantic Analysis and Granular Computing*. ACM Transactions on Asian and Low-Resource Language Information Processing. doi:10.1145/3626319

Cobanoglu, C., & Cobanoglu, N. (2003). The effect of incentives in web surveys: Application and ethical considerations. *International Journal of Market Research*, *45*(4), 475–488. doi:10.1177/147078530304500406

Cobo, M. J., Martinez, M. A., Gutiérrez-Salcedo, M., Herrera, M., & Herrera-Viedma, E. (2014). Identifying citation classics in fuzzy decision making field using the concept of H-classics. *Procedia Computer Science*, *31*, 567–576. doi:10.1016/j.procs.2014.05.303

Dashtipour, K., Gogate, M., Li, J., Jiang, F., Kong, B., & Hussain, A. (2020). A hybrid Persian sentiment analysis framework: Integrating dependency grammar based rules and deep neural networks. *Neurocomputing*, *380*, 1–10. doi:10.1016/j.neucom.2019.10.009

Ehlers, M., Gaehler, M., & Janowsky, R. (2006). Automated techniques for environmental monitoring and change analyses for ultra high resolution remote sensing data. *Photogrammetric Engineering and Remote Sensing*, *72*(7), 835–844. doi:10.14358/PERS.72.7.835

Ersahin, B., Aktas, O., Kilinc, D., & Ersahin, M. (2019). A hybrid sentiment analysis method for Turkish. *Turkish Journal of Electrical Engineering and Computer Sciences*, *27*(3), 1780–1793. doi:10.3906/elk-1808-189

Evans, J., & Mathur, A. (2005). The value of online surveys. *Internet Research*, *15*(2), 195–219. doi:10.1108/10662240510590360

Fenton, K. A., Johnson, A. M., McManus, S., & Erens, B. (2001). Measuring sexual behaviour: Methodological challenges in survey research. *Sexually Transmitted Infections*, *77*(2), 84–92. doi:10.1136/sti.77.2.84 PMID:11287683

Harper, F. M., & Konstan, J. A. (2015). The MovieLens datasets. *ACM Transactions on Interactive Intelligent Systems*, *5*(4), 1–19. doi:10.1145/2827872

Hu, D., Chen, S., Qiao, K., & Cao, S. (2017). Integrating CART algorithm and multi-source remote sensing data to estimate sub-pixel impervious surface coverage: A case study from Beijing Municipality, China. *Chinese Geographical Science*, *27*(4), 614–625. doi:10.1007/s11769-017-0882-x

Ikart, E. M. (2019). Survey questionnaire survey pretesting method: An evaluation of survey questionnaire via expert reviews technique. *Asian Journal of Social Science Studies*, *4*(2), 1–17. doi:10.20849/ajsss.v4i2.565

Immonen, A., Ovaska, E., & Paaso, T. (2018). Towards certified open data in digital service ecosystems. *Software Quality Journal*, *26*(4), 1257–1297. doi:10.1007/s11219-017-9378-2

Janssen, M., Charalabidis, Y., & Zuiderwijk, A. (2012). Benefits, adoption barriers and myths of open data and open government. *Information Systems Management*, *29*(4), 258–268. doi:10.1080/10580530.2012.716740

Ji, P., Zhang, H. Y., & Wang, J. Q. (2018). A fuzzy decision support model with sentiment analysis for items comparison in e-commerce: The case study of http://PConline. com. *IEEE Transactions on Systems, Man, and Cybernetics: Systems, 49*(10), 1993-2004. doi:10.1109/TSMC.2018.2875163

Ju, Y., & Wang, A. (2013). Projection method for multiple criteria group decision making with incomplete weight information in linguistic setting. *Applied Mathematical Modelling*, *37*(20-21), 9031–9040. doi:10.1016/j.apm.2013.04.027

Kirchner, K., Zec, J., & Delibasic, B. (2015). Facilitating data preprocessing by a generic framework: A proposal for clustering. *Artificial Intelligence Review*, *45*(3), 271–297. doi:10.1007/s10462-015-9446-6

Li, X., Ju, Y., Ju, D., Zhang, W., Dong, P., & Wang, A. (2019). Multi-attribute group decision making method based on EDAS under picture fuzzy environment. *IEEE Access : Practical Innovations, Open Solutions*, *7*, 141179–141192. doi:10.1109/ACCESS.2019.2943348

Lietz, P. (2010). Research into questionnaire design: A summary of the literature. *International Journal of Market Research*, *52*(2), 249–272. doi:10.2501/S147078530920120X

Liu, X., He, J., Yao, Y., Zhang, J., Liang, H., Wang, H., & Hong, Y. (2017). Classifying urban land use by integrating remote sensing and social media data. *International Journal of Geographical Information Science*, *31*(8), 1675–1696. doi:10.1080/13658816.2017.1324976

Ma, X., Zeng, J., Peng, L., Fortino, G., & Zhang, Y. (2019). Modeling multi-aspects within one opinionated sentence simultaneously for aspect-level sentiment analysis. *Future Generation Computer Systems*, *93*, 304–311. doi:10.1016/j.future.2018.10.041

Maslej-Kresnakova, V., Sarnovsky, M., Butka, P., & Machova, K. (2020). Comparison of deep learning models and various text pre-processing techniques for the toxic comments classification. *Applied Sciences (Basel, Switzerland), 10*(23), 8631. doi:10.3390/app10238631

Molloy, J. C. (2011). The open knowledge foundation: Open data means better science. *PLoS Biology, 9*(12), e1001195. doi:10.1371/journal.pbio.1001195 PMID:22162946

Nandhini, M., & Pradeep, G. C. M. (2020). A hybrid co-occurrence and ranking-based approach for detection of implicit aspects in aspect-based sentiment analysis. *SN Computer Science, 1*(3), 128. Advance online publication. doi:10.1007/s42979-020-00138-7

Nandwani, P., & Verma, R. (2021). A review on sentiment analysis and emotion detection from text. *Social Network Analysis and Mining, 11*(1), 81. doi:10.1007/s13278-021-00776-6 PMID:34484462

Nasukawa, T., & Yi, J. (2003, October). Sentiment analysis: Capturing favorability using natural language processing. In *Proceedings of the 2nd international conference on Knowledge capture* (pp. 70-77). ACM. 10.1145/945645.945658

Platts, K., Probert, D., & Canez, L. (2002). Make vs. buy decisions: A process incorporating multi-attribute decision-making. *International Journal of Production Economics, 77*(3), 247–257. doi:10.1016/S0925-5273(00)00177-8

Pu, X., Wu, G., & Yuan, C. (2019). Exploring overall opinions for document level sentiment classification with structural SVM. *Multimedia Systems, 25*(1), 21–33. doi:10.1007/s00530-017-0550-0

Rahman, A., & Hossen, M. S. (2019, September). Sentiment analysis on movie review data using machine learning approach. In *2019 International Conference on Bangla Speech and Language Processing (ICBSLP)* (pp. 1-4). IEEE. 10.1109/ICBSLP47725.2019.201470

Regmi, P. R., Waithaka, E., Paudyal, A., Simkhada, P., & Van Teijlingen, E. (2016). Guide to the design and application of online questionnaire surveys. *Nepal Journal of Epidemiology, 6*(4), 640–644. doi:10.3126/nje.v6i4.17258 PMID:28804676

Sanchez-Nunez, P., Cobo, M. J., Vaccaro, G., Pelaez, J. I., & Herrera-Viedma, E. (2021). Citation Classics in Consumer Neuroscience, Neuromarketing and Neuroaesthetics: Identification and Conceptual Analysis. *Brain Sciences, 11*(5), 548. doi:10.3390/brainsci11050548 PMID:33925436

Shao, H., Li, Y., Ding, Y., Zhuang, Q., & Chen, Z. (2020). Land use classification using High-Resolution Remote Sensing images based on structural topic model. *IEEE Access : Practical Innovations, Open Solutions, 8*, 215943–215955. doi:10.1109/ACCESS.2020.3041645

Stewart, K., & Williams, M. (2005). Researching online populations: The use of online focus groups for social research. *Qualitative Research, 5*(4), 395–416. doi:10.1177/1468794105056916

Sudhakaran, P., Nair, P. K., & Suraj, A. (2022, October). Music Recommendation using Emotion Recognition. In *2022 IEEE 2nd Mysore Sub Section International Conference (MysuruCon)* (pp. 1-7). IEEE. 10.1109/MysuruCon55714.2022.9972635

Taherdoost, H. (2016). Validity and reliability of the research instrument; how to test the validation of a questionnaire/survey in a research. *International Journal of Academic Research in Management (IJARM), 5*(3), 28-36. https://hal.science/hal-02546799

Tan, R., Chen, C., Zhang, W., Yang, L., & Ma, H. (2023). Intelligent acquisition of single-valued neutrosophic numbers based on emotional tendency analysis and its application in emergency decision making. *Journal of Intelligent & Fuzzy Systems, 45*(6), 11247–11268. doi:10.3233/JIFS-231039

Tang, D., Qin, B., Wei, F., Dong, L., Liu, T., & Zhou, M. (2015). A joint segmentation and classification framework for sentence level sentiment classification. *IEEE/ACM Transactions on Audio, Speech, and Language Processing, 23*(11), 1750–1761. doi:10.1109/TASLP.2015.2449071

Tiwari, P., Mishra, B. K., Kumar, S., & Kumar, V. (2020). Implementation of n-gram methodology for rotten tomatoes review dataset sentiment analysis. In *Cognitive analytics: concepts, methodologies, tools, and applications* (pp. 689–701). IGI Global. doi:10.4018/978-1-7998-2460-2.ch036

Uhlir, P. F., & Schroder, P. (2007). Open data for global science. *Data Science Journal, 6*, OD36–OD53. doi:10.2481/dsj.6.OD36

Van Oudenhoven, A. P., Schröter, M., Drakou, E. G., Geijzendorffer, I. R., Jacobs, S., van Bodegom, P. M., Chazee, L., Czúcz, B., Grunewald, K., Lillebø, A. I., Mononen, L., Nogueira, A. J., Pacheco-Romero, M., Perennou, C., Remme, R. P., Rova, S., Syrbe, R., Tratalos, J. A., Vallejos, M., & Albert, C. (2018). Key criteria for developing ecosystem service indicators to inform decision making. *Ecological Indicators, 95*, 417–426. doi:10.1016/j.ecolind.2018.06.020

Van Selm, M., & Jankowski, N. (2006). Conducting online surveys. *Quality & Quantity, 40*(3), 435–456. doi:10.1007/s11135-005-8081-8

Wang, W., Zhan, J., & Zhang, C. (2021). Three-way decisions based multi-attribute decision making with probabilistic dominance relations. *Information Sciences, 559*, 75–96. doi:10.1016/j.ins.2021.01.028

Wei, G. (2017). Picture fuzzy aggregation operators and their application to multiple attribute decision making. *Journal of Intelligent & Fuzzy Systems, 33*(2), 713–724. doi:10.3233/JIFS-161798

Wettergren, L., Eriksson, L. E., Nilsson, J., Jervaeus, A., & Lampic, C. (2016). Metadata and Title Correction: Online Focus Group Discussion is a Valid and Feasible Mode When Investigating Sensitive Topics Among Young Persons With a Cancer Experience. *JMIR Research Protocols, 5*(2), e5971. doi:10.2196/resprot.5971 PMID:27183496

Wright, K. (2005). Researching Internet-based populations: Advantages and disadvantages of online survey research, online questionnaire authoring software packages, and web survey services. *Journal of Computer-Mediated Communication, 10*(3), JCMC1034. doi:10.1111/j.1083-6101.2005.tb00259.x

Wu, C., & Zhang, D. (2019). Ranking products with IF-based sentiment word framework and TODIM method. *Kybernetes, 48*(5), 990–1010. doi:10.1108/K-01-2018-0029

Wu, J., Zhang, G., Xing, Y., Liu, Y., Zhang, Z., Dong, Y., & Herrera-Viedma, E. (2023). A sentiment analysis driven method based on public and personal preferences with correlated attributes to select online doctors. *Applied Intelligence*, *53*(16), 1–22. doi:10.1007/s10489-023-04485-9 PMID:36844914

Yang, Z., Li, Q., Charles, V., Xu, B., & Gupta, S. (2023). Supporting personalized new energy vehicle purchase decision-making: Customer reviews and product recommendation platform. *International Journal of Production Economics*, *265*, 109003. doi:10.1016/j.ijpe.2023.109003

Yaqoob, I., Hashem, M., Gani, A., Mokhtar, S. B., Ahmed, E., Anuar, N. B., & Vasilakos, A. V. (2016). Big data: From beginning to future. *International Journal of Information Management*, *36*(6), 1231–1247. doi:10.1016/j.ijinfomgt.2016.07.009

Zahedi-Seresht, M., Mehrabian, S., & Jahanshahloo, G. R. (2016). A new method for ranking distribution companies with several scenarios data by using DEA/MADM. *International Journal of Applied Operational Research-An Open Access Journal*, *6*(3), 11–24. http://ijorlu.liau.ac.ir/article-1-518-en.html

Zanakis, S. H., Solomon, A. W., Wishart, N., & Dublish, S. (1998). Multi-attribute decision making: A simulation comparison of select methods. *European Journal of Operational Research*, *107*(3), 507–529. doi:10.1016/S0377-2217(97)00147-1

Zhang, C., Bai, W., Li, D., & Zhan, J. (2022). Multiple attribute group decision making based on multigranulation probabilistic models, MULTIMOORA and TPOP in incomplete q-rung orthopair fuzzy information systems. *International Journal of Approximate Reasoning*, *143*, 102–120. doi:10.1016/j.ijar.2022.01.002

Zhang, C., Li, D., Kang, X., Liang, Y., Broumi, S., & Sangaiah, A. K. (2020a). Multi-attribute group decision making based on multigranulation probabilistic models with interval-valued neutrosophic information. *Mathematics*, *8*(2), 223. doi:10.3390/math8020223

Zhang, C., Li, D., & Liang, J. (2020b). Interval-valued hesitant fuzzy multi-granularity three-way decisions in consensus processes with applications to multi-attribute group decision making. *Information Sciences*, *511*, 192–211. doi:10.1016/j.ins.2019.09.037

Zhang, C., Li, D., Sangaiah, A. K., & Broumi, S. (2017). Merger and Acquisition Target Selection Based on Interval Neutrosophic Multigranulation Rough Sets over Two Universes. *Symmetry*, *9*(7), 126. doi:10.3390/sym9070126

Zhang, C., Li, D., Zhai, Y., & Yang, Y. (2019). Multigranulation rough set model in hesitant fuzzy information systems and its application in person-job fit. *International Journal of Machine Learning and Cybernetics*, *10*(4), 717–729. doi:10.1007/s13042-017-0753-x

Zhang, C., Zhang, J., Li, W., Castillo, O., & Zhang, J. (2024). Exploring static rebalancing strategies for dockless bicycle sharing systems based on multi-granularity behavioral decision-making. *International Journal of Cognitive Computing in Engineering*, *5*, 27–43. doi:10.1016/j.ijcce.2024.01.001

Zhang, C., Zhang, J., Li, W., Pedrycz, W., & Li, D. (2023). A regret theory-based multi-granularity three-way decision model with incomplete T-spherical fuzzy information and its application in forest fire management. *Applied Soft Computing*, *110539*, 110539. Advance online publication. doi:10.1016/j.asoc.2023.110539

Zhang, H., Zhang, R., Huang, H., & Wang, J. (2018). Some picture fuzzy Dombi Heronian mean operators with their application to multi-attribute decision-making. *Symmetry*, *10*(11), 593. doi:10.3390/sym10110593

Zhang, L., Zhang, L., & Du, B. (2016). Deep Learning for Remote sensing Data: A technical tutorial on the state of the art. *IEEE Geoscience and Remote Sensing Magazine*, *4*(2), 22–40. doi:10.1109/MGRS.2016.2540798

Zhang, X. (2008a). On multi-period multi-attribute decision making. *Knowledge-Based Systems*, *21*(2), 164–171. doi:10.1016/j.knosys.2007.05.007

Zhang, X., & Yager, R. R. (2008b). Dynamic intuitionistic fuzzy multi-attribute decision making. *International Journal of Approximate Reasoning*, *48*(1), 246–262. doi:10.1016/j.ijar.2007.08.008

Chapter 10
Research on Knowledge Representation and Reasoning Based on Decision Implication

Shaoxia Zhang
Shanxi University of Finance and Economics, China

ABSTRACT

Knowledge representation and reasoning based on decision implication is to perform an extremely compact representation of the decision information implied in data, and obtain all decision information in data by means of reasoning, based on the current representation. The existing research in logic and data aspects of decision implication proposes a set of decision implications with information integrity and extreme simplicity (non-redundancy and optimality), i.e., decision implication canonical basis (DICB), which lays a solid foundation for constructing a knowledge representation and reasoning framework in formal contexts. This chapter conducts a systematic and in-depth study on the important issues of knowledge representation capability, and incomplete formal context adaptability of decision implication, and reasoning based on decision implications.

INTRODUCTION

A Brief Review of Formal Concept Analysis

Formal Concept Analysis (FCA) is an order-theoretic method for concept analysis and visualization, pioneered by Wille (Wille, 1982) in the mid-80s. A concept is a pair constituted by its extent and intent. The extent of a concept is a collection of all objects belonging to that concept and its intent is the set of all attributes common to all objects of the extent. FCA establishes the relationships between intents and extents and visualizes the generalization and specialization of concepts by means of concept lattices. Because of its strengths, FCA has been become a powerful tool for data mining (Mouakher and Yahia, 2019; Bartl and Konecny, 2019), social networks (Roth et al., 2008), software engineering (Tilley et al.,

DOI: 10.4018/979-8-3693-1582-8.ch010

2005), cognition-based concept learning (Kuznetsov and Makhalova, 2018) and knowledge reduction (Konecny and Krajca, 2019; Cornejo et al., 2018).

In the study of knowledge representation and reasoning in FCA, (attribute) implication (Ganter and Wille, 1999; Qu and Zhai, 2008; Zhai et al., 2012; Ma et al., 2011; Zhai and Li, 2019) is proposed in the form of $A \rightarrow B$, meaning that if all the attributes in A are satisfied, then all the attributes in B are satisfied. Duquenne etc. (V and J-L, 1986) constructed the so-called canonical basis, which turns out to be complete and non-redundant w.r.t. implication logic (Ganter and Wille, 1999; Stumme, 1996), and minimal among all complete sets of implications. Starting from a canonical basis of a formal context, one can obtain all implications in this context by applying Armstrong rules (Armstrong, 1974).

A Brief Review of Decision Implication

Decision implication, revealing the dependency between conditions and decisions, is a knowledge representation and reasoning theory that has been developed within the case of decision-making (Zhai et al., 2014, 2015b; Li et al., 2017; Zhang et al., 2021; Zhai et al., 2015a). Compared with other decision knowledge representations, such as concept rule (Wu et al., 2009; Li et al., 2013a) and granule rule (Wu et al., 2009), decision implication has been demonstrated to possess a stronger representation ability (Zhang et al., 2020).

Zhai et al. (Zhai et al., 2014, 2015b) conducted decision implication logic, encompassing both semantic and syntactic aspects. In the semantic aspect, the research considers the soundness, completeness, and non-redundancy of decision implications, as well as decision implication basis (a most compact set of decision implications) (Zhai et al., 2015b; Nanjia et al., 2019). In a given dataset, the soundness of decision implications means that the decision implications are valid within the data, the completeness of a decision implication set implies that all sound decision implications in data can be derived from this set, and the non-redundancy of a decision implication set means that no decision implication within the set can be deduced from other decision implications in the set. In the syntactic aspect, two inference rules, namely *Augmentation* and *Combination*, are proposed, which have been demonstrated to be sound and complete w.r.t. the semantic aspect. The logic research results of decision implication can be applied to data (i.e., decision context) research (Li et al., 2017; Zhang et al., 2021; Zhai et al., 2015a). Methods for generating decision implications basis in decision contexts can be found in (Li et al., 2017; Zhang et al., 2021). Additionally, the inference strategies based on decision implications basis and inference rules are explored in (Zhai et al., 2022, 2015a; Nanjia et al., 2019).

A Brief Review of Concept Rule and Granular Rule

Granular computing is a collective term referring to theories, methodologies, techniques, and tools for the analysis of information granules encountered in problem solving (Wu et al., 2009; Li and Wu, 2017). Wu et al. (Wu et al., 2009) brought a perspective of granular computing into FCA based on the fact that concept lattice extracted from data is capable of representing all the information implied by data (Ganter and Wille, 1999). Thus, it is expected that decision implications extracted from concept lattices are also capable of representing all the information implied by decision implications. Wu et al. (Wu et al., 2009) considered such special decision implications, called concept rules, by requiring that the premises and consequences of decision implications must be intents from condition and decision concepts respectively1 . The relationships between concept rules and decision implications, however, remain untouched in (Wu et al., 2009).

Another important result of FCA is that any concept can be represented by the join of some object concepts (Wille, 1982). Inspired by the result, Wu et al. (Wu et al., 2009) considered the special concept rules between object concepts, called granular rules, and expected that all concept rules can be represented by granular rules. Li et al. (Li et al., 2013a) achieved the goal by defining the non-redundancy on concept rules and proving that the non-redundant concept rules can be represented by merging the corresponding granular rules. In addition, Li et al. (Li et al., 2011) proposed a method for deriving all non-redundant concept rules from a decision context and optimized this method with less time complexity in (Li et al., 2013a). Li et al. (Li et al., 2013a) also performed a comparison between the concept rule oriented knowledge reduction (Li et al., 2011) and the granular rule oriented knowledge reduction (Wu et al., 2009).

A Brief Review of Knowledge Acquisition Within Incomplete Formal Contexts

Incomplete data is a common occurrence in real-world scenarios. In FCA, incomplete formal context is employed to formally describe the situations where a complete description of individuals is unavailable. Burmeister and Holzer, among others, have pioneered the development of attribute exploration within incomplete formal contexts (P and R, 2000; Holzer, 2001; Carpineto and Romano, 2004a,b; Ganter, 1999). Additionally, (Holzer, 2004a,b) proposed an algorithm for attribute exploration. Furthermore, attribute exploration delves into the ideas of interactive collaborative exploration, as extensively researched in (Ganter and Wille, 1999).

Despite the lack of information in information system, from a knowledge acquisition perspective, there is an expectation to represent the knowledge initially implied in incomplete information and discover automatic inference rules that require no prior knowledge (Wasserkrug et al., 2008). In fact, substantial work has already been undertaken in modeling incomplete knowledge within the domain of incomplete formal context(S, 2002; P and R, 2000). Differing from formal contexts where knowledge can be precisely described, implications in incomplete formal contexts are semantically assessed by evaluating their validity within completions, which represent the distinct formal contexts an incomplete formal context could be (P and R, 2000). This means that an implication is considered to be necessary when it holds in all completions of the incomplete formal context, while an acceptable implication is said to hold in at least one completion. Both acceptable implications and necessary implications are available for practical applications and can be effectively employed in decision-making and problem-solving in real-world scenarios. Sergei Obiedkov (S, 2002) proposed a deduction mechanism that allowed for the deduction of all necessary/acceptable implications from a basis.

Motivations and Contributions of The Chapter

Comparatively, decision implication is more general than concept rule and granular rule, and hence has a wider application (Zhai et al., 2015b, a, 2014). Concept rule and granular rule, which reveal the dependencies between intents (Wu et al., 2009), are more special than decision implication, and are usually useful and easily obtainable when only concepts or object concepts are provided. This is the case for such practical applications as ontology, where knowledge is generally described by concepts, so considering the decision implications between concepts, i.e., concept rules or granular rules, may be more preferable. A decision implication, however, might not be a concept rule or a granular rule, since its premise or consequence might not be an intent or a granular intent. All the results are basic but insufficient to clarify the essential issue that whether concept rules and granular rules have the power of representing all the information in decision implications, because according to decision implication logic, a subset of decision implications may keep all the decision information of decision implications and thus may be complete w.r.t. a closed set of decision implications (Zhai et al., 2014).

From the perspective of incomplete formal contexts, attribute exploration relies on the prior knowledge of experts, and the correctness and completeness of the knowledge mastered by experts significantly affect the quality of knowledge reasoning. In this case, this paper intends to research the automatic inference rules to completely deduce knowledge applied in knowledge bases without prior knowledge. In the existing deduction mechanism, the basis of necessary implications and that of acceptable implications are inconvenient as it recursively involves the bases of all its completions, resulting in exponential time complexity in generation and inference processes. A concise knowledge basis presentation is needed to enable the streamlined generation of the basis and facilitate the reasoning process. Another critical issue we revealed in our paper is that while necessary and acceptable implications in incomplete formal contexts can be represented by the implications within (complete) formal contexts, the inference rules originally apply to formal contexts may yield invalid implications when they are applied to these two types of implications. In this case, a new form of knowledge representation and inference rules needs to be reformulated for the two types of implications.

Actually, although an incomplete formal context can potentially extend to a vast number of formal contexts, it can be effectively modeled by employing two completions: one for attributes that an object certainly possesses and another for attributes that an object may possibly possess (Ganter, 1999). In this sense, an intriguing concept arises wherein the modeling of an incomplete formal context is based on the two completions. Consequently, knowledge representation and reasoning within an incomplete formal context are transformed into those within two formal contexts. This transformation offers more general and efficient methods for knowledge acquisition. Furthermore, another issue cannot be ignored is that, even with small-scale data, there may exist extensive sets of implications, making them impractical for direct applications. Therefore, it becomes imperative to seek a compact representation for implications. These sets are expected to significantly reduce the number of implications comparing to the closure sets, while still retaining all the information implied in the closure sets.

This chapter conducts a comparative study of decision implication, concept rule and granular rule, and that of decision implication-based knowledge re-representation and reasoning within incomplete formal contexts. The originality and contributions are as follows:

(1) It is exemplified that both concept rules and granular rules are not complete w.r.t. decision implications, and that granular rules are not complete w.r.t. concept rules. This implies that there exists information loss when studying decision implications by using only concept rules or granular rules, or when studying concept rules by using only granular rules. With the help of decision implication logic, we uncover the information loss by identifying the decision implications that cannot be deduced from concept rules or granular rules, and the concept rules that cannot be deduced from granular rules.

(2) We advance the modeling of incomplete formal contexts by introducing specially constructed decision contexts that connect the minimal and maximal completions. This approach enables us to

re-represent both necessary and acceptable implication based on decision implication within the specialized decision contexts.

(3) We extend the applicability of inference rules, specifically *Augmentation* and *Combination*, initially designed for decision implications, to necessary/acceptable implications. Furthermore, we introduce *Reflexivity* rule to jointly define the completeness and non-redundancy for sets of necessary and acceptable implications, working in conjunction with *Augmentation* and *Combination* to effectively eliminate redundancy within these sets. Necessary implication basis and an acceptable implication basis are established, with preserving all the information implied in necessity/acceptable implications while minimizing the number of implications.

The Arrangement of This Chapter

The remainder of this chapter is organized as follows. The basic notions and properties in FCA are reviewed in Section 2. Section 3 conducts a comparative study of decision implication, concept rule and granular rule. Section 4 conducts a comparative study of decision implication-based knowledge re- representation and reasoning within incomplete formal contexts. Conclusions and future work end the chapter in Section 5.

BASIC NOTIONS AND PROPERTIES IN FCA

This section gives a brief overview over some basic notions and properties in FCA.

Formal Context, Implication, And Concept Lattice

Definition 2.1 (Wille, 1982). A formal context is a triple $K=(G,M,I)$, where G and M are the object set and the attribute set respectively, and $I \subseteq G \times M$ is a set of incidence relations between objects and attributes. For $g \in G$ and $m \in M$, $(g,m) \in I$ expresses "the object g has the attribute m".

A formal context is generally represented by a two-dimensional table, in which row headers are object names, column headers are attribute names and a "1" indicates the row object has the column attribute.

Example 2.1 A formal context $K=(G,M,I)$ is given in Table 1, where $G=\{g_1,g_2,g_3,g_4,g_5,g_6\}$ and $M=\{a_1,a_2,a_3,a_4,a_5\}$.

Table 1. A formal context

	a_1	a_2	a_3	a_4	a_5
g_1	1	1	0	0	1
g_2	0	0	1	0	0
g_3	1	0	1	0	0
g_4	0	1	0	0	1
g_5	0	1	1	1	1
g_6	0	0	1	0	1

Definition 2.2 (Wille, 1982). Let $K=(G,M,I)$ be a formal context. For $A \subseteq G$, we define:

$$A^I = \{m \in M \mid (g,m) \in I, \forall g \in A\}$$

Correspondingly, for $B \subseteq M$, we define:

$$B^I = \{g \in G \mid (g,m) \in I, \forall m \in B\}$$

For $g \in G$, $\{g\}^I$ is written as g^I for notational simplicity.

Proposition 2.1 (Wille, 1982). Let $K=(G,M,I)$ be a formal context. For $A,A_1,A_2 \subseteq G$, and $B,B_1,B_2 \subseteq M$, we have:

(1) $A_1 \subseteq A_2 \Rightarrow A_2^I \subseteq A_1^I$ (1') $B \subseteq B_2 \Rightarrow B_2^I \subseteq B_1^I$

(2) $A \subseteq A^{II}$ (2') $B \subseteq B^{II}$

(3) $A^I = A^{III}$ (3') $B^I = B^{III}$

(4) $(A_1 \cup A_2)^I = A_1^I \cap A_2^I$ (4') $(B_1 \cup B_2)^I = B_1^I \cap B_2^I$

(5) $A \subseteq B^I \Leftrightarrow B \subseteq A^I$

Definition 2.3 (Wille, 1982). Let $K=(G,M,I)$ be a formal context. For $A \subseteq G$ and $B \subseteq M$, $C=(A,B)$ is a formal concept of K if $A^I=B$ and $B^I=A$. In this case, A is the extent of C and B is the intent of C.

Definition 2.4 (Wille, 1982). Let $K=(G,M,I)$ be a formal context and $C_1=(A_1,B_1)$, $C_2=(A_2,B_2)$ be two concepts of K. We define:

$$C_1 \le C_2 \Leftrightarrow A_1 \subseteq A_2 \,(\Leftrightarrow B_1 \supseteq B_2)$$

Then, all the formal concepts of K ordered in this way constitute a complete lattice, called the concept lattice of K and denoted by $L(K)$.

Proposition 2.2 (Wille, 1982). Let $K=(G,M,I)$ be a formal context and $L(K)$ be the concept lattice of K. Then, $L(K)$ is a complete lattice, and the supremum and infimum of any pair of concepts (A_1,B_1) and (A_2,B_2) are given by:

$$(A_1,B_1) \vee (A_2,B_2) = \left((A_1 \cup A_2)^{II}, B_1 \cap B_2\right)$$

$$(A_1,B_1) \wedge (A_2,B_2) = \left(A_1 \cap A_2, (B_1 \cup B_2)^{II}\right)$$

Implication reveals the dependency relationship between attributes. An implication is an expression in the form of $A \rightarrow B$, meaning that if all attributes in attribute set A are satisfied, then all attributes in attribute set B are also satisfied. Formal concept analysis can obtain implications from the formal context.

Definition 2.5 (Wille, 1982). Let $K=(G,M,I)$ be a formal context. For $A \subseteq G$ and $B \subseteq M$, if $A^I \subseteq B^I$, then $A \rightarrow B$ is called an implication of K.

Example 2.2 (Continuing Example 2.1). It is verified that

$$\{a_2\}' = \{g_1, g_4, g_5\} \subseteq \{g_1, g_4, g_5, g_6\} = \{a_5\}',$$

then $\{a_2\} \rightarrow \{a_5\}$ is an implication of K.

Decision Implication Logic

Decision implication is an extension of implication in the case of decision, which studies the dependencies between attributes of different domains (such as causes and effects, conditions and behaviors). Similar to the study of implication (Ganter and Wille, 1999), decision implication can be studied from two perspectives, namely the logical way and the data-driven way (Zhai et al., 2015b, 2014, 2015a). By the logical way, we mean decision implication logic, which has the semantical and syntactical aspects. By the data-driven way, one extracts decision implications from a given decision context and discusses the completeness and non-redundancy of the decision implications w.r.t. the decision context. It has been shown in (Zhai et al., 2014) that the results obtained by the logical way can be directly applied to the data-driven way.

The definition of decision implication in decision implication logic is firstly given in Definition 2.6.

Definition 2.6 (Zhai et al., 2014). Let C be a set of condition attributes and D be a set of decision attributes such that $C \cap D = \varnothing$. If $A \subseteq C$ and $B \subseteq D$, then $A \rightarrow B$ is called a decision implication, where A is the premise of $A \rightarrow B$ and B is the consequence.

In the semantic aspect of decision implication logic, the soundness of decision implications and the completeness and non-redundancy of decision implication sets are studied.

Definition 2.7 (Zhai et al., 2014). Let C be a set of condition attributes, D be a set of decision attributes, and L and L_1 be sets of decision implications. We define:

1. For a set $T \subseteq C \cup D$ and a decision implication $A \rightarrow B$, if $A \subsetneq T \cap C$ or $B \subseteq T \cap D$, then T respects $A \rightarrow B$ (or T is a model of $A \rightarrow B$), denoted by $T \models A \rightarrow B$. If for any $A_1 \rightarrow B_1 \in L$, $T \models A_1 \rightarrow B_1$ holds, then T respects L, denoted by $T \models L$.
2. For a decision implication $A \rightarrow B$, if for any $T \subseteq C \cup D$, $T \models L$ implies $T \models A \rightarrow B$, then $A \rightarrow B$ can be semantically deduced from L, denoted by $L \vdash A \rightarrow B$. If for any $A_1 \rightarrow B_1 \in L_1$, $L \vdash A_1 \rightarrow B_1$ holds, then L_1 can be semantically deduced from L, denoted by $L \vdash L_1$.
3. If for any $A \rightarrow B \in L, L \setminus \{A \rightarrow B\} \nvdash A \rightarrow B$ holds, then L is non-redundant.
4. If any $A \rightarrow B$ that can be semantically deduced from L is contained in L, then L is closed.
5. If L is closed, $L_1 \subseteq L$ and $L_1 \vdash L$, then L_1 is complete w.r.t. L.

Given a data set, the soundness of a decision implication means that the decision implication holds in the data. The completeness of a decision implication set is that all sound decision implications in data can be derived from this set. The non-redundancy of a decision implication set means that any decision implication in the set cannot be derived from other decision implication in the set.

From Definition 2.7, we can see that $T \models A \rightarrow B$ means that $A \rightarrow B$ holds in T, i.e., if $A \subseteq T$, then $B \subseteq T$, and that $T \models L$ means that L holds in T, i.e., all the decision implications in L hold in T. Thus, $L \vdash A \rightarrow B$ means that if L holds, then $A \rightarrow B$ also holds, i.e., $A \rightarrow B$ is a decision information implied by L. In this sense, L is non-redundant if and only if any decision implication in L is indispensable, i.e., any decision implication is not implied by other decision implications in L. Furthermore, from Definition 2.7, it is easy to verify that, a decision implication $A \rightarrow B$ is redundant w.r.t. L if and only if $A \rightarrow B$ can be semantically deduced from other decision implications in L, i.e., $L \backslash \{ A \rightarrow B \} \vdash A \rightarrow B$.

The closure of a condition attribute set A w.r.t. a set of decision implications L is given in Definition 2.8, which is actually the maximal consequence deduced from L based on A, as verified in Proposition 2.3 .

Definition 2.8 (Zhai et al., 2014). Let C be a set of condition attributes, and L be a set of decision implications. A closure of $A \subseteq C$ w.r.t. L is defined as

$$A^L = \cup \{ B_i \mid A_i \rightarrow B_i \in L, A_i \subseteq A \}$$

Proposition 2.3 (Zhai et al., 2014). Let L be a set of decision implications, and $A \rightarrow B$ be a decision implication. Then we have that $L \vdash A \rightarrow B$ if and only if $B \subseteq A^L$.

In the syntactical aspect, one studies the soundness, completeness, and redundancy of inference rules (Zhai et al., 2014). Zhai et al. (Zhai et al., 2014) proposed two inference rules, *Augmentation* and *Combination*, by which, one can obtain decision implications from the given decision implications:

Augmentation

$$\frac{A \rightarrow B, A_1 \supseteq A, B_1 \subseteq B}{A_1 \rightarrow B_1} \tag{1}$$

Combination

$$\frac{A \rightarrow B, A_1 \rightarrow B_1}{A \cup A_1 \rightarrow B \cup B_1} \tag{2}$$

Augmentation means that if T is a model of $A \rightarrow B$, $A_1 \supseteq A$ and $B_1 \subseteq B$, then T is also a model of $A_1 \rightarrow B_1$. Similarly, *Combination* means that if T is a model of $A \rightarrow B$ and $A_1 \rightarrow B_1$, then T is also a model of $A \cup A_1 \rightarrow B \cup B_1$.

The following theorems show the soundness, completeness and non-redundancy of *Augmentation* and *Combination*.

Theorem 2.1 (Zhai et al., 2014). (Soundness)*Augmentation* and *Combination* are sound, i.e.,

1. If $A \rightarrow B$ $A_1 \supseteq A$ and $B_1 \subseteq B$, then $A \rightarrow B \vdash A_1 \rightarrow B_1$.
2. If $A \rightarrow B$ and $A_1 \rightarrow B_1$, then $\{A \rightarrow B, A_1 \rightarrow B_1\} \vdash A \cup A_1 \rightarrow B \cup B_1$.

The soundness of the inference rules ensures the semantical compatibility of syntactical deduction, i.e., if a decision implication $A \rightarrow B$ can be obtained from L by iteratively applying the inference rules, then $A \rightarrow B$ can be semantically deduced from L.

Theorem 2.2 (Zhai et al., 2014). (Completeness)*Augmentation* and *Combination* are complete w.r.t. the semantical aspect, i.e., for any closed set L and complete set $L_1 \subseteq L$, we have $A \rightarrow B \in L$ if and only if $A \rightarrow B$ can be obtained from L_1 by applying *Augmentation* and *Combination*.

The completeness of the inference rules ensures the completeness of syntactical deduction, i.e., if a decision implication $A \rightarrow B$ can be semantically deduced from L, then $A \rightarrow B$ can be obtained from L by iteratively applying the inference rules.

Theorem 2.3 (Zhai et al., 2014). (Non-redundancy)*Augmentation* and *Combination* are non-redundant, i.e., they cannot be replaced by each other in deduction process.

Decision Implications Within Decision Contexts

The section studies decision implication in the data-driven way, where the data is represented in the form of decision context.

Definition 2.9 (Zhai et al., 2014). A decision context is a triple $K=(G,C\cup D,I_C\cup I_D)$, where G is the object set, C is the condition attribute set, and D is the decision attribute set such that $C\cap D=\varnothing$. In this case, $I_C\subseteq G\times C$ is the set of condition incidence relations and $I_D\subseteq G\times D$ is the set of decision incidence relations. For $g\in G$ and $m\in C\cup D$, $(g,m)\in I_C$ or $(g,m)\in I_D$ denotes "the object g has the attribute m".

A decision context can also be represented by a two-dimensional table, in which row headers are object names, column headers are attribute names, and a " 1 " indicates the row object has the column attribute.

Example 2.3 A decision context $K=(G,C\cup D,I_C\cup I_D)$ is given in Table 2, where $G=\{g_1,g_2,g_3,g_4,g_5,g_6,g_7\}$, $C=\{a_1,a_2,a_3,a_4,a_5,a_6\}$ and $D=\{d_1,d_2,d_3\}$.

Table 2. A decision context

	a_1	a_2	a_3	a_4	a_5	a_6	d_1	d_2	d_3
g_1	1	1	0	0	1	1	1	0	1
g_2	0	0	1	1	0	1	0	1	0
g_3	1	0	1	0	0	1	0	0	1
g_4	0	1	0	1	0	1	1	0	0
g_5	0	1	0	1	1	1	1	1	0
g_6	1	0	1	0	1	1	0	1	1
g_7	0	1	1	1	0	0	1	1	1

Definition 2.10 defines operators $(.)^C$ and $(.)^D$ in decision contexts.

Definition 2.10 (Zhai et al., 2014). Let $K=(G,C\cup D,I_C\cup I_D)$ be a decision context. For sets $A_1\subseteq C$, $A_2\subseteq D$ and $B\subseteq G$, we define:

$$A_1^C=\{g\in G\mid (g,m)\in I_C,\forall m\in A_1\}$$
$$A_2^D=\{g\in G\mid (g,m)\in I_D,\forall m\in A_2\}$$
$$B^C=\{m\in C\mid (g,m)\in I_C,\forall g\in B\}$$
$$B^D=\{m\in D\mid (g,m)\in I_D,\forall g\in B\}$$

For $g\in G$ and $A\subseteq C,\{g\}^C,\{g\}^D$ and $(A^C)^D$ are abbreviated to g^C, g^D and A^{CD}, respectively. Obviously, Proposition 2.1 is also appropriate for the operators in Definition 2.10. For example, for $A_1\subseteq A_2\subseteq C$, we have $A_1^C\supseteq A_2^C$ and hence $A_1^{CD}\subseteq A_2^{CD}$.

Definition 2.11 introduces decision implication within decision context.

Definition 2.11 (Zhai et al., 2015a). Let $K=(G,C\cup D,I_C\cup I_D)$ be a decision context. For $A\subseteq C$ and $B\subseteq D$, if $A^C\subseteq B^D$, then $A\rightarrow B$ is called a decision implication of K, where A is the premise of $A\rightarrow B$ and B is the consequence.

Example 2.4 (Continuing Example 2.3). We can verify that $\{a_2,a_4\}\rightarrow\{d_1\}$ is a decision implication of K, since we have $\{a_2,a_4\}^C=\{g_4,g_5,g_7\}\subseteq\{g_1,g_4,g_5,g_7\}=\{d_1\}^D$.

We denote by $K_{\mathbb{D}}$ the set of all the decision implications of K, and it can be verified that $K_{\mathbb{D}}$ is closed.

Proposition 2.4 (Zhai et al., 2015a). Let $K=(G,C\cup D,I_C\cup I_D)$ be a decision context, $A\subseteq C$ and $B\subseteq D$. Then we have:

1. $A\rightarrow A^{CD}$ is a decision implication of K;
2. $A\rightarrow B\in K_{\mathbb{D}}$ if and only if $B\subseteq A^{CD}$.

Decision Implication Canonical Basis

Zhai et al. (Zhai et al., 2015a) proposed a most compact set of decision implications, i.e., decision implication canonical basis.

Definition 2.12 (Li et al., 2017; Zhang et al., 2021; Zhai et al., 2015a). Let $K=(G,C\cup D,I_C\cup I_D)$ be a decision context. A set $A\subseteq C$ is called a decision premise of K, if A is proper, i.e.,

$$A^{CD}\supset\bigcup\left\{A_i^{CD}\mid A_i\subset A, A_i \text{ is a decision premise of } K\right\}$$

The set

$$K_{\mathbb{D}}^{*}=\left\{A\rightarrow A^{CD}\mid \text{A is a decision premise of } K\right\}$$

is called the decision implication canonical basis (DICB) of K.

A decision implication in DICB takes decision premise as its premises and the closure of the decision premise w.r.t. the decision context as its consequence. DICB is proven to be complete, non-redundant, and optimal, i.e., it is of minimal cardinality among all complete sets of decision implications, as shown in Theorem 2.4.

Theorem 2.4 (Zhai et al., 2015a). Let $K=(G,C\cup D,I_C\cup I_D)$ be a decision context. Then, $K_{\mathbb{D}}^{*}$ is complete w.r.t. $K_{\mathbb{D}}$, non-redundant and optimal.

Example 2.5 (Continuing Examples 2.3 and 2.4). The DICB of Table 2 is shown in Table 3.

Table 3. The DICB of Table 2

$\{a_1\}\rightarrow\{d_3\}$	$\{a_4,a_5\}\rightarrow\{d_1,d_2\}$
$\{a_2\}\rightarrow\{d_1\}$	$\{a_3,a_4\}\rightarrow\{d_2\}$
$\{a_1,a_4\}\rightarrow\{d_1,d_2,d_3\}$	$\{a_3,a_5\}\rightarrow\{d_2,d_3\}$
$\{a_2,a_3\}\rightarrow\{d_1,d_2,d_3\}$	

All decision implications in Table 2 can be deduced from that in Table 3, by applying *Augmentation* and *Combination*. Take the decision implication $\{a_2,a_4\}\rightarrow\{d_1\}$ for an example. It is derived from $\{a_2\}$ $\rightarrow$ $\{d_1\}$ in Table 3 by applying *Augmentation.*

Furthermore, it can be verified that the DICB in Table 3 is non-redundant, meaning that any decision implication in Table 3 cannot be derived from other ones in the DICB. Take $\{a_3,a_5\} \rightarrow \{d_2,d_3\}$ as an example. The derivation of $\{a_3,a_5\} \rightarrow \{d_2,d_3\}$ only requires the decision implications that contain the consequences $\{d_2\}$ and $\{d_3\}$, namely $\{a_1,a_4\} \rightarrow \{d_1,d_2,d_3\}$ and $\{a_2,a_3\} \rightarrow \{d_1,d_2,d_3\}$ in Table 3. However, since *Augmentation* and *Combination* always expand (or maintain) the consequence of a given decision implication, when they are applied to $\{a_1,a_4\} \rightarrow \{d_1,d_2,d_3\}$ and $\{a_2,a_3\} \rightarrow \{d_1,d_2,d_3\}$, they cannot produce a decision implication with the premise $\{a_3,a_5\}$, and therefore, $\{a_3,a_5\} \rightarrow \{d_2,d_3\}$ cannot be obtained.

A COMPARATIVE STUDY OF DECISION IMPLICATION, CONCEPT RULE AND GRANULAR RULE

Concept Rule and Granular Rule

Decision implication, concept rule and granular rule are considered and extracted from consistent decision contexts (Wu et al., 2009; Li et al., 2013; Zhai et al., 2014).

Definition 3.1 (Wu et al., 2009). Let $K=\left(G,C\cup D,I_C\cup I_D\right)$ be a decision context. *K* is consistent if for any $g\in G, g^{CC}\subseteq g^{DD}$ holds.

Example 3.1 (Continuing Example 2.3). Consider the decision context *K* in Example 2.3. Since

$$\{g_1\}^{CC}=\{g_1\}\subseteq\{g_1\}^{DD}=\{g_1,g_7\}$$
$$\{g_2\}^{CC}=\{g_2\}\subseteq\{g_2\}^{DD}=\{g_2,g_5,g_6,g_7\}$$
$$\{g_3\}^{CC}=\{g_3,g_6\}\subseteq\{g_3\}^{DD}=\{g_1,g_3,g_6,g_7\}$$
$$\{g_4\}^{CC}=\{g_4,g_5\}\subseteq\{g_4\}^{DD}=\{g_1,g_4,g_5,g_7\}$$
$$\{g_5\}^{CC}=\{g_5\}\subseteq\{g_5\}^{DD}=\{g_5,g_7\}$$
$$\{g_6\}^{CC}=\{g_6\}\subseteq\{g_6\}^{DD}=\{g_6,g_7\}$$
$$\{g_7\}^{CC}=\{g_7\}\subseteq\{g_7\}^{DD}=\{g_7\}$$

by Definition 3.1, we know *K* is consistent.

In Section 3, we always assume that the decision contexts we are handling are consistent.

By using the operators in Definition 2.10, we can obtain the concept lattices of the condition and decision parts of *K*, denoted by $L(G,C,I_C)$ and $L(G,D,I_D)$, respectively. Wu et al. (Wu et al., 2009) proposed concept rules by requiring the premises and consequences of decision implications to be intents of $L(G,C,I_C)$ and $L(G,D,I_D)$, respectively, and expected that concept rules are capable of representing all the information implied by decision implications.

Definition 3.2 (Wu et al., 2009). Let $K=(G,C\cup D,I_C\cup I_D)$ be a decision context, $(A^C,A)\in L(G,C,I_C)$ and $(B^D,B)\in L(G,D,I_D)$, where $B\neq\varnothing$. If $A^C\subseteq B^D$, then $A\to B$ is called a concept rule of K, where A is the premise of $A\to B$ and B is the consequence.

Since concept rules reveal the dependencies between intents, it is easy to see that concept rules are special decision implications, and are more easily obtainable than decision implications when providing concept lattices. We denote by K_C the set of all concept rules of K.

Example 3.2 (Continuing Example 2.3). All concept rules of Table 2 are shown in Table 4.

Table 4. All concept rules of Table 2

$\{a_2\}\to\{d_1\}$	$\{a_2,a_3,a_4\}\to\{d_2\}$	$\{a_2,a_4,a_5,a_6\}\to\{d_1,d_2\}$
$\{a_3,a_4\}\to\{d_2\}$	$\{a_2,a_3,a_4\}\to\{d_3\}$	$\{a_1,a_2,a_5,a_6\}\to\{d_1\}$
$\{a_2,a_6\}\to\{d_1\}$	$\{a_2,a_3,a_4\}\to\{d_1,d_2\}$	$\{a_1,a_2,a_5,a_6\}\to\{d_3\}$
$\{a_2,a_4\}\to\{d_1\}$	$\{a_2,a_3,a_4\}\to\{d_2,d_3\}$	$\{a_1,a_2,a_5,a_6\}\to\{d_1,d_3\}$
$\{a_1,a_6\}\to\{d_3\}$	$\{a_2,a_3,a_4\}\to\{d_1,d_3\}$	$\{a_1,a_2,a_3,a_4,a_5,a_6\}\to\{d_1\}$
$\{a_2,a_5,a_6\}\to\{d_1\}$	$\{a_2,a_3,a_4\}\to\{d_1,d_2,d_3\}$	$\{a_1,a_2,a_3,a_4,a_5,a_6\}\to\{d_2\}$
$\{a_2,a_4,a_6\}\to\{d_1\}$	$\{a_1,a_3,a_5,a_6\}\to\{d_2\}$	$\{a_1,a_2,a_3,a_4,a_5,a_6\}\to\{d_3\}$
$\{a_3,a_4,a_6\}\to\{d_2\}$	$\{a_1,a_3,a_5,a_6\}\to\{d_3\}$	$\{a_1,a_2,a_3,a_4,a_5,a_6\}\to\{d_1,d_2\}$
$\{a_1,a_5,a_6\}\to\{d_3\}$	$\{a_1,a_3,a_5,a_6\}\to\{d_2,d_3\}$	$\{a_1,a_2,a_3,a_4,a_5,a_6\}\to\{d_2,d_3\}$
$\{a_1,a_3,a_6\}\to\{d_3\}$	$\{a_2,a_4,a_5,a_6\}\to\{d_1\}$	$\{a_1,a_2,a_3,a_4,a_5,a_6\}\to\{d_1,d_3\}$
$\{a_2,a_3,a_4\}\to\{d_1\}$	$\{a_2,a_4,a_5,a_6\}\to\{d_2\}$	$\{a_1,a_2,a_3,a_4,a_5,a_6\}\to\{d_1,d_2,d_3\}$

Proposition 3.1 states that if A is an intent, then $A\to A^{CD}$ is a concept rule.

Proposition 3.1 Let $K=(G,C\cup D,I_C\cup I_D)$ be a decision context. Then, $A\to A^{CD}$ is a concept rule of K if and only if A is an intent.

Proof. It is straightforward.□

In addition, Wu et al. (Wu et al., 2009) also considered granular rules by requiring the premises and consequences of decision implications to be granular intents.

Definition 3.3 (Ganter and Wille, 1999)(Wu et al., 2009). Let $K=(G,C\cup D,I_C\cup I_D)$ be a decision context. For $g\in G$, we call $(g^{CC},g^C)\in L(G,C,I_C)$ and $(gg^{DD},g^D)\in L(G,D,I_D)$ object concepts (or granule concepts), and call g^C and g^D a condition attribute granule and a decision attribute granule, respectively. Both condition attribute granule and decision attribute granule are called granular intents.

Proposition 3.2 (Wille, 1982). Let $K=(G,C\cup D,I_C\cup I_D)$ be a decision context. Then any concept can be represented by the join of some object concepts, i.e.,

1. If $(A,B)\in L(G,C,I_C)$, then $(A,B)=\vee_{g\in A}(g^{CC},g^C)$;
2. If $(A,B)\in L(G,D,I_D)$, then $(A,B)=\vee_{g\in A}(g^{DD},g^D)$.

Definition 3.4 (Wu et al., 2009). Let $K=(G,C\cup D,I_C\cup I_D)$ be a decision context. For $(g^{CC},g^C)\in L(G,C,I_C)$ and $(gg^{DD},g^D)\in L(G,D,I_D)$, if $g_1^{CC}\subseteq g_2^{DD}$, then $g_1^C\to g_2^D$ is called a granular rule of K.

From Definition 3.4, it is easy to see that granular rules are special decision implications and special concept rules. We denote by $K_{\mathbb{G}}$ the set of all granular rules of *K*.

Proposition 3.3 Let $K = (G, C \cup D, I_C \cup I_D)$ be a decision context. Then we have:

1. For any $g \in G$, $g^C \rightarrow g^D$ is a granular rule.
2. $A \rightarrow A^{CD}$ is a granular rule of *K* if and only if *A* is a condition attribute granule.

Proof. (1) Since we are considering consistent decision context, by Definition 3.1, we have $g^{CC} \subseteq g^{DD}$, and therefore $g^C \rightarrow g^D$ is a granular rule by Definition 3.4.

(2) " ⇒ ". By Definition 3.4, it is straightforward.

" ⇐ ". Because *A* is a condition attribute granule, then there exists $g \in G$ such that $A = g^C$. Next, we will prove $A^{CD} = g^D$, i.e., $g^{CCD} = g^D$ since $A = g^C$. Because $g^{CC} \subseteq g^{DD}$, we have $g^{CCD} \supseteq g^{DDD} = g^D$, i.e., $g^{CCD} \supseteq g^D$. On the other hand, because $\{g\} \subseteq g^{CC}$, we have $g^D \supseteq g^{CCD}$. Thus, we have $g^D = g^{CCD}$. Now, taking $A = g^C$ and $A^{CD} = g^D$ into account, $A \rightarrow A^{CD}$ can be reformulated as $g^C \rightarrow g^D$, a granular rule proven by (1).□

Example 3.3 (Continuing Examples 2.3). All granular rules of *K* are shown in Table 5 .

Table 5. All granular rules of K

$\{a_2,a_3,a_4\} \rightarrow \{d_1\}$	$\{a_1,a_3,a_5,a_6\} \rightarrow \{d_3\}$	$\{a_2,a_3,a_1\} \rightarrow \{d_2,d_4\}$
$\{a_2,a_3,a_4\} \rightarrow \{d_2\}$	$\{a_2,a_4,a_5,a_6\} \rightarrow \{d_1\}$	$\{a_2,a_3,a_4\} \rightarrow \{d_1,d_3\}$
$\{a_2,a_3,a_4\} \rightarrow \{d_3\}$	$\{a_2,a_4,a_5,a_6\} \rightarrow \{d_2\}$	$\{a_2,a_3,a_4\} \rightarrow \{d_1,d_2,d_3\}$
$\{a_3,a_4,a_6\} \rightarrow \{d_2\}$	$\{a_1,a_2,a_5,a_6\} \rightarrow \{d_1\}$	$\{a_1,a_2,a_5,a_6\} \rightarrow \{d_1,d_3\}$
$\{a_1,a_3,a_6\} \rightarrow \{d_3\}$	$\{a_1,a_2,a_5,a_6\} \rightarrow \{d_3\}$	$\{a_2,a_4,a_5,a_6\} \rightarrow \{d_1,d_2\}$
$\{a_2,a_4,a_6\} \rightarrow \{d_1\}$	$\{a_2,a_3,a_4\} \rightarrow \{d_1,d_2\}$	$\{a_1,a_3,a_5,a_6\} \rightarrow \{d_2,d_3\}$
$\{a_1,a_3,a_5,a_6\} \rightarrow \{d_2\}$		

Since concept lattices can retain all information in the data (Wille, 1982), the rules obtained from concept lattices, known as concept rules, are also expected to capture all the information in decision entailments (Wu et al., 2009). Furthermore, since all concepts can be represented by the join of some object concepts (see Proposition 3.2), it is also expected that granular rules are capable of representing all the information implied by concept rules and decision implications (Wu et al., 2009; Li and Wu, 2017).

As mentioned previously, granular rules are special concept rules and concept rules are special decision implications; therefore, we have $K_{\mathbb{G}} \subseteq K_{\mathbb{C}} \subseteq K_{\mathbb{D}}$. A decision implication, however, might not be a concept rule or a granular rule, since its premise or consequence might not be an intent or a granular intent. It is thus essential to clarify the relationships between decision implications, concept rules and granular rules.

Concept Rule and Decision Implication

We will discuss the relationships between concept rules and decision implications in this section. Although concept rules are just special decision implications, from the perspective of decision implication logic, concept rules may be complete w.r.t. decision implications (see Definition 2.7). The following example, however, shows that this is not always true.

Example 3.4 (Continuing Examples 2.3). Consider $\{a_1\} \to \{d_3\} \in K_{\mathbb{D}}$. By Definition 2.8 and $K_{\mathbb{C}}$ (cf. Table 4), we know $\{d_3\} \subsetneq \varnothing = \{a_1\}^{K_{\mathbb{C}}}$, which implies $K_{\mathbb{C}} \nvdash \{a_1\} \to \{d_3\}$ by Proposition 2.3. Thus, in this example, $K_{\mathbb{C}}$ is not complete w.r.t. $K_{\mathbb{D}}$.

Since $K_{\mathbb{C}}$ may not be complete w.r.t. $K_{\mathbb{D}}$, there are some decision implications in $K_{\mathbb{D}}$ that cannot be deduced from $K_{\mathbb{C}}$. We will identify those decision implications, and the following proposition provides some clues.

Proposition 3.4 Let $K = (G, C \cup D, I_C \cup I_D)$ be a decision context and $A \to B \in K_{\mathbb{D}}$. Then, $K_{\mathbb{C}} \nvdash A \to B$ if and only if there exists $d \in B$ such that $K_{\mathbb{C}} \nvdash A \to d$.

Proof. " $\Rightarrow$ ". If $K_{\mathbb{C}} \nvdash A \to B$, by Proposition 2.3, we have $B \subsetneq A^{K_{\mathbb{C}}}$. In this case, there must exist $d \in B$ but $d \notin A^{K_{\mathbb{C}}}$. The latter, by Proposition 2.3, implies $K_{\mathbb{C}} \nvdash A \to d$.

" $\Leftarrow$ ". Because $K_{\mathbb{C}} \nvdash A \to d$, by Proposition 2.3, $\{d\} \subsetneq A^{K_{\mathbb{C}}}$ holds; considering $d \in B$, we have $B \subsetneq A^{K_{\mathbb{C}}}$, and hence $K_{\mathbb{C}} \nvdash A \to B$ by Proposition 2.3.□

Proposition 3.4 says that if we have $K_{\mathbb{C}} \nvdash A \to B$, then there must exist $A \to d (d \in B)$ such that $K_{\mathbb{C}} \nvdash A \to d$; in other words, the reason for $K_{\mathbb{C}} \nvdash A \to B$ is that $A \to d (d \in B)$ cannot be deduced from $K_{\mathbb{C}}$. Thus, it is essential to consider the special case $K_{\mathbb{C}} \nvdash A \to d$.

We define:

$$I_{\mathbb{D}}^{A \to d} = \{A_i \to B_i \in K_{\mathbb{D}} \mid A_i \subseteq A, d \in B_i\}$$

and determine by $I_{\mathbb{D}}^{A \to d}$ whether $A \to d$ can be deduced from $K_{\mathbb{C}}$.

Theorem 3.1 Let $K = (G, C \cup D, I_C \cup I_D)$ be a decision context and $A \to d$ be a decision implication of K. Then we have that $K_{\mathbb{C}} \nvdash A \to d$ if and only if for any $A_i \to B_i \in I_{\mathbb{D}}^{A \to d}$, A_i is not an intent of (G, C, I_C).

Proof. " $\Rightarrow$ ". Suppose that there exists $A_i \to B_i \in I_{\mathbb{D}}^{A \to d}$ such that A_i is an intent of (G, C, I_C). On the one hand, because A_i is an intent, by Proposition 3.1, $A_i \to A_i^{CD}$ is a concept rule and hence $A_i \to A_i^{CD} \in K_{\mathbb{C}}$. On the other hand, by $A_i \to B_i \in I_{\mathbb{D}}^{A \to d}$, we conclude $A_i \to B_i \in K_{\mathbb{D}}$, $A_i \subseteq A$ and $d \in B_i$. Because $A_i \to B_i \in K_{\mathbb{D}}$, by Proposition 2.4, we have $B_i \subseteq A_i^{CD}$ and thus $d \in A_i^{CD}$ since $d \in B_i$. Taking $A_i \subseteq A$ and $d \in A_i^{CD}$ into consideration, by the soundness of *Augmentation* in Theorem 2.1, we conclude $A_i \to A_i^{CD} \vdash A \to d$, and hence $K_{\mathbb{C}} \vdash A \to d$ since $A_i \to A_i^{CD} \in K_{\mathbb{C}}$, a contradiction with $K_{\mathbb{C}} \nvdash A \to d$.

" $\Leftarrow$ ". Suppose that $K_{\mathbb{C}} \vdash A \to d$. Then, by Proposition 2.3, we have $d \in A^{K_{\mathbb{C}}}$. By the definition of $A^{K_{\mathbb{C}}}$ (Definition 2.8), there must exist $A_1 \to B_1 \in K_{\mathbb{C}}$ such that $A_1 \subseteq A$ and $d \in B_1$, and hence $A_1 \to B_1 \in I_{\mathbb{D}}^{A \to d}$. Since $A_1 \to B_1 \in K_{\mathbb{C}}$, we conclude that A_1 is an intent of (G, C, I_C), a contradiction with the condition that for any $A_i \to B_i \in I_{\mathbb{D}}^{A \to d}$, A_i is not an intent of (G, C, I_C).□

Example 3.5 (Continuing Example 2.3). Consider the decision implication $\{a_1, a_2, a_5\} \to \{d_3\}$ of K. We can compute the set $I_{\mathbb{D}}^{\{a_1, a_2, a_5\} \to \{d_3\}}$ and list it in Table 6 .

Table 6: Set $I_{\mathbb{D}}^{\{a_1,a_2,a_5\}\to\{d_3\}}$

$\{a_1\}\to\{d_3\}$	$\{a_1,a_2\}\to\{d_1,d_3\}$
$\{a_1,a_2\}\to\{d_3\}$	$\{a_1,a_2,a_5\}\to\{d_3\}$
$\{a_1,a_5\}\to\{d_3\}$	$\{a_1,a_2,a_5\}\to\{d_1,d_3\}$

It can be verified that none of the premises in Table 6 is an intent. In this case, $\{a_1,a_2,a_5\}\to\{d_3\}$ cannot be deduced from $K_{\mathbb{C}}$ by Theorem 3.1.

Now, let us explain Proposition 3.4 and Theorem 3.1 from the perspective of information loss. From this perspective, any decision implication $A\to B\in K_{\mathbb{D}}$ can be viewed as a decision information extracted from *K*, by which one can make all decisions in *B* when all conditions in *A* occur. In this sense, if a decision implication *A*→*B* can be deduced from $K_{\mathbb{D}}$, i.e., $K_{\mathbb{D}}\vdash A\to B, A\to B$ is available in $K_{\mathbb{D}}$; equivalently, from the syntactical aspect, if one can obtain *A*→*B* by applying *Augmentation* and *Combination* to $K_{\mathbb{D}}, A\to B$ is available in $K_{\mathbb{D}}$.

From this perspective, Proposition 3.4 says that if *A*→*B* is an information loss of $K_{\mathbb{C}}$ w.r.t. $K_{\mathbb{D}}$, then there must exist another information loss *A*→*d*(*d*∈*B*) of $K_{\mathbb{C}}$ w.r.t. $K_{\mathbb{D}}$; in other words, the reason for *A*→*B* being an information loss is that there exists an information loss *A*→*d*(*d*∈*B*). Thus, any information loss *A*→*B* can be reduced to a special information loss *A*→*d*. Similarly, Theorem 3.1 says that *A*→*d* is an information loss of $K_{\mathbb{C}}$ w.r.t. $K_{\mathbb{D}}$ if and only if for any $A_i\to B_i\in I_{\mathbb{D}}^{A\to d}, A_i$ is not an intent of (G,C,I_C).

Now, let us explore the underlying reason behind the information loss *A*→*d* of $K_{\mathbb{C}}$ w.r.t. $K_{\mathbb{D}}$.

First, we claim that the decision information *A*→*d* is available in $I_{\mathbb{D}}^{A\to d}$ but unavailable in $K_{\mathbb{D}}\setminus I_{\mathbb{D}}^{A\to d}$. Let us verify the former. Because $A\to d\in K_{\mathbb{D}}, A\subseteq A$ and $d\in\{d\}$, we conclude $A\to d\in I_{\mathbb{D}}^{A\to d}$. Therefore, the decision information *A*→*d* is contained and thus available in $I_{\mathbb{D}}^{A\to d}$. The most important thing, however, is to be aware that even for any decision implication $A_i\to B_i\in I_{\mathbb{D}}^{A\to d}$ such that $A_i\neq A$ or $B_i\neq\{d\}$ (i.e., $A_i\subset A$ or $d\in B_i$ by the definition of $I_{\mathbb{D}}^{A\to d}$), the decision information *A*→*d* is still available in $A_i\to B_i$. This is a result following from Theorem 2.1 since $A_i\subset A$ and $d\in B_i$. Thus, any decision implication in $I_{\mathbb{D}}^{A\to d}$ carries the decision information *A*→*d*. On the other hand, *A*→*d* is unavailable in $K_{\mathbb{D}}\setminus I_{\mathbb{D}}^{A\to d}$, i.e, $K_{\mathbb{D}}\setminus I_{\mathbb{D}}^{A\to d}\nvdash A\to d$, as verified by the following proposition.

Proposition 3.5. Let $K=(G,C\cup D,I_C\cup I_D)$ be a decision context and *A*→*d* be a decision implication of *K*. Then we have $K_{\mathbb{D}}\setminus I_{\mathbb{D}}^{A\to d}\nvdash A\to d$.

Proof. By the definition of $I_{\mathbb{D}}^{A\to d}$, we have that for any $A_i\to B_i\in K_{\mathbb{D}}\setminus I_{\mathbb{D}}^{A\to d}, A_i\subseteq A$ implies $d\notin B_i$. In this case, by Definition 2.8, we conclude $d\notin A^{K_{\mathbb{D}}\setminus I_{\mathbb{D}}^{A\to d}}$ and thus $K_{\mathbb{D}}\setminus I_{\mathbb{D}}^{A\to d}\nvdash A\to d$ by Proposition 2.3.□

Example 3.6 (Continuing Example 3.5). Take the decision implication $\{a_1,a_2,a_5\}\to\{d_3\}\in K_{\mathbb{D}}$ as an example. The set $I_{\mathbb{D}}^{\{a_1,a_2,a_5\}\to\{d_3\}}$ is listed in Table 6 .

On the one hand, any decision implication in $I_{\mathbb{D}}^{\{a_1,a_2,a_5\}\to\{d_3\}}$ carries the decision information $\{a_1,a_2,a_5\}\to\{d_3\}$. Take $\{a_1,a_2\}\to\{d_1,d_3\}\in I_{\mathbb{D}}^{\{a_1,a_2,a_5\}\to\{d_3\}}$ as an example. By applying *Augmentation* to $\{a_1,a_2\}\to\{d_1,d_3\}$, we obtain $\{a_1,a_2,a_5\}\to\{d_3\}$. Thus, $\{a_1,a_2\}\to\{d_1,d_3\}$ carries the decision information $\{a_1,a_2,a_5\}\to\{d_3\}$.

On the other hand, any decision implication in $K_{\mathbb{D}}\setminus I_{\mathbb{D}}^{\{a_1,a_2,a_5\}\to\{d_3\}}$ does not carry the decision information $\{a_1,a_2,a_5\}\to\{d_3\}$. Consider $\{a_1,a_2,a_5,a_6\}\to\{d_1,d_3\}\in K_{\mathbb{D}}\setminus I_{\mathbb{D}}^{\{a_1,a_2,a_5\}\to\{d_3\}}$. Since $\{a_1,a_2,a_5,a_6\}\subsetneq\{a_1,a_2,a_5\}$, we cannot obtain $\{a_1,a_2,a_5\}\rightarrow\{d_3\}$ from $\{a_1,a_2,a_5,a_6\}\rightarrow\{d_1,d_3\}$ by applying *Augmentation* and/or *Combination*. Thus, $\{a_1,a_2,a_5,a_6\}\rightarrow\{d_1,d_3\}$ does not carry the decision information $\{a_1,a_2,a_5\}\rightarrow\{d_3\}$.

Furthermore, the decision information $\{a_1,a_2,a_5\}\rightarrow\{d_3\}$ is unavailable in $K_{\mathbb{D}}\setminus I_{\mathbb{D}}^{A\rightarrow d}$. Consider $\{a_2,a_5\}\rightarrow\{d_1\}\in K_{\mathbb{D}}\setminus I_{\mathbb{D}}\{a_1,a_2,a_5\}\rightarrow\{d_3\}$. Since $\{d_3\}\not\subseteq\{d_1\}$, we cannot obtain $\{a_1,a_2,a_5\}\rightarrow\{d_3\}$ by applying *Augmentation* to $\{a_2,a_5\}\rightarrow\{d_1\}$. To apply *Combination* and derive $\{a_1,a_2,a_5\}\rightarrow\{d_3\}$ from $\{a_2,a_5\}\rightarrow\{d_1\}$ and the other decision implications in $K_{\mathbb{D}}\setminus I_{\mathbb{D}}^{\{a_1,a_2,a_5\}\rightarrow\{d_3\}}$, we should select the decision implications $A\rightarrow B\in K_{\mathbb{D}}\setminus I_{\mathbb{D}}^{\{a_1,a_2,a_5\}\rightarrow\{d_3\}}$ whose consequences contain d_3. By the definition of $I_{\mathbb{D}}^{\{a_1,a_2,a_5\}\rightarrow\{d_3\}}$, however, we know $A\subsetneq\{a_1,a_2,a_5\}$ (otherwise $A\rightarrow B\in I_{\mathbb{D}}^{\{a_1,a_2,a_5\}\rightarrow\{d_3\}}$) and thus $A\cup\{a_2,a_5\}\subsetneq\{a_1,a_2,a_5\}$, meaning that we cannot obtain $\{a_1,a_2,a_5\}\rightarrow\{d_3\}$ from $A\cup\{a_2,a_5\}\rightarrow B\cup\{d_1\}$ by applying *Augmentation*. Thus, $\{a_2,a_5\}\rightarrow\{d_1\}$ does not carry the decision information $\{a_1,a_2,a_5\}\rightarrow\{d_3\}$.

In conclusion, any decision implication in $I_{\mathbb{D}}^{\{a_1,a_2,a_5\}\rightarrow\{d_3\}}$ carries the decision information $\{a_1,a_2,a_5\}\rightarrow\{d_3\}$, but $K_{\mathbb{D}}\setminus I_{\mathbb{D}}^{\{a_1,a_2,a_5\}\rightarrow\{d_3\}}$ does not.

Since any decision implication in $I_{\mathbb{D}}^{A\rightarrow d}$ carries the decision information $A\rightarrow d$ and $A\rightarrow d$ is unavailable in $K_{\mathbb{D}}\setminus I_{\mathbb{D}}^{A\rightarrow d}$, $A\rightarrow d$ is available in $K_{\mathbb{C}}$ if and only if $K_{\mathbb{C}}$ contains at least one decision implication from $I_{\mathbb{D}}^{A\rightarrow d}$. In other words, $K_{\mathbb{C}}$ loses the decision information $A\rightarrow d$ if and only if none of the decision implications in $I_{\mathbb{D}}^{A\rightarrow d}$ is contained in $K_{\mathbb{C}}$, i.e., none of the decision implications in $I_{\mathbb{D}}^{A\rightarrow d}$ is a concept rule. The following proposition connects the condition with Theorem 3.1.

Proposition 3.6 Let $K=(G,C\cup D,I_C\cup I_D)$ be a decision context and $A\rightarrow d$ be a decision implication of K. Then the following statements are equivalent:

1. None of the decision implications in $I_{\mathbb{D}}^{A\rightarrow d}$ is a concept rule.
2. For any $A_i\rightarrow B_i\in I_{\mathbb{D}}^{A\rightarrow d}$, A_i is not an intent.

Proof. " $\Leftarrow$ ". It is straightforward.

" $\Rightarrow$ ". Suppose that there exists $A_i\rightarrow B_i\in I_{\mathbb{D}}^{A\rightarrow d}$ such that A_i is an intent. Because $A_i\rightarrow B_i\in I_{\mathbb{D}}^{A\rightarrow d}$, we have $A_i\rightarrow B_i\in K_{\mathbb{D}}, A_i\subseteq A$ and $d\in B_i$. On the one hand, we conclude $A_i\rightarrow A_i^{CD}\in K_{\mathbb{D}}$ by Proposition 2.4; on the other hand, since $A_i\rightarrow B_i\in K_{\mathbb{D}}$, we have $B_i\subseteq A_i^{CD}$ by Proposition 2.4 and thus $d\in A_i^{CD}$ since $d\in B_i$. Taking $A_i\rightarrow A_i^{CD}\in K_{\mathbb{D}}, A_i\subseteq A$ and $d\in A_i^{CD}$ into consideration, we have $A_i\rightarrow A_i^{CD}\in I_{\mathbb{D}}^{A\rightarrow d}$. Since A_i is an intent, by Proposition 3.1, $A_i\rightarrow A_i^{CD}$ is a concept rule, a contradiction with the condition that none of the decision implications in $I_{\mathbb{D}}^{A\rightarrow d}$ is a concept rule.□

Proposition 3.6 says that if there exists $A_i\rightarrow B_i\in I_{\mathbb{D}}^{A\rightarrow d}$ such that A_i is an intent, we can find a concept rule $A_i\rightarrow A_i^{CD}$ from $I_{\mathbb{D}}^{A\rightarrow d}$, i.e., a concept rule that carries the decision information $A\rightarrow d$. If, conversely, none of the decision implications in $I_{\mathbb{D}}^{A\rightarrow d}$ satisfies the condition, the definition of concept rule has filtered out all the decision implications in $I_{\mathbb{D}}^{A\rightarrow d}$, and no decision information concerning $A\rightarrow d$ is kept in $K_{\mathbb{C}}$. In other words, it is the restrictions on decision implications imposed by the definition of concept rule that lead to information loss of $K_{\mathbb{C}}$ w.r.t. $K_{\mathbb{D}}$ and cause the incompleteness of concept rules w.r.t. decision implications.

Example 3.7 (Continuing Example 3.5). Consider the decision implication $\{a_2,a_3,a_4\}\rightarrow\{d_2\}\in K_{\mathbb{D}}$. The set $I_{\mathbb{D}}^{\{a_2,a_3,a_4\}\rightarrow\{d_2\}}$ can be computed and listed in Table 7.

Table 7. The set $I_{\mathbb{D}}^{\{a_2,a_3,a_4\}\to\{d_2\}}$

$\{a_3,a_4\} \to \{d_2\}$	$\{a_2,a_3,a_4\} \to \{d_2\}$
$\{a_2,a_3\} \to \{d_2\}$	$\{a_2,a_3,a_4\} \to \{d_1,d_2\}$
$\{a_2,a_3\} \to \{d_1,d_2\}$	$\{a_2,a_3,a_4\} \to \{d_2,d_3\}$
$\{a_2,a_3\} \to d_2,d_3\}$	$\{a_2,a_3,a_4\} \to \{d_1,d_2,d_3\}$
$\{a_2,a_3\} \to \{d_1,d_2,d_3\}$	

For $\{a_2,a_3,a_4\}\to\{d_2,d_3\}\in I_{\mathbb{D}}^{\{a_2,a_3,a_4\}\to\{d_2\}}$, we can verify that the premise $\{a_2,a_3,a_4\}$ is an intent, and thus $\{a_2,a_3,a_4\}\to\{a_2,a_3,a_4\}^{CD}$ is a concept rule and kept in $K_{\mathbb{C}}$. Since $\{a_2,a_3,a_4\}^{CD}=\{d_1,d_2,d_3\}$, we know that $\{a_2,a_3,a_4\}\to\{d_1,d_2,d_3\}\in I_{\mathbb{D}}^{\{a_2,a_3,a_4\}\to\{d_2\}}$ is kept in $K_{\mathbb{C}}$, which implies that the decision information $\{a_2,a_3,a_4\}\to\{d_2\}$ is also kept in $K_{\mathbb{C}}$.

For the decision implication $\{a_1,a_2,a_5\}\to\{d_3\}\in K_{\mathbb{D}}$, from Example 3.5, we know that none of the premises in $I_{\mathbb{D}}^{\{a_1,a_2,a_5\}\to\{d_3\}}$ is an intent. Thus, all the decision implications in $I_{\mathbb{D}}^{\{a_1,a_2,a_5\}\to\{d_3\}}$ are filtered out of $K_{\mathbb{C}}$ by the definition of concept rule and no decision information concerning $\{a_1,a_2,a_5\}\to\{d_3\}$ is kept in $K_{\mathbb{C}}$.

Now, combining Proposition 3.4 and Theorem 3.1, we can present the underlying reason behind the information loss of $K_{\mathbb{C}}$ w.r.t. $K_{\mathbb{D}}$.

Theorem 3.2 Let $K=(G,C\cup D,I_C\cup I_D)$ be a decision context and $A\to B\in K_{\mathbb{D}}$. Then the following statements are equivalent:

1. $K_{\mathbb{C}}\nvdash A\to B$.
2. There exists $d\in B$ such that for any $A_i\to B_i\in I_{\mathbb{D}}^{A\to d}, A_i$ is not an intent.

Proof. It is straightforward.□

Although we have proven the existence of information loss of $K_{\mathbb{C}}$ w.r.t. $K_{\mathbb{D}}$ and explored the underlying reason behind the information loss, it is not clear if the information loss is significant for practical applications. In the following, we provide an inspirational result of the issue.

We have known that the decision implication canonical basis $K_{\mathbb{D}}^*$ of a decision context *K* is complete and optimal by Theorem 2.4. From the perspective of information loss, the completeness of $K_{\mathbb{D}}^*$ implies that $K_{\mathbb{D}}^*$ keeps all the decision information of $K_{\mathbb{D}}$, and the optimality of $K_{\mathbb{D}}^*$ implies that each decision implication in $K_{\mathbb{D}}^*$ contains the most abundant decision information of $K_{\mathbb{D}}$. Proposition 3.7 shows that a decision information $A\to A^{CD}\in K_{\mathbb{D}}^*$ will be lost in $K_{\mathbb{C}}$ if *A* is not an intent.

Proposition 3.7 Let $K=(G,C\cup D,I_C\cup I_D)$ be a decision context and *A* be a decision premise of *K*. Then, *A* is not an intent of (G,C,I_C) if and only if $K_{\mathbb{C}}\nvdash A\to A^{CD}$.

Proof. " $\Leftarrow$ ". Suppose that *A* is an intent. By Proposition 3.1, $A\to A^{CD}$ is a concept rule and hence $A\to A^{CD}\in K_{\mathbb{C}}$, a contradiction with $K_{\mathbb{C}}\nvdash A\to A^{CD}$.

" $\Rightarrow$ ". Because *A* is a decision premise of *K*, by Definition 2.12, $A^{CD}\supset\bigcup\{A_i^{CD}\mid A_i\subset A\}$ and hence $A^{CD}\setminus\cup\{A_i^{CD}\mid A_i\subset A\}\neq\varnothing$. Now, we prove that for each $d\in A^{CD}\setminus\bigcup\{A_i^{CD}\mid A_i\subset A\}$, we have $d\notin A^{K_{\mathbb{C}}}$.

Suppose that $d \in A^{K_{\mathbb{C}}}$. By Definition 2.8, we have $A^{K_{\mathbb{C}}} = \bigcup\{B_i \mid A_i \to B_i \in K_{\mathbb{C}}, A_i \subseteq A\}$, and since A is not an intent, there does not exist $A_i \to B_i \in K_{\mathbb{C}}$ such that A_i=A; we thus obtain

$$A^{K_{\mathbb{C}}} = \bigcup\{B_i \mid A_i \to B_i \in K_{\mathbb{C}}, A_i \subset A\}.$$

Because $d \in A^{K_{\mathbb{C}}}$, there exists $A_j \to B_j \in K_{\mathbb{C}}$ such that $A_j \subset A$ and $d \in B_j$. Since $A_j \to B_j \in K_{\mathbb{C}} \subseteq K_{\mathbb{D}}$, we have $B_j \subseteq A_j^{CD}$ by Proposition 2.4 and thus

$$d \in B_j \subseteq A_j^{CD} \subseteq \bigcup\{A_i^{CD} \mid A_i \subset A\}$$

a contradiction with $d \in A^{CD} \setminus \bigcup\{A_i^{CD} \mid A_i \subset A\}$. Thus, we have $d \notin A^{K_{\mathbb{C}}}$.

Since for each $d \in A^{CD} \setminus \bigcup\{A_i^{CD} \mid A_i \subset A\}, d \notin A^{K_{\mathbb{C}}}$ holds, and then we obtain $A^{CD} \subsetneq A^{K_{\mathbb{C}}}$, thus $K_{\mathbb{C}} \nvdash A \to A^{CD}$ by Proposition 2.3.□

The literature (Zhai et al., 2015b) has shown that a decision premise A must also be a minimal generator (Stumme et al., 2000) of the intent A^{CC}. Generally speaking, however, an intent may own a lot of minimal generators and hence may not be a minimal generator of itself, as verified experimentally in (Zhai et al., 2015a). Thus, if a decision premise is an intent, the decision premise has to be a minimal generator of itself. Therefore, it is reasonable to conclude that nearly all decision premises may not be intents, and by Proposition 3.7, $K_{\mathbb{C}}$ loses nearly all the decision implications in $K_{\mathbb{D}}^*$, each of which contains the most abundant decision information of $K_{\mathbb{D}}$, as illustrated in Example 3.8.

Example 3.8 (Continuing Example 2.3). Consider the intent $\{a_2,a_4,a_5,a_6\}$, where $\{a_4,a_5\}$ is a minimal generator of $\{a_2,a_4,a_5,a_6\}$ and a decision premise of K. Obviously, $K_{\mathbb{C}}$ contains the concept rule $\{a_2,a_4,a_5,a_6\}\to\{a_2,a_4,a_5,a_6\}^{CD}$, i.e., $\{a_2,a_4,a_5,a_6\}\to\{d_1,d_2\}$; however, the decision information $\{a_4,a_5\}\to\{a_4,a_5\}^{CD}$, i.e., $\{a_4,a_5\}\to\{d_1,d_2\}$ is lost in $K_{\mathbb{C}}$. Comparatively, $\{a_4,a_5\}\to\{d_1,d_2\}$ contains more decision information than $\{a_2,a_4,a_5,a_6\}\to\{d_1,d_2\}$, since $\{a_2,a_4,a_5,a_6\}\to\{d_1,d_2\}$ can be obtained by applying *Augmentation* to $\{a_4,a_5\}\to\{d_1,d_2\}$.

In fact, all the decision premises except $\{a_2\}$ in Table 3 are not intents, and all the decision implications except $\{a_2\}\to\{d_1\}$ in $K_{\mathbb{D}}^*$ are lost in $K_{\mathbb{C}}$.

Granular Rule and Decision Implication

In this section, we will study the relationships between granular rules and decision implications. We have shown $K_{\mathbb{G}} \subseteq K_{\mathbb{C}} \subseteq K_{\mathbb{D}}$ and $K_{\mathbb{C}}$ may not be complete w.r.t. $K_{\mathbb{D}}$, so, as a subset of $K_{\mathbb{C}}, K_{\mathbb{G}}$ may not be complete w.r.t. $K_{\mathbb{D}}$, as shown by the following example.

Example 3.9 (Continuing Example 3.4). For the decision implication $\{a_1\} \to \{d_3\} \in K_{\mathbb{D}}$, from Example 3.4, we know $K_{\mathbb{C}} \nvdash \{a_1\} \to \{d_3\}$ and thus have $K_{\mathbb{G}} \nvdash \{a_1\} \to \{d_3\}$, since $K_{\mathbb{G}} \subseteq K_{\mathbb{C}}$. On the other hand, for the decision implication $\{a_2,a_3\} \to \{d_1\} \in K_{\mathbb{D}}$, we know $K_{\mathbb{C}} \vdash \{a_2,a_3\} \to \{d_1\}$ by Proposition 2.3 since $\{d_1\} = \{a_2,a_3\}^{K_{\mathbb{C}}}$, but $K_{\mathbb{G}} \nvdash \{a_2,a_3\} \to \{d_1\}$ since $\{d_1\} \subsetneq \varnothing = \{a_2,a_3\}^{K_{\mathbb{G}}}$.

From Example 3.9, it is easy to see that there may exist information loss by means of $K_{\mathbb{G}}$ to represent all decision information of $K_{\mathbb{D}}$. The following proposition, similar to Proposition 3.4, reduces the information loss to the special case.

Proposition 3.8 Let $K=(G,C\cup D,I_C\cup I_D)$ be a decision context and $A\rightarrow B\in K_{\mathbb{D}}$. Then the following statements are equivalent:

1. $K_{\mathbb{G}}\nvdash A\rightarrow B$
2. There exists $d\in B$ such that $K_{\mathbb{G}}\nvdash A\rightarrow d$.

Proof. It is similar to the proof of Proposition 3.4.□

The information loss of $K_{\mathbb{G}}$ w.r.t. $K_{\mathbb{D}}$ is identified by Theorem 3.3.

Theorem 3.3 Let $K=(G,C\cup D,I_C\cup I_D)$ be a decision context and $A\rightarrow d$ be a decision implication of *K*. Then the following statements are equivalent:

1. $K_{\mathbb{G}}\nvdash A\rightarrow d$;
2. For any $A_i\rightarrow B_i\in I_{\mathbb{D}}^{A\rightarrow d}$, A_i is not a condition attribute granule.

Proof. " ⇒ ". Suppose that there exists $A_i\rightarrow B_i\in I_{\mathbb{D}}^{A\rightarrow d}$ such that A_i is a condition attribute granule. On the one hand, because A_i is a condition attribute granule, by Proposition 3.3, $A_i\rightarrow A_i^{CD}$ is a granular rule and hence $A_i\rightarrow A_i^{CD}\in K_{\mathbb{G}}$. On the other hand, by $A_i\rightarrow B_i\in I_{\mathbb{D}}^{A\rightarrow d}$, we obtain $A_i\rightarrow B_i\in K_{\mathbb{D}}$, $A_i\subseteq A$ and $d\in B_i$. Because $A_i\rightarrow B_i\in K_{\mathbb{D}}$, by Proposition 2.4, we have $B_i\subseteq A_i^{CD}$ and thus $d\in A_i^{CD}$ since $d\in B_i$. Taking $A_i\subseteq A$ and $d\in A_i^{CD}$ into consideration, by the soundness of *Augmentation* in Theorem 2.1, we conclude $A_i\rightarrow A_i^{CD}\vdash A\rightarrow d$, and hence $K_{\mathbb{G}}\vdash A\rightarrow d$ since $A_i\rightarrow A_i^{CD}\in K_{\mathbb{G}}$, a contradiction with $K_{\mathbb{G}}\nvdash A\rightarrow d$.

" ⇐ ". Suppose that $K_{\mathbb{G}}\vdash A\rightarrow d$. Then, by Proposition 2.3, we have $d\in A^{K_{\mathbb{G}}}$. By the definition of $A^{K_{\mathbb{G}}}$, there must exist $A_1\rightarrow B_1\in K_{\mathbb{G}}$ such that $A_1\subseteq A$ and $d\in B_1$, and hence $A_1\rightarrow B_1\in I_{\mathbb{D}}^{A\rightarrow d}$. Since $A_1\rightarrow B_1\in K_{\mathbb{G}}$, we conclude that A_1 is a condition attribute granule, a contradiction with the condition that for any $A_i\rightarrow B_i\in I_{\mathbb{D}}^{A\rightarrow d}$, A_i is not a condition attribute granule.□

Example 3.10 (Continuing Example 2.3). Consider $\{a_3,a_4,a_5\}\rightarrow\{d_2\}$, a decision implication of *K*. The set $I_{\mathbb{D}}^{\{a_3,a_4,a_5\}\rightarrow\{d_2\}}$ is computed and listed in Table 8 .

Table 8. Set $I_{\mathbb{D}}^{\{a_3,a_4,a_5\}\rightarrow\{d_2\}}$

$\{a_4,a_5\}\rightarrow\{d_2\}$	$\{a_4,a_5\}\rightarrow\{d_1,d_2\}$	$\{a_3,a_4,a_5\}\rightarrow\{d_1,d_2\}$
$\{a_3,a_5\}\rightarrow\{d_2\}$	$\{a_3,a_5\}\rightarrow\{d_2,d_3\}$	$\{a_3,a_4,a_5\}\rightarrow\{d_2,d_3\}$
$\{a_3,a_4\}\rightarrow\{d_2\}$	$\{a_3,a_4,a_5\}\rightarrow\{d_2\}$	$\{a_3,a_4,a_5\}\rightarrow\{d_1,d_2,d_3\}$

It can be checked that none of the premises in Table 8 is a condition attribute granule. In this case, by Theorem 3.3, $\{a_3,a_4,a_5\}\rightarrow\{d_2\}$ cannot be deduced from $K_{\mathbb{G}}$.

To clarify the reason behind the information loss $A\rightarrow B$ of $K_{\mathbb{G}}$ w.r.t. $K_{\mathbb{D}}$, by Proposition 3.8, it is essential to explore the underlying reason of the special information loss $A\rightarrow d$.

As analyzed in Section 3.2, $A\rightarrow d$ is available in $I_{\mathbb{D}}^{A\rightarrow d}$ and each decision implication in $I_{\mathbb{D}}^{A\rightarrow d}$ carries the decision information $A\rightarrow d$; $A\rightarrow d$ is unavailable in $K_{\mathbb{D}}\setminus I_{\mathbb{D}}^{A\rightarrow d}$. Thus, $A\rightarrow d$ is available in $K_{\mathbb{G}}$ if and only if $K_{\mathbb{G}}$ contains at least one decision implication from $I_{\mathbb{D}}^{A\to d}$. In other words, $K_{\mathbb{G}}$ loses the decision information $A\to d$ if and only if none of the decision implications in $I_{\mathbb{D}}^{A\to d}$ is contained in $K_{\mathbb{G}}$, i.e., none of the decision implications in $I_{\mathbb{D}}^{A\to d}$ is a granular rule. Proposition 3.9 connects the condition with Theorem 3.3.

Proposition 3.9. Let $K=(G,C\cup D,I_C\cup I_D)$ be a decision context and $A\to d$ be a decision implication of K. Then the following statements are equivalent:

1. None of the decision implications in $I_{\mathbb{D}}^{A\to d}$ is a granular rule;
2. For any $A_i\to B_i\in I_{\mathbb{D}}^{A\to d}$, A_i is not a condition attribute granule.

Proof. "⇐". It is straightforward.

"⇒". Suppose that there exists $A_i\to B_i\in I_{\mathbb{D}}^{A\to d}$ such that A_i is a condition attribute granule. Because $A_i\to B_i\in I_{\mathbb{D}}^{A\to d}$, we have $A_i\to B_i\in K_{\mathbb{D}}$, $A_i\subseteq A$ and $d\in B_i$. On the one hand, we conclude that $A_i\to A_i^{CD}\in K_{\mathbb{D}}$ by Proposition 2.4; on the other hand, since $A_i\to B_i\in K_{\mathbb{D}}$, we have $B_i\subseteq A_i^{CD}$ by Proposition 2.4 and thus $d\in A_i^{CD}$ since $d\in B_i$. Taking $A_i\to A_i^{CD}\in K_{\mathbb{D}}$, $A_i\subseteq A$ and $d\in A_i^{CD}$ into consideration, we have $A_i\to A_i^{CD}\in I_{\mathbb{D}}^{A\to d}$; since A_i is a condition attribute granule, by Proposition 3.3, $A_i\to A_i^{CD}$ is a granular rule, a contradiction with the condition that none of the decision implications in $I_{\mathbb{D}}^{A\to d}$ is a granular rule.□

Similar to Proposition 3.6, Proposition 3.9 says that if there exists $A_i\to B_i\in I_{\mathbb{D}}^{A\to d}$ such that A_i is a condition attribute granule, we can find a granular rule $A_i\to A_i^{CD}$ from $I_{\mathbb{D}}^{A\to d}$, which carries the decision information $A\to d$ and will be kept in $K_{\mathbb{G}}$. If, conversely, none of the decision implications in $I_{\mathbb{D}}^{A\to d}$ satisfies the condition, all the decision implications in $I_{\mathbb{D}}^{A\to d}$ will be filtered out of $K_{\mathbb{G}}$ by the definition of granular rule, and no decision information concerning $A\to d$ is kept in $K_{\mathbb{G}}$. In other words, it is the restrictions on decision implications imposed by the definition of granular rule that lead to information loss of $K_{\mathbb{G}}$ w.r.t. $K_{\mathbb{D}}$ and cause the incompleteness of granular rules w.r.t. decision implications.

Example 3.11 (Continuing Examples 3.7 and 3.10). Take $\{a_2,a_3,a_4\}\to\{d_2\}\in K_{\mathbb{D}}$ as an example. For $\{a_2,a_3,a_4\}\to\{d_2,d_3\}\in I_{\mathbb{D}}^{\{a_2,a_3,a_4\}\to\{d_2\}}$ (cf. Table 7), from Table 2, we can verify that $\{a_2,a_3,a_4\}$ is a condition attribute granule, and thus $\{a_2,a_3,a_4\}\to\{a_2,a_3,a_4\}^{CD}$ is a granular rule and kept in $K_{\mathbb{G}}$. Since $\{a_2,a_3,a_4\}^{CD}=\{d_1,d_2,d_3\}$, $\{a_2,a_3,a_4\}\to\{d_1,d_2,d_3\}\in I_{\mathbb{D}}^{\{a_2,a_3,a_4\}\to\{d_2\}}$ is kept in $K_{\mathbb{G}}$, and thus the decision information $\{a_2,a_3,a_4\}\to\{d_2\}$ is also kept in $K_{\mathbb{G}}$.

Consider $\{a_3,a_4,a_5\}\to\{d_2\}\in K_{\mathbb{D}}$. From Example 3.10, we know that none of the premises in $I_{\mathbb{D}}^{\{a_3,a_4,a_5\}\to\{d_2\}}$ is a condition attribute granule. In this case, all the decision implications in $I_{\mathbb{D}}^{\{a_3,a_4,a_5\}\to\{d_2\}}$ are filtered out of $K_{\mathbb{G}}$ by the definition of granular rule and no decision information concerning $\{a_2,a_3,a_4\}\to\{d_2\}$ is kept in $K_{\mathbb{G}}$.

The underlying reason of information loss $A\to B$ of $K_{\mathbb{G}}$ w.r.t. $K_{\mathbb{D}}$ is summarized in Theorem 3.4.

Theorem 3.4. Let $K=(G,C\cup D,I_C\cup I_D)$ be a decision context and $A\to B\in K_{\mathbb{D}}$. Then the following statements are equivalent:

1. $K_{\mathbb{G}}\nvdash A\to B$;
2. There exists $d\in B$ such that for any $A_i\to B_i\in I_{\mathbb{D}}^{A\to d}$, A_i is not a condition attribute granule.

Proof. It is straightforward.□

As discussed in Section 3.2, $K_{\mathbb{D}}^{*}$ keeps all the decision information of $K_{\mathbb{D}}$, and each decision implication in $K_{\mathbb{D}}^{*}$. contains the most abundant decision information of $K_{\mathbb{D}}$. The following proposition shows that the decision information $A \to A^{CD} \in K_{\mathbb{D}}^{*}$ will be lost in $K_{\mathbb{G}}$ if *A* is not a condition attribute granule.

Proposition 3.10. Let $K = (G, C \cup D, I_C \cup I_D)$ be a decision context and *A* be a decision premise of *K*. Then we have that *A* is not a condition attribute granule if and only if $K_{\mathbb{G}} \nvdash A \to A^{CD}$.

Proof. "⇐". Suppose *A* is a condition attribute granule. By Proposition 3.3, $A \to A^{CD}$ is a granular rule and hence $A \to A^{CD} \in K_{\mathbb{G}}$, a contradiction with $K_{\mathbb{G}} \nvdash A \to A^{CD}$.

"⇒". Similar to Proposition 3.7.□

Similar to the case of concept rules, $K_{\mathbb{G}}$ will lose nearly all the decision implications in $K_{\mathbb{D}}^{*}$, each of which contains the most abundant decision information; moreover, since the definition of granular rule requires a decision premise to be not only an intent but also a condition attribute granule, more decision implications in $K_{\mathbb{D}}^{*}$ will be lost in $K_{\mathbb{G}}$ than in $K_{\mathbb{C}}$.

Example 3.12 (Continuing Example 3.8). By Example 3.8, we know that all the decision premises except $\{a_2\}$ in Table 3 are not intents and thus are not condition attribute granules (because a condition attribute granule must be an intent). In fact, it can be verified that $\{a_2\}$ is not a condition attribute granule either. Thus, none of the decision premises in Table 3 is a condition attribute granule and all the decision implications in $K_{\mathbb{D}}^{*}$ are lost in $K_{\mathbb{G}}$.

Granular Rule and Concept Rule

We will discuss the relationships between granular rules and concept rules in this section. We know $K_{\mathbb{G}} \subseteq K_{\mathbb{C}}$ and Example 3.9 shows that there may exist information loss of $K_{\mathbb{G}}$ w.r.t. $K_{\mathbb{C}}$ (i.e., the decision information $\{a_2, a_3\} \to \{d_1\}$). Similarly, the information loss $A \to B$ of $K_{\mathbb{G}}$ w.r.t. $K_{\mathbb{C}}$ can be reduced to a special information loss $A \to d (d \in B)$.

Proposition 3.11. Let $K = (G, C \cup D, I_C \cup I_D)$ be a decision context and $A \to B \in K_{\mathbb{C}}$. Then the following statements are equivalent:

1. $K_{\mathbb{G}} \nvdash A \to B$;
2. There exists $d \in B$ such that $K_{\mathbb{G}} \nvdash A \to d$.

Proof. Refer to the proof of Proposition 3.4.□

By $I_{\mathbb{D}}^{A \to d}$, we denote all the decision information concerning $A \to d$ in $K_{\mathbb{D}}$; similarly, we denote all the decision information concerning $A \to d$ in $K_{\mathbb{C}}$ by $I_{\mathbb{C}}^{A \to d}$:

$$I_{\mathbb{C}}^{A \to d} = \{A_i \to B_i \in K_{\mathbb{C}} \mid A_i \subseteq A, d \in B_i\}$$

We know that $I_{\mathbb{D}}^{A \to d}$ contains all the decision information concerning $A \to d$. Thus, $A \to d$ is available in $K_{\mathbb{G}}$ if and only if $K_{\mathbb{G}}$ contains at least one decision implication from $I_{\mathbb{D}}^{A \to d}$. The latter is equivalent to the condition that $K_{\mathbb{G}}$ contains at least one concept rule from $I_{\mathbb{C}}^{A \to d}$, as the following proposition shows.

Proposition 3.12. Let $K=(G,C\cup D,I_C\cup I_D)$ be a decision context and $A\to d$ be a decision implication of *K*. Then the following statements are equivalent:

1. $A_i\to B_i\in I_{\mathbb{D}}^{A\to d}$ and $A_i\to B_i\in K_{\mathbb{G}}$;
2. $A_i\to B_i\in I_{\mathbb{C}}^{A\to d}$ and $A_i\to B_i\in K_{\mathbb{G}}$.

Proof. By comparing the definitions of $I_{\mathbb{D}}^{A\to d}$ and $I_{\mathbb{C}}^{A\to d}$, it is easy to see that we only need to prove that for $A_i\to B_i\in K_{\mathbb{G}}$, $A_i\to B_i\in I_{\mathbb{D}}^{A\to d}$ if and only if $A_i\to B_i\in I_{\mathbb{C}}^{A\to d}$. This is obvious, since $K_{\mathbb{G}}\subseteq K_{\mathbb{C}}\subseteq K_{\mathbb{D}}$ and $A_i\to B_i\in K_{\mathbb{G}}$.□

Example 3.13 (Continuing Examples 3.3 and 3.7). Take $\{a_2,a_3,a_4\}\to\{d_2\}\in K_{\mathbb{D}}$ as an example, where $\{a_2,a_3,a_4\}$ is an intent. The set $I_{\mathbb{C}}^{\{a_2,a_3,a_4\}\to\{d_2\}}$ can be computed and listed in Table 9.

Table 9. Set $I_{\mathbb{C}}^{\{a_2,a_3,a_4\}\to\{d_2\}}$

$\{a_3,a_4\}\to\{d_2\}$	$\{a_2,a_3,a_4\}\to\{d_1,d_2\}$
$\{a_2,a_3,a_4\}\to\{d_2\}$	$\{a_2,a_3,a_4\}\to\{d_1,d_2,d_3\}$
$\{a_2,a_3,a_4\}\to\{d_2,d_3\}$	

We can verify that $\{a_2,a_3,a_4\}\to\{d_1,d_2\}$ is a granular rule (cf. Table 5), i.e., $\{a_2,a_3,a_4\}\to\{d_1,d_2\}\in K_{\mathbb{G}}$. In this case, we have that $\{a_2,a_3,a_4\}\to\{d_1,d_2\}\in I_{\mathbb{C}}^{\{a_2,a_3,a_4\}\to\{d_2\}}$ if and only if $\{a_2,a_3,a_4\}\to\{d_1,d_2\}\in I_{\mathbb{D}}^{\{a_2,a_3,a_4\}\to\{d_2\}}$ (cf. Table 7).

Now, we know that $A\to d$ is available in $K_{\mathbb{G}}$ if and only if $K_{\mathbb{G}}$ contains at least one concept rule from $I_{\mathbb{C}}^{A\to d}$. In other words, $K_{\mathbb{G}}$ loses the decision information $A\to d$ if and only if none of the concept rules in $I_{\mathbb{C}}^{A\to d}$ is contained in $K_{\mathbb{G}}$, i.e., none of the concept rules in $I_{\mathbb{C}}^{A\to d}$ is a granular rule.

Theorem 3.5. Let $K=(G,C\cup D,I_C\cup I_D)$ be a decision context and $A\to d$ be a decision implication of *K*, where *A* is an intent of (G,C,I_C). Then the following statements are equivalent:

1. $K_{\mathbb{G}}\nvdash A\to d$;
2. for any $A_i\to B_i\in I_{\mathbb{C}}^{A\to d}$, A_i is not a condition attribute granule.

Proof. Because $K_{\mathbb{G}}\nvdash A\to d$ if and only if none of the concept rules in $I_{\mathbb{C}}^{A\to d}$ is a granular rule, thus, to prove this theorem, we just need to prove that none of the concept rules in $I_{\mathbb{C}}^{A\to d}$ is a granular rule if and only if for any $A_i\to B_i\in I_{\mathbb{C}}^{A\to d}$, A_i is not a condition attribute granule.

"$\Leftarrow$". By Definition 3.4, it is straightforward.

"$\Rightarrow$". Suppose that there exists $A_i\to B_i\in I_{\mathbb{C}}^{A\to d}$ such that A_i is a condition attribute granule. Because $A_i\to B_i\in I_{\mathbb{C}}^{A\to d}$, we have $A_i\to B_i\in K_{\mathbb{C}}$, $A_i\subseteq A$ and $d\in B_i$. On the one hand, we conclude that A_i is an intent since $A_i\to B_i\in K_{\mathbb{C}}$, and hence $A_i\to A_i^{CD}\in K_{\mathbb{C}}$ by Proposition 3.1; on the other hand, since $A_i\to B_i\in K_{\mathbb{C}}\subseteq K_{\mathbb{D}}$, we have $B_i\subseteq A_i^{CD}$ by Proposition 2.4 and thus $d\in A_i^{CD}$ since $d\in B_i$. Taking $A_i\to A_i^{CD}\in K_{\mathbb{C}}$, $A_i\subseteq A$ and $d\in A_i^{CD}$ into consideration, we have $A_i\to A_i^{CD}\in I_{\mathbb{C}}^{A\to d}$; since A_i is a condition attribute granule, by Proposition 3.3, $A_i \to A_i^{CD}$ is a granular rule, a contradiction with the condition that none of the concept rules in $I_{\mathbb{C}}^{A\to d}$ is a granular rule.□

Theorem 3.5 says that if there exists a concept rule $A_i \to B_i \in I_{\mathbb{C}}^{A\to d}$ such that A_i is a condition attribute granule, we can find a granular rule $A_i \to A_i^{CD}$ such that $A_i \to A_i^{CD} \in I_{\mathbb{C}}^{A\to d}$, i.e., a granular rule that carries the decision information $A\to d$ and will be kept in $K_{\mathbb{G}}$. If, conversely, none of the concept rules in $I_{\mathbb{C}}^{A\to d}$ satisfies the condition, the definition of granular rule has filtered out all the concept rules in $I_{\mathbb{C}}^{A\to d}$. In other words, it is the restrictions on concept rules imposed by the definition of granular rule that lead to information loss of $K_{\mathbb{G}}$ w.r.t. $K_{\mathbb{C}}$ and cause the incompleteness of granular rules w.r.t. concept rules.

Example 3.14 (Continuing Examples 2.3 and 3.13). Consider $\{a_2,a_5,a_6\} \to \{d_1\} \in K_{\mathbb{D}}$, where $\{a_2,a_5,a_6\}$ is an intent. We can compute

$$I_{\mathbb{C}}^{\{a_2,a_5,a_6\}\to\{d_1\}} = \{\{a_2\} \to \{d_1\}, \{a_2,a_6\} \to \{d_1\}, \{a_2,a_5,a_6\} \to \{d_1\}\}$$

It can be verified that none of the premises in $I_{\mathbb{C}}^{\{a_2,a_5,a_6\}\to\{d_1\}}$ is a condition attribute granule. In this case, by Theorem 3.5, we know $K_{\mathbb{G}} \nvdash \{a_2,a_5,a_6\} \to \{d_1\}$, i.e., the decision information $\{a_2,a_5,a_6\}\to\{d_1\}$ is lost in $K_{\mathbb{G}}$.

Consider $\{a_2,a_3,a_4\} \to \{d_2\} \in K_{\mathbb{C}}$. For $\{a_2,a_3,a_4\} \to \{d_1,d_2\} \in I_{\mathbb{C}}^{\{a_2,a_3,a_4\}\to\{d_2\}}$ (cf. Table 9), it can be verified that $\{a_2,a_3,a_4\}$ is a condition attribute granule, and thus the concept rule $\{a_2,a_3,a_4\}\to\{a_2,a_3,a_4\}^{CD}$ is a granular rule and kept in $K_{\mathbb{G}}$. Since $\{a_2,a_3,a_4\}^{CD}=\{d_1,d_2,d_3\}$, we know $\{a_2,a_3,a_4\} \to \{d_1,d_2,d_3\} \in I_{\mathbb{C}}^{\{a_2,a_3,a_4\}\to\{d_2\}}$ is kept in $K_{\mathbb{G}}$. In this case, the decision information $\{a_2,a_3,a_4\}\to\{d_2\}$ is also kept in $K_{\mathbb{G}}$.

Based on the above discussions, the underlying reason of information loss $A\to B$ of $K_{\mathbb{G}}$ w.r.t. $K_{\mathbb{C}}$ is summarized in Theorem 3.6.

Theorem 3.6. Let $K = (G, C \cup D, I_C \cup I_D)$ be a decision context and $A \to B \in K_{\mathbb{C}}$. Then the following statements are equivalent:

1. $K_{\mathbb{G}} \nvdash A \to B$;
2. There exists $d \in B$ such that for any $A_i \to B_i \in I_{\mathbb{C}}^{A\to d}$, A_i is not a condition attribute granule.

Proof. They are straightforward.□

DECISION IMPLICATION-BASED KNOWLEDGE RE-REPRESENTATION AND REASONING WITHIN INCOMPLETE FORMAL CONTEXT

Implication in Incomplete Formal Contexts

When incidence relations loss occurs in a formal context, the context is referred to as incomplete formal context, with being formally defined by a three-values context (P and R, 2000).

Definition 4.1 (P and R, 2000). Let M be a set of attributes. An incomplete formal context on M is a quadruple 𝕀𝕂=(G,M,{+,-,?},I), where G is a set of objects, M is a set of attributes, and $I \subseteq G \times M \times \{1,0,?\}$ is a ternary relation with the following interpretation:

- $(g,m,+) \in I$: g has attribute m;
- $(g,m,-) \in I$: g does not have attribute m;
- $(g,m,?) \in I$: it is unknown whether g has attribute m.

Example 4.1. An incomplete formal context is given in Table 10.

Table 10. An incomplete formal context

	a_1	a_2	a_3	a_4	a_5
g_1	1	1	?	0	0
g_2	1	0	?	1	1
g_3	1	1	1	?	0
g_4	?	1	1	1	0
g_5	1	1	0	0	0
g_6	1	1	1	1	?

Within incomplete formal contexts, the values of some attributes may be unknown for some objects, and we have to consider two possibilities for an incomplete entry "?": this entry should be filled with either "1" or "0". In this sense, an incomplete formal context can be translated into a complete one by filling the items "?" with "1" or "0".

Definition 4.2 (P and R,2000). Let 𝕀𝕂=(G,M,{+,-,?},I) be an incomplete formal contexts. We call the formal context 𝕂i=($_G$,M,Ii) $_a$ completion (formal context) of 𝕀𝕂, if

- $(g,m,+) \in I$ implies $(g,m) \in I_i$;
- $(g,m,-) \in I$ implies $(g,m) \notin I_i$;
- $(g,m,?) \in I$ implies $(g,m) \in I_i$ or $(g,m) \notin I_i$.

An incomplete formal context corresponds to multiple completions. Definition 4.3 gives two important completions of incomplete formal contexts.

Definition 4.3. Let 𝕂K=(G,M,{+,-,?},I) be an incomplete formal context. The minimal completion and the maximal completion are respectively defined as:

- $\mathbb{K}_{min}$={G,M,I_{min}} where I_{min}={(g,m)|(g,m,+)∈I};
- $\mathbb{K}_{max}$={G,M,I_{max}} where I_{max}= {(g,m)|(g,m+)∈I or (g,m,?)∈I}.

By Definition 4.3, $\mathbb{K}_{min}$ collects all necessary attributes of objects by replacing all "?" with "0", while $\mathbb{K}_{max}$ gathers all possible attributes that objects might possess by replacing all "?" with "1".

Remark 4.1. Here are some symbol denotations to be used in this chapter:

- The operator $(.)^I$ conducted in $\mathbb{K}_{min}$ and $\mathbb{K}_{max}$ is respectively denoted as $(.)^{I_{min}}$ and $(.)^{I_{max}}$.
- For a set $A \subseteq M$, we denote $I_{min}^A = \{(g,m) \in I_{min} \mid m \in A\}$ and $I_{max}^A = \{(g,m) \in I_{max} \mid m \in A\}$.

Example 4.2 (Continuing Example 4.1). Consider the incomplete formal context $\mathbb{IK}$ in Example 4.1. $\mathbb{K}_{min}$ and $\mathbb{K}_{max}$ are respectively shown in Table 11 and 12.

Table 11. The minimal completion $\mathbb{K}_{min}$

	a_1	a_2	a_3	a_4	a_5
g_1	1	1	0	0	0
g_2	1	0	0	1	1
g_3	1	1	1	0	0
g_4	0	1	1	1	0
g_5	1	1	0	0	0
g_6	1	1	1	1	0

Table 12. The maximal completion $\mathbb{K}_{max}$

	a_1	a_2	a_3	a_4	a_5
g_1	1	1	1	0	0
g_2	1	0	1	1	1
g_3	1	1	1	1	0
g_4	1	1	1	1	0
g_5	1	1	0	0	0
g_6	1	1	1	1	1

Differing from formal contexts where implications can be determined as holding or not, in an incomplete formal context, the lack of incidence relations may lead to uncertainty regarding whether implications hold in the data.

Example 4.3 (Continuing Example 4.1). Consider the incomplete formal context $\mathbb{IK}$ in Example 4.1. It is confirmed that $\{a_2,a_4\}\to\{a_3\}$ always holds in $\mathbb{IK}$, regardless of the values represented by the symbol "?".

On the other hand, there exist implications that cannot be verified as either holding or not. Consider the implication $\{a_2,a_4\}\to\{a_1,a_3\}$. By Table 10, it holds for objects g_1, g_2, g_3, g_5, and g_6, while cannot be determined whether it holds for g_4, and we can only confirm that $\{a_2,a_4\}\to\{a_1,a_3\}$ holds in $\mathbb{IK}$ when g_4 has a_1.

There are also exists invalid implications $\mathbb{IK}$. For example, $\{a_2\}\to\{a_3,a_4\}$ does not hold in $\mathbb{IK}$ since it is invalid for g_1.

The literature (P and R, 2000) evaluates the availability of implications based on their validity within completions. In other words, an implication necessarily holds in an incomplete formal context when it holds in all completions of the incomplete formal context. Similarly, an implication is considered potentially valid when it holds in at least one completion.

Definition 4.4 (P and R, 2000). Let $\mathbb{IK}$=(G,M,{+,-,?},I) be an incomplete formal contexts. For a given implication A→B, we define:

1. A→B is necessary in $\mathbb{IK}$ if and only if A→B holds *in* all completions of $\mathbb{IK}$.
2. A→B is in $\mathbb{IK}$ if and only if A→B holds in a*t* least one completion of $\mathbb{IK}$.

Proposition 4.1 provides the equivalent conditions for determining acceptable implications and necessary implications.

Proposition 4.1(P and R,2000). Let $\mathbb{IK}$=(G,M,{+,-,?},I) be an incomplete formal context. Then,

1. $A \to B(A \cap B = \varnothing)$ is necessary in $\mathbb{IK}$ if and only if $A^{I_{\max}} \subseteq B^{I_{\min}}$.
2. A→B is acceptable in $\mathbb{IK}$ if and only if $A^{I_{\min}} \subseteq B^{I_{\max}}$.

acceptable implications and necessary implications are two categories of knowledge, with possessing varying degrees of knowledge validity; overall, both are available for practical applications, and can be effectively applied to decision-making and problem-solving in real-world scenarios. In this chapter, we intend to seek a more general representation of incomplete formal contexts. This will allow us to transform the process of knowledge acquisition from incomplete formal contexts into a more manageable task by utilizing the general representation.

Decision Implication-Based Knowledge Representation and Inference Rules

A straightforward approach to deducing necessary or acceptable implications involves applying the inference rules within formal contexts to both types of implications.

Example 4.4 (Continuing Examples 4.1). Take the incomplete formal context $\mathbb{IK}$ in Example 4.1 as an example. Let us consider a significant inference rule:

Pseudo-transitive:

$$\frac{X \to Y, W \cup Y \to Z}{X \cup W \to Z}$$

in Armstrong's Axiom System (Armstrong, 1974), which initially applies to formal contexts in FCA (Wille, 1982). Take the acceptable implications $\{a_4\}\to\{a_3\}$ and $\{a_3\}\to\{a_2\}$ in Table 10 as an example. The application of Pseudo-transitive to $\{a_4\}\to\{a_3\}$ and $\{a_3\}\to\{a_2\}$ yields $\{a_4\}\to\{a_2\}$, seemingly a logical progression. However, as we verified in Table 10, it is discovered that $\{a_4\}\to\{a_2\}$ is invalid within $\mathbb{IK}$.

Example 4.4 shows that, as we intend to apply the inference rules in formal contexts to acceptable implications, an unexpected outcome emerges, i.e., the inference rules may lead to invalid results. This phenomenon arises from the incompatibility of acceptable implications; in other words, when these implications do not simultaneously exist in any completion, they fail to collaboratively work in the inference process. This section embarks on an exploration of decision implication-based knowledge representation and reasoning rules. This innovative approach offers a smoother, more effective solution to the challenges outlined above.

By the definitions of $\mathbb{K}_{max}$ and $\mathbb{K}_{min}$ (see Definition 4.3), $\mathbb{K}$ can be easily reconstructed by considering the incidence relations in both $\mathbb{K}_{max}$ and $\mathbb{K}_{min}$. That is to say, the pair ($\mathbb{K}_{max}$, $\mathbb{K}_{min}$) stores all details in $\mathbb{IK}$. Motivated by this discovery, we design a unique formal context:

$$\mathbb{K}^{\uparrow\downarrow} = (G, M \cup \mathring{M}, I_{\max} \cup I^{\circ}_{\min}) \tag{3}$$

by connecting $\mathbb{K}$max and $\mathbb{K}_{min}$, where $M \cup \mathring{M}$ represents the placement of the set M of decision attributes to the right of an identical set of condition attributes. Similarly, $I_{\max} \cup I^{\circ}_{\min}$ signifies the appending of the set Imin to the right of I_{max}. Likewise, another formal context can be constructed:

$$\mathbb{K}^{\downarrow\uparrow} = (G, M \cup \overset{\circ}{M}, I_{\min} \cup I^{\circ}_{\max}) \tag{4}$$

Indeed, $\mathbb{K}^{\uparrow\downarrow}$ and $\mathbb{K}^{\downarrow\uparrow}$, each comprising two components: $\mathbb{K}_{max}$ and $\mathbb{K}_{min}$, can be considered as unique decision contexts. While strictly speaking, the condition attributes and decision attributes of a decision context are distinct, in the case of $\mathbb{K}^{\uparrow\downarrow}$ and $\mathbb{K}^{\downarrow\uparrow}$, the condition attributes align with their corresponding decision attributes. This alignment allows us to loosely interpret them as a form of decision context. Within this framework, both necessary and acceptable implication can be re-presented through decision implication within $\mathbb{K}^{\uparrow\downarrow}$ and $\mathbb{K}^{\downarrow\uparrow}$, respectively.

Theorem 4.1. Let 𝕀𝕂=(G,M,{+,-,?},I) be an incomplete formal context. Then,

1. $A \to B(A \cap B \neq \varnothing)$ is necessary in 𝕂𝕂 if and only if A→B is a decision implication in $\mathbb{K}^{\uparrow\downarrow}$.
2. A→B is acceptable in 𝕀𝕂 if and only if A→B is a decision implication in $\mathbb{K}^{\downarrow\uparrow}$ [2].

Proof. By Proposition 4.1, they are straightforward.□

Example 4.5 (Continuing Example 4.1). Take the incomplete formal context 𝕀𝕂 in Example 4.1 as an example. Decision contexts $\mathbb{K}^{\uparrow\downarrow}$ and $\mathbb{K}^{\downarrow\uparrow}$ are respectively shown in Tables 13 and 14.

Table 13. Formal context $\mathbb{K}^{\uparrow\downarrow}$

	a_1	a_2	a_3	a_4	a_5	a_1	a_2	a_3	a_4	a_5
g_1	1	1	1	0	0	1	1	0	0	0
g_2	1	0	1	1	1	1	0	0	1	1
g_3	1	1	1	1	0	1	1	1	0	0
g_4	1	1	1	1	0	0	1	1	1	0
g_5	1	1	0	0	0	1	1	0	0	0
g_6	1	1	1	1	1	1	1	1	1	0

Table 14. Formal context $\mathbb{K}^{\downarrow\uparrow}$

	a_1	a_2	a_3	a_4	a_5	a_1	a_2	a_3	a_4	a_5
g_1	1	1	0	0	0	1	1	1	0	0
g_2	1	0	0	1	1	1	0	1	1	1
g_3	1	1	1	0	0	1	1	1	1	0
g_4	0	1	1	1	0	1	1	1	1	0
g_5	1	1	0	0	0	1	1	0	0	0
g_6	1	1	1	1	0	1	1	1	1	1

It is seen that $\{a_5\}\to\{a_1\}$, being necessary in 𝕂 (see Table 10), is a decision implication of $\mathbb{K}^{\uparrow\downarrow}$. Similarly, $\{a_2,a_4\}\to\{a_1,a_3\}$ is confirmed to be acceptable in 𝕀𝕂, holding as a decision implication of $\mathbb{K}^{\downarrow\uparrow}$.

Zhai et al. (Zhai et al., 2014) proposed two inference rules *Augmentation* and *Combination* for deduction decision implications (see Formulas (1) and (2)). Proposition 4.2 extends the soundness of *Augmentation* and *Combination* to both necessary and acceptable implications, thereby establishing an inference pathway to obtain the two types of implications.

Theorem 4.2. Let 𝕀𝕂=(G,M,{+,-,?},I) be an incomplete formal context. Then,

1. If A→B is necessary in 𝕀𝕂, $A_1 \supseteq A$ and $B_1 \subseteq B$, then $A_1 \to B_1$ is necessary in 𝕀𝕂.
2. If A→B is acceptable in 𝕀𝕂, $A_1 \supseteq A$ and $B_1 \subseteq B$, then $A_1 \to B_1$ is acceptable in 𝕀𝕂.
3. If A→B and $A_1 \to B_1$ are necessary in 𝕀𝕂, then $A \cup A_1 \to B \cup B_1$ is necessary in 𝕀𝕂.
4. If A→B and $A_1 \to B_1$ are acceptable in 𝕀𝕂, then $A \cup A_1 \to B \cup B_1$ is acceptable in 𝕀𝕂.

Proof. (1) By Definition 4.4, for any completion 𝕂 of 𝕀𝕂, A→B holds in 𝕂, and then $A^I \subseteq B^I$ by Definition 2.5. Because $A_1 \supseteq A$ and $B_1 \subseteq B$, we have $A_1^I \subseteq A^I$ and $B_1^I \supseteq B^I$ by Proposition 2.1. By $A^I \subseteq B^I, A_1^I \subseteq A^I$, and $B_1^I \supseteq B^I, A_1^I \subseteq B_1^I$ holds, i.e., $A_1 \to B_1$ holds in 𝕂 by Definition 2.5. In conclusion, for any completion 𝕂 of 𝕀𝕂, $A_1 \to B_1$ holds in 𝕂, meaning that $A_1 \to B_1$ is necessary in 𝕀𝕂.

(2) Similar to the proof of (1).

(3) By Definition 4.4, for any completion 𝕂 of 𝕀𝕂, A→B and $A_1 \to B_1$ holds in 𝕂, and then $A^I \subseteq B^I$ and $A_1^I \subseteq B_1^I$ by Definition 2.5. In this case, $A^I \cap A_1^I \subseteq B^I \cap B_1^I$ holds, and then $(A \cup A_1)^I \subseteq (B \cup B_1)^I$ by Proposition 2.1, i.e., $A \cup A_1 \to B \cup B_1$ holds in 𝕂 by Definition 2.5. In conclusion, for any completion 𝕂 of 𝕀𝕂, $A \cup A_1 \to B \cup B_1$ holds in 𝕂, meaning that $A \cup A_1 \to B \cup B_1$ is necessary in 𝕀𝕂.

(4) Because A→B and $A_1 \to B_1$ are acceptable in 𝕀𝕂, by Proposition 4.1, we have $A^{I_{min}} \subseteq B^{I_{max}}$ and $A_1^{I_{min}} \subseteq B_1^{I_{max}}$, and hence $A^{I_{min}} \cap A_1^{I_{min}} \subseteq B^{I_{max}} \cap B_1^{I_{max}}$, i.e., $(A \cup A_1)^{I_{min}} \subseteq (B \cup B_1)^{I_{max}}$ by Proposition 2.1. In this case, by Proposition 4.1, $A \cup A_1 \to B \cup B_1$ is acceptable in 𝕀𝕂.□

Although in the previous discussions in the chapter, necessary implications were restricted by having an empty intersection between the condition and consequence (as in Theorems 4.1 and 4.1), it can be observed from Proposition 4.2 that Augmentation and Combination break through such limitation.

We will discuss the reasons behind the applicability of Augmentation and Combination to necessary implications and acceptable implications based on incomplete formal contexts.

Firstly, Augmentation and Combination are applicable to necessary implications. This is due to the fact that necessary implications hold in all completions of the given incomplete formal context. When Augmentation and Combination are applied to necessary implications, it is equivalent to applying the inference rules to the corresponding implications in each completion formal context3. Conse^quently, the implications derived through this process hold in all completions, maintaining their necessity within incomplete formal contexts. Secondly, due to the fact that acceptable implications hold in some completions of the given incomplete formal context, when Augmentation is applied to such an implication, the derived implication remains valid in those complete formal contexts. As a result, these implications also maintain their possibility within incomplete formal contexts.

Next, we will explain the reason behind the applicability of Combination to acceptable implications. The following conclusion is firstly presented.

Proposition 4.2. Let 𝕀𝕂=(G,M,{+,-,?},I) be an incomplete formal context, and A1→B1 and A2→B2 be two acceptable implications of 𝕀𝕂. If

$$B_1 \cap A_1 = \varnothing, B_2 \cap A_2 = \varnothing, B_1 \cap A_2 = \varnothing, \textit{ and } B_2 \cap A_1 = \varnothing,$$

then $A_1 \to B_1$ and $A_2 \to B_2$ hold in some completions of 𝕀𝕂.

Proof. Let $𝕂_1$=(G,M,I_1) and $𝕂_2$=(G,M,I_2) be two completions of 𝕀𝕂 and suppose that $A_1 \to B_1$ and $A_2 \to B_2$ hold in $𝕂_1$ and $𝕂_2$, respectively. The operator (.)I conducted in $𝕂_1$ and $𝕂_2$ is respectively denoted as $(.)^{I_1}$ and $(.)^{I_2}$. In this case, we have $A_1^{I_1} \subseteq B_1^{I_1}$ and $A_2^{I_2} \subseteq B_2^{I_2}$ by Definition 2.5. Because $A_1^{I_{min}} \subseteq A_1^{I_1}$, $B_1^{I_1} \subseteq B_1^{I_{max}}$, and $A_1^{I_1} \subseteq B_1^{I_1}$, we have $A_1^{I_{min}} \subseteq B_1^{I_{max}}$. Similarly, $A_2^{I_{min}} \subseteq B_2^{I_{max}}$ can be easily proved to be true.

Because

$$B_1 \cap A_1 = \varnothing, B_2 \cap A_2 = \varnothing, B_1 \cap A_2 = \varnothing, \textit{ and } B_2 \cap A_1 = \varnothing,$$

we have $(A_1 \cup A_2) \cap (B_1 \cup B_2) = \varnothing$. We construct a completion $\mathbb{K}_3$=(G,M,I_3) where $I_{\min}^{A_1 \cup A_2} \subseteq I_3^{A_1 \cup A_2}$ and $I_{\max}^{B_1 \cup B_2} \subseteq I_3^{B_1 \cup B_2}$. In $\mathbb{K}_3$, we can see that

$$A_1^{I_3} = A_1^{I_{\min}}, A_2^{I_3} = A_2^{I_{\min}}, B_1^{I_3} = B_1^{I_{\max}}, \textit{ and } B_2^{I_3} = B_2^{I_{\max}};$$

and by $A_1^{I_{\min}} \subseteq B_1^{I_{\max}}$ and $A_2^{I_{\min}} \subseteq B_2^{I_{\max}}$, we have $A_1^{I_3} \subseteq B_1^{I_3}$ and $A_2^{I_3} \subseteq B_2^{I_3}$, meaning that $A_1 \rightarrow B_1$ and $A_2 \rightarrow B_2$ holding in $\mathbb{K}_3$.

For the given acceptable implications $A_1 \rightarrow B_1$ and $A_2 \rightarrow B_2$, by applying *Augmentation*, two acceptable implications $A_1 \rightarrow B_1 \setminus (A_1 \cup A_2)$ and $A_2 \rightarrow B_2 \setminus (A_1 \cup A_2)$ can be derived; and by Proposition 4.2, there exists a completion, denoted as $\mathbb{K}$, in which both $A_1 \rightarrow B_1 \setminus (A_1 \cup A_2)$ and $A_2 \rightarrow B_2 \setminus (A_1 \cup A_2)$ hold. In this case, by applying *Combination*,

$$A_1 \cup A_2 \rightarrow (B_1 \setminus (A_1 \cup A_2)) \cup (B_2 \setminus (A_1 \cup A_2)), \text{ i.e.,}$$

$$A_1 \cup A_2 \rightarrow (B_1 \cup B_2) \setminus (A_1 \cup A_2) \tag{5}$$

also holds in $\mathbb{K}$.

On the other hand,

$$A_1 \cup A_2 \rightarrow (B_1 \cup B_2) \cap (A_1 \cup A_2) \tag{6}$$

is necessary in $\mathbb{K}$ since $(B_1 \cup B_2) \cap (A_1 \cup A_2) \subseteq A_1 \cup A_2$, and obviously it holds in $\mathbb{K}$. Then, by applying C***ombination*** to Equations 5 and 6, $A_1 \cup A_2 \rightarrow B_1 \cup B_2$ is obtained, with holding in $\mathbb{K}$, i.e., it is acceptable in $\mathbb{IK}$.

In conclusion, starting from the acceptable implications $A_1 \rightarrow B_1$ and $A_2 \rightarrow B_2$, by applying ***Combination,*** $A_1 \cup A_2 \rightarrow B_1 \cup B_2$ is also acceptable.□

Necessary Implication Basis and Acceptable Implication Basis

Section 4.2 applies the inference rule *Augmentation* and *Combination* for reasoning about necessary implications and acceptable implications. From a perspective of knowledge completeness, the derived necessary/acceptable implications can be considered as redundant knowledge within the data and therefore can be eliminated. Thus, in this section, we address the completeness and non-redundancy of defining sets of necessary implications and acceptable implications based on *Augmentation* and *Combination*, thereby obtaining compact sets of necessary implications and acceptable implications, i.e., necessary implication basis and acceptable implication basis.

However, we find that using only *Augmentation* and *Combination* cannot thoroughly eliminate the redundancy in implications, especially the implications with disjoint sets for premise and consequence.

Example 4.6 (Continuing Example 4.1). Take the incomplete formal context $\mathbb{IK}$ in Example 4.1 as an example. L= {{a_1}→{a_1}, {a_3,a_5}→{a_1}, {a_3,a_5}→{a_1,a_3}} is a set of necessary implications of $\mathbb{IK}$.

Consider the implication {a_1}→{a_1}. Clearly, this implication holds trivially. However, from a decision-making perspective, such an implication is meaningless and redundant, and thus should be removed. Nevertheless, it can be verified that $\{a_1\}\to\{a_1\}$ cannot be derived from other implications in L, i.e., $\{a_3,a_5\}\to\{a_1\}$ and $\{a_3,a_5\}\to\{a_1,a_3\}$, using Augmentation and Combination, preventing the removal of $\{a_1\}\to\{a_1\}$ from L.

Then, Take the implications $\{a_3,a_5\}\to\{a_1\}$ and $\{a_3,a_5\}\to\{a_1,a_3\}$ as an example. For $\{a_3,a_5\}\to\{a_1,a_3\}$, the decision attribute a_3 in the consequence is redundant (as a_3 is already given in the premise). Therefore, for the sake of calculation and analysis efficiency, $\{a_3,a_5\}\to\{a_1,a_3\}$ should be deleted while retaining $\{a_3,a_5\}\to\{a_1\}$. However, we find that using only Augmentation and Combination cannot achieve this effect.

Similar issues arise when applying Augmentation and Combination to acceptable implications, which will not be illustrated. To overcome the shortcomings of Augmentation and Combination, we introduce another inference rule4:

Reflexivity:

$$\frac{}{A\to A}$$

Example 4.7 (Continuing Example 4.6). Consider the set of necessary implications $L=\{\{a_1\}\to\{a_1\}, \{a_3,a_5\}\to\{a_1\}, \{a_3,a_5\}\to\{a_1,a_3\}\}$ from Example 4.6. First, applying *Reflexivity* yields $\{a_1\}\to\{a_1\}$, which can then be removed from *L*. Second, similarly applying *Reflexivity* leads to $\{a_3\}\to\{a_3\}$, and by further utilizing *Combination* to $\{a_3,a_5\}\to\{a_1\}$ and $\{a_3\}\to\{a_3\}$, we obtain $\{a_3,a_5\}\to\{a_1,a_3\}$, leading to the removal of $\{a_3,a_5\}\to\{a_1,a_3\}$ from *L*. In summary, after eliminating the redundant implications, the set *L* simplifies to $\{a_3,a_5\}\to\{a_1\}$.

Consequently, we define the completeness and non-redundancy of sets of necessary/acceptable implications based on the *Augmentation*, *Combination* and *Reflexivity*.

Definition 4.5. Let $\mathbb{IK}=(G,M,\{+,-,?\},I)$ be an incomplete formal context, and L be a set of necessary implications of $\mathbb{IK}$. We define:

1. L is said to be complete, if for any necessary implication A→B of $\mathbb{IK}$, A→B can be deduced from L by applying Reflexivity, Augmentation and Combination.
2. L: is said to be non-redundant, if for any A→B∈L, A→B cannot be deduced from L\{A→B} by applying Reflexivity, Augmentation and Combination, and A→B is called non-redundant in L.

The completeness and non-redundancy of acceptable implication sets are defined in a similar way, and will not be repeated. We then research to construct a set of necessary/acceptable implications with completeness and non-redundancy.

Definition 4.6. Let $\mathbb{IK}=(G,M,\{+,-,?\},I)$ be an incomplete formal context. Then, $A\subseteq M$ is a decision premise of $\mathbb{K}^{\uparrow\downarrow}$, if

$$A^{I_{\max}I_{\min}}\setminus A\supset\bigcup\left\{A_i^{I_{\max}I_{\min}}\setminus A\mid A_i\subset A, A_i \textit{ is a decision premise of } \mathbb{K}^{\uparrow\downarrow}\right\} \tag{7}$$

We denote a set:

$$O_{\mathbb{K}^{\uparrow\downarrow}}=\left\{A\to A^{I_{\max}I_{\min}}\setminus A\mid A \textit{ is a decision premise of } \mathbb{K}^{\uparrow\downarrow}\right\}$$

Lemma 4.1 proves $O_{\mathbb{K}^{\uparrow\downarrow}}$ is a set of necessary implications of $\mathbb{IK}$.

Lemma 4.1. Let $\mathbb{IK}$=(*G*,M,{+,-,?},I) be an incomplete formal context. For $A \to A^{I_{\max} I_{\min}} \setminus A \in O_{\mathbb{K}^{\uparrow\downarrow}}$, $A \to A^{I_{\max} I_{\min}} \setminus A$ is necessary in $\mathbb{IK}$.

Proof. By the conclusion (1) of Proposition 2.4, $A \to A^{I_{\max} I_{\min}}$ is a decision implication of $\mathbb{K}^{\uparrow\downarrow}$; and by the conclusion (2) of Proposition 2.4, $A \to A^{I_{\max} I_{\min}} \setminus A$ is also a decision implication of $\mathbb{K}^{\uparrow\downarrow}$ since $A^{I_{\max} I_{\min}} \setminus A \subseteq A^{I_{\max} I_{\min}}$. In this case, by Theorem 4.1, $A \to A^{I_{\max} I_{\min}} \setminus A$ is necessary in $\mathbb{IK}$.□

Theorem 4.3 proves the completeness w.r.t. the full set of necessary implications, as well as the non-redundancy and optimality of $O_{\mathbb{K}^{\uparrow\downarrow}}$.

Theorem 4.3. Let $\mathbb{IK}$=(*G*,*M*,{+,-,?},I) be an incomplete formal context. Then,

1. (Completeness) A→B is necessary in $\mathbb{IK}$ if and only if A→B can be obtained from $O_{\mathbb{K}^{\uparrow\downarrow}}$, by applying Reflexivity, Augmentation and Combination.
2. (Non-redundancy) For any $A \to A^{I_{\max} I_{\min}} \setminus A \in O_{\mathbb{K}^{\uparrow\downarrow}}$, it cannot be obtained from $O_{\mathbb{K}^{\uparrow\downarrow}} \setminus \{A \to A^{I_{\max} I_{\min}} \setminus A\}$ by applying Reflexivity, Augmentation and Combination.
3. (Optimality) For any complete set L of necessary implications, $|O_{\mathbb{K}^{\uparrow\downarrow}}| \subseteq |L|$ holds.

Proof. (1) "⇐". By Theorems 4.1 and 4.2, it is straightforward.

"⇒". We firstly prove

$$A^{I_{\max} I_{\min}} \setminus A \supseteq \bigcup \{A_i^{I_{\max} I_{\min}} \setminus A \mid A_i \subset A, A_i \textit{ is a decision premise of } \mathbb{K}^{\uparrow\downarrow}\} \tag{8}$$

For any decision premise A_i such that $A_i \subset A$, we have $A_i^{I_{\max}} \supseteq A^{I_{\max}}$ by Proposition 2.1, and then $A_i^{I_{\max} I_{\min}} \subseteq A^{I_{\max} I_{\min}}$, and hence $A_i^{I_{\max} I_{\min}} \setminus A \subseteq A^{I_{\max} I_{\min}} \setminus A$. In this case, Formula 8 holds.

For $A \to A^{I_{\max} I_{\min}} \setminus A$, there are two cases to be considered:

- $A \to A^{I_{\max} I_{\min}} \setminus A \in O_{\mathbb{K}^{\uparrow\downarrow}}$. It is straightforward.
- $A \to A^{I_{\max} I_{\min}} \setminus A \notin O_{\mathbb{K}^{\uparrow\downarrow}}$. Then, A is not a decision premise of $\mathbb{K}^{\uparrow\downarrow}$, and by Equation 8, we have

$$A^{I_{\max} I_{\min}} \setminus A = \bigcup \{A_i^{I_{\max} I_{\min}} \setminus A \mid A_i \subset A, A_i \textit{ is a decision premise of } \mathbb{K}^{\uparrow\downarrow}\} \tag{9}$$

Let

$$L_A = \{A_i \to A_i^{I_{\max} I_{\min}} \setminus A \in O_{\mathbb{K}^{\uparrow\downarrow}} \mid A_i \subset A\}$$

$$P_A = \bigcup \{A_i^{I_{\max} I_{\min}} \setminus A \mid A_i \to A_i^{I_{\max} I_{\min}} \setminus A \in L_A\} \tag{10}$$

It is clear $L_A \subseteq O_{\mathbb{K}^{\uparrow\downarrow}}$. By applying *Combination* to the decision implications in L_A, we obtain

$$\bigcup\left\{A_i \mid A_i \to A_i^{I_{\max}I_{\min}} \setminus A \in L_A\right\} \to \bigcup\left\{A_i^{I_{\max}I_{\min}} \setminus A \mid A_i \to A_i^{I_{\max}I_{\min}} \setminus A \in L_A\right\} \tag{11}$$

where $\bigcup\left\{A_i \mid A_i \to A_i^{I_{\max}I_{\min}} \setminus A \in L_A\right\} \subseteq A$ and $\bigcup\left\{A_i^{I_{\max}I_{\min}} \setminus A \mid A_i \to A_i^{I_{\max}I_{\min}} \setminus A \in L_A\right\} = A^{I_{\max}I_{\min}} \setminus A$ by Equation 9. Then, by applying *Augmentation* to Equation 11, $A \to A^{I_{\max}I_{\min}} \setminus A$ is obtained.

We then prove $A \to B \setminus A$ can be deuce from $A \to A^{I_{\max}I_{\min}} \setminus A$ by applying the inference rules. Because $A \to B$ is necessary, then $A \to B$ is a decision implication in $\mathbb{K}^{\uparrow\downarrow}$ by Theorem 4.1, i.e., $A^{I_{\max}} \subseteq B^{I_{\min}}$; and then $A^{I_{\max}I_{\min}} \supseteq B^{I_{\min}I_{\min}} \supseteq B$ by Proposition 2.1, i.e., $B \subseteq A^{I_{\max}I_{\min}}$. Furthermore, we have $B \setminus A \subseteq A^{I_{\max}I_{\min}} \setminus A$. Then, by applying *Augmentation* to $A \to A^{I_{\max}I_{\min}} \setminus A$, $A \to B \setminus A$ is obtained.

By *Reflexivity*, we have $A \to B$. Then, applying *Augmentation*, we obtain $A \to B \cap A$. By applying *Combination* to $A \to B \setminus A$ and $A \to B \cap A$, we derive $A \to (B \setminus A) \cup (B \cap A)$, which simplifies to $A \to B$.

(2) Assume that there exists $A \to A^{I_{\max}I_{\min}} \setminus A \in O_{\mathbb{K}^{\uparrow\downarrow}}$ that can be obtained from $O_{\mathbb{K}^{\uparrow\downarrow}} \setminus \left\{A \to A^{I_{\max}I_{\min}} \setminus A\right\}$ by applying the inference rules. Clearly, $L_A \subseteq O_{\mathbb{K}^{\uparrow\uparrow}} \setminus \left\{A \to A^{I_{\max}I_{\min}} \setminus A\right\}$ holds. We firstly prove that L_A is sufficient to obtain $A \to A^{I_{\max}I_{\min}} \setminus A$. Assume that there exists another implication such that $A_j \to B_j \in O_{\mathbb{K}^{\uparrow\downarrow}} \setminus \left\{A \to A^{I_{\max}I_{\min}} \setminus A\right\}$ but $A_j \to B_j \notin L_A$ is involved to generate $A \to A^{I_{\max}I_{\min}} \setminus A$, by applying

$$P_A = \bigcup\left\{A_i^{I_{\max}I_{\min}} \setminus A \mid A_i \to A_i^{I_{\max}I_{\min}} \setminus A \in L_A\right\} \tag{12}$$

Reflexivity, *Augmentation*, and *Combination*. By Equations 3 and 4, both *Augmentation* and *Combination* augment the premises of the given implications, in this case, we have $A \supseteq A_j$. Because $A_j \to B_j \in O_{\mathbb{K}^{\uparrow\downarrow}} \setminus \left\{A \to A^{I_{\max}I_{\min}} \setminus A\right\}$, then $A_j \neq A$; because $A_j \to B_j \notin L_A$, $A \not\supset A_j$ holds, and hence $A \not\supseteq A_j$, which contradicts with $A \supseteq A_j$. Thus, L_A is sufficient to obtain $A \to A^{I_{\max}I_{\min}} \setminus A$.

It is easy to see that among all the implications that obtained from L_A, the setis the maximal conclusion. Hence, we have $A^{I_{\max}I_{\min}} \setminus A \subseteq P$. Because A_i is a decision premise of $\mathbb{K}^{\uparrow\downarrow}$, by the definition of DICB, we have $A^{I_{\max}I_{\min}} \setminus A \supset P$, contradicting with $A^{I_{\max}I_{\min}} \setminus A \subseteq P$. Thus, the assumption is wrong, and hence $O_{\mathbb{K}^{\uparrow\downarrow}}$ is redundant.

(3) For $A \to A^{I_{\max}I_{\min}} \setminus A \in O_{\mathbb{K}^{\uparrow\downarrow}}$, let

$$L_A = \left\{A_i \to B_i \in L \mid A_i \subseteq A\right\} \tag{13}$$

We firstly prove $A \to A^{I_{\max}I_{\min}} \setminus A$ cannot be obtained from $L \setminus L_A$. By the definition of L_A (cf. Formula 13) and $A \to A^{I_{\max}I_{\min}} \setminus A \notin L$, we know that for any $A_j \to B_j \in L \setminus L_A$, $A_i \not\subseteq A$ holds. Let $L_1 \subseteq L \setminus L_A$. Because for any $A_j \to B_j \in L_1$, $A_i \not\subseteq A$ holds; and by Formulas 3 and 4, we know by applying *Augmentation* and *Combination*, any $A_k \to B_k$ that deduced from L_1 satisfying that $A_k \not\subseteq A$, and hence $A \to A^{I_{\max}I_{\min}} \setminus A$ cannot be obtained from L_1. In conclusion, any $L_1 \subseteq L \setminus L_A$ cannot deduce $A \to A^{I_{\max}I_{\min}} \setminus A$, and hence $L \setminus L_A$ cannot deduce $A \to A^{I_{\max}I_{\min}} \setminus A$.

Let

$$S = A^{I_{\max}I_{\min}} \setminus A - \bigcup\left\{A_i^{I_{\max}I_{\min}} \setminus A \mid A_i \subset A, A_i \textit{ is a decision premise of } \mathbb{K}^{\uparrow\downarrow}\right\} \tag{14}$$

and let $a \in S$. Then, $a \in A^{I_{max}I_{min}} \setminus A$ holds, i.e., $a \in A^{I_{max}I_{min}}$ and $a \notin A$.

We will prove there exists $A \rightarrow B \in L_A$ such that $a \in B$. Assume that for any $A \rightarrow B_1 \in L_A$, $a \notin B_1$ holds. For any $A_i \rightarrow B_i \in L_A$, there are two cases to be considering:

- $A_i = A$. Because for any $A \rightarrow B_1 \in L_A$, $a \notin B_1$ holds, then $a \notin B_i$.
- $A_i \subset A$. There are two cases to be considered:
  - A_i is a decision premise of $\mathbb{K}^{\uparrow\downarrow}$. Because $a \in S$, by Formula 14,

$$a \notin \cup\left\{A_i^{I_{max}I_{min}} \setminus A \mid A_i \subset A, A_i \textit{ is a decision premise of } \mathbb{K}^{\uparrow\downarrow}\right\} \quad (15)$$

and hence $a \notin A_i^{I_{max}I_{min}} \setminus A$, i.e., $a \notin A_i^{I_{max}I_{min}}$ or $a \in A$, and then $a \notin A_i^{I_{max}I_{min}}$ because we have proven $a \notin A$. Because $A_i \rightarrow B_i$ is necessary, $A_i^{I_{max}} \subseteq B_i^{I_{min}}$ holds by Proposition 4.1, and then $A_i^{I_{max}I_{min}} \supseteq B_i^{I_{min}I_{min}} \supseteq B_i$, i.e., $B_i \subseteq A_i^{I_{max}I_{min}}$, and hence $a \notin B_i$, because $a \notin A_i^{I_{max}I_{min}}$.

- A_i is not a decision premise of $\mathbb{K}^{\uparrow\downarrow}$. By Definition 4.6,

$$A_i^{I_{max}I_{min}} \setminus A \not\subset \left\{A_j^{I_{max}I_{min}} \setminus A \mid A_j \subset A_i, A_j \textit{ is a decision premise of } \mathbb{K}^{\uparrow\downarrow}\right\} \quad (16)$$

For any decision premise A_j such that $A_j \subset A_i$, we have $A_j^{I_{max}} \supset A_i^{I_{max}}$, and hence $A_j^{I_{max}I_{min}} \subseteq A_i^{I_{max}I_{min}}$ by Proposition 2.1, and then $A_j^{I_{max}I_{min}} \setminus A \subseteq A_i^{I_{max}I_{min}} \setminus A$. Thus,

$$A_i^{I_{max}I_{min}} \setminus A \supseteq \left\{A_j^{I_{max}I_{min}} \setminus A \mid A_j \subset A_i, A_j \textit{ is a decision premise of } \mathbb{K}^{\uparrow\downarrow}\right\} \quad (17)$$

And by Formula 17, we have

$$A_i^{I_{max}I_{min}} \setminus A = \left\{A_j^{I_{max}I_{min}} \setminus A \mid A_j \subset A_i, A_j \textit{ is a decision premise of } \mathbb{K}^{\uparrow\downarrow}\right\} \quad (18)$$

By Formula 15, we have

$$a \notin \left\{A_j^{I_{max}I_{min}} \setminus A \mid A_j \subset A_i, A_j \textit{ is a decision premise of } \mathbb{K}^{\uparrow\downarrow}\right\},$$

and hence $a \notin A_i^{I_{max}I_{min}} \setminus A$. Because $A_i \rightarrow B_i$ is necessary, $A_i^{I_{max}} \subseteq B_i^{I_{min}}$ holds by Proposition 4.1, and then $A_i^{I_{max}I_{min}} \supseteq B_i^{I_{min}I_{min}} \supseteq B_i$, i.e., $B_i \subseteq A_i^{I_{max}I_{min}}$, and hence $a \notin B_i$, because $a \notin A_i^{I_{max}I_{min}}$.

From the above, for any $A_i \rightarrow B_i \in L_A$, $a \notin B_i$, holds. In this case, for any $A_k \rightarrow A^k$ which deduced from L_A, $a \notin B_k$ holds. Because $a \in A^{I_{max}I_{min}} \setminus A$, then $A \rightarrow A^{I_{max}I_{min}} \setminus A$ cannot be deduced from L_A.

In conclusion, $A \rightarrow A^{I_{max}I_{min}} \setminus A$ cannot be deduced from $L \setminus L_A$ and L_A, i.e., cannot be deduced from L, contradicting with L is complete w.r.t. all necessary implication of $\mathbb{IK}$.□

The set $O_{\mathbb{K}^{\uparrow\downarrow}}$ is referred to as necessary implication basis of $\mathbb{IK}$. Starting from $O_{\mathbb{K}^{\uparrow\downarrow}}$, by applying the inference rules, all necessary implications in incomplete formal contexts can be derived. At this point, the set $O_{\mathbb{K}^{\uparrow\downarrow}}$ and the set of inference rules (*Reflexivity*, *Augmentation* and *Combination*) form a reasoning system for necessary implications.

Example 4.8 (Continuing Example 4.1). Consider the incomplete formal context $\mathbb{IK}$ in Example 4.1. $\mathbb{K}^{\uparrow\downarrow}$ is shown in Table 13. The set $O_{\mathbb{K}^{\uparrow\downarrow}}$ is shown in Table 15.

Table 15: Set $O_{\mathbb{K}^{\uparrow\downarrow}}$

$\{a_5\} \to \{a_1,a_4\}$
$\{a_2,a_4\} \to \{a_3\}$
$\{a_2,a_5\} \to \{a_1,a_3,a_4\}$

All decision implications in $\mathbb{IK}$, can be deduced from Table 15 by applying the the inference rules. For instance, by applying Augmentation to $\{a_2,a_5\}\to\{a_1,a_3,a_4\}$, we derive another necessary implication $\{a_1,a_2,a_5\}\to\{a_3\}$. Similarly, by employing Combination on $\{a_5\}\to\{a_1,a_4\}$ and $\{a_2,a_4\}\to\{a_3\}$, we initially obtain $\{a_2,a_4,a_5\}\to\{a_1,a_3,a_4\}$, which deduces $\{a_2,a_4,a_5\}\to\{a_1,a_3\}$ through the subsequent application of Augmentation.

Acceptable implication basis is defined as follows:

- $A \subseteq M$ is a decision premise of $\mathbb{K}^{\downarrow\uparrow}$, if

$$A^{I_{\min}I_{\max}} \setminus A \supset \bigcup\left\{A_i^{I_{\min}I_{\max}} \setminus A \mid A_i \subset A, A_i \textit{ is a decision premise of } \mathbb{K}^{\downarrow\uparrow}\right\}$$

- Let

$$O_{\mathbb{K}^{\downarrow\uparrow}} = \left\{A \to A^{I_{\min}I_{\max}} \setminus A \mid A \textit{ is a decision premise of } \mathbb{K}^{\downarrow\uparrow}\right\}$$

Theorem 4.4. Let $\mathbb{IK}$ be an incomplete formal context. Then,

1. (Completeness) A→B is acceptable in $\mathbb{IK}$ if and only if A→B can be obtained from $O_{\mathbb{K}\downarrow\uparrow}$, by applying *Reflexivity, Augmentation* and *Combination.*
2. (Completeness) For any $A \to A^{I_{\min}I_{\max}} \setminus A \in O_{\mathbb{K}^{\downarrow\uparrow}}$, it cannot be obtained from $O_{\mathbb{K}^{\downarrow\uparrow}} \setminus \left\{A \to A^{I_{\min}I_{\max}} \setminus A\right\}$ by applying *Reflexivity*, *Augmentation,* and *Combination.*
3. (Optimality) $O_{\mathbb{K}^{\downarrow\uparrow}}$ is optimal, i.e., for any complete set L of acceptable implications, $\left|O_{\mathbb{K}^{\downarrow\uparrow}}\right| \le |L|$

Proof. Refer to the proof of Theorem 4.3.□

Similar to necessary implications, an inference system for acceptable implications can be constructed based on $O_{\mathbb{K}^{\downarrow\uparrow}}$, and the inference rules *Reflexivity*, *Augmentation*, and *Combination.*

Example 4.9 (Continuing Example 4.1). Consider the incomplete formal context $\mathbb{IK}$ in Example 4.1. $\mathbb{K}^{\downarrow\uparrow}$ is given in Example 4.5. The set $O_{\mathbb{K}^{\downarrow\uparrow}}$ is given in Table 16.

Table 16: Set $O_{\mathbb{K}^{\downarrow\uparrow}}$

$\varnothing \rightarrow \{a_1\}$	$\{a_3\} \rightarrow \{a_1,a_2,a_4\}$
$\{a_2\} \rightarrow \{a_1\}$	$\{a_5\} \rightarrow \{a_1,a_3,a_4\}$
$\{a_4\} \rightarrow \{a_1,a_3\}$	$\{a_1,a_4\} \rightarrow \{a_3,a_5\}$

Consider $\{a_3,a_4\}\rightarrow\{a_2\}$, an acceptable implication in $\mathbb{IK}$. It can be deduced by firstly applying ***Combination*** to ***Augmentation*** to $\{a_3\}\rightarrow\{a_1,a_2,a_4\}$.

CONCLUSION AND FUTURE WORK

This chapter conducts a comparative study of decision implication, concept rule and granular rule, and that of decision implication-based knowledge re-representation and reasoning within incomplete formal contexts, which includes the following contribution:

(1) It is exemplified that both concept rules and granular rules are not complete w.r.t. decision implications, and that granular rules are not complete w.r.t. concept rules. This implies that there exists information loss when studying decision implications by using only concept rules or granular rules, or when studying concept rules by using only granular rules.With the help of decision implication logic, we uncover the information loss by identifying the decision implications that cannot be deduced from concept rules or granular rules, and the concept rules that cannot be deduced from granular rules, and explore the underlying reason behind the information loss in concept rules and granular rules.

(2) We have identified that, while both necessary and acceptable implications can be represented within formal contexts, the inference rules, initial apply to implications within formal contexts, may yield invalid results when they are applied to acceptable implications.To address this issue, we have introduced specially constructed decision contexts that connect the minimal and maximal completions of incomplete formal contexts. These contexts facilitate the re-representation of both necessary and acceptable implications based on decision implications.

(3) We have extended the applicability of inference rules such as *Augmentation* and *Combination*, originally designed for decision implications, to necessary and acceptable implications. Additionally, we have introduced the *Reflexivity* inference rule to enhance redundancy elimination capabilities. The completeness and non-redundancy for sets of necessary/acceptable implications have been defined based on *Augmentation*, *Combination*, and *Reflexivity*. We constructed necessary implication basis and acceptable implication basis, which respectively serve as a compact representation of preserving all information implied in necessary/acceptable implications with minimal implications.

Future work will center on several meaningful aspects:

(1) Potential values exploration of concept rules and granular rules. We will judge whether concept rules or granular rules are complete w.r.t. decision implications in such applications is also a meaningful issue. In fact, it is also worthwhile to study and conduct some experiments to verify if the

information loss in concept rules or granular rules exists or is important in some applications, and if it is the case, to find the approximate and optimal representation types of decision information.

(2) Inference system construction for concept rules and granular rules. It refers to the study concept rules logic, which includes semantical and syntactical aspects. The semantical aspect defines the soundness of a concept rule, and concept rule basis. The syntactical aspect accounts for the inference rules of concept rules, which are sound, complete and non-redundant w.r.t. the semantical aspect.

(3) Uncertain knowledge description in a logic perspective. The semantic investigates the soundness, completeness, and redundancy of implications and the construction of canonical basis. The syntactic focuses on inference rule with semantic consistency, taking cues from the inference rules applied in this chapter.

(4) Incompatible knowledge representation and reasoning. While it has been demonstrated that incompatible knowledge can yield acceptable implications (such as via *Combination*), there may still be incompatibilities between the derived knowledge. Our plan is to explore subsystems of compatible knowledge reasoning and select the appropriate subsystem based on practical scenarios.

ACKNOWLEDGMENT

This work is supported by the Fundamental Research Program of Shanxi Province(202103021223303), the National Natural Science Foundation of China (62072294, 61972238), the Open Project Foundation of Intelligent Information Processing Key Laboratory of Shanxi Province (CICIP2022006), the Scientific and Technologial Innovation Programs of Higher Education Institutions in Shanxi(STIP) (2021L287), NNSFC (62272284), the Special Fund for Science and Technology Innovation Teams of Shanxi (202204051001015), Shanxi University of Finance and Economics Talent Introduction Research Startup Fund (Z18368), Shanxi Province Doctoral Graduates Research Funding (Z24223).

REFERENCES

Armstrong, W. W. (1974). Dependency structures of data base relationships. In IFIP congress, 74. Geneva, Switzerland.

Bartl, E., & Konecny, J. (2019). L-concept lattices with positive and negative attributes: Modeling uncertainty and reduction of size. *Information Sciences*, *472*, 163–179. doi:10.1016/j.ins.2018.08.057

Bartl, E., & Konecny, J. (2019). L-concept lattices with positive and negative attributes: Modeling uncertainty and reduction of size. *Information Sciences*, *472*, 163–179. doi:10.1016/j.ins.2018.08.057

Carpineto, C., & Romano, G. (2004a). *Concept data analysis: Theory and applications*. John Wiley & Sons. doi:10.1002/0470011297

Carpineto, C., & Romano, G. (2004b). Exploiting the potential of concept lattices for information retrieval with credo. *Journal of Universal Computer Science*, *10*(8), 985–1013.

Carpineto, C., & Romano, G. (2004b). Exploiting the potential of concept lattices for information retrieval with credo. *Journal of Universal Computer Science*, *10*(8), 985–1013.

Cornejo, M. E., Medina, J., & Ramírez-Poussa, E. (2018). Characterizing reducts in multi-adjoint concept lattices. *Information Sciences*, *422*, 364–376. doi:10.1016/j.ins.2017.08.099

Cornejo, M. E., Medina, J., & Ramírez-Poussa, E. (2018). Characterizing reducts in multi-adjoint concept lattices. *Information Sciences*, *422*, 364–376. doi:10.1016/j.ins.2017.08.099

Ganter, B. (1999). Attribute exploration with background knowledge. *Theoretical Computer Science*, *217*(2), 215–233. doi:10.1016/S0304-3975(98)00271-0

Ganter, B. (1999). Attribute exploration with background knowledge. *Theoretical Computer Science*, *217*(2), 215–233. doi:10.1016/S0304-3975(98)00271-0

Ganter, B., & Wille, R. (1999). *Formal Concept Analysis: Mathematical Foundations*. Springer Science & Business Media. doi:10.1007/978-3-642-59830-2

Holzer, R. (2001). *Methoden der formalen Begri sanalyse bei der Behandlung unvollst ndigen Wissens*. [PhD thesis, Darmstadt].

Holzer, R. (2004a). Knowledge acquisition under incomplete knowledge using methods from formal concept analysis: Part i. *Fundamenta Informaticae*, *63*(1), 17–39.

Wasserkrug, S., Gal, A., & Etzion, O. (2008). Inference of security hazards from event composition based on incomplete or uncertain information. *IEEE Transactions on Knowledge and Data Engineering*, *20*(8), 1111–1114. doi:10.1109/TKDE.2008.74

Wille, R. (1982). Restructuring lattice theory: An approach based on hierarchies of concepts. In I. Rival (Ed.), *Ordered Sets* (pp. 445–470). Springer Netherlands. doi:10.1007/978-94-009-7798-3_15

Wu, W., Yee, L., & Mi, J. (2009). Granular computing and knowledge reduction in formal contexts. *IEEE Transactions on Knowledge and Data Engineering*, *21*(10), 1461–1474. doi:10.1109/TKDE.2008.223

Zhai, Y., Jia, N., Zhang, S., Li, D., & Weihua, X. (2022). Study on deduction process and inference methods of decision implications. *International Journal of Machine Learning and Cybernetics*, *13*(7), 1959–1979. doi:10.1007/s13042-021-01499-y

Zhai, Y., & Li, D. (2019). Knowledge structure preserving fuzzy attribute reduction in fuzzy formal context. *International Journal of Approximate Reasoning*, *115*, 209–220. doi:10.1016/j.ijar.2019.09.012

Zhai, Y., Li, D., & Qu, K. (2012). Probability fuzzy attribute implications for interval-valued fuzzy sets. *International Journal of Database Theory and Application*, *5*(4), 95–108.

Zhai, Y., Li, D., & Qu, K. (2014). Decision implications: A logical point of view. *International Journal of Machine Learning and Cybernetics*, *5*(4), 509–516. doi:10.1007/s13042-013-0204-2

Zhai, Y., Li, D., & Qu, K. (2015a). Canonical basis for decision implications. *Chinese Journal of Electronics*, *43*(1), 18–23.

Zhai, Y., Li, D., & Qu, K. (2015b). Decision implication canonical basis: A logical perspective. *Journal of Computer and System Sciences*, *81*(1), 208–218. doi:10.1016/j.jcss.2014.06.001

Zhang, S., Li, D., & Zhai, Y. (2021). Incremental method of generating decision implication canonical basis. *Soft Computing*, *26*(3), 1067–1083. doi:10.1007/s00500-021-06452-3

Zhang, S., Li, D., Zhai, Y., & Kang, X. (2020). A comparative study of decision implication, concept rule and granular rule. *Information Sciences*, *508*, 33–49. doi:10.1016/j.ins.2019.08.053

ENDNOTES

1 In the literature (Li et al., 2013b,a, 2011), concept rules are called decision rules.

2 For $A \rightarrow B$, A comes from the condition part of $\mathbb{K}^{\uparrow\downarrow}$ or $\mathbb{K}^{\downarrow\uparrow}$, and B comes from the decision part.

3 ***Augmentation*** and ***Combination*** are applicable to the implications within formal contexts.

4 Clearly, ***Reflexivity*** applies to both necessary and acceptable implications.

Compilation of References

Abdollahzadeh, S., Teymourlu, M., & Amini, A. (2023). Selection of suppliers using FBWM-FGRA hybrid approach in hospital food supply chain. *Journal of Intelligent & Fuzzy Systems*, *45*(6), 9655–9668. doi:10.3233/JIFS-231845

Ahmad, A., Qamar, U., & Raza, M. S. (2020). An optimized method to calculate approximations in Dominance based rough set approach. *Applied Soft Computing*, *97*, 106731. doi:10.1016/j.asoc.2020.106731

Ahmadi, S. A., & Peivandizadeh, A. (2022). Sustainable portfolio optimization model using promethee ranking: A case study of palm oil buyer companies. *Discrete Dynamics in Nature and Society*, *8935213*, 1–11. doi:10.1155/2022/8935213

Akram, M., Zahid, K., & Kahraman, C. (2023). A PROMETHEE based outranking approach for the construction of Fangcang shelter hospital using spherical fuzzy sets. *Artificial Intelligence in Medicine*, *135*, 102456. doi:10.1016/j.artmed.2022.102456 PMID:36628791

Alavi, B., Tavana, M., & Mina, H. (2021). A dynamic decision support system for sustainable supplier selection in circular economy. *Sustainable Production and Consumption*, *27*, 905–920. doi:10.1016/j.spc.2021.02.015

Ali, G., Afzal, M., Asif, M., & Shazad, A. (2022). Attribute reduction approaches under interval-valued q-rung orthopair fuzzy sof framework. *Applied Intelligence*, *52*(8), 8975–9000. doi:10.1007/s10489-021-02853-x

Anastasova, Y., & Yanev, N. (2021). Models and data quality in information systems applicable in the mining industry. E3S Web of Conferences, Sofia, Bulgaria.

Armstrong, W. W. (1974). Dependency structures of data base relationships. In IFIP congress, 74. Geneva, Switzerland.

Atanassov, K. T. (1986). Intuitionistic fuzzy sets. *Fuzzy Sets and Systems*, *20*(1), 87–96. doi:10.1016/S0165-0114(86)80034-3

Awajan, I., Mohamad, M., & Al-Quran, A. (2021). Sentiment analysis technique and neutrosophic set theory for mining and ranking big data from online reviews. *IEEE Access : Practical Innovations, Open Solutions*, *9*, 47338–47353. doi:10.1109/ACCESS.2021.3067844

Azad, P., Navimipour, N. J., Rahmani, A. M., & Sharifi, A. (2020). The role of structured and unstructured data managing mechanisms in the Internet of things. *Cluster Computing*, *23*(2), 1185–1198. doi:10.1007/s10586-019-02986-2

Bai, C., Kusi-Sarpong, S., Ahmadi, H. B., & Sarkis, J. (2019). Social sustainable supplier evaluation and selection: A group decision-support approach. *International Journal of Production Research*, *57*(22), 7046–7067. doi:10.1080/00207543.2019.1574042

Bao, T., Luo, R., & Guo, T. (2022). Analysis of agricultural question classification model based on BERT character vector and TextCNN. *Journal of Southern Agricultural Sciences*, *7*, 2068–2076.

Bargiela, A., & Pedrycz, W. (2008). Toward a theory of granular computing for human-centered information processing, *IEEE.T.Fuzzy. Syst.*, *16*, 320–330.

Barika, M., Garg, S., Zomaya, A. Y., Wang, L., Moorsel, A. V., & Ranjan, R. (2019). Orchestrating big data analysis workflows in the cloud: Research challenges, survey, and future directions. *ACM Computing Surveys*, *52*(5), 1–41. doi:10.1145/3332301

Barlas, P., Lanning, I., & Heavey, C. (2015). A survey of open source data science tools. *International Journal of Intelligent Computing and Cybernetics*, *8*(3), 232–261. doi:10.1108/IJICC-07-2014-0031

Bartl, E., & Konecny, J. (2019). L-concept lattices with positive and negative attributes: Modeling uncertainty and reduction of size. *Information Sciences*, *472*, 163–179. doi:10.1016/j.ins.2018.08.057

Begoli, E., Goethert, I., & Knight, K. (2021). A lakehouse architecture for the management and analysis of heterogeneous data for biomedical research and mega-biobanks. 2021 IEEE International Conference on Big Data (Big Data), Orlando, FL, USA

Behzadian, M., Otaghsara, S. K., Yazdani, M., & Ignatius, J. (2012). A state-of the-art survey of TOPSIS applications. *Expert Systems with Applications*, *39*(17), 13051–13069. doi:10.1016/j.eswa.2012.05.056

Behzadidoost, R., Mahan, F., & Izadkhah, H. (2024). Granular computing-based deep learning for text classification. *Information Sciences*, *652*, 119746. doi:10.1016/j.ins.2023.119746

Bernabe-Moreno, J., Tejeda-Lorente, A., Herce-Zelaya, J., Porcel, C., & Herrera-Viedma, E. (2020). A context-aware embeddings supported method to extract a fuzzy sentiment polarity dictionary. *Knowledge-Based Systems*, *190*, 105236. doi:10.1016/j.knosys.2019.105236

Bisht, G., & Pal, A. (2024). A q-rung orthopair fuzzy decision-making framework considering experts trust relationships and psychological behavior: An application to green supplier selection. *Decision Science Letters*, *13*(1), 67–82. doi:10.5267/j.dsl.2023.12.002

Biswas, T. K., Abbasi, A., & Chakrabortty, R. K. (2022). A two-stage VIKOR assisted multi-operator differential evolution approach for Influence Maximization in social networks. *Expert Systems with Applications*, *192*, 116342. doi:10.1016/j.eswa.2021.116342

Bjeladinovic, S. (2018). A fresh approach for hybrid SQL/NoSQL database design based on data structuredness. *Enterprise Information Systems*, *12*(8-9), 1202–1220. doi:10.1080/17517575.2018.1446102

Błaszczyński, J., de Almeida Filho, A. T., Matuszyk, A., Szeląg, M., & Słowiński, R. (2021). Auto loan fraud detection using dominance-based rough set approach versus machine learning methods. *Expert Systems with Applications*, *163*, 113740. doi:10.1016/j.eswa.2020.113740

Brans, J. P., & Vincke, P. (1985). Note—A Preference Ranking Organisation Method: (The PROMETHEE Method for Multiple Criteria Decision-Making). *Management Science*, *31*(6), 647–656. doi:10.1287/mnsc.31.6.647

Brehmer, B. (1992). Dynamic decision making: Human control of complex systems. *Acta Psychologica*, *81*(3), 211–241. doi:10.1016/0001-6918(92)90019-A PMID:1462786

Cao, F., Xing, B., Luo, J., Li, D., Qian, Y., Zhang, C., Bai, H., & Zhang, H. (2023). An efficient object detection algorithm based on improved YOLOV5 for High-Spatial-Resolution Remote sensing images. *Remote Sensing (Basel)*, *15*(15), 3755. doi:10.3390/rs15153755

Carpineto, C., & Romano, G. (2004a). *Concept data analysis: Theory and applications*. John Wiley & Sons. doi:10.1002/0470011297

Carpineto, C., & Romano, G. (2004b). Exploiting the potential of concept lattices for information retrieval with credo. *Journal of Universal Computer Science*, *10*(8), 985–1013.

Catanzariti, F., Chiaselotti, G., Infusino, F., & Marino, G. (2020). Object similarity measures and Pawlak's indiscernibility on decision tables. *Information Sciences*, *539*, 104–135. doi:10.1016/j.ins.2020.05.030

Chai, N., Zhou, W., & Jiang, Z. (2023). Sustainable supplier selection using an intuitionistic and interval-valued fuzzy MCDM approach based on cumulative prospect theory. *Information Sciences*, *626*, 710–737. doi:10.1016/j.ins.2023.01.070

Chen, C. (2020). *Application research of NLP technology in Agricultural public opinion analysis system*. Beijing University of Technology.

Cheng, Y. T., Zhang, C., Sangaiah, A. K., Fan, X. Q., Wang, A. N., Wang, L. Y., & Liu, Y. X. (2023). Efficient Low-Resource Medical Information Processing Based on Semantic Analysis and Granular Computing. *ACM Transactions on Asian and Low-Resource Language Information Processing*, *3626319*, 3626319. doi:10.1145/3626319

Chen, H., Li, J. H., Min, F., Liu, W. Q., & Tsang, E. C. C. (2017). Optimal scale selection in dynamic multi-scale decision tables based on sequential three-way decisions. *Inf. Sci*, *415–416*, 213–232.

Chen, P., & Guo, X. Y. (2020). Agricultural short text information classification based on Adaboost and Naive Bayes. *Journal of Software*, *41*(9), 13–18.

Chen, T., & Liu, S. H. (2015). Research on agricultural network public opinion monitoring system under cloud environment. *Journal of Agricultural Network Information*, *1*, 41–44.

Chen, Z., Ming, X., Zhou, T., & Chang, Y. (2020). Sustainable supplier selection for smart supply chain considering internal and external uncertainty: An integrated rough-fuzzy approach. *Applied Soft Computing*, *87*, 106004. doi:10.1016/j.asoc.2019.106004

Cherradi, M., & El Haddadi, A. (2022). A Scalable framework for data lakes ingestion. *Procedia Computer Science*, *215*, 809–814. doi:10.1016/j.procs.2022.12.083

Cobanoglu, C., & Cobanoglu, N. (2003). The effect of incentives in web surveys: Application and ethical considerations. *International Journal of Market Research*, *45*(4), 475–488. doi:10.1177/147078530304500406

Cobo, M. J., Martinez, M. A., Gutiérrez-Salcedo, M., Herrera, M., & Herrera-Viedma, E. (2014). Identifying citation classics in fuzzy decision making field using the concept of H-classics. *Procedia Computer Science*, *31*, 567–576. doi:10.1016/j.procs.2014.05.303

Cornejo, M. E., Medina, J., & Ramírez-Poussa, E. (2018). Characterizing reducts in multi-adjoint concept lattices. *Information Sciences*, *422*, 364–376. doi:10.1016/j.ins.2017.08.099

Cortes, C., & Vapnik, V. (1995). Support-vector networks. *Machine Learning*, *20*(3), 273–297. doi:10.1007/BF00994018

Coscia, M. (2022). Generalized euclidean measure to estimate distances on multilayer networks. *ACM Transactions on Knowledge Discovery from Data*, *16*(6), 1–22. doi:10.1145/3529396

Čuš, B., & Golec, D. (2022). Data Lakehouse: Benefits in small and medium enterprises. *Mednarodno inovativno poslovanje= Journal of Innovative Business and Management, 14*(2), 1-10.

Dai, D., Zhou, X. Z., Li, H. X., & Liu, L. F. (2019), Co-training based sequential three-way decisions for cost-sensitive classification, *Proceedings of the 16th International Conference on Networking, Sensing and Control*, 157–162. 10.1109/ICNSC.2019.8743205

Dashtipour, K., Gogate, M., Li, J., Jiang, F., Kong, B., & Hussain, A. (2020). A hybrid Persian sentiment analysis framework: Integrating dependency grammar based rules and deep neural networks. *Neurocomputing*, *380*, 1–10. doi:10.1016/j.neucom.2019.10.009

Das, N. R., Ghosh, S., Mukherjee, I., & Paul, G. (2023). Adoption of a ranking based indexing method for the cricket teams, *Expert Systems with Applications, 213*, 118796. e Costa, C. A. B., & Vansnick, J. C. (1994), MACBETH—An interactive path towards the construction of cardinal value functions. *International Transactions in Operational Research, 1*(4), 489–500.

Das, S. K. (2022). An approach to optimize the cost of transportation problem based on triangular fuzzy programming problem. *Complex & Intelligent Systems, 8*(1), 687–699. doi:10.1007/s40747-021-00535-2

Datablist. (n.d.). *Download Sample CSV Files for free*. https://www.datablist.com/learn/csv/download-sample-csv-files

Dickson, M. S., & Asagba, P. (2020). The Semi-Structured Data Model and Implementation Issues for Semi-Structured Data. *International Journal of Innovation and Sustainability, 3*, 47–51.

Dinh, V.-N., & Nguyen, H.-A. (2022). Data Process Approach by Traditional and Cloud Services Methodologies.

Di, X. K., Zhang, H., & Qin, X. T. (2023). Keywords extraction algorithm in agricultural field based on new word discovery and improved TextRank algorithm. *Journal of Agricultural Engineering, 13*(06), 21–25.

Dogan, O. (2021). Process mining technology selection with spherical fuzzy AHP and sensitivity analysis. *Expert Systems with Applications, 178*, 114999. doi:10.1016/j.eswa.2021.114999

Domingo-Lopez, D. A., Lattanzi, G., Schreiber, L. H. J., Wallace, E. J., Wylie, R., O'Sullivan, J., Dolan, E. B., & Duffy, G. P. (2022). Medical devices, smart drug delivery, wearables and technology for the treatment of diabetes mellitus. *Advanced Drug Delivery Reviews, 185*, 114280. doi:10.1016/j.addr.2022.114280 PMID:35405298

Drury, B., & Roche, M. (2019). A survey of the applications of text mining for agriculture. *Computers and Electronics in Agriculture, 163*, 104864. doi:10.1016/j.compag.2019.104864

Ecer, F. (2022). An extended MAIRCA method using intuitionistic fuzzy sets for coronavirus vaccine selection in the age of COVID-19. *Neural Computing & Applications, 34*(7), 5603–5623. doi:10.1007/s00521-021-06728-7 PMID:35017795

Efe, B., & Efe, L. (2023a). Hastaların Acil Servis Seçimi İçin Q Seviyeli Bulanık MAIRCA Yöntemi Önerisi. *Necmettin Erbakan Üniversitesi Fen ve Mühendislik Bilimleri Dergisi, 5*(2), 288–298.

Efe, B., & Efe, Ö. F. (2023b). Fine-Kinney method based on fuzzy logic for natural gas pipeline project risk assessment. *Soft Computing, 27*(22), 16465–16482. doi:10.1007/s00500-023-09108-6

Efe, Ö. F., & Efe, B. (2022). A decision support model based on q-rung orthopair fuzzy number for glove design application. *Neural Computing & Applications, 34*(15), 12695–12708. doi:10.1007/s00521-022-07118-3

Ehlers, M., Gaehler, M., & Janowsky, R. (2006). Automated techniques for environmental monitoring and change analyses for ultra high resolution remote sensing data. *Photogrammetric Engineering and Remote Sensing, 72*(7), 835–844. doi:10.14358/PERS.72.7.835

Ersahin, B., Aktas, O., Kilinc, D., & Ersahin, M. (2019). A hybrid sentiment analysis method for Turkish. *Turkish Journal of Electrical Engineering and Computer Sciences, 27*(3), 1780–1793. doi:10.3906/elk-1808-189

Evans, J., & Mathur, A. (2005). The value of online surveys. *Internet Research, 15*(2), 195–219. doi:10.1108/10662240510590360

Fang, Y., Gao, C., & Yao, Y. Y. (2020). Granularity-driven sequential three-way decisions: A cost-sensitive approach to classification. *Information Sciences, 507*, 644–664. doi:10.1016/j.ins.2019.06.003

Fang, Y., & Min, F. (2019). Cost-sensitive approximate attribute reduction with three-way decisions. *International Journal of Approximate Reasoning, 104*, 148–165. doi:10.1016/j.ijar.2018.11.003

Feng, F., Zheng, Y. J., Alcantud, J. C. R., & Wang, Q. (2020). Minkowski weighted score functions of intuitionistic fuzzy values. *Mathematics*, *8*(7), 1143. doi:10.3390/math8071143

Feng, S., Xu, T. Y., & Zhou, Y. C. (2021). Rice knowledge text classification method based on deep convolutional neural network. *Nongye Jixie Xuebao*, *3*, 257–264.

Fenton, K. A., Johnson, A. M., McManus, S., & Erens, B. (2001). Measuring sexual behaviour: Methodological challenges in survey research. *Sexually Transmitted Infections*, *77*(2), 84–92. doi:10.1136/sti.77.2.84 PMID:11287683

Fu, L. F., & Zhao, F. F. (2021). Prediction and analysis of agricultural public opinion based on Attention mechanism LSTM model. *Journal of Mathematics in Practice and Understanding*, *51*(17), 64–76.

Fu, Y., Cai, R., & Yu, B. (2022). Group decision-making method with directed graph under linguistic environment. *International Journal of Machine Learning and Cybernetics*, *13*(11), 3329–3340. doi:10.1007/s13042-022-01597-5

Gabarro, J., & Stewart, A. (2021). Modelling web-service uncertainty: The angel/daemon approach. *Computer Science Review*, *39*, 100355. doi:10.1016/j.cosrev.2020.100355

Galo, N. R., Calache, L. D. D. R., & Carpinetti, L. C. R. (2018). A group decision approach for supplier categorization based on hesitant fuzzy and ELECTRE TRI. *International Journal of Production Economics*, *202*, 182–196. doi:10.1016/j.ijpe.2018.05.023

Ganter, B. (1999). Attribute exploration with background knowledge. *Theoretical Computer Science*, *217*(2), 215–233. doi:10.1016/S0304-3975(98)00271-0

Ganter, B., & Wille, R. (1999). *Formal Concept Analysis: Mathematical Foundations*. Springer Science & Business Media. doi:10.1007/978-3-642-59830-2

Gao Q. S., & Zhang X. W. (2011), Implement the traditional/simplified conversion in Java programs. *International Journal of Computer Programming Skills and Maintenance, 13*, 21-24+52.

Gao, C., & Yao, Y. (2017). Actionable strategies in three-way decisions. *Knowledge-Based Systems*, *133*, 141–155. doi:10.1016/j.knosys.2017.07.001

Garg, H., & Rani, D. (2022). Novel distance measures for intuitionistic fuzzy sets based on various triangle centers of isosceles triangular fuzzy numbers and their applications. *Expert Systems with Applications*, *191*, 116228. doi:10.1016/j.eswa.2021.116228

Ghadimi, P., Wang, C., Lim, M. K., & Heavey, C. (2019). Intelligent sustainable supplier selection using multiagent technology: Theory and application for Industry 4.0 supply chains. *Computers & Industrial Engineering*, *127*, 588–600. doi:10.1016/j.cie.2018.10.050

Giebler, C., Gröger, C., Hoos, E., Eichler, R., Schwarz, H., & Mitschang, B. (2021). The data lake architecture framework. *BTW 2021*.

Gilbey, J. (2009). Valuing the digital economy. *Nature*, *462*(7270), 165. doi:10.1038/462165a

Gireesha, O., Somu, N., & Krithivasan, K., & VS, S. S. (. (2020). IIVIFS-WASPAS: An integrated multi-criteria decision-making perspective for cloud service provider selection. *Future Generation Computer Systems*, *103*, 91–110. doi:10.1016/j.future.2019.09.053

Gou, X., Xu, Z., Liao, H., & Herrera, F. (2021). Probabilistic double hierarchy linguistic term set and its use in designing an improved VIKOR method: The application in smart healthcare. *The Journal of the Operational Research Society*, *72*(12), 2611–2630. doi:10.1080/01605682.2020.1806741

Greco, S., Figueira, J., & Ehrgott, M. (2016), *Multiple criteria decision analysis, 37.* New York: Springer.

Greco, S., Inuiguchi, M., & Slowinski, R. (2006). Fuzzy rough sets and multiple-premise gradual decision rules. *International Journal of Approximate Reasoning, 41*(2), 179–211. doi:10.1016/j.ijar.2005.06.014

Greco, S., Matarazzo, B., & Slowinski, R. (1999). Rough approximation of a preference relation by dominance relations. *European Journal of Operational Research, 117*(1), 63–83. doi:10.1016/S0377-2217(98)00127-1

Greco, S., Matarazzo, B., & Slowinski, R. (2001). Rough sets theory for multicriteria decision analysis. *European Journal of Operational Research, 129*(1), 1–47. doi:10.1016/S0377-2217(00)00167-3

Guarnieri, P., & Trojan, F. (2019). Decision making on supplier selection based on social, ethical, andenvironmental criteria: A study in the textile industry. *Resources, Conservation and Recycling, 141*, 347–361. doi:10.1016/j.resconrec.2018.10.023

Gunn S. R. (1998). Support vector machines for classification and regression. *ISIS technical report, 14*(1), 5-16.

Guo S.L., Su X. N., & Fang X. H. (2023), Research on Travel text association knowledge Mining and recommendation service based on NER and Apriori algorithm. *Modern information, 43*(11):123-134.

Guo, D., Jiang, C., Sheng, R., & Liu, S. (2022). A novel outcome evaluation model of three-way decision: A change viewpoint. *Information Sciences, 607*, 1089–1110. doi:10.1016/j.ins.2022.06.022

Guo, X. C., Hao, X., & Yao, X. C. (2023). Research on joint model of intention recognition and slot filling for agricultural pest knowledge answer. *Nongye Jixie Xuebao, 54*(01), 205–215.

Gupta, P. M. (2023). The Role of Big Data in Smart Healthcare. *International Journal of Internet of Things, 2023.* Advance online publication. 10.5923

Han, X. R., Zhang, C., & Zhan, J. M. (2022). A three-way decision method under probabilistic linguistic term sets and its application to Air Quality Index. *Information Sciences, 617*, 254–276. doi:10.1016/j.ins.2022.10.108

Harby, A. A., & Zulkernine, F. (2022). From Data Warehouse to Lakehouse: A Comparative Review. 2022 IEEE International Conference on Big Data (Big Data), Osaka, Japan

Harper, F. M., & Konstan, J. A. (2015). The MovieLens datasets. *ACM Transactions on Interactive Intelligent Systems, 5*(4), 1–19. doi:10.1145/2827872

Hasan, M. M., Jiang, D., Ullah, A. M. M. S., & Noor-E-Alam, M. (2020). Resilient supplier selection in logistics 4.0 with heterogeneous information. *Expert Systems with Applications, 139*, 139. doi:10.1016/j.eswa.2019.07.016

He, K., Zhang, X., & Ren, S. (2016), Deep residual learning for image recognition, In *Proceedings of the IEEE conference on computer vision and pattern recognition,* (pp. 770-778). IEEE.

Hinton, G. E., Osindero, S., & Teh, Y. W. (2006). A fast learning algorithm for deep belief nets. *Neural Computation, 18*(7), 1527–1554. doi:10.1162/neco.2006.18.7.1527 PMID:16764513

Hlupić, T., & Puniš, J. (2021). An Overview of Current Trends in Data Ingestion and Integration. 2021 44th International Convention on Information, Communication and Electronic Technology (MIPRO).

Hobbs, J. (1985), Granularity, *In Proceedings of the Ninth International Joint Conference on Artificial Intelligence (IJCAI)*, 432-435.

Holzer, R. (2001). *Methoden der formalen Begri sanalyse bei der Behandlung unvollst ndigen Wissens.* [PhD thesis, Darmstadt].

Holzer, R. (2004a). Knowledge acquisition under incomplete knowledge using methods from formal concept analysis: Part i. *Fundamenta Informaticae*, *63*(1), 17–39.

Hosseini, S., & Khaled, A. (2019). A hybrid ensemble and AHP approach for resilient supplier selection. *Journal of Intelligent Manufacturing*, *30*(4), 207–228. doi:10.1007/s10845-016-1241-y

Huang, Q., Li, T., Huang, Y., Yang, X., & Fujita, H. (2020). Dynamic dominance rough set approach for processing composite ordered data. *Knowledge-Based Systems*, *187*, 104829. doi:10.1016/j.knosys.2019.06.037

Hu, D., Chen, S., Qiao, K., & Cao, S. (2017). Integrating CART algorithm and multi-source remote sensing data to estimate sub-pixel impervious surface coverage: A case study from Beijing Municipality, China. *Chinese Geographical Science*, *27*(4), 614–625. doi:10.1007/s11769-017-0882-x

Huo, T. T. (2019). *Research on news Text classification based on FastText and its application in agricultural news*. Jilin University.

Hussain, A., Chun, J., & Khan, M. (2020). A novel customer-centric Methodology for Optimal Service Selection (MOSS) in a cloud environment. *Future Generation Computer Systems*, *105*, 562–580. doi:10.1016/j.future.2019.12.024

Ikart, E. M. (2019). Survey questionnaire survey pretesting method: An evaluation of survey questionnaire via expert reviews technique. *Asian Journal of Social Science Studies*, *4*(2), 1–17. doi:10.20849/ajsss.v4i2.565

Immonen, A., Ovaska, E., & Paaso, T. (2018). Towards certified open data in digital service ecosystems. *Software Quality Journal*, *26*(4), 1257–1297. doi:10.1007/s11219-017-9378-2

Isah, H., Abughofa, T., Mahfuz, S., Ajerla, D., Zulkernine, F., & Khan, S. (2019). A survey of distributed data stream processing frameworks. *IEEE Access : Practical Innovations, Open Solutions*, *7*, 154300–154316. doi:10.1109/ACCESS.2019.2946884

Jacquet-Lagreze, E., & Siskos, J. (1982). Assessing a set of additive utility functions for multicriteria decision-making, the UTA method. *European Journal of Operational Research*, *10*(2), 151–164. doi:10.1016/0377-2217(82)90155-2

Janssen, M., Charalabidis, Y., & Zuiderwijk, A. (2012). Benefits, adoption barriers and myths of open data and open government. *Information Systems Management*, *29*(4), 258–268. doi:10.1080/10580530.2012.716740

Ji, P., Zhang, H. Y., & Wang, J. Q. (2018). A fuzzy decision support model with sentiment analysis for items comparison in e-commerce: The case study of http://PConline. com. *IEEE Transactions on Systems, Man, and Cybernetics: Systems*, *49*(10), 1993-2004. doi:10.1109/TSMC.2018.2875163

Jiang, C., Guo, D., & Duan, Y. (2022). Measure effectiveness of change-based three-way decision using utility theory. *Cognitive Computation*, *14*(3), 1009–1018. doi:10.1007/s12559-022-09999-x

Jiang, C., Guo, D., Duan, Y., & Liu, Y. (2020). Strategy selection under entropy measures in movement-based three-way decision. *International Journal of Approximate Reasoning*, *119*, 280–291. doi:10.1016/j.ijar.2020.01.013

Jiang, C., Guo, D., & Sun, L. (2021). Effectiveness measure for TAO model of three-way decisions with interval set. *Journal of Intelligent & Fuzzy Systems*, *40*(6), 11071–11084. doi:10.3233/JIFS-202207

Jiang, C., Guo, D., & Xu, R. (2021). Measuring the outcome of movement-based three-way decision using proportional utility functions. *Applied Intelligence*, *51*(12), 8598–8612. doi:10.1007/s10489-021-02325-2

Jiang, C., & Yao, Y. (2018). Effectiveness measures in movement-based three-way decisions. *Knowledge-Based Systems*, *160*, 136–143. doi:10.1016/j.knosys.2018.07.008

Jiang, H., Zhan, J., & Chen, D. (2021). PROMETHEE II method based on variable precision fuzzy rough sets with fuzzy neighborhoods. *Artificial Intelligence Review*, *54*(2), 1281–1319. doi:10.1007/s10462-020-09878-7

Jin, N., Zhao, C. J., & Wu, H. R. (2020). Research on classification technology of agricultural question Answering based on BiGRU_MulCNN. *Nongye Jixie Xuebao*, *51*(5), 199–206.

Jin, N., Zhao, C. J., & Wu, H. R. (2020). Research on classification Technology of agricultural question Answering based on bigru_mulcnn. *Nongye Jixie Xuebao*, *51*(5), 8.

Jin, N., Zhao, C. J., & Wu, H. R. (2022). Agricultural short text matching Technology based on multi-semantic features. *Chinese Journal of Agricultural Machinery*, *5*, 325–331.

Joshi, B. P., Singh, A., Bhatt, P. K., & Vaisla, K. S. (2018). Interval valued q-rung orthopair fuzzy sets and their properties. *Journal of Intelligent & Fuzzy Systems*, *35*(5), 5225–5230. doi:10.3233/JIFS-169806

Ju, Y. B., Luo, C., Ma, J., Gao, H. X., Gonzalez, E., & Wang, A. H. (2019). Some interval-valued q-rung orthopair weighted averaging operators and their applications to multipleattribute decision making. *International Journal of Intelligent Systems*, *34*(10), 2584–2606. doi:10.1002/int.22163

Ju, Y., & Wang, A. (2013). Projection method for multiple criteria group decision making with incomplete weight information in linguistic setting. *Applied Mathematical Modelling*, *37*(20-21), 9031–9040. doi:10.1016/j.apm.2013.04.027

Kaelbling, L. P., Littman, M. L., & Moore, A. W. (1996). Reinforcement learning: A survey. *Journal of Artificial Intelligence Research*, *4*, 237–285. doi:10.1613/jair.301

Kang, Y., Yu, B., & Cai, M. (2022). Multi-attribute predictive analysis based on attribute-oriented fuzzy rough sets in fuzzy information systems. *Information Sciences*, *608*, 931–949. doi:10.1016/j.ins.2022.07.006

Kasneci, E., Seßler, K., Küchemann, S., Bannert, M., Dementieva, D., Fischer, F., Gasser, U., Groh, G., Günnemann, S., Hüllermeier, E., Krusche, S., Kutyniok, G., Michaeli, T., Nerdel, C., Pfeffer, J., Poquet, O., Sailer, M., Schmidt, A., Seidel, T., & Kasneci, G. (2023). ChatGPT for good? On opportunities and challenges of large language models for educatio. *Learning and Individual Differences*, *103*, 102274. doi:10.1016/j.lindif.2023.102274

Kaya, R., & Yet, B. (2019). Building Bayesian networks based on DEMATEL for multiple criteria decision problems: A supplier selection case study. *Expert Systems with Applications*, *134*, 234–248. doi:10.1016/j.eswa.2019.05.053

Kevin, P., & Ginger, G. (2021). *Managing Data Orchestration and Integration at Scale*. O. R. Media.

Khan, N., Naim, A., Hussain, M. R., Naveed, Q. N., Ahmad, N., & Qamar, S. (2019). The 51 v's of big data: survey, technologies, characteristics, opportunities, issues and challenges. *Proceedings of the international conference on omnilayer intelligent systems*, Crete, Greece. 10.1145/3312614.3312623

Kirchner, K., Zec, J., & Delibasic, B. (2015). Facilitating data preprocessing by a generic framework: A proposal for clustering. *Artificial Intelligence Review*, *45*(3), 271–297. doi:10.1007/s10462-015-9446-6

Koltay, T. (2020). Quality of open research data: Values, convergences and governance. *Information (Basel)*, *11*(4), 175. doi:10.3390/info11040175

Kong, L. Y., & Zhou, Z. P. (2023). Aspect level Sentiment analysis of mixed attention networks based on ELMo. *Journal of Chinese Information Processing*, *37*(06), 147–156.

Krizhevsky, A., Sutskever, I., & Hinton, G. E. (2012). Imagenet classification with deep convolutional neural networks. *Advances in Neural Information Processing Systems*, 25.

Kusunoki, Y., Błaszczyński, J., Inuiguchi, M., & Słowiński, R. (2021). Empirical risk minimization for dominance-based rough set approaches. *Information Sciences*, *567*, 395–417. doi:10.1016/j.ins.2021.02.043

LeCun, Y., Bottou, L., Bengio, Y., & Haffner, P. (1998). Gradient-based learning applied to document recognition. *Proceedings of the IEEE*, *86*(11), 2278–2324. doi:10.1109/5.726791

Lei, W. J., Ma, W. M., & Sun, B. Z. (2020). Multigranulation behavioral three-way group decisions under hesitant fuzzy linguistic environment. *Information Sciences*, *537*, 91–115. doi:10.1016/j.ins.2020.05.025

Leng, Y., Yu, L., & Niu, X. (2022). Dynamically aggregating individuals' social influence and interest evolution for group recommendations. *Information Sciences*, *614*, 223–239. doi:10.1016/j.ins.2022.09.058

Liang, D. C., Liu, D., & Kobina, A. (2016). Three-way group decisions with decision-theoretic rough sets. *Information Sciences*, *345*, 46–64. doi:10.1016/j.ins.2016.01.065

Liang, Y., Ju, Y., Martinez, L., & Tu, Y. (2022). Sustainable battery supplier evaluation of new energy vehicles using a distributed linguistic outranking method considering bounded rational behavior. *Journal of Energy Storage*, *48*(5), 103901. doi:10.1016/j.est.2021.103901

Liao, Q. J., Liu, T., & Zhang, X. Y. (2023). Research on facial expression recognition based on VGGNet. *Software Engineering*, *26*(11), 59–62.

Lietz, P. (2010). Research into questionnaire design: A summary of the literature. *International Journal of Market Research*, *52*(2), 249–272. doi:10.2501/S147078530920120X

Li, H. X., Zhang, L. B., Huang, B., & Zhou, X. Z. (2016). Sequential three-way decision and granulation for cost-sensitive face recognition. *Knowledge-Based Systems*, *91*, 241–251. doi:10.1016/j.knosys.2015.07.040

Li, H. X., Zhang, L. B., Zhou, X. Z., & Huang, B. (2017). Cost-sensitive sequential three-way decision modeling using a deep neural network. *International Journal of Approximate Reasoning*, *85*, 68–78. doi:10.1016/j.ijar.2017.03.008

Li, J., Huang, C., Qi, J., Qian, Y., & Liu, W. (2017). Three-way cognitive concept learning via multi-granularity. *Information Sciences*, *378*, 244–263. doi:10.1016/j.ins.2016.04.051

Lin, T. Y., Polkowski, L., & Skowron, A. (1998). Granular computing on binary relations II: Rough set representations and belief functions, *Rough Sets in Knowledge Discovery. Berlin. PhysicaVerlag*, *1*, 121–140.

Li, P., Xu, Z. W., Wei, C. P., Bai, Q. G., & Liu, J. (2022). A novel PROMETHEE method based on GRA-DEMATEL for PLTSs and its application in selecting renewable energies. *Information Sciences*, *589*, 142–161. doi:10.1016/j.ins.2021.12.090

Liu, D., Liang, D., & Wang, C. (2016). A novel three-way decision model based on incomplete information system. *Knowledge-Based Systems*, *91*, 32–45. doi:10.1016/j.knosys.2015.07.036

Liu, D., Li, T. R., & Liang, D. C. (2014). Incorporating logistic regression to decision-theoretic rough sets for classifications. *International Journal of Approximate Reasoning*, *55*(1), 197–210. doi:10.1016/j.ijar.2013.02.013

Liu, F., Zhang, B., Ciucci, D., Wu, W., & Min, F. (2018). A comparison study of similarity measures for covering-based neighborhood classifiers. *Information Sciences*, *448–449*, 1–17. doi:10.1016/j.ins.2018.03.030

Liu, G., Fan, S., Tu, Y., & Wang, G. (2021). Innovative supplier selection from collaboration perspective with a hybrid MCDM model: A case study based on NEVs manufacturer. *Symmetry*, *13*(1), 143–191. doi:10.3390/sym13010143

Liu, H. B., Han, J. J., & Ma, M. X. (2020). Research on agricultural product price prediction based on EMD-ELM model. *Journal of Agricultural Big Data*, *2*(03), 68–74.

Liu, H. L., Tao, J., & Qin, L. (2021). Implementation of One-hot coding based on Python. *Journal of Wuhan Shipbuilding Technical College*, *20*(03), 136–139.

Liu, J. B., Huang, B., Li, H. X., Bu, X. Z., & Zhou, X. Z. (2022). Optimization-based three-way decisions with interval-valued intuitionistic fuzzy information. *IEEE Transactions on Cybernetics*, *53*(6), 3829–3843. doi:10.1109/TCYB.2022.3151899 PMID:35275831

Liu, P., Loudcher, S., Darmont, J., & Noûs, C. (2021). Archaeodal: A data lake for archaeological data management and analytics. *Proceedings of the 25th International Database Engineering & Applications Symposium*, Lyon, France. 10.1145/3472163.3472266

Liu, X., He, J., Yao, Y., Zhang, J., Liang, H., Wang, H., & Hong, Y. (2017). Classifying urban land use by integrating remote sensing and social media data. *International Journal of Geographical Information Science*, *31*(8), 1675–1696. doi:10.1080/13658816.2017.1324976

Liu, Z. C., Zhao, C. J., & Wu, H. R. (2022). Research on similarity matching method of rice questions based on BiLSTM-CNN. *Chinese Journal of Agricultural Mechanization*, *43*(12), 125–132.

Liu, Z., & Zhang, A. (2020). Sampling for big data profiling: A survey. *IEEE Access : Practical Innovations, Open Solutions*, *8*, 72713–72726. doi:10.1109/ACCESS.2020.2988120

Li, W. (2018). *Semi-supervised agricultural text classification Based on semantic diffusion kernel and support vector Machine*. Gannan Normal University.

Li, X., Ju, Y., Ju, D., Zhang, W., Dong, P., & Wang, A. (2019). Multi-attribute group decision making method based on EDAS under picture fuzzy environment. *IEEE Access : Practical Innovations, Open Solutions*, *7*, 141179–141192. doi:10.1109/ACCESS.2019.2943348

Lu, H., Qiu, Y., & Dai, X. (2021). Chinese Agricultural text classification based on central kernel alignment fuzzy svm. *Journal of Gannan Normal University*, *042*(006), 57–61.

Luo, H., Li, L., Zhang, Y., Fang, S., & Chen, X. (2021). Link prediction in multiplex networks using a novel multiple-attribute decision-making approach. *Knowledge-Based Systems*, *219*, 106904. doi:10.1016/j.knosys.2021.106904

Luo, J. F., Hu, M. J., & Qin, K. Y. (2020). Three-way decision with incomplete information based on similarity and satisfiability. *International Journal of Approximate Reasoning*, *120*, 151–183. doi:10.1016/j.ijar.2020.02.005

Lv, X. C. (2023). *Small-scale Agricultural Product Price Forecast based on the Influence of Network Public Opinions*. Northeast Forestry University.

Mahanti, R. (2019). *Data Quality: Dimensions, Measurement, Strategy, Management, and Governance*. ASQ Quality Press.

Mallak, S., Attili, B., & Subuh, M. (2022). Numerical Treatment of Hybrid Fuzzy Differential Equations Subject to Trapezoidal and Triangular Fuzzy Initial Conditions Using Picard's and the General Linear Method. *Computation (Basel, Switzerland)*, *10*(10), 168. doi:10.3390/computation10100168

Mao, Z. J., Shi, S. J., Li, H., Zhong, J. X., & Sun, J. W. (2022). Landslide susceptibility assessment using triangular fuzzy number-analytic hierarchy processing (TFN-AHP), contributing weight (CW) and random forest weighted frequency ratio (RF weighted FR) at the Pengyang county, Northwest China. *Environmental Earth Sciences*, *81*(3), 86. doi:10.1007/s12665-022-10193-3

Maslej-Kresnakova, V., Sarnovsky, M., Butka, P., & Machova, K. (2020). Comparison of deep learning models and various text pre-processing techniques for the toxic comments classification. *Applied Sciences (Basel, Switzerland)*, *10*(23), 8631. doi:10.3390/app10238631

Ma, X., Zeng, J., Peng, L., Fortino, G., & Zhang, Y. (2019). Modeling multi-aspects within one opinionated sentence simultaneously for aspect-level sentiment analysis. *Future Generation Computer Systems*, *93*, 304–311. doi:10.1016/j.future.2018.10.041

Memory, L. S. T. (2010). Long short-term memory. *Neural Computation*, *9*(8), 1735–1780. PMID:9377276

Meng, Z., Lin, R., & Wu, B. (2024). Multi-criteria group decision making based on graph neural networks in Pythagorean fuzzy environment. *Expert Systems with Applications*, *242*, 122803. doi:10.1016/j.eswa.2023.122803

Mikolov, T., Sutskever, I., & Chen, K. (2013). Distributed representations of words and phrases and their compositionality. *Advances in Neural Information Processing Systems*, 26.

Min, F., Zhang, Z. H., Zhai, W. J., & Shen, R. P. (2020). Frequent pattern discovery with tri-partition alphabets. *Information Sciences*, *507*, 715–732. doi:10.1016/j.ins.2018.04.013

Min, F., & Zhu, W. (2012). Attribute reduction of data with error ranges and test costs. *Information Sciences*, *211*, 48–67. doi:10.1016/j.ins.2012.04.031

Mishra, A. R., Chen, S. M., & Rani, P. (2022). Multiattribute decision making based on Fermatean hesitant fuzzy sets and modified VIKOR method. *Information Sciences*, *607*, 1532–1549. doi:10.1016/j.ins.2022.06.037

Mnich, K., & Rudnicki, W. R. (2020). All-relevant feature selection using multidimensional filters with exhaustive search. *Information Sciences*, *524*, 277–297. doi:10.1016/j.ins.2020.03.024

Molloy, J. C. (2011). The open knowledge foundation: Open data means better science. *PLoS Biology*, *9*(12), e1001195. doi:10.1371/journal.pbio.1001195 PMID:22162946

Moreira, M. Â. L., Gomes, C. F. S., Dos Santos, M., da Silva Júnior, A. C., & de Araújo Costa, I. P. (2022). Sensitivity analysis by the PROMETHEE-GAIA method: Algorithms evaluation for COVID-19 prediction. *Procedia Computer Science*, *199*, 431–438. doi:10.1016/j.procs.2022.01.052 PMID:35136460

Mthembu, Z. K., Patel, S. S., Naicker, N., Joseph, S., Madamshetty, L., Moonsamy, D., Akinola, A. T., & Govender, P. (2024 under review). Developing a Data Lakehouse for a South African Government-Sector Training Authority: Governance Framework Design through Systematic Literature Review and Meta-Analysis. In O. S. Ogunleye (Ed.), *Machine Learning and Data Science Techniques for Effective Government Service Delivery*. IGI Global.

Murat, S., Kazan, H., & Coskun, S. S. (2015). An application for measuring performance quality of schools by using the PROMETHEE multi-criteria decision making method. *Procedia: Social and Behavioral Sciences*, *195*, 729–738. doi:10.1016/j.sbspro.2015.06.344

Nambiar, A., & Mundra, D. (2022). An Overview of Data Warehouse and Data Lake in Modern Enterprise Data Management. *Big Data and Cognitive Computing*, *6*(4), 132. doi:10.3390/bdcc6040132

Nandhini, M., & Pradeep, G. C. M. (2020). A hybrid co-occurrence and ranking-based approach for detection of implicit aspects in aspect-based sentiment analysis. *SN Computer Science*, *1*(3), 128. Advance online publication. doi:10.1007/s42979-020-00138-7

Nandwani, P., & Verma, R. (2021). A review on sentiment analysis and emotion detection from text. *Social Network Analysis and Mining*, *11*(1), 81. doi:10.1007/s13278-021-00776-6 PMID:34484462

Nasukawa, T., & Yi, J. (2003, October). Sentiment analysis: Capturing favorability using natural language processing. In *Proceedings of the 2nd international conference on Knowledge capture* (pp. 70-77). ACM. 10.1145/945645.945658

Opricovic, S., & Tzeng, G. H. (2004). Compromise solution by MCDM methods: A comparative analysis of VIKOR and TOPSIS. *European Journal of Operational Research*, *156*(2), 445–455. doi:10.1016/S0377-2217(03)00020-1

Paiva, F. D., Cardoso, R. T. N., Hanaoka, G. P., & Duarte, W. M. (2019). Decision-making for financial trading: A fusion approach of machine learning and portfolio selection. *Expert Systems with Applications*, *115*, 635–655. doi:10.1016/j.eswa.2018.08.003

Palangetić, M., Cornelis, C., Greco, S., & Słowiński, R. (2021). Fuzzy extensions of the dominance-based rough set approach. *International Journal of Approximate Reasoning*, *129*, 1–19. doi:10.1016/j.ijar.2020.10.004

Pamucar, D. S., Tarle, S. P., & Parezanovic, T. (2018). New hybrid multicriteria new decision-making dematel-maırca model: Sustainable selection of a location for the development of multimodal logistics centre. *Ekonomska Istrazivanja*, *31*(1), 1641–1665. doi:10.1080/1331677X.2018.1506706

Pang, J. F., Guan, X. Q., Liang, J. Y., Wang, B. L., & Song, P. (2020). Multi-attribute group decision-making method based on multi-granulation weights and three-way decisions. *International Journal of Approximate Reasoning*, *117*, 122–147. doi:10.1016/j.ijar.2019.11.008

Pawlak, Z. (1982). Rough sets. *International journal of computer & information sciences, 11*, 341-356.

Pedersen, T. I., & Vatn, J. (2022). Optimizing a condition-based maintenance policy by taking the preferences of a risk-averse decision maker into account. *Reliability Engineering & System Safety*, *228*, 108775. doi:10.1016/j.ress.2022.108775

Pedrycz, W., Skowron, A., & Kreinovich, V. (2008). *Handbook of granular computing*. John Wiley & Sons. doi:10.1002/9780470724163

Peng, G., Privette, J. L., Kearns, E. J., Ritchey, N. A., & Ansari, S. (2015). A unified framework for measuring stewardship practices applied to digital environmental datasets. *Data Science Journal*, *13*(0), 231–253. doi:10.2481/dsj.14-049

Peng, X., & Selvachandran, G. (2019). Pythagorean fuzzy set: State of the art and future directions. *Artificial Intelligence Review*, *52*(3), 1873–1927. doi:10.1007/s10462-017-9596-9

Pınar, A., & Boran, F. E. (2020). A q-rung orthopair fuzzy multi-criteria group decision making method for supplier selection based on a novel distance measure. *International Journal of Machine Learning and Cybernetics*, *11*(8), 1749–1780. doi:10.1007/s13042-020-01070-1

Plano Clark, V. L. (2017). Mixed methods research. *The Journal of Positive Psychology*, *12*(3), 305–306. doi:10.1080/17439760.2016.1262619

Platts, K., Probert, D., & Canez, L. (2002). Make vs. buy decisions: A process incorporating multi-attribute decision-making. *International Journal of Production Economics*, *77*(3), 247–257. doi:10.1016/S0925-5273(00)00177-8

Pratsri, S., & Nilsook, P. (2020). Design on Big Data Platform-Based in Higher Education Institute. *Higher Education Studies*, *10*(4), 36–43. doi:10.5539/hes.v10n4p36

Purohit, L., & Kumar, S. (2018). A classification based web service selection approach. *IEEE Transactions on Services Computing*, *14*(2), 315–328. doi:10.1109/TSC.2018.2805352

Pu, X., Wu, G., & Yuan, C. (2019). Exploring overall opinions for document level sentiment classification with structural SVM. *Multimedia Systems*, *25*(1), 21–33. doi:10.1007/s00530-017-0550-0

Qian, J., Liu, C., Miao, D., & Yue, X. (2020). Sequential three-way decisions via multi-granularity. *Information Sciences*, *507*, 606–629. doi:10.1016/j.ins.2019.03.052

Qian, J., Liu, C., & Yue, X. (2019). Multigranulation sequential three-way decisions based on multiple thresholds. *International Journal of Approximate Reasoning*, *105*, 396–416. doi:10.1016/j.ijar.2018.12.007

Qian, Y. H., Liang, J. Y., Lin, G. P., Guo, Q., & Liang, J. (2017). Local multigranulation decision-theoretic rough sets. *International Journal of Approximate Reasoning*, *82*(C), 119–137. doi:10.1016/j.ijar.2016.12.008

Qian, Y. H., Liang, J. Y., Yao, Y. Y., & Dang, C. Y. (2010). MGRS: A multi-granulation rough set. *Information Sciences*, *180*(6), 949–970. doi:10.1016/j.ins.2009.11.023

Qian, Y. H., Zhang, H., Sang, Y. L., & Liang, J. Y. (2014). Multigranulation decision-theoretic rough sets. *International Journal of Approximate Reasoning*, *55*(1, 1pt.2), 225–237. doi:10.1016/j.ijar.2013.03.004

Rahman, A., & Hossen, M. S. (2019, September). Sentiment analysis on movie review data using machine learning approach. In *2019 International Conference on Bangla Speech and Language Processing (ICBSLP)* (pp. 1-4). IEEE. 10.1109/ICBSLP47725.2019.201470

Raj, A., Bosch, J., Olsson, H. H., & Wang, T. J. (2020). Modelling data pipelines. 2020 46th Euromicro conference on software engineering and advanced applications (SEAA), Portoroz, Slovenia

Regmi, P. R., Waithaka, E., Paudyal, A., Simkhada, P., & Van Teijlingen, E. (2016). Guide to the design and application of online questionnaire surveys. *Nepal Journal of Epidemiology*, *6*(4), 640–644. doi:10.3126/nje.v6i4.17258 PMID:28804676

Ren, X. Y. (2019). *Research on Agricultural public Opinion Monitoring and analysis system*. Henan Agricultural University.

Ridha, H. M., Hizam, H., Mirjalili, S., Othman, M. L., Ya'acob, M. E., & Ahmadipour, M. (2023). Innovative hybridization of the two-archive and PROMETHEE-II triple-objective and multi-criterion decision making for optimum configuration of the hybrid renewable energy system. *Applied Energy*, *341*, 121117. doi:10.1016/j.apenergy.2023.121117

Roy, B. (1991). The outranking approach and the foundations of ELECTRE methods. *Theory and Decision*, *31*(1), 49–73. doi:10.1007/BF00134132

Saaty, T. L. (1977). A scaling method for priorities in hierarchical structures. *Journal of Mathematical Psychology*, *15*(3), 234–281. doi:10.1016/0022-2496(77)90033-5

Saaty, T. L. (2004). Decision making—The analytic hierarchy and network processes (AHP/ANP). *Journal of Systems Science and Systems Engineering*, *13*(1), 1–35. doi:10.1007/s11518-006-0151-5

Sahu, R., Dash, S. R., & Das, S. (2021). Career selection of students using hybridized distance measure based on picture fuzzy set and rough set theory. *Decision Making: Applications in Management and Engineering*, *4*(1), 104–126. doi:10.31181/dmame2104104s

Sanchez-Nunez, P., Cobo, M. J., Vaccaro, G., Pelaez, J. I., & Herrera-Viedma, E. (2021). Citation Classics in Consumer Neuroscience, Neuromarketing and Neuroaesthetics: Identification and Conceptual Analysis. *Brain Sciences*, *11*(5), 548. doi:10.3390/brainsci11050548 PMID:33925436

Sandhu, A. K. (2021). Big data with cloud computing: Discussions and challenges. *Big Data Mining and Analytics*, *5*(1), 32–40. doi:10.26599/BDMA.2021.9020016

Sang, Y.L., Liang, J.Y., & Qian, Y.H. (2015), Decision-theoretic rough sets under dynamic granulation, *Knowl. Based Syst.* 84–92.

Sang, X. Z., Yu, X. Y., Chang, C. T., & Liu, X. W. (2022). Electric bus charging station site selection based on the combined DEMATEL and PROMETHEE-PT framework. *Computers & Industrial Engineering*, *168*, 108116. doi:10.1016/j.cie.2022.108116

Savchenko, A. V. (2016). Fast multi-class recognition of piecewise regular objects based on sequential three-way decisions and granular computing. *Knowledge-Based Systems*, *91*, 252–262. doi:10.1016/j.knosys.2015.09.021

Savchenko, A. V. (2019). Sequential three-way decisions in multi-category image recognition with deep features based on distance factor. *Information Sciences*, *489*, 18–36. doi:10.1016/j.ins.2019.03.030

Seikh, M. R., & Mandal, U. (2023). Interval-valued fermatean fuzzy dombi aggregation operators and SWARA based PROMETHEE II method to bio-medical waste management. *Expert Systems with Applications*, *226*, 120082. doi:10.1016/j.eswa.2023.120082

Shang, K. Y. (2023). European Union accelerates the development of green industry. *Journal of Theoretical Review*, *6*, 62–63.

Shao, H., Li, Y., Ding, Y., Zhuang, Q., & Chen, Z. (2020). Land use classification using High-Resolution Remote Sensing images based on structural topic model. *IEEE Access : Practical Innovations, Open Solutions*, *8*, 215943–215955. doi:10.1109/ACCESS.2020.3041645

Sharma, H. K., Kumari, K., & Kar, S. (2021). Forecasting Sugarcane Yield of India based on rough set combination approach. *Decision Making: Applications in Management and Engineering*, *4*(2), 163–177. doi:10.31181/dmame210402163s

Shi G. F. (2020), Implementation of Chinese text corpus preprocessing module based on jieba Chinese word segmentation, *International Journal of Computer Knowledge and Technology,16*(14), 248-251+257.

Shi Y. L., Cui Y. P., & Du Z. G. (2022). Agricultural News Text Classification Method Based on BERT and Deep active learning, *Journal of agricultural books intelligence 8*, 19-29.

Shin, H., Collier, D. A., & Wilson, D. D. (2000). Supply management orientation and supplier/buyer performance. *Journal of Operations Management*, *18*(3), 317–333. doi:10.1016/S0272-6963(99)00031-5

Singhal, B., & Aggarwal, A. (2022). ETL, ELT and Reverse ETL: A business case Study. *2022 Second International Conference on Advanced Technologies in Intelligent Control, Environment, Computing & Communication Engineering (ICATIECE)*, Bangalore, India 10.1109/ICATIECE56365.2022.10046997

Singh, R. R., Zindani, D., & Maity, S. R. (2024). A Novel Fuzzy-Prospect Theory Approach for Hydrogen Fuel Cell Component Supplier Selection for Automotive Industry. *Expert Systems with Applications*, *246*, 123142. doi:10.1016/j.eswa.2024.123142

Stewart, K., & Williams, M. (2005). Researching online populations: The use of online focus groups for social research. *Qualitative Research*, *5*(4), 395–416. doi:10.1177/1468794105056916

Strijker, D., Bosworth, G., & Bouter, G. (2020). Research methods in rural studies: Qualitative, quantitative and mixed methods. *Journal of Rural Studies*, *78*, 262–270. doi:10.1016/j.jrurstud.2020.06.007

Sudhakaran, P., Nair, P. K., & Suraj, A. (2022, October). Music Recommendation using Emotion Recognition. In *2022 IEEE 2nd Mysore Sub Section International Conference (MysuruCon)* (pp. 1-7). IEEE. 10.1109/MysuruCon55714.2022.9972635

Sutskever, I., Vinyals, O., & Le, Q. V. (2014). Sequence to sequence learning with neural networks. *Advances in Neural Information Processing Systems*, 27.

Taherdoost, H. (2016). Validity and reliability of the research instrument; how to test the validation of a questionnaire/survey in a research. *International Journal of Academic Research in Management (IJARM), 5*(3), 28-36. https://hal.science/hal-02546799

Tam, M. C., & Tummala, V. R. (2001). An application of the AHP in vendor selection of a telecommunications system. *Omega*, *29*(2), 171–182. doi:10.1016/S0305-0483(00)00039-6

Tang, D., Qin, B., Wei, F., Dong, L., Liu, T., & Zhou, M. (2015). A joint segmentation and classification framework for sentence level sentiment classification. *IEEE/ACM Transactions on Audio, Speech, and Language Processing*, *23*(11), 1750–1761. doi:10.1109/TASLP.2015.2449071

Tan, R., Chen, C., Zhang, W., Yang, L., & Ma, H. (2023). Intelligent acquisition of single-valued neutrosophic numbers based on emotional tendency analysis and its application in emergency decision making. *Journal of Intelligent & Fuzzy Systems*, *45*(6), 11247–11268. doi:10.3233/JIFS-231039

Tidke, B., Mehta, R., & Dhanani, J. (2020). Consensus-based aggregation for identification and ranking of top-k influential nodes. *Neural Computing & Applications*, *32*(14), 10275–10301. doi:10.1007/s00521-019-04568-0

Tiwari, P., Mishra, B. K., Kumar, S., & Kumar, V. (2020). Implementation of n-gram methodology for rotten tomatoes review dataset sentiment analysis. In *Cognitive analytics: concepts, methodologies, tools, and applications* (pp. 689–701). IGI Global. doi:10.4018/978-1-7998-2460-2.ch036

Torğul B., Paksoy T., (2023). Smart and sustainable supplier selection using interval type-2 Fuzzy AHP. Politeknik Dergisi, Erken Görünüm Makale.

Torra, V. (2010). Hesitant fuzzy sets. *International Journal of Intelligent Systems*, *25*, 529–539. doi:10.1002/int.20418

Turksen, I. B. (1986). Interval valued fuzzy sets based on normal forms. *Fuzzy Sets and Systems*, *20*(2), 191–210. doi:10.1016/0165-0114(86)90077-1

Uhlir, P. F., & Schroder, P. (2007). Open data for global science. *Data Science Journal*, *6*, OD36–OD53. doi:10.2481/dsj.6.OD36

Van Laarhoven, P. J., & Pedrycz, W. (1983). A fuzzy extension of Saaty's priority theory. *Fuzzy Sets and Systems*, *11*(1-3), 229–241. doi:10.1016/S0165-0114(83)80082-7

Van Oudenhoven, A. P., Schröter, M., Drakou, E. G., Geijzendorffer, I. R., Jacobs, S., van Bodegom, P. M., Chazee, L., Czúcz, B., Grunewald, K., Lillebø, A. I., Mononen, L., Nogueira, A. J., Pacheco-Romero, M., Perennou, C., Remme, R. P., Rova, S., Syrbe, R., Tratalos, J. A., Vallejos, M., & Albert, C. (2018). Key criteria for developing ecosystem service indicators to inform decision making. *Ecological Indicators*, *95*, 417–426. doi:10.1016/j.ecolind.2018.06.020

Van Selm, M., & Jankowski, N. (2006). Conducting online surveys. *Quality & Quantity*, *40*(3), 435–456. doi:10.1007/s11135-005-8081-8

Vaswani, A., Shazeer, N., & Parmar, N. (2017), Attention is all you need, Advances in neural information processing systems, 30.

Vom Brocke, J., Hevner, A., & Maedche, A. (2020). Introduction to design science research. *Design science research. Cases*, 1-13.

Vo, N. N., He, X., Liu, S., & Xu, G. (2019). Deep learning for decision making and the optimization of socially responsible investments and portfolio. *Decision Support Systems*, *124*, 113097. doi:10.1016/j.dss.2019.113097

Wang, F. J., Wei, L. J., & Zhao, X. (2022). Research on agricultural short text classification based on FastText model. *Software*, *10*, 27–29.

Wang, H. R. Q., Wang, X. M., & Miao, Y. S. (2022). Similarity Matching of agricultural question Answering Community Based on BERT-Attention-DenseBiGRU. *Nongye Jixie Xuebao*, *1*, 244–252.

Wang, J., Ma, X., Xu, Z., & Zhan, J. (2022). Regret Theory-Based Three-Way Decision Model in Hesitant Fuzzy Environments and Its Application to Medical Decision. *IEEE Transactions on Fuzzy Systems*, *30*(12), 5361–5375. doi:10.1109/TFUZZ.2022.3176686

Wang, K. Y. (2023). *A BO_SVR Method Based on News Headlines on Soybean Price Forecasting Study*. Jilin Agricultural University.

Wang, P. X., Shi, H., Yang, X. B., & Mi, J. S. (2019). Three-way k-means: Integrating k-means and three-way decision. *International Journal of Machine Learning and Cybernetics*, *10*(10), 2767–2777. doi:10.1007/s13042-018-0901-y

Wang, P. X., & Yao, Y. Y. (2018). CE3: A three-way clustering method based on mathematical morphology. *Knowledge-Based Systems*, *155*, 54–65. doi:10.1016/j.knosys.2018.04.029

Wang, T., Li, H., Qian, Y., Huang, B., & Zhou, X. (2022). A Regret-Based Three-Way Decision Model Under Interval Type-2 Fuzzy Environment. *IEEE Transactions on Fuzzy Systems*, *30*(1), 175–189. doi:10.1109/TFUZZ.2020.3033448

Wang, W. J., Zhan, J. M., & Zhang, C. (2021). Three-way decisions based multi-attribute decision making with probabilistic dominance relations. *Information Sciences*, *559*, 75–96. doi:10.1016/j.ins.2021.01.028

Wang, W. J., Zhan, J. M., Zhang, C., Herrera-Viedma, E., & Kou, G. (2023). A regret-theory-based three-way decision method with a priori probability tolerance dominance relation in fuzzy incomplete information systems. *Information Fusion*, *89*, 382–396. doi:10.1016/j.inffus.2022.08.027

Wang, Z. Q., Zhang, Z., & Xia, Y. F. (2023). Fault Alarm Prediction of CNC Machine Tools Based on Word2vec and LSTM-SV. *Combined Machine Tools and Automatic Processing Technology*, *4*, 71–75.

Wang, Z., Xiao, F. Y., & Cao, Z. H. (2022). Uncertainty measurements for Pythagorean fuzzy set and their applications in multiple-criteria decision making. *Soft Computing*, *26*(19), 9937–9952. doi:10.1007/s00500-022-07361-9 PMID:35966347

Wankhade, M., Rao, A. C. S., & Kulkarni, C. (2022). A survey on sentiment analysis methods, applications, and challenges. *Journal of Artificial Intelligence Research*, *55*(7), 5731–5780.

Wasserkrug, S., Gal, A., & Etzion, O. (2008). Inference of security hazards from event composition based on incomplete or uncertain information. *IEEE Transactions on Knowledge and Data Engineering*, *20*(8), 1111–1114. doi:10.1109/TKDE.2008.74

Watkins, C. J. C. H., & Dayan, P. (1992). Q-learning. *Machine Learning*, *8*(3), 279–292. doi:10.1007/BF00992698

Wei, F. F., Duan, Q. L., & Xiao, X. C. (2015). Classification Technique of Chinese Agricultural Text Information Based on SVM. *Journal of Transactions of the Chinese Society for Agricultural Machinery*, *46*(S1), 174–179.

Wei, G. (2017). Picture fuzzy aggregation operators and their application to multiple attribute decision making. *Journal of Intelligent & Fuzzy Systems*, *33*(2), 713–724. doi:10.3233/JIFS-161798

Wei, L., Liu, L., Qi, J. J., & Qian, T. (2020). Rules acquisition of formal decision contexts based on three-way concept lattices. *Information Sciences*, *516*, 529–544. doi:10.1016/j.ins.2019.12.024

Wei, W., & Liang, J. Y. (2018). Information Fusion in Rough Set Theory: An Overview. *Information Fusion*, *48*, 107–118. doi:10.1016/j.inffus.2018.08.007

Wettergren, L., Eriksson, L. E., Nilsson, J., Jervaeus, A., & Lampic, C. (2016). Metadata and Title Correction: Online Focus Group Discussion is a Valid and Feasible Mode When Investigating Sensitive Topics Among Young Persons With a Cancer Experience. *JMIR Research Protocols*, *5*(2), e5971. doi:10.2196/resprot.5971 PMID:27183496

Wille, R. (1982). Restructuring lattice theory: An approach based on hierarchies of concepts. In I. Rival (Ed.), *Ordered Sets* (pp. 445–470). Springer Netherlands. doi:10.1007/978-94-009-7798-3_15

Wright, K. (2005). Researching Internet-based populations: Advantages and disadvantages of online survey research, online questionnaire authoring software packages, and web survey services. *Journal of Computer-Mediated Communication*, *10*(3), JCMC1034. doi:10.1111/j.1083-6101.2005.tb00259.x

Wu, C., & Zhang, D. (2019). Ranking products with IF-based sentiment word framework and TODIM method. *Kybernetes*, *48*(5), 990–1010. doi:10.1108/K-01-2018-0029

Wu, H. R., Guo, W., & Deng, Y. (2022). A Survey of Semantic Understanding Techniques for Agricultural texts. *Chinese Journal of Agricultural Machinery*, *5*, 1–16.

Wu, J., Zhang, G., Xing, Y., Liu, Y., Zhang, Z., Dong, Y., & Herrera-Viedma, E. (2023). A sentiment analysis driven method based on public and personal preferences with correlated attributes to select online doctors. *Applied Intelligence*, *53*(16), 1–22. doi:10.1007/s10489-023-04485-9 PMID:36844914

Wu, L., & Li, S. (2015). The attempt of text mining data preprocessing in TCM prescription database. *International Journal of Chinese Medicine Library and Information*, *39*(03), 8–11.

Wu, W., Yee, L., & Mi, J. (2009). Granular computing and knowledge reduction in formal contexts. *IEEE Transactions on Knowledge and Data Engineering*, *21*(10), 1461–1474. doi:10.1109/TKDE.2008.223

Xiang, H. M., Bai, T., & Li, Y. D. (2022). Automatic indexing of agricultural text based on word embedding and multi-feature fusion. *Xinjiang Nongye Daxue Xuebao*, *6*, 486–492.

Xie, J., Xia, S. Y., Wang, G. Y., & Gao, X. B. (2023). GBMST: An Efficient Minimum Spanning Tree Clustering Based on Granular-Ball Computing. *Clinical Orthopaedics and Related Research*, *2303*, 01082.

Xue, W. M., & Lu, Y. C. (2005). Dual hesitant fuzzy graphs with applications to multi-attribute decision making. *International Journal of Cognitive Computing in Engineering*, *1*, 18–26.

Xu, J. F., Miao, D. Q., Zhang, Y. J., & Zhang, Z. F. (2017). A three-way decisions model with probabilistic rough sets for stream computing. *International Journal of Approximate Reasoning*, *88*, 1–22. doi:10.1016/j.ijar.2017.05.001

Xu, Y., & Yao, Y. Y. (2019). Partition order product space: Partition based granular computing model. *J. Computer Res. Dev.*, *56*(4), 836–843.

Yager, R. R. (2016). Generalized orthopair fuzzy sets. *IEEE Transactions on Fuzzy Systems*, *25*(5), 1222–1230. doi:10.1109/TFUZZ.2016.2604005

Yang, B., & Li, J. (2020). Complex network analysis of three-way decision researches. *International Journal of Machine Learning and Cybernetics*, *11*(5), 973–987. doi:10.1007/s13042-020-01082-x

Yang, S. Q., Duan, X. L., & Xiao, Z. (2023). Agricultural news text classification based on ERNIE+DPCNN+BiGRU. *Computer Applications (Nottingham)*, (05), 1461–1466.

Yang, X., Li, T. R., Fujita, H., Liu, D., & Yao, Y. Y. (2017). A unified model of sequential three-way decisions and multilevel incremental processing. *Knowledge-Based Systems*, *134*, 172–188. doi:10.1016/j.knosys.2017.07.031

Yang, X., Li, T. R., Liu, D., Chen, H. M., & Luo, C. (2017). A unified framework of dynamic three-way probabilistic rough sets. *Information Sciences*, *420*, 126–147. doi:10.1016/j.ins.2017.08.053

Yang, X., Li, T., Fujita, H., & Liu, D. (2019). A sequential three-way approach to multi-class decision. *International Journal of Approximate Reasoning*, *104*, 108–125. doi:10.1016/j.ijar.2018.11.001

Yang, Z., Li, Q., Charles, V., Xu, B., & Gupta, S. (2023). Supporting personalized new energy vehicle purchase decision-making: Customer reviews and product recommendation platform. *International Journal of Production Economics*, *265*, 109003. doi:10.1016/j.ijpe.2023.109003

Yao, Y. Y. (2009), Integrative levels of granularity, A. Bargiela, W. Pedrycz (Eds.), Human-centric information processing through granular modelling, 182, 31–47.

Yao, Y. Y. (2013), Granular computing and sequential three-way decisions, Proceedings of International Conference on Rough Sets and Knowledge Technology (RSKT 2013), LNCS, 8171, 16–27. 10.1007/978-3-642-41299-8_3

Yao, Y. (2009). Three-way decision: An interpretation of rules in rough set theory. *In LNCS 5589: Proceedings of the 4th International Conference on Rough Sets and Knowledge Technology*, Gold Coast, July 14-16, 2009 (pp. 642-649). Berlin, Heidelberg: Springer. 10.1007/978-3-642-02962-2_81

Yao, Y. (2012). An outline of a theory of three-way decisions. *Lecture Notes in Computer Science*, *7413*, 1–17. doi:10.1007/978-3-642-32115-3_1

Yao, Y. (2021). The geometry of three-way decision. *Applied Intelligence*, *51*(9), 6298–6325. doi:10.1007/s10489-020-02142-z

Yao, Y. Y. (2010). Three-way decisions with probabilistic rough sets. *Information Sciences*, *180*(3), 341–353. doi:10.1016/j.ins.2009.09.021

Yao, Y. Y. (2011). The superiority of three-way decisions in probabilistic rough set models. *Information Sciences*, *181*(6), 1080–1096. doi:10.1016/j.ins.2010.11.019

Yao, Y. Y. (2016). A triarchic theory of granular computing. *Granul. Comput.*, *1*(2), 145–157. doi:10.1007/s41066-015-0011-0

Yao, Y. Y. (2016). Three-way decisions and cognitive computing. *Cognitive Computation*, *8*(4), 543–554. doi:10.1007/s12559-016-9397-5

Yao, Y. Y. (2018). Three-way decision and granular computing. *International Journal of Approximate Reasoning*, *103*, 107–123. doi:10.1016/j.ijar.2018.09.005

Yao, Y. Y. (2019). Three-way conflict analysis: Reformulations and extensions of the Pawlak model. *Knowledge-Based Systems*, *180*, 26–37. doi:10.1016/j.knosys.2019.05.016

Yao, Y. Y. (2020). Three-way granular computing, rough sets, and formal concept analysis. *International Journal of Approximate Reasoning*, *116*, 106–125. doi:10.1016/j.ijar.2019.11.002

Yaqoob, I., Hashem, M., Gani, A., Mokhtar, S. B., Ahmed, E., Anuar, N. B., & Vasilakos, A. V. (2016). Big data: From beginning to future. *International Journal of Information Management*, *36*(6), 1231–1247. doi:10.1016/j.ijinfomgt.2016.07.009

Ye, S. H., Ge, Y. H., & Chen, B. (2023). Cyberbullying detection model based on ELMo-TextCNN. *Journal of Information Security Research*, *9*(09), 868–876.

Yi, J. H., Liu, Y., Forrest, J. Y. L., Guo, X. G., & Xu, X. J. (2022). A three-way decision approach with S-shaped utility function under Pythagorean fuzzy information. *Expert Systems with Applications*, *210*, 118370. doi:10.1016/j.eswa.2022.118370

Yu, B., Cai, M., & Li, Q. (2019b). A λ-rough set model and its applications with TOPSIS method to decision making. *Knowledge-Based Systems*, *165*, 420–431. doi:10.1016/j.knosys.2018.12.013

Yu, B., Guo, L., & Li, Q. (2019a). A characterization of novel rough fuzzy sets of information systems and their application in decision making. *Expert Systems with Applications*, *122*, 253–261. doi:10.1016/j.eswa.2019.01.018

Yu, B., Xu, R., Fu, Y., & Xu, Z. (2022a). A Novel Dominance-Based Rough Set Model with Advantage (Disadvantage) Neighborhoods and Its Applications to Assess Sales Group. *International Journal of Fuzzy Systems*, *24*(8), 3501–3512. doi:10.1007/s40815-022-01342-8

Yu, B., Xu, R., Xu, Z., & Dai, J. (2023b). Optimizing group-oriented multiple attribute decision-making method based on dominance-based rough set model with advantaged (disadvantaged) neighborhoods. *Engineering Applications of Artificial Intelligence*, *124*, 106602. doi:10.1016/j.engappai.2023.106602

Yu, B., Xu, Z., Dai, J., & Yang, T. (2022b). A novel multi-attribute decision-making method based on neighborhood approximations and its application. *Expert Systems with Applications*, *199*, 116946. doi:10.1016/j.eswa.2022.116946

Yu, B., Zheng, Z., Xiao, Z., Fu, Y., & Xu, Z. (2023a). A large-scale group decision-making method based on group-oriented rough dominance relation in scenic spot service improvement. *Expert Systems with Applications*, *233*, 120999. doi:10.1016/j.eswa.2023.120999

Yue, Q., Zou, W. C., & Hu, W. (2023). A new theory of triangular intuitionistic fuzzy sets to solve the two-sided matching problem. *Alexandria Engineering Journal*, *63*, 57–73. doi:10.1016/j.aej.2022.07.018

Yue, X. D., Chen, Y. F., Miao, D. Q., & Fujita, H. (2020). Fuzzy neighborhood covering for three-way classification. *Information Sciences*, *507*, 795–808. doi:10.1016/j.ins.2018.07.065

Yu, H., Wang, X., Wang, G., & Zeng, X. (2020). An active three-way clustering method via low-rank matrices for multi-view data. *Information Sciences*, *507*, 823–839. doi:10.1016/j.ins.2018.03.009

Yu, L. G., Liu, J. T., & Zhu, J. (2022). Effects of the electrical stimulation on the behavioral and physiological performances of the beef cattle [Transactions of the CSAE]. *International Journal of Chinese Society of Agricultural Engineering*, *38*(13), 221–227.

Zadeh, L. A. (1965). Fuzzy sets. *Information and Control*, *8*(3), 338–353. doi:10.1016/S0019-9958(65)90241-X

Zadeh, L. A., Gupta, M. M., Ragade, R. K., & Yager, R. R. (1979). *Fuzzy sets and information granularity*. Advance in Fuzzy Sst Theory and Applications NorthHolland.

Zahedi-Seresht, M., Mehrabian, S., & Jahanshahloo, G. R. (2016). A new method for ranking distribution companies with several scenarios data by using DEA/MADM. *International Journal of Applied Operational Research-An Open Access Journal*, *6*(3), 11–24. http://ijorlu.liau.ac.ir/article-1-518-en.html

Zanakis, S. H., Solomon, A. W., Wishart, N., & Dublish, S. (1998). Multi-attribute decision making: A simulation comparison of select methods. *European Journal of Operational Research*, *107*(3), 507–529. doi:10.1016/S0377-2217(97)00147-1

Zareie, A., Sheikhahmadi, A., & Khamforoosh, K. (2018). Influence maximization in social networks based on TOPSIS. *Expert Systems with Applications*, *108*, 96–107. doi:10.1016/j.eswa.2018.05.001

Zhai, Y., Jia, N., Zhang, S., Li, D., & Weihua, X. (2022). Study on deduction process and inference methods of decision implications. *International Journal of Machine Learning and Cybernetics*, *13*(7), 1959–1979. doi:10.1007/s13042-021-01499-y

Zhai, Y., & Li, D. (2019). Knowledge structure preserving fuzzy attribute reduction in fuzzy formal context. *International Journal of Approximate Reasoning*, *115*, 209–220. doi:10.1016/j.ijar.2019.09.012

Zhai, Y., Li, D., & Qu, K. (2012). Probability fuzzy attribute implications for interval-valued fuzzy sets. *International Journal of Database Theory and Application*, *5*(4), 95–108.

Zhai, Y., Li, D., & Qu, K. (2014). Decision implications: A logical point of view. *International Journal of Machine Learning and Cybernetics*, *5*(4), 509–516. doi:10.1007/s13042-013-0204-2

Zhai, Y., Li, D., & Qu, K. (2015a). Canonical basis for decision implications. *Chinese Journal of Electronics*, *43*(1), 18–23.

Zhai, Y., Li, D., & Qu, K. (2015b). Decision implication canonical basis: A logical perspective. *Journal of Computer and System Sciences*, *81*(1), 208–218. doi:10.1016/j.jcss.2014.06.001

Zhan, J., Wang, J., Ding, W., & Yao, Y. (2023). Three-Way Behavioral Decision Making With Hesitant Fuzzy Information Systems: Survey and Challenges. *IEEE/CAA Journal of Automatica Sinica, 10*, 330-350.

Zhang, C., Bai, W. H., Li, D. Y., & Zhan, J. M. (2022a). Multiple attribute group decision making based on multigranulation probabilistic models, MULTIMOORA and TPOP in incomplete q-rung orthopair fuzzy information systems. *International Journal of Approximate Reasoning*, *143*, 102–120. doi:10.1016/j.ijar.2022.01.002

Zhang, C., Ding, J. J., Li, D. Y., & Zhan, J. M. (2021a). A novel multi-granularity three-way decision making approach in q-rung orthopair fuzzy information systems. *International Journal of Approximate Reasoning*, *138*, 161–187. doi:10.1016/j.ijar.2021.08.004

Zhang, C., Ding, J. J., Zhan, J. M., & Li, D. Y. (2022b). Incomplete three-way multi-attribute group decision making based on adjustable multigranulation Pythagorean fuzzy probabilistic rough sets. *International Journal of Approximate Reasoning*, *147*, 40–59. doi:10.1016/j.ijar.2022.05.004

Zhang, C., Ding, J. J., Zhan, J. M., Sangaiah, A. K., & Li, D. Y. (2022c). Fuzzy intelligence learning based on bounded rationality in IoMT systems: A case study in Parkinson's disease. *IEEE Transactions on Computational Social Systems*, *10*(4), 1607–1621. doi:10.1109/TCSS.2022.3221933

Zhang, C., Li, D. Y., & Liang, J. Y. (2020a). Interval-valued hesitant fuzzy multi-granularity three-way decisions in consensus processes with applications to multi-attribute group decision making. *Information Sciences*, *511*, 192–211. doi:10.1016/j.ins.2019.09.037

Zhang, C., Li, D. Y., Liang, J. Y., & Wang, B. L. (2021b). MAGDM-oriented dual hesitant fuzzy multigranulation probabilistic models based on MULTIMOORA. *International Journal of Machine Learning and Cybernetics*, *12*(5), 1219–1241. doi:10.1007/s13042-020-01230-3

Zhang, C., Li, D. Y., Zhai, Y. H., & Yang, Y. H. (2019). Multigranulation rough set model in hesitant fuzzy information systems and its application in person-job fit. *International Journal of Machine Learning and Cybernetics*, *10*(4), 717–729. doi:10.1007/s13042-017-0753-x

Zhang, C., Li, D., Kang, X., Liang, Y., Broumi, S., & Sangaiah, A. K. (2020a). Multi-attribute group decision making based on multigranulation probabilistic models with interval-valued neutrosophic information. *Mathematics*, *8*(2), 223. doi:10.3390/math8020223

Zhang, C., Li, D., & Liang, J. (2018). Hesitant fuzzy linguistic rough set over two universes model and its applications. *International Journal of Machine Learning and Cybernetics*, *9*(4), 577–588. doi:10.1007/s13042-016-0541-z

Zhang, C., Li, D., & Liang, J. (2020d). Multi-granularity three-way decisions with adjustable hesitant fuzzy linguistic multigranulation decision-theoretic rough sets over two universes. *Information Sciences*, *507*, 665–683. doi:10.1016/j.ins.2019.01.033

Zhang, C., Li, D., Sangaiah, A. K., & Broumi, S. (2017). Merger and Acquisition Target Selection Based on Interval Neutrosophic Multigranulation Rough Sets over Two Universes. *Symmetry*, *9*(7), 126. doi:10.3390/sym9070126

Zhang, C., Li, X. C., Sangaiah, A. K., Li, W. T., Wang, B. L., Cao, F., & Shangguan, X. K. (2023a). *Collaborative fuzzy linguistic learning to Low-Resource and robust decision system based on bounded rationality*. ACM Transactions on Asian and Low-Resource Language Information Processing. doi:10.1145/3592605

Zhang, C., Zhang, H., & Wang, J. (2018). Personalized restaurant recommendation method combining group correlations and customer preferences. *Information Sciences*, *454*, 128–143. doi:10.1016/j.ins.2018.04.061

Zhang, C., Zhang, J. J., Li, W. T., Pedrycz, W., & Li, D. Y. (2023b). A regret theory-based MG three-way decision model with incomplete T-spherical fuzzy information and its application in forest fire management. *Applied Soft Computing*, *110539*, 110539. doi:10.1016/j.asoc.2023.110539

Zhang, C., Zhang, J., Li, W., Castillo, O., & Zhang, J. (2024). Exploring static rebalancing strategies for dockless bicycle sharing systems based on multi-granularity behavioral decision-making. *International Journal of Cognitive Computing in Engineering*, *5*, 27–43. doi:10.1016/j.ijcce.2024.01.001

Zhang, F., Hao, X., Chao, J., & Yuan, S. (2020a). Label propagation-based approach for detecting review spammer groups on e-commerce websites. *Knowledge-Based Systems*, *193*, 105520. doi:10.1016/j.knosys.2020.105520

Zhang, H. (2023). *Research on the forecasting method of China's corn futures market by combining sentiment analysis*. Anhui Agricultural University.

Zhang, H. R., & Min, F. (2016). Three-way recommender systems based on random forests. *Knowledge-Based Systems*, *91*, 275–286. doi:10.1016/j.knosys.2015.06.019

Zhang, H., Zhang, R., Huang, H., & Wang, J. (2018). Some picture fuzzy Dombi Heronian mean operators with their application to multi-attribute decision-making. *Symmetry*, *10*(11), 593. doi:10.3390/sym10110593

Zhang, K. R., Yang, W. S., & Yan, B. (2023). A multi-step forecasting model for airport terminal cooling load based on VMD-IPSO-GRU. *Heating Ventilating & Air Conditioning*, *53*(S2), 84–88.

Zhang, L., Zhang, L., & Du, B. (2016). Deep Learning for Remote sensing Data: A technical tutorial on the state of the art. *IEEE Geoscience and Remote Sensing Magazine*, *4*(2), 22–40. doi:10.1109/MGRS.2016.2540798

Zhang, L., Zhan, J., & Yao, Y. (2020b). Intuitionistic fuzzy TOPSIS method based on CVPIFRS models: An application to biomedical problems. *Information Sciences*, *517*, 315–339. doi:10.1016/j.ins.2020.01.003

Zhang, Q. H., Pang, G. H., & Wang, G. Y. (2019). A novel sequential three-way decisions model based on penalty function. *Knowledge-Based Systems*, *192*, 105350. doi:10.1016/j.knosys.2019.105350

Zhang, Q. H., Xia, D. Y., & Wang, G. Y. (2017). Three-way decision model with two types of classification errors. *Information Sciences*, *420*, 431–453. doi:10.1016/j.ins.2017.08.066

Zhang, R., Xu, Z., & Gou, X. (2023). ELECTRE II method based on the cosine similarity to evaluate the performance of financial logistics enterprises under double hierarchy hesitant fuzzy linguistic environment. *Fuzzy Optimization and Decision Making*, *22*(1), 23–49. doi:10.1007/s10700-022-09382-3

Zhang, S., Li, D., & Zhai, Y. (2021). Incremental method of generating decision implication canonical basis. *Soft Computing*, *26*(3), 1067–1083. doi:10.1007/s00500-021-06452-3

Zhang, S., Li, D., Zhai, Y., & Kang, X. (2020). A comparative study of decision implication, concept rule and granular rule. *Information Sciences*, *508*, 33–49. doi:10.1016/j.ins.2019.08.053

Zhang, X. (2008a). On multi-period multi-attribute decision making. *Knowledge-Based Systems*, *21*(2), 164–171. doi:10.1016/j.knosys.2007.05.007

Zhang, X., & Yager, R. R. (2008b). Dynamic intuitionistic fuzzy multi-attribute decision making. *International Journal of Approximate Reasoning*, *48*(1), 246–262. doi:10.1016/j.ijar.2007.08.008

Zhang, Y. B., Zhang, Z. F., Miao, D. Q., & Wang, J. Q. (2019). Three-way enhanced convolutional neural networks for sentence-level sentiment classification. *Information Sciences*, *477*, 55–64. doi:10.1016/j.ins.2018.10.030

Zhang, Y., Jiang, J., Xiang, Y., Zhu, Y., Wan, L., & Xie, X. (2020c). Cloud-assisted privacy-conscious large-scale Markowitz portfolio. *Information Sciences*, *527*, 548–559. doi:10.1016/j.ins.2018.12.055

Zhao, C. J. (2023). Review on intelligent service technology of agricultural knowledge [Chinese and English]. *Journal of Intelligent Agriculture*, *5*(02), 126–148.

Zhao, Y., & Guo, X. Y. (2020). Research on agricultural text classification method based on Naive Bayes. *Journal of Water Saving Irrigation*, *2*, 98–102.

Zhi, H. L., Qi, J. J., Qian, T., & Wei, L. (2019). Three-way dual concept analysis. *International Journal of Approximate Reasoning*, *114*, 151–165. doi:10.1016/j.ijar.2019.08.010

Zhou, J. M., Li, Y. C., & Lai, C. X. (2022). Research on question classification in question answering system for agricultural field [Natural Science Edition]. *Journal of Henan University of Science and Technology*, *3*, 63–70.

About the Contributors

Chao Zhang, professor of Institute of Intelligent Information Processing, Shanxi University, his main study interests include data mining, granular computing and intelligent decision making. In recent years, he has published more than 80 papers including IEEE Transactions on Computational Social Systems, IEEE Transactions on Fuzzy Systems, IEEE Transactions on Consumer Electronics, Information Sciences, Information Fusion, International Journal of Approximate Reasoning, ACM Transactions on Asian and Low-Resource Language Information Processing, Computers in Industry, Applied Mathematical Modelling. Among them, one paper has been selected as "ESI highly cited paper". He has published 3 academic monographs in national publishers. He has published 2 national invention patents. He has been awarded the first prize of Outstanding Achievements in Scientific Research in Institutions of Higher Learning in Shanxi Province, the second prize of Outstanding Achievement Award in Social Sciences in Shanxi Province, two Excellent Academic Paper Awards in Taiyuan City, ACM Excellent Doctoral Dissertation Award in Taiyuan Chapter, the best student paper award in CGCKD.

Wentao Li received the Ph.D. degree from the Department of Mathematics, Harbin Institute of Technology, Harbin, China, in 2019, and the M.Sc. degree from the School of Mathematics and Statistics, Chongqing University of Technology, Chongqing, China, in 2015. From 2016 to 2018, he was a joint Ph. D student with the University of Alberta, Edmonton, AB, Canada. He is currently an Associate Professor with the College of Artificial Intelligence, Southwest University, Chongqing, China. His current research interests include artificial intelligence, feature selection, and granular computing. In recent years, He has published over 30 articles including IEEE Transactions on Fuzzy Systems, IEEE Transactions on Neural Networks and Learning Systems, IEEE Transactions on Cybernetics, IEEE Transactions on Emerging Topics in Computational Intelligence, Fuzzy Sets and Systems, Information Sciences, Artificial Intelligence Review, and many others. Among them, 3 papers have been selected as "ESI hot paper" and "ESI highly cited paper". He serves on editorial board of several international journals, and successfully held several Special Issues in journals of International Journal of Fuzzy Systems, Wireless Communications and Mobile Computing, Intelligent Automation & Soft Computing, and Frontiers in Neurorobotics. He also served as the reviewer of many journals, such as IEEE TFS, IEEE TNNLS, IEEE TCYB, IEEE TKDE, INS, KBS, AIRE, and granted the certificate of "Outstanding Reviewer" for Knowledge-Based Systems in 2018.

***

Dharmesh Dhabliya is a Professor at Vishwakarma Institute of Information Technology Department of Information Technology with a specialization in research and scientific events. With over 8 years of experience in the field, I have devoted my career to advancing the field of computer engineering through research, teaching, and community involvement. I have a particular interest in exploring the intersection of computer engineering and emerging technologies, and I have published numerous papers in top-tier journals and conferences in this area. In addition to my research activities, I am also deeply committed to mentoring and training the next generation of computer engineers. I have supervised several graduate students and postdoctoral researchers, and I enjoy sharing my knowledge and experience with students through teaching and advising. I am an active member of the computer engineering community, and I frequently participate in scientific events and conferences. I have organized and chaired several workshops and symposiums, and I have served on the program committees of numerous international conferences.

Burak Efe is an Associate Professor at Necmettin Erbakan University Department of Industrial Engineering. He received BSc, MSc and PhD degrees in Department of Industrial Engineering from Gazi University. His interest areas are fuzzy logic, decision making and human factors.

Xueqing Fan is an undergraduate student at the School of Computer and Information Technology, Shanxi University, majoring in Computer Science and Technology. She is pursuing a bachelor degree.

Ankur Gupta has received the B.Tech and M.Tech in Computer Science and Engineering from Ganga Institute of Technology and Management, Kablana affiliated with Maharshi Dayanand University, Rohtak in 2015 and 2017. He is an Assistant Professor in the Department of Computer Science and Engineering at Vaish College of Engineering, Rohtak, and has been working there since January 2019. He has many publications in various reputed national/ international conferences, journals, and online book chapter contributions (Indexed by SCIE, Scopus, ESCI, ACM, DBLP, etc). He is doing research in the field of cloud computing, data security & machine learning. His research work in M.Tech was based on biometric security in cloud computing.

Zesheng Huo is currently pursuing MA.Sc with School of Information Science and Engineering in Yanshan University and with Key Laboratory for information transmission and signal processing of Hebei Province. He current research interests include machine learning, and causal inference.

Chunmao Jiang is currently serving as a professor at the School of Computer Science and Mathematics at Fujian University of Technology, where he also mentors graduate students. With a Master of Science degree from Harbin Institute of Technology (2004) and a Doctor of Philosophy degree in Computer Science from Harbin Engineering University, Professor Jiang has developed a keen interest and expertise in granular computing, three-way decision theory, and cloud computing. As an active member of the academic community, he holds positions as an executive committee member of the CCF Committee on Open Source Development and a member of the CAAI Committee on Granular Computing and Knowledge Discovery. His research interests include intelligent information processing and decision-making, multi-granularity cloud computing, and the development of large-scale Chinese-Russian models. In recent years, Professor Jiang has led significant educational and research initiatives. He has been the principal investigator of one key provincial-level educational reform project and one general project. In the realm of scientific research, he has led and participated in more than ten projects funded by the

National Natural Science Foundation of China, the National Social Science Fund of China, the China Postdoctoral Science Foundation, and various provincial grants. Professor Jiang's scholarly contributions are extensive, with over eighty publications in prestigious journals such as TFS, INS, KBS, and the Journal of Electronics, including more than thirty SCI-indexed articles. His dedication to advancing knowledge in his fields of interest underscores his commitment to both teaching and research excellence.

Kexin Liu is an undergraduate student at the School of Computer and Information Technology, Shanxi University, majoring in Data Science and Big Data Technology. She is pursuing a bachelor degree.

Fanghui Lu is an undergraduate student at the School of Computer and Information Technology, Shanxi University, majoring in Data Science and Big Data Technology. She is pursuing a bachelor degree.

Hatice Kübra Özensel received BSc and MSc degrees in Department of Industrial Engineering from Selçuk University and Necmettin Erbakan University, respectively.

Sabyasachi Pramanik is a professional IEEE member. He obtained a PhD in Computer Science and Engineering from Sri Satya Sai University of Technology and Medical Sciences, Bhopal, India. Presently, he is an Associate Professor, Department of Computer Science and Engineering, Haldia Institute of Technology, India. He has many publications in various reputed international conferences, journals, and book chapters (Indexed by SCIE, Scopus, ESCI, etc). He is doing research in the fields of Artificial Intelligence, Data Privacy, Cybersecurity, Network Security, and Machine Learning. He also serves on the editorial boards of several international journals. He is a reviewer of journal articles from IEEE, Springer, Elsevier, Inderscience, IET and IGI Global. He has reviewed many conference papers, has been a keynote speaker, session chair, and technical program committee member at many international conferences. He has authored a book on Wireless Sensor Network. He has edited 8 books from IGI Global, CRC Press, Springer and Wiley Publications.

Yunsheng Song received his doctor degree from the Key Laboratory of Computational Intelligence and Chinese Information Technology of the Ministry of Education with a doctorate degree in System Engineering, Shanxi University. He joined the Department of Data Science, College of Information Science and Engineering, Shandong Agricultural University in August 2018. His research interests include large-scale machine learning, intelligent data analysis and processing, and agricultural big data.

Anna Wang is an undergraduate student at the School of Computer and Information Technology, Shanxi University, majoring in Data Science and Big Data Technology. She is pursuing a bachelor degree.

Liyin Wang is an undergraduate student at the School of Computer and Information Technology, Shanxi University, majoring in Computer Science and Technology. She is pursuing a bachelor degree.

Yi Xu, professor of School of Computer Science and Technology, Anhui University, her main study interests include intelligent information processing, granular computing and edge computing. In recent years, she has published more than 60 papers including Information Sciences, Artificial Intelligence Review, International Journal of Approximate Reasoning. She has been awarded the Distinguished "Late Breaking Result Paper" in ASE 2020.

Zaifa Xue is currently pursuing Ph.D. degree with School of Information Science and Engineering in Yanshan University and with Key Laboratory for information transmission and signal processing of Hebei Province. His current research interests include machine learning and medical signal processing.

Yinglong Dai received the PhD degree from Hunan University, Changsha, China, in Applied Mathematics. He is a teacher at Hunan Normal University, Changsha, China. His current research areas include Granular Computing, Intelligent Information Processing, Fuzzy Systems, Data Mining, and Topology.

Xiao Zeyu is a student at Hunan Normal University, Changsha, China. His current research areas include Granular Computing, Intelligent Information Processing, Fuzzy Systems, Data Mining, and Topology.

Jiayi Zhang has received the master degree in the School of Computer Science and Statistics, Trinity College Dublin, Ireland.

Shaoxia Zhang received the Ph.D. degree in the School of Computer and Information Technology, Shanxi University, China in 2021. She works at the School of Information, Shanxi University of Finance and Economics, China. Her research interests include formal concept analysis (FCA) and Granular Computing.

Tao Zhang, professor of School of Information Science and Engineering in Yanshan University, and awarded as outstanding young talent in Hebei Province. His research interests include formal concept analysis, machine learning, and causal inference. He proposes the theory of attribute topology and applied it to concept cognitive learning, machine learning, and medical signal processing.

Hansen Zhao received a Master's degree from the Georgia Institute of Technology in the United States.

Xinyue Zhao received the B.E. degree in Data Science and Big Data from University of Shandong Agricultural University, Taian, China, in 2023. She is currently pursuing the M.Sc. degree in Computer Technology of Shandong Agricultural University, Taian, China. Her research interest is agricultural short text analysis.

Index

P

Q

R

S

T

W

www.ingramcontent.com/pod-product-compliance
Lightning Source LLC
LaVergne TN
LVHW080641011026
849160LV00014B/1281